D1525622

THE GERMAN SLUMP

THE GERMAN SLUMP

Politics and Economics 1924–1936

HAROLD JAMES

CLARENDON PRESS · OXFORD
1986

Oxford University Press, Walton Street, Oxford OX2 6DP
Oxford New York Toronto
Delhi Bombay Calcutta Madras Karachi
Kuala Lumpur Singapore Hong Kong Tokyo
Nairobi Dar es Salaam Cape Town
Melbourne Auckland
and associated companies in
Beirut Berlin Ibadan Nicosia

Oxford is a trade mark of Oxford University Press

Published in the United States
by Oxford University Press, New York

British Library Cataloguing in Publication Data
James, Harold
The German slump: politics and economics 1924–1936
1. Germany—Economic conditions—1918–1945.
2. Germany—Politics and government—1918–1933.
3. Germany—Politics and government—1933–1945.
I. Title.
330.943'085 HC286.3
ISBN 0–19–821972–5

Library of Congress Cataloging in Publication Data
James, Harold Douglas.
The German slump.
Bibliography: p.
Includes index.
1. Germany—Economic conditions—1918–1945.
2. Germany—Politics and government—1918–1933.
3. Germany—Politics and government—1933–1945.
I. Title.
HC286.3.J33 1986 330.943'085 85–21529
ISBN 0–19–821972–5

Set by Latimer Trend & Co. Ltd, Plymouth
Printed in Great Britain
at the University Printing House, Oxford
by David Stanford
Printer to the University

Preface

This is an analysis of the inter-war depression in Germany, of its effects on political life, and in turn also of the influence of politics on business. I found setting dates for the title very difficult, since I regard the severe crisis at the end of the 1920s as a product of causes some of which operated over a long chronological span. Whereas economists are able and even eager to be precise when dating business cycles, the economic historian finds it very hard to say when a long-term process of bureaucratisation and rigidification of institutions, a process which is likely to produce structural crisis, began. In this sense every historian is bound to feel some sympathy for the nineteenth-century French writer who set out to produce a history of Napoleon III and only reached the Treaty of Verdun (843). Equally, it is hard to know where to stop. If I have gone on too long, and deal at great length with the Nazi recovery, it is not because my typewriter behaved like the brooms in the hands of the sorcerer's apprentice. I believe that it is absurd to stop accounts of crises at the low point of the crisis (in this case in 1932), as some analysts have done, or at the artificial boundary of 1933 created by the political revolution of National Socialism. Seeing what went on in the recovery offers help in constructing a picture of what was wrong before the Slump.

A sorcerer's apprentice does not thank the sorcerer. In contrast, I should like to express my gratitude and an intellectual debt. In the first place, a book of this kind would not be possible without the enormous volume of recent research on Weimar produced in Germany, USA, and Britain. Secondly, I have specific debts. Professor Knut Borchardt has shaken German historians (and politicians) with his arguments on Weimar. He has been immensely kind in offering me advice, lending me material, and commenting on the manuscript. In Cambridge, Lord Dacre (Professor Hugh Trevor-Roper), Dr Jonathan Steinberg, and Professor Norman Stone, as well as many others, have helped in discussing the ideas of this study.

Mrs Diane Kunz read the manuscript and suggested helpful alterations. Dr Rudolf Tschirbs of Bochum kindly sent me two draft chapters of his dissertation. At a critical stage in the preparation of this work, Agnieszka Kołakowska provided friendship and critical comments. The Master and Fellows of Peterhouse, Cambridge and the staff of the Institut für europäische Geschichte in Mainz have put up with me.

I have had invaluable help from the following archivists: Mr Carl Backlund of the Federal Reserve Bank of New York; Mr Richard Gould of the National Archives, Washington DC; Frau Dr Grahn of the Zentrales Staatsarchiv, Potsdam; Herr Bodo Herzog of the Historical Archive of the Gutehoffnungshütte, Oberhausen; Frau Dr Maria Keipert of the Politisches Archiv des Auswärtigen Amtes, Bonn; Mr John Keyworth of the Bank of England; Frau Dr Renate Köhne and Herr Herwig Müther of the archive of the Fried. Krupp GmbH; and Dr Walter Meis of M.M. Warburg, Brinckmann Wirtz & Co., Hamburg. Frau Dr Gerti Meineke and Herr Eric Warburg very kindly put private papers at my disposal.

The British Academy, the British Council, the Deutscher Akademischer Austauschdienst, the German Historical Institute in London, the Master and Fellows of Peterhouse, and the Volkswagen-Stiftung have provided very generous financial help, without which my archival work would have been impossible. Mrs Hazel Dunn typed the work with her usual efficiency and friendliness.

My greatest debt, however, is to my parents.

HJ

Peterhouse, Cambridge
September, 1984

Contents

List of Tables

Abbreviations

ADAP	*Akten zur deutschen auswärtigen Politik 1918–1945:* Documents on German Foreign Policy
ADGB	Allgemeiner Deutscher Gewerkschaftsbund: Socialist Union Federation
AEG	Allgemeine Elektrizitäts-Gesellschaft
Afa-Bund	Allgemeiner freier Angestellten-Bund: Socialist White-Collar Workers' Federation
AfS	*Archiv für Sozialgeschichte*
AG	Aktien-Gesellschaft: Joint-stock Company
AmEcR	*American Economic Review*
AmHR	*American Historical Review*
b.	Billion (10^9)
BAF	Bundesarchiv Militärarchiv Freiburg
BAK	Bundesarchiv Koblenz
BASF	Badische Anilin- und Sodafabrik
BBB	Bayerischer Bauernbund: Bavarian Peasants' League
BdI	Bund der Industriellen: League of Industrialists
BEWAG	Berliner Elektrizitäts-Werke Aktien-Gesellschaft
BHG	Berliner Handelsgesellschaft Kommandit-Gesellschaft auf Aktien
BIS	Bank for International Settlements, Basel
BoE	Bank of England
BStA	Bavarian State Archive, Munich
BVG	Berliner Verkehrs-Gesellschaft: Berlin Transport Authority
BVP	Bayerische Volkspartei: Bavarian People's Party
CDBB	Centralverein des Deutschen Bank- und Bankiergewerbes: Central Association of German Bankers
CdI	Centralverein deutscher Industrieller: Central Association of German Industrialists
CEH	*Central European History*
Compri	Commerz- und Privatbank Aktien-Gesellschaft
DAF	Deutsche Arbeitsfront: German Labour Front
Danat	Darmstädter- und Nationalbank Kommandit-Gesellschaft auf Aktien

DBFP	*Documents on British Foreign Policy*
DDP	Deutsche Demokratische Partei: Democratic Party
DDS	*Documents diplomatiques suisses*: Documents on Swiss Foreign Policy
DeDi	Deutsche Bank und Disconto-Gesellschaft
DGB	Deutscher Gewerkschaftsbund: Catholic Union Federation
DIHT	Deutscher Industrie- und Handelstag: Federation of German Chambers of Industry and Commerce
DINTA	Deutsches Institut für Technische Arbeitsschulung: German Institute for Technical Work Training
DNHV	Deutschnationaler Handlungsgehilfenverband: Association of Nationalist Shop Assistants
DNVP	Deutschnationale Volkspartei: Nationalist Party
DST	Deutscher Städtetag: Association of German Cities
DVP	Deutsche Volkspartei: People's Party
EcHR	*Economic History Review*
EcJ	*Economic Journal*
FAZ	*Frankfurter Allgemeine Zeitung*
FES	Friedrich Ebert Stiftung archive, Bonn
FRBNY	Federal Reserve Bank of New York
FRUS	*Foreign Relations of the United States*
FZ	*Frankfurter Zeitung*
GHH	Gutehoffnunghütte Aktienverein für Bergbau und Hüttenbetrieb, Nürnberg
GG	*Geschichte und Gesellschaft*
GNP	Gross National Product
GWU	*Geschichte in Wissenschaft und Unterricht*
HA/GHH	Historical Archive of Gutehoffnungshütte
HA Krupp	Historical Archive of Fried. Krupp GmbH, Essen
HJ	*Historical Journal*
HPM	High-Powered Money
HZ	*Historische Zeitschrift*
IfZ	Institut für Zeitgeschichte, Munich
IISG	International Institute for Social History, Amsterdam
IRSG	Internationale Rohstahl-Gemeinschaft: International Steel Cartel
JAmH	*Journal of American History*
JEcH	*Journal of Economic History*

JfN	*Jahrbücher für Nationalökonomie*
JNS	*Jahrbücher für Nationalökonomie und Statistik*
JPolEc	*Journal of Political Economy*
KPD	Kommunistische Partei Deutschlands: Communist Party
L	Litre
m.	Million
MAN	Maschinenfabrik Augsburg-Nürnberg Aktien-Gesellschaft, Augsburg
Mefo	Metallurgische Forschungs-Gesellschaft
MFN	Most Favoured Nation
NA	National Archives, Washington DC
NDP	Net Domestic Product
NNP	Net National Product
NSBO	Nationalsozialistische Betriebszellen-Organisation: National Socialist Factory Cell Organisation
NSDAP	Nationalsozialistische Deutsche Arbeiter-Partei: National Socialist Party
NVO	Notverordnung: Emergency Decree
PA/AA	Politisches Archiv des Auswärtigen Amtes, Bonn
Pf	Pfennig
PRO	Public Record Office, London
PrSA	Prussian State Archive, Berlin-Dahlem
RDI	Reichsverband der Deutschen Industrie: Association of German Industry
RFB	Roter Frontkämpferbund: KPD paramilitary organisation
RFM	Reich Finance Ministry
RGBl	*Reichsgesetzblatt*
RGO	Revolutionäre Gewerkschafts-Opposition: Revolutionary Union Opposition
RKG	Reichs-Kredit-Aktien-Gesellschaft, Berlin
RKW	Reichskuratorium für Wirtschaftlichkeit: Reich Organisation for Efficiency
RLB	Reichs-Landbund: Reich Farmers' League
RM	Reichsmark
RNS	Reichsnährstand: German Food Estate
RWiM	Reichswirtschaftsministerium: Reich Economics Ministry
RWiR	Reichswirtschaftsrat: Reich Economic Council
SA	Sturm-Abteilung: Nazi Storm Troopers

SAA	Werner von Siemens Institut für die Geschichte des Hauses Siemens, Munich
s.f.	Swiss Franc
Sofina	Societé Financière de Belgique
SPD	Sozialdemokratische Partei Deutschlands: Socialist Party
SRSU	Siemens-Rheinelbe-Schuckert-Union
StDep	US State Department
t.	(Metric) ton
TWL	Papers of Thomas Lamont, Harvard Business School Library
VDA	Vereinigung der Deutschen Arbeitgeber-Verbände: Union of German Employers' Organisations
VDESI	Verein Deutscher Eisen- und Stahlindustrieller: League of German Iron and Steel Industrialists
VDMA	Verein Deutscher Maschinenbau-Anstalten: Engineering Association
Vestag	Vereinigte Stahlwerke Aktien-Gesellschaft, Düsseldorf
VfZ	*Vierteljahrshefte für Zeitgeschichte*
VSWG	*Vierteljahrschrift für Sozial- und Wirtschaftsgeschichte*
WTB	Woytinsky-Tarnow-Baade Plan
ZStA	Central State Archive, Potsdam

I

Introduction

> Economic analysis deals with the questions how people behave at any time and what the economic effects are they produce by so behaving; economic sociology deals with the question how they came to behave as they do.
>
> (Joseph Alois Schumpeter: *History of Economic Analysis*)

This study examines the causes and outcome of a specific event, the inter-war depression in Germany. The slump marked a major breach in patterns of economic behaviour: 'the question how they came to behave as they do' started to produce a changing answer. The break in behaviour and expectations involved two processes: the politicisation of the economy and the creation of a committedly interventionist state.

We can find this interventionism already in Weimar. Issues of economic policy—employment, prices, wages, and taxes—were highly controversial. They were frequently resolved, not by economic—market—processes, but by political decisions. Then, at the end of the 1920s, the depression was associated with the breaking up of the political order of Weimar democracy. Cause or consequence? The regimes which succeeded Weimar certainly wanted to draw political lessons about the economy from the story of the Republic's collapse. National Socialist Germany made the restoration of full employment a major policy goal: Hitler announced that he was conducting a war for work. After 1945, many thought that the depression had produced the terrible consequence of Nazism. The Federal Republic's politicians came to believe that political stability required policies which would avoid Weimar levels of unemployment. A recession in 1967 coinciding with the rise in the vote of the radical right produced a serious scare in the political establishment; and the Bonn state became even more committed to the policy priorities set out in the 1967 Law on Stability and Growth. For different reasons, then, the Nazi and Bonn states set themselves goals in economic policy which could, they believed, only be achieved by high levels of state activity. In this way the interventionist state was built up as a product of the politicised economy, and of the belief that economic processes both had political effects and could be determined by political action.

The contrast between the years before 1914 (when the state was small) and those after 1945 (when there was a powerful interventionist state) appears very stark: but both eras evinced a remarkable combination of economic growth and a stable social order. When men in the 1920s looked back to the era before the First World War they saw a period of tremendously secure expectations. True, states were imposing higher taxes to pay for increasingly large armaments programmes and also for social reform; and the size of civil services was increasing all over Europe. However, compared with what was to come, tax levels were not high. In Germany there were no federal income taxes; and in the states of the Reich which did impose their own taxation there was no or only very slight progression in the tax schedule. In 1913 the total burden of *all* taxes in Germany amounted to 8per cent of National Income; in 1925 this proportion had risen to 15per cent. Before the War, *rentiers* were able to live well off an income that they could calculate with more or less exactitude: Charles de Gaulle, the greatest of the nostalgics who could not put out of sight or out of mind the lost glories of the old world, called this the *époque du trois pour cent.*[1] Even socialism posed only a very limited threat to the world of bourgeois stability.

After the end of the Second World War, a new kind of stability was created. Economically, this stability depended on government demand-management, a theory which had only been developed fully as a reaction to the stagnation of the inter-war years. Politically and psychologically, it was different from the kind of stability yearned for by General de Gaulle. For it rested on unusually fast rates of growth and change, on a dynamic instability. This new world was the world of Elvis Presley and the Beatles, and no longer that of the Rosenkavalier and Lehar.

[1] C. de Gaulle, *Le Fil de l'épée*, Paris 1944[2], 56.

In between these two periods of stability and growth lay a world of stagnation and doubt, and frequently of pessimism. There were signs that some men wished to take up the challenge to economic organisation made during the world war, and make the economic planning that had emerged as a necessary response to the war into a permanent feature of social existence. Lloyd George (British Prime Minister from December 1916 to October 1922) introduced a 'new collectivism'. Sir E. H. Carson (Minister without Portfolio) warned that 'British industry would be beaten in a stand-up fight against the organised state–aided efforts of Germany' if the British government continued to adhere 'rigidly to the old system of *laissez–faire* and refused to learn the lesson that in modern commerce, as in war, the power of organised combinations pursuing a steady policy will speedily drive out of the field the unregulated competition of private enterprise'.[2] Étienne Clémentel, the French Minister of Commerce, envisaged economic councils charged with the allocation of raw materials and the fixing of prices.[3] The most well developed plans for economic control came, as Carson knew, from Germany: in particular, from Walther Rathenau and Wichard von Moellendorff. Rathenau was a populist philosopher as well as an economic planner: he interspersed his vision of a *dirigiste* future, where luxury consumption would be heavily taxed, with remarks to the effect that 'the meaning of all economic activity is the creation of ideal values'. In the future, the state alone would control investment: 'The citizen will look with proud pleasure at the state's power, wealth and superabundance, and not any longer at his own hoarded riches.' Individual incomes would fall: but the new state would dispose, no longer of millions, but of milliards.[4] On the basis of Rathenau's and Moellendorff's schemes for planning, the newly created Reich Economics Ministry constructed a basis for economic control: it began systematic observations of the

[2] K. O. Morgan, *Consensus and Disunity: The Lloyd George Coalition Government 1918–1922*, Oxford 1971, 19; P. Cline, 'Winding down the War Economy: British Plans for Peacetime Recovery 1916–1919' in (ed.) K. Burk, *War and the State: the Transformation of British Government 1914–1919*, London 1982, 173–4.

[3] M. Trachtenberg, *Reparation in World Politics: France and European Economic Diplomacy 1918–1923*, New York 1980, 1–10.

[4] W. Rathenau, *Von kommenden Dingen*, Berlin 1925², 102 and 115.

labour market, price and wage movements, foreign trade, and credit. One recent writer has described these plans as representing a 'modern economic policy strategy'.[5]

However, the large post-war schemes for economic control collapsed: their progenitors either became powerless or changed their tune. Clémentel was by 1924–5 arguing for deflation in the most orthodox and traditionalist manner: an increase in the quantity of bank notes that the Banque de France was permitted to issue would be a 'crime against the nation'.[6] Lloyd George still continued to advocate original and interesting economic plans (such as schemes for counter-cyclical spending in the depression); but these plans helped to consign him to the political wilderness. Walther Rathenau ended tragically in a pool of blood in his automobile in the Berlin Grunewald.

The problem was that economic planning was unable to cope with the strains imposed by the contraction of national incomes. Planning was introduced in the very unsuitable environment of the post-war economic dislocation. Because the planners appeared to be advocating new ways of distributing a cake (to use one of the favourite economists' analogies) that was substantially smaller than the accustomed one, they took the blame for the smallness of the cake.

The same fate overtook the corporatist compromise which C. S. Maier describes as being created after the war.[7] Social and economic policy was made through the conflicts and interactions of powerful interest blocs (the state, industrial and agrarian interest organisations, and labour unions). Here it will be argued that the failure of the economy discredited not only the corporatist mechanism of resolving conflicts (since it failed to fulfil this object), but also the interest blocs which used it. A machinery and institutions designed to regulate conflict were in the end destroyed by it.

[5] P.-C. Witt, 'Staatliche Wirtschaftspolitik in Deutschland 1918 bis 1923. Entwicklung und Zerstörung einer modernen wirtschaftspolitischen Strategie', in (eds.) G. D. Feldman, C.-L. Holtfrerich, G. A. Ritter, and P.-C. Witt, *Die deutsche Inflation: Eine Zwischenbilanz*, Berlin and New York 1982, 151–79, especially 166–7.

[6] S. Schuker, *The End of French Predominance in Europe: The Financial Crisis of 1924 and the Adoption of the Dawes Plan*, Chapel Hill 1976, 139.

[7] C. S. Maier, *Recasting Bourgeois Europe: Stabilisation in France, Germany and Italy in the Decade after World War I*, Princeton 1975.

Ways of running the economy—whether Manchesterite, state-socialist, planned as 'economic democracy' on socialist principles, or as a corporatist system of economic estates (*Stände*) as advocated by German and Austrian neo-conservatives—were all incapable of producing stability. The result was pessimism about the economy and about the future. Such sentiments were not confined to Germany. In the USA, the world of what had seemed perpetual prosperity in the mid-1920s was succeeded by 'Buddy can you spare a dime?' Declining industrial Britain appeared to have no future. France's disinvestment experience in the 1930s was variously described as 'a vegetating economy' (C. Rist), 'economic malthusianism' (A. Sauvy), 'eating up one's seed grain' (*Le Temps*), and as an unsuccessful and politically motivated attempt to conciliate *rentiers* and peasants.[8] Italy's birth-rate (taken by Mussolini and others as an indicator of the nation's spiritual, economic, and physical virility) took a sharp dip in the 1930s.

The literary picture of late Weimar Germany is gloomy and familiar. Hans Fallada in 'Little Man—What Now?' (1932) showed the petty bourgeois white-collar worker threatened by pauperisation, or what sociologists such as Theodor Geiger called proletarianisation.[9] Erich Kästner set out to prove that in the new post-war world even a decent sex life was impossible ('Fabian', 1932). Alfred Döblin's 'Berlin Alexanderplatz' (1929) gave a picture of a proletariat slipping into criminality.

These gloomy statements came not only from littérateurs disappointed by the shrinking of the reading public's capacity to pay for its pleasure. Business men were pessimistic too. In the autumn of 1930 Paul Reusch, the Director of the Gutehoffnungshütte—a large steel and engineering combine—told Gustav Krupp von Bohlen und Halbach that he expected that the depression would be an extremely long one.[10] Other

[8] F. Caron (trans. B. Bray), *An Economic History of Modern France*, London 1979, 259. A. Sauvy, *Histoire économique de la France entre les deux guerres*, 2, Paris 1967, 268. J. Jackson, 'The Politics of Depression in France 1932–1936', Cambridge Ph.D. 1982, 429.

[9] T. Geiger, *Die soziale Schichtung des deutschen Volkes: Soziographischer Versuch auf statistischer Grundlage*, Stuttgart 1932, 1967.

[10] HA Krupp FAH IV E 1186 18 Oct. 1930 Reusch to Gustav Krupp von Bohlen und Halbach.

commentators believed that the depression would not come to an end until prices had been reduced to the levels of 1913. The leading liberal economic periodical, *Der deutsche Volkswirt*, found that in its Christmas 1931 number it would be wrong to sound a seasonal note:

> Wartime destruction and military orders, blockade and inflation, the destruction of the old states, the creation of new states with new political machineries, technical revolutions in industry and agriculture, social and moral revolutions: new ways of behaving, new sexual morality, new eating habits, new female clothes, a new relationship with nature, new sports: never in economic history have so many sources of disturbance of such profound impact coincided as over the last decade ...[11]

Germany did in fact have a more severe depression at the end of the 1920s than her western neighbours. We can measure this in statistical terms. Industrial production fell to 61 per cent of its 1929 level at the low point of the depression in 1932. By contrast British industrial production at the lowest point (in 1932) was still at 89 per cent of the 1929 level. French production reached a low in 1935 at 71 per cent of the pre-crisis peak. Only in the United States was the slump in industrial output more severe. As output fell, so did profits; bankruptcies increased, and so did unemployment. At the height of the German depression, 30.1 per cent of the workforce was unemployed (the comparable figure for Britain was 22.5 per cent). In France in 1935 only 464 000 were registered as being out of work.[12]

One of the most important consequences of the German depression was a general political radicalisation, as support for the National Socialist and Communist parties—the parties that seemed to offer the most intransigent opposition to the capitalist order—grew. The growth of these parties weakened the political system of the Weimar Republic, and made it possible for Reich President Paul von Hindenburg to call Adolf Hitler to be Reich Chancellor on 30 January 1933. Germany's answer to the slump—National Socialism—was historically unique.

[11] Quoted in T. Stolper, *Gustav Stolper 1888–1947: Ein Leben in Brennpunkten unserer Zeit*, Tübingen 1960, 287.

[12] From B. R. Mitchell, *European Historical Statistics 1750–1970*, London 1978, 67–9 and 180–1.

Elsewhere, it is true, the depression destroyed democracies and produced authoritarian regimes dominated by experts: bankers, financiers, and generals. Economic troubles undermined the Second Republic in Spain; consolidated the military dictatorship of Pilsudski and his successors in Poland; led to the semi-fascist rule of Gombös and Imrédy in Hungary; and turned King Carol's Rumania into a particularly nasty police state. The slump produced upheavals in South America, too: the fall of the popular Irigoyen regime in Argentina and its replacement by the governments of Uriburu and Justu; and the dictatorship of Getulio Vargas in Brazil. These new regimes of the 1930s looked similar to each other and, at least initially, to the Nazi regime in Germany. They depended on an authoritarian approach to political issues, and they relied on technical experts who believed that they were suppressing corrupt democracies. There was, however, a difference: only in Germany were the experts effectively controlled by a populist mass movement which had a considerable talent for mobilisation and political propaganda, and which in the end demanded a high price from the experts in return for suppressing democracy. The old-style technocrats of the army and finance lost out: the careers of General Ludwig Beck and of Dr Hjalmar Schacht demonstrate how this price was exacted.

In Germany the economy of the later 1930s provided a spectacular justification for the Nazi regime. Hitler loved the publicity that surrounded him as he turned the first spadeful of soil in the battle against unemployment. Other dictators fought battles against unemployment too: but they could never claim to be so successful. Mussolini, like Pilsudski, Gombös, Uriburu, Justu, Vargas, Laval, and MacDonald, thought that the key to recovery lay in wage reductions. He never pretended his recipes would provide for higher standards of living. Indeed Mussolini echoed precisely the prevailing Malthusian doctrine: 'We must rid our minds of the idea that what we have called the days of prosperity may return. We are probably moving towards a period when humanity will exist on a lower standard of living.'[13] Hitler would never have recognised this: and the German economic miracle seemed to bear him out.

[13] D. Mack Smith, *Italy: A Modern History*, Ann Arbor 1969², 405.

In Britain in the 1930s unemployment never fell below 11 per cent (1½ million) of the work-force; while in Germany by 1936 only 8 per cent of the work-force was unemployed. By 1939 only 11 900 were registered as being without jobs. GNP in Germany in constant (1913) prices rose from a depression low (42b. RM) to 81b. RM in 1938: almost a doubling within six years.

The extent of the German recovery elicited a great deal of admiration for Nazi mechanisms of economic control. Often the lesson was drawn that Nazi planning showed how unemployment could be banished by the action of the state. Keynes's Cambridge disciple Joan Robinson made the point in a witty way: 'Hitler had already found how to cure unemployment before Keynes had finished explaining why it occurred ... It was a joke in Germany that Hitler was planning to give employment in straightening the Crooked Lake, painting the Black Forest white, and putting down linoleum in the Polish corridor.'[14]

Even such a brief outline at this raises obvious and important questions: why was the German slump so severe? How far were the Nazis really responsible for the economic recovery? These questions are neither unstudied nor uncontroversial. The controversies arise partly because some see in the experience of the 1920s and 1930s lessons to be drawn for economic policy-making, and partly because of the political issues involved. Since the slump was a major cause of the triumph of Nazism, an analysis of the depression is likely to help to identify those ultimately responsible for causing Hitler's seizure of power. (It is probably not possible to draw a rigid distinction between these sources of dispute and controversy. Some parts of economic theory may be uncontentious or unpolitical, but the vision of Keynes, and of many other economic theorists of this period, was neither.)

In the mythology of the left, Hitler was successful because he was financed by big business, which subsequently benefited

[14] J. Robinson, 'What has become of the Keynesian Revolution?', *Challenge* 16, 1974, quoted in G. Garvy, 'Keynes and the Economic Activists of Pre-Hitler Germany, *JPolEc* 83, 1975, 403.

from the type of recovery he engineered.[15] There is another version current[16]—as it were a minority report of the left—that the Nazis were helped into power by big business and then attacked it. Like the young lady from Riga they returned from a ride, inside the tiger. Neither of these stories is plausible: there were a few enthusiastic Nazis among the business community, and a few more gave money to Hitler in order to insure themselves against the possibility of a successful Nazi revolution; most big industrialists, however, were in 1932 still sceptical of the National Socialist programme and wanted to create a new, non-Nazi, bourgeois party of the right, which would not implement an economically radical doctrine.

In place of this story, however, there is a much sophisticated and convincing interpretation (most extensively elaborated by Bernd Weisbrod) of the role of big business in the political events of 1930–3.[17] According to Weisbrod, heavy industry was engaged in an offensive against the Weimar state, which it blamed for wage rises and for the deteriorating economic situation. This offensive involved not only a demand for anti-parliamentary and anti-democratic rule, but also a preparedness to use the depression to achieve a major change in the distribution of power: to defeat the legacy of the 1918–19 revolution, which had brought to Germany democracy and a social welfare state. Heavy industry did not want an economic recovery to take place under the restrictions such a state imposed. Therefore it used its 'veto-power' to make the slump worse, and to obstruct counter-cyclical policies.

Such an interpretation depends on a fundamental analysis of how the economy could be guided. Weisbrod's picture rests on a belief that there *were* ways out of the German depression, and that there were alternatives to the deflationary course actually pursued by governments during the slump: but that since these alternatives depended on increasing wages and also mass consumption they were politically unacceptable to the

[15] The best example is E. Czichon, *Wer verhalf Hitler zur Macht?*, Cologne 1967.

[16] Argued by T. Mason, 'Der Primat der Politik: Politik und Wirtschaft im Nationalsozialismus', *Das Argument* 8, 1966, 473–94.

[17] B. Weisbrod, *Schwerindustrie in der Weimarer Republik: Interessenpolitik zwischen Stabilisierung und Krise*, Wuppertal 1978; and 'Economic Power and Political Stability Reconsidered: Heavy Industry in Weimar Germany', *Social History* 4, 1979, 241–63.

ruling élites of German society and were rejected for that reason. These élites wanted a large share of a small cake rather than a proportionally smaller share of a larger one for non-economic motives. They might have been better off if the expansionary alternatives had been realised, but their relative share of national income, and with it their social power, would have shrunk. In other words, the right blocked Keynesianism, and were only prepared to accept deficit finance dressed up in clothes (specifically in the 1930s military uniforms) which were acceptable to the German élites.

How extensive in fact was the range of weapons in the arsenal of Germany policy-makers? Were political calculations all that stood in the way of implementing recommendations similar to the conclusions of Keynes's *General Theory*—recommendations which would have led to the creation of a very different economic and political scene in Germany?

Our answer to this question will depend on our view of the nature of the German economy during the 1920s. We need to make a thorough diagnosis before we prescribe a hypothetical cure. The range of problems that can be solved by the injection of Keynesian style demand-management is rather limited both historically and geographically. An important prerequisite for this style of cure is basic political stability: failing this, the prescription might actually make the malady worse. Few, for instance, would wish to recommend 'Keynesianism' as an appropriate solution to Brazilian or Polish economic problems in the 1980s. The German economy of the inter-war years was marked by a high degree of instability and low growth rates; in general by an abnormality in relation both to pre-war history and to the experience of other states. Evidence for abnormality can be derived from studies of inter-war cyclical fluctuations; from consideration of the relationship between German experience and that of the world economy; and from an investigation of the characteristics of inter-war growth.

While before the war there were more or less regular cyclical fluctuations, most commentators agree that the experience of the 1920s and 1930s cannot be accounted for by traditional cycle theory. C. T. Schmidt identifies two cycles between the stabilisation of the mark (1924) and Hitler's seizure of power: the first from December 1923 to March 1926; the second from

April 1926 to August 1932 (dated from trough to trough). The first of these cycles was unusually short, the second unusually long (although the most recent survey of nineteenth-century German business cycles detects a periodicity of 7.2–9.1 years). Schmidt concludes that cycle theory alone does not explain the phenomena of inter-war Germany, and that 'an explanation of these unique characteristics affords an illustration of the influence exerted on an economy by a variety of factors, some of which may not be strictly economic in origin'.[18] Such factors, which we shall consider in greater detail later, include the consequences of war and inflation, the effect of American lending, and the rationalisation mania (the application of the scientific techniques of modern American management—Taylorism and Fordism) to German industry. In addition, the dislocation of the labour market and the loss of confidence on the capital market should be mentioned here.

A further peculiarity of inter-war German behaviour was that the cycles of economic life were not closely correlated with those in other countries. In the nineteenth century, there was an increasing similarity between the phases of the business cycle in different states.[19] There were major international crises in 1900–1 and 1907–8. Inter-war Germany, on the other hand, did not follow world experience. The relatively brief but very severe depression of 1921–2 (usually referred to as 'the collapse of the post-war boom') which affected western Europe and the USA occurred while inflation boosted output and employment in Germany. German's two stabilisation crises (in 1922–4 and 1925–6) were shared only by those countries, chiefly in central and eastern Europe, which faced the same problem of overcoming the legacy of hyper-inflation. The great depression of 1929–32 was a world phenomenon. Germany then recovered and hardly at all shared the major international recession of 1937–8.

More evidence of the peculiarity of the inter-war economy might be derived from a comparison of growth rates with the pre-war Reich or with the Federal Republic. Growth from

[18] C. T. Schmidt, *German Business Cycles 1924–1933*, New York 1934, 266–7. J. A. Schumpeter, *Business Cycles* II, London 1939, 766–7. R. Spree, *Wachstumstrends und Konjunkturzyklen in der deutschen Wirtschaft von 1820 bis 1913*, Göttingen 1978, 172.

[19] W. C. Mitchell, *Business Cycles*, Berkeley 1913, 86–7.

1871 to 1913 was at an annual average rate of 2.9per cent, and from 1949 to 1979 at 5.8per cent; but from 1913 to 1938 growth was only at 2.1per cent.[20] This fall in growth rates was not, however, unique to Germany: the slowing down of growth was more dramatic in both France and USA. And in Britain, the inter-war stagnation appears less severe only because of the very poor pre-war performance of the economy.

Explanations of the slump have approached the issue of German abnormality in two ways: some seek to explain why Germany was particularly vulnerable to an economic stagnation whose causes lay in the international economic order; others prefer to identify purely domestic origins of the slump. These types of account need not, of course, be mutually exclusive. But generally, on both a scholarly and a non-scholarly level, the *international* picture of the slump has been so popular that observers have pushed aside the *domestic* account.

There are three kinds of explanation which place primary emphasis on international considerations: they concern the state of technical advance throughout the world; the development of world trade; and the world financial system.

1. Some writers present the inter-war stagnation and depression as a consequence of world levels of technological advance. Either it is argued that there were not enough new innovations to create new jobs, or that the innovations that predominated in the inter-war period were labour-saving, and not labour-consuming. This analysis was very popular with trade unionists in the 1920s: they thought that technical advance in general was desirable because it offered the prospect of increased wages and reduced hours of work, but believed that employers were introducing the wrong technologies. The theory of technological unemployment has been revived recently in the work of G. Mensch.[21] The German and American depressions were particularly severe, in this account, because these economies were highly responsive to technological innovation.

[20] From A. Maddison, 'Phases of Capitalist Development', *Banca Nazionale del Lavoro Quarterly Review* 121, 1977, 129–31.

[21] G. Mensch, *Stalemate in Technology*, Cambridge Mass, 1979. For an inter-war example, see W. Röpke, *Krise und Konjunktur*, Leipzig 1932.

2. Germany, like Britain, was traditionally an economy which had a high dependence on exports. The export quota (exports as a per cent of NNP) fell in Germany from 17.5per cent in 1910–13 to 14.9per cent in 1925–9. This can be explained by the generally unfavourable conditions for international trade in the 1920s. While world manufacturing output had reached its pre-war level by 1922–3, world trade only came to its old level in 1927. European exports only exceeded the 1913 level in 1929.[22] The particularly unfavourable position of the European exporters can be accounted for in this way: falling rates of population growth, and in Europe the demographic losses caused by war and associated dislocations, caused demand for primary products to decline. The terms of trade shifted dramatically after the mid-1920s against primary producers and in favour of producers of manufactured goods. Producers of manufactured goods found it more difficult to sell in their best historical markets, the primary producing economies engaged in importing capital goods in order to build up their own industrial sectors.

Economies dependent on exporting were likely to be vulnerable, and the vulnerability was reflected in declining export quotas. The depression at the end of the 1920s was characterised by a very sharp fall in the volume of world trade as states attempted to isolate their economies by introducing tariff and non-tariff protection.

3. Capital markets during the international depression were highly unstable, and it became very difficult to borrow. Germany suffered because she had become dependent after 1924 on foreign loans; after 1928, when the Wall Street stock boom began, these loans became hard to obtain. The Wall Street crash of October 1929 ended the stock boom in New York, but it did not dispose American investors to resume lending to Germany or central and eastern Europe.

This account can be taken together with the interpretation of the effects of technical change under paragraph 1. to suggest an additional source of weakness. The relative dearness of

[22] W. G. Hoffmann, *Das Wachstum der deutschen Wirtschaft seit der Mitte des 19. Jahrhunderts*, Berlin, Heidelberg, and New York 1965, 151. I. Svennilson, *Growth and Stagnation in the European Economy*, Geneva 1954, 292, 304–5.

capital meant the desirability of substituting the cheaper factor (labour) for the expensive one (capital). This thesis is corroborated by the declining growth rates of labour productivity during the Weimar Republic. However, there were scarcities of labour in important sectors of the economy that made the factor substitution more difficult. The scarcity of capital was made much more damaging by the structure of the labour market, which required the kind of labour-saving technology that the unions believed was being introduced.

The two most widely read and influential accounts of the international depression have been those of W. A. Lewis and C. P. Kindleberger.[23] Both make a great deal out of the international institutional features that limited the room for manoeuvre of German policy: though both Lewis and Kindleberger also offer specific criticisms of German policy in the depression.

Lewis suggests that Germany should have begun a domestic credit expansion after 1928 and 'at the same time, investment could have been cut to the level of what the country was willing to save, and resources diverted instead towards producing exports and substitutes for imports.'[24] But this suggestion can hardly be serious. In the first place the immediate cause of the slump was the drop in investment, and secondly, the overall theme of Lewis's book is that it was difficult to 'produce exports' because of a global imbalance between supply (which had risen as a result of the wartime development of South America, the Far East, and Australia) and demand (which had fallen because of the demographic consequences of war). Fundamentally, Lewis accepts the propositions set out in paragraph 2.

Kindleberger's account fits best into framework 3. He believes that the USA failed to recognise its responsibilities as the major post-war creditor nation: it should have acted the part of lender of last resort, a part that before the war Britain had filled. As a result, the world lacked economic leadership: an economic leader should, but in the inter-war period did not,

[23] W. A. Lewis, *Economic Survey 1919–1939*, London 1949. C. P. Kindleberger, *The World in Depression 1929–1939*, London 1973.

[24] W. A. Lewis, op. cit., 62.

'provide a market for distress goods'; 'stabilize the international flow of capital'; and, finally, 'provide a discount mechanism for crisis'.[25] An examination of Kindleberger's reasoning offers a way of assessing what the German *domestic* weaknesses were: none of the criticisms of US policy is wholly legitimate or convincing. Thus it is true that the USA had high protective tariffs (the 1922 Fordney–McCumber tariff and the 1930 Hawley–Smoot tariff), but the distress goods of the slump would have had to be agricultural products; and the USA, as a major cereal producer and exporter, could not really be expected to have taken them. American protectionism did not in fact affect the fall of primary product prices except in the notorious case of Japanese silk. Europe had not traditionally had a positive balance of trade with the USA, though of the European economies Germany had been the largest pre-war exporter to the USA. German exports did fall in the 1920s, but rather less as a result of 1920s protectionism than as a consequence of wartime confiscation of German chemical patents (Germany's major export to America).

The second of Kindleberger's points has an obvious direct relevance to the German case, since Germany in the 1920s depended very heavily on international capital flows. Yet Temin has recently argued that there were signs of an economic downturn in Germany *before* the American loan market turned hostile.[26] And after the depression had become severe in Germany, there were still a few American houses willing to lend to Europe (in 1930 and 1931): in these years, for instance, Lee Higginson of Boston contemplated a new loan programme for the German Government. However, these houses were less than firm and less than respectable (to continue this example, Lee Higginson collapsed in 1932 after the suicide of Ivar Kreuger and the breakup of Kreuger's match-monopoly cum government-loan business, with which the Boston bank had been closely associated). Most US banks were worried about the extent of their foreign involvement, and bondholders were unwilling to buy new foreign issues. After December 1930, when

[25] C. P. Kindleberger, op. cit., 307.

[26] P. Temin, 'The Beginning of the Depression in Germany', *EcHR* 2nd Ser. 24, 1971, 240–8.

Bolivia failed to meet sinking fund charges, major defaults on loans occurred in South America and Europe;[27] and the US banks were subjected to a very hostile campaign at home. Many thousand bondholders who had taken the advice of Wall Street bankers on investment now believed they had been swindled. They lobbied their Congressmen for stricter bank control, and leading American bankers such as A. Wiggin and W. W. Aldrich of the Chase National Bank, and C. Mitchell of the National City Bank of New York, had to submit themselves to the questioning of a Congressional committee, and even to criminal proceedings.[28]

In these circumstances Wall Street banks and the Washington Government felt that they could not urge Americans to lend to Europe again. They did not feel willing to lend, for sound business reasons: the general feeling was that grave mistakes had been made in the 1920s by American bankers over-eager to hawk loans around the world, who had lent for unproductive purposes and then sold worthless bonds to a trusting public. The bankers shared this attitude too, though naturally they laid the blame elsewhere, with investors who had been too greedy and had thus created opportunities for sharks to operate. In 1930 one New York banker wrote about the world crisis: 'The remedy is for people to stop watching the ticker, listening to the radio, drinking bootleg gin, and dancing to jazz; forget the 'new economics' and prosperity founded upon spending and gambling, and return to the old economics and prosperity based upon saving and working.'[29] This was the moral lesson of the depression: borrowing was sinful. The bankers were right to point out that it would be foolish to lend irrespective of the credit-worthiness of the borrower, and that emergency aid in the depression might be nothing more than an exercise in throwing good money after bad.

The third of Kindleberger's suggestions—emergency discounting—featured quite prominently in discussions on how to solve the depression. The Bank for International Settlements (BIS), which was originally part of the Young reparations plan

[27] C. Lewis, *America's Stake in International Investments*, Washington DC 1938, 399.

[28] 72 Congress: 1 Session: Sale of Foreign Bonds and Securities in the United States.

[29] Lamont Papers, Baker Library Harvard, 103–14, 14 Aug. 1930. R. C. Leffingwell to T. W. Lamont.

of 1929 and which began operations in 1930, was intended by its founders to be capable of offering discount facilities in a crisis. Sir Charles Addis, an eminently sober and respectable English central banker, told an audience of bankers that there was no harm in the BIS administering 'moderate doses of inflation' by discounting generously bills offered to it;[30] and the BIS was widely expected to use its funds to counteract short-term capital movements. The problems lay—as with the consideration of the issue of long term finance—with the Americans, who believed that the BIS's 'moderate doses of inflation' would only help countries to avoid solving their own problems. If the source of the world malaise lay in too much lending, yet more lending—even if it were only short term—would prove very harmful: Europe should reform itself first and then ask for money. As a Federal Reserve Bank memorandum put it, 'great harm would result if activities on behalf of an international bank fostered the idea that gold losses could be rectified from *without* instead of from *within* the country's inner economy'.[31] The debtor countries should bear the strains of adjustment themselves: the Americans believed it impossible that the structural problems they held responsible for the depression—related in part to agricultural overproduction and in part to wasting and misallocation of credit—could be overcome by a rediscount operation. If 'strong leadership' meant throwing dollars around, it would only shelve a fundamental difficulty for the brief moment when people did not realise that dollars were being thrown around.

By the end of the 1920s, there were in fact many voices, both outside and within Germany, who believed that Germany's economic difficulties were her own, and not international ones. Not all these voices were as condemnatory as that of the prominent American banker who stated that the 'Germans are second-rate people'.[32]

What were the German weaknesses?

1. In the first place, an *industrial sector* which had become so highly organised that it was not prepared to face the reality of

[30] *The Times*, 4 April 1930.

[31] FRBNY BIS 797.3 (2) 19 Feb. 1930 L. Galantiere memorandum: 'Germany and the Bank for International Settlements'.

[32] TWL 181–1, 30 Aug. 1929 J. P. Morgan to T. W. Lamont.

the market. A Marxist school of interpretation follows the explanation offered by Eugen Varga in the 1930s: the severe depression in Germany was the consequence of the high degree of capitalist organisation.[33] German heavy industry (coal, and iron and steel) reacted to the depression not by cutting prices but by restricting production while maintaining prices. In this way monopolisation was responsible for a massive fall in output and for making new investment prohibitively expensive.

2. A similar argument has been applied in the case of *agriculture:* here the political monopoly power of the East Elbian cereal farmers plays the role that economic monopoly power fills in the marxist case about industry. The Junkers used their political muscle to impose ever higher levels of agrarian protection in order to keep up cereal prices: this reduced real purchasing power. An increased real purchasing power might have offered a quicker way out of the slump.

3. Already in the 1920s some observers (Adolf Weber and Robert Liefmann, for example) treated *labour unions* as an example of a producers' cartel.[34] Unions made wages in the depression more rigid, in the same way that heavy industrial organisation produced stickier prices. In discussions at the beginning of the 1930s indeed, the cartel and the union problems were frequently treated as parallel issues.

More generally, business men often complained about the high level of wages in the 1920s.[35] This complaint has recently been examined by Knut Borchardt, who argues that one of the major long-run constraints on Weimar economic growth was a perpetual upward pressure on wages.[36] Real hourly wages

[33] E. Varga, *Die Krise des Kapitalismus und ihre politische Folgen*, Frankfurt 1974.

[34] A. Weber, 'Gewerkschaften und Kartelle als Marktverbände', *Jahrbücher für Nationalökonomie* 79, 1931, 704–23. R. Liefmann (trans. D. H. MacGregor), *Cartels, Concerns, and Trusts*, London 1932, 8, 13.

[35] RDI, *Aufstieg oder Niedergang*, Berlin 1929.

[36] K. Borchardt, 'Zwangslagen und Handlungsspielräume in der großen Wirtschaftskrise der frühen dreißiger Jahre: Zur Revision des überlieferten Geschichtsbilds', *Jahrbuch der Bayerischen Akademie der Wissenschaften* 1979, 18. Also T. Balderston, 'The Origins of Economic Instability in Germany 1924–1930: Market Forces versus Economic Policy', *VSWG* 69, 1982, 488–512; and H. H. Glismann, F. Rodemer, and F. Wolter, *Zur Natur der Wachstumsschwäche in der Bundesrepublik Deutschland. Eine empirische Analyse langer Zyklen wirtschaftlicher Entwicklung* (Kieler Diskussionsbeiträge 55) Kiel 1978.

increased relative to productivity with the result that by the end of the 1920s labour in Germany was too expensive in comparison with other countries. This weakened the German export performance by increasing export prices; and increased German imports because of the income effects of the high wage level. The balance of trade difficulty of the late 1920s was thus a product of the labour market. More generally, the rise in costs caused by higher wage levels led to lower profits and reduced investment. In both the Kaiserreich and the Bonn Republic, the relationship between wages and productivity was more favourable, profits were higher, and economic growth more sustained than in Weimar; although after the mid-1960s the Bonn Republic began to experience the kind of wage pressure familiar from Weimar (along with a slowing of growth and higher rates of unemployment).

The rise in the share of National Income taken by labour and its effects on the economy were not purely German but rather general European phenomena. Real wages in Britain per man-hour

> rose more rapidly between 1913 and 1924 than in any other phase before 1960 ... The extreme labour militancy of 1919 that brought this about was the British counterpart of the unrest that had caused revolution in Russia and soon came near to causing it in Germany. There was thus a large shift in the distribution of income toward labour, a shift only partly reversed later in the inter-war period ... the rise in labour costs immediately after World War I probably did play some independent part in reducing profitability and employment in the following years.[37]

In France, the proportion of National Income paid in wages and salaries increased from below 45per cent before 1914 to around 50per cent in the early 1920s.[38] Generally low investment rates followed from the changed income structure of Europe—including Russia, where the low investment rates were only increased at the end of the 1920s by a massive redirection of resources, associated with wage control that pushed down the share of National Income taken by labour

[37] R. C. Matthews, C. H. Feinstein, and J. C. Odling-Smee, *British Economic Growth 1856–1973*, Oxford 1982, 314–15.

[38] S. Schuker 1976, 71.

(this process was known euphemistically as 'primitive socialist accumulation').

Though labour conflicts were of great political importance in Europe outside Russia, the strengthening of labour need not be explained in purely political terms. The operations of the labour market alone might have produced a similar result (though an assumption that the labour market works exclusively apolitically, particularly in such times of dramatic social upheaval as after the First World War is bizarrely ahistorical). The War had resulted in the deaths of 1.6 million Germans. Four million were wounded, and many of these were left disabled, and fit, if at all, only for light work. Before 1914 and after the Second World War, on the other hand, labour had been relatively abundant. In the nineteenth century there was substantial population movement from eastern Germany to the new industrial centres (or, if industry was not growing fast enough to absorb these rural emigrants, to North America). After 1945, the labour supply in the Federal Republic was fuelled by refugees: at first from the areas in the east lost by Germany at Potsdam, and then, in the 1950s, from the German Democratic Republic (East Germany). So, rather paradoxically, it appeared that a labour scarcity in Weimar Germany led, because of its effects on wage demands, to greater unemployment than Germany had ever known.

4. Employers complained about *taxes and social contributions* almost as bitterly as about wage levels. High tax levels, if not used to finance state investment, would have the same depressing effects on profits as high wage levels. This was one of the reasons also given by Americans for not wanting to lend to Germany at the end of the 1920s: Germany had since 1918 been run by socialists or by people who wanted to buy off discontent by state handouts. This resulted in a gigantic Tammany Hall: 'they put coal in the German Mrs Murphy's cellar by furnishing social aid out of the budget and in addition providing jobs in the government for Mrs Murphy's boys. All this made Germany the most highly taxed nation in the world.'[39] Though this statement exaggerates, it contains an element of truth, for political careers in Germany in the 1920s

[39] FRBNY German Govt. 9 June 1932 L. Galantiere memorandum.

were made by high spending. The most profligate of German mayors (Oberbürgermeister) was Konrad Adenauer of Cologne, whose story illustrates the political gains to be made out of open-handed municipal administration. Taxes for central state expenditure had also risen since the pre-war days; although this was a necessary consequence in part of the reparations bills imposed on Germany, and in part of the expensive social costs resulting from the war.

5. Four major domestic circumstances—the structure of industry, the strength of the unions, the political power of the cereal farmers, and the pressure to increase taxes—may, then, have limited the growth of the German economy. In addition, German nationalists believed that the depression resulted from *reparations*—from the 'tribute payments of Versailles'. One of the few points that employers and trade unions were able to agree over was the intolerable nature of the reparations settlement. They were supported in the protests by the grim prognostications of catastrophe in J. M. Keynes's polemic of 1919, *The Economic Consequences of the Peace*.[40]

Most recent commentators have been less sympathetic to German protests or to Keynes than to Keynes's critic, Étienne Mantoux, who in *The Carthaginian Peace or the Economic Consequences of Mr Keynes* described how trivial was the sum Germany had in fact paid by the time that the 1932 Lausanne Conference effectively ended reparation payments.[41] Lüke, Bennett, Marks, and Schuker believe that the significance of reparations was more psychological than real.[42] However, for a brief moment at the end of the 1920s payments amounted to over 3per cent of GNP (or 7per cent of the German tax bill)—a not insubstantial sum. Fears of future levels of payment may also have had an inhibiting effect on investment decisions: though the Young Plan reduced the reparations annuity in 1930 from 2500m. Gold Marks (in addition to a supplementary sum to be determined in relation to a 'prosperity index') to 2050m.

[40] J. M. Keynes, *The Economic Consequences of the Peace*, London 1919.

[41] É. Mantoux, *The Carthaginian Peace or the Economic Consequences of Mr. Keynes*, London 1946.

[42] R. E. Lüke, *Von der Stabilisierung zur Krise*, Zürich 1958. E. W. Bennett, *Germany and the Diplomacy of the Financial Crisis of 1931*, Cambridge Mass. 1962. S. Marks, 'Reparations Reconsidered: a Reminder', *CEH* 2, 1969, 356–65.

Marks, this was in the middle of a world deflation, in which there seemed to be no end to the fall in prices and to the rise in the value of gold. Many economists, notably the Swede Gustav Cassel, believed that the rise in the gold value was likely to be permanent, as the growth of world output would continually outstrip increases in world gold production.[43] Measured in terms of goods, a Young annuity in 1932 was worth more than a Dawes annuity in 1929.

In addition there was the 'transfer problem'. Reparation payments strained the German budget; but also meant a perpetual outflow of capital from Germany. Since one of the problems of the late 1920s and early 1930s was the growth of protectionism and the stagnation of world trade, it became more and more difficult to export in order to make the transfer of Marks into foreign currency for the reparations account. In 1929, reparation payments accounted for 17 per cent of the total value of German exports, in 1930 14 per cent, and in 1931 10 per cent.[44] The argument often made—that Germany could borrow in order to pay reparations and that the German Government was in effect trying to avoid making serious payment—ignores both the fact that the German Government did not itself borrow very much directly, and the difficulties of the international capital market in the later 1920s (which made the transfer problem so precarious). There was no simple circular flow in which US banks and individuals lent to Germany, which paid reparations to Britain and France, who repaid their wartime debt to the USA, whose government could thus cut the US tax bill and allow its citizens a higher disposable income, which they could lend to Germany etc. For, firstly, American lenders were not *committed* to continue supplying funds, and the net inflow into Germany could be reversed (as it was after 1930) to become a net outflow. Secondly, the main borrowers in Germany were business and local government: the fact that foreign loans provided foreign exchange does not mean that the central (Reich) government did not have substantial difficulties in taxing business or in restricting

[43] G. Cassel, *Die Krise im Weltgeldsystem*, Berlin-Charlottenburg 1933, 23–4.

[44] Calculated from *Die deutsche Zahlungsbilanz der Jahre 1924–1933*, Berlin 1934 (Wirtschaft und Statistik Sonderheft 14), 10–11.

local government expenditure so that the Reich could indeed be in a position to make payments to the Allies.

An analysis of the difficulties caused by reparation payments thus turns out to hinge on the issues already raised: the slow growth of world trade in the 1920s, and the tax burden in Germany. This work examines in turn five aspects of this complex of problems:

1. How prepared were taxpayers to face increases in their burdens? During this century, the state's share of National Income has increased everywhere. Such an increase reflects a new understanding of the roles that the state should be prepared to undertake, but also a willingness on the part of citizens to bear a burden in order to allow the state to perform them. In Germany in the 1920s there appeared to be no such consensus: the only political consensus that could be achieved after 1924 was based on tax reduction, not tax increases. Such considerations placed very narrow limits on state fiscal policy.

2. Why and how did German industrial organisation evolve, and what were the effects of such organisation on the German economy?

3. What effect did the wage push of the late 1920s have on the economic structure of Germany, and what political responses did it evoke?

4. How was German agriculture able to exercise such an influence on the political process as to be able to keep up agricultural prices during the depression? How did the agricultrual sector affect the overall economy?

5. The financial and banking system was highly unstable in the 1920s; and the extent of this instability contributed greatly to the severity of the depression. How far were political calculations responsible for the increase in instability?

All these questions relate to the economic sociology of the slump. In addition to explaining the causes of the slump they help the historian to assess the responses to the depression. Those responses are the subject of the second half of this study. We have described a growing politicisation of the economy: but what kind of politicisation, and what sort of politics? Partly in order to balance the heavily analytical nature of this study, but principally to provide a context for the discussion of public finance, industrial organisation, labour politics, agriculture, and banking, the work begins with a simple chronological sketch of the political development of Weimar Germany.

II

The Political Development of Weimar Germany

Messianic hopes are the counterpart of the sense of despair and impotence that overcomes mankind at the sight of his own failures.

(Leszek Kołakowski, *Main Currents of Marxism*)

The Bismarckian Empire collapsed in 1918 as a consequence of military defeat. In August, First Quarter-Master General Erich Ludendorff told Field Marshal von Hindenburg and the Reich Chancellor, an elderly and colourless Bavarian politician, Count Hertling, that an immediate armistice was needed and that the Allies would be more sympathetic to the request of a representative than of an autocratic government. In this way the Reichstag opposition parties were pushed into office by the military leadership of Imperial Germany. In October labour unrest, which had flared up in April 1917 and January 1918, began again: this time the strikes had a very powerful political motivation, and the strikers called for the end of the monarchy and the creation of a republic. By the beginning of November there was a naval mutiny and the defeated army also began to disintegrate. The army leaders thought that they could no longer maintain discipline in a monarchy, and told the Kaiser to abdicate. He did.

The Republic was proclaimed in two different ways within the space of a few hours on 9 November. From the Reichstag building Philip Scheidemann, a member of the majority SPD, declared a republic under the leadership of the socialist Friedrich Ebert, who had already been appointed as the last Imperial Chancellor. The left-wing socialist Karl Liebknecht announced the creation of a socialist republic from the balcony of the Imperial Palace. In the struggle between the two concepts of the new republic's form, Ebert's won: partly because he had the support of the new Army Supreme Command. General Wilhelm Groener, Ludendorff's successor as Quarter-Master General, who during the War had established a reputation for being able to collaborate with labour unions, placed the army at Ebert's disposal in order to fight Bolshevism: in other words, the Liebknecht movement. In January 1919 the alliance established by the Groener–Ebert telephone call on 9 November was baptised with blood when the Reichswehr put down an attempted revolution staged by the new Communist Party (KPD) under Liebknecht and Rosa Luxemburg.

Elections to a National Assembly (19 January 1919) produced an overwhelming majority for the opposition parties of the Kaiserreich, who had been so abruptly forced into office. The coalition of opposition parties (left liberals, who now formed the Democratic Party, DDP; the Catholic Zentrum or Centre; and the SPD) met in Weimar because Berlin was still unsafe and drew up a constitution, chose a President (Ebert) and ruled, as the 'Weimar coalition', in a government which lasted until March 1920. In that month a military *putsch* under Generallandschaftsdirektor Kapp drove the Reich Government away from Berlin and failed to establish control over Germany only because of a more or less general strike for the Republic. The Kapp *putsch* helped to make many working class Germans feels that they were the real defenders of the Republic; and then that they were betrayed by the republican regime which used the same Reichswehr that had staged the *putsch* to put down strikes that went on too long.

The immediate political consequence of the Kapp *putsch* was the replacement of the discredited Chancellor, Gustav Bauer, who appeared to have lost his nerve when the Reich Government fled to Stuttgart, by another socialist, Hermann Müller. Müller called new elections in order to demonstrate the legitimacy of the Weimar order. After 1920 no Weimar Reichstag came to a natural end as foreseen by the constitution (which provided for elections every four years): all either were dissolved or dissolved themselves prematurely. The outcome of 1920 was a slap in the face for Müller (in subsequent elections, too, the ruling coalition almost invariably did badly). The SPD's vote fell from 37.9 per cent to 21.6 per cent; the DDP's from 18.6 per cent to 8.3 per cent; and the Centre's from 19.7

per cent to 13.6 per cent. The victors of 1920 were the independent (left) socialists; the People's Party DVP (the right-wing liberal party of Gustav Stresemann, a pre-war liberal and wartime annexationist, who had earned himself the reputation of being 'Ludendorff's young man'), which increased its vote from 4.4 per cent to 13.9 per cent; and the Conservative Nationalist DNVP which went from 10.3 per cent to 14.9 per cent.

The Kapp *putsch*, the strikes, the formation of the proletarian brigades in the Ruhr and in Saxony, and the Reichstag elections took place in an apparently deflationary interlude in the long German wartime and post-war inflation. From February 1920 the Mark was rising against the dollar, and prices in Germany were falling (as they were elsewhere in the world, as the post-war boom collapsed). In part these economic developments in Germany were the consequence simply of a world deflation imported into Germany; but in part they followed too from the attempts of Matthias Erzberger, Reich Finance Minister in the Bauer administration, to decrease the size of budget deficits by an overhaul of the tax system. The threat of deflation helped to radicalise industrialists and push them against the Reich Government and against the labour movement (hence some business support for the radical right Kapp *putsch*). Deflation also looked like putting an end to the wage increases of 1919, and provided a ground for labour to defend the Republic against the Kapp rebels: they wanted the Republic to continue increasing wages and improving social conditions. 1920 provided a clear lesson for future governments: that a stabilisation of the currency, or an importation of a world deflation, or an end to the German inflation, was likely to produce class war and destabilise the Republic: and should in consequence be avoided for as long as possible.

After the 1920 elections, the SPD left office and a centre–right coalition including DVP ministers came in under the conservative Catholic politician Constantin Fehrenbach. Fehrenbach gave up serious attempts to balance the budget; but the budget problem only became really acute after the Allies presented a reparations ultimatum (5 May 1921). Fehrenbach's majority then collapsed and the Weimar coalition was set up once more with SPD ministers and a left-centre Chancellor, Joseph Wirth. Wirth and his Foreign Minister Walther Rathenau paid reparations while trying to revise the settlement. The right of the Centre party wanted to take the DVP back into government as the SPD appeared to have too powerful a place within the Wirth coalition, and used the nationalist agitation against reparations as a way of attacking Wirth and Rathenau. Rathenau was assassinated on 22 June 1922. In November 1922 Wirth resigned and Wilhelm Cuno led a rather right-wing Cabinet, which, in the jargon of the time, was called apolitical. Cuno was a Hamburg businessman; the new Foreign Minister von Rosenberg was a career civil servant from the Foreign Office and a former Ambassador; General Groener stayed on in the Transport Ministry; and the Agriculture Minister, Hans Luther, was a professional mayor and not a member of any political party. In January 1923 Cuno's more aggressive foreign policy produced a French occupation of the Ruhr; enormous government budget deficits followed from Germany's attempts to pay those who resisted French military rule; and the hyperinflation, which had already begun in the summer of 1922, accelerated. Cuno's Government collapsed when further resistance on the Ruhr looked impossible. By the middle of 1923, inflation had lost its justification as a political and economic stabiliser. Unemployment rose as the indexation of wages became common practice. Red armies flourished again in Thuringia and Saxony, and in Bavaria 'patriotic associations' planned to use Bavaria as the starting point for a national revolution (which eventually became the fiasco of the Hitler–Ludendorff *putsch* in Munich on 8–9 November). Stresemann formed a Cabinet with the goal of stopping inflation, ending Ruhr resistance, and restoring order. For the first time the SPD and the DVP joined together in a coalition (the Great Coalition).

A key appointment by Stresemann had major repercussions later: the discredited President of the Reichsbank, which had supplied the monetary policy which allowed the inflation to continue, died on 20 November. Havenstein's successor was the DDP banker Hjalmar Schacht rather than the Nationalist Karl Helfferich. Schacht was well regarded in Britain and the USA, and the terms of the 1924 reparations settlement gave the Reichsbank a tremendous power in German affairs. Its independence politically was guaranteed under the terms of the international treaties of 1924.

The full Great Coalition lasted only just over a month, though the Cabinet continued briefly as a centre–right coalition; this became a conventional centre–right alliance at the end of November when Wilhelm Marx (Centre) became Chancellor. In both the second Stresemann and in the Marx administration, the key figure was Hans Luther, the apolitical Finance Minister, now charged with introducing a new currency and producing a budget programme that would avoid a new inflation. Stresemann stayed on under Marx as Foreign Minister; he remained in this post until his death on 3 October 1929. Marx and Luther imposed very heavy taxes and cut back the civil service in order to stabilise public finances. In spring 1924 the Reichstag was dissolved after it voted against the Marx–Luther decrees; in the new Reichstag the Weimar coalition and the DVP had fewer seats. In May, as in a new round of elections called in December, the principal victor was the DNVP, which in May won 5.7m. votes (1920=4.3m.) and in December 6.2m. The smaller parties of the radical right also did well, particularly in May.

During the inflation period, governments had been unstable and short-lived. As a general pattern, the SPD was prepared to take responsibility for foreign policy decisions that were unavoidable but which required the sacrifice of what had been traditionally understood as Germany's national interests: signing the Versailles Peace Treaty, complying with the London reparations ultimatum, and ending the Ruhr conflict. On domestic policy, the right of the Centre disliked working with the SPD and tried to win the DVP as a coalition partner. After 1923 the situation changed. Under Stresemann the DVP took a responsible but mildly revisionist line in foreign affairs: unravelling the territorial settlement of Versailles, it now recognised, would take time.

Between 1924 and 1928 the central issue in politics was no longer whether the SPD should take part in Weimar government, but whether the newly strengthened DNVP should. The DNVP's calculation amounted to a mirror image of the SPD's: the SPD had seen international realism as a *sine qua non* for a stable German domestic political situation in which it could implement its own proposals. The DNVP was reluctant to take responsibility for foreign policy matters and distrusted Stresemann; but it saw major benefits to be derived from being in office. It could work with the right liberals to implement the pro-business tax programme that it wanted, and could use its control of ministries such as Economics and Agriculture to extract benefits from the government for its political constituency. One Reichstag deputy wrote to the DNVP chairman in 1924: 'The Republic is beginning to stabilise itself, and the German people is beginning to accept what has happened. We cannot hesitate longer ... If we want to preserve the party as an influential and powerful movement of the right, we must now take over power in the state.'[1] For the DNVP the difficulty was that a foreign political stabilisation, which would eventually bring badly needed American money into Germany, was a prerequisite for the sort of economic programme the DNVP's backers wanted.

In 1924 some German Nationalists were even prepared on these grounds to make the sacrifice of voting for the reparations plan drawn up by the Dawes Committee and accepted at the London Conference. The party joined the Government in January 1925 (under the new Chancellor, Hans Luther), but left after Luther and Stresemann produced a security pact (Locarno) guaranteeing Germany's western frontier under the terms of Versailles and thus accepting the loss of Alsace-Lorraine. In the same year, 1925, on the death of Ebert, Field Marshal Paul von Hindenburg was elected as Reich President. The election was widely read—as was the DNVP's participation in government—as a declaration that the old order was prepared to come to terms with the new Republic.

After January 1926, the smaller right–centre coalition without the DNVP ruled: first under Luther, then again under Marx. In January 1927 the DNVP was even prepared to come back again (in the fourth Marx Cabinet). There were now DNVP Interior, Agriculture, and Transport Ministers. The way in which Marx and Luther dealt with the very severe recession of 1925–6, when unemployment rose to a peak of

[1] 22 Sept. 1924 von Lindeiner-Wildau to Count Westarp, quoted in A. Thimme, *Stresemann und die Deutsche Volkspartei*, Lübeck 1961, 89.

2.06m. (February 1926), indicated that the worries of the inflation period were over, since the Republic in its right-wing (*Bürgerblock*) version was capable of surviving and dealing with economic squalls. The *Bürgerblock*'s method was to run budget deficits; but this method contained the explosive that eventually blew the *Bürgerblock* apart. The coalition disintegrated apparently because of a dispute between the Centre and the DVP about a school law allowing multi-denominational education (in so-called *Simultanschulen*); but in fact because of the increasing resentment of the working-class left wing of the confessional Centre against the social and economic policies of the *Bürgerblock*. The left of the Centre disliked the 1927 decision to put up civil service salaries, the hand-outs made at the same time to large industrialists, and the attempts of the right-wing Economics Minister Julius Curtius, to block the transition in early 1928 from a two-shift to a three-shift system in parts of heavy industry (in other words, partially to restore the eight-hour day introduced in 1918). In February 1928 the coalition broke up.

In the March elections, the SPD's share of the vote increased to 29.8 per cent (December 1924 26.0 per cent). This looked to the party like the reward for being in opposition for four years. Marx resigned and a government of the Great Coalition under the Chancellorship of Hermann Müller took his place. Müller's Cabinet dealt with the revision of the reparations settlement: at a Conference of Experts meeting in Paris in April 1929 an annuity of 2050m. RM to be paid over 58 years was agreed. The settlement was bitterly criticised by the Nationalists, who under their new leader Alfred Hugenberg had jerked to the right, and who now backed a plebiscite against the 'enserfment' of the Young Plan. During the Experts' Conference, too, one of the German delegates, the heavy industrialist Albert Vögler, resigned from the conference in protest.

The Müller Government also had to deal with an agrarian depression, which had produced considerable rural unrest in late 1927 and early 1928, and with the beginnings of the industrial depression. Share prices had fallen since May 1927. Output of the textile industry, leather and shoes, iron, and building industries fell in 1928. There was a partial recovery in 1929, which was particularly pronounced in heavy industry.

But from 1928 levels of unemployment rose; and the issue that led immediately to the collapse of the Great Coalition was whether rates of contribution by employers and employees to the unemployment insurance scheme should be raised. Behind this dispute lay a deeper division about financial, and particularly about taxation, policy. The Government was under substantial pressure from industry and from the DVP to do what Luther had done to fight the depression in 1925–6 and reduce taxes; but this path seemed ruled out by rising budget deficits, and the more and more violent attacks on the Government by Schacht, who used the existence of deficits as a lever to impose his will on the regime. A first dent in the coalition was made in December 1929 when Schacht published a ferociously critical memorandum which attacked not only the reparations settlement but also the whole conduct of public finance. He forced through the Reichstag legislation limiting government deficits; and the SPD Finance Minister Rudolf Hilferding and the State Secretary in the Reich Finance Ministry, Johannes Popitz, had little choice but to resign.

Müller's successor, Heinrich Brüning (Chancellor March 1930 to May 1932) at first tried to work with Reichstag parties; but essentially his power base lay outside the Reichstag. It lay in the person and confidence of Hindenburg. In the politically difficult winter of 1929–30 the President had been in constant touch with General Groener, and with the ambitious and scheming head of the Ministeramt of the Reichswehr Ministry, General Kurt von Schleicher. These soldiers evolved a strategy for presidential rule, using those emergency provisions of the Weimar constitution which had already been employed extensively by Ebert in the crisis of 1923–4. Brüning, the leader of the Centre Party, was at first reluctant to knife Müller in the back; but he was personally devoted to Hindenburg, whom he revered as a father. So the Centre Chancellor built up a new Cabinet, at first composed of politicians (the veteran Wirth became Interior Minister; Paul Moldenhauer, DVP, was Finance Minister; Hermann Dietrich, DDP, was Economics Minister; and Adam Stegerwald, a Centre trade unionist, was Labour Minister) as well as Groener, who stayed on as Reichswehr Minister from the Müller Cabinet.

On 16 July 1930 the SPD, DNVP, and DVP voted with the

extreme opposition parties NSDAP and KPD against the Brüning administration's financial austerity plans. Brüning then tried to impose the programme by decree in accordance with the methods of presidential rule. The Reichstag majority voted against the decree and Brüning then dissolved the Reichstag. New elections on 14 September produced increases in the KPD vote (from 3.3m. in 1928 to 4.6m.) and above all in that of Hitler's NSDAP (from 810 000 to 6.4m.), whose dramatic rise astonished the political establishment. The Nazis had done well in 1929 and 1930 in Landtag (provincial parliaments) elections in Thuringia and Brunswick, but the scale of the shift to the radical right in 1930 was surprising and terrifying. Literally overnight, the Nazis had become a major political force.

In previous phases of Weimar's political development, the question had been whether the SPD or later the DNVP could be brought into a coalition with the 'bourgeois parties' of the middle: DDP, DVP, and Centre. The September 1930 election created a situation where the inclusion of the NSDAP in government looked, in political arithmetic, the obvious manoeuvre. On 6 October Brüning and his lieutenant Gottfried Treviranus did indeed meet Hitler and two other prominent Nazis, Wilhelm Frick, Minister of the Interior in Thuringia, and Gregor Strasser, the Organisation and Propaganda director of the NSDAP. Though Brüning was appalled by Hitler's hysteria, he did try again one year later (a meeting took place on 10 October 1931) to revive the idea of a Nazi–Centre coalition, but again failed. In consequence the only parties consistently loyal to the Brüning course were the DDP (renamed as the Staatspartei), the Centre (Brüning's own party), the Bavarian People's Party, and a small Treviranus party. These did not represent a Reichstag majority, and Brüning needed to woo DVP support (his Cabinet included DVP ministers) and also that of the SPD. SPD leaders frequently met Brüning, and agreed to 'tolerate' the Chancellor's rule as they feared that his successor might be Hitler. This 'toleration policy' helped to erode further the SPD's electoral support.

More and more the Brüning Cabinet became a cabinet of 'experts' as it moved away from politicians and parties and parliaments. The Justice Minister, Johann Viktor Bredt (from the small Economic Party) left the Government in December 1930 in protest against the austerity decrees, and was replaced on an interim basis by the Permanent State Secretary Curt Joël. Hermann Dietrich moved over to the Finance Ministry after the DVP had demanded the resignation of Moldenhauer because of the latter's budget programme (June 1930), though the Finance Ministry was run in effect by its State Secretary Hans Schäffer. The Economics Ministry remained after Dietrich's departure under the sole control of a State Secretary, Ernst Trendelenburg. The Reich Chancellery and the Foreign Office (Auswärtiges Amt) had powerful State Secretaries too: Hermann Pünder and Bernhard von Bülow. Bülow's power increased in October 1931 when Brüning took over the Auswärtiges Amt in addition to the Chancellorship. These five men—Joël, Schäffer, Trendelenburg, Pünder, and von Bülow—set the tone of the Brüning regime, which looked ever more like a successful version of Cuno's 'apolitical' Cabinet. The most prominent 'apolitication' of all, Hans Luther, completed the picture: he came into the strategically vital post of Reichsbank President after Schacht had finally resigned over the Young Plan (this had solved a great headache for the Reich Government: the Reichsbank President could not in law be dismissed).

Brüning ruled while the depression grew more severe. He responded with a series of austerity decrees: 1 December 1930, 5 June 1931, 6 October 1931, and 8 December 1931. (A further decree of 24 August 1931, the Dietramszeller decree, imposed austerity on the federal states.) These decrees increased tax rates (particularly on indirect taxes), and cut state welfare benefits and civil service pay (details in Chapter III). The Fourth Decree, of 8 December 1931, also tried to impose a *general* deflation on the German economy by decreeing simultaneous cuts in fixed prices (cartellised prices or where there were retail price agreements), wages, and interest rates (see Chapter VI).

Brüning also believed that he could help to solve the German economic problem by tackling reparations again: the 5 June 1931 decree was accompanied by a statement, directed at the Allies, that 'the limits of the privations we have imposed on our people have been reached'. Unfortunately this Emergency Decree and the negotiations in Chequers that followed it were overshadowed by an international financial crisis. The crisis was not ended by the declaration by President Hoover (20 June 1931) of a one year moratorium on all reparation and inter-allied debt payments. On 13 July a major German bank collapsed. Foreign credits were frozen in Germany. The financial crisis spread wider, and led to a government crisis in Britain and then to the devaluation of sterling (September 21). By the end of the year the US dollar was suffering from the jitters. This panic atmosphere did in the end help the Germans to rid themselves of the burden of reparations. When a new centre-left government resulted from the elections to the French Chamber of May 1932, the West European states were prepared in effect to cancel reparations. This is what occurred at the Lausanne Conference (July 1932).

For Brüning, though, it was too late. He fell in his famous phrase of May 1932 'one hundred metres from the goal': before the depression was over and before reparations were cancelled. He had lost the confidence of Hindenburg principally, because as a loyal servant, he had engineered Hindenburg's re-election as Reich President, but with the wrong (of the left rather than the right) majority. Brüning was followed by Franz von Papen, who had virtually no support in the Reichstag. Papen was a Centre deputy, but had to leave the party once he had overthrown Brüning. Then he dissolved the Reichstag in the hope of getting a more sympathetic result and rallying the right around the President, but the July 1932 elections produced a massive NSDAP vote (37.4 per cent of the votes or 13.7m.); and Papen was less able than Brüning to bring the Nazis into government. On 13 August Hindenburg summoned Hitler but then refused to appoint him as Chancellor: for it was only on this condition that Hitler was prepared to move into office. In September the new Reichstag met and voted for a KPD motion of no confidence in the Government before Papen was able to dissolve the Chamber (he tried to dissolve it before the vote was taken, but the President of the Reichstag, traditionally a member of the largest Reichstag party, was Hermann Göring, who simply ignored the practically hysterical Chancellor). New elections (6 November) produced a fall in the Nazi vote by 2 million, and a rise in the KPD and DNVP votes, but did not solve the political problem. On 23 November Hitler reaffirmed his opposition, despite his loss of support, to a coalition which he did not lead. At the same time a non-Nazi coalition was impossible, for the Nazis and the Communists together had over half the seats in the Reichstag.

In December 1932 Schleicher became Chancellor because he told Hindenburg that Papen's Chancellorship meant civil war and that the Reichswehr, restricted in size by the Versailles Treaty, was incapable of fighting at the same time the KPD and the NSDAP, which both had formidable armed organisations. Schleicher has often been depicted as a political general. He was not. Rather he was a back-room boy who was good at throwing spanners into other people's works. When he was in power he was very embarrassed and could only think of putting together a wholly illogical coalition which could only ever exist on paper. He followed the old army tradition of General Groener in the First World War by calling in trade unionists; he also wanted to work with Gregor Strasser, whom he knew to be hostile to Hitler's anti-coalition stance and whom he believed he could lure away from Hitler. Neither Strasser not the unionists were willing to play this armchair politician's game.

At the end of January 1933 the political crisis was at last resolved by the agreement of Papen and the DNVP leader Hugenberg to accept Hitler's terms. The NSDAP coalition at last existed. Hitler was to be Chancellor, there was a Nazi Interior Minister (Wilhelm Frick), and Hermann Göring was appointed as Minister without Portfolio. None of the other ministers was a Nazi, and Papen was to be Vice-Chancellor. In the years since 1930 this was the political action that came closest to being in accordance with the operating rules of a parliamentary system. Together the DNVP and NSDAP did not, it is true, have a Reichstag majority; but they were not far away from one, and they might reasonably expect new elections to improve their position. Presidential intrigues had led in turn to the creation of the Brüning, Papen, and Schleicher Cabinets. Only in January 1933 was Hindenburg prepared to swallow the proud contempt of an aristocratic Prussian for the

'Bohemian corporal' and let democracy work to produce what might be a government with majority support. When in the depression German parliamentarism worked, it produced Hitler.

The next stage in the creation of the Nazi state was essentially a product of the Nazi revolution on the streets, of the application of terror directed primarily against the left but which also frightened the old order so much that it was prepared to make larger concessions to Hitler than those of January 1933. At the election of 5 March 1933, the NSDAP still had no absolute majority even in the Reichstag; but after the election the Reich used force against those Land governments not yet under Nazi control (7 April: Law on the Gleichschaltung of the Länder). Such steps had become possible after the parties, with the exception of the SPD, on 23 March voted an Enabling Law transferring legislative power from the Reichstag to the Reich Government (the communist deputies elected on 5 March were never allowed to take their seats in the new Reichstag). On 2 May non-Nazi trade unions were dissolved; on 23 June the SPD was declared to be a party hostile to the German people and Reich, was dissolved, and its property confiscated. The Staatspartei was also dissolved; the DVP had agreed to end its existence on 29 March; the DNVP collapsed after a catastrophic performance by its leader Alfred Hugenberg at the London World Economic Conference. Finally, on 6 July the Centre party came to an end. It had been, with the SPD, the most stable Weimar party in terms of electoral support; but since March deputies moved out of its Reichstag Fraktion and went over to the NSDAP. Brüning's verdict on the decision of the party executive to dissolve the Centre: 'I was in the end prepared to draw the consequences of the situation and dissolve the party.'[2] There seemed a terrible inevitability: as during Brüning's period of office as Reich Chancellor there was the belief, 'There Is No Alternative'.

A chronology of this kind leaves many unanswered questions: was Brüning right in describing the iron inexorability of affairs? In the first place, there were constraints imposed by Weimar's political framework. What calculations influenced

[2] H. Brüning, *Memoiren 1918–1934*, Stuttgart 1970, 673.

the political parties and how free were they to choose? At times the liberal parties were prepared to work with the socialists; and at other times such a collaboration failed and made necessary other political combinations: first centre–right governments and eventually the right–NSDAP government. Why? How successful were pressure groups (industrial associations, labour unions, agrarian leagues) in determining the course of political developments? And how did they react to the changing economic circumstances: inflation, stabilisation, stabilisation crisis, recovery, depression? In the second place, what constraints did Weimar's economy impose on politicians and on state policy?

III

Public Finance

The government certainly discovered and acted upon the theory of the unbalanced budget.

(Joseph Alois Schumpeter, *Business Cycles*)

The most immediately striking economic consequence of the First World War was the growth of the public sector. That growth was politically highly contentious. Adolph Wagner's famous formulation of the 'law of increasing state expenditure'[1] now appeared to be vindicated. After the War, government expenditure as a proportion of National Income rose from 14.5 per cent (1910/13) to 24.0 per cent (1925/9). Another change that the War brought about was that a greater part of government expenditure was controlled by the central state. Reich expenditure was just over 40 per cent of all government spending in 1913, but by 1925 it represented 45 per cent.[2] In addition, the nature of the Reich's commitments changed: whereas before the War most of Reich spending was military, by 1925 such expenditure accounted for only 9 per cent of the Reich's total.

Both developments (absolute growth; and the rising share of central state expenditure) continued after the stabilisation of the currency. Government spending rose continually until 1929–30; and by 1930 the Reich share had reached 54 per cent, with correspondingly less money being spent by the Länder and the communes. The creation of a centralised system of government finance began in 1919, when the new Republic believed it needed to avoid the paralysis that had afflicted the Empire because of the very limited financial powers given to

[1] A. Wagner, *Finanzwissenschaft* I, Leipzig 1877[2], 68.

[2] P.-C. Witt, 'Finanzpolitik und sozialer Wandel: Wachstum und Funktionswandel der Staatsausgaben in Deutschland 1871–1933', in (ed.) H.-U. Wehler, *Sozialgeschichte heute: Festschrift für Hans Rosenberg zum 70. Geburtstag*, Göttingen 1974, 568. My calculations from S. Andic and J. Veverka, 'The Growth of Government Expenditure in Germany since the Unification', *Finanzarchiv* NF 23, 1964, 244–5.

the central state in 1871. Bismarck's empire depended for revenue on customs duties and some sales taxes. It could not impose direct taxes, which remained exclusively the affair of the states—Prussia, Bavaria, etc. On the other hand, Article 8 of the Weimar Constitution allowed the Reich to lay claim to any tax levied in Germany, while Article 11 empowered the Reich to lay down guide-lines for Länder taxation. The finance reforms of Matthias Erzberger (Reich Finance Minister from June 1919 to March 1920) were built up on this base, and established income and corporation tax as the fundamental sources of Reich income. Subsequent arrangements, known as the Finanzausgleich, provided for the distribution to the Länder and the communes of shares of Reich taxes: from 1 October 1925 the Reich distributed in this way 75 per cent of the revenue from income and corporation taxes, and 35 per cent of the turnover (sales) tax. The share of the turnover tax was later cut to 25 per cent, and in 1930 the share of income tax reduced to 60 per cent. §35 of the Finanzausgleich provided for a redistribution of taxes if Länder raised lower taxes than their proportionate shares of the Reich's population: so that in practice the richer Länder subsidised the poorer ones. These redistributive agreements were provisional: in 1928 a Länder conference met in order to prepare a final version of the Finanzausgleich, but failed to make any recommendation about the distribution of taxes between Reich and Länder. By 1930 Prussia was bringing forward motions in the Second Chamber (Reichsrat) either to end §35 or to apply it to the Prussian provinces as well as the Länder (in this case the impoverished Prussian East would benefit). But the South German states could be relied upon to block an abolition of §35 since they were its beneficiaries.[3]

The constitutional complexities of the Weimar Republic affected public expenditure as well as revenue questions. Reich, Länder, and communes all had their own governments and their own parliamentary institutions keen to make spending decisions. In order to execute these decisions a larger civil

[3] The best survey of the debates about the constitutional implications of *Finanzausgleich* is G. Schulz, *Zwischen Demokratie und Diktatur. Verfassungspolitik und Reichsreform in der Weimarer Republik*, Berlin 1963: on the Länderkonferenz, see 564 ff.

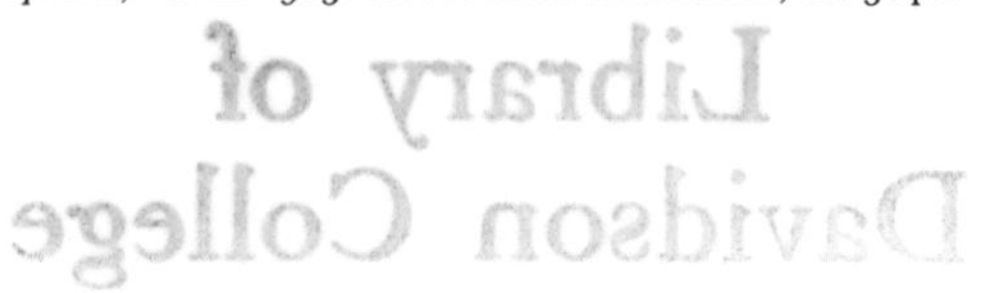

service was needed; and this civil service gave valuable patronage and employment opportunities for the figures who controlled it. From 1907 to 1925 the number of employees in all levels of government administration rose by 66 per cent (from 390 000 to 648 000); while there were lesser but still substantial increases in employment in education and in the postal, telegraph, and telephone services. Increased public ownership of transport (and especially the municipalisation of local transport systems) meant that the number of public transport workers rose from 570 000 to 1 239 000.[4] Such an increase in public employment was not, of course, peculiar to Germany: and indeed the total proportion of the total work-force in public employment remained constant from 1907 to 1925 (at 10.6 per cent) while in Britain there was a substantial *rise* in the equivalent proportion (1911: 6.9 per cent; 1921: 10.0 per cent).[5]

It was not the growth of public employment alone that made the question of public spending in Weimar so thorny. Gigantic sums were needed to pay for the War and its aftermath; but comparatively only a small part of the war effort was paid out of tax revenue. At first money was raised by war loans; but from 1916 the current account budget deficits were covered more and more by the discounting of short-dated Treasury bills (*Schatzanweisungen*) by the banking system backed up by the rediscounting of the Reichsbank. Large budget deficits continued after the Armistice, and provided the major cause of the German inflation.[6] Expenditure had necessarily increased as a consequence of the war: apart from reparations to the western powers, the state now had to pay pensions to one and a half million wounded ex-soldiers and to some of the two and a half million dependants of those killed in the war.[7] The

[4] J. P. Cullity, 'The Growth of Governmental Employment in Germany 1882–1950', *Zeitschrift für die gesamte Staatswissenschaft* 123, 1967, 202–03.

[5] Ibid., 211.

[6] C. Bresciani-Turroni, *The Economics of Inflation: A Study of Currency Depreciation in Post-War Germany 1914–1923*, London 1953, 66–7; S. Webb (Michigan), 'Government Spending, Taxes and Reichsbank Policy in Germany 1919–1923', unpublished paper 1982.

[7] P.-C. Witt, 'Finanzpolitik als Verfassungs- und Gesellschaftspolitik; Überlegungen zur Finanzpolitik des Deutschen Reiches in den Jahren 1930 bis 1932', *GG* 8, 1982, 399.

political disturbances of 1918–19 meant too that the new republican governments were frightened that high levels of unemployment might lead to 'Soviet conditions' in Germany, and spent considerable sums creating or maintaining jobs in order to counter the threat.[8]

On the other hand, the new regime lacked the authority—as indeed the Kaiser's Government had too—to impose high taxes on the German élites. Landowners protested that any kind of taxation amounted to Bolshevism; and industry threatened to go bankrupt if taxes were raised. In consequence taxes were kept low and the public deficit mounted. By default, a policy of unbalanced budgets and consequentially high levels of employment emerged in post-war Germany. But few thought hyperinflation desirable, and after the dramatic experience of 1923 and the complete collapse of the currency there was at last a mandate and a political will to raise taxes. The new taxation programme began to be worked out under the 1923 Stresemann Government; it was finally elaborated under Wilhelm Marx (Reich Chancellor November 1923 to January 1925), in particular by Marx's energetic Finance Minister Hans Luther. Luther's tax increases were, however, presented as part of a general programme which envisaged an eventual return to an old pre-war smaller state. The major feature of the currency stabilisation programme was balancing the budget. This involved reducing expenditure by pegging civil service wages and dismissing many state employees.[9] Only once these spending cuts had been announced was it possible to begin with the other half of the stabilisation package, increasing taxes. In December 1923 a 10 per cent tax was imposed on profits; personal income tax rescheduled to begin from incomes of 600 Goldmarks and over (a very low figure), reaching rates of 40 per cent on high incomes; and a wealth tax of between 0.5 per

[8] The most famous formulation of this view was by Stinnes in a conversation with the US Ambassador on 23 June 1922: 'daß die Waffe der Inflation auch weiter benutzt werden müsse, ohne Rücksicht auf die entstehenden Kapitalverluste, weil nur dadurch die Möglichkeit gegeben sei, der Bevölkerung eine geordnete regelmäßige Tätigkeit zu geben, die notwendig sei, um das Leben der Nation zu sichern.' *Ursachen und Folgen* 5, 515.

[9] A. Kunz, 'Stand versus Klasse: Beamtenschaft und Gewerkschaften im Konflikt um den Personalabbau 1923/4'. *GG* 8, 1982, 55–86.

cent and 5 per cent introduced.[10] In February 1924 debts written off during the inflation were taxed.[11] The combination of tax increases and reductions in expenditure generated a large budget surplus in 1924, but also produced many complaints about the level of taxes. Employers believed that taxes, together with a new restrictive credit policy of the central bank, were damaging business. In 1925 the central employers' organisation, the Reichsverband der deutschen Industrie (RDI) demanded a new 20 per cent cut in public expenditure. The chairman of the liberal industrial organisation, the Hansabund, said that business had lost 2b. RM because of the state's new policy.[12] Since the Government was politically dependent on the parties of the right, it felt obliged to make concessions; and in August 1925 income and wealth taxes were reduced, and the attempt to assess *increases* in wealth in the years of war and inflation was abandoned. Inheritance taxes too were cut.

These industrial demands, and the Government's response, were in part a product of the economic crisis of 1925–6. Other government measures to lessen the impact of the crisis, such as the attempt in late 1925 to impose price cuts, were very unpopular and very unsuccessful. Plans for public works failed to produce a significant economic effect. In consequence, when in 1926 an energetic young Democrat from Saxony, Peter Reinhold, became Reich Finance Minister, he argued in favour of more tax cuts as the best way of dealing with the depression. He even put forward the theory that the state should be prepared to run budget deficits.[13] The new theory was applied in a law on Tax Reduction (31 March 1926): but taxes still remained a favourite target of industrial discontent.

[10] A good source for tax rates is (eds.) G. Colm and H. Neisser, *Kapitalbildung und Steuersystem. Verhandlungen und Gutachten der Konferenz in Eilsen*, Berlin 1930, Vol. II, App. I.

[11] The 3rd Steuernotverordnung: RGBl 1924, I 74 (14 Feb. 1924); K. B. Netzband and H. P. Widmaier, *Währungs- und Finanzpolitik der Aera Luther 1923–1925*, Tübingen 1964.

[12] RDI, *Deutsche Währungs- und Finanzpolitik*, Berlin 1925; D. Hertz-Eichenrode, *Wirtschaftskrise und Arbeitsbeschaffung: Konjunkturpolitik 1925/26 und die Grundlagen der Krisenpolitik Brünings*, Frankfurt and New York 1982, 55.

[13] Hertz-Eichenrode, 99; Reinhold speech in Reichstag 10 Feb. 1926, *Verhandlungen des Reichstages*, III Wahlperiode 1924 Bd. 388, 5402–13. C.-D. Krohn, *Stabilisierung und ökonomische Interessen: Die Finanzpolitik des Deutschen Reiches 1923–1927*, Düsseldorf 1974, 200.

In late 1927, the Hansabund argued, at the height of Weimar's prosperity, that total public spending should be cut by 10 per cent in order to lighten the tax load; and that the Reich Finance Minister should be given a veto over parliamentary proposals which involved increased outlays. The RDI produced memoranda in 1927 and in 1929 (*Aufstieg oder Niedergang?*) arguing the case for public economies and tax cuts.[14]

Business objected, too, to the form that the reductions of 1925–6 had taken. The key element in Reinhold's programme had been the reduction of turnover tax (*Umsatzsteuer*) from 1 per cent to 0.75 per cent (the initial proposal had been to go down to 0.6 per cent, and Reinhold would even have preferred 0.5 per cent). This was a tax which was particularly unpopular with small business, since the tax was on each transaction rather than depending on a value-added principle. Thus every middleman added to the tax bill. Big business did not feel so concerned. Carl Duisberg, the chairman of the Reichsverband, protested that the turnover tax cut had benefited no one, but rather meant a loss of revenue for the state which reduced the scope for other tax cuts. Luther, who by now was Reich Chancellor, also was tremendously critical of the Reinhold measures, which he claimed were not economically stimulating.[15]

By 1927 a new problem arose for financial planners as the size and the expense of the public sector once more increased. After the stabilisation of the Mark, the Government took as one of its foremost priorities the pruning back of the civil service. The number of positions for *Beamte* (permanent public employees) was cut by 13.5 per cent; while the number of non-permanent white collar employees fell from 1 October 1923 to 1 October 1924 by 53 per cent, and the number of manual workers was cut by 26 per cent.[16] As the figures indicate, the cuts in public spending fell most immediately and severely on that vast army of clerks taken on in the inflation to write in all the extra noughts. After the stabilisation, administrative econ-

[14] DST B4472, Oct.–Nov. 1927 Memorandum of Hansabund.

[15] DST B4472, 8 Nov. 1926 Discussion of industrialists with representatives of DST; Colm and Neisser, I 73.

[16] From Reichstag *Drucksachen* III Wahlperiode: 1924 No. 343 (Ergänzung der Denkschrift über den Personalabbau). Figures include employees of Reichspost.

omy was at a premium: whereas administrative costs as a proportion of government expenditure accounted for almost the same amount in 1925 (9.1 per cent) as in 1913 (9.3 per cent), there was then a fall until in 1930 the figure was 6.9 per cent.[17] Between 1924 and 1927 the number of Reich civil servants was cut, but then there was a new increase.

In the fourth Cabinet of Chancellor Wilhelm Marx (formed in January 1927) Heinrich Köhler had been appointed Reich Finance Minister. He was a member of the Centre, had been a civil servant in Württemberg, and believed that the policy of his predecessor as Reich Finance Minister, Reinhold, had been orientated too much towards the interests of big business. Civil service pay, Köhler pointed out, had lagged behind industrial salaries, and he was determined to rectify what he believed to be a major social injustice. So in fulfilment of promises made to a meeting of civil servants in Magdeburg, he pushed through a programme which raised the basic public sector pay by 33 per cent: as a consequence, the income of civil servants in the lower grades in particular was raised dramatically.[18] New jobs were created as part of the same package which brought the *Besoldungsreform*.[19] During the depression, after 1929, there was an attempt to cut the number of posts in the Reich administration, and the communal authorities were severely affected by the crisis in communal finance and were obliged to cut their staff; but the Länder at the same time actually increased the number of permanent officials they hired.[20]

The number and pay of public service workers not employed by the Reich increased throughout the 1920s. Länder policy was in fact much more difficult to control than the Reich civil service, not on the whole because there was much more deliberate waste, but rather because of the uncertainty which surrounded the constitutional future of Germany. There was a great deal of duplication at the Land and communal levels. Communal officials regularly complained of how they were subjected to unneccessary and costly supervision by the Land

[17] Andic and Veverka, 258.

[18] See H. Köhler (ed. J. Becker), *Lebenserinnerungen eines Politikers und Staatsmannes 1878–1949*, Stuttgart 1964, 255–61.

[19] Reichstag *Drucksachen* III Wahlperiode No. 4102.

[20] *Statistisches Jahrbuch* 1932, 476–7; *Statistisches Jahrbuch* 1934, 456–7.

authorities. Great-Berlin, for example, had a Prussian Oberpräsident attached to it simply in order to oversee the city magistracy.[21] Short of a decision to abolish the Länder and create direct links between communes and the Reich authorities, nothing could be done about such a situation. As a result, a great fund of frustration and resentment accumulated. Arnold Brecht, the deputy Prussian representative on the Reichsrat, complained in 1931 that there was 'no one in Germany who has a really objective overview of the whole administration'. Adam Stegerwald claimed in a speech in May 1930 that a simplified Länder system would save 1½–2b. RM a year in administrative costs.[22] Many figures in Reich politics deduced that a unitary state was an urgent necessity simply from the point of view of saving money: the DVP and DNVP both pressed for more centralisation. The DDP had been associated with the centralising proposals of Hugo Preuss in 1919; and the SPD at the 1925 Heidelberg Congress called for a combination of a unitary state with a decentralised administration, in other words, for a virtual abolition of the Länder.

In practice the enthusiasts in the Reichstag parties for the unitary state faced insuperable obstacles: the South German states defended their independence vigorously, and were prepared to join together to thwart any attempts to undermine their solidarity. The Bavarian Minister-President Held tried to defend the idea that a greater decentralisation of decision-making would mean greater direct responsibility and therefore a more economical administration.[23] Only the increasing financial crisis at the beginning of 1930 made Baden and Württemberg prepared to accept a greater degree of Reich control. The SPD Minister-President of Prussia, Otto Braun, thought that the best solution was not to destroy Prussia but to expand it so as to include all the small north German states. In the end, even figures such as Johannes Popitz, who had made it his business as State Secretary in the Reich Finance Ministry to agitate against administrative anarchy, which he termed

[21] C. Engeli, *Gustav Böß, Oberbürgermeister von Berlin 1921 bis 1930*, Stuttgart 1971, 162–3.

[22] A. Brecht, *Mit der Kraft des Geistes: Lebenserinnerungen 1927–1967*, Stuttgart 1967, 60; *Kölnische Zeitung* No. 245b, 5.5.1930.

[23] F. Menges, *Reichsreform und Finanzpolitik: Die Aushöhlung der Eigenstaatlichkeit Bayerns auf finanzpolitischem Wege in der Zeit der Weimarer Republik*, Berlin 1971, 79.

'Polykratie' and which he believed plagued German politics, came to accept the necessity of the existence of the Prussian state because without it everything in Germany would be plunged into chaos.[24]

Often the accusation of too much government in Germany (*Nebeneinanderregieren*) was linked to a critique of parliamentary rule: there were too many parliaments as well as too many governments in Germany. These parliaments had swelled public spending and public sector employment in the style of Reinhold and Köhler. This was the argument presented by the DNVP, whose party Congress in December 1927 launched a campaign against the 'sole rule of parliaments' (*parlamentarische Alleinherrschaft*).[25] During the depression, the progressive rejection of parliamentarism made it much easier to solve the intricacies of the constitutional problem. In the Brüning years, both Brüning and Luther were working for a limitation of the authority of Länder, commune, and local parliaments. Under Papen and Hitler the 'Prussian Problem' was solved by force: on 20 July 1932 the Prussian ministries on one side of the Wilhelmstraβe were occupied by troops directed from the Reich Chancellery on the other side of the street. Hitler completed the Gleichschaltung (or subordination to central control) of the Länder: new elections were called and the results manipulated; and communal parliaments were reconstituted in line with the results of the March 1933 Reichstag elections. Existing Länder governments were deposed as threats to the Reich's security. Hitler's way of resolving the Länder and commune issue did not mean economy of administration or a reduction in the size of the civil service. On the contrary: public employment increased as part of Hitler's 'social revolution', jobs were created for loyal National Socialist supporters, and by 1939 over one million Germans were employed in public administration (this figure does not include those in the armed forces or in education, both of which expanded greatly in the Third Reich).[26]

[24] J. Popitz, *Der Finanzausgleich und seine Bedeutung für die Finanzlage des Reiches, der Länder und Gemeinden* (Speech to RDI Tax Committee, 9 Oct. 1930), Berlin 1930, 6. G. Schulz 1963, 596.

[25] G. Schulz 1963, 580–1.

[26] Cullity, 202: 1939: armed forces 851,000; education 430,000; government administration 1,039,000; postal, telegraph, and telephone 467,000; transport

The bitter constitutional conflicts and struggles, and the clashes over the nature of public administration in Germany, were reflections of a deep division of views about what the state should do. For the function of state expenditure changed dramatically after the War:

1. The proportion of state expenditure devoted to transfer payments to *rentiers* fell. This was directly a consequence of the inflation, which had led to a complete loss of value of government securities, and of the revalorisation legislation of 1924–5, which provided for much less generous treatment of claims against the state than of private loans. Thus after 1924, debt service charges on public budgets were extremely low. Whereas in 1913, 5.6 per cent of public spending was involved in debt service, in 1925 only 0.6 per cent was; the share rose to 2.9 per cent in 1931 as the public debt increased.[27] France and Britain both had much higher debt service charges: in Britain in 1913 6.1 per cent but in 1925 a massive 28.4 per cent was taken in this way.[28] The western states thus made higher transfer payments which did *not* lead to a dramatic social redistribution of incomes. In comparing tax levels of European states in the 1920s, this point should be borne in mind: though public spending had risen dramatically in Britain, those who paid taxes were less resentful than their German counterparts, because they were *qua rentiers* repaid out of the taxes paid.

2. There was in Germany a dramatic growth in the provision of social services. Including housing and education expenditure as social services, the figure rose from 37 per cent of total government spending (1913) to 57 per cent (1925); after this there was a more or less continuous rise to 68 per cent in 1932. If education and housing are removed from the calculation, spending (on social and unemployment assistance, pension and sickness insurance schemes) rose from 19 per cent to 37 per cent to 51 per cent in those respective years.[29] These figures may it is

1,014,047; water, gas, and electricity 173,534; other 485,604; total government employment 4,460,185. See also D. Schoenbaum, *Hitler's Social Revolution: Class and Status in Nazi Germany 1933–1939*, New York 1966.

[27] From Andic and Veverka, 258.

[28] From A. J. Peacock and J. Wiseman, *The Growth of Public Expenditure in the United Kingdom*, London 1967, 184.

[29] Andic and Veverka, 258; see also Witt 1982.

true include some sums that might more legitimately be accounted military expenditure (pensions to war veterans and their dependants): but the main increase represents the creation of the Weimar *Sozialstaat*. In 1927 an attempt was made to take unemployment assistance out of the sphere of the state's responsibilities by setting up an insurance institute (the Reichsanstalt für Arbeitslosenversicherung) which was to finance itself out of employers' and workers' contributions; but in practice this intention was never realised, as rising levels of unemployment required that the state subsidise the Reichsanstalt more and more.[30] In any case, after a certain time, the unemployed were no longer eligible for benefits under the insurance scheme, and became dependent instead on Reich and communal support.

The rising costs of social services until 1928 reflect a determination to increase the stability of the political system of Weimar by the creation of an effective welfare network. After 1928 the increase in costs is largely attributable to the higher unemployment levels with which Weimar now had to cope.

3. Agricultural support represented a major strain on the public purse at the beginning of the 1930s. By the end of 1932 governments had spent 2b. RM on agricultural relief (or *c.*3 per cent of total government spending for the years 1930–2).[31]

These reasons for increases in public spending—a growing bureaucracy, an inability to reform the complex constitutional structure of Germany, increased social and agricultural support—coupled with the reduction in wealth of those who had by tradition lent to the state, and who now had to pay higher rates of tax, made the budgets of public authorities very controversial. Taxpayers believed that increased rates of tax had been responsible for the redistribution of incomes which had taken place during the period of war and inflation; the process of redistribution now seemed to be continuing, even after the stabilisation of the currency. The income pyramid was getting broader: wealthy Germans blamed the state for

[30] L. Preller, *Sozialpolitik in der Weimarer Republik*, Düsseldorf 1949, 371–6.

[31] D. Petzina, 'Staatliche Ausgaben und deren Umverteilungswirkungen: Das Beispiel der Industrie- und Agrarsubventionen in der Weimarer Republik', in (ed.) F. Blaich, *Staatliche Umverteilungspolitik in historischer Perspektive: Beiträge zur Entwicklung des Staatsinterventionismus in Deutschland und Österreich*, Berlin 1980, 102.

this. In the Table 1 income and wealth are compared for the pre- and post-war years. The bands compared are for different levels because of the changed purchasing power of money (the Reich cost of living index with a 1913 base was 141.2 in 1926, 147.6 in 1927, and 151.7 in 1928, the wholesale price index 134.4, 137.6, and 140.0 for these years).[32]

Rises in public expenditure are sometimes believed to be predicated on an increase in the 'tolerable burden of taxation'. Wars involving an agreed national effort justify high rates of tax, which frequently remain after the end of the war, as beliefs as to what levels of taxation are acceptable have changed.[33] Such an explanation might be given about Britain in the 1920s, although British taxpayers also grumbled. But in Germany the War had been paid out of taxation to a much smaller extent than in the UK; and there was a great deal of controversy about public spending, which in the 1920s did not seem to be justified by an agreed national effort. Such controversy about spending created an instability, which increased at the end of the decade as budgets showed more and more strain. The story examined in this chapter might be summarised simply as that of the political effects of borrowing and funding difficulties at all levels of government.

THE REICH

When the German currency was stabilised in 1923–4, an essential part of the package was the imposition of a high tax burden. From 1925–6, however, the surpluses of the stabilisation years were eroded and there were deficits in the Reich budget current accounts. At first they were financed by the use of surpluses accumulated in the two years previous. By 1928–9 the official budget showed deficits; and the Reich's funding difficulties had already begun in 1927. In that year a 500m. RM 5 per cent Government Loan, intended to cover the cost of the large subsidies to industry and agriculture in 1926, proved a failure. The price of the Loan fell from an original 92.00 to 86.90 in July, and the Loan had to be converted up to 6 per cent in order to maintain the prices.

[32] *Statistisches Jahrbuch für das Deutsche Reich*, 1930, 275, 278.
[33] Peacock and Wiseman, 26–8.

ERRATUM

p. 51 Table I: Distribution of tax assessments for wealth and income, by bands as proportion of total wealth and income (in Marks).

Under the heading 'Wealth' 1927 should read 1928.

Table I: Distribution of Wealth and Income in the Weimar Republic

Distribution of wealth 1914 and 1928 (%)

Wealth		Prussia		Saxony		Reich
1914	1927	1914	1928	1914	1928	1928
Less than 20,000	Less than 30,000	12.7	32.3	6.7	31.3	35.1
20,000–70,000	30,000–100,000	21.5	27.4	22.4	29.0	27.3
70,000–700,000	100,000–1,000,000	38.1	30.0	45.4	32.2	28.6
700,000+	1,000,000+	27.7	10.3	25.5	7.4	9.0

Distribution of income 1914 and 1926 (%)

Income		*1914*			*1926*
1914	*1926*	*Prussia*	*Bavaria*	*Saxony*	*Reich*
Less than 2,000	Less than 3,000	47.0	51.2	53.5	55.8
2,000–6,000	3,000–8,000	22.9	26.9	17.9	26.3
6,000–12,000	8,000–16,000	7.5	6.9	7.5	7.5
12,000–35,000	16,000–50,000	9.5	6.0	8.0	6.2
35,000–70,000	50,000–100,000	4.0	2.7	4.1	1.9
70,000+	100,000+	9.1	6.7	9.0	2.3

Source: Colm and Neisser, 528, 533; 1928 figures from *Statistisches Jahrbuch 1932*, 506–9.

Table II: German Government Revenue, Expenditure and Debt 1926/7–1932/3 (m. RM)

	1926/7	1927/8	1928/9	1929/30	1930/1	1931/2	1932/3
Expenditure							
Public Administration	17 201	18 801	20 801	20 872	20 406	16 977	14 535
Reich[a]	6 562	7 155	8 376	8 043	8 163	6 625	5 735
Länder[a]	4 123	4 357	4 585	4 564	4 487	3 907	3 349
Communes[a]	6 734	7 422	8 029	8 461	8 021	6 998	6 289
Hansa Cities[a]	528	595	640	675	647	524	491
Social Insurance[b]	2 843	4 108	4 862	5 314	5 718	5 626	4 168
TOTAL EXPENDITURE[c]	20 397	22 460	25 043	25 736	25 400	21 971	18 168
(as % of GNP)	26.9	26.8	28.4	29.6	32.1	33.3	31.8
REVENUE							
Public Administration	17 286	18 762	19 613	20 082	19 890	16 458	13 780
Reich	6 819	7 113	7 300	7 730	8 041	6 440	5 589
Länder	3 577	3 942	4 144	3 994	3 928	3 432	2 845
Communes	6 387	7 124	7 541	7 713	7 325	6 093	4 952
Hansa Cities	503	583	628	645	596	493	394
Social Insurance[b]	3 371	3 990	5 551	6 029	5 912	5 470	4 390
TOTAL PUBLIC REVENUE[c]	18 412	21 307	22 816	23 205	23 104	20 694	16 684
Increase in Public Debt	1 742[c]	1 075[c]	3 561	3 159	2 704	155	170[d]
Increase in Debt as % of GNP	2.3	1.3	4.0	3.6	3.4	0.2	0.3

Source: Statistisches Jahrbuch, Wagemann 1935, Witt 1982.

[a] Expenditure figures for Reich, Länder, communes, and Hansa Cities include payments to other public authorities: these have been removed in the total.

[b] Calendar year, *not* budget year (1 April–31 March).

[c] P.-C. Witt 1982.

[d] Not including tax certificates (see below, Chapter X).

It was only in 1929, however, that the borrowing crisis began to overshadow every other issue and to produce urgent demands for an economy campaign. A new attempt to fund the government debt failed: only 177m. RM of 500m. RM from the so-called Hilferding Loan was sold, despite tax concessions (freedom from wealth, inheritance, and income tax on the loan) which made a funding operation organised by an SPD Finance Minister look like a hand-out to the rich. Reich expenditure was still rising in 1929, and, unlike in 1926–7 when most of the increases in expenditure had been the consequences of new political decisions on subsidies and civil service pay, the increases of 1928–30 were the virtually inescapable consequences of previous legislation. In addition, by the end of 1929 there was a problem on the revenue side as tax revenue began to fall below the average for previous years because of the impact of the recession.[34]

The budget crisis of late 1929 led to a series of political crises, which were made more acute by the insolvency of the unemployment insurance scheme, by industry's campaign to reduce taxes, and by the international negotiations over a new reparation settlement.

In 1927 the Unemployment Insurance Law had required contributions amounting to 3 per cent of wages, to be shared equally between employer and employee: this figure came from an actuarial calculation that the average number of unemployed eligible for benefit under the insurance scheme would be 800 000. A small emergency fund had also been established to deal with an additional 600,000 temporarily out of work during the winter. However, unemployment almost immediately began to rise above the levels foreseen in 1927. In the winter 1927–8 over 2 million were classified as seeking work, and in the next winter, over 3 million (February 1929). The lowest figure for 1928 (July) was 1 155 000, and for 1929 1 355 000 (again July): this was only just below the maximum figure provided in the 1927 calculations. On 15 January 1928 1.3m. were on unemployment benefit; the figure was 0.6m. in July (with an additional 89 000 on crisis relief). In January

[34] E. Wagemann, *Konjunkturstatistisches Handbuch 1936*, Berlin 1935, 167; H. James, *The Reichsbank and Public Finance in Germany 1924–1933: A study of the Politics of Economics during the Great Depression*, Frankfurt 1985, 98–9.

1929 1.9m. were on unemployment relief, and 138 000 on crisis relief; one year later these figures were 2.0m. and 230 000.[35] Under the terms of Article 163 of the 1927 Law, the Reich was obliged to cover deficits of the insurance institute out of its own budget. In consequence, the Reichsanstalt in March 1929 needed a 288m. RM loan to cover its losses.[36] The Government responded by introducing on 12 October a new regulation for the insurance scheme: this worsened the position of those in seasonal employment (chiefly farm and building workers). But there was no agreement at the end of 1929 to raise the contributions, which would have been the only way of stabilising the Reichsanstalt's position, and the calculation on future requirements made in November was based on an unrealistically low unemployment figure (1.1 million). Thus in the course of 1930 more and more money was required by the Reichsanstalt: a total of 624m. RM in loans was given, and then in 1931 written off by the Government. Additional money was required for means tested 'crisis support' for unemployed workers who had come to the end of their period of eligibility for insurance benefit: by May 1930 an additional 600m. RM was required under this scheme.[37]

The second cause of increased political tension over the Reich budget was the profit squeeze on industry, which by 1929 had led to a general consensus that tax cuts were needed. Some commentators even spoke of a psychosis about tax reduction, *Steuersenkungspsychose*. The RDI published in December 1929 a memorandum *Aufstieg oder Niedergang?* which echoed earlier industrial pleas for the reduction of taxes inhibiting capital formation: capital and corporation taxes, and in particular local, communal, taxes on commerce and real estate. The Reich should force local government to prune its expenditure. Industry's case received substantial academic support. Economists and civil servants as well as bankers and business men met in Bad Eilsen in October 1929 for a conference of the Friedrich-List-Gesellschaft in order to discuss how capital formation in Germany might be encouraged by fiscal

[35] *Statistisches Jahrbuch*, 1929, 274 and 286; and 1930, 316, 323.
[36] Preller, 422.
[37] Ibid., 426–7. IfZ ED93/29 21 May 1930 Schäffer Memorandum: 'Die Entwicklung des Reichshaushalts'.

change.[38] Reich Chancellor Hermann Müller himself argued to his ministerial colleagues that the most important item in the Government's fiscal package was tax-cutting.[39]

The RDI's campaign to cut taxes was supported by the Reichsbank, which produced politically explosive memoranda on this theme. After the end of the Paris Experts' Reparations Conference in spring 1929, the Reichsbank Statistical Department drew up a report calling for a reversal of the Reich's whole economic policy: in particular spending cuts were needed in order to allow the tax bill to be reduced. 'Damaging' taxes (the inheritance and wealth taxes, and the tax on capital gains) and the upper brackets of the progressive income tax should be replaced by taxes on such items of mass consumption as beer and entertainment. The unemployment insurance scheme should be run down. The general post-war development of Germany needed to be put into reverse. At the end of the memorandum came the bald accusing statement that 'Germany instead of allowing the free development of forces in a state based on work (*Arbeitsstaat*) is increasingly a state of pensioners and welfare beneficiaries (*Rentner- und Fürsorgestaat*).'[40]

After the Young plan saved Germany half a billion RM annually in reparations, the theme of tax reductions was brought up again by the Reichstag parties of the centre and right. Such political pressure meant that in 1929 it was impossible to contemplate any measure to deal with the budget deficit except by borrowing.

Even such a step was controversial. The 1929 Loan had met almost universal condemnation. Max Warburg, the Hamburg banker, in December 1928 warned against the damaging effects a new Government Loan would have on the domestic market; he added that a long-term government funding operation would make industrial borrowing in the tightening capital market even more difficult.[41] Hjalmar Schacht too had

[38] RDI, *Aufstieg oder Niedergang?*, Berlin 1929; Colm and Neisser.

[39] (ed.) M. Vogt, *Akten der Reichskanzlei Weimarer Republik: Das Kabinett Müller II*, Boppard 1970, Doc. 363, 25 Nov. 1929 ministerial meeting: 'Er hielt die Steuersenkung für wichtiger als alles andere.'

[40] ZStA Reichsbank 6709, 26 June 1929 memorandum.

[41] Warburg Correspondence 44, December 1928 note of Max M. Warburg.

warned against the Hilferding Loan. However, there was as yet no real difficulty in short-term funding operations, though the Government's desperate bids to raise money helped to make foreigners more pessimistic about the German future and particularly about German financial stability. On these grounds, the banker Rudolf Löb (of Mendelssohn, Berlin) argued that the gap in the budget current account was a serious handicap for the German economy; and Reich Economics Minister Julius Curtius pleaded for a balancing of the budget.[42] The State Secretary in the Reich Chancellery complained during the international scare when the Paris reparation negotiations appeared likely to collapse that the problems (of the short-term debt) 'are such as have not been encountered in the last ten years, not even in the most difficult phases of the inflation'.[43] The confidence of foreigners in German solidity was further dented by the bizarre way in which the Reich and Reichsbank President Schacht conducted separate, rival and conflicting negotiations with foreign banks on the funding issue. While the Reich tried Dillon Read, Schacht was trying to approach the prestigious New York House of J. P. Morgan for a loan on the security of Reichsbahn (railway) preference shares. In July 1929 Schacht invited the Morgan partner Thomas W. Lamont to Berlin, but Lamont evaded the invitation; in September Schacht met an English Morgan partner, but by this time J. P. Morgan himself had condemned the whole operation: 'From what I can see of the Germans they are second-rate people and I would rather have the business done for them by someone else.'[44]

There was a vicious circle: as the short-term debt mounted, foreigners and Germans became more suspicious, and it became more difficult to consolidate the debt, which continued to grow. Thus the Finance Ministry in practice had little choice except to continue to borrow short-term. In May 1929 the Reich loan consortium was required to take 120m. RM short-

[42] IfZ ED93/5 15 March 1929 and ED93/6, 10 June diary entries (Schäffer diary).

[43] BAK NL Pünder 120, 22 April 1929 Pünder memorandum (also in FES NL Müller 307).

[44] Lamont Papers, Baker Library Harvard, 180–23 ff; quote from TWL 181–1, 30 Aug. 1929 J. P. Morgan to T. W. Lamont. Also IfZ ED93/6 11 June 1929 diary entry. Melchior: 'Schacht wants to get the Government and the Reichsbahn in his hand by controlling credit; we must take a firm stand here'.

dated Treasury bills. In addition, large private enterprises with surplus short term funds (IG Farben, Otto Wolff, Fried. Krupp) were encouraged to place these funds with the Reich.[45] A state-owned bank, the Reichs-Kredit-Gesellschaft, was charged in August 1929 with managing a bridging loan for the end of September, without any consultation of the Reich with the Reichsbank. This manoeuvre irritated the already irritable Schacht.[46] In December, the Reich again tried a bridging loan coupled with longer-term credit from Dillon Read. Dillon Read had been involved in German finance for some while, though the centre of its European interests lay in Poland. Dealing with the Polish Government for a period of several years had given the firm experience of the risks, but also of the profits to be made, in European government finance. From June 1929 Dillon Read had helped to manage the German short-term debt (it had opened a credit line of 210m. RM). In December 500m. RM was needed: but the loan was defeated by the intervention of Schacht.[47] On 6 December the President of the Reichsbank published a memorandum which caused a political explosion, as it linked an attack on the Young reparation settlement with a severe criticism of the past record of Reich finance.[48]

This intervention altered the political game: it brought down the Finance Minister, Hilferding, and his *éminence grise*, State Secretary Johannes Popitz. It imposed on the Müller Government a bill—which when enacted became known as the Lex Schacht—which committed the Reich to make a sinking fund payment of 450m. RM over the following year.[49] After the December crisis, Müller became obsessed with avoiding a deterioration of the budget current account, as an increase in the deficit would offer great leverage to opponents of the regime.

In September 1929 the Finance Ministry presented its plans to reduce income tax over the following five years so that

[45] BAK R2/2453, 29 May 1929 Note on Seehandlung consortium; BAK NL Pünder 120, 22 April 1929 Pünder memorandum.

[46] BAK R2/2455, especially 26 Aug. 1929 Reichsbank to Reich Finance Ministry.

[47] PA/AA State Secretary's Papers CF 16.

[48] H. H. G. Schacht, *Memorandum zum Youngplan*, Berlin 1929; also Schacht, *The End of Reparations*, London 1931, 117–21.

[49] RGBI 1929 II 759 (24 Dec. 1930).

eventually the maximum rate would be 35 per cent (rather than 40 per cent), to raise the tax thresholds, to cut communal land and commerce taxes by 10 per cent, to reduce sugar tax, and to increase excise on beer by 50 per cent in order to make up for other tax losses.[50] The whole programme, including additional reductions in the *Industrieumlage,* the industrial levy imposed under the terms of the Dawes Plan, would save German business 910m. RM.

This programme was the basis of a package accepted in December 1929.[51] Customs alterations and increases in tobacco excise imposed an additional burden of 350m. RM. But further increases were needed: in December increases in communal tax were considered (either a tax on drinks, or a general capitation—a scheme particularly popular with the right, since it would educate the German people in how much the expensive state actually cost the citizens). In February 1930 a new series of measures was proposed by Paul Moldenhauer, Hilferding's successor as Finance Minister: the beer excise increase was to be 75 per cent and a mineral water tax was introduced as well as an excise on petroleum and increases in the duties on coffee and tea. Moldenhauer also thought of an Emergency Tax (*Notopfer*) on civil servants and white-collar workers.[52]

The move towards highly restrictive government budgets occurred at the turn of 1929–30. It predated the Brüning regime; but the Hunger Chancellor inherited the obsession of his predecessor. Balanced budgets in Germany were not just a consequence of the capital shortage in Germany or of declining capital imports in 1929 and 1930. Morgan may have had his doubts about the Germans, but firms like Dillon Read and later Lee Higginson had always been prepared to rush in where Morgan feared to tread. The crisis of 1929–30, which had such pronounced long-term consequences, was only so severe because of the rising political tension. This tension alarmed first foreign investors, and then, in the course of 1930, also

50 *Kabinett Müller II*, Doc. 305, 28 Sep. 1929 ministerial meeting.

51 Ibid., Doc. 374, 9 Dec. 1929 ministerial meeting.

52 Ibid., Doc. 442, 11 Feb. 1930 memorandum of Stegerwald; Doc. 454 25 Feb. 1930 Reich Finance Minister to Pünder; Doc. 455, 27 Feb. 1930 ministerial meeting; and RGBI 1930 I 227 ff.

German citizens. Initially, the budget affair was precipitated by nothing more serious than the strained state of Schacht's nerves: Schacht was at this time close to a nervous breakdown, and was behaving with a high degree of irrationality. In January 1930 he sent for the American acting chairman of the BIS Organising Committee and jabbered on about how he was being persecuted: 'he hinted that he was about to be crucified by a gang of corrupt politicians . . . he dwelt at length upon his honesty, truthfulness, and patriotism'.[53] Once the financial instability induced by Schacht's hysteria had set in, however, it was extremely hard to restore confidence.

The long-term effect of December 1929 was that spending cuts became unavoidable. But where should they be made? Already in the spring of 1929 following the international political crisis which broke out over the new reparations plan devised by the international experts in Paris, the Finance Ministry had agreed that there was little alternative in the medium term except to increase taxes.[54] This was a view doubly unpopular: first because of the immense pressure across the political spectrum to reduce taxes; secondly because the reduction in the reparations bill in the Young Plan from the level of the Dawes Plan was expected to be passed on as relief for the German taxpayer.

The necessity of spending cuts combined with pressure for tax reductions and a need actually to *increase* revenue (in order to reduce the scale of the funding problem) imposed great strains on the ailing Great Coalition. The Bavarian People's Party disliked the new beer tax in principle, and resisted a Prussian initiative to reduce the income of the Bavarian state from the tax. In the end it was obliged to vote against the whole of the package of fiscal measures carefully assembled after December 1929; and thus it set in motion the train of events which in March 1930 led to Müller's fall.[55] The DVP rejected the *Notopfer*, and it was not included in the tax measures proposed to the Reichstag. The SPD's union wing on the other hand disliked proposals to increase workers' contributions to unem-

[53] TWL 129-23, 28 Apr. 1934 De Sanchez to Lamont (on events of January 1930).

[54] *Kabinett Müller II*, Doc. 187 app. 27 April 1929 Popitz Memorandum.

[55] See I. Maurer, *Reichsfinanzen und Große Koalition: Zur Geschichte des Reichskabinetts Müller 1928–1930*, Bern and Frankfurt 1973, 113–21.

ployment insurance, and to reduce Reich subsidies for the operation of the insurance scheme.[56] Thus the revised financial programme of 6 March set off an SPD mutiny which destroyed the Great Coalition and so put Brüning into office.

The parties continued to reject any spending cut or tax increase that might affect their electorate particularly severely. Brüning's position was different from that of Müller, since the Cabinet owed its existence to von Hindenburg and was not as dependent on the Reichstag as the Great Coalition had been; but the constant danger of a funding crisis remained. The new team in charge of the Reich Finance Ministry was eager to avoid any humiliation of the kind that had taken place in December 1929. State Secretary Hans Schäffer, Popitz's successor, who until the beginning of 1932 was the most important maker of Reich financial policy, enunciated this view again and again. Short-term borrowing needed to be avoided as a fundamental principle: 'it is quite out of the question that I should let myself be treated as Hilferding and Popitz were treated by the bankers when they wanted money'.[57] There were two reasons for taking this position: one political, the other economic.

Short-term borrowing from the banks laid the Reich open to pressure from the world of high finance at those moments when it was most vulnerable: if civil servants could not be paid and if unemployment pay was not available, there was a risk of the collapse of civil order. Politicians in the early 1930s developed a paranoia about bankers' conspiracies and bankers' 'ramps': a direct product of the financial uncertainty of those years. In Britain, there were stories of how the City had brought down the Second Labour Government in 1931; in France the 'two hundred families' who controlled the Banque de France were meant to be able to manipulate French political life.[58] In Germany, Brüning was convinced that the Deutsche Bank, the largest German bank, had somehow engineered the high Nazi

[56] *Kabinett Müller II*, Doc. 442.

[57] IfZ ED 93/10 25 Feb. 1931 diary entry.

[58] For Britain, see P. Williamson, 'Financiers, the Gold Standard and British Politics 1925–1931', in (ed.) J. Turner, *Businessmen and Politics 1900–1945*, London 1983, 106–29. For France, M. Anderson, The Myth of the Two Hundred Families, *Political Studies* 13, 1965, 163–78; J.-N. Jeanneney, *L'Argent caché: milieux d'affaires et pouvoirs politiques dans la France au XXe siècle*, Paris 1981.

vote in the Reichstag election of September 1930 in the belief that a radical election victory would produce a scare which would weaken the bank's less secure rivals. That the Deutsche Bank's most prominent Director, Oscar Wassermann, was a Zionist did not lessen Brüning's conviction of the bank's unhealthy influence on politics.[59] Dietrich, now Reich Finance Minister, joined Brüning's criticism of the bankers' policies and attitudes, and thought that there would be a popular movement to hang bankers from the lamp-posts of the Behrenstraße (the Berlin street on which all the German Great Banks had their head offices).[60] Schäffer, who was more sober and less prone to paranoid delusions than Brüning and his ministers, merely repeated over and over again that he could not give in to banking pressure for the Reich to impose specific measures by Emergency Decree: 'Even an undertaking of the Reich to German bankers [as opposed to foreigners, who imposed even tougher terms] to enact laws is a questionable proceeding. I am afraid of the dependence of the Government on the Behrenstraße, and I would rather be dependent on the Jägerstraße, though by preference not even that. It would not benefit the standing of the regime.' (The Reichsbank's offices were in the Berlin Jägerstraße).[61]

Schäffer's second argument on short-term deficits was an economic one. Government borrowing in the conditions of the tight capital market would crowd out private borrowers. One of the Schäffer's first memoranda as State Secretary argued that 'crisis of confidence are created or at least made considerably worse if the public *Kassen* [treasuries] resort to the money market at the *Termine* [month-, quarter-, and year-ends] or they call on moneys which, in a normal course, would have been provided by the banks for the economy'.[62] A crisis in confidence would in turn make the problem of funding government debt more acute: and the crisis in public finance and a liquidity crisis for business would each intensify the effects of the other. 'If only a few large firms get into difficulties, or

[59] IfZ ED93/15 20 Nov. 1931 diary entry. Wassermann did in fact believe after September 1930 that the Nazis should be taken into government: ED 93/9 14 Oct. 1930 diary entry.

[60] IfZ ED93/16 2 Dec. 1931 and 4 Dec. 1931 diary entries.

[61] BAK R2/3784 12 Sept. 1930 Meeting of Luther and Schäffer.

[62] IfZ ED93/29 January 1930 memorandum of State Secretary Schäffer.

internal troubles lead to a calling of short-term credit, there is an acute risk that treasury bills cannot be accommodated.'[63] For these reasons the financial policy-makers were primarily concerned with the problem of the *Kasse*, the balance of income and expenditure before borrowing entered the account, rather than the overall budget position.

These warnings were repeated frequently in the course of 1930 and 1931 as the danger grew more acute. Schäffer arrived at the Finance Ministry in early 1930 to discover a cash deficit (*Kassendefizit*) of 1675m. RM. The deficit grew larger throughout the year and led to a political crisis in June and July. The fiscal programme drawn up under Müller and accepted by the Reichstag in April, when the new government was already in office, was not adequate. Tax revenue continued to fall. Brüning's first Finance Minister, Moldenhauer, drew up a programme which involved increasing unemployment insurance contributions by 1 per cent in order to cover a new deficit of 443m. RM in the insurance institute's account, and imposing a *Notopfer* of 4 per cent on civil servants and 2.25 per cent on white-collar workers.[64] He was attacked by the still powerful civil service lobby, but also by some big industrialists (Paul Reusch, Oscar Sempell of the Vestag, Hermann Bücher of AEG) who were disappointed by the moderation of the Brüning regime and by the extent to which it seemed little more than a way of carrying on Müller's measures with a slightly different parliamentary base. The Government's critics saw in the financial embarrassment an opportunity to impose by blackmail a more general alteration of the social welfare system and of the operation of the labour market.[65]

Their strategic consideration followed this line: in March 1930 proposals to increase some taxes had been linked in a package (*Junktim*) with some tax cuts and with an increase in agricultural tariffs designed to please the agrarian representatives in the Reichstag parties.[66] The *Junktim* had been created

[63] IfZ ED93/9, 27 Aug. 1930 'Die Entwicklung der Kassenlage und des Haushaltes 1931'.

[64] (ed.) T. Koops, *Akten der Reichskanzlei Weimarer Republik, Die Kabinette Brüning I und II*, Boppard 1982, Doc. 45, 3 June 1930 Cabinet meeting.

[65] Ibid., Doc. 50, 18 June 1930 ministerial discussion.

[66] (Eds.) I. Maurer and U. Wengst, *Politik und Wirtschaft in der Krise 1930–1932. Quellen zur Ära Brüning*, Düsseldorf 1980, Doc. 56, 16 Apr. 1930 Westarp to Hugenberg.

in order to make the parts of the government programme non-negotiable: to ensure that the parties swallowed the medicine with the sugar lump, and that they did not throw the medicine away. The industrial strategy in dealing with Moldenhauer took the same course: the Government might be levered by its financial difficulties into giving up the system of wage contract (*Tarifvertrag*) agreements and compulsory state arbitration that was an important part of Weimar social legislation, but which stood in the way, business believed, of wage reduction necessary in order to restore Germany's damaged profitability. In addition, some businessmen believed that it was best to keep government, particularly at the Land and municipal levels, starved of funds so that public projects would not compete with or intervene in the operations of the private economy.[67]

When Moldenhauer refused to alter the government programme, his proposals were defeated by a combination of civil servants and businessmen in a vote in the DVP Reichstagfraktion. Disavowed by his own party, Moldenhauer resigned and, in the first reshuffle of the Brüning Cabinet, Hermann Dietrich became Reich Finance Minister. His programme did not differ radically from Moldenhauer's: unemployment insurance contributions were raised by 1 per cent, a 2½–5 per cent *Notopfer* and a general citizens' tax was imposed, and a tax on mineral water introduced. The very minor nature of the changes, and the increase in the proposed *Notopfer*, was in effect a declaration of war on the DVP by the Government; and the DVP responded by joining the DNVP and the SPD as well as the radical opposition parties in defeating the fiscal package in the Reichstag on 16 July.[68] Rather than allow another Finance Minister to go, Brüning applied the financial reform programme through a presidential Decree (*Notverordnung*) under the emergency provisions of the constitution (Article 48) and dissolved the Reichstag when it voted against the decree. From July 1930 Emergency Decrees were exclusively used in the implementation of the fiscal adjustment to falling depression revenues.

[67] HA/GHH 4001012024/7, 5 July 1930 Blank to Reusch (also as Maurer and Wengst, Doc. 105).

[68] Maurer and Wengst, Doc. 96, 25 June 1930 meeting of RDI Präsidium and Vorstand; Kabinette Brüning, Doc. 54, 24 June 1930 ministerial meeting, Doc. 63, 4 July 1930 meeting of Fraktion leaders; and Doc. 71 9 July 1930 ministerial meeting.

The funding of the government debt continued to raise problems: the September elections made the link between funding difficulties and political uncertainty clear.[69] After the elections, State Secretary Schäffer was unable to sell 230m. RM treasury bills required for payments anticipated until January. He was aware at the same time that he needed to build up a certain reserve 'because it is clear that political circumstances affect the capacity of the money market very seriously.'[70] Tax revenue went on falling during the depression, and the revenue–expenditure problem was made more serious by the consistently over-optimistic estimates of revenue produced in the Finance Ministry. Largely for this reason there was by March 1931 a new gap of 430m. RM in the Reich budget.[71] By June 1931 the size of the unfunded deficit was having a very severe effect on the German financial structure, and Schäffer's nightmares now became realities.

Brüning's Government had tried to prevent catastrophe by avoiding short-term deficits. The measures taken to stop the short-term debt increasing were:

Tax increases

Despite a few concessions to the *Steuersenkungspsychose* of the last months of the Great Coalition Government, taxes in the Brüning era were set at new heights. Necessity indicated that there could be no expansionary counter-cyclical fiscal policy of the sort pursued in 1925–6, since such a policy would raise the short-term debt issue in an acute form. However, there were some relatively trivial reductions in those taxes believed to be particularly damaging to capital formation. The level of corporation tax was left unchanged (at 20 per cent of corporate net income); and there were no alterations of basic rates of income and inheritance tax. The property tax of 1929–30 was cut to 3½ per cent of assessed value in December 1930 and to 3 per cent from 1932. On the other hand, a surcharge on income tax for incomes over 8000 RM was imposed (1 May 1930). For both income and corporation tax, payment dates were advanced by a month in April 1932; and the amounts required in

69 BAK R2/3784, 13 Oct. 1930 Mindir. Brecht to Reichsrat.

70 BAK R2/3784, 22 Sept. 1930 Schäffer memorandum on discussion with Brüning.

71 IfZ ED93/10, 6 Mar. 1931 diary entry.

tax pre-payments were raised. In addition there were taxes on single people (from 1 September 1930) amounting to an additional 10 per cent of the income tax bill, and the *Reichshilfe*, a tax on civil servants of 2½ per cent of income imposed from 1 September 1930 but suspended from 31 January 1931 after the first round of civil service pay cuts had been made. There was too a general communal 'crisis tax' or 'citizens' tax' imposed by decrees of 26 July 1930 and 1 December 1930, a progressive tax with a minimum rate of 6 RM for those on incomes under 4500 RM p.a., and rising to 2000 RM for those earning over 500 000 RM.

Indirect taxes were increased in a much more straightforward manner in line with the doctrine of imposing on consumption most of the burden of the depression. Tobacco duties were increased in January 1930 and beer excise (by about 50 per cent) in May 1930 to between 9.50 and 12.00 RPf/Litre, depending upon the quantity of beer brewed. Excise on cigarettes and cigars was raised further from 1 January 1931 (for a cigarette costing 12 RPf, the excise was 45.60 RPf per thousand), and excise on sugar doubled in that year. From May 1930 excise was payable on mineral water (5 RPf/L, for lemonade to 10 RPf/L) and on oil (38 RM/t). The question of the level of turnover tax was much more controversial than that of particular taxes on some items of consumption.[72] After all, the goods selected for excise increases were in some sense luxuries: German citizens did not need to drink beer or mineral water or smoke tobacco or travel in automobiles. Turnover tax, on the other hand, was imposed on almost all goods; and the reduction in the general turnover tax was widely regarded as the most important single measure of the Reich Government's anti-cyclical fiscal policy in 1925–6. It seemed to have worked, although some big business men had complained that the turnover tax reductions were less desirable than changes in rates of corporation tax. There was a political calculation here, too: since the turnover tax was calculated on each transaction, big vertically-integrated concerns or department stores with their own producers paid less tax than small producers and retailers. The turnover tax thus had the political odium of

[72] For a summary of tax changes from 1929 to 1932 see Wirtschaft und Statistik 12/22 (Nov. 1932), 708–13. Detailed information on tax rates from issues of RGBl.

being *Mittelstandsfeindlich,* directed against the middle layers of German society which many politicians considered to be the 'healthy element'.

In 1930 the turnover tax had been put up as part of the original December 1929 Hilferding tax package by 0.1 per cent to 0.85 per cent. Brüning proposed to increase the turnover tax after the September elections again in order to avoid the international humiliation of asking American banks for a bridging loan. The issue arose again in spring 1931 when the government failed to obtain a new bridging loan; an increase in turnover tax was discussed as a way of arresting the rise in Reich short-term debt. Dietrich was prepared to propose an increase to 1.5 per cent while Brüning and Schäffer wanted a more modest 1 per cent.[73] The issue was eventually deferred, with the consequence that the short-term debt became a major source of political instability. Alternatives to turnover tax were only discussed again after the formation in October 1931 of the second Brüning Cabinet and the appointment of a business man, Hermann Warmbold, as Economics Minister. Warmbold strenously resisted any increase in turnover tax and proposed instead a loan, or even a compulsory loan, rather than a tax increase which would either raise prices, or, more probably in the depths of the depression, knock profitability further.[74] Eventually Warmbold lost, and in the December Emergency Decree the turnover tax was increased to 2 per cent.

The tax burden on the German economy also increased because of the action of the Länder. Reich transfers of tax were reduced, and thus the Länder and communes had little choice but to raise their taxes. In Prussia, whose example was followed by many other Länder, building and land taxes were increased from 1 June 1930. Communal commercial tax rates (*Gewerbesteuer*) were also put up in some cases, and the *Gewerbesteuer* was extended to apply to all self-employed persons: another piece of *mittelstandsfeindlich* fiscal policy. Additional taxes were imposed: in Bavaria the 'slaughtered animal tax' from 5 November 1930; in Thuringia an 'administration cost supplement'. Behind these Land tax increases lay the rather cynical calculation

[73] IfZ ED93/10, 17 Apr. and 7 May 1931 diary entries.

[74] BAK NL Luther 367, 4 Dec. 1931 discussion; and IfZ ED93/16, 4 Dec. 1931 diary entry.

on the part of the Reich that it would share the responsibility for unpopular measures with lower levels of government. Such an evasion of responsibility by the Reich was partially successful in embarrassing and discrediting Land governments, and helped to bring nearer the constitutional reordering so desired by Brüning and Luther.

Changes in Unemployment Insurance

The changes in unemployment assistance represented, like the attack on Land revenue, a major undercutting of Weimar's political and social framework. In 1929 and 1930, the Reichsanstalt had required continual support from the Reich, and unemployment insurance was regarded as one of the causes of the Reich's financial difficulties. An obvious response was to cut the expenses involved in running the unemployment assistance scheme. The rates of 'crisis support' (the scheme covering the jobless after they had exhausted their entitlement to insurance benefit) were cut on 11 October 1930; and both insurance benefit and crisis support were reduced by 5 per cent by the 5 June 1931 Emergency Decree. Papen made cuts of up to 23 per cent in June 1932. In addition the period of insurance eligibility was cut in December 1931 to between sixteen and twenty weeks. Finally, and although this step infuriated both workers and employers, the level of contributions—in effect a kind of levy on wages—was raised to $4\frac{1}{2}$ per cent (26 July 1930) and then to $6\frac{1}{2}$ per cent (6 October 1930).[75] As was the case later with increases in the turnover tax, the amount by which the contributions were eventually raised is staggering in the light of the controversy that had initially surrounded the issue: the ostensible reason for the fall of Müller's coalition was the question of whether the rate of unemployment insurance contribution should be $3\frac{1}{2}$ per cent or $3\frac{3}{4}$ per cent.

Civil Service Pay Cuts

Brüning used the pressure on the budget as a reason for cutting civil service pay, freezing vacant posts, and also for dismissing non-permanent public employees (white collar workers—*Angestellte*—who did not have the protection offered by the

[75] Preller 459–73.

status of *Beamter*). These measures certainly produced savings on the budget: the cost of the general Reich administration fell from 1929/30 to 1930/1 by 1.8 per cent, and in the following fiscal year by 12.9 per cent (the equivalent figures for the Länder are 1.0 per cent and 13.5 per cent and the communes 1.5 per cent and 13.8 per cent).[76]

Brüning's campaign to reduce civil service pay also reflected a more general belief that the massive Köhler pay award had been politically maladroit, besides economically disastrous, in that it helped to fuel the general wage push of the late 1920s.[77] One way of tackling the overall wage problem was for the Government to take exemplary action over public sector pay.

Brüning wanted to make it his mission to reverse the 1927 pay award. Reich Labour Minister Adam Stegerwald was very sensitive to the argument that civil service pay had remained high in the slump while workers' earnings had fallen as firms reduced overtime and worked fewer shifts. Civil servants had job security too: they should now be made to accept a cut in salaries in order to 'set a good example'.[78] The free unions were prepared to co-operate in carrying out the pay reduction, which they thought to be a prerequisite for economic recovery, since the 1927 award had, they believed, led to the problems in state finance, which in turn had entailed increasing taxes, lowering benefits, and increasing insurance contributions. In addition, prices were falling in the depression so that some adjustment of nominal income seemed legitimate.

The idea of imposing a special burden (or *Notopfer*) on those with secure jobs had already been floated in the Müller era; then the SPD and Centre unionists had been eager but the proposal had been blocked by the DVP.[79] Brüning was very keen to revive the idea: already on 24 May 1930 he told State Secretary Schäffer that it would be necessary to cut civil service

[76] *Wirtschaft und Statistik*, Sonderbeilage zu 13/20 (1933), 4–5.

[77] See particularly H. Mommsen, 'Staat und Bürokratie in der Aera Brüning', in (ed.) G. Jasper, *Tradition und Reform in der deutschen Politik. Gedenkschrift für Waldemar Besson*, Frankfurt 1976, 81–137.

[78] R. Neebe, 'Unternehmerverbände und Gewerkschaften in den Jahren der Großen Krise 1929–33', *GG* 9, 1983, 309. *Kabinett Müller* II, Doc. 442.

[79] See K. D. Bracher, *Die Auflösung der Weimarer Republik*, Königstein/Taunus 1971[5], 300. But the core of the opposition within the DVP came from the industrial representatives: HA/GHH 400101293/4a, 17 June 1930 Gilsa to Reusch (also in Maurer and Wengst, Doc. 89).

pay in one way or another, despite the persisting and intransigent opposition of the DVP: 'I am not frightened of civil service unrest; at the moment cuts in the public sector are indeed popular.'[80] Brüning's insistence on the *Notopfer* pushed Finance Minister Moldenhauer into a very dangerous position within his party, and led to his resignation. Hermann Dietrich produced a compromise in which a *Notopfer* of 2½ per cent (the DVP's representative in the Cabinet, Julius Curtius, tried to stick at the old figure of only 2¼ per cent) was imposed on those with fixed incomes.[81] The *Notopfer* was tied into a package with a 5 per cent increase in the higher rates of income tax and a general poll tax. (Here there was a highly characteristic Brüning principle of equality of sacrifice: the SPD and the left would dislike the poll tax; the rich would dislike higher income tax; while the poorer civil servants would have their discontent over the *Notopfer* softened by the pleasure of seeing the rich hit).

On 1 December 1930 as a provisional measure, to remain in force until 31 January 1934, civil service salaries were cut from February 1931 by 6%: this step was to affect Länder and communal employees as well as those of the Reich. On 5 June 1931 further cuts of between 4 per cent and 8 per cent were made and child supplements reduced. The Dietramszell Emergency Decree (24 August 1931) allowed the Länder to ignore Land and communal parliaments in the implementation of salary cuts for their employees. Even after Dietramszell, Stegerwald still continued to believe that the civil service pay issue was fundamental: he went on calling for administrative reform and for the simplication of the German bureaucracy. Such proposals were included in the December 1931 Emergency Decree: a new 9 per cent cut in civil service salaries was imposed. In all the Brüning era cost civil servants up to 23 per cent of their nominal income.[82]

State Secretary Schäffer noted how the consequence was a radicalisation of the civil service.[83] Brüning complained that there were two low-grade and two medium-grade civil servants

[80] H. Pünder (ed. T. Vogelsang), *Politik in der Reichskanzlei: Aufzeichnungen aus den Jahren 1929–1932*, Stuttgart 1961, 52–60. IfZ ED93/8, 24 May 1930 diary entry.

[81] *Kabinette Brüning*, Doc. 56, 25 June 1930 Cabinet meeting.

[82] H. Mommsen 1976, 114.

[83] IfZ ED93/19, 4 Mar. 1932 diary entry.

in the Reich Chancellery who were Nazis.[84] A large number of officials in the finance, post, and customs administration became Nazis; and customs officials in Hamburg in 1931 applauded the KPD Reichstag deputy Torgler when he argued that submitting petitions to the German Government would bring no relief, and instead civil servants should imitate the British naval ratings who mutinied at Invergordon or the Polish civil servants who had gone on strike against Pilsudski's austerity decrees.[85] The Deutscher Beamtenbund, the civil service union, called for a revision of the Government's programme and an introduction of an 'active economic policy'; and at the same time it protested against attempts by the Prussian state to make support for the KPD or NSDAP illegal for its employees.[86] But it would be a mistake to see the protests of civil servants as providing a complete alternative to Brüning's policy: rather the protesters wanted a revision of priorities in the deflation. Prices should be cut further and faster than wages. One of the major grievances of the civil servants was that their pay was being used as an instrument in a general policy. Both the cuts in unemployment benefit and the civil service pay strategy were intended to alter the working of the German labour market. Cutting unemployment pay reduced the reserve price of labour and made it easier for firms still offering jobs to pay less, but here the really dramatic cuts came only with the Papen Government. Cuts in civil service pay were the preferred instrument of Brüning's time: they would, it was hoped, alter the expectations of participants in pay talks.

This connection of the specific German budgetary problem with a general complaint of industry about the way the labour market had worked in the 1920s raises the controversial question of whether Brüning 'instrumentalised' the crisis. Did the Chancellor use fiscal deflation, which damaged the economy, in the course of a general employers' offensive against wages?[87] This argument ignores the real budgetary constraints:

[84] Ibid.

[85] U. Büttner, *Hamburg in der Staats- und Wirtschaftskrise 1928–1931*, Hamburg 1982, 390–1.

[86] Ibid., 390–1, 479–80. Also *Die deutsche Beamtenschaft zur Wirtschaftslage: Wirtschaftspolitische Forderungen des Deutschen Beamtenbundes*, Berlin, 3 Sept. 1931.

[87] Argued by H. Mommsen 1976, 111; G. Schulz, 'Reparationen und Krisenprobleme nach dem Wahlsieg der NSDAP 1930: Betrachtungen zur Regierung Brüning',

Brüning was guiding the economy within a very narrow range of options. His high civil servants—Trendelenburg and Schäffer—looked more and more desperately for ways of saving money, even as they realised that the budgetary deflation was helping to undermine political stability as civil servants mutinied and the unemployed took to street warfare. They pressed for very substantial spending cuts in areas where there was no immediate or direct effect on the labour market, as well as asking the civil service to set a good example to the rest of the economy and at the same time accept less pay in order to relieve the strain on the Reich's budget.

Other Spending Cuts

Reductions in other areas of state spending were in fact much more drastic that the pay cuts, largely because they were easier to achieve. Thus administrative costs actually rose as a proportion of total state expenditure. Total public spending on house construction fell from 1 598.7m. RM (1929/30) to 638.3m. RM (1931/2), a fall of 60.1 per cent; and over the same period spending on 'economic purposes' (loans, subsidies, etc.) dropped from 2 202.9m. RM to 1 648.1m. RM (25.2 per cent).[88] These falls provided a stark contrast with the years after the stabilisation of the Mark, when the Reich had responded to economic distress with generous handouts to business men when they complained about their position.

Long-term Funding

In 1930 and 1931 an international loan appeared to be the only realistic way to fund the Government's debt properly in view of the weakness of the German capital market. The Brüning regime negotiated with Lee Higginson and with the Kreuger match monopoly trust; it also tried to raise money through Paul Warburg's International Acceptance Bank, New York, and also through J. P. Morgan. In October 1930 a $125m. loan from a consortium headed by Lee Higginson, Boston, was

VSWG 67, 1980, 220; C.-L. Holtfrerich, 'Alternativen zu Brünings Wirtschaftspolitik in der Weltwirtschaftskrise', *HZ* 235, 1982, 605–31.

[88] *Wirtschaft und Statistik*, Sonderbeilage zu 13/20 (1933) 6–7.

agreed.[89] This Loan was so clearly tied to the Emergency Decree of the same month as to be very humiliating for the German Government: the practice of linking a loan to compulsory reform was reminiscent of the behaviour of late nineteenth-century western governments dealing with Egypt, Turkey, or Morocco. The 6 October Emergency Decree which cut Reich transfers to the Länder and communes and which put up contributions to unemployment insurance was in essence imposed by Germany's creditors.

In the spring of 1931 a new proposal to raise foreign money was worked out: it involved the sale of Reichsbahn preference shares, and depended on a diplomatic *rapprochement* with France to be managed through the good offices of Lee Higginson. But the prospects for this operation were never good, and most Frenchmen remained understandably worried by German motives. France feared that Germany was trying to demolish reparations; on the other hand some Americans thought that she should do just that. American bankers would be prepared to lend more money to Germany only if the reparation issue were finally solved: otherwise they feared that they would find their interests subordinated to those of the reparation creditors. Paul Warburg offered to give a new $500m. loan once the Allies had agreed on reparations;[90] and the prospect of a settlement bringing money into Germany was an important motive for Brüning's fateful step of reopening the reparation issue in the early summer of 1931.

In the financial year 1930/1 the Reich managed to increase its foreign debt from 1b. RM to 3.3b RM, and to reduce its domestic debt slightly. The net credit increase of 2 241 859 RM, equivalent to 27.5 per cent of the Reich's expenditure for that year, allowed the Brüning system to survive.[91] But Brüning was very vulnerable: slight doubts on the part of the creditors would bring the whole flow of funds to a halt. In these circumstances the failure of a new Lee Higginson package and of *rapprochement* with France in spring 1931 was a major

[89] See BAK R2/3784, 23 Sept. 1930 Dreyse note; *Kabinette Brüning*, Docs. 117, 124, Cabinet meetings of 24 and 29 Sept. 1930; IfZ ED93/9, 26 Sept. 1930 and 1 Oct. 1930 diary entries; and McKittrick papers, Baker Library Harvard, Box 23.

[90] IfZ ED93/10, 25 Feb. 1931 diary entry.

[91] *Wirtschaft und Statistik*, Sonderbeilage zu 13/20 (1933) 8–9.

disaster: there was no longer any likelihood of new long-term lending from abroad, and the Reich began to live from hand to mouth again.

In March 1931 53.5m. RM treasury bills were renewed, and a further 71.5m. RM had to be placed on the market.[92] More small cuts in spending became necessary. In June 1931 the Reich forced the commercial banks to take 250m. RM Reich bills under threat of sanctions against them at a time when the Reichsbank was imposing restrictions on its discounting. As a result, the Reichsbank refused to discount some commercial bills, and thus created difficulties for business and strained the liquidity of the banks.[93] Thus began the great disaster of the banking crisis.

The story of the managing of the Reich debt during the depression is a nail-bitting saga of how even relatively small deficits could produce major embarrassment. German deficits were much smaller than those in Britain or the USA at the same time. In part the German exercise was so difficult because of the high level of political uncertainty. What would be the policy of future German governments? Would they repudiate foreign or domestic debts? This uncertainty was a major consideration already in late 1930, following the September elections: Lee Higginson's dette ottomane clauses were an attempt to make their and Ivar Kreuger's money absolutely safe. The German risk was made even higher by the high volume of foreign debt (though no one at this time had a very clear idea of how high it actually was) and by the recency of Germany's inflation experience. It was certain that once there was no longer any prospect of debt security, the German problem would be transformed radically.

THE LÄNDER

Though the position of the Länder was frequently attacked in the course of the 1920s, it was in practice impossible after 1919 to enact any major constitutional reform within the framework

[92] IfZ ED93/30 3 Mar. 1931 Schäffer comment on Kassenlage; ED93/11, 10 and 11 June 1931 diary entries.

[93] See H. James. 'The Causes of the German Banking Crisis of 1931', *EcHR* 2nd Ser. 37, 1984, 79–81.

of the Weimar system, let alone to abolish the Länder. The larger states—Prussia, Saxony, and particularly the South German states, Baden, Württemberg, and Bavaria—had such powerful traditions of their own autonomous political life that any diminution of that autonomy would lead to major disruptions. For the South Germans, almost all political issues of importance were resolved not in Berlin, but in Karlsruhe, Stuttgart, and Munich. Education, church–state relations, police, the administration of justice, and some kinds of economic support were run not by the Reich but by the Länder.

An obvious starting-point for reform would have been to tackle the disparity between the size of the German Länder: in 1925 Prussia included 61.2 per cent of the German population and accounted for 62.5 per cent of the area; Schaumburg–Lippe had 0.08 per cent of the population and 0.07 per cent of the area. For Bavaria, which was by far the largest Land after Prussia, these figures were 11.8 per cent and 17.1 per cent.[94] The Länder Conference of 1928 addressed itself to the problem of a reordering of the Länder, and a final report recommended the creation of a Reichsland or North German unitary state, in practice Great-Prussia, with only Saxony, Baden, Württemberg, and Bavaria being allowed to survive. The old Prussian ministries would be integrated into the Reich's administrative structure on the creation of the new Reichsland. But by the time this report appeared in 1930, the Bavarians had declared their entrenched hostility to a scheme which threatened to be a half-way stage to the creation of a completely unitary state and which thus threatened the autonomy of even the remaining Länder. The Reich Government too now dissociated itself from the proposal to dismantle Prussia.[95]

During the depression, criticism of the Länder became more vociferous. One pressure group which was particularly active in this regard was the 'League for the Renewal of the German Reich' created under Hans Luther's leadership in January 1928 (it was generally known alternately as the Erneuerungsbund and the Lutherbund). Essentially this was an organisation of big business: the Lutherbund's Kuratorium (governing

[94] These figures do not include the Saarland.

[95] *Verfassungsausschuß der Länderkonferenz; Niederschrift über die Verhandlungen vom 21. Juni 1930 und Beschlüsse des Verfassungsausschußes*, Berlin 1930; Schulz 1963, 595–6.

body) was composed of prominent industrialists and merchants: Graf Siegfried Roedern and Heinrich Witthoeft (two leading Hamburg traders and conservatives), Paul Reusch, Carl Bosch, Jacob Goldschmidt, and Paul Kempner (Mendelssohn & Co.). Luther also had excellent contacts with the Fried. Krupp AG; and drew funds from a wider business circle which included the Vereinigte Stahlwerke, Robert Bosch, AEG, Norddeutscher Lloyd, Rheinische Braunkohle, the Bayerische Vereinsbank, and the Deutsche Werft Hamburg.[96] The programme of the League involved a revision of the reparation settlement, and required as a preliminary to this the pruning of German administration. In turn, the simplification of public administration was closely associated with the idea of doing without parliaments: it was widely believed that the log-rolling principle meant that parliamentary activity produced increases in expenditure. The League's annual meeting in February 1930 passed a resolution which, only a month before the end of the Müller Government and the creation of the first presidential Cabinet, emphasised the necessity of the 'activation of the rights of the Reich President as head of the German state and its representative in the eyes of the people, as laid down in the constitution'.[97] Hermann Bücher (AEG) had already written in 1927 to Reusch (GHH) that someone was needed with 'power beyond that of a minister . . . This man really needs to know what he wants, and if he knows what he wants, he would not be supported in a cabinet and probably not in a parliament.' Though Brüning was not involved in the setting up of the Erneuerungsbund, it is not difficult to find the Brüning solution advocated again and again by the League's members. Reusch had argued too that above all it was necessary to avoid the 'hot air of parliamentarism'.[98]

The financial crisis at the end of the 1920s turned into a crisis of Länder parliaments not simply because those parliaments were attacked by influential centralisers. As the Länder faced more and more problems, and were obliged to take more

[96] HA/GHH 400101293/16a, list of contributions.

[97] HA/GHH 400101293/16b, 28 Feb. 1930 proceedings of annual meeting of Erneuerungsbund.

[98] HA/GHH 400101293/15, 28 Oct. 1927 Bücher to Reusch, 8 July 1927 Reusch to Warburg.

and more unpopular steps, the Länder governments lost their majorities in the parliaments. From 1929 Saxony was run by an 'apolitical' Cabinet of civil servants; after 1930 the Held Government in Bavaria was only *geschäftsführend* (i.e. a caretaker regime); and the elections of April 1932 deprived the Prussian and Württemberg Cabinets of parliamentary majorities and turned them too into caretaker regimes.

The Reich did nothing to lessen the discomfiture of the Länder in the depression: on the contrary. Attempts to impose savings in the crisis bore the marks of the Reich's hostility to Land governments. From 1929/30 to 1930/1 Reich tax transfers were cut by 395.3m. RM; and in the following fiscal year by 883.9m. RM.[99] In consequence the Länder and the communes actually had to take steps to increase their own tax revenue in order to make their budgets balance. Revenue from land and building taxes increased by 16.7 per cent from 1929/30 to 1930/1: and revenue from the *Gewerbesteuer* was held at approximately the same level despite the falling volume of business activity. Bavaria, Saxony, and Baden introduced the slaughter taxes. In addition there were new communal taxes on beverages. Between July 1932 and January 1933 the slaughter tax was extended to all German Länder (with the trivial exception of Schaumburg-Lippe, whose cattle population was less than any Land except Lübeck and Mecklenburg-Schwerin).

Increases in Länder and communal taxes helped to fuel the attacks on the Länder by business, which believed that it was being overtaxed chiefly because of the profligacy of the federal states; and this in turn helped to strengthen the Reich in its dealings with the Länder. The Reich Government indeed deliberately pushed responsibility for unpopular measures onto Länder governments struggling to maintain parliamentary majorities. The Bavarian Government complained that 'the Länder are left with odious taxes and falling revenues'.[1] Such designs on the part of Reich authorities had appeared before Brüning's presidential regime: Johannes Popitz in the Finance Ministry had been a powerful, intriguing centraliser, and the

[99] Annual figures from *Wirtschaft und Statistik*.

[1] BStA MA 103331, Oct. 1930 memorandum: 'Wirtschafts- und Finanzprogramm der Reichsregierung'.

Bavarian Minister-President Heinrich Held had already complained in February 1929 that the 'Berliners were trying to push through on the finance-political path the result [the destruction of the Länder] that they could not achieve by force'.[2] The erosion of support in Land parliaments because of tax disputes had begun in 1929: the Berlin Government's representative in Munich for instance wrote (June 1929) that 'it is becoming ever more apparent that a parliament is not the suitable instrument for such wide-ranging and grandly planned measures [expenditure cuts] because deputies cannot be prized away from local interests'.[3]

The tax programme drawn up in December 1929 by Reich Finance Minister Hilferding and then bequeathed to Hilferding's successors placed a further limitation on Land regimes: the Land and communal tax on commerce was to be cut by 20 per cent and the land tax by 10 per cent from April 1930; and these taxes were not to be increased for a ten-year period. Thus Land finance became more and more controlled: the only path for the Länder was the unpopular one of reducing exemptions from Land and commerce taxes, or inventing new taxes altogether. The December 1930 Emergency Decree took over the control clauses of the Hilferding programme, and in addition curtailed the Länder shares in turnover tax.

The same hostile attitude to the Länder characterised the Emergency Decree of 5 June 1931, which imposed crisis supplements as Reich taxes; but although this was in effect a kind of income tax it was not shared under the Finanzausgleich arrangements with the Länder and communes. Neither the June decree, nor the 6 October 1931 Emergency Decree, which restricted the rights of Land and communal parliaments, were preceded by consultation with Land representatives. In June Länder ministers were simply abruptly summoned to Berlin on 2 June to be told the contents of the measures published three days later.[4] The October decree raised profound constitutional implications: the Länder argued that the Reich Constitution did not provide for the Reich to supervise the communes directly, without Land mediation, yet it was precisely this

[2] R2/19980, 5 Feb. 1929 report of Held interview with Edgar Mowrer.

[3] R2/20178, 28 June 1929 report of Reich representative in Munich.

[4] BStA MA 103462, 1 June 1931 meeting of Bavarian Ministerrat.

control that the Decree had established. Under its terms communal building projects were to be cut back, and the purposes for which communal savings on the salaries of the communal employees might be used were centrally defined.[5]

Brüning's imposition of more central control rather curiously alienated those Länder with deep-rooted historical opposition to centralisation rather less than it angered the Prussian Government, which believed itself to be the main target of the Reich's attacks. Held indeed remained in general loyal to the Brüning line, although again and again he sent in objections to what he rightly believed to be its constitutional implications. In Württemberg, the Minister-President from 1928 to 1933 was a Centre politician, Eugen Bolz, who was a friend of Brüning's and whose only criticism of the Hunger Chancellor was that he did not go far enough. He agreed with Brüning that the system of governing bureaucratically by decree law was a way of preserving those parties still loyal to Weimar from the odium of having to impose deflation by parliamentary majority.[6]

In Bavaria Held had already lost his parliamentary majority. In the summer of 1930 the Bayerischer Bauernbund (BBB) refused to support Held's slaughter tax, because this would make meat more expensive for the consumer, would reduce consumption, and depress prices paid to farmers. The government finance bill was defeated in the Landtag, which then went on to pass a motion of no confidence in the Bavarian Government. So Held had to rule by decree law, or give up. The rise of the Nazi vote in the September Reichstag elections frightened the BBB and the Bavarian SPD into taking a more sympathetic stance towards Held's regime: these parties practised a Bavarian version of toleration policy, and the slaughter tax was in practice accepted. Nevertheless Held had to avoid provocation, and tried at all costs to avoid a repetition of the events of the summer. An ideal way of ruling was to allow the Reich to impose its austerity by decree. Thus Held consistently

[5] BStA MA 103463, 6 Oct. 1931 meeting in Reichskanzlei, 13 Oct. 1931 Held to Reich Chancellor; 12 Nov. 1931 memorandum: 'Denkschrift der Bayerischen Staatsregierung über die Aushöhlung der Länder durch die Notverordnungen des Reichs'.

[6] For example, BStA MA 103331, memorandum on 1 Dec. 1931 NVO, 13 Oct. 1930 Held to Reich Chancellor, *Bayerische Staatszeitung*, 29 Oct. 1930 (report of speech by Schmelzle). On Württemberg, see W. Besson, *Württemberg und die deutsche Staatskrise 1928–1933*, Stuttgart, 1959, 176–7, 246.

supported the use of presidential orders in the implementation of Brüning's financial programme. The same calculations about what political parties could be expected to swallow applied to the Reichstag as to the Landtage in Held's eyes: 'in this way those parties in the Reichstag [i.e. the SPD as well as the BVP, the Bavarian equivalent of the Centre], which in their hearts believe that such decisive measures are unavoidable, will be relieved of the responsibility of approving such measures, which might harm part of their electoral support'.[7] Or, as Held told the Bavarian Cabinet, 'We can let ourselves be forced, but should not ourselves collaborate.'[8]

Hostility in Berlin towards Bavaria originated not so much from the Reich Government as from the Reichsbank, which proved to be an ideal base for Luther's campaign against the Länder. The Bavarian state had borrowed abroad in the 1920s, chiefly in order to construct hydro-electric works which would promote the economic development of what had been a rather backward part of Germany. Bavarian indebtedness did not increase significantly during the economic crisis: there was, unlike in Prussia or Saxony, no increase at all in 1929 in the unfunded deficit. Bavarian state finance might well be considered, at least by the standards of the time in Germany, a model of rectitude. Nevertheless when in the middle of the international financial and banking crisis of the summer of 1931 a medium-term credit from the Bankers Trust Company New York fell due, the Reichsbank did its obstreperous best to maximise Bavarian embarrassment. Luther—following the maxims of his Erneuerungsbund—refused to discount bills of the Bavarian electricity works or to assist in negotiations with the Bankers Trust.[9] He believed quite simply that the banking crisis could be used as the ideal opportunity to impose the long-needed Reich reform: snappily, and without reference to parliaments. In the Cabinet he developed this case again and again: 'We must use the extraordinary path of executive force. My suggestion is to take the Prussian executive into the Reich

[7] BAK R2/20178, 26 Sept. 1930 report of Reich representative in Munich. See in general on Bavarian politics: (ed.) M. Spindler, *Handbuch der Bayerischen Geschichte* IV/1, Munich 1974, 484–517.

[8] BStA MA 103734, 6 Oct. 1930 metting of Ministerrat.

[9] Bayerische Staatsbank 153, 4 May 1933 Hammer to Bavarian Minister-President. BAK NL Luther 337, 25 Oct. 1931 Luther conversation with Staatsrat Fritz Schäffer.

so that all civil servants are dependent on the central state.'[10] The only way to stop the 'drift away from private ownership' was by restricting the credit of public corporations.[11]

Prussia rather than Bavaria represented the thorniest problem for both Brüning and Luther. Brüning was a Catholic who was happy to leave sensible conservative Bavaria as it was, while the Protestant zealot Luther would have preferred to subordinate the south German states; but it was clear that at least for the time being South Germany did not present the same range of political problems as Prussia. In the first place, Prussia was ruled still by the parties of the Weimar coalition, and stood in consequence in a rather odd relation to the Reich. Brüning and Luther again took different approaches: Brüning believed that he needed to work with Minister-President Otto Braun in order to secure the continuation of the SPD Reichstag Fraktion's 'toleration policy'. Luther on the other hand gave priority to constitutional reform, and in addition continued to see himself as a rival to Brüning who might well stand to benefit if the Braun–Brüning axis collapsed.

Then there had been a long history of the Reichsbank intervening in Prussian affairs in order to discredit the Prussian Government. Luther's predecessor Schacht was a master of this game. In 1927 he had used his American contacts to stop Prussia issuing an American loan through Harris Forbes.[12] In January 1929 he had stopped a plan to fund the Prussian short-term debt and had offered short-term Reichsbank facilities instead: this proceeding attracted Schacht because it meant keeping the Prussians on a very short leash.[13]

The effect of the slump was particularly severe on Prussia's revenue. Prussia started out from a relatively favourable position in that her debt per capita was lower than that of other Länder (1931: Prussia 13.50 RM; Saxony 38.66; Bavaria 35.44; Thuringia 36.62; Hesse 27.92).[14] But Prussia's income fell particularly sharply: between 1929/30 and 1932/3 the total of

[10] IfZ ED93/15, 18 Nov. 1931 diary entry. Also see BAK R2/4057, 15 Dec. 1930 meeting in Reich Finance Ministry, and Brüning, Memoiren 372.

[11] IfZ ED93/12, 22 July 1931 diary entry.

[12] PA/AA WRep Frage der Aufnahme deutscher Kredite oder Anleihen im Auslande, 27 Sept. 1927 report of German Embassy in Washington.

[13] PrSA Rep 151/63g, Jan. 1929: suggestions for funding of Prussian debt.

[14] BAK R2/19980a, 30 Sept. 1931 middle- and short-term debt of Länder.

Reich taxes transferred to the Prussian state and communes fell by 47 per cent; while Bavaria's revenue from Reich transfers was still 64 per cent of the level at the beginning of Brüning's Chancellorship. So Prussia taxed more, and also used the Reich's ploy of cutting tax transfers to lower administrative levels. From 1929/30 to 1930/1 Prussian tax revenue rose by 1.8 per cent but transfers from the Land to the communes were cut by 8.3 per cent. In the next financial years transfers were cut by 16.6 per cent and then by an astonishing 36.4 per cent.[15] As a result, the Prussian communes were either on the brink of financial collapse, or, more frequently by 1932, actually over it.

The Prussian financial difficulties affected the general political situation in two ways: they determined the responses of the parties in the Prussian Landtag; and they raised the spectre of social disturbance, of a repetition of 1918–19. Observers believed that a severe financial crisis would lead to a premature dissolution of the Prussian Landtag, and this would almost certainly mean that the parties of the Weimar coalition would lose their majority. In order to avoid precisely such a disaster, Braun drafted a scheme to carry out a Reich reform by Emergency Decree and fuse the governments each side of the Wilhelmstraße. The Prussian Minister-President was to become Reich Vice-Chancellor and the Prussian Ministers of the Interior and of Justice would take over the corresponding Reich ministries. In return, the Reich would take care of the administration of finance and therefore of the increasingly desperate communal problem. Prussia's Finance Minister Hermann Höpker-Aschoff was the most enthusiastic proponent of this plan in the Prussian Cabinet (after all it was he who would be relieved of the greatest burden by the scheme) and on 23 August 1931 he announced to the public, prematurely, the details of the fusion of the Reich and Prussia.[16] The financial crisis in Prussia became more and more desperate as these debates went on. On 18 September Höpker-Aschoff told Braun that the Prussian floating debt now amounted to 263m. RM and that Prussia could not survive without the help of the Reich. Even these figures that Höpker-Aschoff found so alarm-

[15] From *Wirtschaft und Statistik*.

[16] H. Schulze, *Otto Braun oder Preußens demokratische Mission: Eine Biographie*, Berlin 1977, 694, 698.

ing were in fact over-optimistic: the total deficit that had not been funded amounted to 451m. RM for 1930 and 1931.[17]

The Prussian state could not make more spending cuts in order to avoid catastrophe. Economies in the Prussian administration appeared to be blocked by the political constellation, as the Centre party consistently refused to support administrative reform and simplification in Prussia.[18] The Reichsbank blocked the implementation of the Braun–Höpker-Aschoff scheme by refusing outright to help with the management of the Prussian debt. Luther refused to give credit to the Prussian communes, and thus made the political future of the Prussian state appear unclear.[19]

In addition, the financial difficulties of Prussia and of the Prussian communes threatened to produce revolution. By the end of 1931 there was a great deal of violence on the Prussian streets, as half-criminal gangs beat each other up in the name of ideologies. The Prussian ministers were terrified: Interior Minister Carl Severing, who controlled the Prussian police, wrote a frightening memorandum. 'If the Oberbürgermeister of Duisburg told the many thousands unemployed that he is not in a position to pay a Pfennig to support them, the consequences would reach beyond Duisburg: the whole industrial area would burst into flames. Such disturbances would damage the Reich's credit.'[20]

Höpker-Aschoff was forced to resign by the Prussian Centre, but his successor Otto Klepper was if anything slightly to the left of Höpker-Aschoff, and resolved to step up the conflict with the Reich. On 23 November Klepper asked for 300m. RM to cover the needs of the Prussian Treasury. The other Länder and the Reich Finance Ministry opposed Klepper's demands, and Held even ran a press campaign in Bavaria supporting the Chancellor in the conflict with Prussia. Klepper retaliated with a public announcement that the Reich was blocking Prussia's plans to spend money to relieve unemploy-

[17] IISG Otto Braun papers 470, 18 Sept. 1931 memorandum of Höpker-Aschoff.

[18] IfZ ED93/17, 6 Jan. 1932 diary entry (on meeting of Klepper and Brüning).

[19] H. Schulze, 712. BAK NL Luther 370, 14 Oct. 1931 meeting of Reichsbank Direktorium.

[20] IfZ ED93/13, 17 Aug. 1931 diary entry. FES NL Severing 47, 5 Mar. 1931 Severing memorandum on Prussian communes.

ment.[21] When the Reich remained uncooperative, Klepper went further and announced in Frankfurt, in a manner calculated to excite international alarm, that Brüning had told him to use deception to balance the Prussian budget and to help the Reich in carrying out a policy of inflation in Germany.[22] Luther told Klepper in January 1932 that the Reichsbank would not handle a Prussian bridging loan if the Braun-Klepper regime did not immediately draw up a plan for budget reform; the Prussian pair then retaliated by accusing Luther of trying to overthrow the Prussian constitutional order.[23]

That order was in grave danger after the elections to the Prussian Landtag on 24 April 1932 deprived the Braun Government of its majority. As there was no other possible majority coalition, since the Centre would not work with the NSDAP, Braun was left in charge of a caretaker government. By now he was suffering from nervous exhaustion and high blood pressure, and withdrew from affairs, taking no part in the government whose Minister-President he remained. The budget situation appeared to be slightly easier after 10 March anyway, since the Brüning Government had agreed to lend 100m. RM to Prussia and pay half this sum by 1 July.[24] However, the Reich did not actually do anything to fulfil its promise, and in June Papen's Finance Minister Schwerin von Krosigk refused to pay: with the result that the Prussian Government was unable to pay its civil servants. In addition, during the summer the amount owed by the Prussian communes to the Prussian state grew: from 61m. RM (30 May) to 130m. RM (31 August).

Communal finance was the weak point at which the Reich and the Reichsbank directed its criticism. At the beginning of 1932 large numbers of communes defaulted on their debts in order to be able to carry on paying wages and social security. As in the summer of 1931, these defaults threatened the

[21] IfZ ED93/15, 23 Nov. 1931 diary entry; and IfZ ZS/A–20 4A 176 (Schwerin von Krosigk).

[22] IfZ ED93/19, 4 Mar. 1932 diary entry.

[23] BAK NL Luther 368, 2 Feb. 1932 meeting of Luther, Warmbold, Braun, and Klepper. FES NL Severing 20, 21 Jan. 1932 Otto Braun to Severing.

[24] H. Schulze, 736.

municipal savings banks and the stability of the financial system. The Reich Economics Minister warned of the consequences of failure to pay interest on the communal debt, but received the answer from Severing that it was more important to prevent revolution by keeping up welfare payments.[25] Luther took up the argument by saying that if the communes were not made by the Land authorities to save their own savings banks, the case for an intervention of the Reich would be strengthened. The Reichsbank itself was no longer prepared to lend on the inadequate security provided by the communes: 'We too are convinced that special measures should be taken by the responsible Reich and Land authorities in order to prevent the special situation of the communes leading to a damaging of the whole credit structure.'[26] Luther also kept up the pressure in other ways: in May 1932, in the middle of the political crisis which followed Brüning's fall, Luther still proclaimed his refusal to help with the management of the Prussian short-term debt.[27] The Prussian Government only weakened its position further by attempts which it could not afford to save Prussian cities from Luther. Later Severing complained of his and Braun's helplessness: 'Whether the system of economy measures was the best way of promoting an economic recovery sometimes seemed doubtful to me. But it was not for Prussia to decide. These were Reich decrees, which had to be put into effect, and Prussia would and could not resist them.'[28]

Pressure on finance softened up the Prussian regime before the *putsch* which on 20 July deposed the Braun Government. The loyalty of the civil service and the police force was placed under strain as uncertainty grew as to whether salary and wage payments would be made at the end of each month. The 'Papen *putsch*' took place on lines envisaged by Luther: the men responsible for its implementation were part of the Herrenklub circle which had supported Luther's scheme for Reich reform. The new Commissary Prussian Interior Minister was Oberbürgermeister Franz Bracht, Luther's successor as Mayor of Essen

[25] BAK R2/20133, 16 Feb. 1932 Reich Economics Ministry circular; 23 Jan. 1932 Prussian Interior Minister to Reich Finance Minister.

[26] BAK R2/20133, 9 Mar. 1932 Reichsbank to Prussian Interior Minister.

[27] BAK R2/19980, 31 May 1932 ministerial meeting.

[28] C. Severing, *Mein Lebensweg II. Im Auf und Ab der Republik*, Cologne 1950, 299.

and his best contact among German mayors. Freiherr von Gayl, the Reich Interior Minister, had delighted Luther in June by declaring his sympathy for the ideas of the Erneuerungsbund. Luther however, was annoyed when the *putsch* actually took place, since it was carried out without his participation, and it meant in practice that he could no longer find a role for himself in German politics.[29]

The *putsch* did not, of course, immediately alter Prussia's financial position: it merely altered the way in which the position might be politically exploited. The Prussian state was used to applying pressure on the communes—which had always been the real enemy of the business world and of the right. By the end of 1932, the financial position was so desperate that Prussia restricted transfers to communes for all payments except 'A' needs (wages and salaries, and social support payments).[30] Gayl and Bracht were no longer prepared to attempt to protect the Prussian communes as Severing had still attempted to do. Indeed Papen's purpose in appointing Bracht was to let a professional mayor smash the powers of the mayors of Germany.

The story of the conflict between the Reich and Prussia from 1930 to 1932 illustrates the way in which the Länder issue was becoming less of a constitutional dispute about the Reich–Land relationship, and more of a clash over the position of the municipalities. It was the communes that looked more and more like the sick men of Germany. Why?

THE COMMUNES

In the Weimar Republic the most immediate, obvious, and active form of governmental authority was not the distant Reich nor even the Land governments, but rather the municipality and the commune. Germany's local government system had originated in the Stein–Hardenberg period: the idea of self-administration (*Selbstverwaltung*) by local notables (*Honoratioren*) was a product of the need to reorganise German local political life in the wake of the terrible defeats inflicted by the Napoleonic armies. Before the First World War, the *Honora-*

[29] IfZ ED93/21, 28 July 1932 diary entry.
[30] BAK R2/20153, 1 Nov. 1932 Mulert to Reich Chancellor.

tioren were giving way to a generation of spectacularly powerful professional Oberbürgermeister, elected by city parliaments but then virtually unsackable and not responsible to the city parliament.[31] These men usually had a determination to modernise civic life at all costs. Often they had little but contempt for the old-fashioned notables and they liked to disregard the civic assemblies. Max Weber referred to 'plebiscitary city dictators'.[32]

After 1918 these great mayors enlarged their powers and their position still further. To begin with, the areas they administered became much larger. A Prussian law of 1920 created Great-Berlin (Groß-Berlin): Berlin annexed seven formerly independent cities and increased its area by a factor of thirteen. The second largest city in the Reich was Hamburg, like Bremen and Lübeck not a city but a Hanseatic state immediate to the Reich: this constitutional peculiarity made it more difficult for Hamburg to swallow the adjacent conurbation of Altona, which belonged to Prussia as part of the province of Schleswig-Holstein. Altona was only handed over to Hamburg in 1938. But there were spectacular cases of city aggrandisement in the Rhineland. In 1922 Cologne swallowed Worringen. In July 1929 the whole Rhineland-Westphalian industrial area was reordered: Düsseldorf was enlarged to include Benrath and Kaiserswerth; Essen was extended to cover Werden, Steele, Karnap, Katernberg, Stoppenberg, Kary, and Kupferdreh. Duisburg was fused with Hamborn, Oberhausen with Sterkrade and Osterheld, Krefeld with Wertingen, Remscheid with Lennep and Lüttringhausen, Rheydt with München-Gladbach, and Barmen with Elberfeld (to form the new city of Wuppertal). In 1928 the area of the city of Frankfurt/Main was increased by 44 per cent as the city was extended to cover Griesheim, Sossenheim, Schwanheim, and Höchst. Stuttgart in 1922 expanded to include Obertürkheim, Hedelfingen, Botnang, and Kaltental; in 1929 Hofen; in 1931 Rotenberg and Münster; and in 1932 Zuffenhausen.[33]

[31] W. Hofmann, *Städtetag und Verfassungsordnung*, Stuttgart 1966, 26–56.

[32] Quoted in (ed.) H. Stehkämper, *Konrad Adenauer, Oberbürgermeister von Köln*, Cologne 1970, 293.

[33] Gesetz über die Bildung einer neuen Stadtgemeinde Berlin, 24 April 1920; Stehkämper 582; D. Rebentisch, *Ludwig Landmann: Frankfurter Oberbürgermeister der*

City administrators had to deal directly with the social problems posed by the German revolution of 1918–19; and the solutions they produced were as characteristic of the nature of the Weimar compromise as the manipulations and intrigues of party leaders in Berlin. Konrad Adenauer, who had become Oberbürgermeister of Cologne in 1917, was acutely aware of the problem faced by city administrators. He believed that it was the activity of the communal officials and the capacity of *Selbstverwaltung* to bring together all classes that had limited the extent of the damage done by the revolution. The cities in his eyes came closest to establishing a real corporatism based on social collaboration. His view of the revolution influenced Adenauer so profoundly that he regarded with horror the policies pursued by Brüning: if there were not immediate and large-scale work creation programmes, Adenauer claimed in the summer of 1930, there would be 'very great political difficulties'.[34] Ludwig Landmann, the Oberbürgermeister of Frankfurt/Main, was eloquent on the theme of how the cities were creating a new German culture and thus a new German stability: 'The justification from a socio-political standpoint of the cultural policy of the large cities in a time of crisis is to help ensure that the leaders rising out of the masses are filled with the spirit which flows from the spirit of art.'[35] Modern historians would describe the process Landmann was speaking of as the imposition of social control: for this task the communes were the most obviously suitable agents.

The cities resisted intervention from the outside with great determination. Adenauer, for instance, always attacked attempts of the Prussian and Reich regimes to 'stick their noses' into the affairs of the Rhenish cities, and he spoke of his fear that a centralised democracy of the type advocated by almost all the political parties except the Centre and the BVP would lead sooner or later to 'autocracy or dictatorship'. Gustav Böß in Berlin tried to run the capital of the Reich and Prussia without intervention from the Reich and Prussian governments.[36]

Weimarer Republik, Wiesbaden 1975, 187; W. Kohlhaas, *Chronik der Stadt Stuttgart 1918–1933*, Stuttgart n.d. (1964?), 130.

[34] Stehkämper, 451. [35] Rebentisch, 217.

[36] Stehkämper, 340; Engeli, 156 ff.

As the cities expanded and as they took on new tasks, their administrations grew larger. Cologne in 1913 employed 2124 officials, while in 1924 there were 4765 (the figure was later reduced, as part of a municipal economy drive, to 4503 in 1928).[37] These officials were generally better paid than their opposite numbers in Reich and Land administrations, and the salaries of mayors were widely and critically discussed. The only way Böß could think of justifying his salary was to say that he was paid less than Adenauer, whose salary was generally believed to be 'somewhere between that of the Reich Chancellor and the Lord God, but nearer the latter's'. In 1929 Adenauer's salary was 33 000 RM but in addition he was paid 4 800 RM for expenses and 43 000 RM as 'living costs'.[38] (The Reich Chancellor was indeed only paid 45 000 RM). During the depression, the Reich Savings Commissar's criticism of municipal life concentrated on the exorbitant incomes of the senior city employees.[39]

The cities of the 1920s embarked on tremendously expensive and ambitious projects, undertaken in accordance with the principle spelt out by Landmann and Adenauer of stabilising social conditions; even in the most extreme and difficult circumstances it was of foremost priority to keep up the ordinary circumstances of bourgeois life. Barmen was a relatively small city (population in 1925: 187 000), but it kept its city orchestra and opera until the worst days of the inflation in 1923, and started municipal culture up again in 1924 as soon as it could.[40] Other considerations guiding the city fathers were the necessity of keeping employment in the city, and a wish to compete with other cities. The favourite areas for municipal activity, and inter-city rivalry, were transport (trams, railways, underground systems in Berlin and Hamburg, and airfields), exhibition halls, sports stadiums, and swimming pools, as well as the more mundane business of municipal gas and electricity supply.

Berlin in the 1920s created a unified transport system. In 1926 the city bought the majority of shares in the Hochbahnge-

[37] Stehkämper, 252. [38] Ibid., 145; Engeli, 212. [39] Kohlhaas, 106.

[40] J. Reulecke, 'Die Auswirkungen der Inflation auf die städtischen Finanzen' in (ed.) G. D. Feldman, *Die Nachwirkungen der Inflation auf die deutsche Geschichte 1924–33*, Munich 1985, 97–116.

sellschaft (underground railway) and in 1927 set up a 'community of interest' between the underground, tram and omnibus systems: this provided the basis for the creation in 1929 of a new company, the Berliner Verkehrs-Aktiengesellschaft (BVG). The BVG's personnel policy proved to be immensely expensive: in order to join different transport systems with different wage structures together into a unified operation, wage increases and reductions of hours of work were needed. In order to make the new company even more attractive for its employees, the BVG set up a subsidiary to construct houses for its workers (the Gemeinnützige Heimstättenbaugesellschaft der BVG GmbH). By the end of 1930 the BVG had put a total of 350m. RM into the construction of a new underground network, although Oberbürgermeister Böß had warned at the beginning of 1929 that in light of conditions on the capital market it would be wise to slow down the construction programme.[41]

In 1926 the city of Berlin took the initiative in constructing a new aerodrome on the site of the Kaiser's old parade ground at Tempelhof: this was supposed to guarantee Berlin's position as a centre of international aviation. Düsseldorf's municipal airport was opened in April 1926; Stuttgart in 1924 founded the Luftverkehr Württemberg AG in order to develop that city's aerodrome.

In 1924 Berlin created the Gemeinnützige Berliner Ausstellungs-, Messe- und Fremdenverkehrs GmbH to build exhibition halls; by 1926 there were three halls and by the end of the decade eight.[42] Exhibitions were just as fashionable in the west of Germany: Cologne was already in 1922 building exhibition halls during the inflation.[43] Neighbouring Düsseldorf in 1921 organised a confectionery exhibition; and after the stabilisation had to reply to Cologne by staging a spectacular health, body culture, and physical exercise exhibition (May–October 1926) which according to the Oberbürgermeister Robert Lehr meant that 'Düsseldorf was no longer merely counted among the great cities of Germany: rather it was weighed and valued

[41] O. Büsch, *Geschichte der Berliner Kommunalwirtschaft in der Weimarer Epoche*, Berlin 1960, 91–2, 94–5.

[42] Ibid., 99–102.

[43] Stehkämper, 570. (Ed.) F. W. Henning, *Düsseldorf und seine Wirtschaft: Zur Geschichte einer Region*, Düsseldorf 1981, 623.

again.'[44] As permanent relics of this exhibition, Düsseldorf kept a municipal planetarium and a Reich Economic Museum. Cologne in 1928 hit on the idea of an International Press Conference. In 1929 there was in Essen the first big gardening exhibition in the world (the Gruga). Stuttgart in 1926 organised an architectural exhibition to celebrate the new ethic: there were buildings by Le Corbusier, Walter Gropius, R. Behrens, and A. G. Schneck.[45] In Frankfurt/Main the cost of the exhibition halls, which required continual subsidies from the city, led to a political crisis in the municipality: Landmann had envisaged fairs as a part of the essential cultural mission of cities for discovering and developing new consumer tastes and demands. But Frankfurt's available fair and exhibition capacity was never used, and important fairs refused to come to Frankfurt: the automobile trade fair preferred to remain in Berlin. In 1928 the majority of the city council voted for the abolition of the Municipal Exhibition Company, the Messegesellschaft. Landmann simply ignored the resolution, and only one year later was prepared to make a compromise restricting Frankfurt to speciality fairs and ending the mass exhibition.[46]

Other aspects of city 'gigantomania' cost money too: Weimar mayors spent large sums lobbying companies to move their headquarters. They offered entertainment to company directors; more expensively, they promised tax concessions and expensive infrastructure constructions. When Frankfurt incorporated Höchst, the centre of an important part of IG Farben's dyestuff business, it needed to make commitments about the future levels of commerce and land tax.[47] Cologne built an expensive new Rhine harbour in the hope of attracting new enterprise; it also tried to award contracts to local firms. The city chose for its new Rhine bridge linking Cologne and Mülheim not a box girder design of Krupp (Essen) but rather a much more costly suspension bridge which would lead to orders for steel cable produced by Felten & Guillaume, Mülheim. It justified the choice on aesthetic grounds.[48]

Finally, some parts of city spending had a purely aesthetic or

[44] Stehkämper, 570–1.

[45] Kohlhaas, 174.

[46] Rebentisch 1975, 237–42.

[47] Ibid., 184–5.

[48] Stehkämper, 164, 289.

environmental intention: Cologne's green belt offered a successful and attractive example of German city planning.[49]

Inevitably, when so much money was being spent, cases of corruption or near-corruption appeared. In light of the zeal with which opposition parties set about collecting examples of corruption, it is actually surprising that there were not more *causes célèbres*. Berlin attracted particular notoriety: it was much more difficult here than in other cities to control the city administration simply because of its enormous size. Some Berlin incidents were relatively harmless: firms were expected to give charitable donations to the city if they were awarded planning permission or if they sought public contracts. Thus when the department store Karstadt built a new branch on the Hermannplatz in 1928 it agreed to pay for the erection of a school retreat house in the country.[50] More sinister was the Sklarek scandal. The Gebrüder Sklarek ran a wholesale textile and men's clothing business. In 1926 they had bought up low quality clothing stocks originally purchased by the city of Berlin for distribution to the needy during the war and inflation. In 1927 they extracted a substantial payment from the city on the grounds that, although there had been a warning that the clothing was of low quality, in fact it was even more shoddy than they had expected. At the same time the Sklareks won a monopoly contract on clothing supplies to the city. The reason was simple: the chairman of the municipal purchasing company, Stadtrat Gäbel, was bribed by the Sklareks. Other leading city officials too bought goods from the Sklareks at absurdly low prices, and the Sklareks also frequently delayed or even forgot to send bills to city employees. The case came into the open in late 1929, and eventually cost Oberbürgermeister Böß his job. Böß's wife had bought a fur coat from the Sklareks for 375 RM although Böβ estimated that the real value was a thousand marks more: in order to make this up Böß had given 1000 RM to charity (or rather he bought a painting from a poor artist for 800 RM and gave 200 RM to some poor relations of his wife's). Böß was clearly not bribed by the Sklareks in the way that Gäbel had been; but he

[49] Ibid., 157–8. [50] Engeli, 142–3.

had acted very incautiously and he had failed to supervise his administration effectively.[51]

In other cases there were accusations of corruption that were much less justified: these accusations belonged to the stock-in-trade of radical politicians. Cologne's Adenauer was frequently blamed for appointing in 1920 his brother-in-law Will Suth Beigeordneter (city director) with special responsibility for financial affairs. This was a key position in the municipal administration. Adenauer justified Suth's appointment on the grounds not only that Suth was extremely capable (he had been offered prestigious posts in many other German towns); but also that it was necessary for Adenauer to have someone he could trust completely in the light of the difficult financial situation created as a result of his spending plans.[52]

This story—and also that of the Brothers Sklarek—illuminates one central difficulty facing municipal administration in the 1920s: the problem of the supervision of city affairs. Böß did not know what his subordinates were doing; and Adenauer needed to have a way of making sure that he did. Such were the problems of big government.

The communes demonstrated in an exceptionally extreme form that rather intractable problem we have diagnosed elsewhere in German public finance in the 1920s: high spending without adequate revenue, meaning a dependence on borrowing, coupled with widespread doubts about the value or purpose of public activity. The immediate consequences were first that the doubts and hostilities made lenders very nervous and lending politically very risky; and second that the critics of high public spending used the existence of an unstable mountain of public debt in order both to drive home their criticism and to exercise a kind of blackmail against the borrowers.

In the mid-1920s the major enemies of city independence were the Land and Reich parliaments; the high Reich civil service (*Ministerialbürokratie*) and the Reichsbank; and heavy industry. The latter mounted a campaign against 'cold socialisation' (*kalte Sozialisierung*) or the peaceful imposition of public ownership through the extension of municipal enterprise.[53]

[51] Ibid., 230–47. [52] Stehkämper, 259–61.

[53] C. Böhret, *Aktionen gegen die 'kalte Sozialisierung' 1926–1930: Ein Beitrag zum Wirken ökonomischer Einflußverbände in der Weimarer Republik*, Berlin 1966.

Industry was not entirely unsuccessful. The Ruhrgas AG, founded in 1927 by the Ruhr Coal Syndicate in order to extend the Syndicate's control over energy markets, managed to dominate the gas market in the Rhineland, Hesse, and North Germany; though in southern Germany the municipally owned Südwestdeutsche Gas AG provided long-distance supplies of gas from a coalfield owned by the city of Frankfurt/Main.[54] By the end of the decade, however, the threat to the communes from larger enterprise had abated, and there were more cases of successful and profitable co-operation between private and municipal enterprise. The Rheinisch-Westfälische Elektrizitätswerke AG, set up in 1893, provided a model for such co-operation; and by 1930 municipalities were represented too on the Supervisory Board of the once so aggressive Ruhrgas AG.

On the other hand, new enemies of municipal administration appeared. As the depression radicalised voters, Nazis and Communists began to disrupt council meetings and unmask real or non-existent corruption.[55] Municipal parliaments frequently faced the same inability to form working majorities as in the Länder and the Reich parliaments; the only majorities possible were negative ones, blocking proposals for financial or other reforms. Civic culture was no longer capable of taming the massive discontent of the German streets. At the same time the enemies of municipal administration in the high civil service became more active as they saw in the economic crisis an ideal opportunity for the realisation of their plans. In autumn 1931, after the banking crisis which severely affected the communes and the communally owned savings banks, Adenauer complained that 'the *Ministerialbürokratie* has now used the circumstances of the time in order to cudgel *Selbstverwaltung* to the floor and has set up the principle of centralisation—i.e. itself—on the throne instead'.[56] These centralisers used the lever of the precarious financial position of the communes: whereas mayors could by and large afford to ignore

[54] D. Rebentisch, 'Städte und Monopol: Privatwirtschaftliches Ferngas oder kommunale Verbandswirtschaft in der Weimarer Republik', *Zeitschrift für Stadtgeschichte, Stadtsoziologie und Denkmalpflege* 3, 1976, 38–80.

[55] In Frankfurt see Rebentisch 1975, 255–9, in Cologne Stehkämper, 449–54.

[56] Stehkämper, 350–1.

Nazi obstruction in city councils, they could not escape the consequences of near or actual financial collapse.

Ambitious projects of the 1920s had been paid for by borrowing, often on the foreign capital market. Cologne had borrowed abroad to build its new Rhine harbour; Dresden to build a new railway bridge across the Elbe; Munich for electricity works and gas and tram installations.[57] From the outset, the Reichsbank had tried to restrict this external borrowing. In December 1924 an Advisory Office for Foreign Credit (Beratungsstelle für Auslandskredite) had been established through agreements between the Reich and the Länder. In its original form, the Beratungsstelle consisted of five permanent members (a representative of the Reichsbank, of the Reich Finance Ministry, and the Reich Economics Ministry, and the Presidents of the Prussian State Bank and the Bavarian State Bank); and in addition there was a representative of the Land involved in the specific credit application. Thus there was numerical parity between the representatives of the Reich and those of the Länder: the State Banks kept in close contact with the Prussian and Bavarian governments. On the other hand, there was no representative of the communes on the Advisory Board. In theory, the Board advised the Land government whether the communes should or should not be permitted to negotiate a foreign loan; in practice its verdict was authoritative. The Board also had the task of advising on the desirability of credit for the Länder.[58]

In its operations, the Beratungsstelle worked against the communes; after 1925 this discrimination was more and more pronounced. While by the end of 1925 the Beratungsstelle had approved 89 per cent of Länder loans and all the applications for Land-guaranteed agricultural and industrial loans, only 65 per cent of the communal applications had been agreed. In 1926 an even lower proportion of communal loans was allowed.[59] But despite the control of the Beratungsstelle, and

[57] See the meeting of the Beratungsstelle of 15 Mar. 1928, BAK R2/2081; also R2/4126, 27 Oct. 1930 meeting.

[58] BStA MA 103859, 5 Dec. 1924 Richtlinien, and 23 July and 12 Nov. 1925 circulars of Reich Finance Ministry. In general see (ed.) K. Hansmeyer, *Kommunale Finanzpolitik in der Weimarer Republik*, Stuttgart 1973.

[59] BStA MA 103859, 18 Dec. 1925 and 1 Apr. 1926 reports of Beratungsstelle meetings.

despite a complete stop on public loans in 1927, German communes accounted for a sizeable part of the German foreign debt: 11.9 per cent of the long-term loans issued in USA between 1924 and 1929 went to German municipalities.[60] The Beratungsstelle did, however, drive the communes to borrow on the domestic market, or to take short-term foreign loans which did not fall under Schacht's control: this may have helped to tighten an already narrow German capital market. In the later 1920s, communal borrowing represented the major part of total public borrowing in Germany. On the eve of the depression the increase in communal indebtedness represented an increasing share of total German investment, as shown in Table III.

Table III: Increase in German Communal Debt 1928/9–1930/1 (m. RM)

	1928/9	1929/30	1930/1
As % of total increase in public debt	62.4	48.1	35.6
As % of net domestic investment in Germany	20.2	26.4	36.6
Increase in Communal Debt (m. RM)	2 221.4	1 521.2	961.5

Sources: Wagemann, *Konjunkturstatistiches Handbuch 1936*, 171–2; Hoffmann 826.

Schacht responded to what he believed was an evasion of the Reichsbank's control mechanism by demanding that the central bank should supervise domestic borrowing by public corporations as well. This principle was accepted, though only after Schacht had ceased to be President of the Reichsbank. In 1930 the Guide-lines on Credit of 1924 were revised: all Länder credit applications were to be submitted to the Beratungsstelle, while a new institution was created to deal with communal borrowing.[61]

There were other ways in which the operation of the Beratungsstelle had been unsatisfactory in the later 1920s:

[60] From Appendix of C. Lewis, *America's Stake in International Investments*, Washington DC 1938.

[61] Hansmeyer, 188 ff.

communes were encouraged to discount in advance the decision of the Beratungsstelle by applying for more funds than they needed. The existence of a central regulating body also helped to fan the inter-city rivalries that plagued German politics anyway: if Munich was allowed to borrow abroad in order to build new tramways, Nuremberg and Chemnitz wanted to be allowed to do the same.[62]

So the Reichsbank resorted to other means to brake communal credit demands. Schacht warned foreign investors directly: in 1925 he publicly attacked loans for Berlin and Cologne. He complained to American bankers about the wastefulness of the administration of Stettin. At the same time, the US State Department, prompted by warnings from Schacht and the Agent-General for Reparation Payments, Parker Gilbert, advised caution to the American public over loans to German Länder and municipalities because Article 248 of the Treaty of Versailles provided for a first claim on the Reich and the Länder by the Allies for reparation for wartime damage.[63] By the end of 1929 the communes were desperate for more funds from America as their expenditure rose uncontrollably. Gustav Böß went with several Berlin officials on a trip to invite the New World to bail out the old. Mulert, the General Manager of the German Association of Cities, the Deutscher Städtetag (DST), told a Reichsrat Committee that 'the more money there is, the more the economic dangers can be avoided'.[64] But at the end of 1929 Schacht made a direct attack, similar to that of 1925, when he criticised the terms of a proposed one-year loan of 120m. RM by Dillon Read to the City of Berlin. Schacht justified his intervention by referring to the dangerously large volume of communal foreign short-term debt.[65] There were no exact figures as to how large this debt actually was in 1929: whereas the Deutscher Städtetag claimed that it amounted to 1050–1100m. RM, the Reich Finance Ministry and industry

[62] BAK R2/4126, 27 Oct. 1930 Beratungsstelle meeting.

[63] DST B2784, 2 Oct. 1925 DST Giro Committee, and 24 Oct. 1925 Stettin to DST. Foreign Relations of the United States 1925 II 177–8; FRBNY Strong papers 1012.1, 18 Oct. 1925 Gilbert to Garrard B. Winston.

[64] Engeli, 227–8.

[65] IfZ ED93/7 4 and 12 Dec. 1929 diary entries.

thought that the amount was nearer to 2000m. RM, and the Reichsbank produced a figure of 3000m. RM.[66]

At the end of 1929 Schacht believed that the only way of reducing this alarmingly large short-term foreign debt was by the drastic means of selective default, which would scare off new creditors. Berlin would be a spectacular case. Schacht suggested that if Berlin wished to save itself, it should privatise the municipal electricity works (the BEWAG) rather than continue to borrow.[67] The case of Berlin raised general issues about the position and future of the communes. The Deutscher Städtetag saw Schacht's action as an attack on all German cities, and Konrad Adenauer made the same point when he told the Reich Finance Minister, 'We must not let Berlin collapse because of the Reichsbank.' Schacht simply retorted by saying that the cities should face the consequences of the actions of 'tricksters and bankrupts'.[68]

That there was now a crisis was recognised by all. Adenauer was even prepared to admit that there had been severe mistakes in the communes' expansionary policies. In spring 1930, he said: 'I must make two critical comments: we [German Oberbürgermeister] have not in the past regarded sufficiently the limits of the financially possible when we made spending decisions (particularly regarding extraordinary expenditures); and secondly, we should have used our rights *vis-à-vis* the communal parliaments more thoroughly.' Adenauer now recognised how thin his defence of the 1925 Cologne $15m. loan had been: then he said that 'the financial and economic circumstances of the City of Cologne are, according to my really detailed knowledge of the situation, as healthy and as favourable as those in Berlin'.[69] By 1929 Berlin was in great trouble; and Cologne's situation was precarious too.

The communes' position at the end of the 1920s was made much worse by the rise in unemployment in Germany: for under terms of legislation providing for the relief of the

[66] DST B4159, 15 Nov. 1929 Bracht to Benecke, BoE CBP 1.1., 30 Nov. 1929 and 1 Dec. 1929 reports of Sir Charles Addis on Reichsbank Generalrat meetings. BStA MA 103861, 13 Oct. 1929 report of von Wolf.

[67] BStA MA 103861, 13 Dec. 1929 report of von Wolf.

[68] IfZ ED93/7, 4 Dec. and 12 Dec. 1929 diary entries.

[69] Stehkämper, 344 and 130–1.

unemployed, substantial financial burdens were imposed on the communes. Under the regulations of February 1924, they were obliged to support the unemployed for 39 weeks. As a result of the 1927 reforms, the communes bore some of the cost of 'crisis relief' after the end of eligibility for unemployment insurance benefit; and after 58 weeks the unemployed were completely dependent on communal welfare relief. In June 1931 the burden on the communes was increased yet further as the eligibility period for insurance relief was cut for some classes of workers to 20 weeks. During the depression, the number of long-term unemployed, and hence the number dependent on communal support, rose:

Table IV: Proportion of Unemployed on Welfare Support in Cities over 100,000 Population[a]

	(%)
30.6.1927	15.5
31.12.1928	18.0
30.6.1929	20.4
31.12.1929	22.3
31.3.1930	23.8

[a] Not including Munich, Karlsruhe, or Lübeck.
Source: BAK R2/20132 June 1930 Memorandum of Dr Köbner, 'Wohlfahrtserwerbslose und Gemeinden'

In August 1930 453 000 workers in Germany depended on welfare support (15.7 per cent of the total registered as unemployed); one year later there were 1 131 000 (26.8 per cent) and in August 1932 2 030 000 (38.9 per cent).[70] Yet it was only in June 1932 that this problem was tackled by setting an upper ceiling for communal liability for welfare relief.

In addition to welfare payments, communes had on the eve of the depression been forced to take over new financial commitments: they complained how they had been forced by the Länder to pay for the building of new police stations, and for new pedagogical and commercial high schools. In Prussia communes were after March 1930 obliged to bid at compul-

[70] Wagemann 1935, 16–17.

sory auctions of over-indebted properties. In fact, an estimated four-fifths of communal expenditure was laid down by law and thus could not be cut at will as part of an economy campaign.[71]

Meanwhile communal tax revenue was falling: particularly sharply, as we have seen, in the case of the Prussian communes. Often communal parliaments obstructed attempts to impose new city taxes.[72]

Table V: Tax Revenue of Communes 1928/9–1932/3 (m. RM)

	Reich tax transfers	Communal taxes and Land transfers	Total
1928/1929	1 649.7 (100)[a]	2 747.0 (100)	4 396.8 (100)
1929/1930	1 595.8 (96.7)	2 794.0 (101.7)	4 390.0 (99.8)
1930/1931	1 427.1 (86.5)	2 877.5 (104.8)	4 333.1 (98.6)
1931/1932	1 009.3 (61.2)	2 649.0 (96.4)	3 676.5 (83.6)
1932/1933	785.0 (47.6)	2 065.0 (75.2)	2 850.0 (64.8)

[a] Figures in brackets as a % of 1928/9 revenue.
Source: Statistisches Jahrbuch, 1930–1935 issues.

Thus the communes were obliged to borrow more. Most of the new debt was funded domestically (though indirectly the money might still come from those foreign bankers who lent to such firms as the Dresdner and the Danat which specialised in communal business); and, although the total volume of debt was still rather smaller than the pre-war communal debt had been, it was predominantly short-term.

Any attempts on the part of the cities to raise taxes in order to cover their deficits were strenuously resisted by pressure both from business and from the Reich. The Deutscher Städtetag noted that '1930 will be first and foremost a year of tax increases':[73] but Brüning did not want the new revenue to go to the communes. Instead the cities had to cut their capital expenditure radically: they drew up their own savings pro-

[71] DST B3328, 13 Oct. 1930 Elsass (DST) to Dorn (Reich Finance Ministry).

[72] Kohlhaas, 105.

[73] DST B2731, 2 Jan. 1930 meeting of Mulert (DST) with Mindir. Hag (Prussian Finance Ministry).

Table VI: Debts of Communes over 10,000 Population 1928–30 (m. RM)[a]

	Cities over 10,000			Cities over 100,000		
	31.3.28	20.9.29	30.6.30	31.3.28	30.9.29	30.6.30
Foreign debt	524 (100)	718 (137)	708 (135)	413 (100)	593 (144)	578 (140)
Internal debt	3 188 (100)	5 317 (167)	6 147 (193)	1 330 (100)	2 654 (200)	3 219 (242)
(of which short- and medium-term)	1 267 (100)	2 338 (185)	2 621 (207)	576 (100)	1 286 (223)	1 585 (275)

[a] (1928 = 100)
Source: DST B 3465, 11.12.1930 Memorandum on 'Level of Debt 1930'.

grammes (Düsseldorf 1930, Munich 1931), or called in the Reich Savings Commissar to advise on cuts (Halle, Mannheim, Stuttgart), or appointed commissions of economy experts (Frankfurt/Main, Ludwigshafen).[74] Though these cuts obviously increased local unemployment, particularly in the building trade, there seemed little alternative, and the communes could only hope that the depression would be short-lived. Most cities waited as long as possible before implementing their retrenchment programmes.[75] Böß had wanted to stop work on the Berlin underground in 1929, but the city council insisted that the project be carried on. Instead Böß tried to raise new funds in America. Landmann in December 1929 asked the Reich Finance Ministry for help in getting foreign funds for building and construction programmes. Adenauer cancelled all building projects only in August 1931, after the banking collapse.[76] Stuttgart continued to build during the depression. The following projects were actually *started* during these dismal years: the construction of a hospital for skin diseases in Bad Cannstadt; the conversion and extension of a midwifery school

[74] D. Rebentisch, 'Kommunalpolitik, Konjunktur und Arbeitsmarkt' in (ed.) R. Morsey, *Verwaltungsgeschichte*, Berlin 1977, 133; and DST B3328, 25 Mar. 1931 Mulert memorandum.

[75] DST B4159, 26 Mar. 1930 meeting in Reich Labour Ministry.

[76] Büsch 186; DST B4159, 4 Dec. 1929 meeting of Landmann and Hilferding (Reich Finance Minister); Stehkämper, 147.

in Berg; and preparations for the grand 1933 German gymnastic festival.[77]

One apparently easy option for the communes was to use the municipally owned savings banks (*Sparkassen*) as a source of funds. The DST repeatedly pressed for a 'consolidation action' to reduce the volume of short-term debt, and the Reich agreed to allow an alteration of the Prussian Savings Ordinance (which also served as a guide-line for other Länder). From December 1929 up to 50 per cent of deposits in savings banks could be used to consolidate communal debt. This step implied a great risk, for the savings of nervous small investors were locked into very long-term funding. More ambitious and wide-ranging plans to consolidate the communal short-term debt ran aground once more on the rocks of Reichsbank policy. The Reichsbank refused to offer Lombard facilities (loans against securities) on communal debt: 'Hoarding of gold and currency in recent months has increased—perhaps because of the discussions about the Young Plan. It is to be feared that an admission of communal loans to Lombard traffic would intensify the hoarding and would be interpreted as a beginning of new inflation methods.'[78]

The savings banks deposits locked into municipal loans in fact caused enough problems on their own: in some parts of Germany, where the mayors had been particularly pressing and powerful, the savings banks had put considerably more than 50 per cent of their deposits into communal business. Savings banks were supposed to hold highly liquid deposits with secondary banks (Girozentralen and Länderbanken) but these institutions had not always pursued conservative investment policies. In eastern Germany, the Länderbanken lent mostly to private firms, and the Landeskreditkasse in Kassel and the Nassauische Landesbank were engaged mostly in mortgages; but in Hanover, Rhineland-Westphalia and Schleswig-Holstein there was a heavy involvement in communal credit.[79] The most notorious case was that of the Rheinische

[77] Kohlhaas, 96.

[78] Negotiations reported in DST B4159; also BAK R2/13446, 6 Feb. 1930 Reichsbank Direktorium to Reich Finance Minister.

[79] BAK R2/13634, 23 Oct. 1931 memorandum of Landeshauptleute in East Prussia and Hesse-Nassau.

Landesbank. At the end of July 1931, when in the banking crisis the whistle had been blown on its activities, it had 250m. RM on deposit from the savings banks, and had loaned a total of 642m. RM of which 522m. RM were credits to the communes. By far the largest of the Landesbank's debtors was the city of Cologne with 94m. RM. Cologne now reaped the harvest of the ambitious expansion of the 1920s.[80]

The 1930 consolidation through the savings banks could work only if the communes did not allow their short-term debt to increase further. Otherwise the effect of the action would be to reduce public confidence in the savings banks and thus undermine the stability of German credit. After September 1930, deposits in savings banks began to be withdrawn, and after May 1931 withdrawals exceeded new deposits.[81] The flow of new funds which might have been available to help the communes had become a trickle. A memorandum of late 1930 recorded that:

> These institutes [savings banks, Länderbanken, and Girozentralen] see the certain and inevitable moment approaching when the liquidity of our organisations will be seriously endangered if the credit demands of the communes resulting from unforeseen expenditure on unemployment relief continue.[82]

An increase in communal debt, the memorandum continued, would lead to a 'danger of financial collapse' of the savings banks. Yet this situation was bound to arise as the communes' optimism about future developments made almost any additional expenditure an unforeseen catastrophe.

The difficulties of the communes were increased too by the Reich's extension of the Beratungsstelle's control in order to eliminate competition for scarce funds:

> The purpose of this extension of the Beratungsstelle's powers is the prevention of disturbances on the capital market as a result of the

[80] BAK R43I/651 (file on Landesbank der Rheinprovinz): especially 14 April 1932 report of Deutsche Revisions- und Treunandgesellschaft.

[81] J. Blatz, *Die Bankenliquidität im Run 1931: Statistische Liquiditätsanalyse der deutschen Kreditinstitutsgruppen in der Weltwirtschaftskrise 1929–1933*, Cologne 1971, 212.

[82] BAK R2/4057, 15 Nov. 1930 memorandum of Deutscher Sparkassen- und Giroverband.

competition of the various borrowing groups. The internal market and the foreign market are to a great extent interdependent.[83]

A new set of Guide-lines laid down the principle that new communal loans should only be taken for productive purposes, and in cases of extraordinary need. The communes should ask permission of the Reich to take foreign loans, and in the case of domestic loans the Land government was to call a meeting of the Beratungsstelle augmented by the addition of a representative from the communes. Even this new system of control did not stop communes making approaches to foreign banks, though the loan contract could not be signed without the approval of the Beratungsstelle. In January 1931, in order to curb the embarrassment caused by such municipal appeals to American banks, the State Secretary in the Reich Finance Ministry sent a circular to the Länder governments asking that in view of the nervous state of the markets German cities should refrain from begging for credit.[84]

Finance Minister Dietrich was fundamentally sceptical about the purpose of much local government expenditure; both he and Luther had been career mayors who had discovered in their own experience that local government required vast sums to grease the wheels of its political machinery. Luther was very frank in expressing his views on communal finance, and his desire for a reform born out of catastrophe:

He did not believe it right always to start from the premise that cities should not be allowed to go bankrupt. The communes had for years had the wrong idea of the world. In his eyes it would be most beneficial for the cities if some of them should go to the wall. From the point of view of self-administration, it was dangerous if communes always had the feeling that they would be helped.[85]

Deprived of loans and of central government support, the German cities started to sell off municipal enterprise. Bremen in January 1931 tried to sell its water and electricity works to a consortium headed by the Société Financière de Belgique (Sofina), but Brüning blocked the sale as it would place an

[83] Hansmeyer 218; and BAK R2/20151, 9 July 1930 meeting in Reich Finance Ministry.
[84] BStA MA 103862, 20 Jan. 1932 Reich Finance Ministry circular.
[85] BAK R2/4057, 15 Dec. 1930 meeting in Reich Finance Ministry.

important part of German industry under foreign control. The French aluminium and electrical industrialist Louis Marlio declared an interest in buying German municipal water and electricity works, and the Reich Finance Ministry's expert Norden warned that French financial imperialism was looking to the Rhenish cities.[86] Berlin had in June 1930 again been prevented from taking a $10m. credit by the Reichsbank's intervention, and had borrowed instead from the Danat bank: but it was clear that the Danat was not able to agree a renewal of this 150m. RM loan due on 31 July 1931. So in March the Berlin electricity works were sold to a foreign consortium in which the Sofina played a major role.[87] (The city overcame the political objections to a sale abroad by creating a holding company in which Berlin still held shares with especially privileged voting rights.)

The crisis for the German cities came with the general banking crisis: by 4 July 1931 there were signs of an imminent collapse of the credit of the big Rhenish cities. 75m. RM of the short-term deposits of the Rheinische Landesbank were withdrawn, as panic spread concerning the solvency of the cities. Düsseldorf needed to borrow 50m. RM to make payments due at the end of June, and Münster took 10m. RM. In June the temporary embarrassment of the Landesbank had been solved by a loan from the Prussian State Bank (Seehandlung), but the funds were exhausted by the middle of July. Luther was then called on to save the Landesbank, but was horrified at the amount of money involved, and in addition still believed that it was his mission to punish past municipal extravagance.[88]

But even the affair of the Landesbank and the similar difficulties of the Hanseatic banks did not deter the high spenders: Breslau was still suggesting at the end of July that a massive foreign loan could be raised on the security of communal enterprise.[89] The lenders however learnt the lessons of the summer of 1931, that over-enthusiastic borrowing caused

[86] BAK R2/4057, 17 Mar. 1931 report of von Hoesch (German ambassador in Paris).

[87] NA StDep 862.51, 19 Feb. 1931 W. E. Beitz memorandum 'Berlin's Financial Problems'; Büsch 163 ff.

[88] IfZ ED93/11, 6 July 1931 diary entry; and PrSA Rep 109/6016 (Landesbank der Rheinprovinz) and BAK R43I/651.

[89] BAK R2/4057, 27 July 1931 Stadtrat Przbilla to Reich Chancellor.

spectacular collapses. Cities were no longer able to find sources of loan money, even when conditions on the credit market gradually improved in 1932 and 1933. Too many black marks had been made against municipal activity. In addition, the Reich Government stepped in, and the Dietramszell decree of October 1931 forbade the savings banks to lend to municipalities and provided for the banks to have greater political independence.

The financial erosion of the position of the cities continued in 1932; a combination of the alteration of tax rates by decree and a reduction in income from transfers of income and corporation tax cost the communes a total of 815m. RM. By the beginning of 1932 many cities were either in arrears on debt service, or had stopped payments altogether: Cologne, Dortmund, Gesenkirchen, and Altona were in this situation. Luther, still following the course of using the crisis to push the Prussian state and the Prussian communes into accepting administrative reform, refused to help the communes by taking their bills for discount in the Reichsbank.[90]

A similarly dilatory and unhelpful approach was taken by the Reich authorities to a suggestion to solve the communal finance problem by consolidating the short-term debt. Such proposals involved the use of the communal house tax (*Hauszinssteuer*) as a pledge for a conversion loan: but this scheme produced fierce resistance from house owners who feared that they would for ever be burdened with the house tax as a result of the new plans. Most communes also preferred voluntary agreements with banks to convert short into long credits rather than compulsory rescheduling which would limit their future freedom of action.[91] In general the banks were co-operative in maintaining communal loans, despite the bitter experience of 1931. They actually preferred to keep their loans on a short-term basis because this meant that they could show the loans at par in their accounts, whereas they would have had to set a long-term consolidation loan at its market value. Moreover, they did not want to commit themselves to writing off parts of the communal loans as they believed that the position of the

[90] BAK R2/20133, 21 Mar. 1932 Mulert to Reich Finance Minister, and 16 Jan. 1932 Deutsche Centralbodenkredit AG to Prussian Minister for Welfare.

[91] BStA MA 103862, 4 Nov. 1931 memorandum of Bayerischer Städtebund.

communes might improve quickly if the various government recovery programme showed signs of being successful.[92] Thus the hope of an economic upswing in this case helped to obstruct consolidation measures which might well have increased the chances of such an upswing.

There were much more fundamental and political objections to a stabilising or rescheduling of the communal debt: the high debt levels had been a lever used by central governments in their efforts to control the political course of the communes. After the Nazi seizure of power in January 1933, dramatic changes took place in local politics. Nazi *Unterführer* demanded the resignation of mayors, and new communal elections in Prussia (12 March) in many cases produced Nazi majorities. In other Länder the pace of change was slower, but in the end the results were similar. By the end of the year, there had been an almost complete change in the administration of German communes. In towns with a population over 200 000 only 14 per cent of the Oberbürgermeister in office in January 1933 were still there twelve months later. There were also large-scale dismissals of communal officials: in Leipzig 1600 were sacked and replaced by 1150 loyal old party members. Such changes were often justified by the need to implement 'savings' in municipal administration and by reference to the old Nazi polemics against wasteful local government.[93]

The victors were not usually, however, the enthusiastic local Nazis who now saw an opportunity to build up their own style of municipal corruption or *Vetternwirtschaft*. In Prussia, the guiding hand behind the change of communal administration was not Minister-President Hermann Göring but the Prussian Finance Minister, Johannes Popitz, the centralising State Secretary of the late 1920s. In October 1930 Popitz had proposed to the Tax Committee of the RDI that communes should be subject to much tighter control from the centre: they should have uniform budget plans, tax schedules and auditing systems, and should required central permission to take up credit or to start public work programmes.[94] In 1931 Popitz set out a

[92] *Der deutsche Volkswirt* No. 16 (20 Jan. 1933); BStA MA 103862, 3 Sept. 1932 report of von Hammer.

[93] H. Matzerath, *Nationalsozialismus und kommunale Selbstverwaltung*, Stuttgart 1970, 79, 86.

[94] Popitz 1930, 10–11.

plan to reduce the communal *Realsteuern* (land and commerce taxes) by two-fifths. In 1933 he welcomed Hitler's Chancellorship as a step towards the 'overcoming of pluralistic forces tied to material interest'.[95]

A new Prussian Communal Law (15 December 1933) provided for a very close state supervision of communal administration. It was opposed in vain by a large number of influential Nazis including the Director of the Kommunalpolitisches Amt of the NSDAP and new mayor of Munich, Karl Fiehler, and Gauleiter Florian of Düsseldorf, as well as by non-Nazi mayors such as Carl Goerdeler of Leipzig, who protested that the 'idea of self-regulation has been completely ended by the Prussian regulation'.[96]

The new constitutional settlement, which ended local elections, at first resembled much more closely the ideas of the Weimar centralisers than it did those of the new power-hungry local Nazi enthusiasts. Later the Nazis made up ground; by 1935 they had secured the appointment of a NSDAP party representative as first Beigeordneter, i.e. deputy mayor.

After the political uncertainty of 1931–3 had been ended by the Nazi local elections and the Nazi revolution in the communes, the question of debt rescheduling, so thorny in the past, became a trivial issue which was easily solved. Under the provisions of the Law of 21 September 1933, interest rates on the new conversion loan were set at 4 per cent, and all payments on non-converted short-term debt were blocked for five years.[97] In consequence, virtually all the 2.8b. RM short-term communal debt was converted. At the same time regulations for unemployement relief were amended so as to lift the burden from the communes altogether.

These were not important decisions: for from the end of May 1933 communes had ceased to play an important role in German politics. Of the numerous opponents of communal administration of the 1920s, it was not the big industrialists nor even the refractory local parliamentary bodies, the city coun-

[95] H. Dieckmann, *Johannes Popitz: Entwicklung und Wirksamkeit in der Zeit der Weimarer Republik*, Berlin 1960, 113–14 and 139–40.

[96] Matzerath, 126.

[97] RGBl 1933 I 647.

cils, that had won a victory: it was the central state. In order, however, for the plans of a Popitz to be implemented, the fomentation of discontent that produced the upheavals of the first half of 1933 was required. Communal administration had been the most obvious and the most disliked form of government intervention in the 1920s: it disappeared as a result of the tensions produced by the economic crisis.

The issues raised by the budgets of the Reich, Länder and communes were so politically divisive and led to such profound instability because the Weimar economy did not grow quickly enough to sustain a rapidly rising level of public spending. One of the reasons why the economy grew slowly was in turn the high level of taxation. In the depression the tensions became worse as revenues fell while it proved difficult to adjust many items of expenditure to the new circumstances. Such cuts in spending as were made produced a fiscal deflation and made both the depression and also distributional conflicts more severe. This led to an attack on the constitional position of the Länder and communes. As an alternative to spending cuts, tax revenue could be raised by increasing tax levels: this depressed profits, and intensified depression and political conflict too. The only way of avoiding either tax increases or spending cuts—external borrowing—depended on foreign assessments

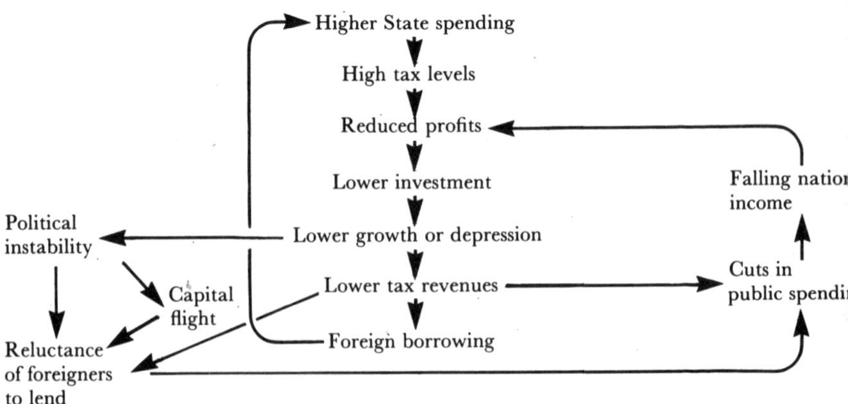

Fig. 1. *The Low-Growth Economy*

of the degree of economic and particularly of political risk in Germany.

These relationships formed a complex network of vicious circles, which are depicted graphically in Fig. 1.

The weak performance of the Weimar economy, which is at the centre of this pictorial representation of instability was not, however, explained by contemporaries in the 1920s or by subsequent analysts *solely* in terms of suffering resulting from over-taxation. There were other forces making for the secular stagnation which made the fisc particularly feared and hated.

IV

The Structure of Industry: Stagnation and Retardation

Wir leben provisorisch, die Krise nimmt kein Ende

(Erich Kästner, *Fabian*)

In what ways was the inter-war slump a product of a flawed economic structure? Theories of the business cycle sometimes attempt to link cyclical depressions, not merely with fluctuations on credit markets or inventory cycles, but with structural crises and structural shifts. This view is at the heart of Schumpeter's famous theory: capitalism is a form of private property economy in which innovations are carried out by means of borrowed money. This in general, though not of necessity, involves the creation of credit. The upswing in a Schumpeterian cycle consists of an expansion generated by borrowing to finance new investment: the building up of promising industrial ventures. In the downswing, borrowing is repaid, and there are no new borrowers because the opportunities for new ventures have shrunk. Entrepreneurial possibilities are restricted, and profits fall as the existing opportunities are fully exploited.[1] Profits in fact are a reward solely for creativity: without innovations—not necessarily technical but also institutional, in labour relations or in marketing—in a market economy profits would disappear. The falling rates of profit have a purging effect: less efficient businesses, which might have been able to survive in the expansion phase, have to close. Only the more progressive firms survive the depression, and in this way this phase of the cycle generates technical, and other, progress.

Much more than most business cycle theory, explanations of economic development in terms of long waves or of 'phases of capitalist development' depend upon accounts of profound

[1] Schumpeter 1939, 223.

structural change between phases.[2] In this sort of story, the inter-war slump represents a caesura in a low-growth phase separating two periods of higher growth: it was so severe because it was a major crisis of readjustment. This interpretation is often applied to the story of technical development. The inter-war slump stood at the beginning of an era of growth and revolutionary development in electrical goods industries, synthetic fibres, and in automobiles; and at the end of an era for iron and steel and the classical products of the early industrial revolution—cotton and woollen fabrics. Keynes put the inter-war problem in this way: 'We are suffering, not from the rheumatics of old age, but from the growing-pains of over-rapid changes, from the painfulness of readjustment between one economic period and another.'[3]

Such an analysis depends on an assessment of the relationship between new (rising) and old (declining) industries: it assumes first that the intensity of the depression was a consequence of the existence of structurally weak declining industries whose markets were collapsing; and secondly that the reduction of demand in the slump helped to deal a knock-out blow to these industries, and thus clear the ring for new kinds of growth. Those historians who believe that politics affect the course of economic development might add three further considerations. Politically the depression radicalised the producers in declining industries, who blamed labour for their difficulties; radicalised the workers, particularly those who lost their jobs in the old industries, and who now blamed capital for their difficulties; and thus produced a new political situation which affected the future rate of growth.

This chapter examines these hypotheses about structural change in German industry and its effects, and challenges them. The major theme is that the depression was far more a phenomenon of general stagnation than it was a consequence of war between sunrise and sunset industries. One of the causes of the general stagnation was an investment ratio much lower than that of the pre-war growth period after the mid-1890s (1910/13: 15.2 per cent of NNP at market prices; 1925/9: 11.1

[2] A. Maddison, *Phases of Capitalist Development*, Oxford 1982.
[3] J. M. Keynes, *Essays in Persuasion* 1928 (*Collected Writings* IX) London 1972, 321.

per cent).[4] This interpretation of the German crisis has important implications for the kind of recovery that might be expected. If a structural crisis did not produce a structural purge, perhaps the opportunities for dramatic new departures were limited.

RISK AVOIDANCE THROUGH THE ORGANISED ECONOMY?

In industry there was no marked regional structural problem. Here the German experience was quite different to that of inter-war Britain, where the slump highlighted the contrasts between an 'old' and declining North and a 'new', rising, South. In Germany there was a far better regional mix of industries. Saxony, for example, was a centre of the ailing textile industry, but also a location for fine mechanical engineering. The older towns of the Ruhr valley (Essen, Bochum, and Dortmund) had well-developed consumer industries (such as brewing), and were not exclusively dependent on coal and steel. The major ship-building centres—Hamburg, Bremen, and Kiel—were either centres of trade as well, or close enough to the centre of trade to allow some regional mobility (an exception to this was the ship-building industry in Elbing: but this had been established as a response to political pressure to create industry in the German East for reasons of national, anti-Polish, policy). By and large there were no single-industry cities—no German Detroits and no German Tyneside or Clydeside. The few German exceptions did in fact suffer badly at the beginning of the 1930s: the mining towns in the belt on the more recently opened coalfield north of the Ruhr river—Herne, Bottrop, and Gladbeck—and the Saxon textile centre of Zwickau. The town with the highest unemployment rate in 1932 was Germany's most famous one-industry site: Solingen, which produced steel goods, and where in May of that year 47 per cent of the work-force had no job.[5]

There are some regional variations in unemployment figures: in general the situation was worse in the East than in the West. On the other hand this distinction is reduced by the

[4] Hoffmann, 104–5 (current prices).

[5] K. Werner, *Die deutschen Wirtschaftsgebiete in der Krise: Statistische Studie zur regional vergleichenden Konjunkturbetrachtung*, Jena 1932, 47, 70.

Table VII: September 1930: Unemployment and Short Work (as % of union membership)

	Unemployment	Short Work
East Prussia	21.7	4.4
Pomerania	21.9	7.6
Silesia	20.3	19.5
Nordmark	16.0	3.5
Brandenburg	16.1	7.8
Saxony	22.5	20.5
Central Germany	21.9	19.7
Hesse	21.3	21.7
Bavaria	18.7	21.8
Lower Saxony	18.2	13.1
Westphalia	15.1	26.1
Rhineland	17.7	19.2
South-West Germany	14.9	31.6
National Average	18.8	17.5

Source: Berliner Tageblatt, 25 Nov. 1930.

consideration that there was a great deal of short-time working in the Rhine-Ruhr, but relatively little in the eastern Prussian territories—East Prussia, Pomerania, the Nordmark, and Brandenburg. In fact few observers spoke in the early 1930s of a specifically regional problem in German industry.[6] There was a regional problem, but that was in agriculture.

So the regional balance of Germany industry was well suited to any needs that structural change might produce: but unfortunately there were few signs in the later 1920s of such transformation. This becomes clear when we look at the rates of growth in sectors of industry.

Defining old and new industries is notoriously problematical. If we believe that industries follow growth paths similar to each other in shape (typically, an S-shaped or saturation curve), but temporally dispersed so that overall growth is a summation of these different sectoral growth paths, we should expect to find in the old industries lower growth rates and lower rates of productivity change. Using these criteria to identify

[6] Ibid. for a general argument on regional variations in levels of unemployment.

the 'old' and the 'new' we have a working, but tautological, definition. New industries are the ones which grow quicker.

Sadly for this case, in practice there do not appear to be such regular growth paths of production; and higher rates of productivity change may not be the result of the 'newness' of a sector (of it being further back along the hypothetical growth path), but may simply be the result of higher rates of output growth (the so-called Verdoorn effect). Thus the greatest caution is needed in identifying industrial decline; and most recent writers on structural change have been very sceptical. 'It is not clear how a new industry should be defined, or how, having defined it, its contribution to growth should be measured ... An alternative approach is simply to identify certain named industries on the basis of casual empiricism.'[7] The casual approach does get us somewhere. Even a cursory analysis of German inter-war development shows stagnation in coal-mining, pig-iron, textile, leather, and construction industries; and that there were exceptionally high growth rates in the chemical sector and in gas and electricity production. Somewhere in between come clothing and steel, where there was modest growth (between 1913 and 1938 at an average rate of over 1 per cent).

The figures in Table VIII indicate an important and interesting peculiarity of the mid-Weimar years. In the period usually known as the 'relative stabilisation' (between inflation and depression, 1924–9), sectoral growth rates were much closer together than rates for those sectors over a longer time period. 1924–9 was when the steel and coal industries looked relatively dynamic; and when there was little difference between the growth of output of hard coal and of lignite (which was in the inter-war period in general a 'growth industry' since it supplied the expanding electricity industry). Even textiles, leather, and clothing, generally poor performers, experienced a short-lived boom, which is only partially represented in Table VIII because their peak production was not in 1929 but in 1927. So the distinction between growth and non-growth industries appears particularly difficult in the stabilisation period.

[7] Matthews, Feinstein, Odling-Smee, 256–7.

Table VIII: Average Annual Growth Rates of Industrial Ouput in Inter-war Germany (%)

	1913–38	1913–25	1925–9	1929–32
Metal Production	0.8	−2.9	5.1	−28.1
Pig Iron	−0.1	−2.9	5.3	−13.8
Steel	1.0	−3.0	7.3	−29.4
Metal Working	4.2	2.3	6.7	−20.9
Stone and Earth extractive industries	0.8	0.6	5.9	−31.3
Hard Coal	−0.1	−2.9	5.3	−13.8
Brown Coal	3.3	4.0	9.6	−11.0
Chemical	5.0	2.4	8.8	−9.4
Oil Refining	10.5	1.9	17.0	11.6
Rubber	8.7	7.1	3.4	−3.8
Sulphuric Acid	0.3	−2.8	8.7	−18.1
Soda	2.2	−0.1	10.4	−8.4
Nitrates	8.5	35.2	11.0	−8.4
Artificial Fabrics	7.1	15.5	24.2	−0.5
Textiles	0.1	−1.7	−0.4	−6.8
Clothing	1.6	−0.1	−2.1	−0.9
Leather	−0.8	−1.8	−2.4	−4.0
Gas, Water, and Electricity	5.8	5.8	7.7	−7.8
Building industries	0.2	—	—	−29.9

Source: Calculated from Hoffmann, 352–4, 362, 390–1.

Optimists would describe the middle years of Weimar as years of stable and balanced growth. Pessimists paint a different picture: these were years in which declining industries, through a unique combination of circumstances, experienced an Indian summer. But both accounts stress the peculiarity of the mid-Weimar period. This peculiarity was geographical as well as chronological, and was a consequence of Germany's stagnation. In France, for instance, where the 1920s were years of significant growth, and of high investment levels (in 1913 investment was 16.8 per cent of National Product, in 1930 20.8 per cent), there were dramatic changes in industrial structure as the share of the engineering trades surged ahead.[8]

[8] Caron, 194, 231.

There is an additional problem—particularly significant when it comes to any analysis of the 1920s, and particularly important for the German case—which concerns all attempts to examine rise and decline by industrial sector: this is the changing effect of economic organisation on inter-sectoral differentiation. The analysis by industries as in Table VIII is too crude and unspecific. In one sense it does not disaggregate enough; in another it disaggregates too much and ignores the emergence of high degrees of vertical, cross-sectorial organisation. Very often the trust provided a bridge between old and new products. How far such organisation of the economy stabilised growth is a controversial question. In some cases there seems little doubt that organised capitalism smoothed structural transformation.

Thus not all the chemical industry expanded at the same rate, and chemicals had their fair share of old trades and sunset branches. Dyestuffs—in the production of which Germany had led the world before the War—should be put into the category of only very modest growth, partly because during the War foreign states, particularly Britain and the USA, had confiscated many German patents. The production of sulphuric acid, which before the War had been the backbone of the German chemical industry, did not rise markedly in the inter-war years. The new chemical products were nitrates, rubber (and later synthetic rubber), and petroleum products. They were largely sold on domestic markets, and they developed in spite of high rates of tariff and non-tariff protection in the world already from the early 1920s (nitrates and explosives were strategically vital industries).[9]

In Germany after 1925 the German chemical industry was dominated by the giant chemical trust IG Farben, which was formed from the fusion of the major pre-war producers: Bayer, Hoechst, Agfa, Weiler-ter Meer, and the Chemische Fabrik Griesheim-Elektron were merged into the BASF. New and old parts of the same industry, although located in different parts of Germany, now shared a common ownership. There were still tensions within the trust's management, as older figures

[9] L. F. Haber, *The Chemical Industry 1900–1930: International Growth and Technical Change*, Oxford 1971, 219–20, 239–46.

from dyestuffs such as Carl Duisberg, the Chairman of both the Executive Board and the Supervisory Board, clashed with a new entrepreneurial élite associated with synthetic fibres and petroleum products. But in this case the high degree of economic organisation almost certainly helped the transition from one set of technologies to another. The rapidly growing parts of IG Farben suffered very high losses during the depression, and were only kept from going under by capital movements witin the firm: the dyestuffs branch was less cyclically vulnerable.[10]

Similar benefits of industrial concentration can be observed in the case of the steel industry: here, ownership was extended to more than one industrial sector. By the 1920s many of the big German steel firms had moved into mechanical engineering. Such diversification offered a better path to new technologies as well as, from the point of view of the owners, a better distribution of risk. The unpredictable circumstances of the war and post-war period made it important to eliminate as many risks as possible. At times when raw or semi-finished products could only be sold at a loss, or at prices controlled by the state, there were still opportunities in the less regulated finishing trades. In addition, finished products could be sold on foreign markets for foreign exchange: this was a highly attractive undertaking in the conditions of the post-war inflation.[11]

Already before 1914 the steel and coal Gutehoffnungshütte (GHH) had acquired interests in wire production. During and after the War, the process of vertical concentration was accelerated. All the major steel firms now had participations in the shipbuilding trade: the GHH bought itself into a new shipyard on the Elbe near Hamburg (the Deutsche Werft, Finkenwerder) as well as buying shares in an old one (the Hamburger Werft). The Deutsch-Luxemburgische Bergwerks- und Hütten AG had a shipyard in Emden; the Thyssen concern took a share in the Vulkan-Werft; and Fried. Krupp AG had long owned the Germania-Werft. Machine tools and engineering firms were other favourite targets for heavy industrial

[10] H. Tammen, *Die IG Farbenindustrie Aktiengesellschaft (1925–1933): Ein Chemiekonzern in der Weimarer Republik*, Berlin 1978, 87–90, 115–16, 143.

[11] See G. D. Feldman, *Iron and Steel in the German Inflation 1916–1923*, Princeton 1977, 120–1, 183.

expansionism. The GHH acquired a substantial mechanical engineering base in south Germany: first in J. Tafel Eisenwerk Nürnberg (1919), then the Maschinenfabrik Esslingen (1920), Fritz Neumeyer AG and Zahnräderfabrik Joh. Renk AG, Augsburg; and, after a dramatic struggle, MAN (1920).[12]

In other cases, steel firms were taken over or created by engineering or trading companies concerned to guarantee their own supplies. A good example is the way in which Otto Wolff built up a steel empire on the basis of a Cologne metal trading business. This wholesale outlet, together with excellent contacts in the civil service (Wolff's fellow director Ottmar Strauss was an official in the Commissariat for Public Security), allowed him to develop a position in exporting. Thus he earned hard currency and made foreign connections which he later used to raise more money to further the cause of vertical integration: Wolff sold shares in Phoenix Stahl to the Kgl. Niederländische Hochofen- und Stahlfabriken AG.[13]

Thus a relatively static steel industry was coupled via ownership with 'dynamic' industries, such as mechanical engineering and trading. It was particularly important in the case of the steel industry that these dynamic sectors had contacts with export markets (here there is an obvious contrast with the chemical industry, where the newest technologies were least concerned with exporting). In many cases the alliance of static and dynamic business also provided for the transfusion of new entrepreneurial talent: Wolff, for instance, was a flamboyant buccaneering type who made his mark in a world dominated by older-style figures such as Fritz Thyssen and Emil Kirdorf, and even older ones such as the aristocratic Gustav Krupp von Bohlen und Halbach. The GHH's engineering works lay mostly in the south, and not in the Ruhr; and the management of these south German plants (figures such as Richard Buz and Ludwig Endres) had a different mentality to that of the old steel men.[14] A concern provided—as was the case in the

[12] Ibid., 213–19, 224–39; and E. Maschke, *Es entsteht ein Konzern. Paul Reusch und die GHH*, Tübingen 1969, 137–62.

[13] F. Pinner, *Deutsche Wirtschaftsführer*, Berlin-Charlottenburg 1925, 59–64. W. Herrmann, 'Otto Wolff', in *Rheinisch-Westfälische Wirtschaftsbiographien*, 8, Münster/Westf. 1962, 123–56.

[14] Maschke, 160–1. HA/GHH 40010220/7b, 10 Dec. 1929 Reusch to Kastl (on attitude of Buz).

chemical industry—a means of linking the generations in Germany's economic development.

The alliance of old and new was often, then, thought of as a way of stabilising the German economy by opening up wider markets and by facilitating capital transfers within the structure of the concerns. The best theoretical exposition of the view that vertical concentration ('organised capitalism') and trustification represented an economic stabiliser was made by the socialist economist Rudolf Hilferding:

> Free capitalism has undergone a transformation into organised capitalism... The uncertainties of the capitalist mode of production are reduced, and the impact of crises, or at least the effect of these on the workers, minimised. A planned distribution of investment by the big trusts, a restraint in the investment of new fixed capital during the boom and a postponement of investments until the recession, a regulated credit policy of the big banks supported by a corresponding monetary policy of the central bank, are the chief instruments of such a policy.[15]

In practice this vision of the crisis-free economy was painfully distant from the realities of the slump at the end of the decade. One problem was that the German slump was made much more severe by the collapse of export markets: but for heavy industry, a major consideration promoting the cause of vertical integration had been a belief in exports as the key to stabilising the development of the economy. It was the access to export markets that had made the engineering firms so attractive to the steel magnates during the war and inflation. The trusts of the 1920s saw export trades as a way of diminishing the risks inherent in dependence solely on domestic orders. This doctrine was known as the *Exportventil* (export stabiliser).[16]

Political calculations reinforced the export ideology. In order to service Germany's growing foreign debt, and in order to pay reparation, it was necessary to export.[17] The Dawes

[15] R. Hilferding, 'Probleme der Zeit', *Die Gesellschaft* 1/1, 1924, 2.

[16] For the concept of the 'export-regulator' (*Exportventil*) see R. Wagenführ, *Die Bedeutung des Außenmarktes für die deutsche Industriewirtschaft: Die Exportquote der deutschen Industrie von 1870 bis 1936*, Sonderhefte des Instituts für Konjunkturforschung No. 41, Berlin 1936.

[17] K.-H. Pohl, *Weimars Wirtschaft und die Außenpolitik der Republik 1924–1926; Vom Dawes-Plan zum Internationalen Eisenpakt*, Düsseldorf 1979, 30.

reparation plan had set out the principle that in the long run reparation payments could only be made if Germany achieved export surpluses. German policy-makers saw in this doctrine a potentially useful weapon in their struggle to reduce the reparations bill; and underpinning the 1920s 'policy of fulfilment' (*Erfüllungspolitik*) was the idea that by pushing German goods out into the world, Germany could cause difficulties for other states, and particularly for the reparation creditors. British shipbuilders, steel-makers and textile manufacturers, for instance, would find that reparations were bad for the world and not just for Germany.

The Reich thus tried to encourage the export drive, and foreign policy in the 1920s demonstrated a fine mixture of public and private goals. Both ending reparations and exporting more became national tasks of great importance and urgency. In 1918–20 the German diplomatic service was reorganised (the Schüler reforms) in order to integrate consuls in the regular diplomatic career structure; and a Trade Political Department (Handelspolitische Abteilung) created.[18] Already before the First World War, German exporters had had more assistance from diplomats than business men in any other country; and after the War this aid was extended. State export insurance (through a newly created company, Hermes), and favourable credits (from a subsidiary of the Reichsbank, the Deutsche Golddiskontbank) were intended to spread 'Made in Germany' throughout the world. The major beneficiaries of the state's export aid and credit insurance schemes were neither the dynamic 'new' trades nor the traditional heavy industrial power bloc, but rather old-style, and smaller, producers: the largest single part (30 per cent of the total) of state export credit went to textile producers, the second largest part (10 per cent) to toy exporters.[19]

Between the stabilisation of the currency and the beginning of the depression, Germany's position on world export markets did indeed improve significantly; while in Germany's rival, Britain, exporters were in difficulties as a consequence of the decision to return to the gold standard at the over-valued

[18] F. G. Lauren, *Diplomats and Bureaucrats: the first institutional responses to twentieth-century diplomacy in France and Germany*, Stanford 1976, 128–31.

[19] Petzina 1980, 82.

parity of \$4.86.[20] German heavy industry tried to maintain its export lead through participation in international cartels, though sometimes there were problems. Steel producers in Germany were so successful in finding export markets that they regularly had to make penalty payments for exceeding the quotas allotted to them in the International Steel Cartel. In the depression, in accordance with the notion that export markets could compensate for domestic inadequacies, steel producers and light industry began to turn eagerly to markets in south-east Europe. Civil servants in the Auswärtiges Amt and in the Reich Economics Ministry joined business leaders in warming up once more the dated idea of an economic Mitteleuropa. Heavy industry also ran its own foreign policy trying to build up German trade with the USSR, which in the depression was by far the most important customer for steel and engineering products. Thus a visit in 1931 of eighteen leading industrialists to the Soviet Union included six steel men (and in addition, a representative of the MAN, which was owned by the GHH).[21]

At first Weimar's experience seemed to bear out the theory of the 'export stabiliser'. The economic recovery of 1926 was led by a very strong export performance; and in the later 1920s exports went on growing when there were clear signs of recession in the domestic economy. It was only in late 1929 that the (seasonally adjusted) peak in exports occurred. After 1928, the *export quotas* of the big steel trusts increased. In 1930/1, for instance, almost half the GHH's sales were on foreign markets (see Table IX).

Export dependence was the rule even in the largest German steel concern, the Vereinigte Stahlwerke (set up by the fusion in April 1926 of the Rheinische Stahlwerke, Phoenix AG, the Rhein-Elbe-Union and Thyssen). The Vestag was unlike the GHH or Krupp in that it exhibited a high degree of horizontal rather than vertical concentration. It was not heavily involved in mechanical engineering, but in 1929 it controlled 43 per cent

[20] See D. E. Moggridge, *British Monetary Policy 1924–1931: the Norman Conquest of \$4.86*, Cambridge 1972.

[21] H. Pogge von Strandmann, 'Industrial Primacy in German Foreign Policy: Myths and Realities in German–Russian Relations at the end of the Weimar Republic', in (eds.) R. Bessel and E. J. Feuchtwanger, *Social Change and Political Development in Weimar Germany*, London 1981, 251.

Table IX: Gutehoffnungshütte Exports as a Proportion of Total Sales 1925/6–1933/4 (%)

1925/1926	34
1926/1927	31
1927/1928	25
1928/1929	31
1929/1930	36
1930/1931	49
1931/1932	47
1932/1933	35
1933/1934	29

Source: GHH Annual Reports

of German crude steel production.[22] It was very keen to put its steel products on the export markets, and sold 61 per cent of German exports of universal iron and 35 per cent of strip steel exports. This search for export markets became more desperate later in the depression. While in a year of strong domestic boom (1927) 53.1 per cent of German pipes, 25.9 per cent of cast iron, and 34.9 per cent of steel wire and plate were sold abroad, at the height of the depression in 1932, these figures were respectively 80.6 per cent, 65.9 per cent, and 51.1 per cent.[23] In other sectors there were similar degrees of export dependence: thus in the later 1920s 55 per cent of IG Farben's sales were abroad, despite widespread foreign fears, which found their expression in protective tariffs, of German chemical strength.[24] In 1929 21.4 per cent of German hard coal, 38.4 per cent of cotton woven fabrics and 23.0 per cent of woollen fabrics, and 56.9 per cent of German toys were exported.

Big business was particularly keen to sell to foreigners. Within each sector, large firms usually had higher export quotas than small firms. They had better marketing and credit facilities, which gave them an advantage on distant markets. Thus while the whole electro-technical industry in 1933 exported 23 per cent of its products, AEG had a quota of 38

[22] R. Brady, *The Rationalisation Movement in German Industry: A Study in the Evolution of Economic Planning*, Berkeley 1933, 108.

[23] HA/GHH 400123/9, memorandum 'Gelsenkirchen'; export quotas calculated from *Statistisches Jahrbuch*, various issues.

[24] Enquête-Ausschuss, *Die deutsche chemische Industrie*, 121.

per cent, Siemens–Schuckert of 42 per cent, and Siemens und Halske of 41 per cent.[25]

On the other hand, these high export quotas should not disguise the catastrophic German export performance in the second half of the slump, after 1930. The combination of the rising tide of world protectionism and then, in September 1931, the devaluation of sterling, ensured that exports now fell *more* quickly than industry's domestic sales. This disaster jolted the doctrine of the *Exportventil*, though it did not destroy it completely. Rather it meant the new export markets had to be found, urgently; this desperate search showed how far the aim of industry in building vertical empires to allow a spreading of risk had failed.

There were other signs too that vertical concentration was a poor way of solving problems: 'organised capitalism' was becoming more rather than less rent by factionalism than unorganised market capitalism. As IG Farben moved into synthetic energy sources and thus nearer to the concerns of the Ruhr coal men, and as Ruhr coal firms used American loans to build up a company, the Ruhrchemie AG, engaged in synthetic nitrate production, the two sides' mutual antagonism increased.[26] As the GHH built up a vertical empire, its Director Paul Reusch started to oppose the system of rebates paid by steel producers to the manufacturing consumers of steel. These rebates had been agreed under the Avi settlement, which came into force on 1 March 1925, as a way of compensating manufacturing industry for the high domestic price of German steel, which otherwise would have produced competitive disadvantages relative to British or Belgian producers. In the depression Reusch wanted to reduce these rebate payments so as to strengthen his mixed steel and engineering concern against other engineering producers.[27]

Organisation may have smoothed the way for some transfers of capital and technology, but it failed in the main task of economic stabilisation, and also of a stabilisation of inter-industry political relations.

[25] R. Wagenführ 1936, 14, 17. E. Wagemann in *Wochenbericht des Institutes für Konjunkturforschung* 4/36, 2 Dec. 1931.

[26] Tammen, 61–3.

[27] HA/GHH 400101290/32, 19 June 1931 Reusch to Ernst Poensgen.

THE CHRONOLOGY OF GROWTH AND CHANGE

The explanations that have been advanced for the peculiarity of mid-Weimar need to be cast in terms of a historical analysis of economic development that goes back at least to the changes wrought by the First World War. Here the investigation is descriptive rather than econometric: for there are great difficulties involved in using econometric models to test hypotheses concerning the economic troubles of Weimar. To start with, this is a period in which there were a large number of external shocks experienced in the course of a relatively brief time-span. There is no long-running development interrupted by one single disturbance. Secondly, despite a great deal of recent research, the war and post-war periods contain many empirical lacunae. There are no reliable figures on industrial investment either overall, or by sectors, between 1914 and 1924. W. G. Hoffmann simply misses out this period from his depiction of the pattern of German economic growth. As a result of the statistical difficulties and neglect, historians have perhaps been over-impressed by the developments of the later 1920s (for which we have abundant statistical material) and have not been sufficiently mindful of wartime changes.

It was in fact during the War and the inflation that the 'newer' industries demonstrated faster growth rates, while 'older' industries (mainly coal and steel, but also textiles) suffered. During the War, the German chemical industry started to develop large-scale nitrates production: later this might have extensive peacetime applications. The Allied blockade had cut Germany off from South American sources of nitrates: synthetic substitutes were developed in response. Rubber production was an important part of the wartime economy.

On the other hand, the iron and steel industry was badly affected by the initial wartime dislocation of the market; later there were difficulties in securing labour as well as with increasing labour radicalism. Particularly bitter conflicts broke out in the metal trade: there were major strikes in the Berlin metal industry in April 1917 and January 1918, as workers suffered from the erosion of differentials and from the general food shortages of wartime Germany. Steel production fell as a consequence of the dislocations at the beginning of the war, and, despite attempts by the military authorities (notably the unsuccessful Hindenburg programme of 1916) to boost production, never recovered. Peacetime industries such as textiles and garments were affected by the rationing of raw materials and by the fall in real wages during the war; and the military demand for uniforms during the war did not provide as adequate an alternative stimulus as in Britain (this impression is confirmed by—admittedly very subjective—comments on the poor standards of clothing among German soldiers in the First World War).[28] A recovery of demand after the conclusion of the armistice (real wages rose in 1918/19) did not result in great increases in textile output.[29] Other traditional trades—such as toy and musical instrument manufacture—also suffered during the war.[30]

What happened in the German Inflation?

Recently, there has been a great deal of discussion concerning the issue of how much investment occurred during the inflation. Related to this is the issue of whether the investment that did take place was misdirected, with the effect that many creations of the inflation period proved to be useless once a sound money regime was restored. In 1930 a commission set up be the German Government concluded that it was 'the capital investments undertaken mainly in the years of inflation' that had been responsible for the massive substitution of machines for labour. A recent general overview of the inflation (by C.-L. Holtfrerich) also presents a picture of substantial and useful investment taking place with finance from foreign funds pouring into Germany as speculative hot-money flows. On the other hand, K. Borchardt, using Hoffmann's figures on capital stock after the stabilisation, is sceptical of the notion of an investment boom. The most detailed empirical work so far of firms' investments (by D. Lindenlaub for the engineering industry) appears to support Borchardt and the sceptics.[31]

[28] For example, E. M. Remarque, *Im Western nichts Neues*, Berlin 1929.

[29] C.-L. Holtfrerich, *Die deutsche Inflation 1914–1923: Ursachen und Folgen in internationaler Perspektive*, Berlin and New York 1980, 230–1.

[30] J. Kocka, *Klassengesellschaft im Krieg 1914–1918*, Göttingen 1973, 29–33.

[31] Enquête-Ausschuß, IV Unterausschuß *Arbeitszeit, Arbeitslohn und Arbeitsleistung. Zusammenfassender Bericht*, Berlin 1930, 2. Also D. Petzina, *Die deutsche Wirtschaft in der Zwischenkriegszeit*, Wiesbaden 1977, 14. Holtfrerich 1980, 202. K. Borchardt,

If there was indeed substantial investment in the inflation era, it must have been motivated to a substantial extent by expectations of future opportunities existing in a relatively long-term perspective. There are many famous inflation stories of the following type: a father leaves equal sums to two sons, one thrifty and hard-working, the other feckless and spendthrift. The thrifty son deposits his money with the bank and soon finds that it is worth less than the empty beer bottles left over after his brother's conspicuous consumption. Spendthrift behaviour of this kind may have been a reasonable choice for private citizens, but it did not make much sense as a business strategy. The brothers would not have been well advised to embark on the construction of an enormous bottle-manufacturing plant. It made no sense to invest in new capital equipment merely to reap the gains offered by a period of instability which no one expected to be long-lasting. Indeed from the end of 1918 onwards, almost everyone expected, wrongly, that the inflation would soon be over. The short inflation illusion of 1918–19 should indeed be reckoned—with the short war illusion of 1914—as a major socio-psychological phenomenon of recent German history. When industrialists decided to use the inflation in order to build, they were building for the years *after* the end of currency instability.

These considerations applied to even the most spectacular of the unwieldy giant concerns created during the inflation: these were designed to knock out commercial enemies during the inflation process in order to win the stabilisation peace. In practice, the schemes of the founders often turned out to be unsound and based on miscalculation. The largest inflation concern, whose founder won notoriety as the incarnation of the inflation mentality, was the Stinnes empire. This was a product of the fusion in 1920 of the coal mining and steel interests of Hugo Stinnes (the Rheinelbe-Union) with the electrical concerns Siemens und Halske and Siemens–Schuckert into the Siemens–Rheinelbe–Schuckert-Union (SRSU). The SRSU

'Wachstum und Wechsellagen 1914–1970', in (eds.) H. Aubin and W. Zorn, *Handbuch der deutschen Wirtschafts- und Sozialgeschichte*, Stuttgart 1976, 701. D. Lindenlaub, 'Maschinenbauunternehmen in der Inflation 1919–1923: Unternehmenshistorische Überlegungen zu einigen Theorien der Inflationswirkungen und Inflationserklärung', in *Die deutsche Inflation: Eine Zwischenbilanz*, 49–104.

proved to be unworkably and uncontrollably large: the managements of the old parts tried to maintain their positions within the new concern, and decision-making turned into a series of undignified tussles. How investment resources should be allocated within the firm was never settled, since the overlarge bureaucracy involved in management got in the way of any discussion of this issue. Carl Friedrich von Siemens later looked back with regret: 'If these conditions were to come out into the open, then it would be a disgrace of the first order for all who bear responsibility for them.'[32] Faults in the execution, and the unwieldiness of the management structure, should not obscure the long-run rationality of Stinnes's concept: his wish to diversify away from a concentration on coal and steel was essentially sound.

A great deal of the answer to the question about the rationality of inflation investment hangs on the issue of *how* new investment was financed. One explanation gives a fundamentally rational account of inflation finance; the other picture of sources of investment makes much more out of inflation madness. In the first version, there was a profit inflation in which wages lagged behind industrial prices; employers' profits were higher in the more dynamic industries; and these employers could afford to invest more. The second version stresses how monetary depreciation aided investment: firms borrowed cheaply and were able to repay their loans in depreciated currency. At the same time they reduced their cash holdings, and followed the line taken by other economic agents: a flight into real values (*Flucht in die Sachwerte*), regardless of how useful the *Sachwerte* in fact were (this is the empty-beer-bottle calculation). In the case of firms, the *Flucht in die Sachwerte* meant investment.

The second, irrational, account, depicts the inflation as primarily a credit inflation, fuelled by political calculations that were economically dysfunctional. The money supply expanded rapidly because of the generosity of bank lending and of the policy of the central bank (Reichsbank) of discounting commercial bills liberally. The Reichsbank was obliged to support the great commercial banks in this way because it

[32] Feldman 1977, 242.

feared that otherwise there would be a credit crisis and social revolution. Rudolf Havenstein, the Reichsbank's President, was so aware of the responsibility of his institution for maintaining social order that he boasted about the Bank's success in buying up paper factories and printing works in order to supply Germany's need for paper money.[33]

However, this 'irrational' account of inflation greatly exaggerates: the whole of the inflation cannot be described as an engineered credit inflation. The Reichsbank was perfectly well aware of the dangers of a liberal rediscounting policy, and in fact was not prepared to discount all bills brought to it by the commercial banks. Several times it tried to enforce a credit squeeze: in the summer of 1922 (until it began generous rediscounting again on 19 August); and again in the spring of 1923. When it did discount liberally, the Reichsbank knew that it was in practice subsidising industrial investment: 'it cannot be denied', an internal memorandum said, 'that a large proportion—perhaps an overwhelming proportion—of credits are only requested because the borrower can make an unusual profit because of the rapidly falling currency and the rapidly rising prices'.[34] It did not believe such operations should be carried on for long; and the periods of generosity in rediscounting were exceptional.

At other times, there were complaints about credit shortages and of banks refusing to over-commit themselves to particular borrowers. The formation of the large concerns was indeed in part a reaction to the problems caused by the credit shortages: industry was trying to free itself from bank tutelage and control.[35] Once banks tried during and after the War to limit their risks by lending only for short periods (and thus no longer for whole investment cycles as in the past), enterprises tried to create their own house banks (Konzernbanken), or to form trusts intended to facilitate capital movements within large

[33] Bresciani-Turroni, 1937, 75–9. *Ursachen und Folgen* 5, 543–5, 25 Aug. 1923 Havenstein speech to Reichsbank Zentralausschuß.

[34] H. Habedank, *Die Reichsbank in der Weimarer Republik: Zur Rolle der Zentralbank in der Politik des deutschen Imperialismus 1919–1930*, Berlin 1981, 74–5.

[35] J. Kocka, 'Entrepreneurs and Managers in German Industrialisation', in (eds.) P. Mathias and M. M. Postan, *The Cambridge Economic History of Europe* VII/1, Cambridge 1978, 570: Hilferding's theory of finance capitalism 'was already basically outdated when it was formulated' (in 1910).

industrial structures. One banker now commented that 'the great industrial corporations generally dominate the banks and not the reverse'.[36]

Until 1922 self-investment of the kind that the trusts and concerns were designed to facilitate was the characteristic form of inflation investment. Only in 1922 did falling profits drive industry back in desperation to the banks and to the Reichsbank, whose credit policy *then* became the most important determinant of economic developments. Industry next lobbied in order to make the Reichsbank relax its policy whenever there was an attempt to slow down the inflation by monetary stringency. The massive borrowing from banks in the hyperinflation period (1922–3) was necessary from industry's point of view in order to finish off investment projects already begun: this was the only phase of the inflation which can properly be described as credit inflation.

That these investment projects had been commenced at all reflected the high level of actual profits (as well as the high level of anticipated profits) in the earlier post-war period. Even in the engineering industry, where there were in general very low rates of profit, in 1920–1 profits were recycled into investment: after those years, however, while other industries looked more and more to bank finance, the engineers cut back severely their investment programmes.[37]

Self-financing out of profits was encouraged by a tax system which failed to impose effective tax rates on industry. Reich Finance Minister Erzberger's reform proposals of 1919–20, which involved new taxes on business as well as higher rates of income tax and a wealth tax, were never systematically implemented. All that remained of the Erzberger scheme was a centralised system which took away from the Länder the right to impose supplements on Reich taxes. Some of the changes in tax administration also helped to concentrate resources in the hands of industry. Thus a wage tax collection by the employers was only required to be paid into the Finanzamt months later: in this way enterprises were given large liquid balances with which they could play. The difficulties of adjusting tax rates during an inflation in which prices fluctuated wildly also meant

[36] Feldman 1977, 256. [37] Lindenlaub, 71–2, 80.

that there was a great deal of scope for appealing against tax assessments, and then for slow payment of sums due.[38]

Stabilisation and Stagnation

The conditions in which industry operated during the stabilisation period after 1924 were entirely different from those of the inflation years.

1. The Impact of the Sozialstaat In the 1920s the importance of taxation in the national economy increased. Taxes represented an important element in the increased costs borne by Weimar business;[39] particularly in years of recession such as 1925 or after 1929, business pressure groups mounted a vigorous campaign to secure cuts. The campaign was highly successful in 1925–6, but, as we have seen, unsuccessful later.

High levels of tax, combined with the effects of the inflation and the redistribution of income that resulted from the War and its social changes, were held to be responsible for the low rates of capital formation, and thus for the absence of sustained economic growth and the threat of falling sales and rising bankruptcies. Falling savings ratios were not in the 1920s a peculiarity of the German economy: Britain, which had had no inflation, but where the tax bill rose after the War, had the same experience. German business men were, however, particularly keen to blame the post-stabilisation tax levels for their difficulties. At a conference of the Friedrich-List-Gesellschaft in Bad Eilsen in October 1929, leading industrialists, bankers, civil servants, politicans, and academics analysed the causes of the German capital shortage. There was a general agreement, Bernhard Harms reported, that 'every tax reduction helps capital formation, irrespective of whether it affects high or middle incomes. There is no complete agreement about the extent of the effects of each of these reductions, but it may be

[38] P.-C. Witt, 'Tax Policies, Tax Assessment and Inflation: towards a Sociology of Public Finances in the German Inflation 1914–1923', in (eds.) N. Schmukler and E. Marcus, *Inflation through the Ages: Economic, Social, Psychological and Historical Aspects*, New York 1983, 450–72.

[39] The cost argument was used in *Aufstieg oder Niedergang?*; and also in standard complaints by business men in the world economic crisis, e.g. 11 Feb. 1931 A. Vögler to Brüning, in SAA 4/Lf 811 (C. F. v. Siemens).

assumed that the cutting of high tax rates has an especially significant effect.[40]

Secondly, German taxes affected not only the overall level of capital formation, but also the financial structure of business. The effect of corporation tax was particularly damaging. The penalisation of declared corporate profits made it more attractive to borrow, even at high interest rates, than to raise capitalisation: profits attracted higher tax rates than interest payments. The high gearing of industry, which proved to be a crucial weakness during the depression (see Chapter VIII), was in part at least a consequence of the German tax system. There may even have been an assumption on the part of the Finance Ministry that dependence on external finance was the best way of achieving a rational allocation of scarce capital: the creation of the large trusts—such as IG Farben and the Vestag—was facilitated by tax concessions precisely on the grounds that larger units had better contacts with overseas sources of finance.[41] The Finance Ministry's policy-makers assumed consistently that foreign capital would be the major, and most promising, source of industrial investment funds. This may have been a correct assumption; but the policy implications, particularly as regards corporation tax, helped to make the financial structure of German companies more unstable.

Tax policy also produced a rather peculiar third consequence. Comparisons of tax levels consistently showed much higher levels of both personal and corporate taxation than in Britain or France. Yet the revenue from taxes in Germany was not as high as the tax level figures implied.

The explanation for this discrepancy lies in the extent of tax evasion in Germany: mostly this took the form of capital export abroad. By the end of the 1920s, attempts to control the volume of capital flight formed a central part of any new tax programme.[42] The Reich Finance Ministry was aware of the extent of the problem, but found itself powerless to act. Many of the worst offenders were the largest German concerns. The

[40] Colm and Neisser, I 388.

[41] ZStA RFM B7710, 2 July 1929 memorandum (on fusion of Vereinigte Glanzstoffabriken AG with NV Nederlandsche Kunstzijdefabriek).

[42] FES NL Müller 179, 8 Sept. 1929 Müller to F. Stampfer.

Table X: Taxation and Social Payments as a Proportion of National Income in Britain, France, and Germany 1925–29 (%)

	Britain	France	Germany
1925	21.9	20.0	22.2
1926	23.4	19.4	24.2
1927	21.6	20.9	25.1
1928	21.9	21.1	25.4
1929	20.7	22.5	25.6

Source: Sonderbeilage zu Wirtschaft und Statistik 12 Jg. No. 12, 1932, 12.

chemical combine IG Farben used its Swiss subsidiary IG Chemie Schweiz, Basel, to avoid high German taxes; so did the state-owned Prussian electricity supply company.[43] Any attack on such giants would lead to terrible political consequences, and would also severely damage the profitability of these large concerns. So tax evasion and capital flight came to be built into the Weimar system. They were the consequence of a society's decision to impose taxes which were higher than the level the taxpayers believed that they could afford.

2. Credit Constraints A second constraint on the development of German industry in the late 1920s was imposed by the availability of external credit. In contrast to the situation prevailing during most of the inflation, external finance was now an important source of investment funds. Some investment was still paid out of undistributed profits: between 1925 and 1928 an estimated annual 1.5b. RM, or 12.5 per cent of the total, capital formation was financed in this way (*Selbstfinanzierung*). After 1929 the volume of investment ploughed back fell off abruptly.[44] But corporate profits in the mid-Weimar years were eroded by the high level of taxation, and firms were obliged to look to the capital market for funds. After 1924 bank lending expanded dramatically.

From 1925 to 1929 bank loans accounted for the major part of industrial investment, and a large proportion of these funds came, indirectly via the banks, from abroad. Many commenta-

[43] ZStA RFM 7710, 11 Nov. 1929 and 4 Dec. 1930 memoranda.

[44] W. Prion, *Selbstfinanzierung der Unternehmungen*, Berlin 1931, 20f. E. Schmalenbach, *Finanzierungen*, Leipzig 1937[6], 7–9.

Table XI. Loans of Major Credit Groups (not including advances on goods or bills discounted) (m. RM)

	Great banks	Other banks	State and Länder banks	All credit Institutes
31.12.1913	2 949	3 348	—	6 297
31.12.1924	1 478	617	846	2 941
31.12.1925	2 301	837	1 828	4 966
31.12.1926	2 849	1 058	2 645	6 552
31.12.1927	3 796	1 473	3 532	8 801
31.12.1928	4 651	2 345	2 662	9 658
31.12.1929	5 762	1 986	2 813	10 561
31.12.1930	5 832	1 921	2 561	10 314
31.12.1931	4 727	1 620	2 640	8 987
31.12.1932	4 382	1 237	2 527	8 146
31.12.1933	4 064			

Source: Untersuchung des Bankwesens 1933 Vol. II, 138 ff.

tors now lamented the weakness of the bourse as a source of funds and the consequent dependence of industry on borrowing. Jacob Goldschmidt of the Darmstädter Bank said 'we must sooner or later reach the limit. There is a certain gearing that a decent firm cannot exceed.'[45] Bank debts were a much more common phenomenon in business in the late 1920s than before the War. For instance, in the iron and steel goods trade, out of a total sample of 60 firms, in 1913, 6 were indebted and owed 2m. M; in 1927, 13 firms owed 5m. RM.[46] In addition, it should be remembered that these published figures on company indebtedness were usually deceptive: firms often financed themselves through commercial bills, which were not included in statements of indebtedness, but which were renewed at maturity so as to provide what in effect was long-term credit.

Immediately after the end of the inflation, there was an acute shortage of loan funds. When in the spring of 1924 there were signs of a new credit-based inflation, the Reichsbank imposed strict quality restrictions on its bill portfolio. During the period from April 1924 until the end of 1925 the central bank discounted at a rate below the market, but discriminated.

[45] Enquête-Ausschuß, *Die deutsche eisenerzeugende Industrie*, 170.
[46] Enquête-Ausschuß, *Die deutsche Eisen- und Stahlwarenindustrie*, 212–15.

Table XII: Industrial Investments of Corporate Enterprise 1924–1931 (m. RM)

	New Plant	Replacement	Total investment	Investment as percentage of new bank loans (Grossbanken)
1924	193	513	706	
1925	574	574	1 148	71.7
1926	301	647	948	57.8
1927	535	721	1 256	75.4
1928	711	789	1 500	57.0
1929	327	841	1 168	95.1
1930	116	791	907	7.7
1931	21	501	522	—

Source: Untersuchung des Bankwesens 1933 Vol. I, 571 ff; II, 138 ff; Landes 371.

This twenty-one-month period was supposed to restore a 'normal' economy and to purge the excesses of the inflation from the German system. Schacht spoke of using harsh monetary policy in order to 'shake the bad . . . apples out of the tree'.[47] He subscribed to the notion that the inflation had been marked by massive misinvestment, and that too many trusts had been created in heavy industry. Lacking any personal experience of industry or of the credit side of the operations of the German banks (he had been a banker, but worked as a public relations man, not as a lender), he felt a deep suspicion and hostility towards that excessive organisation that had been the characteristic of German industrial and financial development.

On the other hand, he felt that 'legitimate' industry and agriculture could not be penalised without leading to injustice and also social discontent.[48] The Reichsbank discounted bills at an artificially low rate—10 per cent to February 1925 and 9 per cent to January 1926—but only took bills from favoured industries. The discriminatory restriction was politically highly contentious.[49] A large number of small business men, deprived

[47] FRBNY Strong papers 1012.4, 28 Jan. 1925 Shepard Morgan to Strong. See G. Hardach 1976, 64.

[48] ZStA Reichsbank 6440, 5 May 1924 memorandum of Dr Natrop (Reichsbank) and comments of Schacht. *Berliner Tageblatt* No. 445, 19 Sept. 1925.

[49] L. A. Hahn in *Frankfurter Zeitung* No. 215, 4 June 1924; also *Frankfurter Zeitung* No. 16, 7 Jan. 1926.

of easy access to the Reichsbank or the commercial banking system, believed that credit restriction worked against them. They also felt later in the decade that they had less access to the foreign markets for capital: they were betrayed by over-centralisation within Germany and internationalism outside. Schacht was frequently attacked by small business: thus when one clothier asked his banker why interest rates were so high and credit so difficult to obtain, he was told 'because of the inadequate credit of the Reichsbank'.[50] The Reich Economic Ministry was sympathetic to this sort of complaint and in 1925 even won over Reich Chancellor Luther: both now pressed for a relaxation of the Reichbank's restrictions.[51] Instead of borrowing abroad, Germany should expand her credit domestically: since, if the money was foreign, big business would have favoured access, but if the increase was managed domestically, thousands of small firms would benefit. From 1925/6, this political pressure appeared to achieve results, and there was a modest credit inflation. This was derived partly from the Reichsbank's abandonment of its restrictive stabilisation policy, and partly from the surge of foreign capital.

Foreign lending to Germany began very hesitantly after the London Conference of 1924 which accepted the reparation proposals made by the Dawes Committee, and which also recommended a major international loan to help the German Government begin payments. The Dawes loan was also intended to 'raise the wind' for foreign lenders, though it was the summer of 1925 before long-term loans to German business, usually bonds issues, became common. Lending reached a peak by the middle of 1927, and then, in July and August, fell off badly.[52] This falling off was only to a small extent due to pessimistic assessments abroad of business conditions in Germany. Most American bankers still sent home ecstatic reports about German industry. Rather, the reduction in foreign lending was the intended consequence of a powerful political campaign to reduce the extent of long-term German borrow-

[50] Enquête-Ausschuß, *Einzelhandel mit Bekleidung* 284. Big industry was on the whole sympathetic to the combination of low discount rates with discriminatory restrictions: *Deutsche Bergwerkes-Zeitung* No. 48, 26 Feb. 1925.

[51] BAK R43 I/634, 17 April 1925 Report of the Reichsbank and subsequent discussion.

[52] Summary in G. Hardach 1976, 70–84.

ing. At the end of 1926, exemption from capital yield tax was ended for foreign investors. In April 1927 the Reichsbank engineered a fall in quotations on the Berlin stock exchange in order to discourage foreign purchasers. In June 1927, a memorandum of the Agent-General for Reparation Payments criticised German public finance in strong terms; and this report temporarily affected foreign confidence in Germany.[53]

The slowing-down of long-term borrowing was, however, followed by a growth of short-term borrowing. This was for the most part under the direct control of foreign banks. Some of the loans went to German banks; quite a substantial amount went direct to German business. The foreign bankers calculated that high interest rates in Germany provided immediate returns; and also that short-term lending was a way of cultivating the German loan market for the future, when the market for long-term bonds issues might have improved again. In 1929 and 1930, there were signs that such an improvement on the bonds market was indeed occurring. After the September 1930 elections, however, when there were large increases in the Nazi and communist votes, long-term lending effectively stopped.[54]

German business had become very dependent on the inflow of foreign funds. A RDI Presidential Committee warned in

[53] *Report of the Agent-General for Reparation Payments*, 10 June 1927, Berlin 1927, particularly 47–53.

[54] The only exact figures on the nature of foreign short-term loans we have relate to July 1931:

Short-term loans to Germany 31 July 1931 (m. RM)

	USA	UK	Others	Total
Banks to German banks	1 724	1 083	2 087	4 894
Banks to German industry, agriculture, and commerce	389	506	1 490	2 385
Banks to German public corporations	116	65	124	305
Total from foreign banks	2 229	1 654	3 701	7 584
Loans from foreign industry and commerce	692	356	2 564	3 612
Other lending	12	23	108	143
Total	3 143	2 054	6 772	11 969[a]

[a] Includes 630m. RM Central bank credit.

Source: BoE OV34/149 1 Dec. 1931 Nordhoff to Layton.

July 1928 of the consequences of a halt in foreign lending, and at the same time pointed out that the continuing flow on which the German economy depended was by no means assured.[55] An even more striking demonstration of industry's dependence on foreign money was given in 1929: in June the Krupp directors were reminded of the need to borrow in order to rationalise the production of the Essen Gußstahlfabrik as an argument for the abandonment of the initially very vociferous opposition of heavy industry to the Young reparations plan.[56] Without the Young plan, there would be no more American funds.

Where did the American money go? It is easiest to trace the path of the long-term loans and investments. Direct investment by American firms amounted by 1930 to $216.5m. (909m. RM).[57] Often direct investment was associated with technological transfers: a major beneficiary was the German automobile industry. Ford owned a plant in Berlin from 1925 and from 1929 in Cologne; in 1929 General Motors, after having worked several smaller factories, bought up Adam Opel AG of Rüsselsheim near Frankfurt/Main.

A total of 5922m. RM German shares (nominal value) was registered as being purchased by foreigners from 1924 to 1930, though the *net* movement of share ownership in this period was very much smaller (+847m. RM).[58] The difference reflects the considerable amount of capital moving out of Germany in the later 1920s.[59] In the case of share transactions, many German firms used foreign subsidiaries to purchase shares of the parent company: these shares were now registered as foreign domiciled, and the whole arrangement brought tax advantages. Tax on commercial paper (*Wertpapiersteuer*) was reduced; and the foreign-domiciled shares were also often

[55] SAA Haller 344, 12 July 1929 RDI Präsidialausschuß.

[56] HA Krupp WA IV 2887, 22 June 1929 discussion in Gußstahlfabrik. Also *Deutsche Bergwerks Zeitung* No. 239, 11 Oct. 1929, *Frankfurter Zeitung* No. 459, 22 June 1929, and *Magazin der Wirtschaft* No. 27, 4 July 1929.

[57] W. Link, *Die amerikanische Stabilisierungspolitik in Deutschland 1921–1932*, Düsseldorf 1970, 375.

[58] Ibid., 356. C. Lewis, 620. *Deutsche Zahlungsbilanz* 10–11.

[59] See F. Machlup, 'Die Theorie der Kapitalflucht', *Weltwirtschaftliches Archiv*, 36, 1932, 512–29.

guaranteed a fixed return which might be deducted from domestic German corporation tax liability.

Most long-term foreign investment in Germany took the form of bond sales: from 1924 to 1930 Germany borrowed a total of 7174m. RM; and of this sum 62 per cent came directly from the USA.[60] The big east coast issuing houses sold their bonds to the investing public fairly quickly, and, although the purchasers were not always the proverbial widows and orphans, they generally lacked information about European or South American conditions. It is difficult to avoid the conclusion that some banks took the American investors for a ride. Many bonds carried high issue commissions for the bankers but interest rates that were low relative to the risk involved.[61] Germany accounted for a large proportion of total American bond lending: 18 per cent of the measured US capital export. The major German bond borrowers turned out to be municipalities (apart from the international loans of 1924 and 1930, the Reich and the Länder were largely excluded from the US market), a few large firms (GHH, AEG, Siemens), and the Roman Catholic Church (this consideration made the Catholic Centre party more favourably disposed than it might otherwise have been to the blandishments of international finance).

Thus, though there were some cases of waste (particularly in municipal and church finance) the American funds did contribute to the development of German industry in the later 1920s. There were American domestic pressures on lenders not to give money that would create competition for American industry: the Director of the Bureau of Foreign and Domestic Commerce, Julius Klein, for instance warned that loans such as that of 1926 to the new German steel trust, the Vereinigte Stahlwerke, were creating trouble for America.[62] Generally, however, these considerations played little role in the 1920s as Republican administrations on the whole continued to believe that European prosperity was good both for American political influence and for American business.[63]

[60] Link, 356. C. Lewis, 620. *Deutsche Zahlungsbilanz* 10–11.

[61] This was a popular argument in the USA, whose most important political advocate was Senator Louis McFadden. C. Lewis's book provides academic support for this criticism of American banks.

[62] Link, 362.

[63] M. Leffler, 'The Struggle for Stability: American Policy towards France

It was the activities of the German banks, not of the foreign lenders, that did most to impose a conservative bias on the pattern of investment in the Weimar Republic. Instead of looking for new opportunities, most bankers preferred the safe bets of the pre-war days; and many indeed even abandoned the more enterprising activities of the Kaiserreich's banking system.

Bank lending policy had traditionally been surrounded by great controversy. Before the war, small industry complained that it had been neglected by the banks; and this criticism was taken up by a few self-critical bankers and particularly by Alfred Lansburgh's influential periodical *Die Bank*.[64] In the inter-war period, the controversy became more acute: the German Great Banks appeared more and more to be unlovely and ungainly 'dinosaurs'. From 1927 to 1929, a subcommittee of the Inquiry into German Conditions of Production and Sale (the Enquête-Ausschuß) examined the state of the German banking industry. Its statistical investigations proved unambiguously that the major banks concentrated their loans with big borrowers.[65] Small trade and industry had to rely on alternative sources: on state banks, and co-operative and savings banks.

The Great Banks were acutely aware of these criticisms: some, like the Deutsche Bank, staged public-relations exercises to counteract their image. In September 1927 the Deutsche Bank raised a 6 per cent five-year $25m. loan in USA which was to be re-lent at advantageous rates to German small business.[66] But despite such exercises, by the end of the 1920s accusations about bank conservatism had become part of the political stock-in-trade. Complaints came from all quarters: a liberal journalist on the *Vossische Zeitung*, Reiner, thought the big banks had caused the economic crisis by neglecting the industrial *Mittelstand* (small craftsmen and traders). The Ver-

1921–1933', Ohio State University Ph.D. 1972, 10, quotes Herbert Hoover: 'Our export trade does not grow by supplanting the other fellow but from the increased consuming power of the world.'

[64] See a recent presentation of a similar argument in H. Neuburger and H. T. Stokes, 'German Banks and German Growth: an empirical view', JEcH 34, 1974, 710–31.

[65] Enquête-Ausschuß, *Der Bankkredit*, 162, 167–8.

[66] F. Seidenzahl, *Hundert Jahre Deutsche Bank 1870–1970*, Frankfurt 1970, 288–90.

ein Deutscher Maschinenbau-Anstalten (VDMA), the interest organisation of the engineering industry, where there were a large number of small and medium firms, protested that big firms had been given favourable access to credit by the Great Banks, and that the funds supplied had been used by the 'large enterprises and the individual directors associated with them in order to carry out financial transactions of the most various sorts, which, as has been demonstrated by many events of the recent past, were partly economically of dubious value'.[67] The NSDAP was particularly energetic in taking up the theme. Wilhelm Keppler, Hitler's economic adviser, said that banks had become too bureaucratic;[68] the Nazi expert on retail trade also argued that large banks had been unable because of their size to see that the risks involved in lending to small firms were in fact lower than the risks of lending to giants.[69]

The savings banks (Sparkassen) found it difficult to provide large volumes of industrial finance. They had developed as a major source of funds before the First World War, but found it much more difficult to rebuild their position than the banks had done. Sparkassen relied on small deposits: but after 1924 the small depositors, frightened by the experience of the German inflation and having lost almost everything, were reluctant to lend again. While Prussian savings banks had 909m. RM deposits in 1913 at the end of 1928 they had only 589m. RM. Whereas in 1929 the balances of the Berlin Great Banks amounted to 164 per cent of the 1913 level, the savings banks had only reached 61 per cent.[70] Moreover, the Sparkassen committed a large proportion of their funds to public sector lending. This was the objection made at the Friedrich-List-Gesellschaft Bad Eilsen conference on capital shortage when proposals to raise the rate of capital formation through tax reductions at low and middle incomes were discussed; such reductions would increase savings, but they would then be

[67] BAK R2/13633, 17 Aug. 1931 VDMA to Reich Finance Minister; IfZ ED93/13, 24 Aug. 1931 diary entry.

[68] Born 1882, a chemical industrialist from 1912, and in 1932 adviser to Hitler on economic policy.

[69] BAK R2/13682, 6 Sept. 1933 Meeting of Bank-Enquête.

[70] Deutsche Bundesbank, *Deutsches Geld- und Bankwesen in Zahlen, 1876–1975*, Frankfurt 1976, 78–9, 102–3.

channelled in an irrational way into the quagmires of municipal finance.[71] Thus there was a further limitation on capital formation in Weimar.

The survey produced by the Enquête-Ausschuß revealed that at the end of 1928 76.4 per cent of the total loaned by Great Banks was in loans over 100 000 RM (and 40.3 per cent over 1 000 000 RM); whereas only 3.4 per cent of their credits were under 10 000 RM. By contrast the Sparkassen put 57.8 per cent of their private loan funds into packages under 10 000 RM. At the Enquête, the Banks did not try to justify their concentration of loan funds by referring to a better risk calculation with big loans. The Enquête's report, which was published in 1930, made on the other hand a great deal out of the risks involved in over-commitment to individual borrowers. Rather, the banks concentrated on big customers partly out of tradition, and partly because they hoped to be involved in profitable side-business such as the issue of new shares where the banks won higher profits than on loans.[72]

In the light of these considerations, it appears unlikely that the distribution of bank credit was in accordance with strictly rational market criteria. Which industries were particularly favoured by the Great Banks? Not, curiously, traditional heavy industry. Coal mining and iron and steel accounted for a total of only 8.7 per cent of the banks' credits; though metal finishing took a relatively high share (7.6 per cent). Relatively little went to the 'dynamic' industries: the chemical industry accounted for only 3.6 per cent of bank credit; engineering and automobile construction 2.9 per cent; and the electro-technical industry—which before the war had been a major area for bank involvement—with 2.3 per cent took less than the wood industry. Instead the major recipients were the food industry (11.2 per cent) and textiles (11.8 per cent). These were industries where there were few innovations in the 1920s.[73] A concentration on older branches is just as evident in the lending of the large regional banks. The ADCA (Allgemeine Deutsche Credit Aktiengesellschaft, the major Saxon bank) and the

[71] Colm and Neisser, I 98 (Professor H. v. Beckerath).

[72] Enquête-Ausschuß, *Der Bankkredit*, 162, 156.

[73] Ibid., 168.

Bayerische Vereinsbank (Munich) both put more into textiles than the Great Banks.[74]

The Enquête drew the conclusion that banks had pressed credits on static industries with which they felt familiar, and that they had as a result been responsible for over-production during the period when demand fell and prices slumped. Another criticism was that banks continued to lend to their customers even when these were in difficulties: so that in the end the scale of bank losses became greater.[75] The bankers themselves showed little confidence in their own judgments. In 1925 at the Bankers' Conference Oscar Wassermann of the Deutsche Bank told of how faulty the banks' credit distribution had been.[76] After the inflation, the banks began to engage themselves in an ever more desperate search for safe investments: in practice this meant investment in older industries.

The poor identification by German bankers of entrepreneurial opportunities can be explained partly in sociological terms. Before the war, when banks had developed as major sources of finance for German industry, bankers had been intimately associated with business life, and had developed specialities in particular fields. Men such as the great mid-nineteenth-century bankers, Mevissen, Camphausen, and Hansemann, had a very detailed knowledge of the Rhineland economy. David Hansemann (1790–1864), the founder of the Disconto-Gesellschaft, had originally been a dealer in woollens in Elberfeld; he sent his son and successor Adolph (1826–1903) into apprenticeship in a Leipzig textile firm. Then Adolph Hansemann became very closely involved with mining in the Gelsenkirchenbergwerks AG. Georg von Siemens, the founder of the Deutsche Bank, was a nephew of the inventor Werner von Siemens, and spent his early professional life constructing telegraphs in Persia.[77]

However, as banks grew bigger and spread their attentions more widely, their relations with industry became more and

[74] *Untersuchung des Bankwesens* 1933, Berlin 1933, I 82. But see the defence of the banks: December 1931 Report of Centralverband des Deutschen Bank- und Bankiergewerbes (copy in BAK NL Silverberg 302).

[75] *Untersuchung des Bankwesens 1933*, I 526–7.

[76] *Verhandlungen des VI. Allgemeinen Deutschen Bankiertages in Berlin*, Berlin 1925, 29.

[77] E. W. Schmidt, *Männer der Deutschen Bank und der Disconto-Gesellschaft*, Düsseldorf 1957.

more formalised. Bankers appeared only on the Supervisory Boards of firms (*Aufsichtsräte*): these did not meet regularly enough to be able to control the day-to-day running of the enterprise. Leading bankers acquired too many Supervisory Board seats to be able to supervise effectively: there were cases of bankers holding over forty seats before 1914, and over a hundred by 1930. Thus the often-remarked fact that Berlin banks dominated the Supervisory Boards of German business by the beginning of this century may be not so much a reflection of the strength of the banks (which is how it is usually presented), but rather a comment on the slightness of banks' acquaintance with industry.[78] In the Bank Inquiry of 1933, one bank director admitted that 'in the case of good companies today the executive decisions are made by the directors (*Vorstand*). The most important task of the Supervisory Board is to appoint good directors.'[79]

The Directors of the Great Banks of the Weimar Republic were, with a few exceptions, solid and decent men who lacked any sense of exploring risks.[80] They looked for safe bets: brewing and textiles. These were investments that were considered 'safe' by grandmothers playing the stock exchange; and there was indeed a certain grandmotherly quality about Weimar bankers' preferences. Such attitudes encouraged the unscrupulous in business; the worst fraudulent loans were taken by Nordwolle (textiles) and Schultheiß–Patzenhofer (brewing). Most Weimar bankers had not studied economics; and in general the foundation for a banking career was either a study of law or a banking apprenticeship, rather than any experience of industry. Already in the second generation of bankers after the Gründerzeit there were many lawyers: these included Adolph Salomonssohn of the Disconto-Gesellschaft (he left the bank in 1888 in order to spend the last twenty years of his life studying philosophy and natural sciences: a real Buddenbrook career), Emil Russell (Disconto), Paul David Fischer (Disconto), E. E. Russell (Disconto), Carl Michalowsky (Deutsche Bank), Georg von Simson (Darmstädter Bank), and Gustav Simperin (Berliner Handelsgesellschaft). Legally

[78] Kocka 1978, 568.
[79] BAK R2/13683, 24 Nov. 1933 statement by Otto Christian Fischer.
[80] See Pinner, 222 for the argument that Weimar bankers lacked creative energy.

trained minds began to run the German Great Banks; and men like Ludwig Bamberger resigned from the Deutsche Bank because they believed that there would shortly follow 'an era in which business activity and business life would become unpopular'.[81]

An additional problem for Weimar banking was that the best training for bankers in the Kaiserreich had been believed to be experience of overseas banking in the powerful South American and oriental subsidiaries of the Great Banks. Men trained in this way who were at the top of their banks in the 1920s included Gustav Schlieper (Disconto), Franz Urbig (Disconto), Paul Millington-Hermann (Deutsche), and Albert Blinzig (Deutsche). Unfortunately training in pre-war overseas banking did not prepare bankers well for a world in which Germany was a debtor rather than a creditor. There was little experience among the bank directors of the 1920s of North American banking: an experience which would have been altogether more useful.

In fairness to the bankers of the 1920s, it should be added that there were some able men who had had some experience of business life: Oscar Schlitter (a member of the Deutsche Bank's executive from 1906 to 1908 and from 1918 to 1932) came from the Bergisch-Märkische Bank and understood West German industry and the gathering process of industrial concentration well. Georg Solmssen spent a great deal of effort trying to rationalise agricultural production and introduce uniform systems of standards. Eduard Mosler (Disconto) was good at dealing with other banks and pushed through the successful fusion of the Disconto Gesellschaft with the Deutsche Bank. But even these men were no more than competent operators of an already well-established, well-oiled system that glided along in smooth routine.

Much more famous in the 1920s were the wild men of the Behrenstraße: foremost among the new school of dynamic bankers was Jacob Goldschmidt, the creator of the Darmstädter- und Nationalbank. His speciality originally lay in making a quick Mark out of mergers. He was genuinely entrepreneurial in the way in which after the stabilisation of

[81] E. W. Schmidt: quotation from 87.

the Mark he discovered two growth areas: municipal finance and rationalisation of textile production.[82] Both these strategies initially produced very high profits, but in the end both proved to be costly mistakes: lending to municipalities was by the end of the 1920s enveloped in acute political controversy. Lending to new textile producers was risky because the new works only proved cheaper to run if they could work at full capacity. At less than capacity, they were more expensive per unit output than the old-fashioned works.

Perhaps the most prominent bankers of Weimar were not the representatives of the Great Banks at all, but private bankers: in particular those associated with two houses, M. M. Warburg & Co., Hamburg, and Mendelssohn & Co., Berlin. Warburg specialised in making contacts with American business and in issuing German loans abroad: before the War, the bank had more or less restricted itself to the financing of foreign trade.[83] Mendelssohn, which before the War had concentrated on foreign government finance, particularly Russian state loans, now looked to international currency dealings and loans for the German Government. The head of Mendelssohn's Amsterdam branch, Fritz Mannheimer, was probably the most gifted and certainly the most colourful of the international speculators of the 1920s. His exuberant personal life, paid for from the gains of speculation, scandalised the decent Calvinist burghers of Amsterdam.[84] Warburg and Mendelssohn were operating in growth areas for banking business in the 1920s: international loan finance and government funding operations. However, these areas were clearly vulnerable to political disturbances. It is significant that the most successful bankers operated now as political entrepreneurs, and did not work in the rational assessment of commercial opportunity and risk. This they left to the unambitious and the conservative, for there were fewer quick gains to be made there.

The capital market, and in particular the German domestic capital market, was not good at developing new sectors of the

[82] H. Schäffer, 'Marcus Wallenberg und die deutsche Bankenkrise' (5 March 1939), MS in IfZ ED93, 132.

[83] E. Rosenbaum and A. J. Sherman, *M. M. Warburg & Co. 1798–1938: Merchant Bankers of Hamburg*, London 1979, 135–43.

[84] Schuker 1976, 92–3; personal information from J. Houwink ten Cate.

German economy: a conservative bias was imposed on German industrial development, and as a result new industries grew successfully only when they were integrated in already existing structures (as was the case with the new chemical products or with the development of mechanical engineering).

CONCLUSION: THE MANIA ABOUT THE RATIONALISATION MANIA

The economic recovery of the later 1920s involved rather little structural differentiation. The prominence of heavy industry in the Weimar years of prosperity should be attributed as much to economic (though partially politically determined) causes—including the nature of the tax structure and the operation of the credit system—as to the directly political causes identified by many historians (see Chapter V).

Nevertheless, Weimar prosperity was later often curiously described as a 'rationalisation boom'. Many German managers did indeed make pilgrimages to the USA to study new management techniques. Carl Köttgen (Siemens) wrote a book entitled *Economic America*.[85] During and after the economic crisis, many observers described the rationalisation boom as the fundamental cause of the massive misdirection of resources. In a book published in 1931, the liberal economist Wilhelm Röpke wrote about the 'folly' of substituting capital (which in Germany, unlike the USA, was dear) for labour: 'in a rationalisation "complex" costly installations were made which were as admirable technically as they were commercially unviable.'[86] The socialist theoretician Emil Lederer put forward a very similar account of the consequences of misinvestment.[87] Generally, there was a collapse of the confident belief that the imposition of increased economic organisation was leading inevitably to the introduction of rational investment planning.

The most distinguished German business economist, Eugen

[85] C. Köttgen, *Das wirtschaftliche Amerika*, Berlin 1925.

[86] W. Röpke, *Der Weg des Unheils*, Berlin 1931, 63.

[87] E. Lederer, 'Die Weltwirtschaftskrise—eine Krise des Kapitalismus: Ursachen und Auswege' (1932), reprinted in (ed.) J. Kocka, E. Lederer, *Klassenstruktur und Probleme der Demokratie in Deutschland 1910–1940*, Göttingen 1979, 210–31, especially 216–17, 225.

Schmalenbach, wrote devastating accounts of the absurdity of many of the investments that had been carried out in the name of 'rationalisation'. He attributed a structural weakness in Germany to the over-representation in the German managerial class of technically trained men who were fascinated by innovation but who had little sense of accounting realities. The depression was the price for technical hubris. Thus the textile works J. P. Bemberg AG continued building large new plant for the production of artificial silk from copper ammoniac in 1929–30, only to find that there was no market for its products. A Frankfurt clothing firm, Bender und Gattmann, collapsed in 1930 as a consequence of having adopted an over-ambitious scheme for assembly-line production.[88]

Technical hubris was only part of the story, however. There was, Schmalenbach believed, an irrational pursuit of bigness: 'Many expansions were carried out only for prestige reasons. Managements could not resist the drug of expansion, although their firms were operating well in the market and did not need to fear a serious competitive battle. But they desired a monopoly position. This was enough to produce a clamour for unprofitable investments and purchases.'[89] As this irrational expansion occurred, the costs of capital increased. There emerged a problem of 'fixed costs': the variable part of the costs of production (chiefly raw materials, fuel, and also wages) fell. If the large modern works operated at well below capacity, they faced a competitive disadvantage because of the burden of the fixed costs. The Vereinigte Stahlwerke, which instituted a substantial modernisation programme, calculated that its colliery costs would rise in the following way if the mines worked at below full capacity:[90]

Capacity used (%)	*Additional costs* (*RM/t*)
90	0.55
80	1.27
70	2.10

Thus, a slight recession might produce a major crisis of overcapacity, falling profits, and then bankruptcies and increased

[88] E. Schmalenbach, *Finanzierungen*, Leipzig, 1937^{6}, 19, 308.
[89] Ibid., 309.
[90] Enquête-Ausschuß, *Die deutsche Kohlenindustrie*, Berlin 1929, 341.

unemployment. Only financially very sound large firms would be able to stand the costs of producing at well below capacity levels.

Schmalenbach's analysis amounts less to a criticism of the whole Weimar economy than to an exposure of mistakes in specific areas. Most of his examples are taken from textiles and clothing, where a few innovating firms, particularly in synthetics (such as Bemberg), were in trouble at the end of the decade. He ridiculed efforts to apply modern management techniques to products like textiles, and he found troubles in other new industries too. Consumer industries producing automobiles or household electrical goods had difficulties because they were unfamiliar with the problems of consumer credit. Joseph Schumpeter indeed believed that a quarter of German investment after 1924 was in fact misinvestment.[91] However, these are examples of individual miscalculation and should not form a general indictment.

The general indictment of over-investment and the pernicious effects of the substitution of capital for labour has been popular with historians. Even such a cautious student as Balderston accepts the rationalisation hypotheses, but paints a slightly subtler picture than Röpke or Lederer. In the absence of sustained economic growth, Balderston says, new or technically interesting, but patchy, investment ('rationalisation') was all that was possible. This argument deals with the apparent objection to Röpke's and Lederer's over-investment analysis, namely that Weimar profit and investment levels were in fact very low.[92]

The thesis that there was too much technical progress in Weimar is, however, misleading and fundamentally wrong. In part the appearance of over-enthusiastic investment was an illusion produced by the statistical uncertainties of the inflation period. It was easy for observers to underestimate the amount of existing fixed capital in 1924.[93] Moreover, it is almost impossible to detect what the alleged rationalisation wave of

[91] J. Schumpeter, 'Wenn die Finanzreform mißlingt...' *Der deutsche Volkswirt*, 4/22, 28 Feb. 1930, 695.

[92] T. Balderston, 'The Beginning of the Depression in Germany 1927–1930: Investment and the capital market', *EcHR* 36, 1983, 404–5.

[93] Case argued by J. W. Reichert, in *Stahl und Eisen* 51/34, 20 Aug. 1931, 1056.

the later 1920s actually consisted of. Much of the boom probably never existed at all. A contemporary English account of 'rationalisation' argued very wisely that in Germany rationalisation 'only had an accidental and temporary meaning'.[94] The American author Robert Brady, whose book described the rationalisation movement in most detail, concludes in a semi-apologetic manner: 'In as much as the technical reorganisation necessarily required some years to be carried through and rounded out, even with continuation of prosperity, an increase in net efficiency for the steel industry as a whole could scarcely be expected to show by now.'[95] 'Rationalisation' in retrospect turned out to be simply a vogue-word used to describe the mistaken investments made in the 1920s and should not lead to a conclusion that there was too much capital investment or too much investment in Weimar.

Rather than a general wave of technical advances and improvements there was simply a sectoral maldistribution of investment that created overcapacity in some basic heavy industries and in textiles. According to Jakob Reichert, the General Manager of the VDESI (League of German Iron and Steel Industrialists) Gruppe Nordwest, there had been a 44.7 per cent increase in steel capacity from the outbreak of the War until the late 1920s. Thus there was a great deal of spare capacity: even in the boom year of 1927 the steel industry was only working at 77 per cent capacity (in the same year overall an estimated 89 per cent of mining and manfacturing capacity was in use).[96] In steel—Brady's favourite case—there was, however, little technical modernisation.

The major technical improvements in the steel industry involved the saving of energy, and were a logical reaction to the fuel shortages of the immediate post-war period. These fuel savings (known as *Wärmewirtschaft*) were possible largely because of the concentration of ownership which led to the formation of such giant concerns as the Vereinigte Stahlwerke.

[94] D. H. Macgregor, *Enterprise, Purpose and Profit*, Oxford 1934, 33. H. Levy, *Industrial Germany: a Study of its Monopoly Organisations and their Control by the State*, Cambridge 1935, 202–3.

[95] Brady, 122.

[96] Weisbrod 1978, 47–8. T. Balderston, 'Cyclical Fluctuations in Germany 1924–1929', Edinburgh Ph.D. 1979, Appendix V/6.

Blast-furnace gas largely replaced coke-oven gas (which might now be sold commercially) in heating. The integrated steel works, which had begun to be prominent in the 1900s, now achieved a complete victory—thanks largely to fuel economy: rolling-mills were almost invariably sited next to iron-smelting works, and were usually very close to coal-mines and coke ovens. Improved layouts resulted in major financial savings: only very small stocks needed to be held.[97] The large scale of the German works and the economies that resulted contrasted dramatically with the sad history of the British steel industry in the inter-war period, where even new projects were not constructed in the right geographical location or on a scale sufficient for the technically available economies to be realised.

Rationalisation in German steel also involved the closure of small-scale plants (this was termed 'negative rationalisation'). Between 1913 and 1928 the number of blast furnaces in Rhineland-Westphalia fell from 118 to 72, while the average weekly production rose from 1491 to 3207 tons). Such closures were not carried out very effectively in the later Weimar years, however. Even in the most modern steel concern, the Vereinigte Stahlwerke, there were major inefficiencies remaining. Albert Vögler described how the founders of the Vestag had wanted to create a 'completely integrated work' (*eine absolute Betriebseinheit*). Those plants 'which did not seem to be technically first-rate or which did not fit geographically into the combination' were to be closed. The Hörde and Dortmund groups concentrated on the export of workshop products, and no longer exported any rolled products; 80–90 per cent of rail production was concentrated in one plant.[98] But in 1933, when the Vestag needed to be reorganised once more and decentralised, Vögler admitted that the plans had not been carried out successfully. Thus, as part of the scheme for the rational integration of the Vestag's steel capacity, speciality steel was centred from 1926–7 at Krefeld; but in fact the production of speciality steels did continue elsewhere. Only one of the five furnaces at Bochum was closed down, even though none of the

[97] Brady, 107–12.

[98] G. H. Seebold, *Ein Stahlkonzern im Dritten Reich; Der Bochumer Verein 1927–1945*, Wuppertal 1981, 34. Brady, 110. Levy, 207. Enquête-Ausschuß, *Die deutsche eisenerzeugende Industrie*, 24

works had ever operated at over 75 per cent capacity. Between 1926/7 and 1928/9 labour productivity at the Vestag's Bochum plant remained more or less constant despite increases in production; and from 1930 productivity fell dramatically as the level of output dropped.[99]

This story of productivity is quite characteristic. A leading banker concerned with industrial finance complained that 'the iron industry has been unable to put the real meaning of rationalisation ideas into effect: that is to increase profitability so that price rises on the domestic market can be halted, and so that Germany can compete again on export markets'.[1] There were very great improvements in productivity from 1924 to 1926, but these owed much more to the ending of the destabilising effects associated with the inflation (such as the very high rates of labour turnover, and, associated with these, decreased skill levels) than to technical improvements. During the war and the inflation there had been a substantial modernisation of the work process; but after the stabilisation, with a few exceptions, chiefly in the automobile industry and in coal-mining, the rate of technical change slowed down. Most of the modern steelworks of the 1920s were built *before* the stabilisation crisis of 1925. The Enquête-Ausschuß listed improvements to a representative sample of western steel works: one Thomas steel works introduced a new system of ladle charges in 1921, and went over to piece-rate calculation of wages (*Akkord*) after 1924. The western Martin work increased its furnace capacity in 1921–2 and again in 1923. The rolling-mill abandoned coal heating in 1922–3 in favour of a mixture of commercial gas and gaseous by-products from the blast furnace, and built a new furnace in 1924–5. It doubled too the number of rolls on the fast and medium roll trains. One of the sheet works installed a new conveyor furnace and introduced an electrical crane before 1921. Only a very few improvements came after 1926; an additional heating furnace in one of the sheet mills in 1926; and an additional casting trolley for the second of the survey's Thomas works in 1925–6.[2]

The same chronology holds outside the steel industry too: the

[99] Seebold, 42–3

[1] Enquête-Ausschuß, *Die deutsche eisenerzeugende Industrie*, 169.

[2] Enquête-Ausschuß, *Arbeitsleistung in Stahl- und Walzwerken.*

war and the inflation were the great time for technical modernisation. Daimler cars were produced on an assembly line after 1919; Carl Zeiss (Jena) introduced motion studies in 1921; and Siemens–Schuckert electric motors were built according to Taylor management principles after 1920.[3]

In the machine industry, according to Brady, the 'rationalisation movement, except in certain technical branches, cannot be said to have made any considerable progress in any of its many branches'.[4] In textiles and clothing, commentators took great pains to explain why there was no technical change: the vagaries of fashion meant that it was senseless to introduce large-scale production or assembly lines. Productivity per hour of work in many branches of the textile trade had actually, according to the Enquête, fallen below pre-war levels.[5] In the electro-technical industry, the changes referred to under the umbrella heading of 'rationalisation' related less to labour-saving technology than to either organisational streamlining and new ways of calculating wages or the introduction of new product lines. These included domestic radios, movies, medical electrical technology (in particular X-ray diagnosis and treatment equipment), and electric locomotives. Such new lines did not always bring commercial success. Siemens misjudged the radio market and employed an artist to promote radios as a replacement for the piano in the home (1932). He designed an elegant black box with folding doors as a luxury radio: it barely sold.[6]

The organisational streamlining in the electro-technical industry was often nothing more than a way of getting rid of technically interesting but commercially diverting sidelines: thus in 1927 Siemens stopped producing automobiles and then

[3] G. Stollberg, *Die Rationalisierungsdebatte 1908–1933; Freie Gewerkschaften zwischen Mitwirkung und Gegenwehr*, Frankfurt and New York 1981, 44–5. E. Schöck, *Arbeitslosigkeit und Rationalisierung: Die Lage der Arbeiter und die kommunistische Gewerkschaftspolitik 1920–1928*, Frankfurt and New York 1977, 172.

[4] Brady, 142.

[5] G. Müller-Oerlinghausen, 'Rationalisierung und Textilwirtschaft', in *Industrie- und Handelskammer Berlin, Die Bedeutung der Rationalisierung für das deutsche Wirtschaftsleben*, Berlin 1928, 341–58. Enquête-Ausschuß, *Die Arbeitsleistung in der Textilindustrie*, Berlin 1930.

[6] S. von Weiher, H. Goetzeler, *Weg und Wirken der Siemens-Werke im Fortschritt der Elektrotechnik 1847–1980*, Munich 1981[3], 91. G. Siemens, *Der Weg der Elektrotechnik: Geschichte des Hauses Siemens II*, Munich 1961, 127–32.

later sold their aero-engine works. Even the organisational revolution in the Siemens und Halske technical office (1924 and 1930) was less inspired by a desire to imitate American management techniques than by the discovery of a massive fraud in the old office.[7] In these circumstances it is hardly surprising that Carl Friedrich von Siemens was sceptical about the economic benefits of rationalisation, and stressed that rationalisation was not a patent medicine which might cure all of Germany's ills.[8]

There was a powerful rationalisation movement in two industries:

1. The automobile industry: here Ford and Opel were still building highly modern, labour-saving plants well into the economic crisis; but labour-saving technology was combined with dramatic economic growth (despite high rates of tax on motor vehicles), so that rationalisation created *more* employment.[9]

On the other hand, these American-style giant plants were rather untypical for Germany. The car was still a luxury product, and consumers demanded individually differentiated toys rather than finalized mass products. In 1929 there were still seventeen major producers of automobiles. The small firms did not try to develop mass markets; rather, mass enterprises such as Opel actually looked for ways to engage the top end of the market. For as a mass product, the German car was not really competitive: Germany's roads were poor, whereas she had a first-rate, and cheap, railway system. Here there was a case of a heavy investment in an older form of enterprise making competitive disadvantages for a potential growth industry.[10]

2. Coal-mining: here too 'rationalisation' continued well into the depression, and included a major technical as well as organisational and financial component. Between 1924 and 1928, 76 Ruhr collieries were closed; and in the remaining

[7] Weiher, 91. Siemens 271.

[8] SAA 61/Lf 109, 2 Apr. 1925, C. F. v. Siemens speech to Reichskuratorium für Wirtschaftlichkeit.

[9] *Wirtschaft und Statistik* 1933, 595.

[10] See F. Blaich, 'Die "Fehlrationalisierung" in der deutschen Automobilindustrie 1924 bis 1929', *Tradition* 18, 1973, 18–33.

collieries equipment was standardised and simplified. Drill hammers and pneumatic mining hammers were now widely used: in the five major mining areas of Germany (Upper and Lower Silesia, The Lower Rhine, the Ruhr, and Aachen) in 1927 72.2 per cent and in 1929 83 per cent of the coal was raised by mechanical means. Electrical and mechanical hoists replaced horses; and there were more efficient boring, water-pumping, ventilation, and compressed-air systems. Technical improvements led to increased productivity and to labour-shedding: not just in the period 1924–6, when increasing productivity was primarily a consequence of the return to stability and occurred elsewhere in the German economy; but also in a 'second wave' between the middle of 1928 and 1930.[11]

With these exceptions, in general, after an initial period (1924–7) of working inflation out of the economic system, Germany was faced by low rates of technical change and productivity growth, combined with over-capacity in some branches. This combination made the search for export markets vital and left Germany at the end of the decade very vulnerable to the collapse of world trade.

These difficulties also induced an increase in the degree of horizontal economic organisation. Sometimes, and particularly in Marxist but also in some liberal historiography, this increase has been wrongly described simply as the cause rather than the consequence of the economic problems. According to this analysis, cartels stopped a 'natural' price decline in the depression, and thus obstructed a 'natural' readjustment through a rise in real incomes and then of consumption. Cartels were indeed a favourite weapon used in price maintenance, particularly in industries facing stagnant technology and a tendency towards over-production. Historically they had been described as 'children of necessity' (*Kinder der Not*).[12] But in the past they had actually rarely survived the 'necessity' they were supposed to remedy. In major depressions, cartels had been blown apart as there were powerful motives for firms to break price

[11] Brady, 76. Also R. Tschirbs, 'Der Ruhrbergbau zwischen Privilegierung und Statusverlust: Lohnpolitik von der Inflation bis zur Rationalisierung (1919 bis 1927)', in *Die deutsche Inflation: Eine Zwischenbilanz*, 308–45.

[12] The phrase is F. Kleinwächter's. R. Liefmann, *Cartels, Concerns and Trusts*, London 1932, 21. H. J. Flechtner *Carl Duisberg: Vom Chemiker zum Wirtschaftsführer*, Düsseldorf 1959, 191.

Table XIII: Ruhr Hard Coal-Mining 1913–1931

	Production (tons)	Number employed	Production per employee
1913	114 550 153	409 183	279.9
1920	88 255 780	496 559	177.7
1921	94 114 785	547 330	172.0
1922	97 346 176	552 188	176.3
1924	90 969 875	452 317	201.1
1925	104 335 566	433 879	240.5
1926	112 192 119	384 507	291.8
1927	118 022 353	407 577	289.6
1928	114 577 050	381 950	300.0
1929	123 603 160	375 970	328.8
1930	107 183 040	334 233	320.7
1931	85 637 584	251 034	341.1

Source: Ruhr und Rhein: Wirtschaftszahlen 'Westen', various issues. 1913–26 figures from Tschirbs 1982, 337.

discipline in an attempt to maintain higher levels of production. After the War there was a higher degree of economic organisation, and also of cartellisation. The depression at the end of the 1920s was new in that at least at first there was no serious weakening of the cartel structures in many branches of industry, particularly in heavy industry. In 1925 there were 2500 cartels in Germany, in 1930 3000.[13] Their strength came partly from the influence of state-created institutions with price-setting functions, such as the Reich Coal Council in the case of the mining industry. But it was also a result of the decisive difference made by the development of the big trusts. Cartellisation only survived if it was linked with trustification. The two best known German cartels, the Rhenish-Westphalian Coal Syndicate and the Pig-Iron Syndicate, were dominated by the large mixed steel works. Here the big trusts could suppress quite effectively threats from outsiders to the cartel's price discipline; and at least until the 1931 banking crisis there seemed to be no threat to the cartels' position.

The power of the cartels is illustrated by the story of the steel industry. Until the autumn of 1931 there was considerable

[13] H. König, 'Kartelle und Konzentration', in (ed.) H. Arndt, *Die Konzentration in der Wirtschaft*, I, Berlin 1960, 304. Also M. Sweezy, *The Structure of the Nazi Economy*, Cambridge, Mass. 1941, 94.

price stability: Rhine-Westphalian pig-iron sold at 85 RM/t until July 1930, when it was cut to 83 RM, and at 78 RM from January 1931. Wrought iron was similarly reduced from 141 RM/t to 137 RM/t and 128 RM/t. But in September 1931, the devaluation of sterling led to a fall in world market prices; and although the German steel syndicate, the Rohstahlgemeinschaft, tried to keep up the prices for standardised products, it was, for the first time since its creation, unable to prevent widespread discounting from cartel prices.[14] Thus steel industrialists were scarcely in a position to be able to resist the 10 per cent cut in cartellised prices decreed by the Brüning Government in December 1931; and they were weak too in the face of pressure by small producers directed against the cartels. Oskar Funcke, a Hagen producer of screws and metal goods, was particularly vigorous in making the case against the Weimar cartels: it was the cartels which had given the state the opportunity of interfering in pricing decisions (as in 1930 and 1931 when the Reich had insisted on the steel men discussing their prices at the same time as they talked about wage levels); cartels also provided the Reich Finance Ministry with material which could be used in making tax assessments. But above all, cartels had been turned from instruments which could be used to protect small firms into the agents of the big trusts.[15] Funcke's arguments were logically quite sound: for if the cartels had not been the agents of the large trusts, they would not have survived as along as they did in the conditions of the depression. However, the remedy that Funcke proposed, compulsory state-organised cartellisation, was a very peculiar one. Other steel consumers, including the powerful Engineering Trade Association (VDMA) argued instead for a state-led demolition of cartels.

The December 1931 measures to reduce cartel prices reflected a general and widespread hostility to cartels, born of the feeling that the price rigidity that they imposed had worsened the slump. This cry was taken up by small business pressure groups; as well as by the SPD and the unions. The cartel issue

[14] R. Schindler, *Die Marktpolitik des Roheisenverbandes während der Weimarer Republik*, Bielefeld 1978, 252–3.

[15] BAK NL Silverberg 249, 6 Oct. 1932 RDI Präsidial- und Vorstandsbeirat für allgemeine Wirtschaftspolitik.

in fact helped to crystallise the anti-business front created by the depression. Cartel critics supposed that price maintenance had restricted demand and provoked a drastic fall in production, which had increased unemployment. The trade union ADGB Jahrbuch in 1931 welcomed the fall of 'free prices' as a possible base for a recovery, but criticised the government for failing to act against cartel prices.[16] In this form the argument was too polemical: the difference in price behaviour should not be ascribed entirely to cartels.

How much price stickiness was in reality caused by the cartels? Cartels operated most effectively in basic goods industries and in some kinds of raw material. The Institut für Konjunkturforschung highlighted the power of cartels by producing price series for 'fixed' and 'free' raw materials. 'Fixed' prices included coal, iron ore, pig iron, semi-manufactured steel, rolled steel, nickel, aluminium, artificial fertilizers, benzol fuel oil, cellulose, newsprint, cardboard, bricks, roof tiles, lime, cement, pipes, window glass, and roofing felt. The 'free' prices were drawn from world coal prices, cast metal scrap tin-plate, fine steel-plate, scrap, lead, tin, zinc, textiles, skins, leather, gasoline, lubricating oil and fat, palm oil, linseed oil, paraffin, rubber, and wood. The latter fell dramatically from a peak in 1928 until 1932, when the index stood at less than half its 1926 value. On the other hand, 'fixed' prices were only 84 per cent of the 1926 level at the beginning of 1932, though they continued to fall until the spring of 1933.[17]

One reason for the fall in 'free' prices was the high representation of commodities suffering from the world slump. But there were dramatic falls too in textile prices: the weakly cartellised industries had to face the problem of falling demand, and they responded by price-cuts. In the textile trade there were a large number of weak cartels which were not capable of controlling prices (mostly the cartels only existed to regulate qualities, and not to fix prices or production). Though there were some large firms (ten of the hundred largest German firms were in textiles), production was still dominated

[16] *ADGB Jahrbuch 1930*, Berlin 1931, 10–12. Also Lederer, 221–2.

[17] H. Wagenführ, 'Kartellpreise und Tariflöhne im Konjunkturverlauf', *Jahrbücher für Nationalökonomie und Statistik* 138, 1933, 501–17. *Wochenbericht des Instituts für Konjunkturforschung* 4/51–2, 24 Mar. 1932, and 6/36, 6 Dec. 1933.

by small family firms with limited product ranges. They faced competition from synthetic fibre producers (the Vereinigte Glanzstoff-Fabriken AG, and J. P. Bemberg AG), and from some of the large-scale rationalised works: the Norddeutsche Wollkämmerei und Kammgarnspinnerei AG had started up major worsteds production.[18] The shoe industry was in a similar position: in 1925 the 360 000 employed in the German shoe industry (including only leather shoe production) worked almost entirely in small workshops. Only one firm (Salamander) employed over 2000 workers. Small-scale industry was again faced with the threat posed by a few major producers (the German Salamander works, and much more dangerously the Czech Bat'a shoe producers).[19]

Textile and shoe industries responded to the crisis in a different way to that of the large heavy industrial trusts. There was a weakness in the consumer market already by 1928; the production of shoes showed a downward trend already after spring 1928.[20] The producers responded by cutting prices. Retail sales of textiles and clothing fell in value from 10b. RM in 1929 to 5.9b. RM in 1932 (a 43 per cent fall). Most of this fall was accounted for by the price decline. The volume of retail sales fell by only 9 per cent, and the volume of textile production by only 15 per cent. The demand for textiles and clothing, which is income-elastic, thus remained surprisingly high, although there are signs of a decline in quality which may not be wholly taken into account in the calculation of volume cited. Demand remained at high levels for foodstuffs too: the total fall 1929–32 in value terms was by a third, but output fell by only 10 per cent over this period.[21]

However, the severity of the price decline in many of the weakly cartellised industries does not prove the success of cartels in price maintenance. Sticky prices were characteristic of much of German big industry, whether cartellised or not. They were a reflection of the growth of 'fixed costs', of capital

[18] List of 100 largest firms in H. Siegrist, 'Deutsche Großunternehmen vom späten 19. Jahrhundert bis zur Weimarer Republik', *GG* 6, 1980, 60–102. Brady, 265.

[19] Enquête-Ausschuß, *Die deutsche Schuhindustrie*, 6 ff.

[20] Ibid., 120.

[21] *Wochenbericht des Instituts für Konjunkturforschung* 5/41, 11 Jan. 1933, and 6/30, 25 Oct. 1933; Wagemann 1935, 283.

intensity: in other words, of the process of modernisation that had begun not after the stabilisation of the Mark but before the First World War.

Even in investment goods industries where there was little cartellisation, for instance where the range of products made cartellisation much more difficult than in steel or coal, there were major falls in production and only small price cuts. Engineering production in 1932 was 38 per cent of the 1928 level in quantity, automobile production 33 per cent. Here calculations of unit costs made price-cutting irrational, despite a rapidly shrinking market as the level of investment in Germany declined.[22] In the latter half of the depression especially, though, price-cutting began; and then industrial cartels were no more effective than cartels in the labour market (unions) in holding up prices (see Chapter VI). In the only area where there was some success in price maintenance—agriculture—that success sprang not from the power of cartels but from the politically motivated actions of the state (Chapter VII).

Prices in general in Germany were stickier than in the west European economies. The stickiness was equivalent to that of the USA (where there was also highly capital intensive production) and less than in some of the poorly-developed east and central European economies. 45 per cent of the decline in the US nominal income during the depression was due to price changes, and 43 per cent in Germany, whereas the comparable figures for Britain and Italy were 71 per cent and 89 per cent respectively.[23]

On the other hand, it would be odd to describe German prices as downwardly inflexible. A fall of 21.9 per cent in the GNP deflator would pose a strain for any social and political system, and the price-falls produced terrible conflicts in Germany. In Britain, where a higher proportion of the decline in nominal national income can be explained by price changes, the fall in prices (7.1 per cent) was very much less substantial, and thus less socially damaging, than in Germany. Only in

[22] Ibid.

[23] See on USA R. J. Gordon and J. A. Wilcox, 'Monetarist Interpretations of the Great Depression: An Evaluation and Critique', in (ed.) K. Brunner, *The Great Depression Revisited*, Boston 1981, 89.

Table XIV: Price and Production Falls in Five European Economies during the Inter-war World Economic Crisis (%)

	Depression	Price Fall	Production Fall	Fall in GNP	Fall in GNP due to: Production	Prices
Great Britain	1928–32	7.1	3.3	11.4	28.9	71.1
Italy	1929–34	25.9	3.8	33.7	11.3	88.7
Germany	1928–32	21.9	22.6	39.5	57.2	42.8
Austria	1929–34	5.0	21.9	25.7	85.2	14.8
Hungary	1929–34	32.5	+2.0	31.1	−6.4	106.4

[a] + indicates *rise* in volume of production

Italy and Hungary were there more severe price declines during the depression: but both these states had authoritarian governments far more capable of warding off challenges to their legitimacy than was the tottering Weimar Republic. Democracies, such as Britain and Austria, would have found a price decline of German proportions an intolerable political burden.

In the light of these considerations, the arguments about German price rigidity can be summed up as follows. There was a considerable price decline. Where there was a stickiness it was the consequence of

> cartels in association with concentrations of ownership;
>
> the prominence in the German economy of investment goods industries;
>
> agrarian protection, which affected food prices;

and more generally,

> a vulnerable political system, which could not afford the political consequences of very great price-falls.

Of these four reasons, the fourth explains why there was no political process capable of doing anything about the other three (and particularly about the first and third reasons).

Only in part then was the severity of the slump in output and employment the consequence of the rise of a highly trustified and cartellised organised economy; there was a more general weakness. After the stabilisation of the Mark, the rate of investment slowed down, implying a reduction in the expectations for future growth. Business men believed that growth would no longer take the path followed by the Weimar economy, but they could not yet identify a new track. This is what we mean by describing the slump as a 'crisis of transition'. Business did not know what transition lay in the future. It had invested a great deal in the past: first, in capital expenditure, which sometimes made the new less attractive. Thus there was a crisis at the end of the 1920s in synthetic textiles because of the favourable cost position of older textile firms; and the well-developed railway system seemed to leave the motor car behind. Secondly, there was a similar institutional effect: Germany had created powerful institutions, such as the investment banks, which were far more suited to a previous stage of development.

This type of explanation is far more encompassing than that which presents the depression as 'the crisis of a highly organised economy', parts of which explanation we have accepted. One of the reasons for the high degree of organisation indeed was the prevailing uncertainty about the future. This discussion also sheds light on a third interpretation of the slump as a 'crises of under-consumption', an interpretation which gained popularity at the end of Weimar particularly with trade unionists. In terms of long-run statistics, this case always looked slightly peculiar. Throughout the whole Weimar period (with the exception of 1929, when there was a pronounced recession in consumer products while producer goods were still in a phase of prosperity), consumer-goods industries produced higher quantities relative to investment-goods industries than before 1914. There was a failure in Weimar, not to consume, but to consume the right kind of new good, where consumption would in turn have had accelerator effects on investment industries. Here again we see Weimar in a transition crisis, where the right kind of transition was not identified. The result was stagnation.

V

The Politics of Business in Weimar Germany

Wir haben nicht zu viel, sondern zu wenig Kapital und große Unternehmer.

(Max Weber, 1916)

Some of the causes of German economic weakness in the 1920s may have been non-economic in origin. Markets experience disruption from those who believe that they are suffering from the way in which those markets operate; and there are also often bundles of attitudes taken from the past which limit the rationality of economic decisions. The power and the behaviour of industry in Weimar has often been taken as a fine example of such a lag in attitudes: an atavistic paternalism and a ferociously embittered hostility to the labour movement stood in the way of economic rationality, and obstructed the development of a 'modern' economy. Recently not only the political collapse of the Republic but also Brüning's deflationary course and, more generally, the stagnation of Weimar's economic development has been attributed to the political influence of heavy industry: in particular of the coal and steel producers of Rhine–Ruhr.[1] This chapter examines this case; and tries to assess the reasons for the increasing hardening of business attitudes at the end of the 1920s, and also the general question of the political effectiveness of Weimar business men.

[1] The idea that the conflict of new and old industries was political as well as economic was set out by R. Hilferding, 'Politische Probleme: Zum Aufruf Wirths und zur Rede Silverbergs', *Die Gesellschaft* 3/II, 1926, 289–302. For recent literature on this theme, Weisbrod 1978 and 1979; and H. Pogge von Strandmann, 'Widersprüche im Modernisierungsprozeß Deutschlands: Der Kampf der verarbeitenden Industrie gegen die Schwerindustrie', in (eds.) D. Stegmann, B.-J. Wendt, and P.-C. Witt 1978, particularly 240. The division between old and new industries is made in a particularly crass way by D. Abraham, *The Collapse of the Weimar Republic: Political Economy and Crisis*, Princeton 1980.

BUSINESS ATTITUDES

The early twentieth-century economy in Germany resembled much more a managerial capitalism dominated by large concerns with rationally organised management systems, the administrative co-ordination of multi-unit enterprise, and ambitious marketing strategies, than it did the buccaneering capitalism of the mid-nineteenth century.[2] True, there were still many small family firms, and industries such as brewing still responded chiefly to local markets; and in some cases smaller units were protected by the exceptionally high degree of cartellisation in the German economy. But the picture was dominated by the big concerns and trusts, who had come to dominate the cartels as well. The development of a 'modern' industry did not produce a climate of social consensus; the salaried entrepreneurs who ran this new industry may have been 'particularly disposed to rational, objective, and systematic behaviour', but they were not at all 'suitable people for solving or at least soothing social conflict and for holding leading positions in society and the state in general'.[3]

The reasons for the high propensity of German managers in Weimar Germany to seek conflict rather than consensus are:

1. Many 'modern' business men absorbed to a high degree the latest anti-labour ideology, which, under the label of Taylorism, and disseminated by institutions such as the RKW (Reichskuratorium für Wirtschaftlichkeit) and DINTA (Deutsches Institut für Technische Arbeitsschulung), enjoyed a vogue among employers in the 1920s.[4]

2. There were economic as well as ideological reasons: some of the most 'modern' industries (e.g. synthetic oil) suffered most from the disturbance of markets in the 1920s: this made rational planning very difficult. The managers responded by an intense hostility to the state which appeared to be partly responsible for the economic malaise.

[2] See J. Kocka, 'The Rise of Modern Industrial Enterprise in Germany', in (eds.) A. D. Chandler and H. Daems, *Managerial Hierarchies: Comparative Perspectives in the Rise of the Modern Industrial Enterprise*, Cambridge Mass. 1980, 77–116.

[3] Kocka 1978, 579–80.

[4] Brady, Stollberg, and U. Stolle, *Arbeiterpolitik im Betrieb: Frauen und Männer, Reformisten und Radikale, Fach- und Massenarbeiter bei Bayer, BASF, Bosch und in Solingen 1900–1933*, Frankfurt and New York 1980.

3. There were political reasons too: the newer managers were flexible figures, who were prepared to compromise with all sorts of political movements, including those on the radical right. Such compromises might well be more attractive than compacts with trade unionists.

In these respects, the development of managerial capitalism in Germany took a different course from that in the United States: in the USA the managerial revolution had been in substance completed and its liberal ideology fully in place *before* the union movement started to play a substantial part in large industrial organisations in the 1930s and particularly during the Second World War. In Germany strong unions had arrived, at the latest by the First World War, and represented a more dangerous threat to emerging managerial strategies than in the USA. The managers often reacted by identifying unionists as enemies. Moreover, the rise of managerial capitalism in Germany coincided with a period of dramatic economic fluctuation: in the USA it had preceded it. Again this increased the potential for an anti-democratic direction of managerial capitalism. Finally, in Germany there was a well-established cultural tradition which dictated how big business men should behave: in the USA there had been no such leading entrepreneurs in *early* industrialisation as Borsig or Krupp in the first half of the nineteenth century in Germany.

Thus the emergence of trusts and large vertical interests, did not bring about a fundamentally new style of conducting business or of labour relations. *Novi homines*, frequently technical experts, had come to the fore: but there was no sign of an overthrow of old ideas about business life and the way it should be organised. Some prominent Weimar figures, like Emil Kirdorf and Fritz Thyssen, both enthusiastic supporters of National Socialism in the 1920s, looked rather bizarrely conservative because of the wish to return to patriarchal and authoritarian labour relations (which were generally termed the *Herr-im-Hause* attitude).[5] They should not be taken as embodying the 'old' business view: either of these two men

[5] Hilferding 1926, 292. For Thyssen and Kirdorf, see the studies in H. A. Turner, *Faschismus und Kapitalismus in Deutschland: Studien zum Verhältnis zwischen Nationalsozialismus und Wirtschaft*, Göttingen 1972. Also Pinner, 71–91.

would have looked eccentric and out of place in any society, and it did not take the Weimar Republic to bring out their quirkiness. Kirdorf was very proud of his status as a self-made entrepreneur, who had risen through management and who had little family wealth. His pride made him turn into an embittered reactionary: even before 1914 he had appeared to be a political eccentric who believed that Kaiser Wilhelm's policy was dangerously radical.[6] Thyssen was a diminutive man, who suffered, as such men often do, from an inferiority complex. This became worse as he came to realise that he could never play the entrepreneur in the way that his great father, August Thyssen, had done. To compensate for his multiple personal inadequacies, Fritz Thyssen took up a personal political philosophy—the *Ständeideologie*, or theory of economic estates, that had been propounded by Othmar Spann—and urged its application to German economic problems. After 1933 he became disillusioned and cross once the Nazis refused to take Spann as seriously as Thyssen believed he should be taken.

Some of the older men were reactionaries because they had defective personalities; but the young men were not particularly liberal either in their approach to management and labour problems. Carl Duisberg of IG Farben is a good illustration of the new-style entrepreneur. He was a second-generation business man (his father had been a textile manufacturer in Barmen): but he rose in the firm of BASF on the strength of his gifts as an academic chemist. Technologists were in general beginning to play an important role in German management. Politically, Duisberg had a liberal's commitment to free trade; but he believed that the economic crisis which broke out at the end of the 1920s had been caused by excessively high wages and taxes. He joined in an industrial attack on the Brüning regime for being too dependent on and too sympathetic towards labour unions; and he promoted the idea of a united front against Marxism (i.e. the SPD and the labour unions). A drastic government cost-cutting programme was, he believed, the only way of restoring economic health and the principle of *Individualwirtschaft*.[7]

[6] H. A. Turner 1972, 61.

[7] Flechtner, 357. M. Wolffsohn, *Industrie und Handwerk im Konflikt mit staatlicher*

Carl Köttgen, of the Siemens–Schuckertwerke GmbH, was another technocrat influential in German business politics: he was a clever engineer, who came from a Barmen engineering firm. He was educated at the Berlin Technische Hochschule and was then responsible for developing mineshaft hoisting machinery and a reversing rolling-mill for Siemens und Halske. His contacts with the Anglo-Saxon world were close: in 1907 he had been appointed managing director of the Siemens Brothers Dynamo Works, London; and he was interned in Britain during the War. In 1924 he visited the USA and wrote a highly enthusiastic book about his experience. He was one of the prime exponents of the rationalisation ideology of improved efficiency, higher wages, and greater prosperity, though even in the mid-1920s he admired America more for the freedom of hiring and firing than for the high wage levels. Yet by 1930 he was talking like a very old-fashioned business man:

> Personally, I do not believe that the hard times we are facing at present are to be explained solely or to a large extent by the world crisis. What we have experienced over the last ten or twelve years presents a quite different picture. We have not only lost a war, but we have had a fundamentally new government, which has been concerned for ten or twelve years to distribute charity to all sides, and that with a generosity which could not have been greater if the war had been won.

A rather similar case to Duisberg was Paul Reusch. He presided over the great vertical concern of the GHH, but had originally come from outside the Ruhr (he was a Swabian, born in Königsbronn, Württemberg), and from rather humble circumstances. He had been a gifted practical engineer, and won his spurs constructing plant in Bohemia and Hungary; and politically he was much more than a naïve reactionary of the Thyssen type. His political programme in the depression, however, was extreme: it involved the exclusion from political responsibility of parliaments and parties. 'We can only ad-

Wirtschaftspolitik? Studien zur Politik der Arbeitsbeschaffung in Deutschland 1930–1934, Berlin 1977, 184, 286. IfZ ED93/14, 18 Sept. 1931 diary entry. HA Krupp FAH IV E 499, Dec. 1930 Duisberg memorandum, 'Die Zukunft der deutschen Handelspolitik'.

[8] C. Köttgen 1925, 18. SAA 11/Lf 374, 11 Dec. 1930 speech of Köttgen to VDA on 'Lohn und Preis'. Biographical details: G. Wenzel, *Deutsche Wirtschaftsführer: Lebensgänge deutscher Wirtschaftspersönlichkeiten*, Hamburg 1929.

vance in Germany if the parties are in future excluded from negotiations on the formation of governments. So much reform is needed that we cannot think of allowing the parties to have any sort of power in Prussia or the Reich.'[9]

Paul Silverberg was a younger man in the expanding browncoal industry, and was unusual among Rhineland business men in that he was Jewish. Lignite was a major source of fuel for the rapidly developing electricity generating industry. He had created a major sensation in 1926 when at a meeting of the RDI he had openly advocated an acceptance of the Republic and its institutions—even if this acceptance meant working with the SPD. Yet in 1922 and 1923 he had been very prominent in industrial attempts to end the application of the eight-hour day; and in the slump he changed his mind about what he now called 'Weimar collectivism'. By the early 1930s he wanted the NSDAP to come into government in order to take 'unpopular' but necessary measures such as the implementation of further wage-cuts.[10]

Silverberg's flexibility—his passionate advocacy of republican solutions in the mid-1920s and of authoritarian ones in the early 1930s—may have derived from his youth. He was ten years younger than Reusch and six years younger than Gustav Krupp von Bohlen und Halbach. The younger chemists of IG Farben too—men like Bütefisch and Gattineau—often became intoxicated with the romantic-reactionary vision of a 'works community'; and this turned them towards the romantic notion of a regeneration of capitalism offered by the NSDAP.[11]

It was the younger men, often in the newer industries, who were particularly likely to be tempted to explore the possibilities offered by new political movements. Hermann Bücher, who was first employed by the RDI, then worked until 1928 in IG Farben and from then in AEG (in other words, in classically 'expansive' industries), paid money to the Nazi rebel Wilhelm Stennes. An electrical-power man who became Chairman of the Federation of Saxon industries, Wilhelm Wittke,

[9] R. Neebe, *Großindustrie, Staat und NSDAP 1930–1933: Paul Silverberg und der Reichsverband der Deutschen Industrie in der Krise der Weimarer Republik*, Göttingen 1981, 131. Also HA/GHH 400101220/11c, 6 Sept. 1931 Reusch to Kastl.

[10] Neebe 1981, particularly 159.

[11] Tammen, 282–5.

was very early in taking an extreme radical stance politically and led the call at the end of the 1920s for the exclusion of parliament from economic decision-making. In the coal industry, too, younger managers put in by the large steel concerns were much more hostile to the labour movement than old-style independent mine owners. They were the most eager to introduce new technologies in the mine and saw the unions as obstructing attempts to rationalise production. Some, like Wilhelm and Walter Tengelmann and Erich Winnacker, became Nazis.[12]

These considerations cast great doubts on attempts made by historians to dinstinguish politically between business men on the basis of their economic position. Export producers were frequently as hostile to unions as producers for a domestic market. Even employers in industries which might have been expected to benefit from a general increase in real incomes, such as the building trade, thought that wages that were too high were crippling Germany. In so far as it is possible to generalise at all about differences in the style of entrepreneurship between 'old' and 'new' industry, the most significant distinction is the rather banal one that, as young industries grew more quickly they could take on more young managers, and these tended to be politically mobile: their commitment to *any* form of political system was weak. It would certainly not be correct to conclude with the socialist theoretician Hilferding, and others since, that the electrical and chemical industries produced managers who liked working with democratic politics.

Rather, all employers changed their political orientation continually; and those who were least committed to a stereotyped vision of pre-war stability changed most, and changed most radically. Hugo Stinnes is a good case: unconventional personally (he wore a beard and synthetic clothes), he welcomed co-operation between employers and unions in 1918–19; his influence was crucial in the founding of the Zentralarbeitsgemeinschaft (the central body composed equally of employer and labour representatives, and charged with regulating social

[12] H. A. Turner 1972, 23. Neebe 1981, 63. Also IfZ ED93/9, 4 Dec. 1930 comments of Paul Silverberg. H. A. Turner, *German Big Business and the Rise of Hitler*, New York 1985, 234.

conflict). At the end of the inflation the Zentralarbeitsgemeinschaft and its ideals collapsed.[13] In 1922 and 1923 Stinnes was working hard to eliminate union influence. Silverberg's performance, hovering between republicanism and its rejection, is equally characteristic.

INDUSTRIAL CORPORATISM AND THE COURSE OF POLITICAL AND ECONOMIC DEVELOPMENT

How successfully was industry able to play the political game in Weimar Germany; and what results did it get out of that game? Maybe the fact that industry was obliged to change its political stance so often should alone make us sceptical of theories that either claim too powerful a role for industry in the Republic or assert that the preponderance of heavy industry dictated a conservative growth path of the Weimar economy. The claim that the conservative bias of Weimar economic development was the result of political influences depends on three premises: (1) that the whole of the Weimar economy was very highly politicised; (2) that economic and political power do not always coincide; and (3) that political power can be used to dictate the outcome of distributional conflicts, and thus, in the end, also the course of economic development. None of these premisses is obviously false: and they have been used, notably by Gerald Feldman and Bernd Weisbrod, to explain the ascendancy of big industry in the late Weimar period.[14]

Before the War, both the Reich and the federal states had devoted large amounts to the subsidisation of agriculture: the so-called *Liebesgaben* (love gifts) from the proceeds of sugar and brandy taxes to the big estate farmers of East Elbia. 500m. M was paid out of the brandy tax between 1871 and 1908, more than the annual Prussian army budget in the 1880s.[15] On the

[13] P. Wulf, *Hugo Stinnes: Wirtschaft und Politik 1918–1924*, Stuttgart 1979, 425–52. Feldman 1977, 336–44; and G. D. Feldman and I. Steinisch, 'Die Weimarer Republik zwischen Sozial- und Wirtschaftsstaat: Die Entscheidung gegen den Achtstundentag', *AfS* 18, 1978, 353–439.

[14] Feldman 1977, 468. Weisbrod 1978, 17–18, 28.

[15] P.-C. Witt, *Die Finanzpolitik des Deutschen Reiches von 1903 bis 1913: Eine Studie zur Innenpolitik des Wilhelminischen Deutschlands*, Lübeck Hamberg 1970, 46. W. Abelshauser, 'Staat, Infrastruktur und regionaler Wohlstandsausgleich im Preußen der Hochindustrialisierung', in (ed.) Blaich 1980, 26–34.

other hand, there were few direct subsidies to industry: the nearest the Reich and Prussian governments came was in the development of branch lines at a great loss to the state in order to stimulate the eastern economy generally, and the strategy of placing as many naval orders as possible under the Tirpitz rearmament drive in times of slack demand.[16] Rather, the state confined itself to setting a broad legislative framework within which business could operate: regulating sickness, accident, and old age insurance, or fixing maximum hours of work.

The First World War changed this. The state became a major source of demand: access to state orders became an ideal opportunity for the realisation of some of industry's grandiose expansion plans. This outlook on the part of business remained after the end of the War. Feldman has examined the way in which industry used the inflation to build up its power. Many steel industrialists were paid large sums by the Government in compensation for losses of plant in the territories ceded to France (Alsace-Lorraine) and Poland (Silesia): Lorraine and Silesia had been major industrial centres of the Kaiserreich. The compensation could be used to build up powerful positions within the new German frontiers. Fritz Thyssen and Peter Klöckner did particularly well here; the Stumm family raised money in a slightly different way: by selling 60 per cent of their Saar Neunkirchener, Dillingener, and Halbacher works to the French, they raised money to buy the Niederrheinische Hütte, the Stettiner Eisenwerk, the Norddeutsche Hütte Bremen, the Lübecker Hochofenwerk; and to gain control of the Gelsenkirchener Gußstahl- und Eisenwerke, the Annener Gußstahlfabrik, the Stahlwerk Oeking, the Eisen-Industrie zu Merden und Schwerte, the Gußstahlfabrik Witten, and the Vereinigte Press- und Hammerwerke.[17]

Heavy industry too was able during the inflation to use its influence within institutions such as the Reich Coal Council—which had price-controlling responsibilities—to obtain favourable prices: though there were also purely economic reasons for the power of the producers on the Coal Council as Germany suffered from a severe coal shortage in the immediate post-war

[16] V. Berghahn, *Der Tirpitz-Plan: Genesis und Verfall einer innenpolitischen Krisenstrategie unter Wilhelm II*, Düsseldorf 1971, 129–57.

[17] Pinner, 92–104.

period.[18] After the end of the inflation, German Government compensation for damage inflicted by the French during the Ruhr occupation provided another bonanza for big business. Moreover, the location of much of German heavy industry near politically sensitive frontiers (in the West in the partially occupied Rhineland; in the East in German Silesia near the bitterly contested Polish frontier) guaranteed that the Government could be pressed into giving financial support for strategic reasons. This last consideration assumed great importance in the last phase of the inflation and during the stabilisation, when there was a threat that the French occupiers might set up an independent Rhineland state, and Rhineland industry had gone along with the French plans with considerable enthusiasm. Business then demanded from the Reich a substantial price for abandoning its collaboration. Later, Röchling and Stumm in the Saar, and Flick and Georg von Giesches Erben in Silesia extracted considerable funds from the Reich and Prussia.[19]

After the end of the inflation and the stabilisation of the currency in 1924, heavy industry tried to play an active role in making both foreign and domestic policy. Discussions between Rhineland business and France did not come to an end with the collapse of the 1923–4 scheme for a separate Rhineland currency; and many of the major acts of economic diplomacy in the mid-1920s were not the product of the official German foreign policy manufactured in the Wilhelmstrasse, but rather of the negotiations of the economic interest groups. The international steel cartel (IRSG) of November 1926, for instance, was an economic version of Locarno, guaranteeing the permanence of the Versailles German–French frontier economically as well as politically. The IRSG ended the war of German and French steel producers for each other's markets by allocating quotas to the member countries.[20] In the depression, some German heavy industrialists, notably Otto Wolff, renewed attempts to bring about a Franco-German economic *détente*, and in spring 1932 a group of promiment

[18] Feldman 1977, 111, 289–92.

[19] Krohn 1974, 216–21. F. Blaich, *Grenzlandpolitik im Westen 1926–1936: die 'Westhilfe' zwischen Reichspolitik und Länderinteressen*, Stuttgart 1978.

[20] K.-H. Pohl, 233.

French, German, and Belgian business men met in Luxemburg for discussions on future west European economic collaboration.[21] The theory of the *Exportventil* provided an ideological justification for industry's attempt to gain leverage over the bureaucracy.

In domestic politics, the situation is more complicated, and the leverage of big industry over government decisions was in general slighter. After 1923/4 the Weimar Republic continued to have many of the characteristics of an inverventionist welfare state (*Sozialstaat*); and many features of the *Sozialstaat* angered business. The 1927 Law on Unemployment Insurance required costly contributions from employers and workers, and also appeared to increase wages because the existence of unemployment benefits raised the reserve price of labour. In October 1923 a system for the arbitration of wage disputes was created, under the supervision of the Reich Labour Ministry. This too appeared to promote the push for higher wages in the later 1920s, since the interventions of the Reich Labour Ministry in labour disputes were not blatantly partisan and did not in every case help the employers. In consequence industry thought that the Labour Ministry was too sympathetic to labour and not mindful enough of the needs of the economy. Business men also continued to believe that tax levels were unacceptably high. Thus they concluded that they were operating in an unsympathetic environment, and they devoted their energy to improving that environment.

In fact, business did extract some advantages from the Republic. Large subsidies were paid out, especially before 1928, and the big firms particularly gained from this *Subvention*. The beneficiaries included the Fried. Krupp AG, the Schichau shipbuilding yard in Elbing, and the Silesian steel industry.[22] To ensure that government policy worked to their advantage, business men lobbied the ministries, and they also made extensive use of their contacts in the political parties. Frequently, industry financed political life. Most business money

[21] J. Bariéty and C. Bloch, 'Une tentative de réconciliation franco-allemande et son échec 1932–33', *Revue d'histoire moderne et contemporaine* 15, 1968, 433–65. James 1985, 241–3.

[22] See in general C.-D. Krohn, *Stabilisierung und ökonomische Interessen: Die Finanzpolitik des Deutschen Reiches 1923–1927*, Düsseldorf 1974.

went to the DVP (right liberals) and the DNVP (nationalists), though there were also Catholic industrialists, who within the Centre party organised special trade and industry councils (*Handels- und Industriebeiräte*).[23] From 1924 to 1928 Germany was run by centre–right coalitions, in which big business could exercise considerable leverage, and even after 1928 the Great Coalition could be influenced by pressure on the DVP.

Weisbrod has argued that as a result both of its economic position, and of its political contacts, heavy industry held a 'veto position' in domestic politics which actively restricted the range of political options. Big business used its powerful position first to impose economic rationalisation, and then, from the end of 1927, to embark on a campaign of social confrontation. In this way it wrecked the basis of Weimar corporatism—a corporatism that had depended for its legitimacy on the regulation of disputes between organised social groups.

Heavy industry's power was indeed very clearly visible in some areas of public policy formulation. Cartel policy is the best example. In the aftermath of the inflation there was a great popular hostility to cartels, which were widely blamed for the pace of the price increases. A 'Cartel Decree' (2 November 1923) of the Stresemann Government allowed the Reich Economics Minister, acting through a cartel court, to alter cartel contracts and change cartel prices if prices were artificially put up or production cut in a 'manner which could not be economically justified'.[24] This was a vague and unsatisfactory phrase—cartels were after all designed to stabilise prices by means of cutting production in order to prevent extreme market fluctuations—and the cartel decree was not in fact used against the numerous cartels of the later 1920s. From 1926 a cartel inquiry operated as part of the general Enquête: but its proceedings were dominated by the RDI. The Chairman of the Enquête Committee was Clemens Lammers, a Centre Reichstag deputy, paper manufacturer, and member of the Präsidium and Executive of the RDI. The majority of the 59

[23] L. Döhn, *Politik und Interesse: Die Interessenstruktur der Deutschen Volkspartei*, Meisenheim am Glan 1970. W. Liebe, *Die Deutschnationale Volkspartei 1918–1924*, Düsseldorf 1956, 82. On Zentrum, see BAK NL ten Hompel 11, meetings of Zentrum Handels- und Industriebeiräte.

[24] RGBI 1923, I 1067–71.

experts giving evidence to the Committee were sympathetic to cartels; and, partly in consequence, the report concluded that there was no case for a state suspension of cartels.[25] Only in late 1931 did Chancellor Brüning revive, in the peculiar circumstances of the economic crisis, the threat to take action against cartels.

There is, however, something slightly strange about the notion of 'veto power'. Mid-Weimar corporatism depended on reconciliation by means of the buying off of interests. An important illustration of the way in which corporatism operated, and of the preconditions for successful operation, was provided during the depression of 1925–6. At the end of 1925, Reich Chancellor Luther supposed that the best way of tackling the depression was to force prices down; such actions would also help to check the inflationary development Luther believed to be occurring. Such a policy, however, was highly unpopular with business, and the price reductions proved to be nearly impossible to implement.[26] In 1926 an alternative policy was tried: tax reductions coupled with an increase in *Subvention*. This was much more attractive: and in 1926 the Weimar system was stabilised on the basis of such state hand-outs. Business men now had to jockey with each other, and not so much with competing social groups, for their place in the queue for these state hand-outs.

In an environment which was fundamentally so favourable, there was no point as far as industry was concerned in trying to exercise a power of veto. Industry had quite enough wind in its sails. The RDI had been so influential in the cartel inquiry because the opponents of cartels were relatively few and weak: indeed even some socialists were quite eager to accept cartels as planning instruments. The problem came when the state was no longer in a position to give. While the state could give, its action helped to create the corporatist consensus; but when it stopped giving the corporations began to break up. *Then*, however, industry stopped being able to impose a 'veto' chiefly because it stopped being able to act in a manner sufficiently co-ordinated for it to be able to represent its interests effectively.

[25] F. Blaich, *Staat und Verbände in Deutschland zwischen 1871 und 1945*, Wiesbaden 1979, 71–2.

[26] Hertz-Eichenrode, 59–77.

This story can be clarified by an examination of the politics of the central interest groups. The major central organisation, the Reichsverband der Deutschen Industrie, was vocal during the later 1920s, and then became effectively powerless during the slump. The Reichsverband had originated from a trade-off entirely characteristic of the compromise nature of mid-Weimar corporatism. A traditional division in German industrial politics had been between the heavy industry (coal and steel) of the Rhine-Ruhr, and the lighter exporting industries of central and southern Germany. This division had taken institutional form in two rival interest organisations. The Centralverein deutscher Industrieller (CdI) arose out of the need to apply political leverage in the protectionist cause during the economic crisis of the 1870s. In 1895 a rival organisation, the Bund der Industriellen (BdI), set itself to speak on behalf of the lighter exporting industry that was harmed by the tariff. The tension between exporting and heavy industry reached a height in the decade after 1895; for after the beginning of the twentieth century heavy industry began to behave in a more responsible way towards manufacturing interests. Thus, for instance, subsidies were then given on heavy industrial products used in producing manufactures for export.

By 1914 the conflicts that had led to the split between the two organisations were no longer as acute: on 8 August 1914 they formed the 'War Committee of German Industry' (Kriegsausschuß der deutschen Industrie) together; in February 1918 this evolved an 'Industrial Council' to consider problems of transition to the peacetime economy; and after the war, the CdI and BdI, faced by a new political situation and by the rise of labour unrest, fused into the Reichsverband (February 1919). The RDI's structure reflected the importance that dealings with the state had taken on for industry in the new Republic: the permanent manager of the Reichsverband (Geschäftsführendes Präsidialmitglied) always came from the higher civil service. Hermann Bücher (1921–5) had been in the administration of the Cameroon until 1914; from 1915–18 he was the German representative in the Turkish trade ministry, and after the Revolution went back to the Auswärtiges Amt. His successor in the RDI was Ludwig Kastl, who from 1907–20 had been in the colonial administration of German South West

Africa, and in 1921 was appointed to a post as Ministerialrat in the Reich Finance Ministry. (Alternatives to Kastl who had been considered in 1925 by the RDI included Karl Ritter of the Auswärtiges Amt, and Gustav Brecht and Hans Posse from the Reich Economics Ministry.)[27]

The nature of the compromise involved in founding the Reichsverband became clearer in December 1924 when Carl Duisberg of BASF was chosen as Chairman of the RDI: this choice is sometimes described as a reflection of the growing ascendancy of the lighter and newer industries within the Reichsverband. Duisberg replaced a 'heavier' industrialist, Kurt Sorge of the Fried. Krupp AG; and some 'heavy' men, such as Paul Reusch, would have preferred a more sympathetic Chairman. Duisberg's goal, however, was not to represent light industry, but rather to bridge over differences within the Reichsverband. He was a rather apolitical scientist with traditionalist leanings.[28] There was never any secret about his admiration for the old order of the Kaiserreich. After 1925, however, he increasingly lost interest in his work in IG Farben and in the Reichsverband, and wished for nothing more than a peaceful retirement.[29] Duisberg's appointment did not mean a dramatic change in the goals of the industrial pressure group. Throughout the Weimar Republic there was in fact a relatively fixed idea of what business wanted in economic terms (the restoration of profitability) and there were few disputes about government economic policy that divided the ranks of industry (as the debate about the tariff had in the Kaiserreich). Only the question of *how* these broad goals of industry should be implemented continued to receive differing answers.

In 1925 there was general agreement that the priority in any government economic programme should be the reduction of taxation, and particularly of direct taxation.[30] This was a goal which heavy industry believed could be best achieved through the creation of a broad united industrial front in the RDI. In 1929 again Rhine-Ruhr used the RDI as a platform to set out its proposals for tax reform and for a revision of social legislation (the result was the pamphlet *Aufstieg oder Nieder-*

[27] Weisbrod 1977, 222. [28] Ibid., 220–2. [29] Flechtner, 401–3.
[30] RDI, *Deutsche Wirtschafts- und Finanzpolitik*, Berlin 1925 (December), 14.

gang?). When it came to more concrete issues of political or economic policy, however, the heavy industrialists looked to much more specific pressure groups: the Gruppe Nordwest of the VDESI, the Langnamverein (a long-established club for Rhineland-Westphalian business), and the Ruhrlade (an influential discussion circle in which only twelve representatives of the very large Ruhr firms participated).[31] In addition, there were country house parties at the seats of the major industrialists: at Thyssen's Stahlhof, Krupp's Villa Hügel, and Reusch's Katherinenhof; and also informal discussions on how big business's party-political funds should be distributed.

The flight away from the RDI as a suitable instrument for heavy industry's political ambitions began with the humiliating affair of the Ruhr iron lock-out of November 1928: in this case the iron and steel men had attempted to break the state's wage arbitration. Ruhr industry tried to enlist the support of other business men; but it failed and instead ran into a barrage of criticism—from the Reichstag parties, including the right-liberal DVP (two-thirds of whose deputies voted to give financial support for the locked-out workers) and from other industries.[32] This experience made the Ruhr men more eager to follow their own path. In 1929 the steel men took an independent line over the question of opposition to the new reparations settlement proposed under the Young Plan; and in debates within the bourgeois parties, and particularly the DVP, on the political future.

The DVP was the most pro-industrial party in Weimar Germany, and was dominated in the Reichstag by representatives of the business world: of 51 DVP deputies in the Reichstag in the legislative period 1924–8, 20 came from big or middle industry; out of 45 in 1928–30, 23. Only civil servants were anything like so powerfully represented in the party.[33]

There was one particular moment in the history of Weimar when industry had a great political influence: the winter of

[31] On the Gruppe Nordwest, see Weisbrod 1978; on the Ruhrlade, H. A. Turner, 'The Ruhrlade: Secret Cabinet of Heavy Industry in the Weimar Republic', *CEH* 3, 1970, 195–228.

[32] Weisbrod 1978, 415–56. U. Hüllbüsch, 'Der Ruhreisenstreit in gewerkschaftlicher Sicht', in (eds.) H. Mommsen, D. Petzina, B. Weisbrod, *Industrielles System und politische Entwicklung in der Weimarer Republik*, Düsseldorf 1974, 271–89.

[33] Döhn, 348.

1929–30. Before and after that influence was comparatively weak—perhaps surprisingly so, in the light of the amount of historical literature that has since been devoted to the subject. By 1932, there were signs that even the very tight pressure groups, such as the Langnamverein and the Ruhrlade, were so rent by internal divisions that they were incapable of operating effectively. Some of these internal divisions were economic in origin: the large, efficient, modern Vestag wanted to solve the over-capacity problem by shutting down entire works. Less modern enterprises objected less strongly to operating at below capacity.[34] In part there were political difficulties as well: as the political situation became ever more fluid in 1931–2 the number of political choices—and thus the scope for disagreement—became bigger. As politics and also very specific economic conflicts intruded into the world of the pressure groups, they stopped operating efficiently; and their organisers complained more and more of a general *Verbandsmüdigkeit* (disillusionment with interest groups).[35]

The high-point of the political influence of big business came after Stresemann's death (3 October 1929). Stresemann himself had, by an enormous effort of will, which in the end cost him his life, provided a counterbalance to the influence of industry within the DVP. He had kept the DVP in the Great Coalition under Hermann Müller; had stopped the DVP using its position in Reich politics to bring down the left-centre Weimar coalition (SPD-Centre-Democrats) in Prussia; and had even been able to prevent the DVP industrial wing's potential leader, Hans Luther, being placed in a winning position on the party's electoral list in the 1928 Reichstag election.[36] When Stresemann died, the links binding the DVP to the Great Coalition Government were weakened appreciably. The DVP pressed for cuts in unemployment benefit as a way of solving the financial crisis in the unemployment insurance system; while the union wing of the SPD tried instead to

[34] HA/GHH 40010124/14, 12 Jan. 1932 Karl Haniel to Reusch (description of Ruhrlade meeting on 11 Jan.), and 18 Jan. 1932 Springorum to Reusch; 400101290/27a 15 Nov. 1932 Reusch to Krupp von Bohlen und Halbach.

[35] See for example HA/GHH 400101220/12a, 20 May 1932 Reusch to Kastl.

[36] HA Krupp FAH IV E 1186, 7 March 1928 Reusch to Krupp von Bohlen und Halbach.

raise insurance contributions. The DVP also pressed for massive tax cuts as part of the Young Plan package.[37] In essence these disputes reflected a conflict of views on how the costs of the depression should be distributed: should labour pay (through decreased benefits as unemployment mounted) or should capital receive tax relief? Eventually it was the intransigence of the SPD unionists in refusing the Government's proposals for benefit reductions in March 1930 that brought the Müller Government down: but much of the provocation had come from the DVP.

The industrialists' hostility to 'socialist' finance policy was, however, only one of a number of causes of the breakdown of the Great Coalition. The most intransigent opposition to the Stresemann line had always come not so much from the industrialists in the party, but from DVP deputies in the Prussian Landtag, who resented the way in which the SPD and the Centre were able to control the immense patronage resources of the powerful Prussian state. Industry was not able to choose Müller's successor, either. Heinrich Brüning came from the union wing of the Centre party, but the DVP industrialists' favourite candidate, Hans Luther, was not available as he had just accepted the post of Reichsbank President.

After March 1930 when the Müller Great Coalition was replaced by Brüning's rule through presidential emergency decree, it proved almost impossible either for the DVP industrialists to control their party effectively, or for them to succeed in their attempt to build up a coherent right-wing bloc that could carry pro-business policies. The reasons for both failures were similar: they stemmed from the widespread hostility to the business world. Even within the DVP there were strong Mittelstand elements who resented the idea of the party being over-committed to the interests of big business. The meeting of the Central Executive of the Party in Berlin on 4 July 1930 underlined the difficulties that the post-Stresemann DVP faced: speakers such as Otto Thiel from white-collar organisations (the DNHV) argued that the DVP was losing support because it had attacked high wages and the principle of the wage contract (*Tarifvertrag*), but had not mentioned cartellised

[37] Maurer, 80–94.

prices. It had ceased to be a 'genuine Volkspartei'. Hippe took up the theme: 'what we are doing at the moment in our People's Party [Volkspartei] is fighting an unconscious class war'. Another speaker made the same complaint: the different social groups within the DVP were now fighting each other.[38]

The one success of the DVP industrialists—the removal of the DVP Reich Finance Minister, Moldenhauer, from the Brüning Government—was illusory. Moldenhauer's successor, Dietrich, produced a harsher programme, and when the DVP voted against this, the result was a dissolution of the Reichstag and an election which reduced the number of the DVP's seats from 45 to 30. As a consequence of the election results, the DVP industrialists found themselves defending the record of the Brüning regime against the attacks of the non-industrial Volksparteiler, and of the new DVP leader Dingeldey. DVP business men were frightened of the political consequences of a fall of Brüning (the new government might be very radical); and also of the economic consequences (political uncertainty had already led once, in the spring of 1929, to a currency crisis which made things worse for industry).[39] The chemical industrialist Wilhelm Kalle defended the Brüning system in this way in the debate within the DVP on 4 July: 'the seriousness of the situation demands that we participate for as long as possible in the last bourgeois government ... the Brüning–Stegerwald construction was born of the necessity of showing the social democrats that we can rule against their left wing'. Ludwig Kastl for instance told the RDI executive that although there might be disagreements about parts of the Government's programme, the general line was correct. The DVP's industrial wing secured the support of the party for the Economic Emergency Decree of 1 December 1930; and in June 1931 when the DVP leadership had called for a summoning of the Reichstag (which almost certainly would have led to a vote of no confidence and thus to the collapse of the regime), the industrial wing was again crucial in making the party alter its stance.[40]

More and more however, there was scepticism about the

[38] BAK R45II/46, 7 July 1930 DVP Zentralvorstand (Central Executive).

[39] M. Grübler, *Die Spitzenverbände der Wirtschaft und das erste Kabinett Brüning: Eine Quellenstudie*, Düsseldorf 1982, 414.

[40] Ibid., 421, 451.

ability of Brüning to tackle the fundamental problem of wage costs of German industry; and the calculation that kept DVP business men with Brüning was simply a fear of the economic consequences of a *politique du pire*. Within the DVP, the path taken by industry in 1930 and 1931 was a reflection of a realisation of the hopelessness of implementing industrial plans: the days when *Aufstieg oder Niedergang?* had made a big political splash were over. The disastrous election result of July 1932 (when the Volkspartei only won 7 seats) came at the end of a long process of party disintegration and increasing powerlessness.

Other parties did not serve industry's interests any better, however. The industrialists in the Centre complained that they lacked sufficient influence to be able to oppose the powerful trade unionist and civil service wings of the party. Already in 1928 the chairman of the Reich Committee of the Centre Handels- und Industriebeiräte said that it was becoming more and more difficult to keep religious business men politically close to the Centre because of the party's neglect of their interests.[41] Later he was more explicit:

> the mad policy of the unions was backed and actually carried out by the Centre and by the clergy. It was they who accepted seven million unemployed and talked about the just wage, while not understanding that that wage is most just which secures jobs and bread for the most workers, i.e. does not price labour out of employment.[42]

In the DNVP the position of industry was even more hopeless. The DNVP turned itself, much more obviously than the DVP, in an anti-capitalist, anti-industrial direction. In the mid-1920s the party had done its best to present itself as as 'social' a party as the next. Its propaganda pamphlets proudly announced that it was the largely DNVP Luther–Schiele cabinet which had re-introduced the eight-hour day in blast furnaces.[43] Then in 1928 Count Westarp was replaced as party leader by Alfred Hugenberg. After this date most Nationalist business men spent their energies trying to remove Hugenberg.

[41] BAK NL ten Hompel 29, 19 Nov. 1928 ten Hompel speech to Zentrum Handels- und Industriebeiräte.

[42] BAK NL ten Hompel 23, 9 Dec. 1933 ten Hompel to Hackelsberger.

[43] Deutschnationale Schriftenreihenstelle, Rüstzeug Nr. 12, *Sozialpolitische Praxis der Deutschnationalen*, 1929, 27.

They tried to create a large united bourgeois party of the right on an anti-Hugenberg basis. The initial step in the creation of this new political movement was the splitting-off from the DNVP of a group of conservative deputies around Gottfried Treviranus: this became the Konservative Volksvereinigung, but failed ever to achieve significant electoral success.[44] Later in 1930, another group of conservative deputies, this time centred around the former leader, Count Westarp, left the Hugenberg party: again there was no substantial change in the political landscape as a result of the defection. In January 1931, Paul Reusch spoke of the need to create a 'national right', 'free of the petty interest representation which at present characterises the bourgeois [i.e. non-Nazi] right'. Reusch was still writing in September 1932 that it was vital for the health of the right to 'remove Hugenberg from his throne': 'then the DNVP will do considerably better in the Reichstag election'.[45] But Hugenberg remained leader until the DNVP dissolved itself in 1933.

After 1931, the story of the political connections of industry becomes much more complicated. There were both economic and political reasons for this: the worsening of the depression, and the further disintegration of political stability. The banking crisis of June–July made the depression much worse: firms had their credit lines cut, and even fundamentally sound enterprises suddenly found themselves in liquidity difficulties. Some of the best known names in the German economy were in trouble: the engineering and locomotive firm A. Borsig GmbH, the brewery Schultheiss–Patzenhofer, and the iron and steel empire of Friedrich Flick (the AG Charlottenhütte etc.). There was a widespread belief that the Reich Government and the Reichsbank had been responsible for the severity of the banking crisis. Reichsbank President Luther particularly was criticised for applying once again quota restrictions to the number of bank bills the Reichsbank would rediscount: it was this action that was believed to be immediately responsible for the weakness of the Darmstädter and the Dresdner Banks and thus

[44] G. Treviranus, *Das Ende von Weimar: Heinrich Brüning und seine Zeit*, Düsseldorf 1968, 112–16.

[45] HA/GHH 400101293/11, 2 Jan. 1931 Reusch to Edgar Jung; 4001012024/10, 21 Sept. 1932 Reusch to Blank.

for the 1931 bank crisis. Prominent industrialists and bankers wanted to remove Luther from the Reichsbank.[46]

Brüning responded to the criticism not by sacking Luther but by remodelling his Cabinet: a business man (Hermann Warmbold, a member of the Executive of IG Farben) became Minister of Economics, after Brüning had unsuccessfully approached several of the major figures of Rhine-Ruhr (Silverberg, Albert Vögler of the Vestag, and Hermann Schmitz, of IG Farben).[47] In addition, business men as well as unionists were prominent in a Presidential Economic Committee summoned to function as an ersatz parliament in economic affairs in the authoritarian environment of the Brüning regime. This Committee debated proposals which eventually formed part of what was to be the Fourth Economic Emergency Decree (8 December 1931), which decreed a general reduction of prices and wages by 10 per cent (or to the level prevailing in 1927), and also a cut in interest rates. The Reichsbank responded to pressure from the industrialists, and also from Brüning, who had promised business that he would put pressure on Luther to adopt a more flexible credit policy. The new discounting policy of the Reichsbank worked particularly in favour of big business.[48]

Such measures may have done something to win industrialists back to the Brüning camp; although the December Emergency decree was criticised by many business men. More and more too the fear of agrarian protectionism led industrial interests to cast around for a way of blocking the farmers' campaign, which, if successful, would have ruined Germany's relationship with major export markets. The Netherlands and the Baltic states in particular were good German customers: but they wanted to sell dairy and pig products to North German consumers. In late 1931 and 1932 fear of the autarkists and protectionists did for Brüning what fear of financial crisis had done one year earlier: but only a few business men gradually returned to the fold.[49] Brüning's policies did not in fact

[46] K. E. Born, *Die deutsche Bankenkrise 1931: Finanzen und Politik*, Munich 1967, 110.

[47] Maurer and Wengst Doc. 339, 12 Oct. 1931 Silverberg to Krupp von Bohlen und Halbach.

[48] James 1985, 295–9.

[49] For trade policy, see: BAK R43I/2546 Warmbold memoranda; and HA/GHH

involve one-sided concessions to the business case, and the Emergency Decree of 8 December aimed specifically at imposing an equality of sacrifice: it was fear of who Brüning's successor might be that kept industry from mutiny.

Brüning's fall did indeed lead to a strengthening of the protectionist forces in Germany. Franz von Papen aimed to implement a substantially pro-industry policy, but the industrial interest groups were frightened by the influence of agrarians and the possibility of a trade war. Business was scarcely consulted while economic policy was worked out, and indeed was taken by surprise by the Papen decrees of 4–5 September 1932.[50] These decrees had the goal of promoting economic recovery. In general they favoured business at the expense of labour. There was a tax reduction. Tax certificates (*Steuergutscheine*) were issued against turnover, commerce, and land taxes paid between October 1932 and October 1933. The certificates could be used to pay tax from 1934 to 1938, and the government hoped they would be traded commercially. In this way, business would receive instant tax relief; but the government would only have to face the cost of the subsidy later, when economic recovery had already increased tax yields.

In addition, there were two, more controversial, provisions which involved the creation of work by means of state intervention in the labour market. Tax certificates of 400 RM were to be issued as a premium to the employer of each additional worker hired: a total of 700m. RM was to be made available in this way. Secondly, firms were in addition given permission to reduce wages in proportion to the extent that they hired more labour. The results were disappointing. By the middle of December, a mere 62,500 extra men had been employed as a result of the premium: so only 25m. RM of the 700m. RM envisaged had been used.[51] The second part of the programme was positively harmful: its implementation demonstrated how real were the limits on any restorationist scheme for labour relations, even under as authoritarian a régime as von Papen's.

400101220/7a 29 Oct. 1931 Reusch to Kastl. HA Krupp FAH IV E 18, 27 June 1932 RDI Präsidialausschuß on Trade Policy.

[50] The measures are conveniently summarised by H. Marcon, *Arbeitsbeschaffung der Regierungen Papen und Schleicher*, Frankfurt 1974, 78–80.

[51] *FZ* 942, 17 Dec. 1932.

In the Berlin metal industry, attempts to use the Papen decree to cut wages provoked strikes (at the Niles-Werke Weißensee, the Maschinenfabrik Stock Marienwerder). There were also strikes in the Berlin spinning and printing trades.[52] In the Ruhr, there was no attempt at all to enforce the wage cuts which were legally possible. Most businesses were reluctant to spark off a class war, even though the chairman of the RDI, Gustav Krupp von Bohlen und Halbach, had one year earlier suggested exactly such a provision linking wage reductions with additional employment.[53]

At the same time as Papen's political base was crumbling, the social provisions of his September decrees appeared less and less useful. After the November Reichstag election his days were numbered. His successor, General Kurt von Schleicher (Reich Chancellor December 1932 to January 1933) was not really successful in winning over industry to a programme he believed would be more realistic than that proposed by Papen. He planned for a much more *étatiste* direction of state work creation programmes; and some business men feared that he was too eager to set up a populist anti-capital consensus around the union wings of the major parties; NSDAP, Centre, and SPD (the *Gewerkschaftsachse*). Even those business men who in 1930 had still argued for an agreement with the unions were sceptical, since the unions had been severely weakened politically by the scale of unemployment, and were less attractive now as negotiating partners. But the *Gewerkschaftsachse* was not killed by big business: rather it died because it never had a chance of life. Gregor Strasser was well regarded by many business men: Paul Silverberg argued that the NSDAP could be turned into a Volkspartei that might co-operate within the existing political system, just as the SPD had been brought into responsibility after 1919. No one imagined, however, that Strasser was any good without Hitler, and the aim of the Silverberg calculation was to make Hitler *salonfähig*. There was the additional problem that Silverberg was personally hostile to Schleicher. Strasser was unable to convince Hitler that the project was sound, and he could not rebel against Hitler either,

[52] *FZ* 714/5, 24 Sept. 1932.

[53] Marcon, 202–3. Wolffsohn 1977, 193–5. HA Krupp FAH IV E 152 7 Feb. 1931 Krupp von Bohlen und Halbach to Brüning.

partly because he was under the spell of the Führer's charismatic personality, and partly because he had little independent support within the Nazi party.[54]

The second arm of the *Gewerkschaftsachse* collapsed just as quickly; the SPD refused to let the trade unionist Theodor Leipart participate in Schleicher's Government at the beginning of January 1933. Schleicher was thus left without a political base.[55] And at the same time as the support for the Schleicher regime collapsed, Schleicher's enemies worked out their own plans. Alfred Hugenberg had on 22 November 1932 refused to join a Hitler Government. After this he was pushed towards Hitler by the threat of insalubrious revelations about DNVP politics: many eastern landowning conservatives had been involved in a scandal arising out of the administration of agricultural emergency relief. By the beginning of December, Hugenberg had become willing to bring the DNVP into a coalition with the NSDAP. The political game was complete when Papen met Hitler on 4 January 1933. From then it was only a matter of time until Hitler was appointed Chancellor.

What is striking about the frenetic political negotiations of December and January is the very limited role that industry played. The Chairman of the RDI, Gustav Krupp von Bohlen und Halbach, was away in Switzerland at the time of the crucial talks of January 1933.[56] For a short time after January he tried to resist the Nazi attempts to control industrial interest organisations. The papers of the most politically active heavy industrialist, Paul Reusch, testify to a resigned pessimism, not to an active attempt to mould the German future. Though there was a time in the spring of 1932 when he imagined that the Nazis could be harnessed, later in the summer and autumn he became frightened of the social radicalism of the movement. Reusch disliked Nazi collaboration with Communists in the Berlin transport strike of November 1932; and he was appalled by the Nazi economic Sofortprogramm (Kampfschrift Heft

[54] Neebe 1981, 162–4. U. Kissenkoetter, *Gregor Strasser und die NSDAP*, Stuttgart 1978, 166–76. P. D. Stachura. *Gregor Strasser and the Rise of Nazism*, London 1983, 103–20.

[55] R. Neebe, 'Unternehmerverbände und Gewerkschaften in den Jahren der Großen Krise 1929–1933', *GG* 9, 1983, 323–6.

[56] This theme is emphasised in the study of V. Hentschel, *Weimars letzte Monate: Hitler und der Untergang der Republik*, Düsseldorf 1978, 136.

16) which he described as containing 'much nonsense'.[57] In fact, neither the upsurge in industrial hopes for National Socialism in spring 1932, nor industry's subsequent disillusionment, had very much real effect on the Nazi political success.

The one figure who did try to bring business and Nazism together was the ex-president of the Reichsbank, Hjalmar Schacht. His story is revealing. Schacht had an office run by a young Hamburg economic journalist, Carl Krämer, which was supposed to make political contact with the National Socialists. This office ran, for the whole of its brief life, on a shoe-string, financed by industrial Pfennige and not Marks. Its operations were scarcely successful. Hitler and the party suspected and ignored Schacht, and kept their own economic advisers. Schacht did not get much encouragement from business either. He continued to make vitriolic complaints about the pusillanimity of the German industrial world. Already in March 1930, as he struggled with the Müller Government, he believed that he had been betrayed by industry. In 1931 he attacked business for not having 'the courage of its convictions' to be present at the Harzburg rally of the National Opposition.[58] In September 1932 he accused business of merely 'running behind every government'.[59] The Schacht office did produce one concrete policy plan—a scheme for the introduction of monopoly trading organisations—which was pooh-poohed by Krupp and Reusch, and which never was used as a basis for any government action after 1933 when Schacht was in power.[60]

30 January 1933 did help business only in that it ended the political confusion and uncertainty that had prevailed since Brüning's fall. At least a stable environment was created within which business could act. Hitler proved able to give a guarantee that his wild supporters would behave, and the initial rowdy demonstrations of the SA were curbed. Furthermore there was a promise that after March 1933 there would be no

[57] HA/GHH 400101290/33a, 20 March and 27 July 1932 Reusch to Schacht.

[58] HA/GHH 400101220/8a, 10 March 1930 Herle (RDI) telephone conversation with Reich Finance Minister Moldenhauer; 400101290/33a, 20 Oct. 1931 Schacht to Reusch.

[59] HA/GHH 400101290/33a, 12 Sept. 1932 Schacht to Reusch.

[60] HA/GHH 400101290/27a, 10 Jan. 1933 Krupp von Bohlen und Halbach to Schacht.

more elections. Business men like Krupp, who before 30 January had been reluctant to co-operate with Nazis, gradually became prepared to accept the new political order. If they showed any hesitation, they were bullied. The RDI functionaries were purged before the RDI was converted into the Reichsstand der Deutschen Industrie.[61] Schacht raised money from industry for the Nazi Party by a fairly straightforward strong-arm technique. At a meeting of Nazi leaders and business men there was little discussion. The Nazis first made speeches; then Schacht stood up and said seven words: 'And now you must pay up, gentlemen' ('*Und nun, meine Herren, an die Kasse*').[62]

German industry was obliged thus to readjust its political orientation rapidly in the 1920s and 1930s as political circumstances changed. It had accepted a pluralist democracy after 1924 in the same way and with the same arguments as it accepted totalitarian control in the 1930s, and, in due course, liberal democracy in the western zones after 1948–9, and even the beginnings of Soviet-style planning in the East. In none of these cases was business openly enthusiastic about the nature of the political alteration at first: industrialists loved pointing out the way in which *all* political solutions—even, bizarrely, Ludwig Erhard's deregulated free market solution—were contrary to the course of what they believed to be Germany's 'natural development'. The major changes in business behaviour were forced on business by exogenous political considerations.

The story told here emphasizes the limits on industry's power to influence political events. That power varied, however. It was greatest in the winter of 1929–30 as the political system began to shift from a system of interest brokerage—in which organised industry had some role, but had to engage itself in conflict with other social groups—to one where a very small number of people (Hindenburg, the camarilla around him, Brüning and his ministers, and the top civil servants) tried to remain in control, while the mass parties proposed radical alternatives to the Weimar system. Like a lever arm suspended

[61] U. Wengst, 'Der Reichsverband der Deutschen Industrie in den ersten Monaten des Dritten Reiches', *VfZ* 28, 1980, 94–110.

[62] L. P. Lochner, *Die Mächtigen und der Tyrann: Die deutsche Industrie von Hitler bis Adenauer*, Darmstadt 1955, 172.

horizontally as two power systems held each other in check, German politics at this turning point could be very easily influenced.

What caused the transition between these two differently operating systems? The answer is: the depression. It was much more difficult to arrange interest politics when the pressure groups themselves became the locus for acute conflicts in a struggle for influence. The records of negotiations between big concerns in 1931–2 are filled with the documentation of dispute: over labour policy, marketing, and competition for export orders. Until the beginning of the Brüning era, industrial interests had kept together, as there were advantages in using concerted pressure—as in 1929 over the tax issue—to press home a case. After that, it was unclear in what form such massive pressure should most appropriately be applied. Consequently, the rifts between different firms began to become visible: and the influence and power of business collapsed yet further.

Some of the conservatism and inflexibility of the German industrial structure in the later 1920s might perhaps then be attributed to the political influence of big business; though there were also economic and institutional reasons for the slow rate of change in German economic life and for the failure to generate growth through structural alteration (Chapter IV). It is much harder to blame the events of and the decisions taken during the economic crisis itself on 'organised capitalism' or on the corporate economy: for that is the period when the corporate economy began to disintegrate. Historians have recently tried to describe the Weimar economic and political system as 'organised capitalism';[63] such a system was in fact only capable of surviving in an environment of growth. When growth stopped and contraction set in, the organisations designed to organise the market and to arbitrate disputes were no longer capable of doing that. This chapter has examined the disintegration of industry's political force; the next chapter echoes this story in the case of labour organisations.

[63] (Ed.) H. A. Winkler, *Organisierter Kapitalismus: Voraussetzungen und Anfänge*, Göttingen 1974.

VI

Labour Problems: Consequences or Causes of the Stagnant Economy?

'Ich glaube, daß in diesem Fall nicht nur Menschen versagt haben, sondern auch die Ideologie sich als unzulänglich erwiesen hat.

(W. Woytinsky to Schorsch, 16 August 1933)[1]

The main impetus behind the increasingly radical political attitude of business was the belief that wages were too high, and that pressure from the labour unions had pushed up industrial costs, making German industry internationally uncompetitive. The Ruhr iron and steel magnates were especially vociferous in this regard; but they were, as we have seen, not alone. A carefully worked out memorandum produced in the office of Carl Friedrich von Siemens spoke of the

impression that in countries outside Germany, and particularly in America, there has been in the last years an increase in electrotechnical production, while in Germany especially in the last business year production stagnated. It may be deduced that German production has fallen relative to world production ... Herr von Siemens here points out that the frequent wage increases have not affected our turnover, which remains at a steady level; so that the external picture appears to justify the attitude of the trade unions that wage increases raise purchasing power and thus have a beneficial effect on sales. But Herr von Siemens believes this to be a false conclusion and wants to investigate whether the frequent wage increases over the last years have not been the reason why our production relative to world levels has not increased.[2]

Rhine-Ruhr did draw very radical conclusions, however. In September 1931, for instance, Paul Reusch wrote to Ludwig Kastl that the proposed statement on the economy drawn up jointly by the economic interest groups suffered from a major omission:

[1] FES NL Woytinsky 4.
[2] SAA 4/Lf 811 (C. F. v. Siemens), 10 Aug. 1929 memorandum of von Witzleben.

there is no attack on the unions, who in the end have controlled every government since the end of the war and are chiefly responsible for the tragedy that has broken over the German economy . . . I am fully aware that an important section of the interest groups are not willing to conduct open war against the unions because of cowardice. Therefore one day it will be necessary for [heavy] industry to go its own way, separately, on this issue.

In another letter, Reusch wrote that 'we have made the mistake in the past of fighting the government, not the unions'.[3]

These attitudes may have reflected in part an a priori assumption about the nature of the economic problem. Already at the time of the stabilisation in 1923–4 many industrialists argued that future prosperity could not be guaranteed unless wage rises were limited and hours of work extended.[4] Those who like Hugo Stinnes had in the inflation been prepared to make compromises with labour now preferred conflict in order to hold down the level of wages.[5] Hopes that wage levels would not change significantly after 1924 soon proved to be illusory. Many figures in the business world began to feel that a favourable solution to the economic problem was impossible because of labour control of key institutions in the Weimar state, notably the Ministry of Labour; and thus that an attack on the wage issue required a political battle. This point was often made by referring to the theory set out at the SPD's Heidelberg Congress in 1925 that there was a 'political wage': the working class, so the theory went, should use its control of the state in order to influence the operation of the economic process. Hilferding told the delegates that the fight for control of the state's power resources 'makes even the most indifferent worker aware of the importance of the conquest of political power . . . since today the economic fate of every citizen depends on state decisions: down to the size of the weekly pay-packet, the price of foodstuffs, and the hours of work'.[6] This argument was used here by Hilferding to justify

[3] HA/GHH 40101220/11c, 6 and 30 Sept. 1931 Reusch to Kastl.

[4] H. Hartwich, *Arbeitsmärkte Verbände und Staat 1918–1933: Die öffentliche Bindung unternehmerischer Funktionen in der Weimarer Republik*, Berlin 1967, 321–8.

[5] Feldman 1977, 323.

[6] *Protokoll über die Verhandlungen des sozialdemokratischen Parteitages Heidelberg 1925*,

the acceptance of democracy by a labour movement which had previously been at least nominally committed to the idea of revolution as the only possible way of effecting social change. The SPD's opponents however turned it into a powerful polemical point against Weimar democracy.

This chapter examines first the reasons why the wage issue led to such bitter conflict; and then looks at attempts by the state, and by the unions themselves, to find ways of defusing the conflict in the period of the depression, at the moment when disputes about wages threatened to blow apart the Weimar political system. Unfortunately these attempts to defuse the wage conflict succeeded eventually only in adding new incendiary material.

WAGES AND THE NATIONAL ECONOMY

Recent economic research, summarised for instance in the (British) Treasury's 1985 paper on employment and wages, argues that real wage increases, because of their effects on employers' costs, are responsible for lower growth rates and higher levels of unemployment. For Britain in the 1980s a fall of 1 per cent in real wages increases the demand for labour by between $\frac{1}{2}$ per cent and 1 per cent, and increases real GDP by $\frac{1}{2}$ per cent.[7]

A similar analysis has been applied to Weimar by Knut Borchardt. Two macro-economic indicators point accusingly at a politically inspired wage push: the 'cumulative real wage position'; and labour's share of national income. The 'cumulative real wage position', measured from a base year, represents the difference between the growth rate of real gross wages and salaries per annum and per employee, and the growth of output.[8] A few caveats should be made about this calculation before we use it to interpret wage behaviour. The real wage

Berlin 1925, 282–3. See also K. Borchardt, 'Die deutsche Katastrophe', *Frankfurter Allgemeine Zeitung* 24, 29 Jan. 1983.

[7] HM Treasury, 'The Relationship between Employment and Wages', January 1985. Also S. J. Nickell and M. Andrews, 'Unions, Real Wages, and Employment in Britain 1951–79', *Oxford Economic Papers*, November 1983.

[8] Borchardt 1979, 42–3. Glismann, Rodemer, Wolter 1978 (Kieler Diskussionsbeiträge 55) 29.

Table XV: Cumulative Real Wage Position 1925–1933 (Base 1938)

1925	20.8	1930	17.3
1926	20.1	1931	12.5
1927	18.2	1932	8.9
1928	20.8	1933	5.9
1929	23.3		

Source: Glisman, Rodemer, Wolter, 29.

ratio was first calculated for the Bonn economy by the Sachverständigenrat zur Begutachtung der gesamtwirtschaftlichen Lage: but there is no unanimous agreement on the implications of the ratio, and particularly on the question of whether it provides a means of explaining unemployment. The intention of the calculation is to establish a measure of industrial costs, and thus of the circumstances surrounding investment decisions, and consequently growth rates and levels of employment. Wage costs only provide one element in such calculations. The original formula for Bonn, used by Glismann and Borchardt for Weimar, has since been modified considerably in order to allow for changes in capital costs and for the effects of taxes and subsidies. As a consequence the Sachverständigenrat's real wage position has been recalculated for the 1970s, and the revision no longer shows so dramatic an increase from the 1960s levels: so it is not as easy as before to present the increase as offering an explanation of why levels of unemployment in the Federal Republic are so high in the 1970s. More generally, there is little positive evidence of a correlation over long periods between the real wage position and overall levels of employment: the same real wage position can correspond to several different employment levels.[9] The inference originally made from the calculation, that a high real wage position slowed down growth and reduced employment in the 1970s, seems weakened in the light of the decline since 1975 of the real wage position, which has fallen to the level of the early 1960s at the same time as unemployment has reached heights unprecedented for Bonn. We lack sufficient evidence about capital

[9] See 1980/1 Sachverständigenrat: *Verhandlungen des Deutschen Bundestages*, Anlage 268 (1980), 81; and also criticism of the argument in the minority opinion of Werner Glastetter, ibid., 200–8.

costs and corporate taxation to be able to apply the revised (1980/1) Sachverständigenrat formula from Bonn to Weimar: but it is possible to make a few impressionistic comments. In Chapter IV we examined non-wage costs for industry: the high costs of capital, and the increased rates of taxation.[10] This rise in non-wage costs was held by many business men to be the major threat: while, for instance, in small-scale metal goods production, taxes in 1913 were estimated at 4.4 per cent of costs, in 1928 they accounted for 10.8 per cent. In the shoe manufacturing industry, pre-war taxes were only 1 per cent of costs, in 1927 2–3 per cent. Taxes on each ton of steel produced had risen by the late 1920s to five times their pre-war level.[11]

A second observation might be made: the real wage position is a ratio, and does not necessarily imply any causal mechanism. It is not by itself, without any further corroboration, a confirmation of the wage-push hypothesis about Weimar development. One reason why it appears so high for Weimar is the decline in the growth rate of labour productivity (an issue which will be investigated in more detail later in this chapter). Productivity per man-hour rose for Germany at the following rates (per cent p.a.):[12]

1880–1913	1.99		
1913–1938	1.73	(1913–1929	1.37)
1938–1973	2.36	(1929–1938	2.36)

Thus the Weimar Republic experienced the slowest growth of any period over the last century; and productivity per man-week was even poorer still, because of the reduction in hours worked after 1918–19.

Did wages rise faster than productivity growth as the employees claimed? In a criticism of Borchardt, C.-L. Holtfrerich argued that productivity per hour, calculated from a basis of NDP (at factor cost), was above the pre-war level every year after 1925, and that productivity per employee reached the pre-war level in 1927 and did not subsequently fall below it. He

[10] H. Glismann, H. Rodemer, and F. Wolter, *Zur empirischen Analyse langer Zyklen wirtschaftlicher Entwickling in Deutschland: Datenbasis und Berechnungsmethode* (Kieler Arbeitspapiere 72) Kiel 1978, 22.

[11] Enquête-Ausschuß, *Eisenerzeugende Industrie*, 215; *Schuhindustrie*, 105.

[12] From Maddison 1982, 212.

concludes that it is incorrect to describe the Weimar economy as one of high wage demands and low labour productivity.

Even Holtfrerich's figures on productivity, however, suggest that in 1925/6, 1926/7, and especially 1927/8 productivity increases were *less* than increases in real wages. Employers obviously did not have this macro-statistical material available, but they did present a case which might have been based on it: that wages in the later 1920s represented higher costs and eroded profitability. The gap between the massive wage rises in 1928 and the falling productivity in that year is particularly striking. In 1929 productivity increased again, but most of this increase was simply making good the losses of 1928 (see Table XVI). Thus even given these caveats about the real wage position, it is clear that Weimar labour costs might quite reasonably be seen as threatening profitability. Changes between the years are as significant for gauging responses of labour and capital in both economic and political terms as the overall real wage position: and the Glismann–Borchardt calculation shows very clearly the dramatic improvement of labour's position in 1927–9. There the development is supported by Hoffmann's material on productivity, which Holtfrerich cites, and by the calculation on yield of capital, which show a falling-off of profitability after 1927.[13] Labour thus managed to appropriate the fruits of the Weimar boom.

Another indication of the structural strength of labour's position in Weimar Germany is given by the second piece of evidence in Borchardt's argument: allowing for changes in employment structure, labour's share of national income was 10 per cent higher in the later 1920s (66.75 per cent for 1925–9) than before 1914 or in the 1950s.[14]

To some extent the macro-economic calculations on wage levels reflect just the change in occupational structure as the German economy was modernised. A higher proportion of the population was in employment in the 1920s than before the war, and the share of self-employment fell slightly. Another consequence of the modernisation of the economic structure

[13] C.-L. Holtfrerich, 'Zu hohe Löhne in der Weimarer Republik? Bemerkungen zur Borchardt-These', *GG* 10, 1984, 122–41. Hoffmann 503, 509.

[14] Borchardt 1979, 43–4 (footnote 69).

Table XVI: German Industry and Artisan Production 1925–1932: Hourly Wages and Productivity.

	% nominal wage increase[a]	% real wage increase[b]	Labour productivity[c]	Labour productivity increase[d]
1925			100	
1926	6	6	104	3.6
1927	9	5	109	5.0
1928	12	10	104	−4.8
1929	5	4	111	7.7
1930	−3	1	117	5.2
1931	−7	1	118	0.9
1932	−16	−5	122	3.4

[a] Effective hourly wages.
[b] Deflated by Reich cost of living index.
[c] 1925 = 100.
[d] Increases calculated over previous year.

Source: Calculated from tables in Holtfrerich 1984, 130–1

was the growth of relatively well-paid employment in the service sector, which pushed up averages for wages.

The argument about wages in fact needs to be broken down according to industrial sectors, as well as chronologically, if the effect of actual and expected wage charges on investment decisions is to be determined. On the level of an analysis of firms' costs, there were plenty of reasons to be concerned with wages. A frequent complaint of industrialists in the post-war period was that wages formed a higher proportion of their costs than before the War. For the shoe industry, wages in 1927 represented 20–5 per cent of costs, while before the War this proportion had been below 20 per cent. German shoemakers complained about competition from the Czech Bat'a factory, where production was decentralised in small groups of self-regulating co-operatives, and where wages were not fixed by contract and there was neither arbitration nor trade unionism.[15] Even business men with little interest in ideology took to complaining about the level of wages: Robert Bosch was well known as an industrialist with left-wing sympathies who was impressed by the consumer prosperity generated by American capitalism: but he wrote in 1927 in his house magazine, the *Bosch-Zünder* (i.e. at a time *before* the slump ate into profits) that German wages could never be as high as in America, because

[15] Enquête-Ausschuß, *Schuhindustrie*, 15, 161, 168.

otherwise German industry would perpetually be making losses on the scale of 1926.[16]

WAGES AND TECHNOLOGY

The material on wages we have examined so far offers only one possible explanation of Weimar economic weakness. The relatively high overall level of wages might have been a consequence, not of union strength, as the shoemakers frightened by Bat'a suggested, but of difficulties encountered by German industry in finding markets; or of low productivity growth. The labour unions certainly did not feel that they had achieved a great victory in the 1920s, and to support their case they provided what was in the long run a misreading of productivity changes in Germany. How did they come to such a misassessment of the effects of rationalisation in Germany?

Unions pointed out that although real wages were rising in the second half of the 1920s, not until 1927–9 were these rises as fast as productivity growth (this presented a contrast to Britain, where real wages over the same period grew consistently faster than productivity gains). Thus, although by the end of the decade real wages in some industries in Germany were approaching the British level, this superiority was believed to be a compensation for the scale of the German rationalisation drive.[17]

Secondly, the unions claimed that comparisons with 1913 wages were not appropriate for there had been no substantial increase in real wages in the decade before the First World War. Money wage rises at that time had, the unions said, been balanced by increases in the cost of living as food producers imposed the Bülow tariff (1902) on the nation, and as international cereal prices rose. So there was a lag in the trend of growth in real wages, stemming from before the war, that needed to be made up. It is indeed true that real wages, having grown by 1.7 per cent annually in the 1880s and 1890s, grew from 1900 to 1913 by less than 1 per cent per annum.[18]

[16] Stolle, 201.

[17] E. H. Phelps Brown, 'Levels and Movements of Industrial Productivity and Real Wages Internationally Compared 1860–1970', *Economic Journal* 83, 1973, 67.

[18] D. Groh, *Negative Integration und revolutionärer Attentismus: Die deutsche Sozialdemokra-*

The combination of these two considerations makes it clear why the German unions in the 1920s endorsed what they believed to be a rationalisation wave so unequivocally and with so little hesitation. Rationalisation provided a sure path to increases in working-class incomes. Rarely has a labour movement been so enthusiastic about the possibilities offered by technical change. It is true that during the high unemployment immediately after the stabilisation, and again during the depression, some unionists expressed their hostility to a development which appeared to threaten some jobs; and there was always more opposition to rationalisation from the shop floor than from the union leaderships.[19] Most union leaders believed, however, that rationalisation was nothing more than a logical continuation of man's assertion of his mastery over the natural world. Some even added the more general argument that technical change and improved social organisation were the prerequisites for the introduction of socialism.[20]

In August 1925 the German mineworkers union (Verband der Bergarbeiter Deutschlands) called for the implementation of an extensive rationalisation programme in the mines under the supervision of the state authorities, who were to make sure that rationalisation was not turned against the working class.[21] In 1926 a group of union leaders toured the United States and returned moved by the high living standards provided by large-scale modern industry. Wilhelm Eggert reasoned that 'this ambition of the human species to create instruments, equipment, and machines, to reach into the secrets of nature, and to gather together and control natural energy in the service of economic progress, is to be found as a more or less powerful drive in every historical epoch'. The Fourth Congress of the International Federation of Factory Workers in Hanover (July 1929) passed a resolution arguing that the process of rationalisation was not basically harmful to the working class, as long as it was subject to control by political institutions:

tie am Vorabend des Ersten Weltkrieges, Frankfurt 1973, 127–8. A. V. Desai, *Real Wages in Germany 1871–1917*, Oxford 1968, 125.

[19] *Rote Fahne* 63, 16 March 1927. More generally Stollberg, 120 and Stolle, 96–7.

[20] P. Hertz and R. Seidel, *Arbeitszeit, Arbeitslohn und Arbeitsleistung*, Berlin 1923. W. Woytinsky in *Gewerkschaftszeitung* 29, 18 July 1932, 453.

[21] ZStA RFM B776, 20 Aug. 1925 VBD Memorandum: 'Denkschrift zur Umstellung des Ruhrbergbaues'.

> Our objective is to influence technical progress and fight against the greater exploitation of labour by false methods of rationalisation; to increase the consumption of the surplus products of industry by raising real wages; and to prevent the working class being plunged into the miseries of unemployment in consequence of the appropriation of the fruits of rationalisation by the minority that controls the means of production.[22]

Some workers knew that they had a particularly strong interest in rationalisation: the car workers' union conference in Frankfurt/Main 1930 set out the theory that rationalisation would lead to increased wages, and this would increase the consumption of new kinds of goods. Thus 'the revolutionary automobile will serve the cause of the revolutionary workers'.[23]

The July 1929 Factory Workers' resolution makes clear that there were worries about some aspects of rationalisation. Fritz Naphtali, who was a leading proponent of the thesis that rationalisation was bringing with it socialism, spoke of *Pseudo-rationalisierung* in the cases where the workers did not benefit.[24] There were two particular sources of concern: employees were worried about increases in the pace of work and consequently rising accident rates as operatives became exhausted; and about the 'control of the work place'. The word *Tempo* stood for many of the malaises of the 1920s. Chemical reaction times were cut in nitrate production in Bayer, Leverkusen;[25] new assembly lines demanded faster working; and special institutes such as the REFA were created to study timing in industry. Between 1924 and 1931, 10 000 time-and-motion specialists were trained to assess the performance of workers in the metal and electrical industries.[26] The idea that man had become a slave to machines forcing an ever and ever faster pace was a cliché of the time, which was explored in literature and in films: most famously in Fritz Lang's *Metropolis* (1926). The second problem, which was raised already by the *Tempo* issue, was that of control of the work-place. *Tempo* subordinated the worker to a technically forced pace and to the time-and-motion men, while an increase in the proportion of workers paid piece-rate (*Akkord*) strengthened the power of central computing offices, who worked out their own systems of

22 Brady, 328.
23 Stollberg, 90.
24 Ibid., 93–4.
25 Stolle, 104.
26 Stollberg, 52–3.

assessing efficiency and calculating rewards. Many younger managers adopted the fad for modern management that came from the USA and had as its patron saint F. W. Taylor. Taylor had already set out before the War an ideology of modern management which involved more management control and higher speeds of work: 'most of us remain, through a great part of our lives, in this respect grown-up children, and do our best only under pressure of a task of comparatively short duration'.[27]

There had been disputes before the War as *Tempo* was increased and as new methods of calculating *Akkord* were implemented: there was a strike in Robert Bosch (Stuttgart) in 1913 after a new, central *Akkord* office was set up and the management limited the right of workers and unions to contest *Akkord* calculations.[28] Curiously, though, in the light of the discussion in Chapter IV about *when* rationalisation actually occurred, it was after 1925, when the rate of technical change was slowing down, that the most passionate discussions about the rationalisation drive took place. Perhaps this was because the American influence over Germany was now embodied for all to see in the reparations plan of the summer of 1924, in the American Agent-General for Reparations Payments in Berlin, and in the hundreds of American bankers hawking loans round Germany and bringing in their wake thousands of American tourists. After 1924, American lending to Germany was well publicised, and some politicians and business men ran campaigns warning of the dangers of *Überfremdung*.

More importantly, though, only after 1924 could the effects of technical change be isolated from other dislocating moments. The very high rates of labour mobility during the inflation period meant that the labour-saving effects of technical change were not really apparent, and that productivity was very low: workers did not stay in their jobs long enough to maximise their speed of work. Many of the new processes demanded long acclimatisation times: thus in Bosch in 1933 a

[27] F. W. Taylor, *Shop Management*, New York 1911, 69. Taylor's *Principles of Scientific Management* (1911) was translated into German two years later: (trans.) R. Roesler, *Die Grundsätze wissenschaftlicher Betriebsführung*, Berlin 1913.

[28] H. Homburg, 'Anfänge des Taylorsystems in Deutschland vor dem Ersten Weltkrieg: Eine Problemskizze unter besonderer Berücksichtigung der Arbeitskämpfe bei Bosch 1913', *GG* 4, 1978, 170–98.

semi-skilled worker after four months' employment was still only producing 85 per cent of the output of a well-established worker.[29] Workers after 1924 stayed in employment longer: and as the high rates of turnover slowed down, fewer workers were needed. The steel, chemical, and mechanical engineering industries all laid off large numbers of unskilled and semi-skilled workers.[30]

Secondly, stable currency conditions permitted a much more rational framework for *Akkord* calculations. Complicated differential payments systems had made little sense as wages were adjusted frequently during the inflation; the managers' schemes could be realised, however, once monetary conditions became relatively stable. These new schemes often led to resentments within the work-force. The issue of differentials was thus a key one in conflicts in the Berlin metal and electrical industries in 1924–5. Skilled workers were encouraged to negotiate their pay outside the framework of union contracts; and high levels of output were now generously rewarded.[31] *Akkord* rates were increasingly set by central technical offices rather than individually at the discretion of foremen: thus the Siemens Berlin Wernerwerk counting and meter department abandoned *Akkord* fixed by foremen at the beginning of 1927.[32] Such an exercise might have made sense technically for a long time before the stabilisation, but Taylor's modern management principles had in practice been impossible to implement during the inflation.

Rationalisation appeared suddenly to create an environment in which it made sense for workers to press wage claims. Other considerations worked in the same direction:

1. After the stabilisation, the sensitivity to labour-saving rationalisation increased because of the number of lay-offs. Left-wing oppositions to union leaderships emerged, and were particularly powerful among those groups of workers (usually the unskilled, where there had been the very high rates of labour turnover during the inflation) who were threatened by redundancy. Unions were in difficulties. Threats of unemployment had weakened the union structures; and the membership

[29] Stolle, 199. [30] Ibid., 96. [31] Hartwich, 127–8.
[32] SAA 11 Lf/100 (Köttgen), 25 Jan. 1928 Aktennotiz.

of the free (socialist) unions had fallen from 7.8m. in 1922 to 4.0m. in 1924.[33] The union leaderships came to believe that successful performances in wage bargaining provided the best means of buying off the opposition movements, and indeed opposition collapsed during the mid-Weimar stabilisation, even though unemployment levels continued to be very high throughout the 1920s. The union reaction to internal opposition produced a wage push that surprised classically trained economists: high levels of unemployment led to a search for greater security, which involved paradoxically *upward* rather than downward pressure on wages.

2. Weimar wage demands also reflected a wish to be compensated for another type of uncertainty which posed a threat in the stable currency world. Labour was still terrified of falling real wages as a result of its experience in the inflation—in the course of which the relationship between wages and prices had fluctuated very wildly.[34] A particularly sensitive issue was that of food prices. Until 1925 German tariffs were prohibited under the terms of the Versailles Treaty; but after Germany's sovereignty in this area was restored, concern about food prices became as urgent a political issue as it had been in the days of the Bülow tariff. After the increases of 1925 and 1928, labour was frightened by the rising tide of agrarian protectionism.

Moreover, there was the question of what kind and what amount of food should be included in household calculations. During the inflation, food supplies had been limited, and hours of work short. The increases in the hours worked after the stabilisation meant that workers had to eat more. The testimony of steel workers to the Enquête-Ausschuß is very expressive in this regard: 'I need to eat more in order to carry out my work . . . I need to eat more, more meat. I can't eat dry bread, because then I wouldn't be able to work . . . Even if we didn't earn so much before, we didn't need to work so much and we didn't give as much money out on food.'[35]

[33] H. Grebing, *Geschichte der deutschen Arbeiterbewegung: Ein Überblick*, Munich 1970, 179.

[34] Balderston 1982, 502–4.

[35] Enquête-Ausschuß *Arbeitszeit, Arbeitslohn und Arbeitsleistung im Hochofenbetriebe*, Berlin 1929, 48–50.

So at the same time as food prices increased, workers needed to buy more and better quality food because of the conditions of work. And at the end of the 1920s, observation of increases in retail prices frequently led to general fears of a renewal of the inflationary mechanism. In 1927, the Nazi Party in Bremen was able to use the likelihood of a new inflation as an occasion for making a propaganda point.[36] In April 1929, when it appeared that the breakdown of the Paris Experts' Reparations Conference would be accompanied by a currency and exchange crisis, trade union leaders warned of the danger of inflation, and stressed the importance of keeping transfer protection in order to secure the value of the German currency.[37] Again and again in the depression labour politicians warned of the disastrous consequences of inflation.[38] Before that, and throughout the later years of the Republic, safeguards in the forms of wage increases against the effects of both agricultural demands and general price inflation were powerful considerations in labour bargaining.

3. Finally, the issue of *net* wage levels was important. Wages were subject to more deductions in the 1920s than before the war. Although almost all skilled workers actually paid lower rates of income tax than they had done in the Kaiserreich (because Weimar taxation was more progressive), they made much larger social insurance contributions. A skilled worker in a rolling mill paid 5.1 per cent of his wages in income tax and 2.5 per cent in social contributions in 1913/14; in 1928 these figures were 3.9 per cent and 8.6 per cent respectively.[39] Though social insurance contributions of course represented a good—increased security—they did immediately lower disposable incomes.

These three additional considerations ensured that the issues raised by rationalisation became politically acute at exactly the time when the real impact of rationalisation in the sense of technical improvement was softening: during the economic

[36] M. H. Kater, *The Nazi Party: a Social Profile of Members and Leaders 1919–1945*, Oxford 1983, 188.

[37] IfZ ED93/5, 2 April 1929 diary entry.

[38] See for example, *Vorwärts* 4 Oct. 1931: inflation was 'eine abscheuliche indirekte Steuer'.

[39] Enquête-Ausschuß, *Eisenerzeugende Industrie*, 56.

recovery of 1926–9 when production was increasing but wage productivity was not. One final suggestion: perhaps the unions were just impressed by the scale of the rise in German industrial output.

Wage rates continued to climb until 1930; and there were few cases of cuts in wage rates until March–April 1931, when reductions were made in many industries, although in some cases the old rates were retained even longer. There were falls in earnings already in 1930, however: an arbitration award for the steel industry, the Oeynhausen settlement, and allowed cuts in piece rates paid over the wage contract (*Tarif*) level.[40] In addition, weekly earnings had fallen already from 1929 as overtime was reduced.

THE STRUCTURE OF WAGES

Employers blamed unions for misinterpreting the effects of rationalisation, and for first pushing wages upward and then countering the 'natural' tendency for wages to fall in a depression. Already in 1925 the economic crisis made business adopt a harsher anti-union line.[41]

In fact, however, upward pressure on wages in the initial stages of depression was not a phenomenon new to the Weimar Republic. Already in the Kaiserreich there had been a lag between indices for output and employment and a wage index: before unions were either well organised or powerful. In the Kaiserreich in the most spectacular case of boom and bust—the *Gründerjahre* of the 1870s—the boom collapsed in 1873, but the peak of building wage rates was reached only in 1876.[42] Some features of the Weimar economy thus predated unions and collective wage agreements.

There was a peculiarity in Weimar that might at first be taken to support the thesis that there was an increased political determination of wage behaviour. This was the remarkably uniform behaviour of rates in different industries. Table XVII shows the hourly rates which applied, using 1925 as a base.

A caveat: wage rates, usually determined by contract (*Tarif*-

[40] Grübler, 157–63.

[41] Hartwich, 292. Hertz-Eichenrode, 44.

[42] G. Bry, *Wages in Germany 1871–1945*, Princeton 1960, 137.

Table XVII: Hourly Wage Rates (Yearly Average) 1925–1932

	Building	Woodworking	Metal products	Textiles	Chemicals	Brewing	Hard coal
1925	100	100	100	100	100	100	100
1926	110.4	109.4	108.9	105.4	107.2	104.0	108.7
1927	114.9	115.3	113.1	114.9	114.3	111.4	116.2
1928	122.9	127.8	124.0	127.0	124.2	123.2	121.3
1929	131.0	133.9	132.9	131.6	131.4	130.2	126.1
1930	133.2	139.0	134.6	133.3	133.9	133.2	127.0
1931	124.1	134.4	127.6	127.0	129.3	132.0	117.7
1932	97.9	108.2	110.4	113.7	108.7	114.4	100.4

Source: Bry, 376–83.

vertrag) between employers and workers, were usually well below hourly earnings and the extent of the difference between effective hourly wages and wage rates increased during the upswing 1926–8: by 1928 this 'wage drift' for male workers was sometimes as high as 80 per cent (for skilled workers in rolling-mills). The difference diminished again during the depression, but the effect of wage drift is to make inter-industry comparisons for *skilled* workers hard. There is much less difficulty in the case of unskilled workers.[43]

Two industries behaved significantly out of line with the general trend: construction and hard coal-mining. Construction showed a particularly heavy cyclical fluctuation, which was accentuated by the heavy political element in demand for building labour. This was one of the areas in German economic life where public sector involvement was greatest: 50 per cent of the construction of dwellings in the later 1920s was paid for from public funds. Building was very severely hit by the crisis in public finance in the later 1920s; and large numbers of building projects were cancelled abruptly.[44] Thus there was the odd consequence that building wages lagged less behind general output indicators than they had in the 1870s. Until 1929, however, there were substantial rises in building wages, and the sharp fall in building wages after 1929 did not stop employers in the building (and related) trades from blaming excessive pay for their problems.[45]

[43] Enquête-Ausschuß, *Eisen- und Stahlwaren*, 182; *Schuhindustrie*, 83. *Wirtschaft und Statistik* 1932, 375–7.

[44] Enquête-Ausschuß, *Wohnungsbau* 12; and below.

[44] From Bry, 376–83. BAK NL ten Hompel 11, 21 Feb. 1930 ten Hompel speech to

The second abnormal industry was coal. Low wages were partly a reflection of over-capacity and over-production, but also followed from a lowering of skill levels. The coal industry was one of the few where capital was being substituted for skilled labour during the 1920s. A consequence was that surface workers now overtook the previously highly paid pit workers in monthly or annual earnings because they worked longer shifts. In general, miners lost the position that they had previously held at the top of the wages league, a loss which was very bitterly resented.[46] The Christian Mineworkers' Union argued again and again that the wage differentials of the Kaiserreich represented an ideal of social justice, a 'just price' for labour. The miners were particularly unhappy after the big civil service pay award of 1927, which they knew that they were in no position to emulate.[47]

In other industries where wage statistics are available, there appear to be few inter-sectoral differences, and a surprising uniformity of behaviour. There was a particularly striking upsurge after the 1927 civil service pay award, which most workers found that they *could* emulate. Wages in textiles and chemicals behaved almost identically: a striking confirmation of the analysis offered in Chapter IV of the structural stagnation of the Weimar economy,[48] and of the similarity in growth patterns in the later 1920s. There are specific characteristics of the labour market which should be added to the general explanation of Weimar stagnation.

Weimar had very low rates of labour mobility. This was in large part a consequence of the post-war scarcity of housing: by 1927 Germany was suffering from a deficit of some 800 000 housing units.[49] Rent control, introduced on 18 August 1914, helped to restrict the supply of new accommodation; and the control was kept long after other prices were decontrolled after

General Meeting of Zentrum Handels- und Industriebeiräte. Ten Hompel was a cement producer.

[46] C. Wilhelms, *Die Übererzeugung im Ruhrkohlenbergbau 1913 bis 1932*, Jena 1938, 3–4. R. Tschirbs, 'Tarifpolitik im Ruhrbergbau 1918–1933', Bochum Ph.D. dissertation 1984.

[47] Tschirbs 1982, 309. M. Schneider, *Die christlichen Gewerkschaften 1894–1933*, Bonn 1982, 601–2.

[48] See Stolle, 29 ff for low wages in the chemical industry.

[49] Preller, 483.

the war. Rents on old accommodation were set by the stabilisation financial decrees at 100 per cent of the 'peace' (1913) rent for the beginning of 1927, and 120 per cent in October, while the cost of new accommodation was substantially higher. So tenants stayed in 'old' houses, and landlords found it unprofitable, despite large state building subsidies, to embark on new construction. The state subsidies in fact came out of a tax on property values, which varied from Land to Land, and which had a depressing effect on the property market.[50] Just as the communes were beginning to tackle the problem of the housing shortage in a serious way, they were hit by the depression, and they stopped construction and diverted the revenue from the property tax to general administrative purposes.

The housing shortage had significant effects on wage negotiations: it was difficult to import new labour to a region. But where employers did control their own housing stock (as in the Ruhr coal industry, where employers had 157 024 houses for workers in the late 1920s),[51] they could use this stock to put pressure on wages.

Nationwide *Tarifverträge* increased the extent of the problem by decreasing incentives for mobility. In addition they forced up costs in areas where wages had traditionally been low in a national comparison, and thus altered the regional balance of unemployment. The severe crisis in Saxony was often blamed on high wage increases stemming from the evening-out of wages after the War. Traditionally lower Saxon wages were taken almost to the levels of the West and the Rhineland. (High wage increases were not, of course, the only problem: Saxony also suffered in the later 1920s because of her exceptionally high degree of dependence on exports.) However, even when the coal market was buoyant, a Saxon coal-owner told the Enquête Committee that he had had to lay off miners as he could not afford wages comparable to those in the Ruhr.[52]

The poor labour mobility stemming from the housing shortage and from national *Tarifverträge* made the impact of the

[50] Ibid., 68, 286, 334, 384, 386.

[51] Brady, 81.

[52] Werner, 29. C. Brückner, 'Die sächsische Industrie' in (ed.) K. Diehl, *Wirkungen und Ursachen des hohen Zinsfußes in Deutschland*, Jena 1932, 209. Enquête-Ausschuß, *Die deutsche Kohlenwirtschaft*, Berlin 1929, 311.

Table XVIII: Urban Population Employed in Industry and Services: Selected European States (m.)

					% Increase	
		1920	1930	1940	1920–30	1930–40
UK and Ireland	I[a]	9.4	10.0	10.8	6	8
	S[b]	9.5	10.9	11.9	15	9
Germany	I	13.2	13.3	15.0	1	13
	S	8.4	9.7	11.7	15	21
France	I	6.5	7.3	6.1	12	−16
	S	6.2	6.6	6.8	6	3
Eastern Europe and Italy	I	9.9	12.8	—	29	—
	S	9.6	11.7	—	22	—

[a] I = Employment in industry.
[b] S = Employment in services.
Source: Svennilson, 76.

demographic losses of the world war more severe. Rent control and demographic loss, of course, were phenomena which affected most of Europe: but their effects were more severe in Germany than elsewhere. Whereas industrial and service employment grew only slightly in Germany in the 1920s, there were higher growth rates in Britain and even in Malthusian France (and much higher rates in the industrialising economies of central and eastern Europe and Italy: see Table XVIII).

Reactions to the new levels of uncertainty in the 1920s and the problem of labour supply were likely to create both a wage push, and a relatively uniform behaviour of wages in different sectors. Did political calculations play a role here too? Most commentators have been careful to be agnostic on this issue. The leading authority on German wage behaviour writes:

> Large-scale unemployment, coupled with the maintenance of wage-rate levels, was historically a new experience. This became the basis for business claims that wage-rate behaviour had acquired characteristics which interfered seriously with the mechanisms normally relied on to bring about recovery. Whether or not such assumptions were sound, there can be no doubt that both union rates and effective rates did resist downward adjustment in the face of widespread unemployment.[53]

[53] Bry, 158.

There may be a more definite answer: first, employers, since they saw the state acting in the market, assumed when the market worked unfavourably for them that the state was responsible for such an unfavourable operation. This accounts for the psychology of the response to state action. Secondly, the unions' strength was not constant throughout the later 1920s, and the strengthening of the unions coincides very remarkably with both the height of the wage push and the most dramatic state action in the labour market: the 1927 pay award for the civil service.

THE ORIGINS OF STATE INTERVENTION IN THE LABOUR MARKET

Before the war, *Tarifverträge* were concluded in some industries: book printing was organised by collective contract from 1873, though the printers had tried to impose contracts as early as 1848. By 1914 contracts had been extended to the construction industry, and also partially to the wood, paper, leather, cleaning, and tailoring industries. In total, 1 574 285 workers were covered by wage contracts in 1912 (i.e. 6 per cent of those employed).[54] Employers in heavy industry rejected the concept, however, until the wartime dislocation of the labour market brought the state into the wage-bargaining process. A combination of the mobilisation for the army and the expansion of the armaments industries led to labour shortages in some areas, and by 1916 many business men were worried that workers were being lured away to other firms by offers of higher wages. The Patriotic Auxiliary Service Law (14 December 1916) was intended to control this wage inflation:[55] it provided for the arbitration of wage claims by boards composed equally of representatives of employers and unions under the presidency of a state-appointed chairman (a representative of the War Office). In this way wage contracts

[54] Hartwich, 19. *Die deutsche Sozialpolitik: Eine Materialsammlung (Nach dem Stande vom 15 Januar 1926)*, Berlin 1926, 27. *Deutsche Sozialpolitik: Erinnerungsschrift des Reichsarbeitsministeriums*, Berlin 1929, 73. P. Ullmann, *Tarifverträge und Tarifpolitik in Deutschland bis 1914*, Frankfurt/Main 1977.

[55] G. D. Feldman, *Army, Industry, and Labour in Germany 1914–1918*, Princeton 1966, 197–249.

became a general feature of German economic life. The Law was dressed up as a wartime measure, intended to deal only with the exceptional situation of the armaments economy, which would be repealed immediately on the 'return to normalcy'. This repeal was indeed one of the first acts of the revolutionary regime in Germany (12 November 1918): though soon afterwards there followed a declaration that privately negotiated settlements were to be regarded as legally binding (23 December 1918).

After the Revolution, wage contracts became a standard part of employer–labour negotiations. At the end of 1918 only 1.1m. workers were covered by contracts; one year later the figure was 6m., and at the end of 1920, 9.6m. The institution survived the inflation and the stabilisation: at the beginning of 1924 13m. workers had negotiated contracts, and although the figure fell to 10.97m. in January 1927, the system spread again, and the number of workers affected rose by a million.[56] Most of these contracts were on a company or plant basis: but there were also nationally and regionally negotiated arrangements. In January 1928 out of a total of 17m. employed in Germany, 1.4m. workers were covered by Reich contracts and 3.4m. by regional agreements.[57]

There were many bitter wage disputes during the German inflation: though the peak year for strikes was 1920, with 8 000 strikes affecting 8m. workers, there were conflicts in 1921 and 1922 as workers tried to keep up wages in the face of price rises.[58] 1923, when there were no accurate records of the number of strikes, was a year of exceptional social violence. The combination of a threat of anarchy and a desire to stabilise wage negotiations as part of the process of monetary stabilisation prompted the Government to reintroduce the wartime arbitration system. A decree of 30 October 1923 provided for arbitration committees under the direction and supervision of the Reich Labour Ministry. If the workers' or the employers' representatives failed to agree to an arbitration award, the chairman could still impose the award himself (decree of 29 December 1923). This right of the chairman to make an award single-handed (the *Einmann–Schiedspruch*) was abolished by a

[56] Hartwich, 430. [57] *Deutsche Sozialpolitik* 1929, 47.
[58] J. Kuczynski, *Die Lage der Arbeiterklasse 1917–1933*, Berlin 1966, 245.

court ruling in January 1929, but was subsequently reintroduced, in defiance of the judicial decision, on 9 March 1931 as part of the Brüning system of austerity emergency measures.

After arbitration, the Reich Labour Minister had the right to impose a *Verbindlichkeitserklärung*: this made the award legally binding and subsequent strikes or lock-outs illegal. This element of compulsion, and the general increase in the scope for state intervention in the economy, led some labour lawyers to describe the Weimar system as Fascist; and indeed the Weimar Republic bore a strong resemblance to Italy where the process of wage determination was worked out in the aftermath of the Pact of the Palazzo Vidoni (October 1925). There disputes were to be resolved by negotiations between the Fascist unions and the employers' associations, and in 1926 the system was complemented by the power of the labour magistracy (the equivalent of the German Reich Labour Ministry) to make binding awards.[59] The effect of the German arbitration decree was to impose through collective agreements

> a conscious attempt by the state to use the organisations to carry out its own social policy objectives. . . . The state no longer leaves a large area of working life to the autonomous regulation of the organisations, intervening only to assist them in achieving their objectives; on the contrary the organisations enter into the service of the state in the very process of carrying out their autonomous role. They become public institutions.[60]

In fact the organisations of employers and workers found it very difficult to reach autonomous agreements in the slow-growth Weimar economy, and as a consequence called the state in more and more frequently.

In addition to the *Verbindlichkeitserklärung*, the Reich Labour Ministry used other mechanisms in attempting to control the social process. After the stabilisation of the Mark, for instance, the Ministry recommended that wages should initially be set at 70–80 per cent of their 1913 value.[61] Later the Ministry declared that it had the general aim of creating social justice. For most of the Weimar Republic, the Ministry was in the

[59] A. Lyttleton, *The Seizure of Power: Fascism in Italy 1919–1929*, London 1973, 319 ff.

[60] O. Kahn-Freund (eds. R. Lewis and J. Clark), *Labour Law and Politics in the Weimar Republic*, Oxford 1981, 179–80.

[61] Hartwich, 38.

hands of members of the Centre party; and there was considerable ministerial stability. It was in the Labour Ministry—together with the Army Ministry—that ministers lasted longest. Heinrich Brauns (1920–8) and Adam Stegerwald (1930–2) came from a Catholic tradition which stressed social corporatism and the importance of 'just wages' as a prerequisite for social stability, a tradition which went back to the days of Bishop Ketteler. Stegerwald believed that a general rise in wages, coupled with the security from unemployment and with improved education, would bring the working class into the state and create more responsible citizens.[62] The interlude between the Centre ministers was filled by the SPD trade unionist, Rudolf Wissell, who was as attached as Brauns and Stegerwald to the creation of a *Sozialstaat*, but who—since he had much closer connections with the free unions—roused the immediate antipathy of business. Wissell's unpublished memoirs are filled with accounts of how he fought over major and minor issues for the improvement of working class conditions. Often his campaigns turned out to be bizarre: as when he invited the bewildered cleaning ladies to receptions in the Labour Ministry.[63] In 1929 and 1930 Wissell's Cabinet colleagues put pressure on him to slow down the rate of wage increases, and he felt greatly pained by these requirements dictated by the Economics and Finance Ministries. He wrote to Hermann Müller to complain about the attacks of his union colleagues who believed that 'the scales had turned against them once the Minister of Labour was a social democrat'.[64] These attacks led Wissell to adopt in the winter of 1929–30 a line more and more opposed to concessions to the Volkspartei.

In 1929 the Labour Ministry published a commemorative volume to celebrate the first ten years of its existence. Ex-Minister Brauns described in the preface how the 1918 Revolution had 'demanded a wide-ranging socio-political transformation'.[65] The book put forward two very controversial ideas: first, that wage increases were in general good for the economy, since they raised purchasing power.[66] Secondly, and this raised

[62] Schneider 1982, 557.

[63] BAK NL Wissell, MS memoirs.

[64] FES NL Müller II, 177, 29 Aug. 1929 Wissell Memorandum for Hermann Müller.

[65] *Deutsche Sozialpolitik* 1929, 1.

[66] Ibid., 105–7.

even more fury, the book claimed that state policy had had an important effect on the outcome of wage settlements.[67]

The Reich Labour Ministry was not the only Reich institution to impose politics on to wage bargaining. The officials of the Reich Economics Ministry occasionally took the side of labour too. For instance in 1925 when the Finance Office in Beuthen (Silesia) produced a memorandum urging concessions in the form of *Subvention* to the mines of the Schaffgotsch'sche Werke, where the hours of work had been increased from twelve to fourteen hours, the Reich Economics official who was responsible refused, on the grounds that 'such an exploitation of human labour is not possible under present social legislation'.[68]

On the basis of observation of state interventions it might well have been held that the state was making things difficult for business: the Labour Ministry, in particular, was a constant thorn in industry's side.

THE DEVELOPMENT OF WAGES AFTER THE STABILISATION

There were five phases in the development of a wage structure in Germany after the stabilisation of the Mark.[69] In the first, wages moved up quickly from their initially very low level (1924–5); then there was a temporary slowing down during the recession (mid-1925–6); in the third phase wages were pushed up by the example of the civil service pay increase (1927–8); in the fourth employers tried desperately, but on the whole unsuccessfully, to resist the wage pressure (1928–30); and finally from 1931 wage rates moved decisively downwards.

The first period set the tone for Weimar's poor labour relations. Employers immediately used the opportunity offered by economic reconstruction to attack the eight-hour day established in November 1918. In consequence, the length of the working day became a major issue in labour politics. Whereas before 1923 relatively few strikes occurred over hours, and strikes over wages were ten times as frequent, in 1924 this

[67] Ibid., 108–9.

[68] ZStA RFM B776, 31 Oct. 1925 Memorandum of Hans Schäffer (Reich Economics Ministry).

[69] For a slightly different chronology, see Hartwich, 294.

ratio fell to four times.[70] Ruhr industrialists had already in 1922 foreseen the end of the inflation and wanted to secure favourable terms for their operations in a stabilised economy. At Unna on 30 September 1923 mine owners met in order to agree an increase in shifts from 7 to 8½ hours. The Reich authorities—faced by a threat from western industry to break away from the Reich and negotiate with France—gave in, and on 17 November 1923 the revolutionary decree on hours was allowed to lapse. As well as by the desire to guarantee order in the crucial phase of transition to the stabilised economy, the arbitration decree of 30 October had been motivated by the need to provide employees with some counter-concessions once the end of the eight-hour day was acknowledged. On 21 December the final blow to the eight-hour system was dealt by a new decree which, while recognising the 'principle' of eight hours, allowed widespread exceptions if these could be justified (as they almost invariably were) on 'economic grounds'.

Steelworks almost everywhere replaced three-shift operations by two-shift systems in January 1924: new hours of work were calculated to allow what was in practice, including pauses, a twelve-hour shift. From January 1924 to July 1927 Thomas steelworkers in Rhineland-Westphalia worked sixty-eight or sixty-eight and a half hours a week (and seventy-two hours if on night-shifts).[71] The insistence with which employers in the stabilisation period demanded—particularly in the coal, steel, and metal industries—increases in the hours of work reflected the major shortage of skilled labour which Germany experienced. Training had been neglected during the war and inflation eras (a major loss of capital in terms of human skill should be included in the balance sheet of economic gains and losses from Germany's inflation).[72] After 1924 the proportion of older workers in plants increased dramatically as business looked for higher skill levels.[73]

The new hours led to a great deal of labour unrest. There was a strike in May 1924 when Ruhr miners refused an

[70] *Deutsche Sozialpolitik* 1929, 63–7, 96. G. D. Feldman and I. Steinisch 1978, 353–439.

[71] Enquête-Ausschuß *Arbeitsleistung in Stahl- und Walzwerken*, 24, 48.

[72] (Ed.) G. Abramowski, *Akten der Reichskanzlei Weimarer Republik, Die Kabinette Marx I und II*, Boppard 1973, doc. 358, 21 Nov. 1924 letter of August Thyssen Werke.

[73] Enquête-Ausschuß *Arbeitsleistung im Hochofenbetriebe*.

arbitration award of an eight-hour shift coupled with a 15 per cent pay increase. Those who refused the new shift—they amounted to about 90 per cent of the work-force—were locked out; and the Labour Ministry then declared a new (and slightly more generous) arbitration award binding. The new award allowed extra pay for overtime and a general 5 per cent additional increase in pay. The strike then collapsed.[74] A strike from March to May in the chemical works of BASF (Ludwigshafen) against the nine-hour day failed too in the end because of the scepticism of the union involved about the use of going on strike, and because of the intervention of the German police and the French army.[75] Protests against the new hours of work proved futile: the textile industry now worked a fifty-four to fifty-six-hour week; and the Berlin metal and electrical industries imposed an extra hour of overtime.[76] Those works where the old hours were kept did this not because of labour protests, but because of technical conditions. In fine sheet metal production, continuous working in eight-hour shifts with no pauses provided an optimal mode of production in very modern plants.[77] In other industries, where there was no labour shortage, the eight-hour day was kept: this was the case in the shoe and wood industries.

Such fundamental changes in the working week were possible initially only because of the momentary confusion and weakness in the ranks of the labour movement. In the case of the largest of the 1924 disputes, the Ruhr coal conflict, the socialist union leadership opposed acceptance of the arbitration award, while the Christian unions accepted the second of the two awards.[78] The free unions felt they were not strong enough to carry on the dispute on their own when the award was declared binding. In the chemical industry, the Fabrikarbeiterverband was not reluctant to accept lengthened hours. In these cases, labour union compliance eventually solved the problem for the Labour Ministry and for the employers; while in other cases employers tempted workers away from the

[74] Feldman and Steinisch, 413–34.
[75] Stolle, 120–2.
[76] Preller, 305. Hartwich, 106.
[77] Enquête-Ausschuß *Arbeitsleistung in Stahl- und Walzwerken*, 268–72.
[78] Schneider 1982, 610–11.

unions by promises of increased differentials. This happened in the Berlin metal industry, where the union (the Deutsche Metallarbeiterverband) tried to impose an overall wage increase, but skilled workers (reacting to the scarcity of skills) preferred to negotiate on an individual factory basis. In February 1925 an arbitration award formally recognised that for the Berlin metal trade an overall contract was not appropriate.[79]

Unions were thus in a very unpleasant dilemma: where arbitration awards turned out satisfactorily, some workers felt that they could negotiate better by themselves, or that they could derive the benefits of union negotiating without joining themselves (on a 'free rider' calculation). Where, on the other hand, arbitration awards were unsatisfactory, the unions were held to be responsible. The decline in union membership in 1924 has already been commented on. Some of the workers who left unions in 1924 formed radical alternatives: in the chemical industry there was the left-wing Industrieverband. In metals and mining, strong radical wings were built up after 1928.[80] These groups were generally linked to the KPD, although there were sometimes quarrels over tactics between the party and the unionists. The opposition groups, known generally as the Revolutionäre Gewerkschaftsopposition, RGO, dominated labour representation in many industries by the time of the depression. The RGO was particularly powerful among building, metal, coal, dock, agricultural, and unskilled clerical workers: in the Bochumer Verein (steel) the RGO won 43 per cent of votes to the works councils in 1929 and 35 per cent in 1930. In March 1931 the RGO had 40 per cent of the votes in the works council elections in Bayer Leverkusen.[81] These opposition groups enthusiastically endorsed the KPD's 'social fascism' line as set out in 1928 by Comintern. They saw in the reformist trade unions the major enemy which had organised the betrayal of the working class. All this, together with weak finances after the inflation,[82] worried the unions.

The SPD too shared the unions' concern. Both SPD and

[79] Hartwich, 108–9.
[80] See in general Schöck and Stolle.
[81] Seebold, 47. Stolle, 106–7.
[82] Hartwich, 137.

unions needed to look around for a new ideal. Fritz Tarnow of the Wood Workers' Union said at the Socialist Union Federation (ADGB) conference in Breslau in 1925:

Each of us knows, on looking at the developments of the last year, that something in the spirit of the German labour movement has been broken. An illusion has burst . . . It is always necessary to ask whether this situation must remain, or whether we cannot introduce into our labour movement and particularly into our trade union movement an ideology in which the masses can believe, an ideal.'[83]

Rudolf Hilferding expressed a very similar thought when he wrote in a letter to the veteran socialist philosopher Karl Kautsky of the need to put more emphasis on 'moral and spiritual elements' in socialist agitation.[84] Presumably it was easier to invent new ideals and new ideologies than to transform the world.

The theories developed by Hilferding and Naphtali—the assertion of the existence of organised capitalism, the necessity of the political wage, and the possibility of economic democracy—were responses to the union crisis: how could socialist and union action still be effective when the unions seemed to be retreating on all fronts?[85] Thus the notorious phrases of the late 1920s were born as an instrument for agitation, intended to remotivate and remobilise the unions and hold the labour movement together. Since the unions on their own had not been successful, the argument ran, it was necessary to look to the state as the defender of labour's interests. The system of wage arbitration and binding declarations had been the one area where labour in 1924–5 had appeared to do well, a compensation for the set-backs over the hours of work.

In 1926–7 an economic revival did not appreciably strengthen the power of the unions. There were still a large number of unemployed, and skilled workers still preferred to negotiate for themselves. The number and the extent of strikes had fallen from 1924 with the recession; and arbitration and the use of

[83] Quoted by J. A. Moses, *Trade Unionism in Germany from Bismark to Hitler 1869–1933*, London 1982, 357.

[84] IISG Kautsky papers KD XII 636, 19 July 1924 Hilferding to Kautsky.

[85] F. Naphtali, 'Debatten zur Wirtschaftspolitik', *Die Gesellschaft* 6/1 1929, 210–19.

binding declarations also fell dramatically from 1925 to 1926.[86] As a result, employers were not unhappy with the status quo, although they were aware that there were many unsolved issues, and that wages continued to rise in the recession despite the fall in the number of strikes (see Table XIX).

Table XIX: Days Lost Through Labour Disputes: Germany 1924–1932

1924	36 360 134	1929	4 489 870
1925	17 113 886	1930	3 935 977
1926	1 325 309	1931	2 001 976
1927	6 043 698	1932	1 137 890
1928	20 288 211		

Source: Hartwich, 433.

In 1927 the situation changed: the number of strikes shot up again, and arbitration awards and binding declarations were more frequently imposed. This development cannot simply be attributed to the restoration of prosperity: the upswing that had lasted until the middle of 1925 had had no such effects. Rather the new labour conflicts resulted from the politicisation of pay. This politicisation stemmed partly from the SPD's new theory of the political wage (a theory which served as self-defence since it gave both the unions and the SPD a new function).[87] An additional major cause of the new conflicts was, however, the development of public sector pay under Reich Finance Minister Köhler, for in 1927 civil service salaries were raised by up to 33 per cent.

Trade unionists—particularly Catholic unionists, but also members of the free unions—and SPD leaders were infuriated at the size of the Köhler settlement. After a speech from Adam Stegerwald, the Catholic union federation DGB resolved to refuse support in the future to any Reichstag deputy who voted for the pay award. The DGB proposed as an alternative that civil service pay should be linked to an index measuring the general level of German prosperity. Rudolf Hilferding described the pay award as a 'crime' and the SPD Minister-

[86] Hartwich, 434–7.

[87] *Protokoll über die Verhandlungen des Sozialdemokratischen Parteitages Kiel 1927*, Kiel 1927, 165–84.

President of Prussia, Otto Braun, tried to hold up the civil service reform in the second chamber, the Reichsrat. In the Reichstag debate, the SPD speaker complained that Köhler's Magdeburg speech had overtones of inflationism, and that it had led to immediate price increases because of prevailing attitudes to inflation. However, the SPD was still slightly cautious in public, and tried to avoid the appearance of attacking the civil service by blocking the Köhler proposals *tout court*.[88]

The unions responded to Köhler by increasing their demands: this became all the more urgent as there were indeed signs of a general price rise. In the Berlin metal industry, two separate demands each of an additional 5 Pfenning per hour, were met in 1927; elsewhere wages rose and unions wanted short-term wage contracts so that they might be speedily revised. But it was the white-collar employees who did best. For white-collar workers in Siemens und Halske sales departments in Berlin, wages rose in 1927 by 20.2 per cent (for a lower grade female employee) and by 17.2 per cent (for a man in a higher position). Metal workers' contract wages in Berlin by comparison increased by 13.6 per cent (Class IV) and 15.6 per cent (Class V).[89]

Some industries tried to pass on the wage rises as price increases: but these attempts were not always successful, and in some branches (such as the Berlin low voltage electrical industry), prices actually fell continuously between 1926 and 1928.[90] These links between wage and price movements became very important in the public discussions of the developments of 1927: who was racing ahead of whom in the inflationary spiral?

The sector where this conflict took its most acute form was the Rhineland-Westphalian metal industry. At the heart of the controversy was the issue of what proportion of industrial costs were represented by wages, and consequently what kind of price increases might be justified by reference to wage behav-

[88] Brüning 1970, 127–8. Schneider 1982, 601–2. *Verhandlungen des Deutschen Reichstages. III Wahlperiode 1924*, 394 11624A (21 Oct. 1927).

[89] From SAA C. Köttgen 11 Lf/100. Hartwich, 416–17.

[90] P. Czada, *Die Berliner Elektroindustrie in der Weimarer Zeit: Eine regionalstatistische-wirtschaftshistorische Untersuchung*, Berlin 1969, 185, 188.

iour. The answer to this question is surprisingly difficult to find, for two reasons: the first was the political sensitivity of the issue. Industry was unwilling to release statistical material which did not fully support the bombastic case about wages that its spokesmen were continually making in the press. Secondly, the release of such material raised sensitive questions about inter-industrial politics: many firms, particularly those controlling both mixed steel works and coal mines (a not uncommon arrangement), sometimes strayed beyond the bounds set by cartels for their internal price calculations. Prices within vertical concerns often did not correspond to those laid down in cartel conditions.[91] In addition, information about wage costs gave away secrets about levels of efficiency and modernisation.

Weisbrod, in the most exhaustive recent account of the subject, uses material offered to the Enquête-Ausschuß, and to the Commission on Industrial Costs headed by the economist Eugen Schmalenbach.[92] Weisbrod estimates that the share of wages in industrial costs remained approximately constant throughout the later 1920s: and that in 1929 it amounted to 51 per cent of the costs in hard coal mining, 13.2 per cent in steel rolling-mills, and approximately 67 per cent in combined works.

Internal memoranda, worked out for use within the big companies, do not support such a picture unambiguously. A memorandum prepared for company use within the Fried. Krupp AG shows that for the Essen works (the Gußstahlfabrik) wages as a proportion of non-material costs did *not* indeed change substantially during the Weimar Republic; but it also shows that as a proportion of *total* costs, wages *rose* considerably every year from 1927 to 1930, and that they were higher than before the war.[93] The Krupp case shows very well how a fall in raw material prices combined with difficulties in finding markets for steel, focused the attention of employers on wage costs (see Table XX).

[91] C. Wilhelms, 82, 92.

[92] Weisbrod 1978, 63–7. Enquête-Ausschuß, *Die deutsche Kohlenwirtschaft*, 128; and *Eisenerzeugende Industrie*, 76f. *Gutachten über die gegenwärtige Lage des rheinisch-westfälischen Steinkohlenbergbaus. Dem Reichswirtschaftsminister erstattet durch Prof. Dr. Schmalenbach, Dr. Baade, Dr. Lufft, Dr. Ing. Springorum, Bergassessor Stein*, Berlin 1928, 62.

[93] HA Krupp FAH IV C 73(b) 'Allgemeine Fragen der Geschäftsleitung der Firma 1908–32'.

Table XX: Fried. Krupp AG: Gußstahlfabrik Essen: Calculation of Costs

	1913/14	1927/28	1928/29	1929–30
Total costs (m. M/RM)	147.7	158.0	143.7	144.2
Non-material costs	43.2	51.6	60.9	66.1
(% of total)	29.2	32.7	42.4	45.8
Of which:				
Wages	11.2	13.1	15.9	16.9
General services	8.9	5.2	6.7	8.1
Taxes	4.0	5.0	7.1	7.6
Social expenditure	1.8	3.0	3.4	3.9
Voluntary welfare	3.8	2.8	3.1	3.3
Interest payments	3.7	2.6	5.3	4.8

Source: HA Krupp FAH IV C 73 (b).

A calculation by the GHH's Economic Department put the point in another, much more contentious and polemical, way: the wage increases awarded between 1925 and 1928 'cost the economy' 19–25b. RM: this was 7 per cent of national income and was roughly equivalent to the fall in investment from the pre-war level. Put in this way, the case is economic nonsense (it assumes a fixed sum for national income): but the calculation does reveal how the employers were thinking. The blame was attributed in the GHH's calculation to political events, particularly after the 1927 civil service pay episode. Scherer, the head of the GHH's Economic Department, concluded that the only way out of a system which caused such a vigorous wage push was a 'quick and thorough alteration of our whole parliamentary system (parliamentarism)', though he also added that at present such a goal would be difficult to achieve.[94]

For heavy industry there was an additional grievance: wages were politically determined, but so also were prices. The Reich Coal Council had been established in March 1919 as an alternative to the socialisation of the mines. It included representatives of the Reich, the Länder, of coal consumers, and trade unionists, as well as of the coal employers. Its primary function was to set prices. In Rhine-Ruhr in 1927 the show-

[94] HA/GHH 400127/0, 9 Dec. 1927 memorandum 'Wie steht es mit dem deutschen Wiederaufbau?' 400127/1, 4 Mar. 1929 memorandum: 'Belastung der deutschen Wirtschaft durch Steuern, Löhne und Gehälter, Soziallasten, Frachten'.

down began between heavy industry and the Government over the related issues of prices, wages, and employment policy. In May the Coal Council blocked an application of the Rhenish-Westphalian Coal Syndicate to increase prices on the provocative grounds that 'although Ruhr coal is not as prosperous as the public believes, a price increase must be rejected in consideration of the interests of the economy as a whole'.[95] The mine owners—often the owners of large integrated steel works—were furious. Steel industrialists reacted by ignoring the objections to price rises put by the Reich Economics Ministry and based on similar grounds to those put forward by the Coal Council. They were concerned too to make a point about the 'economy as a whole', namely that wage rises could not go on for ever. A price hike would teach the unions, and the politicians, a lesson.

After an arbitration award of 15 December 1927 laid down that overtime (over eight hours) was to be paid at a rate increased by 12½–25 per cent, iron and steel employers took the offensive for a second time. Prices for steel were increased again in January by 3RM/t. for cast iron, and then by another 4 RM/t. in May, despite renewed objections from the Reich Economics Ministry, hostile articles in the liberal press (particularly the *Frankfurter Zeitung* and the *Vossische Zeitung*), and falling steel sales. Indeed the third consideration—the declining market position of steel—increased the desperation with which the wage struggle was fought. Steel producers described the price increase as 'forced on us by the Reich Labour Ministry'.[96] The victory of the SPD in the election to the Reichstag in May, the formation of the Great Coalition Government, and the appointment of Wissell as Reich Labour Minister all helped to increase tension further; and in November the employers began the Ruhr iron lockout. This was a campaign directed primarily against state arbitration, and against the power of the Reich Labour Minister to declare awards binding. The conflict did not end with a clear victory for either side. The original arbitration award was revised downwards by the intervention of a second arbitrator, the

[95] C. Wilhelms, 82 f.

[96] Weisbrod 1978, 357, 373–85; and SAA 4/LF 716 (monthly reports of Vestag) (C. F. v. Siemens) Apr. 1928.

Reich Interior Minister, Carl Severing. Initial increases of 2–3 per cent were reduced to 1.5 per cent. On the other hand, the original arbitration award was left in force for a month to make the political point that it had been valid; and the employers encountered a great deal of unpopularity. The Reichstag voted, for instance, to provide financial support for the locked-out workers. And finally, the employers' front had broken up. Some industrialists, such as Gustav Krupp von Bohlen und Halbach had never been enthusiastic about the action. Krupp was terrified that the Klöckner works would steal a march on the Fried. Krupp AG's markets as Klöckner lay outside the Ruhr *Tarif* area, and was thus not affected by the lock-out. So he set out to weaken the employers' resistance, and in the end won: the Severing award was accepted. The men most discredited by the affair were the hardliners such as Paul Reusch, who contemplated resigning his office as Chairman of the Gruppe Nordwest of the VDESI and of the Langnamverein in protest against the pusillanimity of the employers.[97]

Reusch recognised that the 'moderates' such as Krupp had not won by discrediting the state or by intimidating the Interior Minister. Severing had revised his award on economic grounds: he had believed that the original arbitration award was too generous to the unions, and that the decline of world steel prices meant that a halt had to be called to the wage rises.[98] In other words, he was impressed by the employers' arguments, and not by Krupp's rather puny muscles. So the Severing award was a defeat for industry's political pretensions.

BRÜNING'S WAGE REVOLUTION

The wage increases continued in 1929, but although these were more frequently the result of arbitration than in the past, the number of cases in which the Reich Labour Minister imposed the awards as binding fell slightly from the high levels of 1927.[99] Wissell became much more cautious in his interven-

[97] Weisbrod 1978, 440–8. M. Schneider, *Unternehmer und Demokratie: Die freien Gewerkschaften in der unternehmerischen Ideologie der Jahre 1918 bis 1933*, Bonn 1975, 78–83.

[98] Severing II, 175.

[99] Figures given in Hartwich, 433–7.

tions in the labour market. A major break in policy occurred only after the replacement of the Great Coalition by the Brüning Government, however. From the middle of 1930 arbitration began to be used with a different policy goal. No longer would a Reich Labour Minister declare that he wanted to erect the *Sozialstaat*; instead the aim of state intervention was to achieve parallel reductions in prices and wages. The proposed means, however, caused friction with the employers, as well as with the unions.

The immediate background to the new policy was falling employment. Total employment declined from the middle of 1929; and March 1933 was the first month since February 1930 in which employment was greater than in the corresponding month of the previous year.[1] Employers believed that the level of wages was chiefly to blame as a cause of low investment, and hence of low output and declining employment; and at the same time they saw that the turnaround in the labour market could be used as a way of putting pressure on wages.

The socialist and liberal press sometimes voiced the suspicion that mass dismissals, which began to be common in 1930 at the time of the political change-over from the Great Coalition to presidential government, were being used as a tactic in wage negotiations. Labour Minister Stegerwald repeated the accusation, though business men not surprisingly tried to deny the charge; and Stegerwald tried to use the Labour Ministry's influence in awarding public contracts under work creation schemes only to firms which were not making mass dismissals or allowing high levels of overtime and thus exhibiting an 'anti-social behaviour'.[2]

The use of dismissal as a weapon in wage conflicts was particularly clear in the case of white-collar workers. Here the number of employees was less directly related to current levels of output than was the case for manual workers: clerical and technical employees were rather a kind of overhead charge. In addition, the high levels of skill in many cases, particularly with technical employees, made employers in general eager to keep their employees on as long as possible. Siemens reduced its

[1] Wagemann 1935, 12.

[2] *Frankfurter Zeitung*, 27 July 1930. WTB Agency report, 1 Aug. 1930.

blue-collar work-force from the beginning of 1929: by January 1930 there had been a cut of 12.4 per cent, while over the same period the number of white-collar workers *rose* (by 6.0 per cent); in the next year (to January 1931) these figures were respectively −20.4 per cent and −13.6 per cent; from January 1931 to January 1932, −25.6 per cent and −12.9 per cent; and January 1932 to January 1933, −13.5 per cent and −20.9 per cent. It was thus only at the end of the depression that really severe reductions in the number of white-collar workers were made (see Table XXI).

The same story is true in the case of IG Farben, though the contrast between dismissal of blue- and white-collar workers is less dramatic here. From January 1930 to July 1931 the

Table XXI: Employment at Siemens und Halske and Siemens–Schuckertwerke 1928–1934

	1928	1929	1930	1931	1932	1933	1934
Manual Workers							
January	71 042	72 173	63 244	50 371	37 477	32 430	39 435
February	70 432	71 394	61 085	48 829	35 599	31 988	40 718
March	70 695	70 026	59 023	47 494	34 393	31 834	42 754
April	69 667	69 636	57 487	46 647	33 665	31 565	44 511
May	70 236	69 585	55 503	45 784	33 447	31 575	46 339
June	71 167	70 186	54 955	45 625	33 742	32 252	48 146
July	72 042	70 990	54 195	45 487	34 455	33 683	50 867
August	72 879	71 266	53 849	45 458	34 042	34 424	52 869
September	73 198	70 841	54 257	45 199	34 535	35 697	53 948
October	71 772	69 958	53 688	44 152	34 748	35 522	53 809
November	71 662	69 084	54 003	42 444	33 895	36 966	53 311
December	72 188	67 192	53 401	40 830	32 430	38 650	52 969
White-Collar Workers							
January	28 398	31 338	33 210	28 681	24 971	19 762	20 302
February	28 706	31 564	33 163	28 431	24 553	19 676	20 541
March	29 196	31 725	32 989	28 276	24 165	19 636	20 792
April	29 419	32 040	32 711	27 839	22 980	19 343	21 323
May	29 256	32 251	33 361	27 747	22 607	19 339	21 701
June	29 531	32 329	32 058	27 721	22 523	19 463	22 057
July	29 780	32 503	31 646	27 429	21 502	19 435	22 474
August	30 145	32 677	31 265	27 307	21 337	19 578	22 847
September	30 322	32 817	30 504	27 119	21 214	19 725	23 191
October	30 633	33 032	30 126	26 471	20 535	19 608	23 411
November	30 928	33 191	30 056	26 118	20 336	19 798	23 621
December	31 114	33 264	29 734	25 906	20 259	20 046	23 898

Source: Compiled from SAA 29/Ls 774.

number of blue-collar workers fell by 23.1 per cent; the number of white-collar workers fell by 16.2 per cent.[3]

The decision to begin dismissing clerical employees in Siemens sprang directly from the frustration of its management over the issue of wages. In the summer of 1930 Köttgen, negotiating on behalf of Siemens–Schuckert, made a threat that the number of white-collar workers would be cut by 10 per cent if there was not agreement to work shorter hours without compensation for the loss of hours of work; the threat was put into effect when the unions failed to agree to the management proposal.[4]

Falling employment in heavy industry also affected wage negotiations there. In the western iron and steel industry, the number of jobs had been falling since the autumn of 1929 (see Table XXII). However, a major problem for the steel industry was that plants, and particularly the most modern works, operated very inefficiently at low output levels. The state's arbitration system recognised this problem, and in the summer of 1930 struck the first blow at the 1920s wage push. In July an arbitration award at Bad Oeynhausen removed the requirement previously in force as part of the December 1928 Severing award, that piece rates could not be altered in the light of productivity changes. Since productivity fell as levels of output declined, the application of the Oeynhausen principle meant a reduction of wage rates by 5–7 per cent: from 98.8 to 92.6 Pf/hr in foundries, and from 88.1 to 84.1 Pf/hr in the further stages of metal production.[5] These levels remained in force in the steel industry until July and August 1931 when further cuts were made.

As part of the settlement, price cuts were to accompany the wage cuts. After the clashes of 1927 and 1928 the connection between price and wage movements had been a major theme for political argument. The employers' organisation Arbeitnordwest in July 1930 agreed to a price cut in steel simultaneously with the reduction of wage rates, although the reduction eventually made was not as great as that originally

[3] Tammen, 78–9.

[4] SAA 11/Lf 430 (Köttgen), 28 July and 7 Aug. 1930 discussions in Reich Labour Ministry.

[5] *Ruhr und Rhein*, Wirtschaftszahlen 'Westen', 8 Jan. 1931 and subsequent issues.

Table XXII: Rhine-Ruhr Industry: Employment 1927–1932

		Coal	Iron and Steel
1927	January	415 496	185 145
	July	404 659	206 512
1928	January	398 140	216 961
	July	377 260	216 103
1929	January	365 104	207 605
	July	378 834	218 367
1930	January	383 478	200 441
	July	327 108	173 362
1931	January	287 956	145 615
	July	248 312	133 923
1932	January	220 054	105 646

Source: Compiled from *Ruhr und Rhein*, 'Wirtschaftszahlen Westen'.

demanded by some industrialists and by some consumers of steel. The debate on the extent of price reduction in the summer of 1930 reveals a great deal about inter-industrial disputes: the Vestag had modernised its plant in order to concentrate on the bulk production of steel, while the big vertical firms like the GHH worked much more with speciality steels and with a much more skilled labour force. Thus the Vestag was particularly keen to cut its costs by reducing wages, while it was happy to reduce prices substantially in the hope that this might keep up sales. The other works were much more reluctant to make large price cuts. Ernst Poensgen of the Vestag wanted a much more substantial cut than the 4RM/t. (=3 per cent) eventually agreed by the steel cartel, but only because he liked the theory of simultaneous large wage and price cuts as a way of dealing with the slump.[6] 4 RM/t. was too little to have a substantial effect either on demand or on the general price level.

The discussion on pricing was even more sensitive for the coal industry: for coal, unlike steel, was sold directly to a wide range of customers and affected the politically sensitive retail price index directly. In December 1930 coal prices in the Ruhr were cut by 9 per cent (from 16.89 RM/t. to 15.40 RM/t.) on the understanding that the state would use its authority to

[6] HA/GHH 400101293/10b, 10 June 1930 Reusch telephone conversation with Blank.

force a wage reduction. There was an element of bluff in this demand of the mine owners, for market forces meant that in practice they had little choice but to lower their prices. Director Lübsen of the GHH argued indeed that in making the coal price cut, 'we are sacrificing nothing: the reduction was long needed'.[7] In January 1931 mining wage rates in the Ruhr were cut by 6 per cent by an arbitration award after a very bitter conflict. Originally in December the mine owners had believed that they could cut the wage rates by 12 per cent. In January they thought that 8 per cent was reasonable, and that the 6 per cent figure represented a deception by the politicians and the wage arbitrators. One coal-owner went on arguing that economic considerations made a 20 per cent reduction necessary. As a countermeasure in reply to the arbitration award, the employers laid off all Ruhr miners from 15 January. They were then compelled by the Government's Emergency Decree to abandon their resistance and accept the 6 per cent award: this struggle damaged Brüning's relations with the Ruhr coal owners.[8]

The mine owners' offensive against the unions and also against the state continued throughout 1931. First they tried to use the threateningly high level of unemployment in order to worsen the miners' production quotas (*Gedinge*). In June they opposed the continuation of the existing wage rates, and in September they again demanded a 12 per cent cut. The urgency of their pleas increased after the devaluation of sterling in September strengthened the competitive position of British collieries. Brüning reacted to the massive pressure from the coal employers by stalling: he used an Emergency Decree in September to impose a cut, but only of 7 per cent. The cut was so small because both Brüning and Stegerwald were frightened by the increasing radicalisation of the miners. As an alternative to a larger reduction, the Government freed both employers and workers from unemployment and sickness insurance payments, thus making the reduction in wages less unpleasant for the workers and improving the cost position of the employers by means of what was effectively a subsidy.[9] Nevertheless, the mine owners continued to object that they had not been

[7] Tschirbs 1984. [8] Grübler, 173–6, 301–17, 330–5. [9] Tschirbs 1984.

compensated for the advantage achieved by the English through devaluation, and they tried to move quickly with yet another wage cut *before* the Government decreed a general round of wage reductions at the end of the year.

In the steel industry in 1931 a similar strategy was followed: prices were reduced just before the wage contracts were due for renegotiation. As in 1930, though, cast steel was reduced by a much smaller amount than had been demanded by the largest steel producer, the Vestag, which had been concerned to keep up sales and production figures at any cost. Whereas the Vestag had pressed for a reduction of 25 RM/t., the cartel price was eventually only cut by 9 RM/t.[10] Sales at below the syndicated price level did in fact become more common, but these did not have the obvious and immediate impact on wage negotiations of overall cartel cuts.

In the course of the year, Brüning grew more and more angry at the greed and obstructionism of the Ruhr coal and steel men. Sometimes he argued that the economic crisis was their fault anyway, a penalty for the irrational grandiose over- and misinvestments of the 1920s.[11] In the face of the protests of industry on the one hand and of the unions on the other he found it impossible to pursue a consistent course or to formulate clearly policy goals over the wage–price issue. The government spoke repeatedly of the need to reduce the costs of production, but almost as frequently it referred to the need to maintain working class incomes. These two arguments counterbalanced each other in a terrible stalemate, and what emerged in practice was often simply a muddle. Thus in the course of *one* conversation in August 1931 Stegerwald said first that it was impossible to cut wages any further; then he backtracked a little and agreed to accept a 10 per cent cut in wages; and then at the end of the discussion he told the employers that they should 'proceed vigorously so that they might achieve as much as possible [in wage reductions]'.[12]

[10] *Ruhr und Rhein*, Wirtschaftszahlen 'Westen'. Grübler, 307–8. HA/GHH 40101220/9a, 5 July 1930 Reusch to Kastl; 4 Oct. 1930 Scherer memorandum.

[11] *Kabinette Brüning* Doc. 312, Brüning in ministerial meeting 29 May 1931: 'industry had misdirected more capital than public authorities, with the exception of the communes' (1137).

[12] BAK NL ten Hompel 32, 21 Aug. 1931 meeting of Fonk, Horster, and Stegerwald.

Such was the confusion that the 'parallel policy' of simultaneously deflating wages and prices in the end produced. It was a policy guided by the intention of imposing sacrifice with a heavy-handed fairness. An alternative to using wage contracts and state arbitration as a way of imposing this sacrifice was for the state to take the indirect course of using public sector employment to set an example: this was also highly desirable from the budgetary point of view, as it helped to provide a solution to the problem of the deficits. Brüning believed that he might begin the process of adjustment of German costs to the changed world economic environment by attacking civil service pay: the Emergency Decrees imposed spectacular and exemplary cuts here.[13]

Brüning's 'parallel action' also involved pressure from the Government on German prices. Price cuts would affect wage negotiations through their effect on real wages. An Emergency Decree of 16 January 1931 lifted retail price maintenance on those brand goods not reduced in price by at least 10 per cent by the beginning of February.[14] In this case the Government was trying to manipulate the retail price index with an eye to wage bargaining, though agricultural products remained outside the scope of the Government's price reduction campaigns for fundamentally political reasons concerned with the powerful position of the large East Elbian landowners (this problem will be examined in the next chapter). Many big industrialists did in fact complain that food prices had not fallen fast enough, and that the failure to cut the cost of living had resulted in greater labour resistance to wage cuts. They argued too that costs in Germany were kept up because there were too many small tradesmen (*Übersetzung des Handels*); and they observed that this problem had become more severe in the depression as the number of small traders increased. Small barrow and peddling operations were run by those who had lost their jobs and who could not find other employment.[15]

Brüning succeeded in the immediate goal of cutting prices in

[13] See above, Chapter III.

[14] Grübler, 311.

[15] Examples in C.-D. Krohn, D. Stegmann, 'Kleingewerbe und Nationalsozialismus in einer agrarisch-mittelständischen Region: Das Beispiel Lüneburg 1930–1939', *AfS* 1977, 45–9.

the depression: perhaps too well. Falling demand produced a powerful reaction on retail markets. Special offers proliferated; free gifts were given by traders, and some shops (usually the larger retail units) offered up to 5 per cent or 6 per cent discounts for cash payments.[16] Small shopkeepers with low turnovers were horrified by these developments: they attributed more of the price collapse than they logically should have done to the Government's price reduction programme. Once the state started to intervene in the market, it had to take the blame for any unfavourable evolution.

Small shopkeepers and retail traders had suffered in the same way as larger industries from the rise in wages during the 1920s and from high levels of taxation. Overhead costs as a proportion of sales rose throughout the stabilisation period in retail business:[17]

1925	19.7 per cent
1926	21.0 per cent
1928	22.2 per cent

In the depression it proved extremely difficult to reduce overhead costs in retail business: at the end of 1932 costs in the textile trade were 90.2 per cent of their 1929 level, while turnover had fallen to 72.3 per cent.[18] Small shopkeepers blamed higher wages more generally too, for their difficulties: and believed that Brüning was unfairly trying to force shops, not workers, to make the major sacrifices of the slump. The 1920s had, they thought, brought higher incomes for the wrong people: and this had damaged rather than helped their businesses. The income distribution of the population had shifted so that the 'solid' public had disappeared and been replaced by fashion-conscious working class customers with a taste for shoddy goods and volatile fashions.[19] Small business in particular complained about the volatility of tastes: holding inventories had become very hard, and much greater capital outlays

[16] H. Uhlig, *Die Warenhäuser im Dritten Reich*, Cologne-Opladen 1956, 44–5.

[17] Ibid., 30.

[18] BAK NL Silverberg 641, 17 Dec. 1932 DIHT memorandum: 'Möglichkeiten der Hilfe für den Einzelhandel'.

[19] Enquête-Ausschuß, *Einzelhandel mit Bekleidung*, I 284 and II 197.

were required than in the days when shops could have been sure of being able to sell their goods at some time. Large stocks of very uncertain saleability had to be maintained now: 'It is difficult to sell a suit that has become unfashionable ... the public is not solid and wants trashy finery ... the old housewives' virtues have disappeared ... there has been a shift to better qualities if [textile] goods are visible, and a shift to lower qualities for less visible textiles' (i.e. showy blouses and skirts but shoddy knickers).[20]

These small shopkeepers would have had difficulty in adjusting to the new markets and the new ethos of the 1920s anyway. They found, though, at the end of the decade that the Government had set about reducing prices, and that the decent Catholic Chancellor Brüning was taking the side of the modern world against the solid bourgeois values which small retailers believed that they embodied perfectly. Thus they voted in droves for the Nazis.

Direct pressure on the labour unions thus began to look like a much simpler political approach to the economic problems of Germany than the indirect courses of attacking the civil service and retail trade. In the first place, the unions were politically and ideologically on the defensive. Their theories of the mid-1920s about a self-regulating capitalist economy moving inexorably towards greater social justice collapsed in the face of the slump.[21] Secondly, as unemployment grew, the negotiating power of the unions became weaker. Employers were aware of this weakness, but did not succeed in formulating coherent strategies to take advantage of their position. While some thought that they could use the wage contract negotiation system in order to enforce reductions, others wanted to use the depression to get rid of the contract and arbitration system altogether. In particular there was an attempt to appeal to the interests of the skilled workers. The Berlin metal industry abandoned contracts in the world depression: as in 1924–5, skilled workers saw advantages in being treated outside the framework of general wage negotiations, and the employers found it easy to break the solidarity of their work forces. The

[20] Ibid., I 79, 105–6.

[21] See E. Heupel, *Reformismus und Krise: Zur Theorie und Praxis von SPD, ADGB, und AfA-Bund in der Weltwirtschaftskrise 1929–1932/3*, Frankfurt and New York 1981.

Vereinigte Stahlwerks in 1930–1 similarly introduced a complicated system of differential wages in an attempt to break up the front of the steel workers.[22] Robert Bosch made a point of keeping on skilled workmen, despite low order books, even if this meant relegating them temporarily to less skilled jobs.[23]

The unions found it difficult to respond to the weakening of their position, and to the collapse of their political and economic dreams. Some unionists suggested ways of alleviating the effects of the crisis: Fritz Naphtali found it difficult to sacrifice his optimistic theory of the 1920s, and argued that new capital imports would restore economic prosperity.[24] This theme was quite often taken up in union demands: the Government should make political concessions, primarily on the security and disarmament issues, to France, so that political stability might encourage foreign capital to move in again. Wladimir Woytinsky, the statistician employed by the ADGB, believed that only international co-operation and international capital movements could bring the European economies out of depression.[25] In January 1931 Brüning summoned a commission of experts under the chairmanship of the former Centre Labour Minister Heinrich Brauns, to explain the causes of high unemployment and to suggest remedies. It included a distinguished socialist economist, Eduard Heimann. The Brauns Commission too saw as the major solution to Germany's economic ills an increase in capital imports from abroad.[26]

Other union proposals for solving the crisis depended on drastic price cuts. In particular a reduction in agricultural tariffs would reduce the cost of living, and increase purchasing power and demand. As with the international loans suggestions, however, the unions believed that such a proposal was frustrated by political calculations: in this case, by the power of the agrarians. The economist A. Löwe argued that it was necessary to cut prices in basic industries; Naphtali thought

[22] Seebold, 44. [23] Stolle, 211.

[24] F. Naphtali, 'Neuer Angelpunkt der aktiven Konjunkturpolitik oder Fehlleitung von Energien', *Die Arbeit* 7 (July 1931), 485–97.

[25] W. Woytinsky, 'Ausweg aus der Krise? Internationale Arbeitsbeschaffung', *Paneuropa* 7/9, Nov. 1931, 270–7.

[26] G. Kroll, *Von der Weltwirtschaftskrise zur Staatskonjunktur*, Berlin 1958, 377–80. *Gutachten zur Arbeitslosenfrage* Teil I–III, Berlin 1931 (Veröffentlichung des Reichsarbeitsblattes).

that a way of ending the crisis was to allow prices to fall further than wages.[27] Again there were thought to be political obstacles: the power of big capital. The union leaders could not believe that this power of big capital—like their own power—was vanishing to be replaced by the power of the street and of the ballot box.

Lying behind the union price argument was a more general theory about the economic effects of higher wages. The unions' proposals were often represented in a caricatured simplicity as a 'purchasing power theory': a universal increase in wages would raise purchasing power and thus restore prosperity. Woytinsky, for instance, argued that the economic crisis was caused by a disproportionality resulting from a reduction in the wage quota as a consequence of the rationalisation movement.[28] Other socialist theoreticians put forward an exactly contrary account of why increased wages would generate recovery. Jakob Marschak and Alfred Braunthal suggested that higher wages would lead to higher savings ratios: the Sparkassen and insurance funds would benefit and the funds available for capital investment would rise.[29]

Neither of these theories was completely absurd. There was indeed a shortage of capital in the 1920s; and there was a shortage of demand during the depression. But neither of the arguments solved the immediate question that employers believed they faced: the lower rates of profitability in the economic crisis. To improve these, prices would have to be cut *less* than costs.

Brüning's 'parallel policy' ran here into a major obstacle: despite the weakness of the unions, it was impossible to obtain their consent for the parallel reduction of wages and prices. In conditions of falling output and a radical and ideologically structured disagreement between unions and employers on how the fall could be reversed, the prospects for collaboration between employers and unions were poor. Two attempts to restore something similar to the Zentralarbeitsgemeinschaft of

[27] A. Löwe, 'Lohnabbau als Mittel der Krisenbekämpfung', *Neue Blätter für den Sozialismus*, 1930, 289–95. F. Naphtali, *Wirtschaftskrise und Arbeitslosigkeit*, Berlin 1930, 27. See also Heupel.

[28] W. Woytinsky, 'Ein Jahr der großen Not', *Vorwärts*, 31 Dec. 1930.

[29] Heupel, 75–6.

the immediate post-war period when unions and employers' organisations had worked together in the face of a major challenge, were made in 1930: in June, and then after the Reichstag election, in November and December. In the unions' draft for a joint programme of employers and employees, prices should be cut by the reduction of middlemen's profits (this was a way of avoiding a direct confrontation over the problem of industrial costs): and there should be no reduction in nominal wage rates until prices were cut. The RDI and the Employers' Federation VDA replied that the primary requirement for recovery was a reduction in industrial costs.[30]

New attempts to bring labour and capital together in the winter of 1930–1, this time in response to an initiative of Reich Labour Minister Stegerwald, broke down as the summer talks had already done, and for similar reasons. Only this time the sticking point came from the union side. Most employers were still prepared to make compromises in the face of an official initiative, such as Stegerwald's, simply to keep the Brüning regime alive. At a meeting of the ADGB's Federal Committee, however, only a minority of union leaders (Eggert and Tarnow) accepted the recommendation of the Chairman of the Committee that wages and prices should be cut in parallel. Brandes, Scheffel, Feinhals, Balleng and Bernhard stated that wages had already been savagely cut. Tarnow, of the Wood Workers' Union, pleaded in reply that it was nevertheless necessary to make 'a marriage of convenience' with the employers; but the other unionists beat him down, arguing that the employers' intentions were not serious.[31] The industrial interest groups were in fact negotiating in a vacuum, since they were powerless to commit their member firms on matters of price, whereas unions might bargain on behalf of their members. Neither the RDI nor the VDA had the authority to determine either prices or wages; and many firms and even regional interest groups (for instance, the Saxon Industrialists' Federation) opposed the RDI's conciliatory attitude to the

[30] Maurer and Wengst, Doc. 87c, June 1930 draft declaration of union representatives; Doc. 87d, June 1930 draft of union representatives for joint declaration of unions and employers; Doc. 99b, 26 June 1930 press release of RDI and VDA on discussions with unions.

[31] Ibid., Doc. 176, 14–15 Dec. 1930 ADGB Bundesausschuß; Doc. 183, 14 Jan. 1931 ADGB Vorstand.

Brüning regime. State Secretary Schäffer noted that he was not surprised that the unions were reluctant to trust employers in the negotiations, since industry had 'let itself in with a horde of White Guards'.[32]

Furthermore the unions felt themselves to be vulnerable, and this reduced rather than increased their preparedness to make concessions to capital. In 1929 there were 4.9m. free union members, but by 1931 only 4.1m. Unions would only weaken their grass-roots organisations and strengthen the RGO by conceding wage cuts; and the membership fall forced unions to become very defensive, as in 1924–5.

All the elements in the 'parallel policy' had thus collapsed by the summer of 1931. The worsening of the depression which followed after the banking crisis diminished even further the likelihood of co-operation between the representatives of different economic interests. When the idea of parallel action was revived at the end of 1931, it came in a very different and much more authoritarian guise. A voluntary agreement between unions and employers was now clearly out of the question. Brüning's new approach was akin to the schoolmaster knocking together the heads of two fractious boys in order to produce sense. On 13 October a letter from Hindenburg to Brüning was published which called for the creation of an 'Economic Advisory Council' (Wirtschaftsbeirat der Reichsregierung): the Council was designed to provide a replacement to the Reichstag, in which the parties were too strong. It met from 21 October to 23 November. Its members represented industry (five delegates), the unions (six), small employers (five), and banks, agriculture, and artisan producers (three each). This forum worked out the provisions of the Fourth Emergency Decree (8 December) which characteristically distributed sacrifices: wages, cartellised prices, and interest rates were all cut.[33] This new way of proceeding allowed Brüning to go ahead without the local consensus implied in the acceptance of arbitration awards: the experiences of the winter 1930–1 had been very painful when unionists and employers had defied the Government in this regard. The device of the Presidential

[32] IfZ ED93/18, 11 Feb. 1932 diary entry.

[33] See BAK R43I/1166, R43I/660, and R2/13640.

Emergency Decree also meant that the participants in the Advisory Council were not required to bear public responsibility for the consequences of their deliberations, for such responsibility would have rendered the Council ineffective immediately. And finally, the state no longer needed to stake its reputation in every labour dispute by declaring arbitration awards as binding: thus the December decree marked a decisive step away from the arbitration award and contract system of Weimar wage bargaining.

A twenty-one-member 'Central Committee' of the Provisional Reich Economic Council (Reichswirtschaftsrat) charged with producing schemes for public employment and work creation served in Brüning's eyes a similar function to that of the Advisory Council. The Committee was a way of bringing together unions and employers in a relatively harmless way, and thus in the end of providing some kind of legitimation for Brüning's rule.[34] It would not be divisive, since it need never refer to either the price or the wage issue; and it provided another forum for discussing economic issues without involving the Reichstag, which could not be relied upon because of the powerful position of the extreme parties. In this way a substantial part of economic policy-making might be effectively depoliticised. The Committee's meetings occurred between December 1931 and March 1932. Often they were depressing: as when a Director of the Reichsbahn explained that there would be little point in work-creation programmes designed to modernise the Reichsbahn, since the Reichsbahn was already the most modern railway system in Europe.[35] Eventually the Committee did draw up a list of labour-intensive projects, intended to reduce unemployment. The major schemes involved road building (for 800m. RM), flood protection (150m. RM), agricultural improvements (200m. RM), and house repairs (where the Reich would give credits of 300–500m. RM). The final report was, however, very unspecific about how these schemes might be financed: it was clear that the private banking sector could not be expected to form a consortium to lend the amounts of money required by

[34] ZStA VorlRWR 616, 618–19, meetings of Zentralausschuß.

[35] Ibid. 618, 25 Feb. 1932 (fifth meeting).

the Council's proposals. On the other hand, it was emphasised in the course of the discussion that the Reich budget could not stand the strain of a large work-creation programme, and that the Central Bank was not prepared to monetise the public debt.[36]

The Reichswirtschaftsrat Committee's plan was thus in practice consigned to Cloud-cuckoo-land. It had attempted to resurrect the collapsed corporatism of the mid-Weimar years, without making an attempt even to discuss the reasons that kept the parties of that corporatism apart in the depression; and, very importantly, the Council had not been able to work out a financing scheme. A similar air of unreality hung, for comparable reasons, about the union schemes of 1932. The political background of these resembled that of the deliberations of the Reichswirtschaftsrat Committee: both the Reichswirtschaftsrat and the unions were not trying to look for a way out of the crisis which would help everyone and offend no one.

After the financial crisis of 1931, unionists began to draw up proposals for 'alternatives' to the Brüning course. Such alternatives usually rested on a combination of monetary expansion with large public-works programmes. The proposals appeared to offer a way out of the union leaders' dilemma: they brought back the possibility of an agreement with industrial leaders and co-operation between opposing interest groups, while they did not depend on the acceptance of wage cuts.

These calculations arose out of the political context in which the unions functioned. Communist, and also to some extent Nazi, successes derived a great deal of support from unemployed workers. There were street battles, especially in Berlin and Hamburg, between the followers of the radical political parties; and the KPD had evolved its own paramilitary organisation—the Rot Frontkämpferbund (RFB)—in imitation of the Nazi SA.[37] The violence of the unemployed appeared to undermine the legitimacy of the Weimar political system: the Woodworkers' Union newspaper addressed itself to this prob-

[36] Ibid. 619, 4 and 8 Mar. 1932 (ninth and tenth meetings).

[37] E. Rosenhaft, *Beating the Fascists? The German Communists and Political Violence 1929–1933*, Cambridge 1983.

lem, and complained that the unemployed were being used as 'the tools of movements directed against the working class and against trade unions'. In order to prevent a permanent split, and a consequent weakening, of the working class, the unions believed that the level of unemployment needed to be reduced quickly: or at least, the unions needed to be seen trying to reduce the level of unemployment quickly.[38]

A second consideration influenced figures such as Woytinsky and Tarnow. The radical demands of some unionists for a complete overthrow of capitalism—these demands were propagated vigorously in the DMV (Metal Workers' Union) and by the AfA-Bund (the White Collar Workers' Union)—might well have a propaganda success with parts of the working class, and even attract back some of the lost support. But they would also antagonise the traditional political establishment. Just as critical for Tarnow's case was the need to make agreement with the old order: otherwise the establishment might turn, out of fear of a socialist transformation of society and economy, to the Nazis for help.[39]

The union programmes of 1932—first the so-called WTB (Woytisnky–Tarnow–Baade Plan) and then the plan accepted at the Extraordinary Union (ADGB) Congress of 13 April 1932, corresponded in other words to an urgent political necessity: they were intended as anti-fascist programmes, having the goal of bringing the working class and the unions back into the Weimar fold, and at the same time as ways of appeasing the grass-roots membership.

The building unions had already argued for government-financed work creation in 1930. In their industry employment depended very much on government orders anyway. Other trade unionists only took over the theme after 1931 and the collapse of employer–union negotiations, and after hopes for international action against the slump had faded.[40] Woytinsky, Baade, and Tarnow worked out their proposals at the

[38] W. Zollitsch, 'Einzelgewerkschaften und Arbeitsbeschaffung: Zum Handlungsspielraum der Arbeiterbewegung in der Spätphase der Weimarer Republik', *GG* 8, 1982, 103.

[39] U. Wengst, 'Unternehmerverbände und Gewerkschaften in Deutschland im Jahre 1930', *VfZ* 25, 1977, 114. Maurer and Wengst Doc. 176, 14–15 Dec. 1930 ADGB Bundesausschuß meeting.

[40] Zollitsch, 91.

turn of 1931–2. Initially Woytinsky still argued that a big international loan and international credit creation would be the best way of relieving unemployment in Germany.[41] Since this was no longer practicable in the light of the collapse of international capital markets in 1931, Germany should go it alone. One million men, Woytinsky calculated, could be employed for a year from the expenditure of 2b. RM. In March 1932 Woytinsky put the final stone of his proposal in place by tackling the problem that had perplexed the Reichswirtschaftsrat Committee: he now argued that a domestic credit creation within reasonable bounds would not be inflationary, and he calculated that as a result of his proposals only an additional 200–300m. RM would need to be placed in circulation by the Reichsbank.[42] Tarnow complemented this argument by explaining that cheap credit alone would no longer be sufficient to produce an economic upturn (*Konjunkturwende*) and that the state would have to use the additional credit to create supplementary demand in order to achieve an economic stimulus.[43]

The WTB plan was taken up as union policy at the 13 April Union Congress. Like the Reichswirtschaftsrat Committee's plan, the WTB proposals were labour-intensive and involved road building, agricultural improvements, flood protection, the construction of small dwellings, and Reichsbahn and Reichspost orders. They were to be financed through a general loan, and from long-term credits of the state-owned Reichskreditgesellschaft and other financial institutions.[44]

In the light of the fundamentally political purpose of the union plan, criticisms which show that the proposed expenditure would not in fact be likely to produce one million jobs are perhaps beside the point. More importantly, the plan also failed to meet the objections of union members tired of the conservatism, immobility, and lack of imagination of the union

[41] W. Woytinsky, 'Wann kommt die aktive Wirtschaftspolitik?' *Die Arbeit* 9/1, Jan. 1932, 11–31.

[42] W. Woytinsky, 'Arbeitsbeschaffung und keine Inflationsgefahr!' *Die Arbeit* 9/3, Mar. 1932, 142–54.

[43] ZStA VorlRWR 618, 21 Jan. 1932 Tarnow in meeting of Zentralausschuß.

[44] Reprinted in (ed.) W. Luthardt, *Sozialdemokratische Arbeiterbewegung und Weimarer Republik: Materialen zur gesellschaftlichen Entwicklung 1927–1933*, Frankfurt 1978, I 257–8.

leaders. It may thus not be a valid objection to the WTB plan to say that it demonstrated too much imagination: but the Union Congress was bitterly attacked within the labour movement and the April plan failed entirely to slow down the process of political radicalisation. Theodor Leipart, the ADGB's Chairman, complained in August 1932 that the 'union radicals are now abandoning evolutionary for revolutionary socialism ... he believed that the economy and the workers would be the ones to suffer most from this radicalisation'.[45]

The radicalisation continued because at a local level the issue of wage reduction still appeared to be the fundamental one. There was a successful strike against wage cuts in the Weissenfels shoe industry: and from 3 to 7 November 1932 the Berlin transport workers went on strike against the advice of the socialist union (the Gesamtverband). The strike in the Berliner Verkehrs-Gesellschaft was led—to the horror of Leipart and the union leaders—by both the RGO and NSBO, the Nazi shop-floor cell movement. The Berlin police arrested Communist and Nazi pickets alike as they stood side by side.[46]

Both the Metal Workers and the Factory Workers Union were so frightened by the continuing radicalisation that they dropped their commitment to the union work-creation programme.[47] Even at the time of the April Congress, many unionists had only swallowed the work-creation scheme because it had been presented as part of a package together with a more general plan for the reordering of the economy (*Umbau der Wirtschaft*): Tarnow had had to commit himself to schemes for the extension of socialisation (which he privately dismissed as 'music of the future') in order to rescue his ideas at the Congress. In June the ADGB and the AfA-Bund together produced a new programme which drowned the idea of work creation in a flood of much more far-reaching proposals. At the head of the new list stood the traditional demand for an 'increase of mass purchasing power', coupled with the complete restoration of the forty-hour week. Then followed the nationalisation of key industries; coal, iron and steel, cement, large chemical works, and electricity; the nationalisation of

[45] IfZ ED93/22, 10 Aug. 1932 diary entry.
[46] Heupel, 192–3. [47] Zollitsch, 106.

banks and insurance companies; the creation of a state trading monopoly for agricultural products, and state 'organisation' of trade in general; and finally the combination of a democratisation and decentralisation of industry with the erection of a central planning office.[48]

One way of expressing the criticism that the work-creation programme represented too much of a concession to Weimar, to industry, and to corporatism, was the argument that the real enemy of the working class was inflation. Inflation would strengthen the power of big business and agriculture; and inflation would be an inevitable result of the co-operation of labour unions with big business or agriculture during the depression. Max Cohen, for instance, argued that 'if it is not possible to raise new capital by the normal methods (loans), and if there is an artificial credit creation, ... there will be an inflation'.[49] Naphtali believed that the 2b. RM spending proposed in the WTB plan severely underestimated the amount required to find jobs for one million workers: an additional 1b. RM would be needed, and there would be inflationary consequences. Hilferding warned against inflation as 'the most terrible indirect tax'. The English devaluation of September 1931 'has made the crisis much worse and strengthened the social-reactionary tendencies which increase anyway in a crisis'. The threat of inflation was just an additional proof of the need for a change in economic organisation: 'for us socialists, this new and most pronounced appearance of capitalist anarchy, this failure of the credit organisations of the world ... is the new proof of the necessity of another and superior form of organisation'.[50]

In the end, neither the unions nor the SPD were able to produce immediate workable alternatives to Brüning's policy. The demands that the labour movement had to respond to—on the one hand conserving the loyalty of the grass roots, on the other negotiating in the political world of the early 1930s—contradicted each other too severely. The consequent demora-

[48] *Sozialdemokratische Parteikorrespondenz* 6–7, June–July 1932, plan of 21 June 1932.

[49] ZStA VorlRWR 618, 23 Feb. 1932 meeting of Zentralausschuß.

[50] *Vorwärts* 21 Sept. and 4 Oct. 1931. See also M. Schneider, *Das Arbeitsbeschaffungsprogramm des Allgemeinen Deutschen Gewerkschaftsbundes: Zur gewerkschaftlichen Politik in der Weimarer Republik*, Bonn 1975, 74 ff.

lisation was evident in December 1931, in a broad acceptance of the Emergency Decree by the SPD despite the wage reduction provisions. Wilhelm Keil, one of the SPD's finance experts and someone who in 1929–30 had been bitterly critical of the party's leadership for making too many concessions to the right, commented after Naphtali had attacked the Brüning measures at a meeting of the SPD Reichstag Fraktion: 'What is Naphtali's programme? I can see none. One should not overlook that the Emergency Decree contains, besides unsocial measures, also price cuts, rent cuts, and an interest reduction on the 30 billion borrowed capital. Above all—would the Decree be cancelled if we vote against it? Not at all. No government today would cancel the decree'.[51] This strange mixture of political calculation and respect for the symmetry with which Brüning had shared out the burdens of the depression was highly characteristic of a party and a labour movement resigned to failure and impotence. In a private letter, Rudolf Hilferding wrote rather sadly: 'there is no socialist solution to the crisis, and this makes the situation unprecedentedly difficult and allows the Communists and National Socialists to grow stronger'.[52]

The demoralisation of the union and socialist leaders, which first of all gave birth to the work creation programme and then strangled the infant in its cradle, started *before* the political events of the summer of 1932 which effectively ended the SPD's political chances. The SPD and the unions had justified their tacit support for Brüning by the need to 'stop fascism'. Their line was known as *Tolerierungspolitik*. But in May 1932 Brüning fell. On 20 July 1932 Reich Chancellor von Papen took over the Prussian ministries ('the Papen *putsch*') which had previously been controlled by an SPD coalition under Otto Braun: the union leaders advised against a general strike of the sort that in 1920 had defeated the Kapp *putsch*, since the Reich and the employers were likely, given the state of the labour market, to win.[53] Unionists wondered about the lessons to be learnt from this defeat: some were prepared to consider abandoning the SPD and joining the Christian and liberal

[51] W. Keil, *Erlebnisse eines Sozialdemokraten*, Stuttgart 1948, 407.

[52] IISG Kautsky papers KD XII 653, 2 Oct. 1931 Hilferding to Kautsky.

[53] Severing, II 357.

(Hirsch–Duncker) unions in an attempt to conserve what strength remained. The ADGB hesitated over the timing of such a merger, and the opportunity passed. Later, in December 1932, Leipart negotiated via intermediaries with Reich Chancellor von Schleicher about participation in government, but by the beginning of 1933 the talks had broken down.[54]

After the appointment of Hitler as Chancellor, the unions beat a retreat again. First they discussed with the Christian unions the formation of a unitary organisation appropriate for the new corporative state; this Einheitsgewerkshaft would also include representatives of the Nazi party. In April 1933 free trade union leaders (W. Leuschner, Theodor Leipart, Peter Graßmann) joined Christians (Jakob Kaiser, Bernhard Otte, Adam Stegerwald) and nationalist unionists (Anton Erkelenz, Max Habemann, Ernst Lemmer) in a union 'circle of leaders' (*Führerkreis*).[55] That such attempts of unionists to compromise with the Nazis were vain is demonstrated by the dissolution of the non-Nazi unions on 2 May 1933. The attempt to compromise was, however, nothing more than the logical outcome of an attitude which since 1931 had raised the question of the political survival of unionism to a position of primacy at a time when union support was disintegrating, and when the political system was less and less susceptible to the influence of unions.

The question of the strength of unions offers a curious mirror image to the question of the strength of employers: in the depression, employers remained obsessed with union power as a cause of the wage push; and unions were frightened of constructive economic programmes that might strengthen the might of the Ruhr barons. The trade unionist Feinhals for instance warned against a civil truce (*Burgfrieden*) that might benefit the employers. Both images, it has been suggested here, were almost grotesque exaggerations.[56] The unions were economically and politically emasculated by the depression; and the employers' organisations were rapidly breaking apart. But what survived longest in the debris of Weimar corporatism was

[54] Hentschel, 65. H. Mommsen, *Arbeiterbewegung und nationale Frage: Ausgewählte Aufsätze*, Göttingen 1979, 367.

[55] H. Mommsen 1979, 369.

[56] Wengst 1977, 113.

the image of the enemy. These images had corresponded to reality at particular, and relatively short-lived, moments: the image of powerful business men owed a lot to the political intrigues of 1929–30, and to the circumstances of Hermann Müller's fall. The picture of powerful and greedy unions was the creation of the period 1927–9 when wage rises were not matched by increases in productivity, and when political events and in particular the Köhler civil service pay increase fuelled wage demands.

The threat to profitability posed by the wage increases of 1927–9, which occurred in the phase when unions were most involved in negotiation procedures, and arbitration awards and binding declarations were most frequent, created a political climate unsympathetic to unionism: not just among big business, but especially with small producers and retailers. This climate put the unions on the defensive in the initial discussions in 1930 and 1931 over whether wages or prices should be cut first. The embarrassment about how to tackle the problem of whether to put wages or prices first caused the unions to retreat later, in 1931 and 1932, into proposals which they wanted to draw up, not primarily because they were practicable, but rather because they were ways of avoiding tackling practical problems.

VII

Agriculture

> In der Mark [Brandenburg] ist alles Geldfrage. Geld — weil keins da ist — spricht Person und Sache heilig.
>
> (Theodor Fontane, *Der Stechlin*)

In the story of the German economy agricultural politics played a role quite disproportionate to the size of agriculture's economic contribution. In 1925/9 agriculture, forestry, and fishing in fact accounted for only 16.2 per cent of German NDP.[1] Within agriculture, large-estate (chiefly East Elbian) farming enjoyed a political pre-eminence that also did not match its economic importance: only 10.9 per cent of German cattle and 26.2 per cent of cereal production were on farms of over 100 ha.[2] These two statements help to account for a major part of Weimar's economic difficulties.

THE LEGACY OF THE KAISERREICH, WAR, AND INFLATION

One of the simplest explanations for the political importance of agriculture in the Weimar Republic is that it still employed a very large work-force. In 1925 30.5 per cent of the economically active population was engaged in agriculture, forestry, and fishing.[3] Agriculture thus represented Germany's major low-productivity occupation, whose size gave it political significance. There was in Weimar an additional problem: policy-makers were burdened by the legacy of what had been at least partially successful solutions to the agrarian problem in the past.

Here the Kaiserreich cast a long shadow. The Empire's agricultural policy cannot be considered a failure if we wish to measure success in the quantitative terms. German agricultural

[1] Hoffmann, 33.

[2] M. Nussbaum, *Wirtschaft und Staat in Deutschland während der Weimarer Republik*, Berlin 1978, 347.

[3] Calculated from Mitchell, 54.

productivity was low before 1914 only in comparison with other parts of the German economy, but not with other European agricultures. Particularly in cereal farming, Germans had applied modern techniques in a systematic way. By 1907 97.4 per cent of farms over 100 ha. were using machinery; and even small holdings were substantially mechanised (the corresponding figures for farms between 5 and 20 ha. is 72.5 per cent). German farming stood in sharp contrast to the backwardness of her southern and eastern neighbours: for each steam threshing machine there were 111 ha. of land under cereal crops, while in Hungary there were 945 ha. and in Roumania 1194 ha. Even France was substantially less developed: there mechanisation scarcely went beyond the area of intense capitalistic cultivation of the northern plain.[4] Germany's lead in fertilizer consumption—partly a consequence of the existence of a strong chemical industry—was even more striking than her high degree of mechanisation. As a result of high levels of fertilizer application, yields rose spectacularly after the 1880s.

The introduction of a protective tariff on 1 January 1880 helped to keep up prices of grain: though they never reached the heights attained in the 1850s and 1860s, which looked in retrospect like the golden years of German agriculture. Farm prices rose too from the 1880s. The protective tariff kept things sweet not only for the big landowners of East Elbia—who in the 1890s were the main campaigners for the restoration of a higher tariff after Caprivi's reductions—but also for smaller farmers, both in cereal and mixed farming areas. It was actually the southern and western farmers who in the late 1870s had been the loudest advocates of tariff protection. In addition, the higher costs of animal feedstuffs which followed from the tariff were compensated by a system of strict veterinary regulation that kept out South European, Scandinavian, and Baltic animal and dairy products.[5] Indeed in many cases the smaller farmers, rather than the great

[4] D. Baudis and H. Nussbaum, *Wirtschaft und Staat in Deutschland vom Ende des 19. Jahrhunderts bis 1918/19*, Berlin 1978, 210. I. T. Berend and G. Ránky, *Economic Development in East-Central Europe in the 19th and 20th Centuries*, New York 1974, 49.

[5] J. C. Hunt, 'Peasants, Grain Tariffs, and Meat Quotas: Imperial German Protection Reexamined', *CEH* 7, 1974, 311–31.

Junkers, were the beneficiaries of the Government's agrarian policy: in areas such as the Lausitz small farmers bought and divided up the old great but unprofitable estates.[6] In general, agriculture was moving towards a greater degree of parcellisation rather than to the concentration of ownership which was occurring at the same time in other sectors of the economy. The knowledge that large estates were being broken up did not help to endear the modern world to the politically influential Junkers; they became more and more suspicious of technical change which they believed to be causing the demise of their class.

The 1880 tariff resulted in a politicisation of the countryside. Peasants came to believe that any difficulty that they might encounter could and should be overcome by the action of the state.[7] This lesson was learnt very effectively in the early 1890s, when a reduction of the tariffs on agricultural goods coincided with a sharp drop in cereal and hop prices and with an epidemic of foot-and-mouth disease among pigs and cattle. These agrarian catastrophes were not the result of Chancellor Caprivi's actions (even the reduction of grain prices was much too severe to be explained by the effect of the tariff reduction)[8]; but it appeared to many peasants that they were. Thus voting for the liberal Volkspartei finally ended in Württemberg; and the East Elbian Agrarian League (Bund der Landwirte), founded in 1893, won a substantial number of South German members.[9] From the 1890s the politics of the farm and the politics of the Reich became inseparably entangled.

The disputes about the tariff presented the most crippling of the legacies of the Kaiserreich. The tariff had been a suitable weapon in the war against the international price decline of the 1870s, but protection did not provide answers for every agrarian crisis. The price fall of the 1890s was only short-lived, but for reasons unconnected with the increase in protection levels in 1902 (the Bülow tariff). The general international price level

[6] J. Šolta, *Die Bauern der Lausitz: Eine Untersuchung des Differenzierungsprozesses der Bauernschaft im Kapitalismus*, Bautzen 1968.

[7] See D. Blackbourn, *Class, Religion and Local Politics in Wilhelmine Germany: the Centre Party in Württemberg before 1914*, New Haven 1980, 88.

[8] See charts in Baudis and Nussbaum 190–1.

[9] S. R. Tirrell, *German Agrarian Politics after Bismark's Fall: the Formation of the Farmers' League*, New York 1951.

began to rise from the mid-1890s for monetary reasons: the discovery of South African gold was sometimes credited with this world inflation, but a far more likely reason is the money creation of a rapidly expanding financial sector. Urban demand, too, increased and helped to stimulate agriculture: new concentrations of population were made possible by the suburban railway, and towns grew quickly. Politicians, nevertheless, liked to pretend that the tariff worked, and pretended too, like Chancellor Prince Bernhard Bülow, that they cared for the peasants.

Wilhelmine politics had created a nostrum—tariff protection—that was clearly incapable of dealing with the major international price decline which occurred during the 1920s. The tariff and associated measures (veterinary regulation and manipulation of railway freight rates) also allowed some types of agricultural production to survive without being forced to undergo a major change or rationalisation. Agricultural modernisation before the Kaiser's War meant producing more with machines and also meant employing fewer labourers; but it rarely meant modernising product structures. The area of rye cultivation expanded, although the market for rye was disappearing as higher levels of income produced changes in urban taste. However, the most important failures occurred outside cereal farming. There were no uniform standards for milk and dairy products; and modern marketing techniques were made impossible by the diversity of qualities. The co-operative movement on the land was ill-developed and failed to set uniform standards. There were 40 000 different co-operatives in Germany. Of these 8 000 were grouped in the Raiffeisen association, and 12 000 were associated in a Reichsverband; the rest were local.[10] Even in cereals, where standardisation should have been easier, there were problems: 400 varieties of wheat were grown in Germany.[11]

Veterinary health was poor. Those farmers in southern Germany who had benefited so much from the hygiene regulations which excluded south European products were throwing stones in very transparent glasshouses. Tuberculosis was rife

[10] G. Stoltenberg, *Politische Strömungen im schleswig-holsteinischen Landvolk 1918–1933: Ein Beitrag zur politischen Meinungsbildung in der Weimarer Republik*, Düsseldorf 1962, 74.

[11] *Wirtschaftsdienst*, 12, 22 Apr. 1927.

among German cattle. In 1912 one quarter of slaughtered cattle had damaged or unusable lungs.[12] One of the reasons that margarine was so attractive to consumers in the Kaiserreich (to the chagrin of the farmers) was that it was not produced by cows suffering from tuberculosis or brucellosis. Standards did not improve during the War or in the 1920s.

Instead the War and inflation in general weakened German agriculture substantially. Sometimes the farmer has been depicted as one of the major beneficiaries of the price inflation, since the considerable burden of pre-war agrarian debt virtually disappeared. But a substantial volume of agrarian savings (4.5b. M) was wiped out; and the peasants generally felt that they had lost out as a result of the inflationary process.[13] At the outbreak of war agriculture had suffered from a loss of labour as farm workers went to the front. Many smallholdings had to be left in the hands of women and children for the duration; and often this change was permanent, as many peasant farmers did not come back from the war. Fodder, fuel, and fertilizer was expensive and difficult to obtain.[14]

As a result, there were serious falls in productivity; and the quality of land as well as livestock and buildings deteriorated. It took a long time after the end of the inflation for the pre-war yield to be achieved once more (Table XXIII). The average

Table XXIII: Cereal Yields in Germany 1913–1924 (100 kg./ha.)

	Rye	Wheat	Barley	Oats	Potatoes
1913[a]	19.3	24.1	22.0	22.0	157.1
1921	15.9	20.4	17.1	15.8	98.8
1922	12.6	14.2	14.0	12.5	149.4
1923	15.3	19.6	18.1	18.3	119.5
1924	13.5	16.6	16.6	16.0	131.9

[a] Post-war area.

[12] *Statistisches Jahrbuch 1913*, 53.

[13] M. Sering (with F. Neuhaus and F. Schlömer), *Deutsche Agrarpolitik auf geschichtlicher und landeskundlicher Grundlage*, Leipzig 1934, 113.

[14] Recently: J. Osmond, 'Peasant Farming in South and West Germany during War and Inflation 1914 to 1924: Stability and Stagnation', in *Die deutsche Inflation: Eine Zwischenbilanz*, 289–307.

Table XXIV: Average Weight of Slaughtered Animals 1906–1924 (kg.)

	Oxen	Cows	Calves over 3 months	Pigs
1906	330	240	185	85
1921/2	306	209	161	83
1922/3	278	206	156	87
1923/4	294	220	166	88

weight of slaughtered animals (particularly in the case of beef and veal) fell; and the animal population fell too, and only began to rise again after the stabilisation of the currency in 1923–4 (Tables XXIV and XXV).

Table XXV: Number of Animals in Germany (December) 1913–1924 (m.)

	Cattle	Pigs	Poultry
1913[a]	18.5	22.5	71.9
1922	16.8	15.8	67.8
1923	16.3	14.7	65.2
1924	17.3	16.9	71.7

[a] Post-war area.
Source of Tables XXIII–XXV: Statistiches Jahrbuch 1927, 56–7, 66, 62–3.

The position of the farmer was made worse by the price controls which were applied from an early stage in the War. Rye, wheat, barley, yeast, potatoes, feedstuffs, and sugar were controlled from 1914. Food controls remained in force longer than any other wartime price ceilings. Butter and milk were deregulated only in the summer of 1921. Some sales of food occurred, it is true, at black-market prices: particularly towards the end of the War, when one-third to one-half of fruit, meat, and eggs were sold on non-official markets.[15] The social upheavals of 1918–19, however, meant that the authorities were particularly eager to enforce controls on food prices in order to minimise urban discontent. Cereal products in particular could be very carefully controlled, with inspectors measuring the total area of production and taking samples in order

[15] Holtfrerich 1980, 84, 89, 91.

to assess the yield before the harvest was taken in: this made it difficult to divert food from the controlled market.[16]

Furthermore, peasants were often slow to react to such economic activities as the inflation offered. Black-market activities usually required more skill than traditional German blunt peasant cunning. Often peasants complained that they were victimised by middlemen: and in those areas where rural small traders were almost exclusively Jewish (Franconia and Thuringia) the anti-Semitic flame was fanned.[17] In fact the peasants were complaining about nothing more irrational and nothing more exploitative than the rational operation of a market. The price scissors had moved, largely as a result of the fallen income levels during and after the War, against agriculture. A contemporary survey of 1920 showed that crop prices were seven to eight times the pre-war level, while farm production costs were ten to sixteen times higher.[18]

It is easy to see why peasants felt victimised by the state, by middlemen, and by the consumers: they blamed the way the market operated on the machinations of all of these. As a result they flocked to the Freikorps and the so-called Patriotic Associations. These organisations set out to attack not only the principle of revolution, but also the Republic which permitted inflation profiteers to operate. They denounced their enemies as international: on the one side the Red International of the workers, on the other the Golden International of (Jewish) finance. In June 1921 30 000 peasants from all over Germany gathered in Rendsburg (Schleswig-Holstein) to hear the Bavarian 'peasant doctor' Georg Heim denounce the Berlin authorities as *volksfremd* (alien) because they had imposed a regime of economic control (*Zwangswirtschaft*). In 1922 and 1923 widespread tax boycotts were organized on the land. Schleswig-Holstein 'werewolves' (rural terrorists) announced in 1923–4 that they were fighting a war against Marxism and against the

[16] R. G. Moeller, 'Winners and Losers in the German Inflation: Peasant Protest over the Controlled Economy', in *Die deutsche Inflation: Eine Zwischenbilanz*, 263–75.

[17] M. Sering, *Die deutsche Landwirtschaft unter volks- und weltwirtschaftlichen Gesichtspunkten*, Berlin 1932, 340. H. H. Hofmann, 'Ländliches Judentum in Franken', *Tribüne: Zeitschrift zum Verständnis des Judentums*, 1968, 2890–904. G. Pridham, *Hitler's Rise to Power: the Nazi Movement in Bavaria 1923–1933*, New York 1973, 240.

[18] Hugo Hagemann, quoted in Osmond, 295.

'mammonistic self-interest of the entrepreneurial representatives of economic liberalism'.[19]

On the big cereal estates the same bitter atmosphere prevailed. The latifundia provided the secret meeting places for the Freikorps and the terror organisations; and East Elbian barns were the ideal place to store arms in preparation for a rising against the state. Particularly where widows (in many cases war-widows) entrusted their estates to so-called estates administrators (*Gutsverwalter*), violence was the order of the day. The *Gutsverwalter*, like the new managers in Ruhr collieries, were politically more radical than the old Junkers: the Freikorps Rossbach, for instance, was largely run by *Gutsverwalter*. In 1920 and 1923 after the failure of attempts at a *putsch* by the right, the *putschists* slipped back into the countryside of Mecklenburg and Pomerania,[20] where they continued to dream up irrational politics while actually applying more and more irrational economics.

The only kind of hope that German governments were able to hold out to the angry disillusioned farmers was the promise that, once the currency was stabilised and once Germany was free again to reinstitute her own tariff system (the Versailles Treaty placed limits on Germany's sovereignty regarding tariffs until January 1925), the old protective mechanism might be brought once again into play. Tariffs were still treated as the cure-all for agrarian problems. One Minister of Agriculture in the inflation reminded farmers of their dependence on the state: 'the agricultural sector should not forget that some day it will not be able to live without the protection of the Government'.[21] He meant tariff protection.

STABILISATION PROBLEMS

The process of stabilising the currency in 1923–4 dealt a further blow to German agriculture, and particularly to cereal farmers. The harvest of 1923 was gathered and sold during the final weeks of the hyperinflation, when money was at its

19 Stoltenberg, 61–2 and 81.

20 R. G. L. Waite, *Vanguard of Nazism: the Free Corps Movement in Postwar Germany 1918–1923*, New York 1952, 190 and 228.

21 R. G. Moeller, 274.

maddest. Only in some cases was the crop sold for dollars or other fixed values.[22] The Mark was stabilised in November, when the exchange rate of 4.2 billion in the European sense (10^{12}) to the dollar was established and held. In December and January a heavy tax programme was devised to remove one of the major causes of the German inflation, the unbalanced budget. The tax levels of the Second Tax Emergency Decree (December 1923) and the Third Decree (February 1924) were a shock to an agricultural sector that had been treated with extraordinary leniency under the Kaiserreich. Overall for the period 1924–30 tax levels on agriculture were estimated at 3.7 times the pre-war level.[23]

Farmers often borrowed to pay these taxes. They also borrowed in order to buy seed corn, fertilizer, and badly needed new implements.[24] In consequence the pre-war debt was quickly re-established. Finally, some farmers borrowed because inflation had at last established itself so much as part of their pattern of expectations that they could not believe that the stabilised currency would last: they thought that a new inflation would once more favour those who borrowed most. Such calculations in fact appeared reasonable once rather dramatic price rises occurred again in the early months of 1924. Later, when enquiries were made as part of the investigations into the Osthilfe scandal, it emerged that many large farmers had borrowed in the immediate post-stabilisation period in order to buy automobiles or to take holidays on the French Riviera. One Weimar Agriculture Minister, Hermann Dietrich, who was himself a farmer, estimated that of the debt incurred by farmers between 1924 and 1930 (8b. RM), only 3b. RM had been used for productive purposes.[25] This agrarian debt problem, which came to overshadow all discussion of agricultural policy in the Weimar Republic, originated in 1924 and in the adjustment to the world of a stabilised currency.

[22] Enquête-Ausschuß, *Untersuchung zur Lage der Landwirtschaft in den Provinzen Pommern, Niederschlesien, Oberschlesien und Grenzmark Posen-Westpreussen*, 15–16.

[23] Sering 1932, 41.

[24] For example, BAK R43I/634 6 Dec. 1925 meeting: statement by Minister of Agriculture of Mecklenburg-Schwerin.

[25] B. Buchta, *Die Junker und die Weimarer Republik: Charakter und Bedeutung der Osthilfe in den Jahren 1928–1933*, Berlin 1959, 31. E. Welter, *Die Ursachen des Kapitalmangels in Deutschland*, Tübingen 1931, 170–1.

When in spring 1928 peasants all over Germany refused to pay tax and boycotted suppliers of agricultural equipment, a survey found that the substantial tax arrears went back to 1924–5.[26] The short-term agricultural debt, which later proved so difficult to handle, was in the main contracted in 1924–5, when farmers borrowed short because the long-term market was not operating well and because they expected interest rates to fall (see Table XXVI).

Table XXVI: German Agricultural Debt 1925–1930 (m. RM)

	Secured loans	Medium-term loans	Short-term credits	Total
31.12.1925	1 011.3	25.8	2 186.1	3 223.2
31.12.1926	2 048.5	101.8	2 127.0	4 277.3
31.12.1927	2 814.4	304.4	2 565.8	5 684.6
31.12.1928	3 623.3	318.0	2 889.8	6 831.1
31.12.1929	4 117.1	360.4	2 865.2	7 342.7
31.12.1930	4 373.0	330.2	3 088.1	7 791.3

Source: Reichskreditgesellschaft, *Deutschlands wirtschaftliche Entwicklung im ersten Halbjahr 1931*, 39.

On the other hand, no one was very worried by agricultural debt in 1924–5. On the contrary, the Government tried to follow a strategy of encouraging agricultural investment, in order to make up for the long period of neglect during the War and the inflation. This involved encouraging farmers to borrow more; and credit policy was biased towards agriculture through conscious decision. In the initial years when the Reichsbank imposed a severe credit restriction (1924–5) it aimed to make cheap money available to agricultural borrowers. To its critics the Reichsbank replied that additional investment in agriculture would reduce the amount of food that Germany needed to import and would thus improve the balance of trade.[27] As the period of credit restrictions drew to an end, new institutions were set up to lend to agriculture on privileged terms: in July

[26] ZStA RFM B778, 2 May 1928 Reich Agriculture Ministry memorandum: 'Richtlinien zum landwirtschaftlichen Notprogramm'.

[27] E. Salin, *Staatliche Kreditpolitik*, Tübingen 1928, 18–20. BAK R43I/634, 5 Dec. 1925 Schacht address to representatives of Länder on finance programme; R43I/2538, 9 June 1926 Discussion in Reichsbank with leaders of RLB.

1925 the Rentenbank-Kreditanstalt began to supply long-terms loans. In 1926 the Deutsche Golddiskontbank, which originally had been an instrument to obtain foreign loans for the mark stabilisation, was transformed into an agricultural loan bank. Both these institutions sought loans for agriculture from abroad. In Prussia, the Preußische) Zentralgenossenschaftskasse (Preußenkasse) lent to farmers; and the large Berlin banks were encouraged to become involved too.[28] Already before the War, the Dresdner Bank had had an agricultural mortgage department; its activity here now expanded.

The effects of these operations can be gauged by the fact that the post-stabilisation period is the only time in modern German history when the share of agriculture in the national capital stock *rose*.[29] Their success might also be measured by the rise in agricultural yields, so that the set-backs of war and inflation were made good. The figures expressing debt as a proportion of tax-assessed value indicate how serious the debt problem had become in East Prussia and Silesia. But by 1929 very few farms were profitable; and high interest payments represented a major cause of farm unprofitability (see Tables XXVII and XXVIII).

Agricultural credit appears to be another case of the bias in lending in the 1920s in favour of big units. The bias meant the encouragement of the least efficient forms of agricultural enterprise: and the number of large units in agriculture continued to fall in the 1920s, despite the peculiar distribution of credit. It also allowed the dedication of an excessive area to rye cultivation, although the market for rye went on shrinking. The area under rye rose from the end of the inflation until 1926, and did not decline significantly until 1930.[30]

The debt situation became so difficult because of the development of agricultural prices. The price scissors which in the War and inflation had moved against agriculture remained unfavourable. Agricultural prices were relatively lower than industrial prices as a consequence of a new economic structure, and not merely of peculiar circumstances prevailing during the inflation. According to the Statistisches Reichsamt, artificial

[28] See Schacht's statement to German bankers in 1925: *Verhandlungen des VI. Allgemeinen Deutschen Bankiertages zu Berlin 14–16 September*, Berlin 1925, 294–6.

[29] Hoffmann, 44.

[30] Ibid., 274.

Table XXVII: Debt of German Farms on 1 July 1929 (RM/ha.)

Size of farm (ha.)	East Prussia	Silesia	East Central Germany	Central Germany	North-west	Rhineland and South-west	Bavaria
5–20	—	528	558	521	536	366	518
20–50	555	612	520	514	576	469	429
50–100	550	853	583	709	641	690	563
100–200	645	826	734	795	827	—	—
200–400	650	840	703	916	705	—	—
over 400	506	801	584	—	—	—	—
Average	570	666	599	611	583	414	497
As percentage of tax value of 1928							
5–20	—	37	59	26	31	28	43
20–50	68	37	47	28	33	31	34
50–100	64	52	57	34	34	35	41
100–200	79	56	73	39	42	42	—
200–400	76	57	71	48	43	—	—
over 400	68	61	57	—	—	—	—
Average	69	45	59	31	33	30	40

Source: Sering 1932, 53.

Table XXVIII: Proportion of Farms operating at a loss or with Interest Payments higher than 105% of Net Return, 1 July 1929 (%)

Size of farm (ha.)						
	5–20	20–50	50–100	100–200	200–400	400+
East	66.9	72.2	80.3	83.8	86.6	85.9
South and West	63.3	61.5	65.5	78.2	84.4	—

Source: Sering 1932, 48.

fertiliser prices remained at their pre-war level; but buildings and agricultural machinery increased in price more than agricultural products.[31] Taxes and social welfare contributions pushed up farm costs; and wages on the land were substantially increased. By 1927/8 rural wages were 50 per cent above the pre-war level. Wages continued to rise until 1929. This rise affected East Elbia more severely than south-west Germany, where smaller units relied much more on family labour.[32]

As long as agricultural prices rose, there appeared to be no real debt problem, however: even if, as was the case, the price rise was less than increases in industrial products. A price fall would be disastrous; and in 1927–8 there were indeed the first signs of difficulty. This was the beginning of the German agrarian crisis. Since 1925, the world wheat price had fallen; but because of Germany's tariff, German prices were sheltered and cereal prices only began their decline in the middle of 1927.[33] In late 1927, farmers argued that the tariff was no longer working: for, as a consequence of the expansion of German production, German wheat prices actually lay *below* world market prices, while rye prices fell to only just above the world level.[34] There was a set-back at the end of 1927 in livestock (especially pig) prices also.[35]

As the price dip began to be pronounced, the credit difficulty became acute. In addition, the rise in short-term interest rates at the end of 1927 raised costs; and in 1928 it became more difficult for farmers to borrow for the long term. In June

[31] Sering 1932, 40–1. [32] Ibid., 41, 141–3 (Table 44).
[33] Kindleberger, 88; Svennilson, 92.
[34] *Statistisches Jahrbuch 1928*, 350–1. Sering 1932, Stat. Appendix 60–1.
[35] Ibid., 352–3.

1928 the Ostpreußische Generallandschaftsdirektion found itself unable to raise money for German farmers on the American market. Absolutely characteristically, the farmers blamed the allegedly anti-agrarian policies of the Reich Government.[36] In reality, the credit difficulty of 1928 was a consequence of a growing scepticism about agricultural loans: farmers were now borrowing at a substantial premium over the costs of credit for German industrial borrowers or municipalities. The premium reflected a realisation on world financial markets that agriculture had a murky future: the signs of a major and continuing decline in world prices were too clear to be ignored.

AGRARIAN RADICALISM: THE RESPONSE TO THE FARMERS' CRISIS

The voting behaviour of the non-Catholic peasantry in Weimar Germany was highly unstable. Turn by turn peasants were disappointed by their elected representatives, who failed to do anything about their miserable economic position; and at the next opportunity they voted for different representatives. The DNVP had replaced the liberal parties and sometimes even the SPD in peasant favour by 1924; but from 1928 the Nationalists' hold on the land was eroded. The major cause of this was the developing debt and price crisis.

A farming sector that had survived in 1924–7 by borrowing more and more, in 1928 found its means of salvation cut off, and it became radicalised. On 28 January 1928, 140 000 peasants marched in protest in Schleswig-Holstein.[37] The march was followed by tax boycotts. By April 1928 only 36 per cent of the tax due in Schleswig-Holstein had in fact been collected. Despite official concessions (in February the Finance Ministry agreed to allow a postponement of payments to the Rentenbank in cases of particularly high debt) the unrest continued.[38] The Reichstag elections of May 1928, which in urban Germany reflected the relative stability of the prosperity phase of Weimar democracy, in the countryside were held

[36] e.g. BAK R2/2065, 27 June 1928 Prussian Minister of Agriculture to Reich Finance Minister.

[37] Stoltenberg, 111.

[38] ZStA RFM B780, 10 Feb. 1928 circular.

under the shadow of the agrarian crisis. The victors of 1928 on the land were to some extent the small peasant parties: the Christlich-Nationale Bauern- und Landvolkpartei won 1.8 per cent of the Reich vote (and was represented by ten deputies in the new Reichstag), the Landbund won 0.6 per cent, and the Deutsche Bauernpartei 1.5 per cent. These peasant parties still did well in the next Reichstag election (September 1930); after that the protest vote was taken over by the NSDAP. Peasant votes for some of the larger parties increased too in 1928: particularly if those parties had been involved in opposition to the right-wing *Bürgerblock* governments of 1924–8. The SPD was equipped after the 1927 Kiel Congress with a new agrarian programme which spoke of a 'deep solidarity of the interests of the workers and of the working peasantry'; and which promised the peasants free legal aid (to sort out their credit and tax problems) and free technical advice in order to raise the productivity of German agriculture.[39] In 1928 the SPD increased its rural vote. In some areas the KPD (Communist Party), too, managed to get votes out of rising rural discontent. The peasant wings within the Centre, the Bavarian People's Party, (BVP) and the Democratic Party were also strengthened.

As the SPD, Centre, BVP, and DDP were in the government coalition after 1928 and could only partially solve the agrarian question, peasants continued to shift their political allegiance. In Schleswig-Holstein a new organisation, the Landvolkbewegung, established itself: the leaders of this new movement were hostile to any form of central state control or taxation and began in 1928 a campaign of direct action.[40] This started with the use of violence against bailiffs attempting to confiscate cattle in order to claim tax arrears; but by 1929 the direct action developed into a series of bombings carried out with the help of explosives experts from the terror organisation of the early 1920s, Organisation Consul.[41]

The new peasant movements were radical and hostile to all established political parties. Some of their members believed that even the NSDAP was 'too soft' and 'not revolutionary

[39] IISG NL Braun 7/370, 3 Jan. 1927 Baade to Braun (draft report of SPD Agrarian Commission).
[40] Stoltenberg, 113.
[41] Ibid., 124, 137.

enough'. Nazism and Communism both tried to embrace the peasant unrest:[42] when one of the bombers of 1929 was on trial both the KPD and the NSDAP tried to persuade him to stand as a Reichstag candidate. Peasant communism was still in evidence in some areas in the 1932 elections (in Kremperheide, Schleswig-Holstein), when almost all the Schleswig-Holstein peasantry had turned Nazi; and there were cases of Nazi agrarians, such as Bodo Uhse and Bruno von Salomon, who joined the KPD.

The exact nature of the political programmes of the KPD and NSDAP played little role in attracting peasants: what mattered was the strength of the parties' opposition to the status quo. Eventually the agrarian radicalism directed against the state, against tradesmen, middlemen, and bankers, worked principally to the advantage of the NSDAP. However, in the early stages of the agrarian crisis, before the Nazi grip on the countryside really tightened, German agrarian radicalism resembled rather strongly the anarchist agrarian unrest common at that time in Europe: in Russia at the end of the First World War, in parts of Italy, and particularly in Spain.[43] These anarchist elements in the peasantry were most in evidence in those areas where there were no big estates: in Upper and Lower Bavaria, and the west coast and the less fertile inland areas (the Geest) of Schleswig-Holstein.

By 1932 the agrarian pressure groups had been taken over by the NSDAP: for once the Nazis noticed the potential peasant protest vote, they began a major propaganda effort in the countryside. But peasant protest antedated the Nazification of the peasantry. It was surprisingly late (March 1930) when the first Nazi agricultural programme was drawn up; and only later in that year was an agrarian political *Apparat* under Walther Darré created.[44] Moreover, the peasant Nazis always looked very different to the urban party members: the semi-anarchist tradition remained. The Schleswig-Holstein NSDAP, for instance, was under the control of the son of a Dithmar-

[42] Ibid., 136.

[43] E. Hobsbawm, *Primitive Rebels: Studies in Archaic Forms of Social Movement in the 19th and 20th Centuries*, Manchester 1959, 57–107.

[44] J. E. Farquharson, *The Plough and the Swastika: the NSDAP and Agriculture in Germany 1928–1945*, London 1976, 15.

schen marsh farmer. Gauleiter Hinrich Lohse had first worked as a bank clerk, and then become the spokesman for the peasantry's hatred of money and of finance capital. A more sophisticated town Nazi sneered at Lohse and his rural friends: 'for people of that sort the idea of "breaking interest serfdom" was just as much a holy conviction as in other places belief in an immediate Second Coming is'. Krebs, who had a Ph.D. and was the Nazi Gauleiter of Hamburg, described Lohse as 'bourgeois': by which he meant, confusingly, peasant. Nazi philosophy mattered little to the peasant Nazis. Lohse 'could have fitted in just as easily with the Economic Party or one of the other middle-class parties', since the peasants of Dithmarschen were 'not concerned about the "Third Reich" as an ideal to be realised in the future. What mattered to them were their farms and freedom from tax officials, which does not mean that they were so narrow minded as not to know that the farm and the Reich were somehow tied up with each other. Lohse too, in my opinion, was concerned about "the farm".'[45]

The Schleswig-Holstein experience was closely paralleled elsewhere. In over-indebted East Prussia the break-through of the radicals came slightly later than in the North-West. By 1929, however, the NSDAP was doing well here out of the discontent of those unable to borrow. In 1930 the Reichslandbund, the successor of the Agrarian League, turned radical in the East and revolted against its President, Martin Schiele, who had become Brüning's Minister of Agriculture. Schiele's successor, Count Kalkreuth, steered the Reichslandbund into complete and intransigent opposition to the Brüning Government.[46]

In some parts of Bavaria, the NSDAP already used the agrarian crisis as early as 1927–8. Julius Streicher in a speech in Ansbach in October 1927 took up the favourite peasant theme of the threats posed by state tax collectors and by grasping creditors: 'the peasantry is without a fatherland, German land is sold and mortgaged to the international Jewish controlling power; today the peasant no longer possesses his own corn for

[45] (Ed.) W. S. Allen, *The Infancy of Nazism: the Memoirs of ex-Gauleiter Albert Krebs 1923–1933*, New York 1976, 269–70.

[46] Grübler, 254 ff.

he must pay four-fifths of his income in taxes, and woe betide him who does not pay, for then the bailiff comes'.[47]

THE GOVERNMENT'S RESPONSE: TARIFF INCREASES OR DEBT REDUCTION?

The combination of agrarian pressure and the changing attitudes of the large parties had a profound impact on the course of government agrarian policy after 1928. Politicians still needed to woo the peasants. Partly as a consequence of the volatility of the peasantry's electoral behaviour and partly also as a result of the confessional split there were many parties which believed that they either had, or needed to cultivate, a special commitment to the land and a special interest in agrarian problems. As a result, no Weimar Cabinet lacked ministers determined to push the case of agriculture (in the Great Coalition, a Baden Democratic farmer, Hermann Dietrich, was Minister of Agriculture).[48] Other, non-agrarian, interest groups had to take notice of the agrarian bias in government policy.

The problem arose of what means could be used to conciliate the peasants' representatives, who were constantly terrified of losing their electoral support. Two alternative approaches to the agricultural crisis each involved the imposition of substantial costs on the rest of society: the first solution was the old favourite of raising prices by tariff or non-tariff (usually quota) protection; the second, reducing or consolidating debt. The first alternative might make food more expensive for the consumer, and if carried far, might provoke retaliation against German exports: but tariffs would bring revenue for the Government. The second course involved the commitment of government funds.

In the aftermath of the stabilisation there were few enthusiastic advocates of high levels of protection. With the exception of a few paid propagandists of the agrarian associations, most agricultural economists even opposed the reintroduction of the Bülow tariff in 1925. Friedrich Aereboe was the most vocifer-

[47] Pridham, 58.

[48] A. von Saldern, *Hermann Dietrich: Ein Staatsmann der Weimarer Republik*, Boppard 1966, 46–77.

ous anti-tariff polemicist. The most influential and most eminent of all the German experts in this field, Max Sering, also in the 1920s opposed all except 'educational tariffs' in a genuinely Listian sense: that is tariffs which were to be used to shield a structural change in agriculture, such as the cultivation of feedstuffs in place of rye (although Friedrich List notoriously never advocated an agricultural tariff).[49] This academic consensus influenced politicians: Brüning stated during the depression that 'even agriculture cannot in the long run keep up such a high level of protection as at present. It cannot bear the cost [because the tariff increased the cost of animal feedstuffs]. Behind the protective tariff, individual farmers are continuing to increase their debt.'[50]

From 1924, however, the tariff was, academic consensus notwithstanding, a political hot potato. In 1924–5 it was the wish to impose tariffs immediately the Versailles restrictions on tariff policy had come to an end that drew the right into supporting the Republic, since the agrarians could hardly influence government policy if they refused to join cabinets. Republicans knew that they could split the DNVP by making tariff concessions: Count Kalkreuth, then President of the Reichslandbund, appeared in 1925 as a 'moderate' conservative, because he knew that the Republic could stand and deliver when he pointed the agrarian pistol at it. He stated his firm belief that 'the main thing is that we enter government'.[51] In this way the revived Bülow tariff played a major role in the political stabilisation of the Republic: it was the economic underpinning of a new quiet conservative republicanism, that style of republicanism which was symbolised by the election of Field Marshall Paul von Hindenburg as Reich President and by Hindenburg's immaculately constitutional behaviour during the first four years of his office. Like other measures which stabilised the Republic politically, however, the tariff imposed an economic price.

The 1925 tariff was a carefully balanced political juggling

[49] Sering 1932, 881 f. F. Aereboe, *Agrarpolitik: Ein Lehrbuch*, Berlin 1928, particularly 453–6.

[50] IfZ ED93/19, 21 Mar. 1932 diary entry.

[51] M. Stürmer, *Koalition und Opposition in der Weimarer Republik 1924–1928*, Düsseldorf 1967, 65.

act. One of the coalition partners of the first Luther Government—the first Weimar regime to include the DNVP—was the Centre Party. The Centre had a strong working-class and union wing frightened of raising food costs which, if pushed too hard by the agrarians, might vote with the SPD on the tariff issue. But the Centre also had a substantial peasant following in Westphalia and Württemberg, which depended on imported feedstuffs and which could not be reckoned to be on the side of the big agrarians of the DNVP in tariff issues. So the agrarians produced a compromise which restored the old tariff only for some cereals, and which would allow barley into Germany at a cheap price. The Reich Interior Minister, Schiele, one of the agrarian representatives in the Cabinet, argued that a general agricultural prosperity could be achieved by this partial tariff if it were combined with cheap interest loans: 'As long as feedstuffs come to Germany duty free or with only low duties, all other agricultural tariffs do not increase prices, but only switch demand from the foreign to the domestic market'. As an economic argument, this was, needless to say, specious.[52]

A law of 17 August 1925 imposed a 30 RM/t. duty on rye, 30 RM on oats, and 35 RM on wheat, but only 22 RM on maize; two years later the duties on oats, rye, and maize were raised to 50 RM.[53] The tariff isolated Germany for some time from developments on the world market, but an increased volume of German production depressed prices and led to the crisis of 1927–8. This was the problem that the new Great Coalition Government faced after the election of March 1928. The Minister of Agriculture, Dietrich, produced a few constructive measures: the long-needed Reich Milk Law of 1930 for the first time regulated dairy standards.[54] Despite Dietrich's Baden origins, most of his measures seemed to favour the eastern latifundia: these appeared, because of their high indebtedness, to be at the centre of the agrarian crisis.

At the centre of Dietrich's programme lay trade policy. In December 1928 the sugar duty was raised; in December 1929, after rises in the wheat and rye duties earlier in the year, a so-

[52] (Ed.) K. H. Minuth, *Akten der Reichskanzlei Weimarer Republik, Die Kabinette Luther I und II*, Boppard 1977, doc. 141, 5 Aug. 1925 Schiele: 'Thesen zur Wirtschaftspolitik'.

[53] RGBl 1925 I, 261–311; RGBl 1927, I 180.

[54] Saldern, 67.

called 'gliding tariff' was approved (and was subsequently extended to oats and barley). As world prices continued their slide, new tariff increases could be put through without new legislation being required. By January 1930 the duties were 90 RM (rye) and 95 RM (wheat). Tariffs were also extended to encompass non-cereal products: a butter tariff was swallowed by the socialist and Centre Ministers on the grounds that it represented an 'educational' tariff protecting a new industry that was being reorganised.[55] There were foreign political complications. In June 1929 the Cabinet voted, as part of a tariff package, to annul the Swedish trade treaty of May 1926 as the Swedish Government would not permit an alteration of the terms of the treaty to encompass the German 'gliding tariff'. German–Polish relations were soured by the militant opposition of German agrarians to Polish meat exports: the farmers thus got in the way of the Allied requirement at the Hague Conferences of 1929–30 that a new reparations settlement should be accompanied by a German–Polish *détente*.[56]

Dietrich experimented with debt relief as well as with trade-political measures. Since 1922 there had been a very limited form of interest subsidy for frontier regions, justified on defence grounds as the Reichswehr was so severely limited by the reduction in manpower imposed at Versailles that it needed the assistance of frontier farmers. In 1928 a more far-reaching scheme was established to supply the East with cheap, subsidised, foreign loans: however, the sums were still comparatively small. 29m. RM was given to small and medium-sized farms under 100 ha. (6.7 per cent of these farms in the eligible area were subsidised), while 66m. RM went to the large estates (46 per cent of which received the cheap loans).[57] In May 1929 the next stage in the creation of a bonanza for large estate owners was completed: a programme to deal with the 'Emergency Area' of East Prussia created a special agricultural fund to reschedule loans and provide interest supplements.

The Great Coalition laid down a path which its successors followed. Dietrich had begun to polemicise against free trade. In the Reichstag in March 1929, he made a statement which

[55] *Kabinett Müller II*, doc. 216, 1 June 1929 Stegerwald in Cabinet meeting.

[56] Ibid., doc. 310, 3 Oct. 1929 Cabinet meeting.

[57] Buchta, 45–6.

was remarkable for the leader of the party that had inherited the mantle of German left liberalism: 'among the Democratic deputies there is not a single free trader'.[58] After 1928–9 the problems of agricultural policy-making became more acute: but they remained essentially the same. Ever and ever more extensive solutions failed, and they produced more and more acute political tensions.

Interest payment by agriculture measured as a proportion of agricultural sales continued to rise until 1931 (Table XXIX).

Table XXIX: German Agricultural Interest Payments 1924–1932

Year (1 July–30 June)	Agricultural sales (m. RM)	Agricultural interest payments (m. RM)	Sales/Interest payments (%)
1924/5	7 590	425	5·6
1925/6	8 130	610	7·5
1926/7	8 590	625	7·3
1927/8	9 440	785	8.3
1928/9	10 300	920	8.9
1929/30	9 750	950	9·7
1930/1	8 890	950	10.7
1931/2	7 270	1 005	13.8
1932[a]	7 000	795	11.4

[a] Estimate.
Source: Wochenbericht des Institutes für Konjunkturforschung, 5 Oct. 1932.

A great difficulty for the Great Coalition's successors was that the Dietrich measures appeared to have enjoyed a partial success. In 1928–9 income from agriculture increased, but the improvement was in reality limited to northern and eastern Germany. In southern Germany losses and debts continued to rise. Agrarian radicalism in the north and east only waned temporarily: it revived in 1930 as the crisis intensified once more. Then the agrarians demanded a repetition of the Müller–Dietrich solution.

Industrialists, however, who were largely dependent on the integration of Germany in world trade and in the world economy, regarded the agrarians' tariff demands with alarm.

[58] Saldern, 52.

Raising German tariffs posed a threat of retaliation from important German customers: the Netherlands, the Scandinavian states, and Poland. All the main industrial interest associations—the RDI, the VDA and the DIHT (the Federation of Chambers of Commerce and Industry)—opposed proposals to leave a 'Most Favoured Nation' system of trade relations through the imposition of agrarian quotas.[59] The unions and the SPD agreed about the damage done by agrarian protectionism. They added a further element: tariffs reduced living standards, because they increased food prices. Before the War, the campaign against the Bülow tariff and against excessive bread prices had been a central part of the SPD's programme.[60] In Weimar Germany, food was still the major item in working-class budgets, although its share gradually fell as living standards improved in the 1920s. The Hamburg Statistical Office's survey of family budgets showed the proportion of income spent in a working class household on food, drink, and tobacco as 48 per cent in 1925 and 43 per cent in 1929.[61] SPD and Catholic politicians realised the significance of food costs: even the authors of the pro-peasant SPD programme of the Kiel Congress agreed that 'for the SPD as the party of the urban masses, the agrarian question is in the first place a stomach question'.[62] Several times the Minister of Labour in the Brüning era, Adam Stegerwald, threatened to resign if tariffs were put up.[63]

Tariffs had also represented an argument deployed by the labour movement in the major wage push of the later 1920s. Wage rises represented nothing more, the unions said, than a compensation for agrarian protection. For most business men, the tariff increases agreed in December 1929 appeared to be both from the standpoint of trade and labour relations a final concession: more could not and should not be done to help the

[59] *Kabinett Müller II*, doc. 54, 1 Nov. 1928 Müller to Braun. RDI, *Beiträge zu einem Agrarprogramm*, Berlin 1930.

[60] Groh, 127–8.

[61] 'The Hamburg Family Budget Enquiry of 1925–1929', *International Labour Review* 24, 1931, 742–7.

[62] *Protokoll über die Verhandlungen des SPD-Parteitages Kiel* 22–7 May 1927, Kiel 1927, 119 (Baade).

[63] *Kabinette Brüning*, doc. 244, 17 Feb. 1931 ministerial meeting. See also Grübler, 264.

farmers. Yet unless the world agricultural crisis ended, agrarian conditions in Germany would continue to worsen, and German farmers would agitate for new measures.

This was the background to the proposals made at a meeting of the RDI in December 1929 by the Rhineland brown coal industrialist Paul Silverberg: and also to the Osthilfe (help for the east) plans of the Brüning Government. Silverberg's suggestion was that the industrial contributions required under the Dawes reparations Plan (the *Industrieumlage*) should be used to relieve agriculture, since they no longer formed a part of the Young Plan. Industrial money would be used in debt relief. The purpose was twofold: to stop tariff increases by providing an alternative source of relief, and to set up a basis for industry to co-operate with labour in cutting wages on the grounds that food prices had fallen.[64] The negotiations of 1930 concerning industrial co-operation with labour always produced agreement that prices and wages should be reduced, but always reached an impasse over the question of which should be reduced first: a fall in food prices would offer a way out.

Silverberg's scheme was not at first accepted by many of his industrial friends: in part this was simply because of the cost involved. Gustav Krupp von Bohlen und Halbach wanted the end of the Dawes Plan to bring tax relief for industry, not debt relief for agriculture. Clemens Lammers thought that money from the *Industrieumlage* could better be used to relieve the strain on the Reich budget. Small industry disliked the thought of continuing to pay the *Umlage*.[65] (In the version of the Silverberg scheme that was eventually adopted, in 1931, this issue was solved by raising the threshold for liability to the industrial levy from a capitalisation of 20 000 RM to 500 000 RM. Thus the number of firms paying the levy was reduced dramatically, and artisan and medium-sized enterprises could no longer complain that they were being unfairly penalised in order to aid an inefficient primary sector.)[66] There was in 1929 a second objection to the Silverberg plan: the proposed pro-

[64] RDI Extraordinary meeting of 12 Dec. 1929: RDI Schriftenreihe no. 50, Berlin 1930, 31–6. Also Neebe, 52.

[65] BAK NL Silverberg 574, 29 Mar. 1930 Lammers to Vögler, and 14 April 1930 Silverberg to von Braun. IfZ ED93/8, 12 May 1930 diary entry.

[66] See in general BAK NL Silverberg 574.

gramme had a strong political purpose, namely that of bringing 'moderate' industry together with agriculture in order to produce realistic political solutions based on a right bloc. Economic programmes were often regarded with suspicion as a result of the political messages they might contain; and this persistently helped to vitiate economic policy-formulation during the depression. In 1929 the DNVP industrialists saw in Silverberg's programme not a positive scheme but rather a torpedo directed against them and their influence: and thus they attempted to frustrate its implementation.

Agrarians too were worried by the plan. Some of them feared that the institution (later known as the Industriebank) created to apply debt relief might actually attempt to implement a dangerous mixture of commercial principle and social policy. Already in 1919 a law on Settlements (*Siedlung*) had used land from large estates to create small farmsteads. Since 1928 Eastern farmers had been waging a bitter campaign against the Prussian State Land Bank, the Preußenkasse, which they regarded as the instrument of the social democratic Prussian Government and whose aim they thought was the breaking up of large estates. The Director of the Preußenkasse had indeed written an article arguing that small peasant farming represented the 'most rational agrarian policy'.[67] The Industriebank, some feared, might take up some of the anti-Junker policies of the Preußenkasse. On the other hand, if treated in the right way, an industrial lending programme might offer an ideal means of breaking the grip of the Preußenkasse and thus also of the Prussian Government, and of committing big business to the defence of the Junkers. Richard von Flemming, the President of the Pomeranian Chamber of Agriculture and holder of a Fideikommiß (entailed estate) in Paatzig, Drammin, and Ribbertow, wrote encouragingly to Silverberg that the best solution was to avoid any possibility of state interference (which might be guided by the 'political' principles of the Centre unions and the Centre peasants): 'We need to place the whole action on a purely private economic base so that the action becomes not merely a

[67] O. Klepper, 'Rationelle Agrarpolitik', *Magazin der Wirtschaft* 6, 1930, 223.

support for agriculture but also that industrial funds are used to create a market for industrial products.'[68]

On such a basis a compromise between industry and agriculture might be worked out. On 18 March 1930 Reich President von Hindenburg, who was by now, as a consequence of the political crisis, in close contact with agrarian politicians, sent a letter including the Silverberg proposals for the use of the *Umlage*. By then, too, the Silverberg plan appeared—even to those business men who had initially been sceptical—to be a useful alternative to tariff increases.

While industry vacillated over the amount of the industrial levy, the Reich Agriculture Ministry drew up its own plan for an agricultural relief bank (*Ablösungsbank*). Local producer co-operatives would be made responsible for the repayment of farmers' debts. Creditors would receive in place of second mortgages a Relief Certificate (*Ablösungsschein*) drawn on the co-operative. Silverberg and his associates feared that such a scheme which one-sidedly favoured the agricultural debtor would damage general credit conditions, and make borrowing more difficult in the future; and argued that the *Ablösungsschein* was nothing more than a kind of *Notgeld* (emergency money) of the sort that had been issued by companies, farms, and individuals in the concluding stages of the inflation.[69] Since the mid-1920s the Economics Ministry and the Reichsbank had been involved in a continual, almost obsessional campaign against *Notgeld:* and Brüning and Luther were frightened away from the Agriculture Ministry's plan by the warnings of the industrialists.[70]

The Silverberg scheme now became a way of stopping the state 'controlling credit': in early 1931, when foreign borrowing again appeared possible, the Industriebank tried to obtain initial funds from a consortium including the Skandinaviska Kreditaktiebolaget, Lee Higginson & Co. Boston, and the Schweizerische Kreditanstalt.[71] Foreign loans were, once

[68] BAK NL Silverberg 574, 30 Jan. 1930 Flemming to Silverberg.

[69] Ibid., 235, 27 June 1930 Silverberg to Kastl; 574, 17 Oct. 1930 Flemming to Silverberg and 11 Dec. 1930 Velten news summary of von Braun (Reich Agriculture Minister) plan.

[70] Ibid., 574, 15 Dec. 1930 Flemming to Luther.

[71] Ibid., 578, 2 May 1931 memorandum of Deutsche Bank.

again, to make an appearance as the Germans' fairy godmother. After Brüning's unsuccessful trip to the eastern farming areas in January 1931, the Reich Government too became convinced of the merits of the Silverberg plan. Again the circus of farmers' demonstrations was wheeled out: the Reich Chancellor himself was the target. At Breslau 40 000 farmers demonstrated: some of them threw stones at Brüning, who was terrified and horrified. 'The East was not ready for a particularly favourable treatment ... The East was still, one hundred and twenty years after the war of liberation, not ready for democracy.' Brüning was shocked that the eastern farmers had lost faith in Hindenburg, the victor of Tannenberg, and that they had taken up in the most radical form hostility not only to the Republic, but also to any kind of central government at all. The only consolation, Brüning thought, was that Frederick the Great himself had had difficulties with the Prussian Junkers.[72]

The demonstrations of the East Elbian farmers were in fact brilliantly successful: the East received as a result yet more 'particularly favourable treatment'. The Ablösungsbank was allowed to function, and eventually the Preußenkasse was excluded from the administration of agrarian debt relief. On the other hand, Brüning elevated hostility to further increases in tariffs almost to the status of a dogma, and on several occasions his Cabinet came near to breaking up over this issue. In April 1931 Brüning refused to allow an increase in the butter tariff demanded by the Ministry of Agriculture.[73] Until January 1932 there were no more tariff rises, and on several occasions Brüning even threatened to put the reduction of tariffs on the Cabinet's agenda.[74]

The law of 31 March 1931 (Osthilfe Law) dealt with agrarian debt: it provided for 500m. RM debt relief for agriculture and 150m. RM for commerce to be given over the period 1931–6. Osthilfe aid was limited to Upper Silesia and the Grenzmark, and parts of Pomerania, Brandenburg, and Lower Silesia. The money was to come partly from the *Industrieumlage* and partly from the Reich budget, and was to be managed by the Bank für Industrieobligationen. Long-term

[72] Brüning 1970, 242–4.
[73] *Kabinette Brüning*, doc. 284, 25 Apr. 1931 ministerial meeting.
[74] Grübler, 286.

mortgages were to be substituted for the short-term loans that the eastern farmers had taken in such large quantities. Two months after the original law (21 May 1931) the area covered by the relief scheme was extended to cover the whole of the area to the east of the River Elbe.[75]

One year after it began operations, the Bank für Industrieobligationen had given 41m. RM credit to agriculture and 5.5m. RM to commerce; by 1933 these sums were 130m. RM and 28m. RM respectively.[76] These were relatively small sums in relation to the total volume of agrarian debt, although even this limited approach cost the Reich a great deal of money. Osthilfe had been born as part of a grandiose political vision of Silverberg's; it turned out to be little more than a costly damp squib:

1. The means used in Osthilfe debt relief were insufficient to allow a reduction of cereal tariffs and thus a lightening of the burden on peasant animal husbandry.

2. The consolidation of agrarian short-term debt was not far enough advanced to prevent the high volume of that debt contributing to the undermining of German credit stability in the summer of 1931. The resulting bank collapse made the position of the land much worse, as banks tried to call in loans in order to protect themselves. Gustav Krupp in September 1931 wrote accurately enough that help for the East had been useless and that 'money had been given to those farms where any kind of help was too late': chiefly inefficient and now insolvent large estates.[77]

3. Predictably, Osthilfe failed to appease the rural militants. By the middle of 1931 there was little support left for the original scheme of rallying the moderate right envisaged by the early proponents of Osthilfe, Silverberg, or the dissident agrarian members of the DNVP Treviranus and Schlange-Schöningen (who in November 1931 became the new Commissar for Osthilfe).[78] Prussian agrarian conservatives remained

[75] The Osthilfe provisions are summarised in Sering 1934, 116–27.

[76] BAK NL Silverberg 572, Reports of Bank für Industrie-Obligationen.

[77] Ibid., 578, 16 Sept. 1931 Krupp von Bohlen und Halbach to Silverberg; and copy of 5 Oct. 1931 letter of Paul Hansen to von Fabeck (editor of *Kölnischer Stadtanzeiger*).

[78] BAK NL Passarge 6, 15 Sept. 1931 diary entry.

what they had always essentially been: a collection of short-sighted and intransigent reactionaries, who viewed the state as a gigantic udder which should be squeezed only to their advantage. Their intrigues and their pressure on Hindenburg in May 1932 brought down Brüning along with Schlange-Schöningen and Treviranus.

These conservatives believed that the Prussian state and the Preuβenkasse were still obstructing Osthilfe. An official called Johann-Georg von Dewitz, who acted as Osthilfe Commissar in the Landstelle Köslin, tried to stage an attack on the Prussian role in agricultural relief. Partly at least Dewitz was motivated by the desire to conceal the way in which he had used Osthilfe funds on his father's estate.[79] Dewitz complained to Hindenburg that the Prussian Government regarded large estates as an 'antiquated and economically unprofitable' form of enterprise. Although the investigation of Dewitz's complaint only revealed that the Preuβenkasse was merely objecting to grotesque cases of corruption in the administration of Osthilfe, it was too late. In November 1931 further modifications to the administration of Osthilfe relief were made, largely at the insistence of the Reich President. The Reich took over entirely and excluded Prussia from the operation (Siedlungsverordnung of 17 November 1931).

One of the obstacles in the way of an implementation of the Industriebank scheme was that the original hope of attracting foreign money was—at least after the summer of 1931—vain, while the sums that could be raised by the Reich or by German industry were limited. In February 1932 a partial solution to this problem was found in the form of the mobilisation bonds in vogue elsewhere at that time (see Chapter VIII). On 6 February the Deutsche Rentenbank issued 500m. RM bonds at 4½ per cent on the security of agriculture's Rentenmark debt of 1923–4: this relieved the strained Reich budget, since the Reich was obliged to supply only 100m. RM towards the cost of the scheme. The new debt was used to consolidate the farmers' floating liabilities; and would be serviced from the funds of the Industrieobligationenbank (from 1933–6 with 80m. RM p.a.; the Reich would contribute another 20m. RM p.a.) A further

[79] F. M. Fiederlein, 'Der deutsche Osten und die Regierungen Brüning, Papen und Schleicher', Phil.D. diss. Würzburg 1966, 182–93; Buchta, 116–23.

annual sum of 10m. RM would be contributed from 1935 to 1938 from the profits of the Rentenbank-Kreditanstalt).[80]

This creation of February 1932 was in fact a more effective version of the 1930 proposals for an Ablösungsbank set out by the Reich Agriculture Ministry: both schemes were based on the invention of some kind of bogus paper which could be used to mobilise debt. Thus in the course of 1932 both Prussia and then the Industriebank were excluded from the administration of rural credit; and then in July the Osthilfe scheme was extended to cover huge areas of Prussia and Saxony, and later, in October, also the Bavarian border regions.

The Reich was moving away from the concept of specific regional aid programmes, partly because all of German agriculture was by this time in deep distress, and partly because of the attacks in the press and by the Reichstag parties on the numerous scandals surrounding Osthilfe. A more general programme did not run the same risk of being attacked for corruption. The Fourth Emergency Decree (8 December 1931) decreed a reduction of interest rates (including interests on agricultural loans) over 8 per cent: this was the first step towards the general application of interest relief. Agriculture had suffered more than any other part of the economy from exorbitant interest rates. In September 1932 a decree reduced interest payments on agricultural mortgages again, this time by 2 per cent (the decree left services charges unchanged, but treated the 2 per cent as amortisation rather than as interest payment).[81] It was only a small step further when in July 1933 the debt relief programme was extended to the whole of Germany.

The partial debt relief programmes in 1931 and 1932 polarised politics on the land still further. In the first place, the programmes had been administered in the belief that indebtedness was only a problem where it was highest, and thus that the West and North-west required no relief. Secondly, there was the bitter conflict in the East about who should control the highly sensitive business of debt relief: industry, the Prussian state, or the Reich. On the other hand, depoliticisation of debt

[80] Sering 1934, 120.

[81] Ibid., 121. See also BAK R2/13645, 8 Sept. 1932 Otto Chr. Fischer proposals, and 20–1 Sept. 1932 discussion in Reich Justice Ministry.

in December 1931 by means of a general interest reduction only saved German agriculture 150–60m. RM a year, and helped to increase the pressure from farmers for a more thoroughgoing state intervention in credit markets.[82]

It was after the banking crisis of July 1931, which led to exceptionally high interest rates, that agrarian discontent focused on banks. In the summer of 1931 banks tried to recall loans in order to maintain their own liquidity; and in addition, as farm prices collapsed with falling food prices, the security provided by farmers was no longer adequate in relation to their loans. Thus when loans were called the result was often bankruptcy and compulsory sale. In 1931, 5 765 farms were auctioned by receivers (0.7 per cent of Germany's farm land); in 1932, 7 060 (0.6 per cent):[83] and these figures would have been much higher had it not been for government efforts to prevent such forced auctions.

In late 1931 peasant protest meetings claimed that it was interest rates of 10–15 per cent that had caused the agrarian crisis.[84] In December 1931 a demonstration of peasants at Wertingen (Bavaria) called for the ending of rural usury (*Abbau der Wucherzinsen*), as well as for an increased butter tariff and an extension of Osthilfe to the whole Reich.[85] Petitions from peasant interest groups gave a prominent place to demands for action on the credit issue.[86]

Not all peasant protest was directed against usurious creditors: the willingness of peasants to blame rural usury for their plight depended on long-established habits of thought about what represented justice. Increased taxation was almost as frequently a target for peasant hostility.[87] Behind the peasants' complaints lay a notion of a *just rate* of interest: an inheritance from the past when the Catholic Church had condemned rural

[82] IfZ ED93/14, 2 Oct. 1931 diary entry: Trendelenburg comments on the beneficiaries of interest reductions. Also *Wochenbericht des Instituts für Konjunkturforschung* 5/20, 17 Aug. 1932, 81.

[83] *Statistisches Jahrbuch* 1933, 386.

[84] BAK R2/13640 (filed protests against high interest charges).

[85] BStA MW 457, 29 Sept. 1931 Bavarian Landesbauernkammer to Reich Agricultural Minister; MW 460, Dec. 1931 Peasant demands at Wertingen.

[86] BAK R43I/2549, 17 Nov. 1931 Generalsekretär des Landwirtschaftlichen Hauptverbandes Württemberg und Hohenzollern to Reich Chancellor.

[87] BStA MW 460, 13 May 1929 petition of Christlicher Bauernverein für Schwaben.

money-lenders. It was not only the Nazis who realised the political potential of these rural views. The NSDAP agrarian *apparat* took up the theme of *Brechung der Zinsknechtschaft*: but so did the Centre and even the DDP.[88]

The connection between strength of peasant protest and past traditions of thought meant that often there were violent demonstrations in areas where actual levels of debt were comparatively low. Bavaria was not on the whole highly indebted: only the relatively few large cereal farms faced difficulties here. Of the Bayerische Handelsbank's agricultural mortgages 77 per cent (84 per cent by value) were not in arrears on payments in July 1932.[89] Perhaps Catholic peasants, having been warned over and over again by priests of the dangers of usury, had borrowed less: but they protested more. The Bayerische Gemeindetag told Chancellor von Papen in September 1932 that the Brüning interest rate reduction of December 1931 had been too late, that political upheavals had reduced the beneficial impact of the Brüning measure, and that in consequence further interest reduction was urgently needed.[90] There were more violent expressions of peasants' feelings on this issue too. Banks were attacked by outraged farmers in the Bavarian outback. The Nazis in April 1932 besieged the Bank für Landwirtschaft und Gewerbe in Vilshofen; and mobbed the two bank directors they claimed had pressed excessive loans on otherwise cautious farmers.[91]

The general reduction of debt made the future of agricultural credit insecure: who would lend if they were then prevented by the state from recovering their loans? By February 1932 it had become more or less impossible to enforce payments on mortgages. In addition, some agrarians were setting out schemes involving the cancellation of up to half the existing agricultural debt. It is scarcely surprising that rural tradesmen were very worried by 1932. Even debt reduction

[88] See Saldern, 79 for criticism of DDP's agrarian policy; on DDP agrarian policy see BAK NL Dietrich 331. On the Centre, see G. Plum, *Gesellschaftsstruktur und politisches Bewußtsein in einer katholischen Region 1928–1933: Untersuchung am Beispiel des Regierungsbezirks Aachen*, Stuttgart 1972, 96–9.

[89] *Münchener Neueste Nachrichten* no. 187, 5 Sept. 1932.

[90] BAK R2/13641, 22 Sept. 1932 F. Döhlemann (Bayerische Gemeindebank) to Papen. Also BStA MA 67530, 19 Oct. 1931 Döhlemann to Brüning.

[91] *Vilshofener Anzeiger* no. 82, 6 Apr. 1932, in BStA MW 391.

had failed to remove the sources of agrarian discontent: in the East structural change rather than debt relief was what was required. But Hermann Müller and his successors were so intimidated by the political power of the latifundia farmers—in the DNVP, in the army, and in the circle around Hindenburg—that they were unable to consider a programme to replace rye by animal feedstuffs or by intensive grazing. Moreover, even such a scheme may not have been appropriate in the conditions of the deep depression, as demand for animal products was falling rapidly as living standards worsened.

Debt relief had not succeeded either in reducing agrarian pressure for protection. In spite of Brüning and Stegerwald, German trade policy became more and more restrictive. From the end of 1929 a quota had been applied to imports of Swedish cattle; one year later quotas existed for butter; and by 1932 there were five different levels of butter tariff. In March 1931 the Government was authorised to conclude bilateral trade agreements without consulting the Reichstag, and the first such agreements (with Hungary and Roumania) were made in the summer of 1931. In January 1932 the Government was authorised to ban imports from countries retaliating against German protective measures.

Papen was much less capable of resisting agrarian demands for protection than Brüning had been. The struggle between industry and agriculture over trade policy now flared up again. Papen's Cabinet was divided: a majority, led by von Braun (Agriculture Minister) and von Gayl (Interior Minister) sympathised with the agrarian case. Schwerin von Krosigk (Finance Minister) was uncertain and thought that some concession to the farmers was needed. Warmbold (Economics Minister), Neurath (Foreign Minister), and Hugo Schäffer (Labour Minister) opposed the agrarians. In a speech in Munich on 26 September von Braun brought the internal cabinet conflict into the open by calling for the introduction of a general import quota system.[93]

Most business men were not sympathetic to any compromise with agriculture. Though Germany's trade partners might

[92] HA Krupp FAH IV E 184, 12 July 1932 Industrialists' meeting with Posse.

[93] Von Braun speech reported in *Vossische Zeitung*, no. 463, 27 Sept. 1932.

possibly accept quotas on individual agricultural products, they would never accept the kinds of demands now made by German farmers. Hermann Bücher concluded: 'A pact with agriculture would not be successful . . . An attempted coalition would be disastrous for industry.' Though, for instance, the industrial interest associations were prepared to allow butter quotas, they could never take the terms proposed by farmers. In July 1932 the Green Front suggested a quota of 50 000 tons at a tariff of 1000 RM/t.; industry was only willing to accept 86 000 tons at 750 RM/t.[94] Business men brought out political objections of labour again: 'an increase in the price of edible fats and the associated fall in consumption would have particularly severe psychological consequences, judging by the experience of the war years'. A plan to restrict lard imports was opposed because 'the basic fat foundation of industrial workers' diets must not be made more expensive'.[95] Underlying these arguments was the thought that the struggle to cut wage costs would become much more bitter—indeed almost impossible—if the tariff fanatics had their way.

Industrial trade policy was set out at an Extraordinary Meeting of the Präsidium of the RDI on 17 August 1932: *(a)* the best trade system was one which rested on MFN treatment and which excluded quotas; *(b)* existing German import restrictions should gradually be removed; *(c)* the world economic problem in general, and the German economic problem in particular, might be solved by the creation of *Großwirtschaftsräume* (large economic areas or co-prosperity spheres) through customs unions. Here was a reiteration of the old industrial goal of a German-dominated Mitteleuropa: a goal which had always appeared unattractive to most farmers because of the agrarian nature of the non-German parts of Mitteleuropa.[96] Farmers operating with cheap labour would be able to swamp the German market.

Almost all the political activity of German industry in late

[94] HA Krupp FAH IV E 184, 27 June 1932 RDI Präsidialausschuß für Handelspolitik, 18 July 1932 meeting of Subcommission.

[95] Ibid., 184 27 June 1932 RDI Präsidialausschuß; and 185, 15 Nov. 1932 meeting of industrial and agrarian representatives.

[96] BAK NL Silverberg 249, 17 Aug. 1932 RDI Präsidium (also HA Krupp FAH IV E 184).

1932 reflected the concern over trade policy. There was a danger that if the NSDAP ever came to power it would attempt to impose an autarkic programme. So Jakob Herle of the RDI wrote to the Nazi economic adviser Adrian von Renteln warning against too strong an emphasis in any future Nazi programme on the capacity of the domestic market. Exports were vital to Germany's future.[97] Paul Reusch and Gustav Krupp von Bohlen und Halbach protested against Hjalmar Schacht's December 1932 scheme for the bilateralisation of trade.[98] Industry's commitment to exporting and to a relatively open world economy remained after the political revolution of January 1933. Heavy industry campaigned against the pro-agrarian and pro-autarkic stance of the new Economics Minister (Alfred Hugenberg) and against Hugenberg's attack on MFN.[99] Eventually these business attacks helped to unseat Hugenberg from his ministerial position.

There were only a few dissidents from this line within the industrial camp. J. W. Reichert, the General Manager of the VDESI, sometimes spoke of reviving the old Bismarckian alliance of *Solidarprotektionismus* between agriculture and heavy industry. But even here the motive was a rather cynical one, and not really concerned with the benefits that tariffs might bring for industry. Reichert wanted to end the bitter attacks on big business made by German farmers. After Count Kalkreuth had expressed a cautious dissent from agrarian complaints about the high cost of iron and thus of farm machinery, Reichert wrote to him:

I am pleased to be able to deduce from your latest letters that you are prepared, in the name of the independence of the German economy and of German politics, to allow the steel industry prices which in relation to German production costs can guarantee a satisfactory profit: even if this can only be achieved by the use of trade policy to protect the iron industry. In this statement of the President of the Reichslandbund I see a return to the old tradition, which already

[97] BAK NL Silverberg 232, 23 Sept. 1932 RDI circular; and 8 Sept. 1932 Herle to A. von Renteln, arguing against bilateral trade treaties and against an exaggerated concentration on the domestic market.

[98] HA Krupp FAH IV E 1124, 10 Jan. 1933 Krupp von Bohlen und Halbach to Schacht; and E 1186, 2 Jan. 1933 Reusch to Schacht.

[99] BAK NL Silverberg 235, 9 Feb. 1933 industrialists' meeting with Reich Economics Minister Hugenberg.

under Bismarck bound together most closely the two soil-based [*bodenständisch*] trades: agriculture on the one side and coal and steel on the other.[1]

This Bismarckian alliance never re-emerged, however: in the first place, non-cereal products could not be adequately protected (it was over issues such as the butter tariff that the export-industrialists dug their heels in most). Between 1928 and 1932 the instruments of protectionist trade policy were used chiefly to help cereal growers. Throughout this period the gap between German and world cereal prices continued to grow. Protection was applied not only to rye and wheat but also to animal feedstuffs (which Dietrich as Minister of Agriculture in the Müller Cabinet had originally wanted to leave unprotected). But while feedstuffs were double the world market price, pig prices in Germany in 1931 were actually *below* the English level.[2] Particularly those farmers in north-west Germany who from the last years of the nineteenth century had gone over to intensive animal husbandry were penalised by tariff policy, and would not support it.

Secondly, the hostility of small cultivators to big industry and commerce generated as a result of the debt issue turned into an extreme and militant agrarianism: a hostility to industry and finance on the land that had not been a part of the agrarian discontents of the 1890s. In the 1890s and 1900s it was the big estate farmers who had been the most fanatical opponents of the civilisation of capitalism: it was they who had wanted to introduce stamp duties on the bourse, and turnover taxes on commerce[3] (and they had been successful). For smaller farmers, it required the extreme fluctuations of interest rates and the intervention of the state in the 1920s and then the catastrophe of the financial crisis of 1931 to produce an equally critical reaction against the modern world. But then they did react, and with extraordinary violence.

What effects did the agrarian crisis and government agrarian policy have on the rest of the economy?

[1] HA/GHH 400101024/3, 25 Dec. 1932 Reichert to Kalkreuth.
[2] See Stolper in *Der deutsche Volkswirt*, 5/22, 27 Feb. 1931, 699–701.
[3] Witt 1970, 355.

1. Agricultural debt relief occurred at the expense of the non-agricultural community.

2. The wage push of the late 1920s was given additional momentum by the influence of the tariff on food prices.

3. Debt relief weakened the position of small country traders, who were forced to reduce their claims on farmers.

4. The tariff on wheat, rye, and barley cost German consumers 1 140m. RM in 1930, 1 790m. RM in 1931, and 1,860m. RM in 1932 (or a sum equivalent to 1.6 per cent, 3.1 per cent, and 3.7 per cent respectively of NNP). The transfers to the farmers produced by the higher prices amounted to 1.2 per cent, 2.8 per cent, and 3.3 per cent of NNP.[4]

5. Agrarian pressure damaged German trade relations with other states.

6. Peasant resentments against high interest charges and against middlemen fuelled the movement for economic radicalism.

[4] Cost to consumers: multiplication of the difference between German and world market prices by the volume of German consumption. Subsidy to farmers: multiplication of the difference between German and world prices by the volume of German consumption minus net imports.

VIII

The Banking Crisis

Uns erfreut das bloße Sparen,
Geld persönlich macht nicht froh.
Regelmäßig nach paar Jahren
Klaut ihr's uns ja sowieso.
(Erich Kästner, *Auf einer kleinen Bank vor einer großen Bank*)

It was the outbreak of a banking crisis in the summer of 1931 that made the German depression so severe. Similar crises occurred in other central and east European states: the bank collapses of 1931 hit the Austrian and Hungarian economies very severely. There were fears too of financial instability in France in the wake of the collapse in November 1930 of the Banque Adam, Boulogne-sur-Mer, and the failure of the Banque Nationale de Crédit. Even the very important Banque de l'Union Parisienne needed to be bailed out with Belgian capital.[1] In Italy, a major banking crisis was only avoided by the intervention of the Government to stop publication of bank figures, which looked as bad as, or worse than, those of the ill-fated Vienna Creditanstalt.[2] The banking collapses of 1930–3 made the depression in the USA substantially more severe; and one influential historical account presents the monetary contraction induced by banking failures as the major cause of the US crisis.[3] In eastern and central Europe banking collapses appeared not at the outset, but rather later in the depression. We can speak of a 'two phase depression', the second phase being produced by the effects of severe contraction of the money supply because of banking developments. In the second phase, it is easy to answer the controversial question 'Did monetary forces cause the Great Depression?' with a simple

[1] A. Dauphin-Meunier, *La Banque 1919–1935: Allemagne Angleterre France*, Paris 1936, 224–6.
[2] G. Toniolo, *L'economia dell'Italia fascista*, Rome 1980, 210–19, 228–33.
[3] M. Friedman and A. J. Schwartz, *A Monetary History of the United States 1868–1960*, Princeton 1963, 299–419.

yes.[4] The question as to the effect of monetary forces in the first stage is much more difficult to answer.

In addition, the collapse of the banks in central Europe had a major social psychological and political impact. Capitalism appeared to have crashed with the banks, and this helped to discredit existing political systems. Meanwhile, those politicians actually in power found themselves obliged to demand a greater degree of state intervention in order to prop up and reform the banking system, and in the end also to regulate and control the economy.

In states where there was no great threat of a banking collapse, such as Britain, the inter-war depression was much milder: but even in these cases, financial instability may have had an indirect effect on the economy because of its implications for government policy. Thus in Britain the fear of financial crisis, particularly after the Austrian and German collapses of the spring and summer of 1931, dictated budget economy measures.[5] Here there were political as well as economic effects: the recommendations of cuts in expenditure made in the report of the May Committee broke up the Labour Government.

Financial instability was then for both economic and political reasons a major concern in all states during the inter-war slump, even in those cases where that instability did not erupt as a bank panic. In Germany there were already signs of monetary crisis in spring 1929 when a politically induced foreign exchange run occurred during the meeting of the Paris Experts' Committee on reparations: the international market feared that the Experts would not be able to reach agreement on a new reparations plan. A similar run took place in September 1930, after the Nazi party did unexpectedly well in the Reichstag elections. In each case money flowed out of Germany; and in 1929 bank deposits in Germany contracted (by 5 per cent from the end of March to the end of May), though in autumn 1930 there was no such fall in bank

[4] P. Temin, *Did Monetary Forces Cause the Great Depression?*, New York 1976.

[5] A. Cairncross and B. Eichengreen, *Sterling in Decline: The Devaluations of 1931, 1949, and 1967*, Oxford 1983, 72–83; the authors argue that the threat of financial crisis in Britain was a result of budget difficulties combined with continental financial instability.

deposits.[6] Both exchange crises caused rises in short-term money rates; and in 1929 a moderately important insurance firm, the Frankfurter Allgemeine Versicherungs AG, failed.

In both 1929 and 1930 the crises were controlled by the German Reichsbank in co-operation in the first case with other central banks and in the second with the private American loan consortium led by the Boston investment bank of Lee Higginson & Co. Despite the strain imposed on the world financial system by developments in USA (the Wall Street boom 1928–9 and then, after October, the crash) and in Britain (the constant pressure on sterling) the system of 'central bank co-operation'[7] was still working to control capital and money flows.

In 1931 on the other hand, the failure of a major German financial institution, the Darmstädter- und Nationalbank (or Danat-Bank), on 13 July led to a general run on the banks and forced a closure of all German financial institutions. They reopened for limited business after two days (they were then allowed to pay out money for wages, salaries, and pensions and for tax payments); and normal operations were resumed only on 5 August. Reopening was only possible with large guarantees and capital grants from the Reich. As part of the price for its support, the Reich fused the Darmstädter with another weak bank, the Dresdner Bank; and it demanded an extensive purge of bank directors.

THE BANKING CRISIS AND BUSINESS

The bank crisis in 1931 had an immediately destructive effect on the real economy—unlike the partial and short-lived crises of 1929 and 1930. But financial conditions had already affected industrial and commercial activity before the big crisis of 1931. Firms attempted to adjust their gearing downwards in response to the uncertain conditions prevailing on the financial market. The reduction of the proportion of debt to capital was particularly pronounced in manufacturing industry (especially machinery, the electro-technical industry, foodstuffs, and clothing) and in the building trade. The reduction in short-

[6] James 1984, 85–6 (Statistical Appendix).
[7] S. V. O. Clarke, *Central Bank Cooporation 1924–1931*, New York 1967.

Table XXX: Sample of German Joint-Stock Companies: Debt and Investment 1927–1933

	1927	1928	1929	1930	1931	1932	1933
(a) Long-term Debt as a proportion of Paid-in Nominal Capital (%)							
Extractive Industry:	16.0	17.3	23.1	25.6	22.9	22.5	24.0
Hard coal	12.5	12.2	19.8	24.3	22.4	22.9	27.1
Building materials	7.4	10.2	7.6	7.5	5.2	5.1	6.6
Manufacturing Industry:	8.3	15.9	16.0	16.2	18.3	18.0	16.3
Machinery and vehicle construction	10.9	12.4	14.9	16.5	12.5	12.4	18.3
Electro-technical	20.4	21.5	29.8	28.1	29.4	29.8	23.6
Chemical	1.4	20.5	18.6	18.3	25.1	25.0	19.1
Textile	11.4	11.7	7.8	7.8	7.1	6.7	8.1
Foodstuffs	8.2	9.8	10.2	12.7	9.6	9.3	8.2
Clothing	2.6	5.2	13.0	12.3	7.7	2.1	2.8
Water, gas, and electricity	39.0	54.1	66.8	74.3	55.7	55.4	47.5
Trade	28.0	37.1	24.2	28.6	27.7	26.5	37.3
Banks	297.3	386.4	455.4	557.7	484.7	495.2	682.5
Building industry	8.8	15.2	15.4	13.4	4.9	0.8	15.7
Total (not including banks and insurance)	17.1	24.0	28.5	31.3	26.3	26.1	24.5
(b) Short-term Debt as a proportion of Paid-in Nominal Capital (%)							
Extractive Industry:	38.7	41.2	37.8	38.7	34.9	33.5	36.1
Hard coal	30.3	38.0	30.7	33.9	24.7	22.3	22.7
Building materials	23.1	30.0	33.3	31.7	20.9	19.1	31.7
Manufacturing Industry:	72.7	73.8	68.2	60.4	47.2	42.5	44.6
Machinery and Vehicle construction	82.7	90.1	78.6	71.5	79.0	66.6	51.1
Electro-technical	82.3	68.8	70.8	60.9	53.2	41.5	51.4
Chemical	52.8	53.9	49.6	46.3	33.2	32.7	35.0
Textile	94.0	95.4	94.3	87.4	53.4	52.6	60.4
Foodstuffs	126.5	125.0	105.4	83.3	60.9	52.4	57.9
Clothing	86.7	71.2	108.1	82.3	32.4	31.2	28.7

Water, gas, and electricity	28.7	29.8	43.5	38.7	26.7	21.1	20.4
Trade	96.8	103.4	132.1	113.5	53.2	52.1	67.9
Banks	944.2	1 123.9	1 260.6	1 251.2	1 150.6	1 254.1	1 081.6
Building industry	83.5	88.6	105.9	79.8	73.8	61.3	66.4
Total (not including banks and insurance)	54.2	56.1	55.4	50.5	39.9	36.0	45.0
(c) Net Profit/Loss as a proportion of Capital 1927–1933 (%)							
Extractive Industry:	6.7	6.9	7.0	4.0	−2.6	0.1	2.3
Hard coal	5.3	3.4	5.7	1.8	−2.4	1.9	2.7
Building materials	10.3	9.9	6.7	2.2	−7.5	−9.5	0.3
Manufacturing Industry:	8.1	7.0	4.0	2.4	−3.4	−2.3	3.0
Machinery and vehicle construction	4.8	3.0	2.7	0.2	−7.2	−6.6	0.6
Electro-technical	6.8	7.5	7.3	3.1	−12.4	−13.9	2.6
Chemical	9.1	10.0	8.3	6.9	2.4	1.8	4.9
Textile	9.7	5.7	−8.5	−4.7	−6.6	−5.8	3.5
Foodstuffs	8.1	6.9	6.5	4.6	2.1	4.4	3.8
Clothing	12.9	10.6	3.7	0.4	−6.3	7.1	7.5
Water, gas and electricity	7.1	7.2	6.5	5.7	3.9	5.3	5.6
Trade	8.3	7.6	8.3	6.5	5.7	3.3	6.3
Banks	8.7	8.8	8.0	6.2	−30.6	−4.7	1.7
Building industry	8.5	8.8	9.5	7.6	0.8	−13.7	3.7
Total	7.5	7.1	6.8	4.1	−9.1	−1.2	2.6

Source: Calculated from surveys of companies reporting in the last quarter of the year, *Wirtschaft und Statistik*.

term debt was to a large extent achieved through destocking: inventories were reduced in quantity as far as possible (as well as in value, which occurred automatically as prices fell). There were major falls in inventories in textiles, engineering, and vehicle manufacture already in 1929; in the electro-technical industries inventories began to fall in 1930. In addition, textiles suffered particularly from a fall in value of stocks, and this in turn increased the pressure to throw goods on the market. The industry had been forced to hold large stocks because of the shortage of capital in retail trade and also because of the more rapid shifts in fashion in the 1920s which made retailers eager to avoid holding stocks. These considerations produced very high losses in the textile trade in the slump.

On the other hand, inventories and short-term debt in hard coal-mining were still *increasing* quickly in 1930 and even early

Table XXXI: Coal Inventories 1928–1932 (1,000 t)

	Pithead Stocks			Movement of inventories
	Ruhr	Upper Silesia	Lower Silesia	
1928	1 382	358	111	+105
	1 990	391	119	+269
	2 572	485	163	+226
	3 094	373	69	−158
1929	2 315	241	45	−775
	1 265	153	52	+177
	1 453	239	64	+117
	2 532	361	57	+813
1930	4 511	790	229	+1 730
	6 941	1 002	408	+966
	8 292	1 109	479	+827
	9 656	1 058	539	+620
1931	9 959	1 176	529	+5
	10 226	1 388	505	+31
	10 165	1 471	449	+18
	10 165	1 420	389	+305
1932	10 220	1 565	428	−85
	10 267	1 721	409	+85
	10 098	1 824	437	+374

Source: Reichskreditgesellschaft, *Deutschlands wirtschaftliche Entwicklung*, several issues.

1931. The same held true too in other parts of heavy industry: the Vereinigte Stahlwerke reported in 1930 excessive stocks of coal, coke and ores. Fried. Krupp AG only managed to reduce its inventories in 1931.[8]

The credit crisis of 1931 made the situation for businesses much more acute, and precipitated a second wave of destocking in 1932.

Non-inventory investment was also falling: new investment fell from 1929 (the peak investment for the post-stabilisation period had been reached in 1928). Gross investment did not fall quite so dramatically in 1929 only because of an increasing volume of replacement investment. In 1930 there was net disinvestment in the following industries; textiles, lignite, chemicals, engineering, and building. There was still new investment taking place in the oil industry, hard coal mining (the Harpener Bergbau extended its deep pits: Robert Müner and Gneisenau), and in automobile production: new plants were built for Ford in Cologne and for Adam Opel in Rüsselsheim.[9]

However, some observers trace the weakness of German investment back even earlier than 1928. If we take new domestic orders for the machine industry (the most characteristic investment goods industry) as a proxy for investment decisions and thus as a major *lead* indicator, we find the pre-crisis peak in the autumn of 1927 (Table XXII).

These changes in investment cannot be so directly attributed to credit market changes as the process of inventory destocking and disinvestment. They were responses to overall profitability and to longer-term expectations of how the economy would develop. But in investment the banking crisis of 1931 produced a caesura too: for it precipitated liquidity crises and even bankruptcies, and thus ruled out for many enterprises the idea of any new investment.

In the spring of 1931 there had been signs that a general recovery might begin soon. Interest rates were low; the economic periodicals sounded an optimistic note as to the level of business confidence; and the normal seasonal spring fall in the

[8] *Wirtschaft und Statistik* 1932, 594–7. Also SAA 4/LF 716, Vereinigte Stahlwerke monthly reports and memorandum, 'Lagerbestände: Halbzeug und Walzeisen-Fertigerzeugnisse'.

[9] *Wirtschaft und Statistik* 1932, 594–7.

Table XXXII: New Domestic Orders for German Machine Industry 1927–1932 (1928=100)

Quarters					
1927	1	100	1930	1	72
	2	116		2	61
	3	131		3	55
	4	110		4	41
1928	1	111	1931	1	42
	2	102		2	42
	3	97		3	33
	4	91		4	26
1929	1	92	1932	1	21
	2	96		2	25
	3	87		3	26
	4	77		4	26

Source: Wagemann 1935, 228.

level of unemployment lasted longer than usual. Schumpeter concludes that the German economy had already reached its 'natural' lower limit at this time:

> Some adjustments in the cost structures of the kind noticed in our description of German events of 1930 may have given an impulse to individual firms and industries. If so, subsequent vicissitudes would have to be explained primarily in terms of accidents and external factors and the first half of 1931 would, in this case, give us a fair idea of what the rest of the depression would have been without them.[10]

From June and July 1931, however, banks put up their money rates in order to keep deposits; and cut back their loan business in order to maintain liquidity in the face of deposit withdrawals. As a result of having to repay loans quickly, even firms which would normally have been regarded as healthy moved into difficulties and near to bankruptcy. Small firms were particularly badly hit as banks believed that they would encounter less resistance to loan repayments from them; but even large and well-regulated firms suffered. The Fried. Krupp AG, for instance, had reorganised itself financially in 1925–6. With a capital of 160m. RM it had, on 30 September 1931, debts of 43 162 000 RM to banks and of 29 748 000 RM to

[10] Schumpeter 1939, 930. *Wochenbericht des Instituts für Konjunkturforschung* 3/52, 25 Mar. 1931.

other creditors (largely suppliers); one year later, after the massive bank reduction of credit, these figures were 34 128 000 RM and 9 025 000 RM respectively.[11] Krupp gives a striking example of how the bank crisis affected the abilities of suppliers to give credit, thus forcing destocking. As a consequence of the bank disaster, the German depression thus reached its cyclical low in 1932 rather than 1931.

Two issues are central to a discussion of the German banking crisis:

1. How far was the crisis caused by external influences, and how far did it follow from an internal logic of the German economy? The Germans insisted again and again that it was the withdrawal of French, and more particularly American, short-term loans to Germany that had caused the banking collapse. This explanation has appeared in almost all standard accounts of German developments. Schumpeter—in speaking of 'accidents and external factors' which prompted an 'inexplicable and altogether unique' outflow of money from Germany—is presenting a quite orthodox account: it was impossible for him and for others to imagine that a financial crisis of such magnitude could stem from the workings of the economic system alone. The most thorough early account of the bank panic was written by Hans Priester, a journalist on the *Berliner Tageblatt*, who conceived his work as a polemical attack on the management of the German banks and of the Reichsbank, but nevertheless stresses that the origins of the collapse lay in a failing of foreign confidence, a crisis of confidence so deep-rooted that it could not be dealt with in the way that the scares of 1929 and 1930 had been.[12] It is this version that has been adopted, with minor variations, in the more recent authoritative accounts of Lüke, Born, and Gerd Hardach.[13]

2. What could have been done to prevent such a crisis? Recently this question has become rather controversial. The threat of financial instability has again become more acute since the breakdown of the post-World War II Bretton Woods System in 1971–3, and because of the massive borrowing,

[11] Fried. Krupp AG Annual Reports 1931 and 1932.

[12] H. Priester, *Das Geheimnis des 13. Juli*, Berlin 1931.

[13] Lüke 1958; K. E. Born, *Die deutsche Bankenkrise 1931: Finanzen und Politik*, Munich 1967; G. Hardach 1976.

particularly by newly industrialising countries, to cope with the strains posed by the two oil-price hikes of the 1970s. As a result of the contemporary problem, a substantial amount of attention is now devoted in academic analysis to financial crises as major causes of economic fluctuations.

Hyman Minsky has presented in this context a reinterpretation of Keynes, which correctly situates Keynes in the environment of the inter-war period, an environment characterised by the threat of financial instability.[14] In his model of the Keynesian solution, government expenditure offers the key to the stabilisation of the financial situation.

Minsky's picture involves, as an 'essential and not a peripheral characteristic of the financial structure of capitalism', investment booms in which large projects are financed on a basis of increasing debt levels until a terminal period; only during the terminal period are the current earnings of the finance unit greater than its payments commitments.[15] Thus when a new steel works is built, it takes a long time before the works produce steel which can be sold; in the meantime the enterprise needs to borrow in order to pay large amounts to designers, construction firms, etc.

The present value of units such as the steel works—the basis on which they take up debt—is measured by discounting future returns. As interest rates rise during the investment boom, assessments of the present value of such investments fall. Holders of debt will try to liquidate their assets; and they will be particularly quick in doing this if they have been buying financial assets on margin. Thus the prices of assets in the market fall faster and further sales are forced. The financial crisis that results may take the form of a Stock Exchange crash, or, if banks have been particularly active in the financing of investment, a bank collapse. Such financial and speculative crises, according to Minsky, often mark the upper turning-point of the business cycle. The creation of state debt is the one secure way of preventing such a crisis, since state security

[14] H. P. Minsky, *John Maynard Keynes*, New York 1976.

[15] H. P. Minsky, 'The Financial-Instability Hypothesis: Capitalist Processes and the Behaviour of the Economy' in (eds.) C. P. Kindleberger and J.-P. Laffargue, *Financial Crises: Theory, History and Policy*, Cambridge 1982, 32.

creates a kind of debt that is not vulnerable to overtrading and to the revision of expectations which causes lenders to wish to reduce their holdings of non-state debt. Such a view of financial crisis is based on reflection on the American experience, and particularly on the American inter-war experience, where open market purchases by the Federal Reserve System of government paper did indeed eventually offer a way out of the bank crashes of 1930–3.

For the German case, however—in view of the investigation in Chapter III of the insecurity surrounding public finance at the end of the 1920s—we might be less happy with an analysis of the Minsky type. The post-war rise in state expenditure was politically controversial, and the controversy was sharpened by the constitutional structure and the external political position of the Weimar Republic. If everyone in Germany, and abroad, had accepted that high state expenditure was desirable, the Minsky path might have been suitable. Since there was so much reference to overspending, to slush and corruption, and since these references were picked up by the international financial community, increases in government debt appeared to be, *ceteris paribus*, a destabilising rather than a stabilising influence.

THE STORY OF THE CRISIS

The German money supply began to contract from the summer of 1930. After a more or less uninterrupted rise from 1925, the money supply fell: by 17 per cent to June 1931. The fall was not a consequence of the action of the central bank alone: only a part (8 per cent) of the fall is attributable to the action of the Reichsbank in determining the stock of what Friedman and Schwartz call high-powered money (HPM) (currency in circulation and bank reserves at the central bank). The main cause of the contraction of the money supply 1930–1 lay in the commercial banking sector: in the first place, banks sought to increase their reserves in an attempt to keep up their nominal liquidity in the face of deposit withdrawals; secondly, such withdrawals reduced the ratio of deposits to currency. After May 1931, the fall in the widely defined money supply became very much quicker and assumed a new significance; the attack on the banks meant in July the failure of the Darmstädter Bank, and then a general panic which closed all banks for several weeks. The result of this loss of confidence was a fall in the broad money stock to February 1932 at an annual rate of 24 per cent (during which period HPM actually rose). This was the shock that dealt such a fatal blow to hopes of economic recovery in the spring of 1931.[16]

The question of how the bank and credit crises should be dealt with became rapidly the central issue for economic policy-making: in the aftermath of the collapse, immediately effective short-term measures looked like chimeras, and a much longer-term strategy—involving as a first step the reconstruction of the banking system and a change in the method of handling government debt—needed to be adopted.

The crisis did not look like a classical banking crisis of the type that occurred in Britain in 1847 or 1890 and was occurring in USA after 1930, a type of crisis that might be overcome by traditional remedies, such as a liberal rediscounting policy of the central bank, motivated by a belief in the obligation of central banks to act as lenders of last resort in a crisis. In the first place, the German situation was unusual because of the high foreign short-term indebtedness of the German banking system and of the German economy as a whole. The total German short-term foreign debt was 15½–16b. RM in mid-1930, and 13.1b. RM in July 1931. The German banks alone owed 5.9b. RM in July 1931.[17] Moreover, there were structural weaknesses in the German banking system. The capital and the reserves of the banks had been depleted as a consequence of the inflation; and the dramatic expansion in bank lending in the later 1920s took place as a result on a very narrow capital base. Bank liquidity ratios were very low: much lower than before the War, although even then the banks had relied on the Reichsbank as lender of last resort in crises such as that of 1907.[18] In addition an exaggerated conservatism meant, as we have seen in Chapter IV, that bank lending was

[16] James 1984.

[17] Ibid. 76. Also R2/13651, debt on 28 July 1931.

[18] H. James, 'Did the Reichsbank draw the Right Lessons from the Great Inflation?' in (ed.) G. D. Feldman, *Die Nachwirkungen der Inflation auf die deutsche Geschichte*, Munich 1985, 211–30.

concentrated with big industry and big agriculture, and with traditional products. This helped to slow down the economic development of Germany in the 1920s by causing a misallocation of investment resources; it also contributed to the undermining of the banking system once the weak debtors started to get into difficulties.

A fundamentally unsound structure required only a small push, then, to topple it. Was that push a foreign one? American observers argued that foreign withdrawals should not be held responsible for a crisis produced by German mismanagement. Firstly, they said, the loss of foreign currency in 1930 and 1931 was due to a massive German capital flight tolerated by the German Government; and secondly, the financial position of industry and the banks was made worse by that government's management or mismanagement of its debt.[19] Here it is argued that the American view of the cause of the bank collapse was in substance correct; and that the German Government recognised this when it embarked on a policy of reconstruction.

At the outset of the crisis, the Reichsbank believed that it should confine itself to reassuring statements. German banks were not, it claimed in the face of all truth, fundamentally weak: the affair of the Austrian Creditanstalt (which on 13 May had failed to produce its accounts) could not be repeated in Germany. Reichsbank President Hans Luther told the Governor of the Federal Reserve Bank of New York (FRBNY) George Harrison that: 'Periodical publication of German banks' statements provides safe means for judging their situation which is sound notwithstanding large foreign withdrawals.'[20] Earlier in the year State Secretary Schäffer had told a foreign finance expert that he was not worried about short-term private loans reaching maturity and that indeed matters were now 'on the upgrade'.[21] These claims were not simply the product of a deceptive confidence intended to placate foreigners; rather the Government and the Reichsbank were badly informed about the position of banks and industry. The

[19] This line was consistently argued by the Governor of the FRBNY, George Harrison.

[20] FRBNY Reichsbank file, 11 June 1931 Luther cable to Harrison.

[21] PRO FO 371/15209, 27 Feb. 1931 Rumbold (British ambassador in Berlin) to Sargent.

Finance Ministry found out only three days before the general public about the difficulties which the Bremen firm of Nordwolle had in balancing its account, and it took longer for the Government to realise how much money the Darmstädter Bank had in textiles in general and Nordwolle in particular.[22]

German banks faced regular and seasonal strain, and the first reaction was to treat June–July 1931 as nothing more than a slightly abnormal case of the vulnerability of the German banking system to a shock at the payment date at the month-end when bourse contracts became due ('Report and Deport business'). In the summer of 1931 the banks lost a high proportion of their short-term deposits: the fastest fall was in the volume of eight-day to three-month deposits. These withdrawals affected the Great Banks particularly severely: whereas before the crisis their liquidity had always been superior to that of the small private banks, by the end of 1931 it had fallen below that of the local banks.[23]

Part of the problem was that the Great Banks had proportionately larger foreign commitments than had local or provincial banks. The knowledge of the high level of short-term indebtedness in general in Germany certainly helped to increase the general insecurity. Already in 1927 Hjalmar Schacht, then the Reichsbank President, had sounded an alarm about the overall size of the foreign debt; and in 1929 the Reichsbank and the Government conducted a secret study of foreign lending to banks (the problem was that the published monthly balance sheets of the banks gave no indication of the extent to which deposits were of foreign origin). But the volume of foreign debt actually gives little clue to the relative weakness or strength of the banks. The 1929 figures showed that the Berliner Handelsgesellschaft, which had a reputation for conservatism, actually had a higher proportion of its deposits from abroad than the Deutsche, Dresdner, Darmstädter banks or the Disconto-Gesellschaft.[24] Within the camp of the Great Banks, it is impossible to find a significant division between banks working largely with foreign funds and another group looking more to dom-

[22] IfZ ED93/11, 14 June 1931 diary entry.

[23] F. W. Henning, 'Die Liquidität der Banken in der Weimarer Republik' in (ed.) H. Winkel, *Währungs- und finanzpolitische Fragen der Zwischenkriegszeit*, Berlin 1973, 58, 60.

[24] ZStA Reichsbank 6709: Foreign Deposits in Major German Banks, June 1929.

estic sources of capital. Indeed, the Deutsche Bank, which was relatively strong in the crisis, had a relatively low proportional share of deposits from abroad; but the Disconto-Gesellschaft, with which it fused in 1929, had a much higher share than the Dresdner or the Darmstädter.[25]

The 1929 survey did not offer any indications of overall danger either: and there were only a very few warning voices. A director of the state-owned Reichs-Kredit-Gesellschaft had already argued in 1927 that the high level of short-term debt was dangerous, but on the whole the Economics Ministry, Schacht, and later Luther, believed that the inflow of short-term loans was part of a longer-term flow of investment, and that the short-term credits reflected nothing more than the pre-war custom of using investment funds on the money market when the capital market was unfavourable.[26] Thus if the price of shares were judged too high, the amount lent short-term would increase: for instance in 1926 foreigners had bought shares, but as the bull market developed they sold and placed their proceeds with the banks. This argument looked as if it rested on the assumption that there were no substantial hot-money flows; but it could be argued too that a discount rate rise would be sufficient to retain and attract new short-term money and would also at the same time lower share prices, making the conversion attractive for foreign investors. Even in June 1931 a rise in the Reichsbank discount rate reassured foreign lenders quite effectively (this reassurance was of little avail since it was only at the last moment that *foreign* loss of confidence played a substantial role in events in Germany).[27] Thus the Government and the Reichsbank did not believe that the German system was particularly unstable.

After 1929 and the September 1930 elections, the political calculation increased in significance for investors; and maturities of foreign short-term loans were reduced.[28] Those bankers who feared that something was seriously wrong, however, did

[25] K. Gossweiler, *Großbanken, Industriemonopole und Staat. Ökonomie und Politik des staatsmonopolistischen Kapitalismus in Deutschland 1914–1932*, Berlin 1972, 329 is misleading here.

[26] IfZ ED93/27, 27 Aug. 1927 Schäffer memorandum (on short-term indebtedness).

[27] *Vossische Zeitung*, no. 142, 16 June 1931.

[28] IfZ ED93/9, 1 Oct. 1930 diary entry.

not believe that the malaise lay in the level of foreign investment, but hinted instead at fundamentally flawed bank positions. This was the real German problem. The Swiss banker Friedrich Somary believed—and publicised his belief—that the world economy would not recover its health before the overvalued pound left the gold standard, before the German and Italian banks collapsed as a consequence of the faulty credit policies pursued in those countries, and before the Kreuger concern collapsed.[29]

The apparent withdrawals very frequently marked domestic capital flight: the Reich Statistical Office estimated that, between 1924 and 1930, 4–5b. RM had moved abroad long-term and another 4.5b. RM short-term. The left-wing parties in Germany quoted very high figures for capital flight—Stegerwald (Centre) in spring 1929 said 8b. RM, Severing in June 1930 7b. RM for flight to Switzerland alone. The *Frankfurter Zeitung* in August 1930 estimated the volume more humbly at 5b. RM.[30]

Defining the volume of capital flight is (and was) in fact largely a guessing game. The official statistics provided by the Statistisches Reichsamt provide only a possible upper figure: between 1927 and 1930, 3.9b. RM short-term and 4.9b. RM long-term funds had been moved out of Germany.[31] Of course this sum includes foreign withdrawals and 'genuine' German foreign investment. It is difficult logically to distinguish between legitimate foreign investment and flight capital, since the same sum might be used to protect a German firm against taxes and exchange losses in Germany and also to consolidate that firm's hold over Central Europe. Swiss subsidiaries were set up to take money out of Germany unknown to the German tax-collector and also to conceal from Czech, Hungarian, and Austrian authorities that it was German money that was being invested in their states. We can only look at the kind of use made of German funds abroad and guess: in many cases

[29] IfZ ED93/30, 27 Jan. 1931 Schäffer note on conversation with Somary; also ED93/19, 11 March 1932 diary entry. The Kreuger concern was highly involved with European government finance: including in Germany, where Kreuger had been associated with the Lee Higginson operation.

[30] ZStA RWiM 15060, 24 Oct. 1930 memorandum; *Frankfurter Zeitung* 22 Aug. 1930; PA/AA Sonderreferat W, Finanzwesen 16/11 memorandum (n.d.).

[31] Wagemann 1935, 125 ff.

German money abroad was re-lent into Germany and appeared as a foreign deposit handled on a different tax basis.[32] Such an operation was clearly capital flight.

There were two different kinds of capital flight: first, there was the long-standing export of capital by companies and banks. Banks clearly needed to place a certain amount of money to protect their position, though they kept relatively large sums outside Germany even after June–July 1931 when such reserves should have been used. Industrial capital export had taken place in order to avoid high German taxes; this is why the Bad Eilsen conference of the Friedrich-List-Gesellschaft had insisted on the urgency of tax reduction. In 1929 Hermann Müller spoke of the need to reduce capital flight as a primary consideration in any new tax programme.[33]

The Reich Finance Ministry was aware that this sort of operation was taking place: during the inflation period German firms had become expert in the art of transferring money to Belgium and particularly to the Netherlands and Switzerland. On occasion the Finance Ministry had little alternative except to encourage this flight. When the chemical combine IG Farben founded a Swiss subsidiary (IG Chemie Schweiz) with the sole aim of avoiding the payment of 6–8m. RM tax, the Ministry concluded lamely: 'Such transactions cannot be stopped if the mobility of international capital is not interfered with.' The IG Chemie Schweiz had shares with a guaranteed and fixed dividend: profits were in this way transferred out of Germany.[34] In 1930 the Finance Ministry agreed to Polyphonwerke AG imitating IG Farben, although the Polyphonwerke could not even put up the rather weak case that IG Farben had presented, namely that some of its investors were Swiss. When the Vereinigte Glanzstoff-Fabriken AG fused with the Dutch firm of NV Nederlandsche Kunstzijdefabriek, the Ministry allowed a reduction in bourse turnover tax on the fusion and then also granted a delay in the payment of the tax.[35]

[32] See A. Teichova, *An Economic Background to Munich: International Business and Czechoslovakia 1918–1938*, Cambridge 1974, 127 and 285, for examples of how Germans used foreign interests as a camouflage in expanding into south-east Europe.

[33] FES Müller II 179, 8 Sept. 1929 Müller to Stampfer.

[34] ZStA RFM B7710, 11 Nov. 1929 Finance Ministry memorandum.

[35] Ibid. B7710, 2 July 1929 Finance Ministry memorandum.

The Prussian Ministry of Commerce had tried to stop the Polyphonwerke transaction, but in December 1930 the Prussian state-owned electricity works carried out exactly the same manoeuvre in setting up a Basel firm, the Continentale Elektrizitäts-Union AG. The Reich Finance Ministry commented sourly: 'So the Land is carrying out a similar transaction to that which the Prussian Ministry responsible both for the bourse and for the Preussag holds to be illegitimate.'[36]

Large-scale capital flight could only be controlled effectively through credit policy. If money became scarce in Germany, firms would not be able to afford the luxury of avoiding taxes and of speculating against the Mark, and capital would be repatriated, if only in the form of short-term loans from Swiss or Dutch cover institutions. A very clear indicator of the extent of German capital flight was thus given by the revelation that, of the Dutch short-term credits outstanding on 28 July 1931, 67 per cent were direct to German industrial, agricultural, or commercial undertakings; for Switzerland the figure was 45 per cent while for the USA it was only 28 per cent; a high proportion of these direct loans to German industry represented loans from industry to itself.[37] The Dutch credits were concentrated in a relatively small part of the German economy: 203 German firms accounted for 63.4 per cent of the total volume in 1931; 8 per cent of the Dutch money went to mining, 9 per cent to textile works, 10 per cent to machine-tool producing and 12.6 per cent to food-processing concerns.[38] Tight German credit policies should then keep the Mark stable, and indeed the British consul in Basel did report very favourably in late 1930 on the decline of large-scale capital flight.[39]

The same set of motives did not apply to the other form of capital flight—the movement of relatively small sums across the German border. Banknotes were taken across to Switzerland—the Reichsbank's branches in Lörrach (directly across the river from Basel) and Konstanz (on the Lake) reported to Berlin on the demand for high denomination notes at times of political crisis. During the Paris reparations negotiations, the

[36] Ibid. B7710, 4 Dec. 1929 Finance Ministry memorandum.
[37] BoE OV 34/149, Analysis of the Short-Term Credits granted to Germany.
[38] BAK R2/13651, 7 Nov. 1931 report of Anmeldestelle für Auslandsschulden.
[39] PRO FO 371/14357, 1 Nov. 1930 report of British consulate Basel.

Konstanz branch paid out 460 000 RM in 1,000 RM notes in the course of a single day. Swiss banks told the German consulate in Basel too about the increase in their foreign deposits: in November 1930 Swiss banks reported that foreign deposits had risen by 2.6b. s.f. over the past year, and half of this (or 3.25b. RM) represented German capital flight. In this category fall the purchase of property abroad—in Zürich alone houses to the value of 34m s.f. were bought by foreigners or holding companies from 1928 to 1930—and the buying of foreign life insurance policies.[40] The proportions of life insurance business carried out in RM reveal better than any other indicator the degree of lack of confidence at the grass roots in the long-term stability of the German currency (see Table XXXIII).[41]

Table XXXIII: Life Insurance in Germany: % of New Business denominated in RM

1924	1.95
1925	24.80
1926	51.95
1927	68.92
1928	74.22
1929	62.69
1930	72.54

Immediately after the inflation, only a small minority of new business was conducted in RM; the amount grew until 1929, when the events at Paris and the open struggle between the Reichsbank and the Reich Government undermined public confidence.

Small-scale capital flight could not be controlled at all through changes in the credit market in Germany: it could only be halted, if at all, by legal action. After the banking collapse restrictions were imposed on foreign travel in order to prevent middle-class Germans on their way to cures in Swiss sanatoria taking suitcases stuffed with Marks with them.

Banks and industry were affected also by genuine foreign withdrawals of credit. After September 1930 there had been a

[40] From files of PA/AA Sonderreferat W, Finanzwesen 16, 11–12; 23 April 1929 Report of Reichsbank branches, and 6 May and 8 Nov. 1930 Reports of Zürich consulate-general.

[41] ZStA RWiM 15345.

loss of gold and foreign currency as French banks withdrew money from Germany.[42] The major shock to Germany came, however, in the spring and early summer of 1931. After the Creditanstalt's collapse in May the whole central European situation had been precarious and there had been some withdrawals in Germany. The banks lost 337m. RM (=2.6 per cent) of their deposits in May; those with bad reputations lost most. Thus the Danat lost 97m. RM, the Deutsche 51m. RM, and the Commerzbank (or Compri) 36m. RM, while deposits in the conservative BHG actually increased, though the BHG's cash liquidity and first-degree liquidity were poor in comparison to other banks.[43] The banks had not reduced their short-term borrowing, however, and there are no signs of foreign withdrawals immediately after the Creditanstalt's collapse. Only in the week ending 6 June did the Reichsbank sell foreign currency (73m. RM) in any substantial volume, and serious gold losses only began in the next week. The only sales of gold before the 6 June were to France (45m. RM).[44]

On 6 June, the Brüning Government issued a public appeal which gave the impression that a reparations crisis was about to occur. From this day, withdrawals increased in a *sauve qui peut* of creditors. In June 1931 the Danat lost 847.8m. RM deposits (=40.9 per cent), the Dresdner 218.1m. RM (=10.7 per cent), the BHG 35m. RM (=8.6 per cent), the Deutsche 321.5m. RM (=8.2 per cent) and the Compri 113m. RM (=8.1 per cent).[45]

The initial foreign attack came from France, even though after September 1930 French credit to Germany had not been substantial. It was in fact Germans in France who made the first move. On 13 June, the British ambassador in Paris reported that 'alarming reports have reached government circles in Paris from one Mannheimer, an associate of Mendelssohns, whose motive and general conduct are not considered to be above suspicion', that the Reichsbank might

[42] Weekly statements of Reichsbank: in September the Reichsbank lost 140m. RM foreign exchange, or 5% of its reserves.

[43] My calculations from monthly bank statements published in *Die Bank*; see also Born, 67.

[44] FRBNY Reichsbank file: weekly cables of Reichsbank reporting gold and foreign exchange position.

[45] *Die Bank*.

suspend payment in a few days.[46] At first only Germans and other Europeans got out of the Mark: in the week ending 10 June the Reichsbank sold 20m. RM gold in Britain, 10m. in France, 17m. in the Netherlands, 8m. in Switzerland, and only 6m. in the USA. It was only in the week ending 24 June that most of the gold sales were on the American market.[47]

The evidence of the banks confirms the picture of Uncle Sam joining in a run only at the last moment. It was 23 June before the Bankers Trust Company tried to cut the credit line extended to the Deutsche Bank.[48] On 6 July 1931 the US ambassador cabled to Washington that the Guaranty Trust Company of New York had given notice to the large Berlin banks that it was going to begin immediate withdrawals.[49] In view of the enormous withdrawals other creditors had made from the Danat in June, this decision was surprisingly late.

Foreign observers suspected that Germans were responsible for a domestic panic, and expected the Reichsbank to control the situation by discriminating against those responsible for the domestic capital flight. The FRBNY and Governor Harrison in particular offered continual, rather bad-tempered, advice to Luther on how to manage Germany. Germany lost more and more foreign currency and gold. The alternatives considered by the Reichsbank—new international borrowing from the BIS and the central banks or a rejection of para. 31 of the Reichsbank Law requiring a minimum reserve in gold and foreign currency of 40 per cent of the German note issue—were impracticable: in the first case because no one was willing to lend, in the second because a violation of the Reichsbank Law would also be an attack on the 1930 Hague Treaty. Instead, Harrison insisted that the Reichsbank could only stop capital flight by the application of rigorous restriction in its discounting policy.[50] On 13 June Luther had already put the discount rate up two points to 7 per cent and on 22 June the Reichsbank began selecting the bills it took for discount. This

[46] PRO FO 371/15209, 13 June 1931 Tyrrell cable.
[47] FRBNY Reichsbank file, weekly cables.
[48] BAK R111/108, 23 June 1931 memorandum of C. Wight (Bankers Trust).
[49] NA StDep 862.51, 6 July 1931 Sackett cable.
[50] FRBNY Harrison papers 3115.2, 19 June 1931 Harrison–Norman telephone conversation.

was not enough. Harrison told Montagu Norman (Governor of the Bank of England) that he would not accept that the USA had any obligation to buy bills to help Germany and Europe. He continued to argue that Luther was not doing enough: 'I felt the chief difficulty was a flight from the Reichsmark by German nationals and that the Reichsbank should resort to much more drastic credit control than apparently was the case.' Though Norman took a slightly more sympathetic attitude to Luther, he argued that the main problem was that 'they need Dr Schacht there' since 'Luther does not seem to have the force necessary to do the trick'.[51] Harrison's view was shared by the US State Department. Under-Secretary Castle cabled to the ambassador in Berlin that, 'All reports received here [i.e. from the FRBNY] seem to indicate that instead of instituting the strictest measures of control, the German Government is temporising in the hope of assistance from the US.'[52]

The FRBNY continued to press its argument even after the collapse of the Danat. When Norman tried to explain that the bank's closure showed that restriction had been taken as far as was economically possible, Harrison noted: 'I did not quite follow this statement, nor did I agree with him.' Harrison was supported by the Banque de France, whose Governor believed too that 'a good part' of the German crisis was caused by the actions of German nationals.[53]

American and French policy was in fact based on a realistic assessment of what was going on in Germany, though the capital flight which led to the balance of payments crisis was in fact extraordinarily difficult for a government used to treating capital flight sympathetically to control. At the same time the French and American leaderships believed that an end should be called to the policy of the 1920s, the policy of treating European weaknesses with indulgence. The main European weakness was the failure to stabilise public expenditure.

Many observers saw 1931 as a case of the collapse of public

[51] Ibid. 3115.2, 2 and 8 July 1931 Harrison–Norman telephone conversations.

[52] NA StDep 862.51, 15 July 1931 Castle to Sackett.

[53] FRBNY Harrison papers 3115.2, 16 July 1931 Harrison–Norman telephone conversation; 3125.2, 10 July 1931 Harrison–Lacour–Gayet conversation.

finance rather than an isolated banking upset. Thus one US consular report:

This consistent uncertainty and insecurity with regard to the Reich's finances during the past year seems to have been one of the main reasons for the severity of the economic depression. Not until December did the Government break with this method, but the measures then taken to effect a rehabilitation of its finances, which were generally considered sound, would probably have been more effective if adopted at an earlier date.[54]

The Reich Finance Ministry was aware that the volume of its short-term debt posed a threat to the stability of the currency. Negotiations with German commercial banks on the funding of the government debt would draw attention to the size of the debt and would revive the conflicts of 1929. From January 1931, the Reich Government pressed the Reichsbank to open a credit line with other central banks or with the BIS. Luther was hostile to this idea to the last minute: he continued to block the way until 19 June, only one day before the attack on the Mark made him beg for a central bank loan.[55]

Norman, who for six months had been told by Luther that Germany did not require and would not use a central bank credit, was very surprised when at last Luther made his request; and he then took a hostile stance, as he believed that only political demands, and in particular the French insistence on receiving reparation payments, were responsible for the economic collapse in Germany.[56] Reparations had, he thought, led to the German budget crisis and to bank difficulties.

There were in fact no shocks to the German Finance Ministry in April and May, but a new savings programme was drawn up to provide a protective buffer of cash to prevent a funding crisis similar to that of December 1929 from occurring once reparations negotiations had begun. The new programme, which cut civil service salaries still further and which imposed a small increase in the turnover tax, was to coincide

[54] NA StDep 862.51, 22 May 1931 W. E. Beitz Report; FRBNY German Govt. file, 9 June 1932 memorandum of L. Galantiere.

[55] IfZ ED93/11, 19 June 1931 diary entry (note on meeting in Reichskanzlei of Schäffer with Luther and Brüning).

[56] Bennett 1962, 225 ff. Also FRBNY Harrison papers 3115.1, 9 July Harrison–Norman telephone conversation.

with the German government's statement that 'the limits of the privations we have imposed on our people have been reached'. It was put into effect by NVO on 5 June.[57]

The June NVO was, however, insufficient in its scope and too late in its timing, for on 9 June it became clear that tax revenue for April and May was well below the projected figure.[58] Suddenly, the old funding crisis reappeared. The commercial banks were to be forced to take 125m. RM more treasury bills by 10 June, despite Luther's protests that this operation would strain the banks too much. The problem was that there were no realistic alternatives.[59] The British embassy had suggested that Germany should raise the money in France, but the Reparations Appeal had poisoned the political climate there. A League of Nations loan too would be tied to impossible political conditions. Without loans from somewhere, however, Germany would not be able to make the monthly Young Plan payment due with the BIS on 15 June, and German credit would collapse.[60]

Even borrowing the 250m. RM from German banks risked a repetition of 1929. The DVP had already announced its intention to support the Nazis and the DNVP in forcing the calling of the Reichstag and bringing down Brüning. If the Reichstag were called, 'we would risk the suspension of the NVO and the collapse of world confidence in Germany'. Schäffer was frightened that the DVP would use its contacts in the German banking world as part of its intrigue against Brüning.[61]

The banks allowed the German Government to deal with 15 June, and the problem of making reparations payments appeared to have ended—though only for the course of a year—when on 20 June President Hoover announced a moratorium on international political payments (reparations and war debts). International uncertainty, however, remained as

[57] RGBl 1931 I 279–314. 6 June memorandum quoted in Bennett 1961, 128.

[58] IfZ ED93/11, 9 June 1931 diary entry.

[59] IfZ ED93/11, 10 and 11 June 1931 diary entries.

[60] IfZ ED93/11, 12 June diary entry (Schäffer conversation with Luther and Dreyse).

[61] IfZ ED93/11, 12 June 1931 diary entry; also BAK NL Luther 365, 12 June 1931 negotiations with Dingeldey (DVP); and HA/GHH 4001012024/8b, 11 June 1931 Blank to Reusch.

the French Government hesitated in accepting Hoover's plan.[62] It was now that the international withdrawals from Germany became really significant, and Luther could only persuade western authorities to help if he applied credit restrictions with the aim of preventing German capital flight.[63] Harrison's doctrine was forcing Luther to shut the door after a bolting horse. Restriction was announced on 20 June and put into effect on Monday 22 June. The Reichsbank was no longer prepared to act unconditionally as a lender of last resort. This action raised the spectre of a funding crisis once more, for banks would be less willing to take Reich paper if the number of other bills they might take to the Reichsbank for rediscount were reduced. Luther admitted, 'If restrictions are applied, the private banks cannot be expected to take Reich paper.'[64]

In those circumstances, the Reich's schedule of payments became in the eyes of the Finance Ministry officials a countdown to banking disaster:[65]

	m.RM		m.RM
19–20 June 1931	80	30 June 1931	30
25 June 1931	30	4 July 1931	104
26 June 1931	20	10 July 1931	37.5
27 June 1931	10	15 July 1931	122.5
29 June 1931	30		

On 9 July the Finance Ministry reached an agreement with the Reichsbank. The Reich was to take a credit which was not to be renewable beyond 16 July, and Reichsbank Director Fuchs agreed to renew 35m. RM Reich Treasury bills, but then the arrangement collapsed as the Reichsbank was unable to find rediscounters for the bills.[66]

After the credit rationing was imposed, Luther's resistance to the notion of appealing for a foreign loan crumbled. It no longer seemed of any purpose to use Germany's credit difficul-

[62] Bennett 1961, 169 ff.

[63] Ritscher (RKG) and Löb (Mendelssohn) advocated domestic credit rationing: IfZ ED93/11, 13 June 1931 diary entry.

[64] IfZ ED93/11, 20 June 1931 diary entry.

[65] IfZ ED93/11, 15 June 1931 diary entry: advice of Norden, Weiss, and Bayrhoffer (in Reich Finance Ministry).

[66] BAK R2/3853, 15 July 1931 memorandum.

ties to force the Government to undertake financial reform, since the main cause of the panic was now an external run prompted by concern over the state of German public and private finance. On 20 June Luther received a $100m. credit from the three major western central banks and the BIS, and when this was insufficient to deal with the demand for *Devisen* (foreign exchange) he tried to negotiate a new loan. On 9 July he made an aeroplane journey to London and he quickly went on, without encountering success anywhere, to Paris and Basel.[67]

Lack of Reichsbank support put the banks in a more difficult position, and industry suffered as government bills crowded out private ones.[68] It was widely believed that if any major firm came into difficulties and its bills became frozen that there would be a general catastrophe. Even if only one bank faced a run, the others would be too weak to help.[69] Bankers warned that Germany was not far from a universal collapse,[70] and the Reichsbank had made it clear that it would not give Lombard credit (advances against securities) to the Reich after 16 July.[71]

As a result there was already a nervous atmosphere before the Communist newspaper *Welt am Abend* on 5 June speculated on difficulties in the Danat bank after the Danat had refused to renew a loan to the municipality of Berlin.[72] The Danat issued a *démenti*. On 17 June Nordwolle published accounts revealing a loss of 24.05m. RM, and the close connection of Nordwolle and the Danat further weakened confidence in the bank.[73] It took another two weeks before it was clear quite how large Nordwolle's losses really were. On 1 July they were already estimated at 200m. RM. The next day the Reichsbank discussed the implications of the development of the Nordwolle affair for the Danat, but the first sign of public attention was an article in the Basel *Nationalzeitung* on 5 July which stated

[67] Bennett 1961, 224–30. G. Hardach 1976, 133–6.

[68] BAK R43I/647, Deutsche Bank memorandum: 'Denkschrift über die Juli-Ereignisse im Bankgewerbe', 8 Oct. 1931.

[69] IfZ ED93/11, 16 June 1931 diary entry.

[70] IfZ ED93/11, 19 June 1931 diary entry.

[71] IfZ ED93/11, 24 June 1931 diary entry.

[72] Born 1967, 71.

[73] IfZ ED93/11, 14 June 1931 diary entry.

that a major German bank was 'in difficulties'.[74] The Berlin Government promptly denied that the Reichsbank General Council had discussed the credit position of a Great Bank. On the next day, however, the *Nationalzeitung* defended itself by speaking openly of the Danat, and this started a panic among the Danat's depositors.[75]

Although the Reichsbank was aware of the danger of a general collapse of credit, it did not want to help in an obvious way as it feared that the Nordwolle's foreign (and predominantly British) creditors might spread the panic out of short-term German holdings.[76] The Reichsbank did nothing to make its credit rationing milder, and Goldschmidt, the head of the Danat, later complained that the rationing system had been used deliberately in order to discriminate against his bank.[77] Luther worked on the assumption that the German banking sector should protect itself against the collapse of a major institution.

German banks in the 1920s had been ruthlessly competitive in their drive to take over small provincial institutions. Luther, Brüning, and many commentators believed that in 1931 the other banks allowed the Danat to fall because of a misplaced sense of competition.[78] In addition the other banks were paralysed by fear and by conservatism. The Austrian Creditanstalt, according to popular interpretation, had made its fateful mistake in 1928 by taking over the struggling Bodenkreditanstalt. At the beginning of July, the losses of Nordwolle and of other firms linked to the Danat could not easily be ascertained and the banking system would have had to undertake a limitless risk in supporting the Danat.[79] Goldschmidt had only been willing to ask the Deutsche Bank for aid at the last moment (8 July) and then the Deutsche Bank also felt too weak to take advantage of its apparent strength. Most bankers were suspicious of the Danat's methods—and in particular of

[74] IfZ ED93/31, 29 July 1931 Schäffer memorandum: 'Geheimgeschichte der Bankenkrise', 251.

[75] Born 1967, 87–8.

[76] BAK R43I/1450, 4 July 1931 ministerial meeting.

[77] Schäffer 'Geheimgeschichte' (Fn. 74) 252; also IfZ ED93/11, 8 July 1931 diary entry.

[78] Priester 1931, 8 f.

[79] See 6 Oct. 1931 Deutsche Bank memorandum (Fn. 68).

the way in which it had become more of a *banque d'affaires* than any other German institution. Wassermann of the Deutsche Bank frequently referred to the banking problem as 'the Danat problem'.[80] Secondly, the Danat had specialised in the highly political business of communal finance: it had close connections with the City of Berlin and this had already placed the Danat in an unfavourable limelight in 1929 during the Schachtian struggle with Berlin.[81] Thirdly, the Danat's dividends had been considerably higher than those of its rivals, and this was widely supposed to be the consequence of the higher risks taken under Goldschmidt's management. Though the Danat's inherent position was in fact slightly stronger than that of the Dresdner Bank, it paid a price for its reputation.[82]

On 4 July, Luther attempted to make industry take part, together with the leading Berlin banks, in a 500m. RM guarantee syndicate for the Danat. Some major firms refused to join and on 8 July Luther used an emergency decree to set up the syndicate. In taking this action, Luther made his first major breach with the Harrisonian orthodoxy he had followed until then: the guarantee could only work if the Reichsbank was prepared to undertake to take all offered bills from the enterprises giving the guarantee.[83] In effect, the Reichsbank from then on stood behind the banks, and the ensuing debate about Luther's policy only occurred because on 8 July it was not clear quite how large a commitment the Reichsbank had given.

Luther's decision was not supported by banking orthodoxy. The Reichsbank's gold and foreign exchange cover of its note issue was very close to the legal minimum of 40 per cent (on 30 June it had been 40.1 per cent; by 7 July it had only recovered slightly, to 43.6 per cent),[84] and the general opinion was that the Bank's safety margin should be increased before it indulged in a risky support exercise. One banker, Rudolf Löb (Mendelssohn), thought that the only way to increase the Reichsbank's

[80] Schäffer 'Geheimgeschichte' (Fn. 74) 255. HA/GHH 400101251/Ob, 24 July 1931 Max Warburg to Reusch: in the meeting of 6 July Wasserman had suddenly announced that 'the Danat issue has not been resolved'.

[81] IfZ ED93/7, 12 Dec. 1929 diary entry.

[82] Schäffer 'Wallenberg' (Fn. IV/82) 132.

[83] IfZ ED93/11, 8 July 1931 diary entry.

[84] Reichsbank weekly statements.

gold balance was to float a $375m. German Government loan abroad. Such a project was destined to remain in the realm of fantasy, particularly as the problem was seen both abroad and at home as being fundamentally that of the German budget.[85]

An alternative proposal for an official German guarantee of some kind coupled with a voluntary freezing on the part of foreign creditors was eventually developed into the so-called 'Standstill Agreements'. From 8 July the Reich and the Reichsbank were obliged to play a crucial role in maintaining German stability. Germany was pushed into such an arrangement by reflection on the probable consequences of a collapse of its credit: 'If the foreign credits are not repaid the other credits would be called, there would be a run on the savings banks and in the end revolution.'[86] One of the first necessities was the stabilising of municipal finance. It had been the general American view that the management of German banks had lost its nerve but that the only basic weakness had been over-investment in German city administration. The Danat had notoriously taken too many municipal bills; and by 4 July there were signs of an imminent collapse of the credit of the big cities of Rhineland-Westphalia.[87]

Hamburg and Bremen were in acute difficulties, too, and their finances raised more international problems because of their importance as trading centres. Bremen's difficulties had contributed to the scope of the Nordwolle problems and brought down an old Bremen house, J. F. Schröder Bank. In Hamburg the major bank, M. M. Warburg & Co., was in less immediate danger than J. F. Schröder because Max Warburg could obtain support from Wall Street. Max Warburg's partner, Carl Melchior, reported that Max's American brothers had given personal guarantees, and Max as a result was able to announce that he could survive if only 3.8m. RM of his bank's 5.8m. RM credit to the city of Hamburg were paid back (a further 2m. RM were due from Hamburg to Behrend Söhne and 4m. RM to the Reichspost).[88] At a time when Reichsbank Vice-President Dreyse was pressing the

[85] IfZ ED93/11, 4 July 1931 diary entry.
[86] IfZ ED93/11, 2 July 1931 diary entry (comment of Schäffer).
[87] See Chapter III.
[88] IfZ ED93/11, 2 July 1931 diary entry. See also Büttner 217–33.

Reich to repay its debt in order to save the banks, the Reich was engaged in pumping money into the Rhineland, Hamburg, and Berlin in order to prevent the provincial and regional banks collapsing. The Reich gave 30m. RM as a first step to halt the collapse of the Hanseatic banks.[89]

The Reichsbank needed a new foreign loan if it were to be able to support this ambitious programme of stabilisation. This was the purpose of Luther's aeroplane journey of 9 July. The trip took in London, Paris, and Basel. On 8 July, Dreyse opened negotiations with the FRBNY for a similar credit. The German appeal only helped to sustain Harrison's unfavourable impression of what was happening in Berlin, since the only argument Dreyse advanced was a political one, which by now had become rather hackneyed: that without American help the Brüning Government would fall and Bolshevik or Nazi terror would descend on Germany. The reasoning appeared hysterical and offended Harrison's well-developed sense of the independence of the central bankers from political questions.[90]

On Saturday 11 July Goldschmidt told the Government that he could not open his bank for business on Monday morning. It was clear by Saturday evening that the Reichsbank would receive no help from abroad and thus was condemned to impotence. A new problem appeared: while the Dresdner Bank on Saturday had denied that it was in danger, on Sunday Wassermann (Deutsche Bank) reported that his rival was close to collapse too as a result of the high volume of withdrawals. A new Cabinet meeting on the bank issue then began (at 16.30 hrs.) and two hours later representatives of the banks joined the discussion. Schacht too—as a financial expert and former Reichsbank President—was present for most of that Sunday. There was a great deal of talk about the role of the Reichsbank. The Dresdner Bank argued that its collapse had been caused by the Reichsbank's refusal to take its bills and claimed that it had still had enough bills eligible for Reichsbank discount, while the Reichsbank replied that it had been kept in the dark about the real state of the Dresdner.[91] More or less

89 IfZ ED93/11, 9 July 1931 diary entry: Schäffer–Dreyse meeting.

90 FRBNY Harrison papers 3135.0, 8 and 11 July 1931 Harrison–Dreyse telephone conversation.

91 Schäffer 'Geheimgeschichte' (Fn. 74) 259–60.

continual discussions—lasting until four o'clock in the morning—took place over this weekend.

Everyone agreed on Sunday that the Reichsbank's restriction of discounts should stop. Dreyse was aware of the extent to which the Reichsbank's policies had worsened the bank crisis.[92] Para. 31 of the Bank Law in fact provided for the Reichsbank to go under the 40 per cent reserve requirement in an emergency (and imposed for this a financial penalty, although this was never actually levied in 1931). This step was not enough by itself, and the Government was required to do something directly to save the banks.

Schacht proposed a partial state of guarantee of bank deposits (he proposed a ceiling per account of 10,000 RM). This would protect and reassure the small man and at the same time punish the foreigners who had been aware of the high risk consequent upon the high interest lending to Germany. Foreign credits would be frozen, so that it would not matter if foreigners ceased to trust Germany. Luther welcomed the economic nationalism that Schacht proposed, but he was opposed by State Secretary Schäffer, who in the end won over the Chancellor and the Foreign Minister. Schäffer believed that further foreign loans were possible and that foreigners should be encouraged to co-operate in the conversion of short-term into long-term loans. A complete guarantee would not really be as costly as Schacht had argued, because it would by itself help to restore confidence.[93]

It was French help that Schäffer was proposing to call on: he had spoken on 11 July to Comte de Brinon, the Berlin representative of the French press agency Havas, a man who was a personal friend of the French Prime Minister, Pierre Laval, about the business. Brüning would accept this scheme only if Germany made no political concessions to France on the key issues of disarmament, the German claim to the Polish corridor, or the building of pocket battleship 'B', since such concessions would destroy Brüning's already strained relations with the political right, with the Reichswehr, and with von Hindenburg. As a result Brüning's conversations with Laval when the Chancellor was on his way to London came to

[92] IfZ ED93/11, 11 July 1931 diary entry.
[93] Schäffer 'Geheimgeschichte' (Fn. 74) 260.

nothing, and all Brüning could think of doing was to conjure up a red spectre. 'The French must intervene. If they do not help, something will arise in Europe which will be quite different from capitalism, and it will scare the French stiff. That is why we must not yield an inch on the political issues.'[94] German diplomats had been using this notion ever since 1919 with a monotonous regularity and no one abroad took the argument seriously any more. Thus the Schäffer solution to the bank crisis was adopted in the end—a complete Reich guarantee for the Danat—without the presence of the political willingness that Schäffer would really have required for his plan to work. Brüning would not give in to France.

COPING WITH THE BANK COLLAPSE

A few hours after the banks opened for business on Monday 13 July, the Berlin banks were obliged by the volume of withdrawals to ration payments. In the afternoon, the Central Association of German Banks (CDBB) declared that there would be serious difficulties if banks were to open on Tuesday, and a Bank Holiday was declared—initially for only two days.[95] Money became suddenly scarce. An immense number of Reichsmark must have disappeared under mattresses. The Reichsbank later thought that about 1 billion had been hoarded in this way, and some estimates were even higher: at least one-fifth of the currency in circulation became in this way unavailable.[96]

Analysts of financial crises always suggest that the maxim of a banking system confronted by a major run should be to pay out in the hope of restoring confidence, but the German banks agreed to close. They closed not because they recognised their fundamental illiquidity: the extent of this only emerged later in the year, after careful auditing of their balances. Rather they closed, they thought (like the Dresdner's directors on 12 July), because the Reichsbank would not take their bills. The Reichs-

94 IfZ ED93/11, 13 July 1931 diary entry.

95 Born 1967, 108.

96 The 1b. RM estimate is Luther's: ZStA RWiM 15345, 24 Oct. 1931 Luther to Brüning. In the Reichswirtschaftsrat Committee Kraemer suggested 1500–600m. RM on 21 Jan. 1932: ZStA RWiRat 618.

bank's actions of June–July 1931 were controversial and it is possible to argue that a great deal of misery would have been avoided if the Reichsbank had not allowed itself to be pressed both by Norman and especially by Harrison into pulling the rug out from under a rather shaky house of cards by imposing discount restrictions.

The CDBB representatives saw the Reichsbank and its leadership as being primarily responsible for the calamity. On 15 July Georg Solmssen of the Deutsche Bank carried a letter to the Reich Chancellery requesting the replacement of Luther.[97] Already on 13 July bankers had asked for government authorisation of the issue of emergency money (*Notgeld*) familiar from the inflation period. This course had substantial support outside banking: the steel industrialists Thyssen and Vögler, for instance, argued that bills on exports to Russia might be used as the basis for this issue, and that the emergency programme to deal with the credit crisis might be turned into a broader one to spark off an economic recovery. Both Thyssen and Vögler put this argument forward in the language of social defence: without revival, there would be revolution.[98] Frisch (Dresdner) thought that the Darlehnskassen of the World War, which had lent on the security of public loans and had thus been one of the major engines of the inflation, could be revived; while Kempner (Mendelssohn) and State Secretary Trendelenburg wanted to reissue Rentenmark. The only major banker to oppose these schemes as undermining confidence still further was Wassermann, who did so because he still imagined that the Deutsche Bank could survive the universal crisis. It was the civil service and the Reichsbank, and in particular Luther, Reichsbank Vice-President Dreyse, and Schäffer, who offered the most effective resistance.[99] After Luther's panic air trip to Basel the central bankers at the Bank for International Settlements (BIS), and indeed the whole international financial world, were convinced of the precariousness of Luther's position. Basel thought that Brüning would like to see Schacht at

[97] Born 1967, 110.

[98] BAK R43I/602, 15 July 1931 meeting of Chancellor with iron and steel industrialists.

[99] IfZ ED93/11, accounts of 11–12 July 1931 discussions.

the head of the Reichsbank and that German industry was insisting on his return.[1]

Luther was thus under considerable pressure. His immediate response was to set up a new institution to give an additional signature so that the Reichsbank might take bills drawn between banks. The Akzept- und Garantiebank Aktiengesellschaft was founded at Luther's initiative on 28 July 1931 by the bankers not immediately threatened, and it promptly gave acceptance credit to the Danat and to the savings banks and Girozentralen which had suffered from the high volume of withdrawals by small savers.[2] The savings banks had concentrated on the treacherous business of communal finance and their long-term loans had been based on the assumption—which was not unreasonable in normal times—that their depositors would not suddenly get out. In order to win the support of the Akzeptbank, banks had to demonstrate that 'important economic interests' were at stake and that the credit was not merely required in order to improve the liquidity of the bank. The savings banks could present reasonable cases on these grounds, and indeed 70 per cent of the Akzeptbank's credits were given to them.[3]

Luther's next action was initially an unfortunate one. The Reichsbank discount rate was put up drastically (it reached 15 per cent on 31 July); but the banking world was strongly opposed to the extra costs imposed by such a high rate. At the meeting of the Reichsbank's Central Committee on 31 July which discussed the increase, most of the bankers' representatives argued that Luther's proposed rate was excessive.[4] Bankers powerful enough to sit on the Central Committee could exercise a great deal of influence on the workings of a non-price money system and thus were inclined to favour low discount rates and credit allocations rather than the rationing by price advocated in classical banking theory.[5] In response the rate was taken down to 10 per cent on 11 August and to 8

[1] NA US Treasury (Bureau of Accounts) RG 39 'Germany' 104, 31 July 1931 Cochran report.

[2] M. Pohl, 'Die Liquiditätsbanken von 1931', *Zeitschrift für das gesamte Kreditwesen*, 1974, 928.

[3] Ibid., 930. Born 1967, 118.

[4] BAK NL Luther 365, 31 July 1931 Reichsbank Zentralausschuß meeting.

[5] W. Bagehot, *Lombard Street: a Description of the Money Market*, London 1873.

per cent on 2 September. The subsequent period of non-monetary credit rationing through the Akzeptbank provided an opportunity for the Reichsbank to put into effect an old plan for directing credit to rationalise the German economy. Luther's memoirs describe how credit control was used to restore private industry: the local offices of the Reichsbank calculated figures from statements of 1924 to 1929 and adjusted them for unhealthy expansion in this period in order to provide guide-lines for rationing.[6]

What then emerged was a new *Subventionspolitik* controlled through the Reichsbank and not the Economics Ministry; the same kind of criteria (strategic and national importance) were applied as in the policy of the mid-1920s. An example is the way in which sensitive enterprises in Silesia were treated: the Finance Ministry recommended that the Danat Bank should be allowed to take bills drawn against itself by the firm of Henckel-Donnersmarck in order to save the concern, and also the army, from embarrassment. To make this operation possible, the Danat was given Akzeptbank acceptances.[7]

Together with temporary Reich support, the Akzeptbank was effective enough to enable the banks to reopen for business on 5 August and the savings banks on the 8th. It was also obvious that politically there was a push for a radical reform of the banking system. As the Reichstag could not be called since it could be relied on only to attack Brüning's policy, a committee on banks was set up as a substitute Reichstag to debate the bank problem.[8]

On a personal level, Chancellor Brüning had after 13 July become deeply suspicious of many of the leading bankers. He thought that the Government had been misled and misinformed about the extent of the crisis; and for him bank reform meant a purge. 'The personalities burdened with the guilt of the collapse must be removed if it is in any way possible to assure the continuity of technical direction without them.'[9] The two weakest banks were merged, and on the new board of

[6] H. Luther, *Vor dem Abgrund 1930–1933: Reichsbankpräsident in Krisenzeiten*, Berlin 1964, 216. Luther also cites a memorandum of 24 Oct. 1931: see BAK NL Luther 337, 24 Oct. 1931 Reichsbank to Reich Chancellor.

[7] IfZ ED93/14, 30 Sept. and 17 Oct. 1931 diary entries.

[8] Born 1967, 155.

[9] Born 1967, 171.

directors of the joint Danat-Dresdner Bank the only representatives of the old bank boards were Frisch (Dresdner) and Bodenheimer (Danat). The other big banks were affected too by the Brüning diktat. One-third of the directors of the Deutsche Bank, and half of the Commerz Bank's, were sacked. This was the price for substantial Reich support during reorganisation: by 1932 91 per cent of the Dresdner's capital, 70 per cent of the Commerz Bank's, and 35 per cent of the Deutsche Bank's, was in public ownership.[10]

In economic foreign policy too the state took a more active part. What began as an improvised and provisional holding operation was built up into an ever more complete system of control. There was sharper exchange regulation to attempt to prevent the resumption of capital flight; and foreign credits were locked into Germany through the Standstill Agreements.[11] These originated in the attempts of foreign bankers, at first British and American, to save their positions in Germany by agreeing not to pull out their credits. After 13 July, London and New York, then Paris, Amsterdam, and Zürich formed short-term creditors' committees to ensure that all Germany's creditors were treated equally. At the London Conference (20–3 July 1931), the international statesmen were put under great pressure by the London City and the international financial community. Eventually the Conference recommended not only that the June Central Bank credit to the Reichsbank should be renewed, but also that existing private loans to Germany should as far as possible be maintained. On 13 August 1931 a committee of foreign creditor representatives from eleven countries met in Basel to draw up a Standstill Agreement in accordance with the wishes of the London Conference.

One of the main problems the committee faced was that the technical form of the credit extended to Germany differed between creditors. Most of the American and British credit was in the form of acceptance credit, by which foreign banks

[10] Ibid., 176.

[11] The best survey of the standstill is still C. R. S. Harris, *Germany's Foreign Indebtedness*, London 1935. See also S. Wegerhoff, 'Die Stillhalteabkommen 1931–33: Internationale Versuche zur Privatschuldenregelung unter den Bedingungen des Reparations- und Kriegschuldensystems', Ph.D. Munich 1982.

accepted bills drawn on them by German bankers or industrialists; these could then be discounted outside Germany (i.e. sold to financial institutions with the security of the foreign acceptance). They were short-dated bills (usually three months), but on expiry were usually replaced by new bills. The total possible credit given by any one foreign bank ('credit line') had been negotiated previously, and the bills offered a security for the credit. On the other hand, the Swiss loans usually took the form of short advances, which again were renewable. Usually this form of credit was slightly more expensive, but, as we have seen, in many cases it represented only nominally Swiss loans of what was in fact German money back into Germany.[12]

Another difficulty was that in the late summer of 1931 the exact volume of short-term foreign lending had not yet become clear, and so the bankers had no idea of the relative importance of the loans they were discussing. In particular they did not know the vast extent of non-bank credit to Germany. Nevertheless, already by 19 August a plan had been initialled. It set out an orderly mechanism for the withdrawal of short-term deposits, and for the maintenance of a part of the short-term debt (acceptance lines and time deposits) at the level of 31 July 1931. These provisions covered all credit lines open at that date, not merely those portions which Germans had chosen to use. So in theory the agreement gave German traders the chance of borrowing more in order to finance overseas trade. At the end of the standstill, unused credit lines were merely cut by 10 per cent. The original agreement lasted for only six months. Such a duration was accepted in the belief that in the near future a fundamental alteration of reparations would change financial conditions completely. However, in January 1932 the scheduled reparation conference in Lausanne was postponed until June, and a new credit agreement was concluded for a twelve-month period.

The standstill protected only a part of Germany's foreign debt, and even that only incompletely. Between 31 July 1931 and 30 September 1932 the standstill debt decreased from

[12] *DDS* 10, 1930–1933, 117, 31 Oct. 1931 K. Ritter (German Auswärtiges Amt) to H. Rüfenacht.

6.3b. RM to 4.3b. RM, while the unprotected short-term debt (which was much larger than the creditors in Basel in August 1931 had imagined) fell from 6.8b. RM to 5b. RM.[13] In addition some Germans used scarce foreign exchange to rebuy long bonds on foreign markets at the very low prices that followed the financial panic. Thus the collapse of 1931 and the standstill was not the end of the painful process of debt contraction, but rather simply the end of the beginning. But without the standstill, the damage would have been greater, and there would have been a formal default (which in turn would have caused banks in Britain, Switzerland, and the USA to collapse).[14] The standstill thus reflected the interests both of Germany and of the short-term debtors, a papering over of illusions and difficulties by a mutual consent. On both the German and the western sides the illusion was that short-term credits had been used for the purpose of financing international trade: in fact three-quarters of the standstill-protected loans had been used for fixed investments or for the maintenance of stocks.[15] The difficulty was trying to unfreeze this mass of illiquid credit. But the large frozen debt meant that hopes of new credit from the west were unrealistic (though there were such hopes at least until 1933). Thus Germany no longer needed to manage her domestic monetary policy with an eye to impressing foreigners, and this gave her an unaccustomed degree of flexibility.

THE IMPLICATIONS OF THE BANKING CRISIS

The effects of the banking crisis on public policy-making were:

1. The crisis reinforced the suspicion of government budget deficits. In 1931 state debt had had a highly destabilising effect on the financial system. State Secretary Schäffer set out this view with particular vehemence and clarity. When Reich ministers Stegerwald and Dietrich proposed deficit-financed re-

[13] James 1984, 76.

[14] For fears of a German default bringing down Swiss banks, see *DDS* 10, 1930–1933, 267, 8 May 1933 Directoire de la Banque Nationale to Chef du Département des Finances.

[15] BAK R111/230, 4 Nov. 1931 Eric Archdeacon to Sloan Colt (President of the Bankers Trust Company).

employment programmes at the beginning of 1932, Schäffer blocked the proposals because he believed that they would lead to a new weakening of the banks. In March 1932 Schäffer resigned (with effect from May) because he feared that a failure to balance the budget might lead to a new round of financial panics and bank collapses.[16] But even after Schäffer's departure, the same hostility to public deficits was maintained: particularly by Count Schwerin von Krosigk, who had been a Ministerialdirektor under Schäffer, and who became Minister of Finance in the Papen Cabinet, and then retained the post until 1945; and by Hjalmar Schacht, who returned as President of the Reichsbank in March 1933.

2. In order to avoid new bank collapses following from too restrictive a monetary policy, the Reichsbank followed a course of what might be termed 'private reflation'. After the summer of 1931, the authorities aimed to stabilise the financial sector by the creation of institutions such as the Akzept- und Garantiebank, and later in 1932 the Finanzierungsinstitut AG (Finag) and the Tilgungskasse für gewerbliche Kredite (Tilka).[17] These were intended to provide for a systematic and gradual writing off of banks' illiquid or valueless assets.

The reconstruction of the banks was accompanied by mildly expansionary measures. From the middle of 1931 the Reichsbank tried to bring down the discount rate from the crisis levels of the summer. The Emergency Decree of December 1931 provided for a compulsory cut in interest rates: this provision was bitterly contested and its opponents (most prominently Luther and Schäffer) may have been correct in arguing that it induced *more* rather than *less* uncertainty on the capital market because creditors in the future would be afraid of a second reduction.[18] In the short term, however, it did reduce the burden of debt service.

The central bank now broke many of its old rules. It was prepared to discount large quantities of so-called 'frozen bills' and also to discount paper issued on the security of state export

[16] IfZ ED93/17, 17 Jan. 1932 diary entry; ED93/32, 19 Mar. 1932 Schäffer to Brüning. See also E. Wandel, *Hans Schäffer: Steuermann in wirtschaftlichen und politischen Krisen*, Stuttgart 1974, 223–6.

[17] See Pohl 1974.

[18] IfZ ED93/16, 2 Dec. 1931 diary entry.

guarantees on the long-term credit required to finance German–Soviet trade.

Some quantitative indicators of the degree of success of the Reichsbank's new policy are that from July 1931 the German money supply dropped by only 12.4 per cent to December 1932 (in real, i.e. price-deflated terms, of course, it rose quite steeply); whereas, if foreign bank deposits alone had determined the money supply, the continuing withdrawal of foreign funds after the crisis (in spite of the Standstill Agreements) would have led to a sharper fall in the money supply (of 20.5 per cent).[19] The main cause of the arrest of 1931's decline in the money supply was the increasing willingness of German bank depositors and a willingness of the banks to reduce the reserves that they had been forced to build up as a consequence of the uncertainty of 1931. Thus in 1932 the ratio of deposits to currency in circulation rose. The Deposit/Currency ratio could in general be treated as a measure of confidence in the banking system: 1932 was very unstable politically and signs of political crisis in May and June, and then again in November and December, produced falls of the Deposit/Currency ratio. The ratio rose after Hitler's accession to power, but at moments of uncertainty, such as the coincidence of the exchange rate crisis of mid-1934 with a political crisis as Hitler attacked Röhm and the SA, the deposit level of the German banks fell again temporarily but sharply. From 1933 the real (price-deflated) money supply remained very stable, while the nominal money supply in 1933 continued to decline from the falling level of 1932. After 1933 it rose slowly until the outbreak of war.[20]

3. The events of 1931 and their economic consequences, combined with the massive extent of state aid to banks, led to an outburst of populist discontent directed at the world of finance. As we have seen, politicians such as Brüning and Dietrich were by no means immune, and occasionally let themselves make very wild remarks against the men of money. Business men, too, believed that bankers had cut back their loans too savagely and too unfairly in 1931; and disliked the way in which the calling of loans continued after the bank

[19] My calculations: James 1984, 85–6.

[20] J. J. Klein, 'German Money and Prices 1932–1944' in (ed.) M. Friedman, *Studies in the Quantity Theory of Money*, Chicago 1956, 122.

crisis also, as part of the exercise of restoring financial stability. Between July 1931 and February 1932 the total volume of bank credit in Germany was cut by 16 per cent. An additional source of tension was that, although interest rates were falling, the reduction was balanced by the banks' imposition of very high-risk premiums. The RDI's expert on banks, the textile manufacturer Abraham Frowein, played over this issue with Brüning's quite well-known hostility to banks, and demanded the intervention of a powerful state-appointed banking commissar to ensure that the financial community replaced the funds withdrawn from industry.[21] Finally, many business men also attacked the Finag and the Tilka because they appeared to be institutions subsidised by the state to support banks but not industry.[22]

It was at a more popular level that the really substantive war against banks was waged: it was this war that made Brüning and Dietrich adopt more radical positions. Dietrich, for instance, had a largely farming constituency in Baden: and peasants' and farmers' protest meetings in late 1931 and 1932 made excessive interest charges a central issue when they compiled lists of grievances. Small traders, too, unleashed the resentments that they had long felt against bankers. The banking disaster made the economic crisis seem like a general crisis of capitalism, and it fanned the already burning flame of popular anti-capitalism into a powerful inferno.

[21] BAK NL Silverberg 234, 5 Feb. 1932, Abraham Frowein meeting with Solmssen.

[22] BAK NL Kastl 34, 3 Oct. 1932 Sempell to Kastl and 11 Oct. 1932 Warmbold to Luther. Bak NL Luther 352, 19 Dec. 1932 Lammers to Luther.

IX

Economists and the Depression

Nationalökonomie ist, wenn die Leute sich wundern, warum sie kein Geld haben.

(Kurt Tucholsky, *Tiger, Panther & Co.*)

Was there a bankruptcy of economic theory in the sense that it failed to provide effective guide-lines for the formulation of policy? Many contemporaries, from a wide range of political persuasions, took this stance, which has also been adopted in the writings of subsequent historians. Wladimir Woytinsky said that 'economic science was helpless in the face of the crisis'.[1] According to the Bonn Professor Herbert von Beckerath, 'statesmen, public opinion, and in many cases academics were too slow to identify the causes and the true nature of the present emergency and to draw practical conclusions which might end the crisis or even alleviate the terrible consequences'.[2] Frequently, in fact, academic economists were concerned with giving only long-run explanations of economic development and crisis: they thought that they were more like meteorologists than like physicians, and that their job was not to cure but to observe. Clearly theories which may be scientifically very useful in that they explain, may be useless when it comes to suggesting to practical men how to act. Theories which suggest how to act are of a peculiar category, and necessarily make assumptions about the capacity of the actors to influence events.

The most famous long-run explanation of development was given by Werner Sombart in *Der moderne Kapitalismus*. In his third volume, and more explicitly in his 1928 address to the Verein für Sozialpolitik, he identified a *Spätkapitalismus* in which more and more limits were placed on entrepreneurs, and in which, consequently, individual initiative atrophied. But as entrepreneurs became less influential, the state and big trusts

[1] W. Woytinsky, 'Das Rätsel der langen Wellen', *Schmollers Jahrbuch* 55, 1931, 577.

[2] H. v. Beckerath, 'Politik und Weltkrise', *Schmollers Jahrbuch* 56, 1932, 321.

planned the development of the economy. Markets became more rational as societies became better at communicating information. Moreover, there was more consumption as population growth slowed down and the pressure that growth placed on resources was reduced. On the whole then, this was an optimistic, not a pessimistic, theory. As the relative importance of investment goods industries, which had been chiefly responsible for cyclical fluctuations declined, the growth of consumption helped to stabilise the course of economic development. Sombart made a prediction: capitalism's characteristic cycles would disappear, or at least become very much milder. The Marxists, he said, were wrong to predict ever bigger and more dramatic crises.[3] The third volume of *Der moderne Kapitalismus* appeared in 1927—a very unfortunate timing.

Joseph Schumpeter's work in this period bears some striking resemblances to Sombart's, in spite of Schumpeter's very different intellectual ancestry in Böhm-Bawerk's neo-classical economics. His *Theory of Economic Development* was first published in 1911. Like Sombart he saw entrepreneurial initiative as the key motor of the capitalist dynamic, and the sole source of profit. The diffusion of innovative ideas among a broader group and the consequent erosion of profits was responsible for cyclical downturns. He added the observation that improved communications would smooth out the cycle; 'the most important remedy *à la longue* [for dealing with economic depressions], and the only one which is exposed to no objections, is the improvement of business cycle prognosis'.[4]

This line of argument was fruitful in that it produced a great deal of empirical study of business cycles. Arthur Spiethoff's article on 'Krisen' in the *Handwörterbuch der Staatswissenschaften* (1925) was the most wide-ranging and lucid synthesis.[5] In 1925 Ernst Wagemann set up an Institut für Konjunkturforschung

[3] W. Sombert, *Das Wirtschaftsleben im Zeitalter des Hochkapitalismus: Der moderne Kapitalismus III*, Munich and Leipzig 1927, 702. Also 1928 address: 'Die Wandlungen des Kapitalismus' in *Verhandlungen des Vereins für Sozialpolitik in Zürich 1928*, Munich and Leipzig 1929, 23–40.

[4] J. Schumpeter (trans. R. Opie), *The Theory of Economic Development: An Inquiry into Profits, Capital, Credit, Interest and the Business Cycle*, Cambridge Mass. 1934, 253.

[5] A. Spiethoff, 'Krisen' in (eds.) L. Elster, A. Weber, F. Wieser, *Handwörterbuch der Staatswissenschaften* VI, Jena 1925, 8–91.

(IfK) which produced weekly reports on the state of the market. Wladimir Woytinsky tried to make a logical distinction between cyclical and seasonal or structural unemployment. These men were responding to practical demands: business leaders in the mid-1920s were interested in statistical data on the future. The IfK ran a successful and appreciated statistical service especially for the Rhine-Ruhr industrial area. Governments too wanted to find out more about the trade cycle, since it affected their revenue and their expenditure, and Wagemann was President of the Reich Statistical Office. Woytinsky was the trade unions' statistician. Studies of cycles were usually based on an assumption that to understand cycles was to be able eventually to eliminate them. Spiethoff's article, for instance, had argued that crises were avoidable.[6] But as the depression at the end of the decade grew more severe, the business conditions analysts were subjected to increasing attack, from academics but also from business men who no longer saw the practical point of the analysis.[7]

The left in the 1920s had put forward optimistic theories, too: Sombart's strictures on Marxism and the Marxist catastrophic view of crisis in fact were inappropriate. Even the Comintern developed a theory of the stabilisation of capitalism, and it was only during the 1930s that the Comintern's economists, led by Eugen Varga, started to resurrect the literature of economic crisis.[8] During the 1920s some German socialists (E. Lederer, A. Löwe) went even further and argued that capitalism was becoming more ethical as the influence of the state grew. Other socialists held that the increasing organisation of capitalism—the emergence of trusts and cartels—was leading in the direction of a 'general cartel' which would be able to regulate markets and investment, and ensure the disappearance of cyclical fluctuations. Rudolf Hilferding's theory of organised capitalism, which derived from the Marxist critique of the historical school of German economists, was in this way surprisingly close to Sombart, the heir to the

[6] Ibid., 32, 85–6.

[7] For instance, 'Diagnose oder Prognose', *Ruhr und Rhein* 12/40, 2 Oct. 1931. *FZ* no. 409, 4 June 1931 report of Silverberg speech to Langnamverein.

[8] See R. B. Day, *The 'Crisis' and the 'Crash': Soviet Studies of the West (1917–1939)*, London 1981.

historical tradition.[9] Like Sombart, Hilferding believed that crisis and depression were characteristic of the infant, but not the adult, stages of capitalism.

Hilferding's doctrine required no theory of state interventionism, and in fact the SPD's leadership in the crisis at the end of the 1920s were rather frightened of an expansionist monetary policy. It was frightened of what the social consequences of such a policy might be. Many socialist leaders had matured intellectually in the 1890s, when it had been the reactionary agrarians who had advocated the inflationary bimetallic currency as a replacement for the gold standard. Then the farmers had hoped that inflation would reduce their debt, and that they could win at the expense of the consumer. Most socialists thought too that it had been the agrarians and the big industrialists who had been the major beneficiaries of the post-war inflation. So despite the famous and controversial socialist theory of the 1920s that some state institutions—the judiciary or the arbitration machinery established by the Reich Labour Ministry—might be used to redistribute wealth and economic power, the SPD was on the whole sceptical about state spending and about monetary expansion. Instead the party believed that a new legal and administrative framework, and more equitable taxation, represented far more ethical answers to the question of how to shape the future development of society.

Among non-socialist economists, an emphasis on the limitations being placed on the operation of capitalism more generally produced pessimistic assessments, and Sombart's optimism was highly untypical of the general direction of academic argument. The crises of the 1920s were described as 'crises of interventionism': 'the collapse of interventionist economic policy is clear in the crisis ... The capitalist economic order takes its purpose and sense from the market. If the functioning of the market and of price-determination is interrupted, the consequence is not order, but chaos and economic crisis.'[10] The state's action kept agricultural prices too high (E. Salin, G. Stolper), or wages (L. Mises, A. Weber), or taxes

[9] R. Hilferding, 'Probleme der Zeit', *Die Gesellschaft* I/1, 1924, 1–17.

[10] L. Mises, *Die Ursachen der Wirtschaftskrise: Ein Vortrag*, Tübingen, 1931, 32–4.

(Stolper, Mises). Criticism of the raising of wages and tax for political reasons was so frequent that it passed as a truth generally accepted. In 1931, Mises wrote: 'unemployment, the magnitude and duration of which is now used as a demonstration of the failure of capitalism, is a consequence of the fact that wages are held above the level they would be set at in an unencumbered market because of the influence of trade unions and the existence of unemployment benefit'.[11] Adolf Weber told the story of long-run economic decline resulting from the increased militancy and organisation of labour. His influential book *The Struggle between Capital and Labour* was frequently reissued and revised in the Weimar period. It told the story of how employers' organisations were growing weak and impotent as divisions arose between small and large employers and between Berlin and the provinces, and how these divisions were augmented by the conflicting social and political philosophies held by business men.[12] It was not bureaucratisation or oligopolisation that produced a withering of creativity and a threat to growth. On the contrary, Weber indeed welcomed the decline of small independent business men. In England, where there was no doubt about the strength and independence of small owners and producers, their unbending blinkered conservatism had done great harm.[13] The German problem was rather that business was not sufficiently strong or influential politically to be able to deal with the consequences of the spread of unionisation or the intervention of the Labour Ministry in wage bargaining. It was these political dangers that were producing the 'end of capitalism' which the title of one of Weber's books apocalyptically announced. The implication was that only a political change of a fundamental kind would be able to hold off the otherwise inexorable collapse. Weber was not worried at all by the cyclical problem; Mises, Stolper, and his collaborator Carl Landauer, believed that an end to crisis and upheaval would come only with the dismantling of interventionism.

[11] L. Mises, *Kritik des Interventionismus: Untersuchungen zur Wirtschaftspolitik und Wirtschaftsideologie der Gegenwart*, Jena 1929, 20–1. Also G. Halm, 'Zum Problem der Lohnsenkung', *Schmollers Jahrbuch* 55, 1931, 619–39.

[12] Adolf Weber, *Der Kampf zwischen Kapital und Arbeit: Gewerkschaften und Arbeitgeberverbände in Deutschland*, Tübingen 1921³, 253–4.

[13] Adolf Weber, *Ende des Kapitalismus*, Munich 1930³, 47.

Those theories which did promise most in terms of their implications for practical action were monetary ones. On the whole this was a field of inquiry ignored both by the historical school and by the Marxists. Monetary theorists were probably more significant outside Germany than within the German economic traditions: in the inter-war period it was the great economists outside Germany—Irving Fisher, Maynard Keynes, Knut Wicksell, Carl Snyder—who examined monetary theories. However, this kind of analysis, though subordinate, was not entirely neglected in Germany or Austria: L. Albert Hahn, Walter Eucken, Friedrich Hayek, and Wilhelm Röpke are of special interest because of their importance in developing the ideas of the social market economy after 1945. Of these four men, Hahn and Röpke were the most concerned with exploring the policy implications of theory. Hayek went far in the opposite direction in explaining that crises, though monetary in origin, could not be prevented by monetary policy instruments.[14]

Nevertheless it was foreign writers who most influenced German thinking on monetary policy. This is explicable in terms of the political environment. Keynes was regarded favourably in Germany because of his 1919 attack on the Versailles settlement. His subsequent works were translated into German; and even some politicians read, and were influenced by, the *Tract on Monetary Reform* (1923) and the *Treatise on Money* (1930). The former was, and still is, the most notoriously inflationary of Keynes's works, and was composed under the strange economic and political circumstances of the immediate post-war years. It included the famous statement that 'it is worse, in an impoverished world, to provoke unemployment than to disappoint the *rentier*'.[15] The latter work argued that investment might fall below savings, and that this imbalance, which was a source of crisis, could be corrected by reductions in interest rates. (This was a solution which the Keynes of the 1936 *General Theory*, and also German Keynesians such as Carl Föhl, believed to be inadequate. Föhl in 1937 took the extreme position of maintaining that interest rates had no effect at all on the real economy because they did not

[14] F. Hayek, *Preise und Produktion, Beiträge zur Konjunkturforschung* 3, Vienna 1931.

[15] J. M. Keynes, *A Tract on Monetary Reform*, London 1923, 36.

influence employers' calculations of future profits, and thus their investment decisions.)[16]

The Swede Gustav Cassel was widely read in Germany too. He had a simple, very clear and very political, theory of the monetary origins of depression, which was highly attractive to Germans. For Cassel, regular crises resulted from the fluctuations of the investment goods sector. Firms began investment projects which they subsequently found difficult to complete because they could not borrow enough money. Crises then resulted not from underconsumption, but from shortages of available investment funds at that rate of interest which had been anticipated in advance. Thus these disturbances might actually be avoidable if economic agents became better informed about business conditions; and in general, he thought, economies had a natural tendency to 'develop smoothly'. Consequently, he deduced, economic fluctuations might be avoided by a correct policy choice. Though it was possible that non-monetary influences, emanating from the investment goods sector (for instance a dramatic technological innovation, such as the railway or electricity) might disturb the monetary equilibrium, affect price levels, and produce an economic shock, even these effects could be controlled by choosing the correct monetary policy.[17]

Cassel believed that the cause of the 1920s instability lay in the operation of the gold standard or gold exchange standard mechanism. He was concerned to give an explanation primarily in terms of international rather than domestic monetary influences. In the 1920s the gold standard was responsible for a chronic deflationary pressure, as there was a divergence between the arithmetic rate of growth of the world gold stock and the geometric growth of world production.[18] At the 1922 Genoa Conference, a gold exchange standard had been recommended in order to economise on metallic gold: reserve currencies could be substituted for gold for central bank reserve purposes. But the goals of Genoa had been frustrated by the

[16] C. Föhl, *Geldschöpfung und Wirtschaftskreislauf*, Munich and Leipzig 1937.

[17] G. Cassel, *Theoretische Sozialökonomie*, Leipzig 1932[5], 570–2.

[18] The theory is clearly set out in G. Cassel, *The Monetary Character of the Present Crisis* (Institute of Bankers), London 1931; G. Cassel, *Die Krise im Weltgeldsystem*, Berlin-Charlottenburg 1933, particularly 23–32.

actions of two countries. France and USA accumulated large gold reserves, and refused to allow a domestic monetary expansion which might have counteracted this growth in reserves. In addition, France in the late 1920s started to convert dollar and sterling reserves into gold. The result was that the deflationary pressure on the rest of the world was intensified.

Such an argument had a particular appeal in Germany because the reparations bill was denominated in gold. Cassel's case could be used to prove to the Allies that the real burden of reparations would go on rising and rising over the next half-century of payments under the Young Plan. It had the additional attraction, too, of making France and USA, the two powers who were blocking a downward adjustment of reparations, appear responsible—because of their short-sighted monetary policies—for the collapse of international economic relations, and thus in the end for the breakdown of the Versailles settlement also. Other theories similar to Cassel's were given the same degree of public attention in Germany: the supplement to the London *Economist* on 'The Crisis' by Henry Strakosch (January 1932) was translated into German and was also distributed by the German Government.[19]

Some of the German theorists—Röpke and to a lesser extent Wilhelm Lautenbach—shared this international emphasis on monetary analysis. They believed in the desirability of international reflationary action of the kind proposed by the League of Nations Gold Delegation. Others looked more to national policies: the least international and the most domestic in outlook was Albert Hahn. His main interest was in the way that banks created money by means of a credit inflation, and in the stimulus that this provided. Without credit expansion, there would be no economic development. But Hahn also saw clear limits on monetary policy, and was much less sanguine than Cassel on the theoretical possibilities open to governments and central banks: 'a central bank cannot make it its duty . . . to abolish economic fluctuations'.[20] In the mid-1920s, Hahn had argued that the only way to reduce the damagingly high

[19] *The Economist*, Supplement, 9 Jan. 1932.

[20] A remark of F. Somary's quoted in L. A. Hahn, *Fünfzig Jahre zwischen Inflation und Deflation*, Tübingen 1963, 25.

interest level, which was depressing investment activity, was by cutting wage and price levels, and also by cutting industrial costs in Germany by reducing taxes.[21] An intervention in the real economy was required. This action was a political exercise, since a market course (forcing price reductions by putting up the Reichsbank's discount rate) would have an exactly opposite effect to the one intended.

In the crisis at the end of the decade, Hahn argued like Cassel and Fisher that the rise in the value of gold had been responsible for pushing firms into bankruptcy because it increased the real level of debt. But he believed that there was a domestic remedy. The state could steer against the depression by expanding the money supply.[22] Hahn thought that there was no really severe structural problem in Germany, and in particular no problem of an insufficient demand for money. Work creation projects were useless, and excessive state expenditure would not be an effective contra-cyclical instrument, since it would produce crowding out effects that would damage the credit structure and limit the potential for future credit expansion.[23] There was really no need to worry about what to spend money on: 'the problem is not what to do with the money, but rather how much money we can create'.[24]

In fact the course Hahn was recommending—monetary expansion and fiscal control—was the one Hans Luther was pursuing with sometimes more and sometimes less consistency after the financial catastrophe of 1931. Hahn appeared to be an opponent of Luther's: but the major criticisms Hahn made of the Government and the Reichsbank's policies were voiced between the outbreak of the bank crisis and the beginning of 1932, while the Reichsbank was still groping for a new direction. After that date, he became quieter. Hahn's recommendations do not, then, amount to a real 'alternative' to the economic policies of the presidential governments.

The plan for monetary expansion that attracted the most

[21] Ibid., 41; and L. A. Hahn, *Aufgaben und Grenzen der Währungspolitik: Eine Kritik der deutschen Währungspolitik seit der Stabilisierung (Kiel Vortrag)*, Jena 1928.

[22] L. A. Hahn, *Kredit und Krise*, Tübingen 1931; 'Im Zeichen der Weltdeflation', *FZ*, 4 Sept. 1932; 'Deckungsnebel', *Der deutsche Volkswirt* 6/18, 29 Jan. 1932, 580–2.

[23] Hahn's contribution to discussion in Studiengesellschaft für Geld- und Kreditwirtschaft, reproduced in *Berliner Tageblatt* 22 Feb. 1932 and *Deutsche Bergwerkszeitung* 23 Feb. 1932. Also Hahn 1963, 99–103.

[24] Hahn 1963, 100.

attention was that put forward in January 1932 by Ernst Wagemann of the Reich Statistical Office and the Institut für Konjunkturforschung. Wagemann's proposal is intelligible only in the context of the bank crisis and the monetary collapse that had followed it.[25] He began with an idea for reforming the banking system by splitting banks operating primarily current accounts from the deposit banks. The latter would be allowed to channel long-term deposits into long-term industrial finance. The current account institutes would be required as a safety measure to hold fixed reserves at the central bank. Onto this scheme for a reform to introduce English-style banking practice into Germany he tacked a proposal for using the public debt as security for a substantial part (3b. RM) of the money in circulation (the total circulating in Germany at the beginning of 1932 was 6b. RM). This 'fiduciary issue' (again there was an English model) needed no gold or foreign exchange backing since it represented an absolutely basic minimum circulation. Hence the question of convertibility would not arise.

Though it is not quite clear even from Wagemann's published pamphlet that he intended a major monetary expansion rather than simply a stabilisation and an end to contraction, there was intense discussion of his ideas at a study group on credit reform, the Studiengesellschaft für Geld- und Kreditwirtschaft. The Wagemann proposals aroused a storm of protests from all parts of the political spectrum, left-wing as well as nationalist politicians, liberal newspapers, and academic economists. Thirty-one leading academics signed a public letter denouncing Wagemann.[26] The plan was alleged to be 'inflationary'. The Reichsbank and the Government had to make it clear that they were not associated with the plan, even though Wagemann was employed by the Reich. It became clear that it was very difficult publicly to discuss monetary reform in the tense political climate of Germany in 1931–2.

[25] The plan is set out as E. Wagemann, *Geld- und Kreditreform*, Berlin 1932. On the Wagemann plan see R. Regul, 'Der Wagemann-Plan', in (eds.) G. Bombach, K.-B. Netzband, H.-J. Ramser, M. Timmermann, *Der Keynesianismus III, Die geld- und beschäftigungstheoretische Diskussion in Deutschland zur Zeit von Keynes*, Berlin 1981, 421–47.

[26] A copy of the letter of M. J. Bonn and others of 25 Feb. 1932 is in BAK R2/14525.

Many of the money theorists also believed that there were economic as well as political constraints on action in the depression. There was more room for manoeuvre in an expansion than in a contraction; and much of the discussion was not on how to cure the depression, but on how to manage a new upswing. R. Stucken in 1934 discussing the possibilities for central bank influence on business conditions still thought that the most important contribution a central bank could make was to curb speculative excess in the recovery phase.[27] Such an approach for the most part, then, left the question of policy in the crisis unanswered. There were, however, some bolder voices: Wilhelm Röpke, Hans Neisser, and Gottfried Haberler. It is difficult to be quite sure of what kind of theory was developed by these men, and when—since at first the theory was expounded orally.[28] Röpke was on paper the most expressive of this group. He looked at non-monetary ways of influencing the course of monetary development.

Röpke started from the observation that cyclical fluctuations were quite natural, but that they could be intensified or diminished by monetary or fiscal policy. Depressions comprised two phenomena: a 'primary depression' that no power in the world could alter, since it was a product of the natural course of development; and secondary crises, which could be controlled by public policy. Monetary policy had to be 'neutral', not inflationary: this meant, in Röpke's proposal, that it should have no influence on prices and production.[29] In other words, there should be no attempt in a depression to produce recovery by raising prices through monetary expansion. Röpke often warned about the grim consequences of inflationism, Keynesian-style:

> certainly a credit inflation as such is a thousand times better than a credit deflation; but the decisive point—not emphasised enough by Keynes—is that a credit deflation follows a credit inflation as surely as a hangover follows a drinking orgy. This is crucial, and takes away

[27] R. Stucken 'Konjunkturbeeinflussung durch die Notenbank', *Jahrbücher für Nationalökonomie* 140, 1934, 52.

[28] See W. Röpke, 'Trends in German Business Cycle Policy', *Economic Journal* 43, 1933, 434.

[29] W. Röpke, *Krise und Konjunktur*, Leipzig 1932, 107–8.

the foundation from that subtle form of inflationism represented by Keynes.[30]

However, he also added an explanation which, in its 1933 formulation, looks like that of the *General Theory*, and which stated that 'pumping additional credits into the arteries of the national economy' was not enough. He believed that it was possible to learn from the American experience of attempts to expand credit. US experiments 'have verified the surmise that even a rate of interest which approaches zero may be insufficient, under the conditions of a severe depression, to induce entrepreneurs to enter upon new investment'.[31] So instead the state should invest, since private demand for money for investment was unlikely to be sufficiently great. It was fiscal policy that should have the main contra-cyclical influence.

The actual policy of successive Weimar governments—borrowing in the expansion and attempting to repay from budget surpluses in the depression—had been exactly the wrong way round. Röpke believed, like Hahn, that terrible mistakes had been made in the upswing, when there had been a much greater freedom for manoeuvre. Since the middle of the 1920s, Röpke had attacked the instability caused by fiscal policy. In 1925 he wrote an essay attacking excessively high levels of taxation, and urged that they should be reduced. Later he added other criticisms: in 1929 he said that it was wrong to attempt to use the tax system as an instrument of redistribution, since such a policy was likely to reduce the already low German propensity to save. He added a rider that state welfare payments were 'sapping the feeling of responsibility and the will to increase income by higher productivity'.[32] Not only were the large budget deficits in the expansion damaging in that they restricted future budget policy, but their redistributional effects augmented the damage.

In 1931, however, Röpke took a different tack: a relatively limited state spending programme would produce an initial economic spark (*Initialzündung*) that would halt the secondary depression and allow recovery to take place.[33] But there should

[30] Quoted in *Keynesianismus III*, 312.
[31] Röpke 1933, 436.
[32] W. Röpke, *Finanzwissenschaft*, Berlin 1929, 53–4.
[33] W. Röpke, 'Ein Weg aus der Krise', *FZ* 336, 7 May 1931.

only be a small stimulus, and it should be accompanied by a package of additional measures so that the state's contra-cyclical policy would feed business confidence rather than lead to a further sapping of responsibility. Further economic development could occur untrammelled if 'schematic wage-determination' was ended.[34] It was also crucial that the *Initialzündung* should be given at the right point in the economic cycle: it was useful only at the bottom of the depression, when the 'primary deflation' had played itself out. Otherwise the state stimulus might only delay the necessary process of economic adjustment (*Anpassung*). Other advocates of expansionary state policies made similar points. The socialist economist Gerhard Colm thought that if the point of state spending was not to be lost in an open economy, there needed to be wage cuts and wage controls. After 8 December 1931, though, Colm believed that Brüning had gone far enough, and that no further government action in cutting wages was required.[35]

For Röpke, it was crucial that restrained monetary policy and the modest domestic recovery achieved by the *Initialzündung* should bring a restored foreign confidence in Germany and a new inflow of foreign money. Like the Brauns Commission, and like Woytinsky in 1931, Röpke argued that the basis of a lasting recovery would be state encouragement of further capital inflows.[36] Germany's position as an international debtor was to be maintained for the foreseeable future; and Röpke was very sceptical of purely domestic plans for a big expansion. The period after 1933 confirmed his belief that such expansion was dangerous. Later, when he read the *General Theory*, he wrote from Switzerland in a letter to Gottfried Haberler that 'Keynes is saying very important things that need to be taken seriously: but he is playing with dynamite'.[37]

There were two reasons why so many theorists were frightened of a dramatic fiscal expansion. First there was the problem of what the sums used to create public employment should be spent on. Some of the objections here were of a

[34] Röpke 1932, 120. [35] G. Colm in *Die Arbeit* 4, 1930, 241–7.

[36] 'Ein Weg aus der Krise', *FZ* 7 May 1931; also W. Röpke, *Der Weg des Unheils*, Berlin 1931, 101–7.

[37] W. Röpke (ed. Eva Röpke), *Briefe 1934–1966: Der innere Kompass*, Zürich 1976, 26.

relatively trivial or technical kind: that there were not enough projects sufficiently advanced on the drawing boards to be translated into practice. But there was a real and quite powerful objection to counter-cyclical fiscal policy disguised by this argument. It was not easy for the state to transfer its orders from boom to slump because many state-financed projects were in fact infrastructure investments required as a response to the upswing. New factories meant new roads, schools, and sewers. And if more goods were traded, more railway waggons and locomotives had to be built. On the other hand, roads and sewers constructed at random during the slump might well be in the wrong position, and if there was already a large modern rolling stock, adding more would increase the cost of maintenance needlessly and destabilise the railway's finances.[38] Other objections to state projects were moralistic: the state would be acting unfairly in giving a competitive advantage to particular economic agents if it awarded contracts in so-called direct work creation, rather than giving general tax concessions from which the whole of business would benefit.

Secondly, there was also a general argument about the—under some circumstances—destabilising effects of public spending. The fundamental German economic difficulty was widely held to be a shortage of capital, and interest rates which were consequently, in the 1920s, above those prevailing in France, Britain, or the USA. In 1932 a very long book edited by Karl Diehl set out to list 'the effects of high interest rates in Germany': though the authors were not successful in eliminating from their consideration other causes of economic weaknesses, they did succeed in proving, particularly for agriculture and construction, how much damage dear money had done.[39] Yet F. Neumark wrote in his chapter on public spending that one of the major causes of dear money was the state's demand for money. He argued that public loans, such as the big Reich Loans of 1927 and 1929, had had a crowding-out effect (*ausstechen*) on the public sector. The consequences of state borrowing in the future might be even more serious: it might be

[38] A. Lansburgh, in *Die Bank* 50/50, 14 Dec. 1932, 1748–53 (reproduced in *Keynesianismus III*, 375–81).

[39] (Ed.) K. Diehl, *Wirkungen und Ursachen des hohen Zinsfußes in Deutschland*, Jena 1932.

that rises in interest rates following from expansionary state budgets would fail to attract more funds, since 'there are circumstances in which, as was the case in the inflation, interest rates actually lose their regulatory functions'.[40]

Some theorists of counter-cyclical fiscal policy paid through credit drew the conclusion that their strategy would not make any sense in the early 1930s. Harald Fick, for instance, wanted the state to borrow in order to be able to run deficits; but the credit market now appeared too vulnerable. Fick deduced from this that Brüning was right.[41] This is also why so few writers were prepared to argue that the state should spend large sums on work creation. Indeed, one striking feature of almost all the well-known work creation projects is the energy and effort devoted to explaining how little such schemes would cost the state. Both Woytinsky and Hans Schäffer worked out a form of multiplier-effect argument to support this case. Woytinsky's March 1932 scheme involved spending 2b. RM on work creation: he estimated that this would save 600m. RM in unemployment insurance payments which would no longer need to be made, and that additional income tax would raise 200m. RM. In addition the newly employed would pay their own insurance contributions (100m. RM). Most importantly, consumer industries would be stimulated: here another 200m. RM would be saved on unemployment payments. The secondary effects of work creation were such that 2b. RM spent by the state would produce a gain of 1.6b. RM in additional revenue or expenditure saved: so the real cost was only 400m. RM. Woytinsky's figures could be used to calculate an employment multiplier of 1.33.[42] Schäffer argued a similar case in discussion with Hans Luther in August 1931, when he discussed the hypothetical consequences of spending 3b. RM.[43] In Germany the idea of the multiplier arose as re-employment enthusiasts tried to explain that their ideas would not cost anybody very much.

[40] F. Neumark, 'Der öffentliche Haushalt, insbesondere der Reichshaushalt, unter den Einwirkungen der bestehenden Kreditschwierigkeiten', in (ed.) Diehl 1932, 575, 584.

[41] H. Fick, *Finanzwirtschaft und Konjunktur*, Jena 1932. Also *Keynesianismus III*, 359.

[42] W. Woytinsky, 'Arbeitsbeschaffung und keine Inflationsgefahr', Die Arbeit 9/3 (Mar. 1932).

In the case of Schäffer, the renewed financial instability of September 1931 made him reassess his proposals. In April 1932 he stated that 'work creation can never end the crisis, but only protect men from despair'.[44] When he resigned from the Finance Ministry, he wrote to Brüning that 'the contraction of the German economy, which began in the winter of 1930/1 and then continued with the withdrawal of foreign capital and the subsequent collapse of the banks, was a process which cannot be reversed by domestic means, or even brought to a halt'.[45] Woytinsky did not, of course, reach the same conclusion, and instead reacted to the events of late 1931 by dropping his earlier insistence, which he had shared with Röpke, that international financial assistance was needed. Germany should, the union theoreticians argued in 1932, stand alone: but they stood alone in Germany in saying this.

An interesting example of the intellectual difficulties produced by the question of state budgetary policy and financial instability is the case of Wilhelm Lautenbach, who is sometimes described as 'the German Keynes'.[46] Like many unorthodox economic thinkers, he was not an academic economist but a civil servant (in the Reich Economics Ministry), and he was exposed to all the internal government discussions on fiscal and monetary stability. In June 1930 he had argued, after the iron and steel arbitration award for north-west Germany, that the state should give additional orders to make up for the shortfall in macro-demand caused by wage cuts. This was in 1930 a very radical suggestion: very few thought that there was a fundamental problem of demand, and almost all analysis was concerned with the question of industrial costs.[47] Lautenbach did not oppose the wage cuts as a means of adjusting German costs, but he did worry about the demand side. He thought of ways of trying to increase aggregate demand. In a memorandum of 1932, 'Work creation and contradictions in financing

[43] IfZ ED93/13, 31 Aug. 1931 diary entry.
[44] IfZ ED93/20, 12 Apr. 1932 diary entry.
[45] IfZ ED93/32, 19 Mar. Schäffer to Brüning.
[46] On Lautenbach, see K. Borchardt, 'Zur Aufarbeitung der Vor- und Frühgeschichte des Keynesianismus in Deutschland: Zugleich ein Beitrag zur Position von W. Lautenbach', *Jahrbücher für Nationalökonomie und Statistik* 197, 1982b, 359–70.
[47] BAK NL Lautenbach 31, 2 June 1930 exposé.

it', he claimed that there was no difficulty in creating credit: 'the provision of credit is a purely technical and organisational problem: it is child's play to solve it'.[48] Credit creation did not, however, solve the problem of deficient demand; and then the events of July and September 1931 even made him modify his general policy line. Now he said that interest reduction would be unwise and that rates should instead be kept high in order to attract foreign capital. The budget deficit should not be financed by credit creation, since that 'would damage us in the eyes of foreigners, and for that reason is in practice impossible'. Instead both wages and cartel prices should be cut. In addition to these recommendations, Lautenbach added the comment that the German capital shortage had been caused by excessive public spending 'crowding out' private borrowers.[49] This conclusion, and these policy recommendations, have been described provocatively—but not inaccurately—as blueprints for Brüning's 8 December 1931 Emergency Decree.[50] When examining policy alternatives, Lautenbach did look over his shoulder at British economic policy. He thought that Keynes's recommendations, which were intended to produce economic and political stability, would in Germany only create disorder and instability.

It was not only the monetary theorists who argued for expansionary state budgets: and sometimes those others have been classed in retrospective analysis together with the monetary men as 'reformers'. In his 1954 book on the 'reformers', Grotkopp, who in the depression had been the secretary of the Studiengesellschaft für Geld- und Kreditwirtschaft, wrote that the reformers had had no concept of a new economic order or of reshaping the rules of the game, but that they merely wanted to stabilise the existing system through an 'active policy': a policy which might too have had the desirable function of restoring the tarnished reputation of the democratic state.[51]

[48] BAK NL Lautenbach 31, memorandum 'Die Arbeitsbeschaffung und ihre Finanzierung kontradiktorisch dargestellt'.

[49] BAK NL Lautenbach 31, 17 Sept. 1931 'Möglichkeiten einer aktiven Konjunkturbelebung durch Investition und Kreditausweitung'.

[50] Borchardt 1982b, 368.

[51] W. Grotkopp, *Die große Krise: Lehren aus der Überwindung der Wirtschaftskrise 1929–1932*, Düsseldorf 1954, 70–3.

Such an assessment is true in the case of Grotkopp and of most of the monetary theorists; but other 'active policies' were very heavily ideologically charged. One of the most influential reformers was Robert Friedländer-Prechtl, whose work appeared from 1931 in a periodical, *Die Wirtschaftswende*, and in a book with the same title.[52] He inspired the Nazi economic programmes of 1932, though the Nazis never acknowledged their debt, probably because of Friendländer-Prechtl's Jewish origins.[53] As the title of his work suggests, he wanted a dramatic shift or structural break (*Wende*) in the actual economy, not merely in economic policy. In 1926 he had produced an analysis which suggested that there would be a chronic problem of unemployment because of the changed nature of capitalism.[54] Particularly harmful had been the development of large trusts and concerns. Another reason why private initiative was slowing down was the reduced rate of population growth: and he deduced that large state orders were needed to make up for the falling demand. But these state orders should not leave the structure of ownership or the distribution of wealth unchanged.[55] It was essential to destroy the harmful trusts, which had ruined the Mittelstand by putting up wages to levels that small firms could no longer afford. Only in this way could a healthy and individualistic capitalist economy be restored.

The depression gave Friedländer the opportunity to develop before an interested public the theories he had evolved earlier: 'the principle of the private economy is based on millions of small and medium enterprises, not on the few giant firms which are in their structure and behaviour a kind of state enterprise, only with excessive wages and without control'.[56] This radical individualist saw state counter-cyclical spending as the prime means of readjusting Germany's economic structure.

It is not surprising that those who advocated the most active economic policy were the most keen on destroying what they

55 R. Friedländer-Prechtl, *Die Wirtschaftswende: Die Ursachen der Arbeitslosen-Krise und deren Bekämpfung*, Leipzig 1932.

53 Grotkopp 1954, 36.

54 R. Friedländer-Prechtl, *Chronische Arbeitskrise, ihre Ursprünge, ihre Beseitigung*, Berlin 1926.

55 Friedländer-Prechtl, quoted in Grotkopp 1954, 128.

56 IfZ ED93/32, 6 Dec. 1932 Friedländer-Prechtl to Schäffer.

identified as a corrupt existing order, or that such schemes for destruction should immediately raise fundamental political questions. On the other hand, those who like Hahn and Röpke, or even Fick and Colm, basically accepted the existing economic order found it difficult to make very effective concrete suggestions. Röpke was horrified by those militant ideologues who regarded 'a business cycle policy working within the present economic system and relying on its most elementary reactions' as a 'rather pathetic naivety'. He was frightened of men who believed that 'we must abandon the wreck, leaving it to break up and seek salvation on the shores of the promised land of a planned autarkic economy, with as much agriculture and as little manufacturing as possible'.[57]

The liberal monetary theorists shrank from recommendations which involved too great a degree of control of the capital markets, because of the political implications of such control. They faced a dilemma: only a very unacceptable total control could have prevented the destabilising effects of fiscal expansion. Eucken and Hahn argued that their case was fundamentally directed against interventionism. Röpke was obsessive about getting the timing of his small dosage right so that it should not interfere with the market recovery. Schäffer thought that 'economic action made more sense in a free, not a controlled, environment'. Optimistically he also held that the 'world was moving into a new era of free trade and political liberalism'.[58]

Most economists, then, were in practice useless in the sense that they could offer interesting diagnoses, but no cures. Many Germans in the early 1930s, however, clearly wanted a cure, and wanted it very urgently.

[57] Röpke 1933, 428.

[58] IfZ ED93/20, 28 Apr. 1932 diary entry (conversation between Schäffer and Dietrich).

X

A Nazi Recovery?

> The whole modern world is crazy. The system of closed national barriers is suicidal and we must all collapse here and the standard of living everywhere be reduced. Everybody here is crazy. And so am I. Five years ago I would have said that it would be impossible to make me so crazy. But I am compelled to be crazy.
>
> (Hjalmar Schacht, 17 October 1934)[1]

Why did Germany recover from the depression? Why did she not recover sooner? To most commentators in 1930 and early 1931 these questions would have appeared absurd and bizarre: economies, they held, recovered by themselves as long as the state did not intervene actively and thus make crises caused by government intervention in a market mechanism worse by yet more government intervention. The *Frankfurter Zeitung* in late 1932 still, in the face of ostensibly very active government policies, presented the economic recovery, which some observers were beginning to notice, as an entirely natural phenomenon and not as the product of the efforts of von Papen or his ministers.[2] It was a measure of the extent to which a world view had collapsed that after 1932 many writers started to look for more far-reaching and radical explanations of why recoveries took place. Thus the recovery of the 1930s has attracted a degree of historical attention unprecedented in the literature about economic crisis, while few people bother to ask themselves how Europe recovered after the crisis of 1846–8 or 1873–6 or 1907–8.

Politicians as well as historians have been so fascinated by the recovery because of the change in political systems that occurred during the depression, as well as of the severity of the

[1] (eds.) W. E. Dodd Jr. and M. Dodd, *Ambassador Dodd's Diary*, London 1941, 185.
[2] *Frankfurter Zeitung*, 886–7, 27 Nov. 1932 'Der Weg bis zum Aufstieg'.

depression itself. Did the National Government in Britain after 1931 or Roosevelt's New Deal administration take the right course? Or did France's failure to get out of the depression quickly follow from her unwillingness to abandon Republican government? That there was a new regime in Germany with very radical claims means that the question of the relationship between political change and economic recovery is posed in a particularly acute fashion by the German example.

Nazi economic policy has presented historians with an enigma: it appeared to produce an amazing recovery in which full employment, unknown in Germany since the end of the Great Inflation, was established almost as quickly—in four years—as Hitler boasted it would be.[3] Hitler was certainly a more accurate economic forecaster than the majority of contemporary commentators who predicted economic collapse following from reckless government expenditure. Even after four years of National Socialism, many of these observers could not believe that it worked economically. Hans Priester concluded in 1936 that 'the economic policy of the Third Reich failed, because it only considered the material aspects of economic life. Psychological factors, which are essential to economic calculation, were left out of the plans.'[4] The Hungarian economist Thomas Balogh wrote in 1938 that the Nazi economic miracle had reached a natural limit and was imposing 'an increasing strain on the people which will inevitably have its repercussions in the longer run'.[5]

On the other hand, it is really hard to argue that Hitler deserves any credit as an innovator in economic policy. Perhaps he should get better marks for predicting than for planning. For most of Nazi economics was highly conventional: there was the insistence that budgets should not be too unbalanced, high tax levels were maintained, and saving was encouraged. Alan Milward has recently commented on this 'contradictory aspect' in the historical accounts of German

[3] 1 Feb. 1933 Aufruf der Reichsregierung an das deutsche Volk, in M. Domarus, *Hitler: Reden und Proklamationen 1932–1945. Kommentiert von einem deutschen Zeitgenossen*, Munich 1965, 192.

[4] H. E. Priester, *Das deutsche Wirtschaftswunder*, Amsterdam 1936, 319.

[5] T. Balogh, 'The National Economy of Germany', *EcJ* 48, 1938, 461–97. The quotation is from 496.

recovery, drawing attention to 'the apparent acceptance that in 1933 and 1934 there was both a high savings ratio, a great readiness to release savings for tasks such as house repairs, and taxation so high as to restrict consumption.'[6] The Nazis were keen to claim that they appreciated the importance of innovation and technical change; and they exercised an undoubted attraction for technocrats such as the engineers Feder and Lawaczeck,[7] the chemists Gattineau and Bütefisch,[8] and the architect Albert Speer, who commented on 'the sight of discipline in a time of chaos, the impression of energy in an atmosphere of universal hopelessness'.[9] These were men who believed that their projects or their careers were obstructed by the conventional and conservative corporatism of Weimar. But in practice these Nazi technocrats had a difficult time in the first years of the Third Reich, and it was only really in the exceptional circumstances of wartime that the technocrats were able to realise parts of their dreams.

HITLER'S ECONOMIC PROGRAMME

When Adolf Hitler became Reich Chancellor in 1933 there was still a large question mark over future Nazi policy, and especially over economic policy. Nazi statements had been many and contradictory. The new Chancellor, who now put on a tailcoat and looked like a figure of the old order, was a mystery. The high civil servants, the figures who had been so influential in making policy under Brüning and even under Papen, were puzzled. Arnold Brecht, Prussian delegate to the Reichsrat, described the uncertainty which gripped the official world of Berlin: 'People who believed that they could look into the inner nature of such public figures as Papen or Schleicher, Brüning or Ebert, Hindenburg, Bismarck or Napoleon, or even Lenin or Mussolini, could not penetrate Hitler.' State Secretary Trendelenburg complained that Hitler has 'the empty

[6] A. Milward, Review of R. J. Overy, *The Nazi Economic Recovery 1932–1938*, London 1982, in *EcHR* 36, 1983, 653.

[7] See (ed.) H. A. Turner, *Hitler aus nächster Nähe: Aufzeichnungen eines Vertrauten 1929–1932*, Frankfurt 1978, 255.

[8] Tammen, 282–4.

[9] A. Speer, *Inside the Third Reich*, London 1971 (paperback ed.), 49.

face of a waiter'.[10] Köpke of the Auswärtiges Amt was reassured by discovering that Hitler was more 'moderate' than Göring, but otherwise was unsure.[11]

Nazi pronouncements on the economy did not give any help in understanding what Hitler believed he might do. The twenty-five-point party programme of February 1920, which Hitler had subsequently declared to be 'unchangeable', included pledges to abolish the 'servitude of interest' (Point 11, *Brechung der Zinsknechtschaft*), nationalise trusts (Point 13) and big estates without compensation (Point 17), as well as to attack 'speculators and usurers' (Point 18). However, Hitler had been prepared to say that the party programme was only intended for propaganda purposes and that it did not represent a serious basis for political action.[12] In speeches to business men, Hitler committed himself to the defence of private property.[13] After 1929 he made sure that he told the German peasantry that he did not intend to use his party's power to confiscate land.[14]

Many historians who have attempted to interpret Hitler's views on the economy have given up because the vision they discovered was impossibly vague and nebulous. Bullock believes that 'Hitler neither understood nor was interested in economics'.[15] Jäckel examines Hitler's *Weltanschauung* in terms of ideas about foreign policy and anti-Semitism, and, although a major justification for Hitler's expansionism was fundamentally economic, does not consider the Führer's ideas on how to manage the domestic economy.[16] Other writers have avoided the problem of talking about Hitler's views on the economy in a different way: that is to argue that Hitler merely did the

[10] A. Brecht, *Mit der Kraft des Geistes: Lebenserinnerungen Zweite Hälfte 1927–1967*, Stuttgart 1967, 272.

[11] G. Otruba, 'Die Wirtschafts- und Gesellschaftspolitik des Nationalsozialismus im Spiegel der österreichischen Gesandtschaftsberichte 1933/34', in (ed.) F.-W. Henning, *Probleme der nationalsozialistischen Wirtschaftspolitik*, Berlin 1976, 51–2.

[12] See A. Barkai, *Das Wirtschaftssystem des Nationalsozialismus: Der historische und ideologische Hintergrund, 1933–1936*, Cologne 1977, 23.

[13] See the 1926 speech reproduced in (ed.) W. Jochmann, *Im Kampf um die Macht: Hitlers Rede vor dem Hamburger Nationalklub von 1919*, Frankfurt 1960.

[14] Farquharson, especially 13–15.

[15] A. Bullock, *Hitler, a Study in Tyranny*, Harmondsworth 1962, 152.

[16] E. Jäckel (trans. H. Arnold), *Hitler's Weltsanschauung: A Blueprint for Power*, Middleton Conn. 1974.

obvious. For Mason, Hitler's economics were nothing more than an expression of social defence.[17] Stone concludes that 'it was not that Hitler knew much about economics; on the contrary, he merely acted on common sense'.[18] Yet what did social defence involve in the extraordinary circumstances of 1932, 1933, or 1934? or what was common sense? Only recently have the writings of Turner, Barkai, and Herbst indicated a new interest in the question of Hitler's vision of the economy.[19] Though not many knew about that vision in 1933—*Mein Kampf* is reticent here—it is in fact well documented.

1. There was nothing socialist about Hitler's economics. The NSDAP always placed emphasis on the need for individual initiative and action. It tried to cut itself off from 'Marxism', the SPD's socialism. Nazi collectivism was political, not economic, and left individuals as economic agents. The repeated and famous declarations of the Nazi intention to socialize people rather than factories meant that far-reaching programmes of state control over the economy were unnecessary.

Emphasis on the will in Nazi propaganda led to an insistence—which was not usual in the conventional economic literature of the time—on the importance of innovators and designers. To this extent Hitler's vision was the true product of an economy in transition, groping for a new future. Hitler repeatedly expressed his admiration for men like Ferdinand Porsche, the automobile designer, and the Junkers aero-manufacturers: these genuine entrepreneurs had been threatened by the bureaucratised trusts and had almost gone under in the depression.[20] Innovation was the key to the future: 'it depends on the will. One can't leave things to take their own course. Countries which are rich and have everything don't need

[17] T. Mason, *Sozialpolitik im Dritten Reich: Arbeiterklasse und Volksgemeinschaft*, Opladen 1977, 300.

[18] N. Stone, *Hitler*, London 1980, 26.

[19] H. A. Turner, 'Hitlers Einstellung zu Wirtschaft und Gesellschaft vor 1933', *GG* 2, 1976, 89–117. Barkai 1977a. A. Barkai, 'Sozialdarwinismus und Antiliberalismus in Hitlers Wirtschaftskonzept: Zu Henry A. Turner', *GG* 3, 1977, 406–17. L. Herbst, *Der totale Krieg und die Ordnung der Wirtschaft: Die Kriegswirtschaft im Spannungsfeld von Politik, Ideologie und Propaganda 1939–1945*, Stuttgart 1982.

[20] (Ed.) W. Jochmann, *Adolf Hitlers Monologe im Führerhauptquartier 1941–1944: Die Aufzeichnungen Heinrich Heims*, Hamburg 1980, 289. D. Irving, *The Rise and Fall of the Luftwaffe: The Life of Luftwaffe Marshal Erhard Milch*, London 1973, 36–7.

discoveries any more. What for? Discoveries are uncomfortable. People want to go along in the old way. These rich peoples, England, France, and America, only want to sleep.'[21] This will to invent and create was, Hitler thought, a constant of human nature which could no more be abolished than could the sexual drive. On the other hand, that will might well atrophy: and Germany in the 1920s had been plagued by impotent old entrepreneurs. Hitler was frequently bitterly critical of the German bourgeoisie and of the captains of industry ('gullible fools'). He said that 'the role of the bourgeoisie is played out'.[22] He was cynical, too, of business men's motives: when they talked of idealism and national unity they meant only wage reductions.[23] This not altogether implausible doctrine came out of the experience of the Brüning years. But then Hitler added a sort of Darwinian evolutionism: new classes would emerge to take over the creative role.

This belief made Hitler appear to some of his supporters to be advocating 'liberalism of the purest and crassest kind'. Oddly, Hitler did not mind this accusation. 'To stand still is to retreat ... our state can only evolve through a struggle for existence, in a competitive battle which is as unrestricted as possible and is only controlled by the dictate of the general good: the good of all, of the *Volksgemeinschaft*, of humanity.' Though the state might intervene in exceptional circumstances, Hitler disliked the notion of a long-term control: 'As soon as we return to normal times, we must remove all the restrictions which interfere with the play of natural forces. The state is not a nanny, but rather the embodiment of the ethical consciousness of a people and of the individual.' He concluded that eventually there could only be either a liberal or a socialist solution, that a *via media* was impossible, and that he rejected socialism.[24]

2. Despite Hitler's attack on rich nations as idle and sleepy, he did want the German people to become richer. This indeed was the goal and ultimate justification of entrepreneurial activity. He argued in the terms set by the debate in the later 1920s about rationalisation and technical progress: 'an increase

[21] H. Rauschning, *Gespräche mit Hitler*, New York 1940, 29.
[22] Ibid., 26, 44.
[23] H. A. Turner 1978, 465–6.
[24] Ibid., 215–17, 322.

in the purchasing power of the masses will be an important means of managing economic recovery.' He also told road-workers that 'it is our purpose to raise slowly mass purchasing power in order to provide orders for factories and to bring movement to the German economy again'.[25] Hitler even presented this view to the captains of industry, although it could not really be expected to appeal to men who had spent much of the 1920s attacking the unions' purchasing-power theory. In Hamburg in 1926 he put on a very respectable front when addressing the Nationalklub von 1919, where the conservative élite of Hamburg society had assembled in order to sample the wares of the Bavarian orator. Social concessions to the workers were, he argued, of paramount urgency—although they should not be made as long as there was a 'Marxist threat'. Marxism was not concerned with satisfying the workers' desires, but rather with turning desires into an instrument in the class struggle. Precisely for this reason, Hitler deduced, anti-Marxists should be concerned with material welfare.[26]

This belief was part of a wider high-technology vision of the future: Hitler was far from being a simple straw-chewing romantic agrarian reactionary. Most of his favourite ideas were for new consumer goods: he thought that food could be grown in the sea-bed; and he wanted to revolutionise domestic life.[27]

> Blocks of flats will have kindergartens right next door: the housewife won't even have to bring the toddlers there herself, she'll just push a button and the nanny will call to collect the children. The housewife won't have to carry kitchen and household rubbish down the steps and carrying heating material up: that must all be done by automatic equipment in the flat. The alarm clock that wakes her up in the morning will at the same time boil the water needed for breakfast . . .

There was in fact no limit to the extent to which human society could become richer: 'progress consists in making life more beautiful for people! . . . There was [in the past] the stupid thought that living standards could not be raised further.' Technical change need never cause unemployment: 'I will

[25] Domarus 234, 23 March 1933 Government declaration in Reichstag; see also 302, 23 Sept. 1933 speech to Autobahn workers.

[26] Jochmann 1960, 108.

[27] Turner 1978, 207.

simply build twice the length of Autobahn if we require half the amount of labour previously needed for a certain stretch.'[28]

3. From 1932 the Nazi party attached importance to re-employment projects. Gregor Strasser's Reichstag speech of 10 May 1932 set out an ambitious programme: it was meant to win votes, and the speech was reprinted in the party press and circulated in as high an edition as Hitler's own speeches. The May 1932 *Sofortprogramm* provided for the expenditure of 10b. RM for roads, agricultural improvements, and settlements; and it claimed that these projects would employ up to 2m. labourers. However, after criticism from the old right, which argued that this Strasser plan was too inflationary, it was dropped. In October 1932 a new programme (*Aufbauprogramm*) was launched, which was much less specific about re-employment than the May Sofortprogramm, but still provided for 3b. RM to be spent on work creation.

Although most of the Nazi voters were not workers and were not unemployed, Hitler repeatedly said that the economic hardship of traders and artisans could only be solved by an increase in the general level of employment. This was by no means a conventional pro-business line: both Mittelstand and large industrial interest organisations had argued that the direction of causation was the reverse, and that the way to restore employment in Germany was to raise profitability first. Hitler argued the other way round: 'the fight to preserve the Mittelstand is also and in the first place a fight against unemployment'.[29] Statements such as this were important for the Nazis' claim to be a movement which transcended class divisions. (We might notice an interesting parallel here: in 1931 and 1932 both Brüning and the SPD also treated re-employment projects as a way of healing the social divide in Germany). Re-employment was in general a prime instrument of political integration.

Correspondingly, Hitler boasted of success after January 1933. In October he told a *Daily Mail* correspondent that in eight months 'we have taken two and a quarter million

[28] Jochmann 1980, 256, 306.

[29] Domarus 371, 21 Mar. 1934 speech to Munich-Salzburg Autobahn workers.

unemployed out of a total of six million back into the productive process'.[30] By September 1934 a proclamation drawn up by Hitler and read out by Gauleiter Adolf Wagner stated that Nazi programmes had reduced unemployment by 4.5m.[31]

4. Just as important from the standpoint of social integration was the avoidance of a new inflation. This was for Hitler a vital matter, for in his eyes the Republic had discredited itself because it had allowed the expropriation of the *rentiers*. Hitler said that this expropriation was the consequence of the practical application of the ideas of 'Marxism'. Gauleiter Wagner's 1934 proclamation, after citing the reduction of unemployment as a major Nazi success, added the important rider that 'the German Mark has remained stable, despite all export difficulties'.

The accusation frequently made against the Nazis in 1932 that their programme would mean a new inflation was particularly damaging and dangerous in view of the widespread popular fears of that year of inflation and financial instability. Hitler's speeches again and again tried to refute the accusation: in April he said in Dresden, 'Many say today that we would produce an inflation. We cannot do this, even if we wanted to, for the specialists in inflation are sitting in the parties which today rule the state.'[32] He believed that the SPD had deliberately destroyed the small saver in order to pauperise and proletarianise the German people. In July he cited Friedrich Engels as an example of the socialist argument: 'When capital destroys small artisans and small merchants, it is performing a valuable service, since it is indirectly furthering the goals of social democracy.'[33] The theme that inflation was produced by the connivance of big finance with the SPD also lent itself to an anti-Semitic treatment: Jews in business and in the 'Marxist' movement wanted to destroy the solid values of the German Mittelstand.

The rejection of inflation was far more than merely a public pose. Hitler made the same points in private discussions. In late 1931 when Bernhard Köhler, a Nazi economic specialist,

[30] Ibid. 322, 18 Oct. 1933 interview with Ward Price.
[31] Ibid. 448, 5 Sept. 1934 proclamation.
[32] *Völkischer Beobachter*, 6 Apr. 1932.
[33] *Völkischer Beobachter*, 31 July 1932.

suggested that money could be 'manufactured out of the air' in order to pay for a work creation programme, Hitler replied, 'If I were alone with you, I would say: poor madman.' Köhler answered that the state had always had the right to produce money. Hitler objected violently: 'That's exactly what previous governments have done. *They* pour money for unemployment relief down the drain.'[34]

After January 1933, Hitler continued to insist on the damage done by inflations. In his government declaration after the March elections, he emphasised the need for parsimony in public finance in order to avoid inflationary budget deficits.[35] In private he opposed the thought of a devaluation of the German Mark or of the Danzig Gulden: 'I have pledged my word. I will not make inflation. The people would not understand it.' This view of the pernicious effect of inflation came from Hitler's wartime experience: again and again he came back to the frightening story of Germany's collapse in 1918. This had not been the product of military defeat: here Hitler followed the orthodox view of the German right. Rather 'the last war was lost because of a limitless lack of understanding for the susceptibilities of the masses of small savers and housewives'. Rather than allow such an inflation to occur again, he said, he would prefer to abolish money altogether.[36] In 1933 Hitler thought that it was necessary to appoint as Reichsbank President a conservative economist such as Schacht at least until unemployment was conquered: otherwise there would be an international speculative attack on the Mark and unemployment would rise again.[37]

However, he always rejected the notion that the stability of a currency depended on a certain proportion of metallic reserve for the currency, on the 40 per cent gold minimum, for instance, required by the Weimar Republic's Reichsbank law. Such a view was 'Jewish' or 'plutocratic', a product of the 'golden international'. In attacking fixed reserves, Hitler was well within the old German tradition of conservative currency theory expounded by figures such as G. F. Knapp and K.

[34] Turner 1978, 332–3.

[35] Domarus 233, 23 March 1933 Government declaration: 'The problem of public finance is in fact a problem of making economies in administration.'

[36] Rauschning 195–6.

[37] Turner 1978, 401.

Helfferich. Stability, Hitler believed, was rather a question of the power of the state: 'One has inflation only when one wants it. Inflation is lack of discipline. Lack of discipline on the part of buyers and lack of discipline on the part of sellers. I will ensure that prices remain stable. For that I have the SA. Woe to the man who puts up prices. We don't need any legal measures to stop price rises, we can do this through the party alone.'[38] Much later, he came back to this theme when talking to his wartime cronies: 'Inflation does not arise when money enters circulation, but only when the individual demands more money for the same service. Here we must intervene. That is what I had to explain to Schacht, that the first cause of the stability of our currency is the concentration camp.' It was 'state authority' that stood in the way of an unstable Reichsmark. Abolishing the 'gold currency', Hitler said, meant that without running a risk of currency instability, the state could, as long as there was unemployment, pay easily for the rearmament of Germany.[39]

In practice the business of managing a recovery was not as easy as this. In the initial stages of Nazi rule, the nature of Hitler's vision mattered comparatively little: but then the rise in consumer spending brought, as it already had done in the Weimar years, difficulties. It was at this stage that Nazi ideology dictated how these difficulties were to be resolved. Already before full employment was reached, there were sharp conflicts apparent between Hitler's economic desiderata:

the reawakening of private enterprise;
a rise in national income;
re-employment;
currency stability.

Could this conflict be resolved? Hitler thought not, at least within Germany's current frontiers. The creation of new entrepreneurial opportunities and the rise in national income required *Lebensraum*, the expansion of Germany to the East, an expansion which had already been set out in his writings of the 1920s—*Mein Kampf* and the unpublished *Second Book*.[40] Wei-

[38] Rauschning, 25. [39] Jochmann 1980, 88, 343, 345.

[40] (ed.) G. Weinberg, *Hitlers Zweites Buch: Ein Dokument aus dem Jahr 1928*, Stuttgart 1961.

mar Germany had suffered because it was inhabited by a *Volk ohne Raum*. This 1920s vision had been developed *before* the depression at the end of the decade required a response formulated as economic policy; and *after* Hitler had drawn up his economic programme, the geopolitical vision still remained as the ultimate way of resolving difficulties or contradictions. In that sense, all steps taken before the war of expansion were for Hitler nothing more than provisional *ad hoc* measures.

The difficulty facing Nazi policy-makers can be put another way: like the Weimar governments, Hitler promised more people more. Such promises were hard to fulfil in the real world, and the lack of fulfilment had destabilized Weimar's political system. How could Hitler avoid a destabilisation of his own state—a destabilisation which, particularly in 1933 and 1934, many observers believed they could detect. In October 1933 US Ambassador William Dodd wrote how Hitler 'is surely not so powerful with the people as Mussolini, the Italian despot, has been'.[41] The SPD's Prague exile organisation and the Nazi Sicherheitsdienst both reported widespread discontent in these early years of Nazism.[42] If Hitler is really held to have established his legitimacy by removing unemployment, why was that legitimacy so contested in the early years of the regime when unemployment was falling quickly and when Hitler was able to announce his success over and over again?

In fact the obstacles in the way of an implementation of Nazi policy appeared in 1934 and 1935 very clearly in those areas most important in ideological terms for the new regime:

raising farmers' incomes;
improving the position of the Mittelstand;
making workers wealthier;
financing and managing a rearmament drive;
increasing National Income without running into the balance of trade difficulties familiar from Weimar days.

These problems will be examined in turn.

[41] Dodd, 61.

[42] Quoted in I. Kershaw, *Popular Opinion and Political Dissent in the Third Reich: Bavaria 1933–1945*, Oxford 1983, especially 66–110.

AGRICULTURE

National Socialism explicitly claimed to take the agrarian issue out of the discussion of general economic questions. The economy should be obliged to accept a sacrifice in order to help farmers on national or racial grounds: 'the restoration of the profitability of agricultural enterprise may be hard for consumers. But the fate which would overtake the whole German people if the German peasant went to the wall makes these hardships appear trivial.'[43] Farm incomes should be raised, therefore, at the cost of the rest of the economy. 'It is necessary from now on to separate the peasant economy from the capitalist market economy', the new economic policy asserted.[44] After 1932/3 farm incomes did indeed increase: (see Table XXXIV).

Agriculture benefited from tax cuts (turnover tax on agricultural products was cut by half), and from the continuation of Brüning's policy of interest reduction in the form of a general debt rescheduling (June 1933). Thus in the financial year 1934/5 agriculture as a whole paid only 650m. RM interest; in 1931/2 this sum had been 1,005m. RM. Taxation in 1934/5 amounted to 440m. RM; in 1931/2 agriculture paid 570m. RM and in 1927/8, 730m. RM.[45] The most immediately oppressive, and the most resented, farmers' payments were thus substantially reduced from the Weimar levels. Such relief, however, does not account for all, or even a very large proportion, of the rise in farm income.

While debt relief and even tax help represented developments of policies pursued already by Weimar governments, National Socialism offered two new institutions. The first, the Entailed Farm Law (15 May 1933) was supposed to create stable large peasant units of between 7.5 and 125 ha. by protecting against foreclosure, division among heirs, and even voluntary sales (at least without court permission).[46] The intention was to arrest the flight from the land and to create a racially sound peasant stock. However, the 1930s was a period of fast flight from the land because of the vigour of the urban

[43] Domarus 233, 23 March 1933 Government declaration.

[44] *Die deutsche Volkswirtschaft* 8 1933/4, 387.

[45] *Statistisches Jahrbuch* 1937, 541.

[46] RGBl 1933 I 685.

Table XXXIV: Income and Expenditure of German Agriculture 1928–1936 (m. RM)

	1928/9	1929/30	1930/1	1931/2	1932/3	1933/4	1934/5	1935/6	1936/7
Sales									
Cereals	1 733	1 769	1 592	1 510	1 377	1 457	1 426	1 542	1 497
All vegetable products	3 752	3 564	3 177	2 985	2 645	2 848	3 145	3 355	3 373
All animal products	6 476	6 244	5 469	4 365	3 760	4 561	5 157	5 343	5 488
Total	10 228	9 808	8 646	7 350	6 405	7 409	8 302	8 698	8 861
Expenditure									
Taxes	720	740	640	570	560	510	440	450	480
Interest on loans	920	950	950	1 005	850	730	650	630	630
New buildings	384	366	314	217	160	186	204	206	239
Maintenance on buildings	360	351	314	251	203	217	227	223	242
Machinery	281	242	190	139	138	177	234	327	395

Source: Statistisches Jahrbuch 1937, 541.

economy. Farmers complained that their labour was being attracted away and that young people no longer wanted to till the soil.[47]

The second new creation, the Reichsnährstand (RNS) was a marketing organisation designed to end the 'tyranny of free prices' or 'liberal materialism' which had produced such a catastrophic decline in prices since 1927. It was created in a hurry after the large harvest of 1933 threatened to bring a new price fall. The RNS standardised marketing and fixed prices through regional boards (*Verbände*) for each major agricultural commodity.[48] In some aspects, then, the RNS seemed to be merely a continuation of Dietrich's plans for product standardisation, but other features were more radical. There were fixed quotas for delivery to the RNS boards at specified prices: this institution recalled the highly unpopular *Zwangswirtschaft* that had followed the World War and which had stopped farmers benefiting from food shortages.

In 1933 the RNS may have helped to keep prices up, but by 1935 it proved a useful way of keeping prices down. A Reich Price Commissar was able to use the *Verbände* as executive instruments for the imposition of price maxima. Eventually the peasants noticed the way they had been regulated by the Nazi régime to their own disadvantage. In Bavaria there were even cases of peasant protest against the régime's anti-Semitism, perhaps a product of moral outrage but also of a hope that Jewish middlemen might be able to pay free, unregulated prices.[49] From the end of 1934 the peasant problem turned round: from being one of over-indebtedness and over-exposure to tax it became a resentment of farmers who felt deprived of what they considered to be their legitimate share in Hitler's miraculous economic recovery.

In economic terms, however, we might apply after 1935 the converse of the argument about the Müller–Brüning period. The state's price control now involved a transfer of real resources from a less efficient agricultural sector to a more efficient industrial one; and cheap food after 1934/5 helped to sustain the growth of the 1930s.

[47] Examples in R. Grunberger, *A Social History of the Third Reich*, Harmondsworth 1974, 207–9.

[48] See Farquharson, 71–85.

[49] Kershaw, 242–5.

THE MITTELSTAND

The term Mittelstand was used in the 1920s by sociologists to describe the expanding social group of white-collar workers ('the new Mittelstand') and also the relics of the past, the 'pre-industrial classes' of independent peasant farmers, craftsmen, and small traders ('the old Mittelstand').[50] In the political usage of the time, however, Mittelstand politics meant representation of the interests of craftsmen and traders; and it is in this sense that the word is used here.

There were many National Socialist supporters in the lower grades of the civil service and also, to a lesser extent, among clerical workers and among peasantry; but National Socialism had always made a particular effort to cultivate the traditional Mittelstand. In the party's early years, its radicalism deterred many Mittelständler; but even the party programme of 1920 spoke of the 'creation of a healthy Mittelstand and its maintenance'. By the end of the decade, most politically active Mittelständler were still in the parties of the right: the DNVP or, more and more, regional parties or particular interest parties (the Wirtschaftspartei, or Economic Party, and the Reichspartei für Volksrecht und Aufwertung, a party which called for a better deal for those expropriated during the German inflation).[51] Economically, the Mittelstand suffered in the 1920s. In a fashion-conscious and volatile decade, outmoded smaller producers and sellers had to compete with big producers and with department stores which held larger stocks and which could be flexible in changing product lines more frequently. Then small business men in trade and craft manufacture were affected by the price decline in the economic crisis, and by the credit crisis: many had, as we have seen, borrowed for the first time in the 1920s. After 1931 the complaints of the Mittelstand about the modern world

[50] H. A. Winkler, *Mittelstand, Demokratie und Nationalsozialismus: Die politische Entwicklung von Handwerk und Kleinhandel in der Weimarer Republik*, Cologne 1972, especially 162. See also the recent work of T. Childers, *The Nazi Voter: The Social Foundations of Fascism in Germany 1919–1933*, Chapel Hill 1983.

[51] L. E. Jones, ' "The Dying Middle": Weimar Germany and the Fragmentation of Bourgeois Politics', *CEH* 5, 1972, 36; and L. E. Jones, 'Inflation, Revaluation and the Crisis of Middle-class Politics: a Study in the Dissolution of the German Party System 1923–1928', *CEH* 12, 1979, 146–68.

increased. In addition, both retail trade and craft manufacture were threatened by dilution as unemployed workers looked for new occupations: the number of itinerant traders, house decorators, and builders *increased* during the economic crisis and endangered already established businesses. Consequently craft workers and even retailers, who had previously been reluctant to organise themselves into professional associations, demanded restrictions on entry and certificates of competence (*Befähigungsnachweise*).

The NSDAP built up its Mittelstand *apparat* during the crisis, as it attempted to work against the interest parties and integrate the concerns of the Mittelstand into a general political line. In the Braunes Haus an Economic Policy Department (Wirtschaftspolitische Abteilung) under Otto Wagener began functioning in January 1931 and set out a conservative corporatism based on *Stände* (estates), sympathetic to the Mittelstand and unpopular with big business. Wagener developed plans to break up large concentrations of ownership.[52] Industrial dislike hastened Wagener's dismissal (September 1932), but many aspects of the Nazi economic programme in 1933 were still designed to appeal especially to the Mittelstand. Anti-inflation policies were a long-standing Mittelstand obsession. Interest reductions helped the small business men whose borrowing had led them into trouble in 1931 and 1932. Small building firms profited from house improvement and repair subsidies. But tax rates were not adjusted substantially: between 1933 and 1935 there were changes in agricultural turnover tax, reductions of the automobile and land taxes, and more tax relief for the employment of female domestic servants. The only change that affected small enterprise directly was the reduction of unemployment insurance contributions.[53]

In spring 1933 the Mittelstand enthusiasts in the party thought that they could go further. Some believed that it was up to them to implement what they imagined to be Hitler's programme. On 1 April Jewish shops were boycotted by members of the SA. On the same day, an attack on the interest organisations of big business began. Otto Wagener arrived at

[52] Barkai 1977a, 31.

[53] On taxes under National Socialism, see R. Erbe, *Die nationalsozialistische Wirtschaftspolitik 1933–1939 im Lichte der modernen Theorie*, especially Zürich 1958, 31–2.

the offices of the RDI to demand, in the name of the National Socialist revolution, the removal of the RDI's General Manager Ludwig Kastl, who had been closely associated with Brüning's policy, and of all Jewish directors of the RDI; and also the appointment as political liaison men of two figures with a background in Mittelstand interest politics, Hans von Lucke (NSDAP) and Alfred Möllers (DNVP). In this way the main pressure group of the big firms could be neutralised. Reich Economics Minister Hugenberg gave in to Nazi pressure and appointed Lucke and Möllers as Reich Commissars with responsibility for the RDI. But already on 16 June the RDI conducted a defensive action by fusing with the Weimar Employers' Association VDA into a new Reichsstand der deutschen Industrie.[54] Indeed it was thanks to Nazi radical pressure that life returned to the rather moribund interest associations of Weimar big business: they were now organising themselves in 1933 against the threat of radical Nazism rather as in 1918 and 1919 they had organised to defend themselves against radical socialism. The formation of the Reichsstand was a success from the point of view of big business. It marked the end of the threat of experiments in economic organisation and secured a new corporatist solution. The Reichstand was controlled by very familiar names from Weimar business politics: Krupp von Bohlen was President, Carl Köttgen of Siemens Vice-President, and Jacob Herle, formerly Kastl's deputy, the new General Manager.

The campaign of small traders against large retail units lasted longer than the Nazi Mittelstand's very fleeting attempts to seize the Reichsverband, but in the end it was no more successful. Since the mid-1920s the NSDAP had conducted a campaign against department stores. Some of the biggest department store chains (Leonard Tietz AG and Hermann Tietz & Co., and A. Wertheim GmbH) were owned by Jews. In Königsberg the NSDAP had called for the 'destruction of the enemy of the world, the department store'. A brochure of 1928 described department stores as the creation of Jewish finance capital. Odd details were given to corroborate the Nazi

[54] U. Wengst, 'Der Reichsverband der deutschen Industrie in den ersten Monaten des Dritten Reiches: Ein Beitrag zum Verhältnis von Großindustrie und Nationalsozialismus', *VfZ* 38, 1980, 94–110.

accusations: the *Völkischer Beobachter* claimed that 50 per cent of the salesgirls in department stores had been infected with venereal disease. In the economic crisis the hostility felt by small shopkeepers towards department stores increased, and when in 1932 Nazis took over the Trade Association of Retail Business the department stores were forced to leave the Association (November). In April 1933 the Jewish boycott damaged the business of the stores. Often shop windows were broken, and occasionally the boycott developed into violence against store owners. In Nuremberg the whole management of Schocken & Co. was arrested by the Nazi Factory Cell organisation (NSBO).[55]

The hostility felt by small men was fanned further, and probably not deliberately, by actions of the new Government directed against exactly the small business men who were meant to have been the basis of Nazi support. In line with Hitler's doctrine of preventing inflation by using concentration camps in lieu of disciplined monetary policy, over two hundred small Münich shopkeepers were arrested and notices pinned on the doors of their shops: 'Shop closed by police because of exorbitant prices: shopkeeper in protective custody in Dachau.'[56]

At the same time as the new regime attacked its old supporters, it came under more and more pressure to *help* rather than attack department stores. The stores were defended by labour and finance. The working-class NSBO argued that it would be unwise to increase unemployment by attacking the Tietzs and Karstadts: an estimated 90,000 jobs were at risk. The financial community was worried about the possible knock-on effects of a major bankruptcy in the retail sector: in the still uncertain political climate, such a failure might well unleash yet another round of panics, runs, and bank collapses. In June 1933 the Hermann Tietz chain appealed for state help in rescheduling its debt.[57] Hitler himself was bitterly opposed: 'the banks had given such large credits because of a wrong view of the economy'.[58] They should now pay the price.

[55] H. Uhlig, *Die Warenhäuser im Dritten Reich*, Cologne 1956, 35–7, 87.

[56] Ibid., 106.

[57] Ibid., 112–15. Also BAK R43II/238, 23 June 1933 Cabinet meeting.

[58] Bak R43II/238, 23 June 1933 Cabinet meeting.

However, the new Economics Minister, Kurt Schmitt, the director of the Munich Allianz insurance group, pressed for state action. It was a courageous step for the new minister to make, since Hugenberg had disgraced himself in the eyes of many influential Nazis by appealing for state subsidies for the Karstadt concern; and Schmitt's appointment had been widely regarded as the installation, at last, of a real Nazi in the Economics Ministry. But Schmitt had in fact only joined the party on 1 April 1933, and had been appointed at the instigation of Hermann Göring in order to stop a real Nazi ideologue, Otto Wagener, seizing the Economics Ministry. Soon Schmitt restored a decidedly non-Nazi atmosphere in his Ministry. In July 1933 a new State Secretary was appointed to work alongside the Nazi Gottfried Feder. This was an old Weimar civil servant, Hans Posse, who was an expert on trade relations with Central and Eastern Europe. And Schmitt accomplished his immediate aim in the Tietz case without great difficulty, and despite Hitler's oppostion.[59] The German banks were offered state guarantees to form a holding company to rescue Hermann Tietz (the Hertie-Kaufhaus-Beteiligungs GmbH).

On 6 July Hitler himself gave his blessing to the new (or rather old) economic course when he issued a proclamation to the Reichsstatthalter (the Nazi Reich's envoys in control of Land policy) stating that the Nazi state would only be able to establish itself if it were economically secure.[60] Making the economy stable involved the exclusion of party members from economic policy-making: the Reich Economics Ministry was to be left in charge here. The party hierarchy supported this line. In February 1934 Martin Bormann published a decree prohibiting department stores from advertising and from selling National Socialist uniforms, but at the same time calling for an end to Nazi attacks.[61] There were further restrictive measures (bans on lending libraries and refreshment rooms in department stores, and limits on sales promotions), as well as voluntary agreements by suppliers to limit discounts given to large retailers; but the department store survived the Third Reich.

[59] W. A. Boelcke, *Die deutsche Wirtschaft 1930–1945: Interna des Reichswirtschaftsministeriums*, Düsseldorf 1983, 65–8.

[60] Domarus 287, 6 July 1933 proclamation.

[61] Uhlig, 133.

The Mittelstand Nazis were furious at the preservation of the most unpleasant features of the old economy. On 24 July 1933 Erich Wildt of the Reichsstand des Deutschen Handels (the umbrella organisation of commerce formed in parallel to the Reichsstand der Deutschen Industrie) told a Munich audience how vital it was that

> anonymous finance companies disappear. *We* need no finance-political transactions of the Hertie kind . . . I believe that . . . no one in this room can claim that the Mittelstand ever asked for subventions. Retail trade always suffered all the hardships of a severe depresison without running to the Government; rather it made the heaviest sacrifices and put itself at the disposal of the Government.[62]

The Reichsführer of the German Retail Foodstuffs Traders complained that shopkeepers had been victimised because they had never been able to mobilise the political muscle possessed by farmers or workers:

> because we did not collapse in complete despair like the farmers, and because we did not march in loud demonstrations through the streets of large cities like the workers, because we did not ask for state aid like capitalist big business, because we carried our own burdens on our own shoulders, and because we gritted our teeth, we must now be assured of the full recognition of our importance for state and economy in our National Socialist Germany.

The Third Reich was to be theirs. But at present the Reich Economics Ministry was still too much under the thumbs of big business. One problem was that small retailers proved immensely difficult to mobilise into an effective political lobby. Out of 108 000 retailers in Bavaria, only 15 000 had joined trade associations by 1933; of 300 000 in Germany, only 150 000 were organised.[63] The Nazi Mittelstand organisations had not really been successful in representing the small German trader, whose economic and political conservatism made him distrustful of any kind of political activity. Voting Nazi in protest against the Weimar system was a very different matter to taking an interest in the day-to-day formulation of the Nazi revolution.

[62] Hayler papers.

[63] Hayler papers, 15 April 1934 Franz Hayler speech in Stuttgart; figures from 1 July 1933 speech in Rosenheim.

As they saw their failure, even the Nazi Mittelstand leaders began to sing a different song. The Reichsführer of Retail Foodstuff Traders, Franz Hayler, who later became leader of the Reichsgruppe Handel, told his organisation in 1934 that it would have to accept that some of its hopes would be disappointed. Nazi claims initially had been too large: 'Retail trade was led into the Third Reich by men who in their methods were hardly different from the leaders of industry, the parties and other interest groups (*Interessentenhaufen*). Quite unrealistic promises were made in the course of propaganda actions, which cannot be immediately implemented as was claimed. This must lead to colossal disillusionment.'[64] Nazi Mittelständler would have to tighten their belts and be content with the 'ideal' benefits provided by the new regime. Maybe this turnaround by the leaders of the movement should not be surprising: the Nazi Mittelstand leaders were by definition not characteristic of the apathetic small traders that they claimed to represent. For instance, the new leader of retail trade was an entrepreneurial maverick who in the course of the 1920s had experimented with property dealings, film production, motor manufacture, and hot-wax painting before he came to food retailing.

The Reich Economics Ministry was now firmly in control of policy; its control was extended in 1934, after Schmitt had worn himself out. In June 1934 he had collapsed while giving a speech. His successor was Hjalmar Schacht, who was appointed at first on a temporary basis but who then stayed until November 1937. Schacht was able to use the extensive powers of the Reichsbank in economic foreign policy to augment the control of the Ministry. Under him, there were still only a very few Nazis in the Ministry; most of Schacht's most trusted advisers came from the Reichsbank (Karl Blessing and Rudolf Brinkmann, a Director of the Reichsbank's subsidiary, the Golddiskontbank). In order to protect himself against the party Schacht put in a few Nazis, such as a cousin of Göring's (Herbert Göring) and an ex-Nazi student leader, Dr Heinrich Hassmann, who became Personnel Director. But Hassmann was loyal to Schachtianism and played his excellent

[64] Hayler papers, 1 July 1933 Hayler speech in Rosenheim.

contacts in the Braunes Haus in Munich and in the Gestapo to his master's advantage. In 1936 the party enthusiasts were so incensed that they staged a party trial of Hassmann.[65]

Schacht was never really trusted by the Nazi leadership. Hitler himself was prepared to tolerate him only because he represented the best known safeguard against inflation. Goebbels thought that Schacht was a 'cold unemotional mocking cynic'.[66] When in 1933 Schacht was passed over as a candidate for the succession to Hugenberg as Economics Minister, Goebbels and Hitler laughed together 'until our cheekbones hurt'.[67] In the light of the widespread suspicion of Schacht, the strength and independence of his position until 1936 is remarkable. He could not, however, hold himself above water for ever by shouting about his indispensability. He made more and more enemies.

In general the Economics Ministry under Schacht continued to deal sympathetically with the big industrial interest organisations,[68] although individual firms fell foul of the ever more complicated control regulations, particularly those relating to foreign trade. In consequence, many business men had accumulated such long lists of extremely irritating minor grievances[69] against Schacht that they were in the political conflict of 1936 unwilling to sacrifice themselves to help the Minister who was basically favourable to them. Schacht isolated himself in the other direction too: his contacts with the international financial and business world made him suspect to many Nazis, and Hitler himself raged about how Schacht had been bribed by Henry Deterding of Shell to obstruct plans for greater domestic production of strategic raw materials.[70] In 1936, when the Economics Ministry's control broke, it was over this issue of trade policy: Mittelstand Nazis were able to attack Schacht, and big business, for being too attached to exports and to the world economy. Big firms like the GHH and the Vereinigte Stahlwerke had been unwilling to help in the development of Germany's domestic iron ore resources.[71]

[65] Boelcke, 87–9.

[66] BAK NL Goebbels 64, 24 Jan. 1937 diary entry.

[67] BAK NL Goebbels 82, 27 July 1933 diary entry.

[68] Boelcke, 99.

[69] See for instance HA/GHH 400101290/34, especially 17 Mar. 1936 Schacht to Reusch.

[70] Jochmann 1980, 239.

[71] M. Riedel, *Eisen und Kohle für das Dritte Reich: Paul Pleigers Stellung in der NS-Wirtschaft*, Frankfurt 1973, 152, 193.

The disputes of 1936 were precipitated by the shortage of fats, which had become apparent by the end of 1935. Difficulty in buying butter and meat was taken very seriously, since it threatened to erode popular morale. Hitler was particularly sensitive to this issue. Price Commissioner Goerdeler circulated a memorandum arguing that only well-fed people could be prepared for war.[72] Schacht and Goerdeler blamed the agricultural price controls for the shortages but Darré and the RNS called instead for the release of more foreign currency by the Reichsbank in order that fats could be imported. Darré then formed a peculiar, and brief, alliance with those autarky enthusiasts who wanted more German industrial raw materials to be domestically produced: Germany should import more butter and less iron ore.[73]

Out of this dispute emerged the Four Year Plan, which represented a major defeat for Schacht. The memorandum which introduced the Four Year Plan proposed a readjustment of the relationship of authority between the private economy and the state: 'The Economics Ministry has only to set the national task, and the duty of the private economy is to fulfil that task. If the private sector is not willing to do this, the National Socialist state will accomplish that goal on its own.'[74] However, the hopes of Mittelstand figures such as Keppler and Pleiger that the Four Year Plan would mark the beginning of a new Nazi Mittelstand policy were soon disillusioned too.[75] The beneficiaries of the Plan were the new and highly bureaucratic Reichswerke Hermann Göring, and the chemical concern IG Farben which was responsible for the implementation of the Plan's targets for the production of synthetic products. Some commentators simply called the Plan's administration the 'verstaatlichte IG'.[76] In 1943–4 yet another Mittelstand offensive was launched as part of an attempt to seize control of Nazi economic planning, and this time the Economics Ministry, since 1938 under the control of a rather ineffective economic

72 IfZ Beck papers F40/2, 26 Oct. 1935 report of Goerdeler.

73 BAK R43II/331, 24 Mar. 1936 Schacht to Darré.

74 (ed.) W. Treue, 'Hitlers Denkschrift zum Vierjahresplan 1936', *VfZ* 3, 1955, 209.

75 Riedel, 41. See also R. J. Overy, *Goering: The Iron Man*, London 1984, 49–52.

76 D. Petzina, *Autarkiepolitik im Dritten Reich: Der nationalsozialistische Vierjahresplan*, Stuttgart 1968, 123.

journalist, was taken over.[77] The Mittelstand began to plan for the post-war economy. But the war was lost.

Like the farmers, the old Mittelstand claimed a share in the fruits of National Socialism. Like the farmers, the Mittelständler were generally not heard sympathetically, though the Mittelstand case was put more forcibly and in 1936 and 1943 indeed helped to produce an upheaval in the Nazi power structure. Here too—as with agriculture—it was economically beneficial that an argument which in Nazi ideological terms made good sense was rejected: in both cases the rejection meant that resources were channelled away from inefficient parts of the economy.

LABOUR IN THE THIRD REICH

Labour relations were the sphere in which Nazi economic policy brought the most immediate, dramatic, and visible changes from the Weimar system. The already weakened trade unions were dissolved on 2 May 1933 and replaced four days later by a new compulsory umbrella organisation, the German Labour Front (*Deutsche Arbeitsfront*, DAF). By and large the DAF was ineffective and impotent. It was not concerned with wage negotiations, but tried instead simply to improve conditions of work: redecorating factories, introducing or improving canteens, extending holidays slightly, and organising workers' free time. The leader of the DAF, Robert Ley, was occasionally influential in the political disputes of the Third Reich. Hitler and the Nazi leadership had developed an obsession with maintaining standards of living, and this obsession gave Ley a useful lever to pull in the factional squabbles among the Nazi paladins. In 1933 the victory of the conservatives in the Economics Ministry displeased Ley as much as it affronted the Mittelstand Nazis, though labour's claims were as difficult to reconcile with the interests of small business as with the dictates of conservative economics.[78] Mittelstand enterprise was in fact of all business the least able to afford the investments needed to make improvements in the work climate.

Ley's greatest influence came in 1935–6, when he allied

[77] Herbst, 276–313. [78] On conflicts between Ley and Schacht see Boelcke, 92–8.

himself with Darré against Schacht's attempt to restrict the consumption of fats in Germany. The DAF was always very concerned with the quality of the food supply. Schacht was defeated in the struggles of 1936, but this did not bring victory either for Darré or for Ley: Göring's Four Year Plan brought increasing restrictions on labour rather than improving conditions of work. So both labour and the Mittelstand lost out.

Ley's efforts were not concerned with wages in the German recovery. Wages after 1933 were politically determined, but in a very different manner from that of Weimar. Unions and works councils were excluded from labour negotiations, but so were the *Betriebsführer*, as the employers were termed in Nazi parlance. Instead the *Tarifvertrag* was worked out by newly created 'Trustees of Labour'. In practice, these usually simply renewed the *Tarifvertrag* running in January 1933: after one year of the Third Reich, only 591 out of a total of 6742 *Tarifvertrag* contracts had been set by the Trustees.[79] Thus nominal wage rates barely changed after 1933: only in the cases of domestic workers, and of agricultural and building workers, was there any marked improvement. Raising farm wages corresponded with the Nazi goal of keeping more Germans on the soil; and the rise in building wages was a reaction to market pressures as the big construction projects of Nazism got under way. In general, however, the Labour Trustees preferred non-market ways of dealing with the problems of labour scarcity. In February 1935 a Work Book was introduced. It was to be retained by the employer for the duration of the labour contract and was intended to make it more difficult for workers to move in search of higher wages. On 7 November 1936 a decree forbade newspaper advertisements for building and metal workers. In February 1935 the Reich Labour Minister even suggested that it might be necessary to intervene in order to allow more flexibility in building wages, but the suggestion ran into political obstacles and was blocked by Hess and the party. It was 'agreed to keep to the existing wage levels as rigidly as possible'.[80] Despite such

[79] H. Egloff, 'Gestaltung des Arbeitsverhältnisses', *Jahrbuch für nationalsozialistische Wirtschaft* 1937, 62–3.

[80] BAK R43II/541, 12 Feb. 1935 Reich Labour Ministry to Lammers (State Secretary in Reich Chancellery); 2 May 1935 meeting. See also Mason 1977, 156–7.

attempts to control mobility and wages, in 1935 and 1936 employers in the building, brickmaking, metal, and engineering trades began to have to pay over the level set by *Tarif*. For this reason, official wage statistics based on the *Tarifvertrag* almost certainly give for the late 1930s too unfavourable a picture of the position of labour. Between 1933 and December 1935 actual average hourly earnings (as opposed to the *Tarif* rates) rose by 4.5 per cent; weekly earnings rose much more (13.7 per cent), as longer hours were worked.[81] But the labour market certainly did not succeed in escaping controls sufficiently to produce the very dramatic wage rises that the unions had negotiated in Weimar.

Another area where labour was beaten back was in the factory itself: the elected Weimar councils (*Betriebsräte*) were replaced by 'councils of confidence' (*Vertrauensräte*) nominated by the DAF and only confirmed by election by the work-force. In fact, participation in the *Vertrauensrat* elections was very low (only 40 per cent in the first year), even though non-voting was penalised. From the point of view of the Government's work-creation programme it was particularly embarrassing that some of the lowest voting figures came from factories that had received large state orders. In 1934 and 1935 the Gestapo reports indicated increasingly bitter demands for decent wages.[82] Such a dramatic curtailing of labour activity—the abolition of the unions, of *Betriebsräte*, and the imposition of a longer working day—was only possible because of the widespread disillusion with old-style union activity. Both the leadership and the membership of the unions had suffered from a collapse of morale during the slump: they had been unable to resist Nazism, prevent the savage wage reductions of 1931–3, or act against the rising levels of unemployment. After 1933 Nazism tried to create a new sort of legitimacy by its efforts in work creation.

Work-creation programmes (which will be discussed in more detail below) were, however, not the sole or even the most important element in Nazism's attempt to end unemployment. In May 1934 a new law prohibited the offering of jobs to non-

[81] Calculated from BAK R43II/541, 3 Jan. 1939, Reich Labour Ministry wage statistics. From 1935 to 1939 the respective figures are 5.5% and 8.2%.

[82] Der Deutsche Volkswirt 9, 1934/5, 1421. Gestapo reports in BAK R58/1126–8.

local labour in areas of high unemployment: in this way the Government tried to stop the drift of unemployed workers to big cities—Berlin, Hamburg and Bremen—where their presence would be very obvious, and might also be a potential source of unrest. In January 1935 there were still 303 000 without work in Berlin, but in the autumn of 1936 only 126 000.[83] In this way the problem of unemployment in big cities was solved speedily by administrative action. There were other administrative interventions in the labour market. Married women were officially discouraged from working, and many were dismissed by their employers. Unmarried girls were encouraged to go to the altar by marriage loans, which were turned into grants if the new wife turned herself into a prolific mother. Often dismissals of married women took place not at the command of central government, but at the insistence of local party and SA organisations, though from the end of 1933 these independent local initiatives to implement real Nazism were quite strictly controlled. Those dismissed in 1933 during the political and racial purge of the civil service were not permitted to register as unemployed.[84] In August 1934 a decree provided for the dismissal of workers under twenty-five and their replacement by family fathers: 130 000 jobs changed hands in this way in the course of 1935.[85]

Unemployed young workers were drafted into a work corps: in 1934 on average 240 000 were enrolled in the *Arbeitsdienst*. Two-fifths of these worked on land improvements, a quarter in transport construction, and the rest in forestry or in constructing settlements.[86] In addition, in March 1934 630 000 were employed in emergency work (*Notstandsarbeiten*), though this number fell off very sharply by 1935.[87]

Conscription of labour and the 'fight against double-earning

[83] RGBl 1934 I 381 (15 May 1934). Also F. Syrup, 'Die Regelung des Arbeitseinsatzes', *Jahrbuch für nationalsozialistische Wirtschaft* 1937, 35–49, especially 39.

[84] See in general Mason 1977; A. Schweitzer, *Big Business in the Third Reich*, London 1964; O. Nathan, *The Nazi Economic System: Germany's Mobilisation for War*, Durham NC 1945, 170–213.

[85] RGBl 1934 I 786 (Law of 10 Aug. 1934). Syrup 1937, 41.

[86] H. Egloff, 'Die Arbeit im neuen Reich', *Jahrbuch für nationalsozialistische Wirtschaft* 1935, 148–9.

[87] W. Stothfang, 'Die künftige Gestaltung der öffentlichen Notstandsarbeiten', *Der deutsche Volkswirt* 10, 1935/6, 59–61.

households' in place of a macro-economic counter-cyclical policy had been part of the standard rhetoric of conservative attempts to solve unemployment in the era of the presidential cabinets. Both proposals had, for instance, been advocated in a memorandum sent to Brüning in April 1932 by Carl Goerdeler, the Mayor of Leipzig.[88] After 1933 all that changed was that this sort of policy could be more ruthlessly implemented, because there were fewer restrictions on the Government's freedom of action. But forcible re-employment and statistical manipulation do not explain the rise in employment in Germany after 1933. Jobless figures in fact fell in 1933 far more slowly that the rise in employment. Employment increased from 11.7m. in January 1933 to 16.9m. in July 1935; but unemployment had only fallen from 6.0m. to 1.8m.[89] Part of the explanation for this is that by no means all those willing to work in the depression were in fact registered as unemployed; but the figures also show how little the Nazi recovery was a statistical conjuring trick. The fundamental reason for the reduction in unemployment was not jiggery-pokery with numbers, but rather the dramatic revival in economic activity which turned the labour problem round so that by 1936, and even more so by the end of the decade, there were serious labour shortages. How far was the state responsible for this economic miracle?

THE STATE BUDGET

Fiscal policy may actually have helped to preserve the existing economic structure in Germany. Spending policy did not have a revolutionary impact in quantitative terms: though government spending rose continually under the Third Reich it remained approximately constant as a share of National Product (rising until 1934/5 and then falling, fluctuating between 31 and 34 per cent). On the revenue side, tax rates barely changed from the levels of the Brüning years: and the major, ideologically motivated, recodification of taxes in October 1934 in fact merely copied its detailed provisions from

[88] BAK R43I/2045, Apr. 1932 Memorandum of Goerdeler.
[89] Wagemann 1935, 12, 16.

Weimar. Tax concessions did not encourage many new enterprises or stimulate business, except in automobile production and in private house construction (where there were subsidies for housing improvements). No systematic attempt was made to provide an economic stimulus by reducing the general level of tax burdens, and for this reason the Keynes–Kahn employment multiplier remained at a low level during the Third Reich. Indeed, one of the reasons most frequently given for the Nazis' failure to implement the thoroughgoing tax reform promised by Hitler and State Secretary Reinhardt in 1933 was that nothing should be done about taxation until the first Nazi priority—the reduction of unemployment—had been accomplished.[90] Thus the state was happy simply to take its share in the German recovery when it took place: and the amount of National Income paid in taxation remained approximately constant between 1933 and 1939.

Goebbels sometimes claimed that budget deficits were quite safe since 'no people had ever gone under because of deficits: only because they lacked weapons'.[91] The reality of the Third Reich in peacetime was otherwise. Government deficits did rise continually from 1932, but until the last year of peace, they were always rather conservatively funded. Of an estimated total of *c.* 80b. RM non-regular, 'extraordinary' Reich expenditure between 1933 and 1939, 56 per cent was financed by non-borrowed income (taxes and revenue from public enterprise), 24 per cent was borrowed on the long-term capital market (the first Reich loan since the abortive 1929 loan was successfully floated in 1935), and only 12 per cent borrowed on short-term markets. The other 8 per cent was financed by monetary expansion; but this inflationary financing occurred only at the end of the 1930s.[92] In managing these deficits, the Reich saw to it that the capital market was treated with the greatest care. The Reich ordered the Länder and communes to avoid any expenditure financed by loans in order that the loan market might be reserved for the Reich's rearmament drive.

[90] *Die deutsche Volkswirtschaft 1933*, no. 18, 554. F. Blaich, 'Die "Grundsätze nationalsozialistischer Steuerpolitik" und ihre Verwirklichung im Dritten Reich', in (ed.) F. W. Henning 1976, 99–100.

[91] BAK NL Goebbels 65, 14 Jan. 1938 diary entry.

[92] S. Lurie, *Private Investment in a Controlled Economy: Germany 1933–1939*, New York 1947, 36–7.

The language of the Finance Ministry's circulars was precisely the same as those of the 1920s which had also been directed against Land and communal overspending.[93] This strategy was successful: Table XXXVII shows how for most of the Nazi period the debt levels of Länder and communes actually *decreased*.

From 1932 to 1934, a government deficit was hidden from the public by being redubbed as 'anticipation of future revenue'. A major part of the work-creation programme was financed through certificates (*Steuergutscheine*) which might be used in the future to pay certain Reich taxes, and which in the meantime were discountable by the banking system. These certificates had been used in Papen's September 1932 programme as a subsidy to employers who hired extra workers. In December 1932 Schleicher's programme provided for the use of 500m. RM certificates to pay for public works. Table XXXVII shows how the government's borrowing requirement rose throughout the Nazi years. In the recovery period, up to 1934/5, it was rather restrained, however.

From 1934 a second concealment device was used. Large amounts were directed into the armament economy from the money market rather than the capital market through the notorious mechanism of the Mefo-bill. The use of this type of bill was a consequence of the regime's obsession with avoiding the appearance of strain on the budget. Already under Brüning, the Reich had used a device called pre-financing (*Vorfinanzierung*), which involved the anticipation of future revenue and which had been developed under Brüning to pay for work-creation projects. Bills were given to the contractors by a specially created financing institution, the Deutsche Bau- und Bodenbank, and were provided with a Reich acceptance that meant that the paper could be easily discounted by the commercial banking system and rediscounted by the central bank. The Reichsbank's legal ceiling on discounting Reich treasury bills did not matter here, since the bills were those of the Bau- und Bodenbank and only had a Reich acceptance: this gave them the same status as other genuinely commercial bills guaranteed by the Reich (usually export bills). A similar

[93] BAK R43II/781, 30 Jan. 1936 Reich Finance Ministry circular. Also H. Baumgarten, 'Gemeinden müssen sparen', *Der deutsche Volkswirt* 10, 1935/6, 851–2.

Table XXXV: Government Expenditure and Revenue 1932–1937 (fiscal year) (m. RM)

	Expenditure	Tax Revenue	Taxes			
			Income	Corporation	Turnover	Customs
1932/3	17 684	10 222	1 332.6	105.8	1 354.4	1 106.0
	(31.0)[a]	(17.9)[a]	(13.0)[b]	(1.0)[b]	(13.2)[b]	(10.8)[b]
1933/4	18 376	10 621	1 293.0	210.0	1 516.2	1 065.1
	(30.5)	(17.6)	(12.2)	(2.0)	(14.2)	(10.0)
1934/5	23 756	11 892	1 720.4	319.5	1 872.5	1 148.6
	(34.9)	(17.5)	(14.5)	(2.7)	(15.7)	(9.7)
1935/6	24 675	13 326	2 417.4	592.7	2 020.0	1 249.4
	(32.9)	(17.8)	(18.7)	(4.4)	(15.2)	(9.4)
1936/7	28 099	15 537	3 209.5	1 046.9	2 389.2	1 333.4
	(33.7)	(18.6)	(20.7)	(6.7)	(15.4)	(8.6)
1937/8	29 624	18 599	4 059.2	1 552.8	2 753.6	1 595.2
	(31.8)	(20.0)	(21.8)	(8.3)	(14.8)	(8.6)

Source: Statistisches Jahrbuch, with Mefo-expenditure (see below) added to Reich expenditure.

[a] % of GNP.

[b] % of total tax yield.

Table XXXVI: Government Debt 1931–1938 (31 March) (m. RM)

	Reich					Reich, Länder, and Communes				
	Pre-1924 debt, and fixed value debt	New debt			Total	Pre-1924 debt	New debt			Total
		Total	Foreign	Short-term			Total	Foreign	Short-term	
1931	4 727.8	6 614.5	3 305.5	1 705.1	11 342.2	6 042.2	17 980.0	4 799.2	4 575.8	24 022.1
1932	4 571.3	6 862.6	3 215.2	1 717.8	11 434.0	5 803.9	18 373.3	4 679.6	4 550.1	24 177.1
1933	4 421.5	7 268.5	3 037.2	1 943.8	11 689.9	5 592.3	18 772.6	4 480.3	4 962.8	24 365.0
1934	4 238.5	7 554.2	2 026.2	2 188.1	11 792.8	5 330.5	19 199.4	2 935.3	3 743.3	24 529.9
1935	3 917.4	8 534.9	1 773.0	2 486.8	12 452.3	4 918.9	20 146.5	2 574.3	3 661.9	25 063.0
1936	3 765.6	10 606.2	1 677.9	2 918.3	14 371.7	4 688.1	22 012.7	2 418.1	3 853.3	26 700.8
1937	3 622.1	12 435.9	1 441.9	2 382.9	16 057.9	4 440.5	23 368.1	2 087.4	3 216.4	27 808.5
1938	3 466.6	15 631.7	1 332.9	2 345.2	19 098.3	4 210.8	26 145.7	1 943.1	2 965.4	30 356.5

Source: Statistisches Jahrbuch, various issues.

Table XXXVII: Net Increase in Short- and Long-Term Government Debt 1931–1938[a] *(m. RM)*

Year	Reich			Länder	Hansa Towns	Communes	Total	Total as % of GNP
	Official debt	Mefo-bills	Steuergutscheine					
1931/2	91.8			39.8	2.1	21.3	155	0.2
1932/3	255.9		450	158.3	−1.6	−242.8	620	1.1
1933/4	102.9		1 519	−38.5	−26.6	145.1	1 702	2.8
1934/5	659.5	2 140	−242	−36.3	38.2	−128.4	2 431	3.6
1935/6	1 919.4	2 720	−430	−29.8	−7.5	−244.4	3 928	5.2
1936/7	1 686.2	4 450	−428	−58.1	−19.3	−501.0	5 130	6.1
1937/8	3 040.4	2 690	−869	−122.3	−84.3	−285.8	4 369	4.7

[a] — Indicates net decrease in government debt.

Source: Compiled from issues of *Statistisches Jahrbuch*; Mefo-bills from L. Schwerin von Krosigk, *Staatsbankrott*, Göttingen 1974, 230–1. Hoffmann's GNP figures have been adjusted to a budget-year basis by logarithmic calculation.

small enterprise to the Bau- und Bodenbank, the Metallurgische Forschungsgesellschaft mbH, was created in 1933 to pre-finance rearmament.

Bills drawn on the Mefo by the armament suppliers were accepted by the Mefo and could then be discounted by the Reichsbank. Once they had been discounted, they were provided with an (unwritten) Reich guarantee. Though the bills were usually dated only for three (sometimes it was six) months, they could be provided by the armaments suppliers in bundles of up to twenty. Thus the Mefo remained in debt with the Reichsbank, and the Reich could delay paying, for up to five years. Between 1937 and 1939 payment through Mefo-bill came to be the main way of paying for rearmament.

These bills represented a fundamentally inflationary mechanism of financing public spending: after 1935, government borrowing, though concealed, amounted to between 3 and 6 per cent of the National Product. In 1937 and 1938 the Mefo-bill issue produced bitter conflicts between Schacht and the Government, and in January 1939 most of the Reichsbank's directors, including Schacht himself, protested and were then dismissed by Hitler.

Even in this period of great tension, however, the Government tried to treat the capital market very cautiously. In the later 1930s it was still very concerned to see that its paper was bought by businesses and by private individuals, and not by the financial sector alone. The purchase of state paper was a kind of financial vote of confidence in the regime, and the bitter experience of 1916, when German citizens had stopped being willing to buy Reich Loans, was often recalled. Until the end of 1938 Nazi Germany had no such problem: only then did the quantity of state paper bought by the banks increase dramatically while private purchases fell.[94] After this date openly inflationary finance was needed.

There was a great deal of propaganda for savings. For instance, in 1936 school savings schemes were introduced.[95] The savings increase was not, however, just a consequence of

[94] Surveys by Reichsbank Volkswirtschaftliche und Statistische Abteilung of sales of state paper: BAK R43II/786.

[95] R. Schraut, 'Das Kleinsparwesen—eine bedeutsame Quelle für die Sammlung nationalen Sparkapitals', *Die Deutsche Volkswirtschaft*, 1938, no. 15, 581.

skilful propaganda. The reason for the Reich's relatively great success until 1938 was that the increase in the national wage bill after 1932 occurred at the same time as prices were restrained by state action, and that after 1934 the quality of goods available for purchase started to fall off. State loans, or more usually deposits in savings banks or commercial banks then channelled into state paper, were a way of dealing with the 'purchasing power overhang' that had been created in this way. Even this operation had to be kept very quiet. Price Commissar Goerdeler warned that the consequences would be severe if it were widely known that savings bank deposits were being channelled into the pockets of the Reich: 'if several citizens report that they are not able to obtain loans from the savings banks, savers will become suspicious and frightened. I cannot say to the saver who remembers the experience of the inflation and the 1931 banking crisis, "Save, the Reich needs your money", and hope to be successful.'[96] In this way the dictates of public morale and public confidence shaped the possibilities for the state's budget policy.

At least on the face then, this was a regime of fiscal conservatism, whose policy was spelt out by Schacht: 'while the Reichsbank will expand credit in aid of valuable private enterprise, it would not provide the Government with huge credits to introduce public works on the fallacious theory of providing employment'. Rather the Government would have to embark on an austerity course: 'the German Government must proceed with measures which inevitably will have the effect of reducing the standard of life still further by way of budget economies, which are now in hand, a reduction of social expenditure, and a general levelling at the expense of those that are better off'.[97] This conservative doctrine matched the conservative reality of the early years of Nazism. The periodical *Währung und Wirtschaft*, which was very close to Schacht, argued in 1933 that 'if public finance is to be managed in such a way that there is no threat to the currency, the Reich, Länder, and communes must use all their moral authority to

[96] IfZ Beck papers F40/2, 26 Oct. 1935 Report of Goerdeler.

[97] NA Treasury RG 39, 'Germany' Box 64, 21 Mar. 1933 report of Sackett. BoE OV34/82, 1 Apr. 1933 Siepmann conversation with Schacht.

resist the endless demands made at all times on public funds'.[98] Schwerin von Krosigk, the Reich Finance Minister who remained in office until 1945, also stated his belief in self-induced rather than state-directed economic recoveries: 'work creation is only a help for an economy that can recover by itself anyway'.[99] The National Socialist economic periodical *Die deutsche Volkswirtschaft* made a point of commenting on the ineffectiveness of the Reinhold work-creation programme of 1926 and its disastrous legacy for economic policy: 'Leading figures in the economy until recently still praised the policy of reducing taxes and providing subsidies carried out in the Reinhold era, although these policies led to the undermining of state finance. People then thought that it was necessary to prime the pump.' There were, of course, multiplier effects to be achieved through pump-priming; but the periodical argued that these had generally been exaggerated. 'There is still an overestimation both of what has already been done and of what will be done.'[1]

A total of 5.25b. RM was in fact spent on work-creation projects between 1932 and 1935: as part of these projects, government spending on construction and road building did increase appreciably during the first years of Nazi rule.[2] But levels of investment in housing and transport remained well below Weimar levels. Even roads, which were so important a part of the Nazi vision of the future, received less investment funds in 1934 than in 1927. It was only after 1935 that enormous sums were put into the Reichsautobahnen.[3] Those commentators who have been so impressed by the scale of Nazi public investment in these sectors have been victims of an optical illusion: communes, which had spent heavily on construction in the 1920s, were now forced to cut back their expenditure, while Reich money flowed into building. But the

[98] *Währung und Wirtschaft* 1933 no. 9, 153.

[99] BAK R43I/2045, 21 July 1932 Cabinet meeting.

[1] K. Müller, 'Die Maßstäbe der Arbeitsbeschaffung', *Die Deutsche Volkswirtschaft* 1933, no. 13, 405.

[2] L. Grebler, 'Work-Creation Policy in Germany 1932–5', *International Labour Review*, 35, 1937, 336. See also K. Schiller, *Arbeitsbeschaffung und Finanzordnung in Deutschland*, Berlin 1936, 63.

[3] *Statistisches Jahrbuch* 1938, 564–5. See also Erbe, 112–13.

amount of total government funding did not change very dramatically.

Where the Nazi state did spend much more than Weimar was on rearmament. This corresponded with the ideological and power-political claims of Nazism, though the preparations for a German rearmament were already well under way in the Brüning era. The presidential cabinets had fought tenaciously in the Geneva disarmament negotiations for an increase in the number and type of weapons permitted to Germany.[4] Under the provisions of the Treaty of Versailles only a seven-division army was allowed; but already in 1928 plans for an emergency army of sixteen divisions or more were drawn up. Between 1928 and 1933 camouflaged munitions works were built; 'economic officers' (*Wirtschaftsoffiziere*) toured hundreds of factories looking for potential plants to be used in economic mobilisation. They built up large card indexes of suitable firms. A total of 5,000 were listed in this way. After 1930 there were regular contacts between officers in the Reichswehr Ministry and the Economics Ministry; these were formalised in May 1931 when joint committees (*Arbeitsausschüße*) were established for particular munitions products. The economic crisis brought headaches for the war planners. Many factories with mobilisation potential were threatened by insolvency or bankruptcy.[5] In spring 1932 the Reichswehr Ministry drew up a lengthy list of endangered firms involved in the manufacture of armaments, and requested that they should be given state subsidies or tax concessions so that they might weather the economic storm. The army was particularly concerned that if, as seemed likely, Germany's exports to the USSR declined, there would be a further collapse in the strategically vital engineering trades. An easy way to deal with this threat was to integrate military spending into projects for work creation, projects that were becoming more fashionable politically. This was already happening in the case of the scheme drawn up in the last days of the Brüning administration: the plans for work

[4] E. W. Bennett, *German Rearmament and the West 1932–1933*, Princeton 1979.

[5] G. Thomas (ed. W. Birkenfeld), *Geschichte der deutschen Wehr- und Rüstungswirtschaft 1918–1943/4*, Boppard 1966, 57, 75. In general, E. W. Hansen, *Reichswehr und Industrie: Rüstungswirtschaftliche Zusammenarbeit und wirtschaftliche Mobilmachungsvorarbeiten 1923–1932*, Boppard 1978, 89–91, 111.

creation included help for the Dornier aircraft works. Papen took over these plans. Kurt Schleicher, under Brüning still head of the Ministeramt in the Reichswehr Ministry, evolved there even grander military work-creation projects. The Reichswehr Ministry's Heereswaffenamt, the predecessor of the military economic agency of the Third Reich, Wehrwirtschafts- und Waffenwesen, pushed too for state support for the Borsigwerke, an illiquid armaments-producing Berlin engineering firm.[6]

As a consequence of these preparations, and also of his concern with German expansion, Hitler took up the theme very soon after he had become Chancellor. He believed that a massive rearmament campaign would cure unemployment. On 8 February 1933 he told his Cabinet that 'the next five years must be dedicated to the rearmament of the German people. Every publicly supported work-creation scheme must be judged from this standpoint: is it necessary for the restoration of the military strength of the German people?'[7] On the other hand, the army made it clear that it was unable to define the projects for such a massive programme immediately, and already on 9 February Hitler had accepted the argument that the speed of rearmament could not be increased further.[8]

How successfully was the arms build-up integrated into the Nazi *Arbeitsschlacht*, the war for work? The combination of a National Socialist obsession with total mobilisation for war and disguising of military projects as work creation makes it difficult to present accurate figures for the extent of German rearmament.[9] Some Nazis wanted to see all expenditure as potentially war expenditure, since the whole of society would have to fight a future war. General Georg Thomas, the foremost military expert on the economics of rearmament, quotes with approval the view of Major General Beuther that

[6] BAF RH8 v 959, 17 Feb. 1932 WiL memorandum, 8 Mar. 1932 list of firms; and 23 May 1932 memorandum of Chef of Heereswaffenamt. RH8 v 935, memorandum of Apr. 1933: 'Verkauf der A. Borsig GmbH Tegel an Rheinmetall'. RH8 v 1004, 2 July 1932 memorandum (on Dornier).

[7] BAK R43I/1459, 8 Feb. 1933 ministerial meeting.

[8] BAK R43II/540, 9 Feb. 1933 meeting of Reich Government Committee on Work Creation.

[9] G. Spencely, 'R. J. Overy and the Motorisierung: a Comment', *EcHR* 32, 1979, 105–6.

under National Socialism all government expenditure in the end had a military goal: the 'war economy according to us embraced all branches of the economy in the coming total war'.[10] If there was to be a complete mobilisation of the German people and a 63-division army, the whole economy had to be prepared for conversion into a militarised command system supplying the needs of troops.

Even when Germany withdrew from the Geneva disarmament negotiations (14 October 1933) she still had to take care to conceal rearmament. At least until the remilitarisation of the Rhineland in March 1936 Germany was very vulnerable. A memorandum of 1933 noted that 'perfect disguise is necessary' regarding projected expenditure on road communications around a concealed armaments work at Fürstenberg/Brandenburg, which would also be a base for a push into Poland.[11] Other projects which were dressed up as work-creation projects during the early stages of German rearmament were gas experimentation and training sites (disguised as land reclamation or flood protection), the protection of armaments works against possible air attacks, and the extension of German aluminium production.[12] An estimated 600m. RM of the resources of the Gereke project (the 2b. RM plan worked out under the Schleicher regime) was eventually spent on works closely related to rearmament. In 1935 the Wehrwirtschaftsstab was substantially in control of all work-creation schemes.[13]

'Unreliable statistics, the problems of distinguishing between public posture and private intent, and definitional problems of rearmament'[14] mean that we cannot be sure exactly how in quantitative terms rearmament affected the German economy. But, perhaps surprisingly in the light of the statistical obstacles and questions, most of the academic controversy about the extent of rearmament has centred around the period after 1936, when there was little doubt that Germany was preparing for war; and for the years between 1933 and 1936—the years when Germany returned to full employment—there is little

[10] G. Thomas, 83.
[11] BAF RH8 v 1004, 26 May 1933 memorandum.
[12] Ibid. Also RH8 v 1004, 26 Apr. 1932 Thomas memorandum.
[13] Petzina 1968, 16. BAF RH8/941, 11 June 1935 memorandum.
[14] Spencely, 106.

Table XXXVIII: Armaments Expenditure in Germany 1933–1938 (b. RM)

	Schacht	Statistiches Handbuch	Schwerin Krosigk	Eichholtz[a]	Kuczynski
1933/4	—	1.9	0.746	1.5	3.5
1934/5	2.25	1.9	4.197	2.8	5.5
1935/6	5	4.0	5.487	5.5	10.5
1936/7	7	5.8	10.273	11.0	13.5
1937/8	9	8.2	10.961	14.1	16.5
1938/9	11	18.4	17.247	16.6	26.0

[a] Calendar year; 1933 only February–December.

disagreement about the figures offered for the cost of military expenditure, and little disagreement, too, that that expenditure was relatively small compared with later sums. Schacht's estimates (Table XXXVIII) are entirely fictitious and do not deserve serious consideration; the figures provided by the Länderrat after the Second World War and taken over by Burton Klein ignore Mefo-bill payments and are thus too low. Overy uses the material presented at Nuremberg by Schwerin von Krosigk; the East German historian Eichholtz gives slightly lower set of figures and adjusts these in 1937/8 for expenditure in that year which only appeared in the accounts of the following fiscal year. Another East German historian, Jürgen Kuczynski, taking a much broader definition of what constitutes armaments, had produced higher figures (see Table XXXVIII).[15]

The Schwerin von Krosigk–Overy figures represent a reliable *minimum* spent on rearmament. Until March 1936, then, at least 10.4b. RM was spent, or 5.2 per cent of GNP over the period 1933–5, or more than twice the amount spent on work creation. This money represents a major stimulus given to the economy. Its effect on specific sectors is also critical for an overall analysis of the economic consequences. Expenditure on

[15] International Military Tribunal, *Trial of the Major War Criminals XLI*, Nuremberg 1949, Document Schacht 7, 249. B. H. Klein, *Germany's Economic Preparations for War*, Cambridge Mass. 1959, 16. Schwerin von Krosigk figures from L. Zumpe, *Wirtschaft und Staat in Deutschland 1933 bis 1945*, Berlin 1980, 308. D. Eichholtz, *Geschichte der deutschen Kriegswirtschaft 1939–1945* I, Berlin 1969, 31. J. Kuczynski, *Die Geschichte der Lage der Arbeiter unter dem Kapitalismus* 16, Berlin 1963, 132.

armaments meant orders for engineering works. During the depression, exports to the Soviet Union had kept German engineering above water: this task now fell to rearmament.

By contrast, the very expensive road-building and construction programmes provided few orders for established engineering firms, and posed instead considerable labour problems. Workers on the new Autobahn sites were moved a long way from their homes, housed in primitive huts, and were often faced by very hostile environments. Their wages were lower than those of unskilled female textile workers. Such conditions often led to unrest. Near Aachen, where a dam was being constructed across the River Rur at Schwammenauel, the construction workers were paid only 53 Pfennig an hour, though they came from areas where 61 Pfennig or more was paid for unskilled labour. They complained because they were separated from their families and because they had to pay high charges for accommodation. In Königsberg, the illegal KPD was very active among the emergency workers. In March 1935 the Kiel Gestapo complained that on those sites where 'large numbers of workers are gathered, individual agitators made the NSDAP and its organisations appear ridiculous'.[16] Labour difficulties had already been used in the Brüning period as an argument against work creation: a massive public construction programme on low wages was thought impossible under Weimar conditions,[17] and a more authoritarian system was required to deal with the problems of public order that would be posed.

Armaments manufacture on high wages in clean factories near major population centres raised none of these difficulties (neither did automobile construction: but this was on a relatively trivial scale compared to that of the military economy). Exactly this location of the armament industry imposed limits on economic mobilisation until 1936. Most armaments orders went to old, big firms. In part this was a legacy of the Versailles system which restricted production of certain weapon types to a very small number of firms, so that Allied supervision would

[16] BAK R58/660, 6 Oct. 1934 Aachen Police report to Gestapa; R58/1570 Königsberg report for Feb. 1935; R58/1128, 5 Mar. 1934 Kiel report. See also on Bavaria Kershaw, 81–3.

[17] For example, BAK R43I/2045, Apr. 1932 Goerdeler memorandum.

be easier. Only thirteen firms were allowed to make weapons and munitions. Thus infantry weapons in the later 1920s were made exclusively by Simson-Suhl, and artillery and mine-throwers only by Rheinmetall, BMW Eisenach,and Fried. Krupp. In the late 1920s 'black' factories were created, such as E. Loeffelland (Donauwörth), Schichau (Elbing), and the Metallwarenfabrik Treuenbrietzen, but even after 1933 the main supplies were still the Versailles monopoly factories. Army procurement officers continued to be selective and exclusive. In March 1937 General Thomas complained that although the Wehrmacht's mobilisation plans provided for the use of small factories, and calculations about the interest of the Mittelstand in the National Socialist state added ideological weight to such a strategy, in practice the need to rearm quickly and efficiently had meant that only big enterprise was used to working to military specifications.[18] Discussions that took place in 1935/6 about the relationship between the peacetime and the military economy reveal quite how little rearmament had until then changed Germany's economic structure, and quite how narrow was the base of the military economy.

The army's experts had often warned that if rearmament went ahead too fast and involved too many firms there would be a danger of economic crisis once rearming came to an end. New munitions producers would find their capacity idle before they had been able to write off their new plant. Better not to give such firms orders at all. By 1935, when universal conscription was introduced, there was a fierce debate about what would happen when rearmament stopped. The army leadership was keen to establish as large an army as possible quickly, in order to forestall foreign pressure for limitations on German military capacity; but such a policy contained economic dangers and conflicted with goals of a long, steady mobilisation.[19] Georg Thomas believed that military expenditure had been almost entirely responsible for economic recovery, not only in engineering but also in coal and steel. In February 1934 the coal mines had been still only producing at 30–40 per cent

[18] Hansen 33; BAF Wi/IF 51196, 15 Mar. 1937 Thomas memorandum 'Die wehrwirtschafliche Lage'.

[19] See M. Geyer, *Aufrüstung oder Sicherheit: Die Reichswehr in der Krise der Machtpolitik 1924–1936*, Wiesbaden 1980, 441–4.

capacity; one year later, thanks to the military stimulus, it was at 70–80 per cent.[20] Thomas thought that the only way to prevent major strain was to encourage German heavy industry to look to export markets again. This was a prerequisite for any further rearmament, for as the limits of existing capacity were reached, the vehemence with which the large firms—which until then had been the main beneficiaries of the armaments economy—stated their reluctance to build new plant increased. These firms disliked, too, attempts by some officials in the War Ministry to insist that for strategic reasons new capacity should be located not in the vulnerable old heavy industrial areas but that the whole armaments economy should be moved to Berlin, Hanover, and the Lower Elbe, and to the triangle between Magdeburg, Bitterfeld, and Merseburg, which was to be built up as Germany's new industrial heartland. These disputes brought about a crisis in civil-military relations in 1935. On 18 October the Minister of War, Werner von Blomberg, suddenly abolished all existing budgetary limitations and restrictions on military expenditure. There was an immediate outcry, since it appeared to mean the end of economic rationality in military planning.

A military memorandum of November, submitted to General Keitel, to War Minister Blomberg, and to Luftwaffe Minister Hermann Göring spoke of industrial fears of inflation and worries that Schacht would be sacked and replaced by Popitz, who was believed to be a more pliant figure.[21] Industry was demanding a reduction of government expenditure on rearmament, re-employment, and Autobahn construction; and it feared that the regime was not prepared to authorise such a reduction and that instead it wanted to let the money supply expand. Schacht sharpened the crisis by a speech in the same month to officers of the Wehrmachtsakademie. In this he attacked 'exaggerated' demands for the relocation of the German industrial economy, and argued that Germany could never have autarky. Instead he said that the only way of continuing the armaments economy was to find export markets for German weapons in south-east Europe and South Amer-

[20] BAF Wi/IF 5383, 18 Feb. 1935 Thomas memorandum 'Rüstung und Wirtschaft'.

[21] BAF Wi/IF 51196, 25 Nov. 1935 memorandum. M. Geyer 446.

ica.[22] Here Schacht was echoing the arguments of Thomas who had also seen in the export economy the only hope of carrying on rearmament once full employment had been reached.

The way the polemic was mounted in 1935 put trade policy at the centre of the dispute about what course the German economy should follow in the future. Here all the problems of Nazi policy came together: rearmament demanded large quantities of raw material imports (oil, metal ores, rubber); consumers and farmers were demanding higher imports too. To pay for these imports, higher exports were needed; yet Germany found it more and more difficult to subsidise her exports sufficiently to make them competitive. What options were there?

NAZI TRADE POLICY

The disputes about economic policy between 1933 and 1936 took the form of arguments over trade policy. Before the seizure of power, Hitler had avoided an explicit pronouncement as to whether he would liberalise trade or impose autarky. When he spoke to the leading Ruhr industrialists in 1932, all he promised was a trade policy which would embody 'the political will of the whole nation', but he did not say what that will was.[23] It was inevitable that in time, if the German economy recovered, there would be a trade problem. Imports would increase: German industry was heavily dependent on imported raw materials, and consumers too would want to buy more foreign goods. The increased imports could be paid for either by also increasing exports (difficult in the hostile environment of the world economic crisis) or by borrowing (even harder, given the experience of 1931). The only other course would be to restrict non-essential imports.

In effect a decision to take this line had been made, though not on trade political grounds, already in 1931. The massive movement of funds out of Germany provided an opportunity to use exchange control as a way of controlling imports. On 15 July, in the immediate aftermath of the banking crisis, the

[22] BAF RH8 v 957, 12 Nov. 1935 Schacht speech.

[23] Domarus 85–6, 26 Jan. 1932 Hitler speech to Düsseldorf Industrieklub.

Berlin exchange rate was made legally binding throughout the Reich (in order to prevent a recurrence of the events of 1923 when, during the Ruhr occupation, unofficial markets had quoted lower Mark rates than that established in Berlin). After July 1931, the Reichsbank kept the Mark stable only 'by Emergency Decree'.[24] A decree of 1 August required the registration of all foreign exchange over a certain—very small—sum, and imposed a tax on foreign travel. In a supplementary decree of 1 August exchange control was extended to cover foreign trade: lists of imports were drawn up in order to allow discrimination against unnecessary 'luxury' imports. Three categories were established:

1 Essential: unrestricted allocation of foreign currency;
2 Necessary 'to a certain extent': allocation of up to 10 000 RM;
3 Unnecessary: no allocation.[25]

Such a very simple scheme turned out in the end to be very complicated, for in order to avoid the imputation of discriminatory trade practices—which would provoke retaliation—Germany kept the lists secret from the importers, who were forced to play a guessing game with the new bureaucracy established to superintend *Devisenbewirtschaftung*, and who in consequence complained bitterly. The Stettin Chamber of Commerce, for instance, wondered aloud why Stettin merchants were no longer allowed to import salt herrings.[26] The semi-secret lists proved too confusing and the system was never really implemented. On 1 October 1931 currency was allocated instead on the basis of previous years' requirements. In November 75 per cent of the previous year's sum was allowed; by March 1932 this had been cut to 35 per cent, although the quota was then raised to 50 per cent from May and remained until February 1934 at this level. The purpose of this progressive reduction was to cut unnecessary imports and to oblige importers to use

[24] This was Schacht's accusation in his Harzburg speech on 11 Oct. 1931: text in BAK NL Silverberg 235; also in H. H. G. Schacht, *Nationale Kreditwirtschaft*, Berlin 1934, 5–11. See also H. H. G. Schacht, *Grundsätze deutscher Währungspolitik*, Oldenburg 1932, 41–2.

[25] BAK R11/1385, 'Geschichte der Devisenbewirtschaftung'.

[26] BAK R11/1384, 4 Aug. 1931 Industrie- und Handelskammer Stettin to Reich Economics Minister.

as far as possible the foreign credit lines open to them under the Standstill Agreements on foreign short-term credit.[27]

The system of the allocation of a fixed proportion pleased the North German trading centres, but many German producers wanted freer imports of raw materials and greater restrictions on the import of manufactured goods. This would mean in practice the revival of the list system. Steel producers, too, particularly after the sterling devaluation, felt threatened by imports: British steel was now sold on the German market at prices up to 20 RM/ton below German cartel rates, and German steel suppliers had to respond with discounts that bit further into their already endangered profitability.[28] Even the central industrialists' pressure group, which was extremely hostile to open protectionism, believed there was a case for clandestine protectionism. An RDI memorandum on currency control submitted to the Chancellor in March 1932 argued that while there was no doubt that a tariff war would hurt Germany, underhand methods of import restriction might well be used: 'the principle of not using currency policy in the service of trade policy had been exaggerated'.[29]

In the light of the shock many German export industries suffered after the pound left gold, it is surprising that so few Germans were prepared to consider the possibility of a devaluation of the Mark. Such a course was sometimes proposed by foreigners: Professor Sprague of Harvard, Economic Adviser to the Bank of England, told Brüning and Luther that a Mark devaluation would be the quickest way of bringing Germany back into the world economy.[30] In 1932 officials in the British Treasury believed that Germany would do well to consider joining a sterling bloc.[31] Keynes argued the case in a speech to the Überseeclub in Hamburg in January 1932 and in an interview with Brüning.[32] Brüning, however, replied that he would consider joining sterling only on certain conditions, most importantly that the pound should rise to a rate of 18 RM,

[27] *Berliner Börsen-Courier* 494, 22 Oct. 1931.

[28] Schindler, 253.

[29] BAK R11/1385, 11 Mar. 1932 RDI memorandum.

[30] Harrison papers Columbia, File 20, 20 July 1931 Sprague to Harrison.

[31] PA/AA WRep Friedensvertrag Allg. 20, 2, 15 Mar. 1932 Dreyse memorandum.

[32] *Hamburger Fremdenblatt*, 9 Jan. 1932: report of Keynes's lecture to the Überseeclub on 8 Jan.: 'Die Aussichten des Pfundes und der Goldstandard'.

which at the time appeared unlikely to be fulfilled.[33] One obstacle was the internationally binding treaty commitment to keep the Mark on gold, but there were other reasons why only a small handful of men were prepared in Germany to argue the case for devaluing. Even most of the so-called 'reformers' were worried by the idea of devaluation; the exceptions—Carl Krämer, Rudolph Dalberg, Albrecht Forstmann, and Felix Pinner—carried little weight, and some, like Krämer, soon abandoned their views.[34]

There were widespread fears that a devaluation would lead to an uncontrollable slide of the Mark. These may have been the consequence of the recent and painful memories of the inflation and hyperinflation,[35] although such fears about the consequences of devaluing were present in Britain too, where there had been no such inflation.[36] It was quite realistic to believe that German abandonment of the gold standard would destroy the only precariously restored financial stability of Germany. Even with no German devaluation, the fall of sterling had produced a nervous attack in Germany: the Berlin bourse, which had only reopened for business on 3 September, had to be closed again on 21 September and official dealings were only resumed on 12 April 1932.

Another motive was important in the calculations of many Germans. Business wanted a permanent readjustment of costs and in particular a permanent reduction of wages and taxes *before* Germany allowed herself to rejoin the world economy. This view was very clearly put by the German industrial representative on the Board of the BIS who wrote in July 1932

[33] PRO FO 370/15936, 23 Jan. 1932 Rumbold to Sir John Simon.

[34] *Der deutsche Oekonomist* 49, 11 Dec. 1931; also reprinted in (eds.) G. Bombach, H.-J. Ramser, M. Timmermann, W. Wittmann, *Der Keynesianismus II: Die beschäftigungspolitische Diskussion vor Keynes in Deutschland*, Berlin 1976, 143–51. See also W. Grotkopp, *Die große Krise: Lehren aus der Überwindung der Wirtschaftskrise 1929/32*, Düsseldorf 1954, 207–14.

[35] A general survey of the difficulties and of the advantages of a devaluation is K. Borchardt, 'Zur Frage der währungspolitischen Optionen Deutschlands in der Weltwirtschaftskrise', in (eds.) K. Borchardt and F. Holzheu, *Theorie und Politik der internationalen Wirtschaftsbeziehungen: Hans Möller zum 65. Geburtstag*, Stuttgart 1980, 165–82. Also J. Schiemann, *Die deutsche Währung in der Weltwirtschaftskrise: Währungspolitik und Abwertungskontroverse unter den Bedingungen der Reparationen*, Bern 1980. Schiemann presents a more optimistic picture than Borchardt of Germany's possible gains from devaluing.

[36] D. Marquand, *Ramsay MacDonald*, London 1977, 669.

of the circumstances in which a German devaluation might be effected. Paul Reusch wrote to the Hamburg banker Max Warburg:

> As I have already told you in person, I agree with your view that at present currency experiments cannot be contemplated. But once the German public budgets are set in order, once the internal situation is clarified and stabilised, once England has stabilised her currency, and, above all once the reparations issue is settled, we should devalue as soon as possible to the same extent as sterling is devalued against gold. Only so will industry be capable of exporting again.[37]

In another letter Reusch wrote: 'As long as the public households are not brought into order, the prerequisites for a permanent recovery will not be present.'[38] The General Manager of the RDI argued in a similar vein that 'the answer is not for the world to make a little bit of inflation and thus raise prices: instead the solution can only be for a correct relationship to be established between prices for finished goods and prices for raw materials. That means reducing production costs for finished goods in all areas.'[39]

In the meantime, in order to compensate German exporters for the hardships they suffered as a consequence of the sterling devaluation, a rather complicated system of export subsidies was introduced. The scheme was developed in 1931 and 1932 and was justified by the mistaken belief that it was the nervousness and greed of foreign creditors that had been responsible for the world financial crisis, and therefore that the lenders should now be made to contribute a sacrifice for recovery.[40] The key element in the scheme was the low price of German bonds abroad: after the September 1930 elections, and especially after the bank crisis, German long-term loans fell to very low quotations. Thus while the effective yield on Swiss bonds in May 1932 was only 5.27 per cent, where there were high political or economic risks yields were grotesquely inflated: Austrian bonds yielded 19.86 per cent, Germans 26.12

[37] HA/GHH 400101251/Ob, 3 July 1932 Reusch to Max Warburg. Also 400101290/30a, 20 July and 16 Nov. 1932 letters of Reusch to Luther.

[38] HA/GHH 400101250/1, 8 Nov. 1932 Reusch to Reichsbank Director Hülse.

[39] HA/GHH 40101220/11c, 10 Oct. 1931 Kastl memorandum.

[40] H. H. G. Schacht, *Interest or Dividend? A Question Propounded to the World. 11 Dec. 1933 Address delivered before the German Chamber of Commerce in Switzerland, Basle District Group*, Berlin 1934, 25–6.

per cent, and Hungarians 42.1 per cent. The general average price for German bonds abroad in 1932 was 38.7 (the lowest value was in December 1931: 28.6).[41] German firms could clean up their balance sheets and reduce future expenditure by buying back these bonds at low quotations, but this operation required foreign currency. Permission was given by the Reich Government for proceeds from exports classed as 'additional' to be used in bond repurchases. Such exports were those that because of foreign competition would not have been made without the implied subsidy. How much did this subsidy amount to? By 1933 enough bonds had been repatriated to make a general subsidy of 6.5 per cent of the value of German exports possible: but because in practice permission was not given in the case of *all* exports, but only to exporters dealing with competitive and elastic markets, a higher rate of subsidy, between 9 per cent and 12 per cent, was in fact possible.[42] In this way Germany tried to make good the British advantage while at the same time staying nominally on the gold standard; though in practice the end of free exchange also meant the end of the working of a gold standard system as normally understood.

Frozen exchange and export subsidies were thus inherited and not conceived by the Third Reich. Bond repurchases were still being used to subsidise exports in the autumn of 1933. By this time, however, the quotation of German bonds abroad had risen: the average price in New York went up in late 1932, fell after the Nazi seizure of power, but then rose again to reach 56.99 in January 1934.[43] The rise made the repurchase scheme less attractive. In consequence an alternative plan was launched by the Reich Economics Ministry, involving 'scrips', the part payments of interest and amortisation on long-term debt frozen in German Marks after June 1933. A foreign importer could pay for certain exports in scrips purchased from foreign creditors at a discount. This reduced the cost in foreign currency of the German export, without requiring the use of

[41] Wagemann 1935, 121–4. *Wochenbericht des Instituts für Konjunkturforschung* 5/43, 25 Jan. 1933.

[42] Bond repurchases calculated from BAK R2/13652, 31 May and 7 June 1932 meetings of Committee on Foreign Debts; and ZStA Reichsbank 6778, 30 May 1933 Creditors' Committee meeting in Reichsbank.

[43] Wagemann 1935, 121.

foreign exchange on the part of the German exporter (as the bond repurchase scheme had done).[44]

There were however problems in scrips too: the market failed to develop as the Germans had hoped and expected. In November 1933 there was a shortage of scrips because foreigners were reluctant to sell scrips at a discount to foreign importers and preferred to keep their blocked Mark account in the expectation that things might change in Germany.[45] So subsidies had to be restricted by the imposition of ceilings for specified commodities and specified countries. Thus those countries which had remained—like France and Belgium—on the old gold standard and had not followed sterling or the dollar were excluded from the scheme's operation. On the other hand exports from those industries which were either vital to the new strategy of economic development or which represented important traditional small producer export trades were particularly favoured. While there was a general maximum of 10 per cent on scrip subsidisation, 12 per cent was allowed for iron goods and automobiles, and 15 per cent on aluminium foil, cellulose, dyestuffs and printing paper (industries where it was strategically vital to encourage a greater degree of domestic production), and toys (a traditional German export business).[46] In this way exchange control and export subsidies could be refined until they represented a tool for guiding the future development of the German economy.

There was another use of control of export subsidies: a withholding of permission to sell exports against scrips could be used as a penalty device. Infringement of the by now very complex regulations might bring exclusion from the Economics Ministry's scheme, but there was also another category of offence. If firms produced at costs which meant that German exports were *not* being sold at a loss, they were not eligible for the subsidy. On the other hand those firms which could demonstrate higher than average losses could claim rebates. Essentially this was a device intended to attract less efficient

[44] BAK R7/4727, 22 Sept. 1933 circular of Reichsstelle für Devisenbewirtschaftung.

[45] BAK R7/4727, 18 Nov. 1933 memorandum.

[46] BAK R7/4727, 18 Nov. 1933 secret decree Dev. I 52880/33 'Ausfuhrförderungsliste'.

and smaller firms into production for export markets, and to counteract the advantages that big producers naturally had. One result was that big firms started to dislike the operation of the additional exports scheme,[47] not surprisingly, since by August 1934 the following major German enterprises had been excluded from supplementary export subsidies: Carl Zeiss Jena, Hermann Kolb Maschinenfabrik Köln, IG Farben Industrie AG, Daimler Benz AG, and Humboldt-Deutz-motoren.[48]

Export subsidies did not prevent balance of trade problems from re-emerging. In 1934 and 1935 recoveries in the world and in the German economies placed a new strain on trade policy. German firms were less inclined to export as they found the domestic market becoming more attractive. The Economics Ministry's subsidies were not enough to create a strong interest in exporting among small businesses.[49] At the same time imports increased, as the effects on consumer spending of the reduction in unemployment became apparent.[50] Imports of raw materials also became more expensive as the world terms of trade began to turn against the manufacturing countries. Rising imports and difficulties in exporting exhausted the small remaining gold and foreign currency reserve of the Reichsbank. In December 1933 the reserve had still been 395m. RM. By June 1934 it had fallen below 100m. RM.[51] Further regulation of trade was urgently needed. The currency allocation quotas for importers established in 1931 were pushed back to 5 per cent. A currency decree banned the import of wool and animal hairs. This step was complemented by direct state action to restrict textile output and thus consumption of raw materials: in July 1934 hours of work were reduced for clothing and textile production, and the construction of new factories prohibited. Raw material imports as a whole were regulated by a new administrative apparatus, and in September the transition in trade policy was completed with

[47] BAK R7/3441, 15 Apr. 1937 M. Ilgner (IG Farben) to Schacht.

[48] BAK R7/4729, 8 July 1934 circular of Reichsstelle für Devisenbewirtschaftung.

[49] BAK R7/4657, 19 July 1935 circular of Economics Ministry.

[50] D. Doering, 'Deutsche Aussenwirtschaftspolitik 1933–35: Die Gleichschaltung der Aussenwirtschaft in der Frühphase des nationalsozialistischen Regimes', Berlin Ph.D. 1969, 64.

[51] Figures from ZStA Reichsbank 6778, 27 Mar. 1934 Reichsbank memorandum.

a 'New Plan' which set up twenty-five supervisory centres responsible for the allocation of foreign exchange for imports.[52]

In practice the New Plan led to a bilateralisation of trade. Exchange was allocated only to the extent that it was available in a particular foreign currency for all except the most urgent imports. As a result differing Mark rates began to develop for each currency. Trade with south-east Europe and South America expanded as Germany appeared more and more as a major customer, and as small and relatively powerless states built up substantial claims against Germany. These were areas of the world where Germany could afford to let an unfavourable trade balance develop. In some states—Yugoslavia and Roumania—the value of the blocked Mark accounts was allowed to depreciate, and thus incentives to buy more from Germany were created.[53] Yugoslav and Roumanian importers were not always free to dispose of their blocked accounts as they wanted: German firms were reluctant to sell goods in which there was a strong domestic market, and offered instead alternative products. The German exports of thousands of mouth organs to Yugoslavia is one of the most famous stories (though probably apocryphal) of the working of the exchange control economy.[54]

Where such specific advantages for German exporters did not exist, the old additional export subsidisation scheme continued to operate. From spring 1935 it was financed by a general levy on the whole of German industry. About 60 per cent of German exports received some kind of subsidy after this as compensation for the maintenance of the Mark at the old parity against stable currencies where no clearing agreements existed.[55] But complaints multiplied: the blocked accounts, scrips, and repurchased bonds required immense bureaucracies—not only on the part of the state, but also on the part of

[52] On the New Plan, see Doering 246–62; and H. S. Ellis, *Exchange Control in Central Europe*, Cambridge Mass. 1941, 211–33.

[53] See L. Neal, 'The Economics and Finance of Bilateral Clearing Agreements: Germany 1934–8' *EcHR* 32, 1979, 391–404.

[54] E. N. Peterson, *Hjalmar Schacht, For and Against Hitler: A Political-Economic Study of Germany 1923–1945*, Boston 1954, 236.

[55] BAK R26 IV/36, 15 May 1936 Reichsbank Director Brinkmann in meeting of Experts Committee on Exports.

exporters. In 1936 Göring complained when he was trying to replace export subsidies by a more rational form of control that a textile firm with a monthly turnover of 60 000 RM had to fill in 15 000 forms requiring 10 900 signatures (or one form for every 4 RM exported).[56] Despite the occasional and irritating penal measures, the bureaucratism tended to work in favour of bigger firms with administrations better used to filling in forms and dealing with the state. Thus the defenders of the old system were the big steel men who in 1936 rejected the alternative of a completely state-controlled export economy in which orders would be directed to smaller enterprise. The workings of additional export subsidisation had already provided a taste of the way in which state schemes tried to work against big business.[57]

Why was devaluation not contemplated in 1934, nor again in a new crisis over foreign trade and imports in 1936? Partly there was still the old obsession about inflation: in February 1934, as the foreign exchange shortage began to develop, Schacht made the theme of his speech to a Congress of German bankers the need to avoid at all costs a new expropriation of workers' savings.[58] In October 1933 a British banker visiting Germany noted that although the 'obvious' course for Germany to take was to devalue the Mark, 'in all my interviews I found only one man who advocated this course, and his view was grounded upon his position as export manager [of the Vereinigte Stahlwerke]. Over and over again the conviction was reiterated that the internal risks were too great.'[59] These internal risks were even greater in 1936: only a 50 per cent or even 70 per cent devaluation would have brought Germany back into the world of free exchange. The consequences of such a devaluation on German prices and wages would have been appalling, however: the demons of the First War and the inflation haunted Germans, as they haunted Hitler. In Düsseldorf in early 1935 the Gestapo reported rumours of a new inflation: Schacht's speeches were being interpreted as an

[56] BAK R26 IV/36, 30 June 1936 meeting of Experts Committee on Exports.
[57] Ibid. Statements of Vögler, Lange, and Klöckner.
[58] *Die Deutsche Volkswirtschaft* 1934, no. 18, 547. Doering, 220.
[59] Midland Bank archives, 30/207, 13 Oct. 1933 W. F. Crick, 'Report on Visit to Germany'.

acknowledgement that the German currency 'was without real backing, only a fiction'.[60]

The discussions of 1934 and 1936 revealed how devaluation was considered less in terms of its effects on the balance of trade than as a device to stimulate the economy by increasing prices and thus cutting the real value of debt. Schacht's adviser, Rudolf Brinkmann, argued that the British sterling devaluation had not produced major benefits for British exports; and that the monetary policy which had been implemented after the devaluation was restrictive.[61] Grotkopp argued that those who had wanted devaluation in 1931 and 1932 had never believed that it would really stimulate exports, but rather wanted a domestic monetary expansion. Devaluing just to set the balance of trade right he described as the harmful practice of 'Valuta-dumping'.[62] This sort of devaluation was unnecessary in 1934 because a German monetary expansion could take place behind the sheltering wall of exchange control.

Bilateral trading, on the other hand, offered all the advantages of an effective devaluation against those countries' currencies whose exports Germany was particularly interested in buying. It presented a solution which gave priority to the kinds of import Germany's planners thought desirable. By 1939 German academic economists agreed that exchange control was a stable and long-term policy instrument for general economic planning.[63] And the complicated regulations affecting currency, exports and debt repayment also gave Germany a useful level to pull on in international diplomacy. Already in the 1920s under Stresemann, Germany had used her economy as a weapon in foreign policy; and in the 1930s this tradition of instrumentalising economic affairs in the service of diplomacy was continued.

[60] H. Brüning (ed. C. Nix), *Briefe und Gespräche 1934–1945*, Stuttgart 1974, 105, 119–20. BAK R58/1127, 5 Mar. 1935 Düsseldorf Gestapo report.

[61] R. Brinkmann, 'Kampf im Welthandel' (1936) in *Wirtschaftspolitik aus nationalsozialistischem Kraftquell: Eine Sammlung ausgewählter Vorträge, Reden und Ansprachen*, Jena 1939, 50–1. Brinkmann worked in the Economics Ministry until 1937, and then became a Director of the Reichsbank.

[62] W. Grotkopp, 'Devalvation', *Die Deutsche Volkswirtschaft* 1934, no. 7, 210–13.

[63] F. Meyer, 'Devisenbewirtschaftung als neue Währungsform', *Weltwirtschaftliches Archiv* 49, 1939, 415–72.

GERMANY'S DEBTS

Like the story of covert export subsidisation linked with covert import control, the story of the instrumentalisation of Germany's high foreign debt begins with the credit crisis of 1931. Weimar's great Foreign Minister, Gustav Stresemann had been aware in the 1920s that the high level of foreign lending might one day give Germany an argument against reparations.[64] In the summer of 1931 that day arrived. Large amounts of foreign money were locked up in Germany by exchange control or by voluntary agreement.[65] These sums could only be gradually recovered even in the best circumstances, and—if Germany had to go on paying reparations—might well never be recovered.

In the course of the early months of 1932 Germany set out to isolate France by playing on British and American feelings of insecurity regarding their German debt. At the beginning of 1932 two major obstacles still existed to the settlement of the reparation issue, and meant that Germany felt it better to agree to the postponement of the reparations conference in Lausanne originally scheduled for January. In the first place, France and Belgium still demanded a surplus beyond the amount they were required to repay to their wartime allies on inter-allied debt. In the second place, the USA did not appear to be sympathetic to the idea of cancelling or substantially reducing inter-allied debt payments;[66] but without help over this from America, Britain and France could scarcely afford to be generous over reparation. The USA indeed refused to attend the reparations conference at Lausanne as they were not direct recipients of reparation and as they maintained what Secretary of State Henry Stimson called the 'historic attitude' of denying a connection between war debts and reparations.[67] Despite these American statements, all the parties at Lausanne continually looked over their shoulder to see what Uncle Sam would do. As the settlement was reached, a 'Gentleman's

[64] Link, especially 397–400.

[65] On the standstill, see Wegerhoff 1982.

[66] For instance see the joint declaration by Herbert Hoover and Laval after Laval's visit to the USA in October 1931, *FRUS* 1931 II, 252–3.

[67] *FRUS* 1932 I, 637, 29 Dec. 1931 Stimson *aide-mémoire* for the French Ambassador in Washington.

Agreement' was appended: the treaty on reparation should not be ratified until the USA had revised the war-debt repayment schedule. Such a revision could not be expected until after the US presidential elections in November; in the meantime it was crucial that not even a slight American note of dissent about the Europeans' action should reach the conference. There was no such note, and American officials in fact privately advised Britain's Ambassador in Washington that Europe should go ahead and settle reparations and that the USA would then fall into line,[68] though later Stimson tried to deny that his men had ever expressed such opinions.[69]

Why did the USA display this admittedly slightly muted enthusiasm? There were powerful farming interests in the South and the Mid-West opposed to any relaxation of the tough position towards Europe that constituted 'the historic policy'. The Hearst press made an uproar about concessions to Germany.[70] However, Lausanne was the last major instance of the application of pressure from the New York financial community on a Republican adminstration. President Hoover himself was sceptical about the bankers' plans, particularly after the failure of his one-year debt moratorium to solve the world's problems, and he continued to press—even after the presidential elections—for debt repayment. The State Department was much more vulnerable, however: Morgan partner Thomas Lamont wrote to Stimson that it was certain that American public opinion would accept a statement from the President that the health of the economy required a major reduction of inter-allied debt.[71] Under this kind of pressure the State Department ignored Hoover's personal scepticism about German motives and intentions.

The views of America's unofficial policy makers were equally influential in European capitals. Lamont urged Ramsay MacDonald, the British premier and Chairman of the Lausanne Conference and a regular correspondent of his, to work together

[68] *DBFP* Ser. II, vol. 3, doc. 2, 28 Dec. 1931 Cable of Sir R. Lindsay (British Ambassador in Washington); doc. 105, 25 Apr. 1931 cable of Sir R. Lindsay.

[69] *FRUS* 1932 I, 673, 1 June 1932 Stimson to Mellon (Secretary of the Treasury).

[70] For example, Garet Garrett, *Other People's Money! The Great American Racket*, New York 1931; and Garet Garrett, *A Bubble that broke the World*, Boston 1932 (reprinted from the *Saturday Evening Post*).

[71] TWL 181–25, 23 May 1932 Lamont to Stimson.

with France in a radical reduction—though not a complete cancellation—of reparations.[72] In this way was created a climate that allowed the assumption of American generosity in the 'Gentleman's Agreement' to seem reasonable.

British policy was subjected much more directly to the same kind of pressure from financial interests, and in Britain there was no farming lobby opposed to reparations cancellation. At the beginning of 1932, the Treasury and the Bank of England, which were both soft towards Germany, believed that the most favourable solution that Lausanne could reach was an extension for five years of the Hoover moratorium, long enough to allow the world to recover from the slump.[73] Germany opposed this view, as Chancellor Brüning made it clear that he believed that even a long moratorium would be of little help and would only prolong the uncertainty under which the world economy was suffering.[74] The situation changed as Germany's gold and foreign currency reserves started to drop again in 1932: between the end of July 1931 and the beginning of the Lausanne meeting Germany lost over 40 per cent of her holdings. The worsening reserve position meant that a moratorium on all foreign payments became much more likely. British financial interests now pressed for a more radical solution: the cancellation of reparations with only a token final payment. The Treasury was bombarded with grim warnings of what would happen if Lausanne failed: 'there would. . .be some form of transfer moratorium on all debt repayment [both long- and short-term] during the summer, if possible in agreement with Germany's creditors'. The Dutch central banker Bruins had told the British financial adviser in Berlin that there was a strong possibility of a fully planned exchange economy with Schacht as 'economic dictator'.[75] The City wanted to avoid this. R. H. Brand of Lazard Bros. & Co., London, set out the majority view of the British financial community in a memorandum for the Foreign Office: 'If the foreign banking world see an additional liability [i.e. continued reparation

[72] TWL 181–24, 13 May 1932 Lamont to MacDonald.

[73] PRO Treasury T160/450 F 13050, 1 Jan. 1932 Leith-Ross memorandum.

[74] *DBFP* ser. II, vol. 3, doc. 10, 8 Jan. 1932 cable of Sir H. Rumbold.

[75] PRO Treasury T160/437 F 12630/02/3, 30 May 1932 Rowe-Dutton to Leith-Ross.

payments] placed on Germany, which there is no sign at present of her being able to meet, confidence in her stability will certainly not grow and the moment when exchange freedom can be given will be still further and indefinitely postponed.'[76]

At the conference itself, the German delegation knew that the best way to guarantee British and American sympathy was to cast doubt on the stability of the German economy.[77] These arguments, as well as the plea that if Germany were not treated sympathetically she would be radicalised politically, were quite traditional in the German reparations case, and had been presented many times during the 1920s. What was new was that the British now stated the case with equal force:

> They knew the state of Germany and Central Europe, and they must make it possible for the banks etc. to reinvest there. If there is still uncertainty regarding future payments, whether to be based on capacity or the attainment of certain indexes, the same conditions as in the past would prevail. There would be no firm foundation or any foothold for future business. There would be no confidence, no lending, no necessary investments; it would be impossible for European trade to recover.[78]

The British premier MacDonald put pressure on France to modify the old French opposition to reparation cancellations. He imposed a deliberately tight timetable: MacDonald had to return to London before 13 July 1932, when the British delegation was due to sail to the Imperial Conference at Ottawa. Thus if France remained inflexible, Britain threatened to allow the Lausanne conference to collapse, and France could not afford to let this happen as the breakdown would be held to be a consequence of French, not German, actions. MacDonald kept to this line throughout the conference, although he was disgusted when he actually saw the German delegation, and particularly when he encountered Chancellor von Papen ('fussy, emotional, unintelligent, confused'). He always stressed that he wanted a settlement based on economic

[76] PRO FO 371/15936, 31 Mar. 1932 R. H. Brand memorandum on trip to Germany.

[77] *DBFP* ser. II, vol. 3, doc. 138, 198, 17 June 1932 Papen declaration.

[78] *DBFP* ser. II, vol. 3, doc. 140, 226, 20 June 1932 Great Britain and France conversation, statement of W. Runciman (President of Board of Trade).

rationality. 'Very much struck by the fact that in reality both Germans and French think only of themselves in all this and of politics more than economics and trade which are the deepest rock foundations of politics.'[79]

Germany still needed to bully or lure France into an acceptance of the 'reasonable' scheme worked out by MacDonald which reflected what the London City perceived as its interests. Papen offered France a carrot as well as a stick: again the carrot depended on the political manipulation of Germany's debts. French creditors were willing to agree to write off part of their German loans if they might receive preferential and speedy repayment through increased German exports to France.[80] This scheme was a revised version of the older idea that Germany should make payments in kind to France: such a notion had been an integral part of every reparations plan between 1919 and 1929. Alternatively, Papen bluffed, if Germany should not be well treated at the conference, she would devalue the Mark and join an anti-French sterling bloc.[81]

This combination of strategies—one directed at the Anglo-Saxons, one at France—produced a success for Germany at Lausanne. A final payment of 3b. RM in 5 per cent bonds was to be deposited with the BIS in Basel. These bonds would be presented to Germany for issue once, and if, the Young Loan rose above 90 per cent of its nominal price. Thus reparations were in effect at an end: Germany could, if she manufactured constant political uncertainty, see to it that the price of the Young Loan on foreign markets remained low. If the Lausanne bonds were not issued they were to be destroyed fifteen years after the ratification of Lausanne, and though the settlement was never in fact ratified because the USA refused to give debt relief on inter-allied debt, the bonds were solemnly burnt in 1948.

French commentators in 1931 and 1932 often argued and warned that the Germans were following an 'artichoke policy', pulling one leaf after another off the security system that had

[79] Marquand, 720–1.

[80] Speech of Schwerin von Krosigk on 27 June 1932: text in ZStA RWiM 15059. Also *FRUS* 1932 I 678–9, 23 June 1932 Cochran cable.

[81] ZStA RWiM 15059, 28 June 1932 meeting of Bülow and Laboulaye, and 24 June 1932 Bülow cable.

been created at Versailles.[82] The next step, after reparations were ended, would be to free Germany of the burden of commercial debt repayment which remained after the 6b. RM short-term credits were frozen under the Standstill Agreements (first in September 1931 for six months; then for a year in the German Credit Agreement of 1932, which was subsequently renewed annually). The British and American creditors in fact pulled the first new leaf off themselves: when in September 1931 the pound, and then—more importantly for Germany—the dollar, left the gold standard, in April 1933, German debts expressed in gold Marks were automatically reduced. Between February and September 1933 Germany's external debt was reduced from 19.0b. RM to 14.8b. RM. 3.2m. of this reduction was a consequence of the currency movement.[83] The value of credits maintained under the standstill, and of long term loans, had fallen by over a quarter.

Schacht was resolved to take advantage of the international financial anarchy that followed the completely unexpected dollar decision, and the subsequent failure of the London World Economic Conference to develop proposals for international financial and economic co-operation. He was eating more of the artichoke. His first step in the Reichsbank had been to free Germany from foreign ties by paying back *en bloc* the emergency Central Bank credit originally given to Germany in the crisis of June 1931. In May 1933 he invited international bank representatives to Berlin in order to intimidate them into accepting a new settlement on the servicing of long-term debt. What form this settlement would take was until 9 June unclear, although the bankers were sure that it would hurt them. The 'Law on Payments Due Abroad' provided that from 1 July interest and amortisation on all non-standstill debts, but not including the Dawes or interest on the Young Loans, would be paid through a 'Konversionskasse'. Fifty per cent of the debt service should be transferred if the service did not amount to more than 4 per cent of the principal. The rest would be paid in 'scrip' in RM; the Reichsbank agreed to buy this scrip for foreign exchange at a discount of 50 per cent.[84] Thus the

[82] IfZ ED93/20, 19 April 1932 diary entry: statement of Masson (Crédit Lyonnais).

[83] *Wirtschaft und Statistik* 1934 (Mar.), 134–5.

[84] *RGBl* 1933 I 349 (9 June 1933).

Table XXXIX: Germany's External Debt 1931–1939 (b. RM)

	July 1931	Nov. 1931	Feb. 1932	Sept. 1932	Feb. 1933	Sept. 1933	Feb. 1934	Feb. 1935	Feb. 1936	Feb. 1937	Feb. 1938
Standstill credits	6.3	5.4	5.0	4.3	4.1	3.0	2.6	2.1	1.7	1.2	1.0
Other short-term credits	6.8	5.2	5.1	5.0	4.6	4.4	4.1	4.6	4.6	4.2	4.0
Long-term credits	10.7	10.7	10.5	10.2	10.3	7.4	7.2	6.4	6.1	5.4	4.9
Total	23.8	21.3	20.6	19.5	19.0	14.8	13.9	13.1	12.4	10.8	9.9

Source: Statistisches Jahrbuch 1939/1940, 582.

German service on long-term debt was in practice reduced to 77 per cent of the level of June 1933, though German firms continued to pay the same amounts of RM. At the end of 1933 the quota paid in foreign currency was cut to 30 per cent, but in January the Reichsbank announced that it would now buy scrip at 67 per cent of the nominal value. The intended effect was to encourage foreigners to sell scrip: if they did they would receive 77 per cent of the service charge, but all converted into foreign exchange. In 1934 the Dawes and Young Loans were also blocked.

The 1933 partial blocking of transfers of debt service also opened the way to special agreements. In December 1933 at the same time as the foreign currency quota was reduced, Germany allowed a complete payment on frozen Dutch and Swiss assets in return for additional German exports. On 4 July 1934 Germany reached a special agreement with Britain.[85] On the other hand, the USA—which did not take substantial amounts of German exports—could not come to similar terms with Germany. US representatives at the German Creditors' Congress in January 1934 tried to explain that the USA bought natural rubber from Dutch Indonesia and that the Netherlands were a major purchaser of German goods, but the appeal to triangular trade principles did not work. With characteristic effrontery the Germans replied that it was Roosevelt who had been responsible for pushing the world back into bilateralism.[86]

There were other reasons besides the American failure to buy German goods why the USA was treated so badly after 1933. The special agreements of 1933 and 1934 were carefully tailored to suit the sort of political and economic power structure that Germany believed she was dealing with. Thus Britain was handled very differently from the USA because it was thought that Britain was run by financiers and America was not. The appeal to Germany of 'economic appeasement' was that it offered a strategy for dividing her foreign political

[85] C. R. S. Harris, *Germany's Foreign Indebtedness*, London 1935, 66–71. B.-J. Wendt, *Economic Appeasement: Handel und Finanz in der britischen Deutschland-Politik 1933–1939*, Düsseldorf 1971, 187–216.

[86] ZStA Reichsbank 6778, 25 Jan. 1934 International Creditors' Meeting. *The Economist*, 3 Feb. 1934.

opponents. While political issues—concern about the pace of German rearmament, about the nature of German goals in south-east Europe, or about the treatment of German Jews—might pull the Western powers together, and create alliances such as the 'Stresa Front' (of Britain, France, and Italy: April–May 1935), economic themes had the reverse effect. Foreign Minister von Neurath explained in November 1933 how economic measures might be used 'in order to avoid under all circumstances warlike complications, which at the present time we cannot cope with . . . By means of a statement that the objectives of our policy are exclusively economic and financial we can succeed in breaking up the front that has now been formed against us because of concern about the possibility of surprise actions on the part of Germany.'[87] Neurath rather than Schacht was indeed the real instigator of the course of special agreements with the Swiss, the Dutch, and the British, and Schacht actually complained that these agreements were wrecking his economic policy.

Nevertheless, Schacht emphasised again and again the great political influence in Britain of the City and his own determination to play his contacts there to the advantage of German policy. Schacht's son-in-law, Hilger von Scherpenberg, worked in the German Embassy in London, and Scherpenberg's son was Montagu Norman's godchild. Norman and Schacht met regularly at Basel at the BIS meetings, and Norman made no attempt to conceal his 'unbounded admiration' for the German central banker.[88] Thus the political crisis which followed such events as the December 1933 reduction of cash transfers of interest and amortisation could, Schacht argued, be handled by his friends.

The British Embassy in Berlin, and the Board of Trade, in December supported the idea of retaliation against Germany by means of a compulsory clearing agreement which would bilateralise trade and reduce German exports to Britain and the Empire. Since every import and export would have to be balanced, Germany could in this case no longer run a trade

[87] Quoted in G. Schmidt, *England in der Krise: Grundzüge und Grundlagen der britischen Appeasement-Politik 1930–1937*, Opladen 1981, 223.

[88] A. Boyle, *Montagu Norman: A Biography*, London 1967, 281. Also Brüning 1974, 33.

surplus with Britain. The City and the Bank of England were in consequence opposed to compulsory clearing because it meant endangering the British standstill debts, which could only be paid out of an export surplus.[89] Thus the pre-eminent position of the City in the financing of German trade was at risk. Schacht and Germany were prepared to recognise this concern of London bankers, and the required standstill repayments were made regularly and without fuss until the outbreak of war. The standstill credits were an important weapon for German diplomacy in dealing with Britain. Whereas Germany ran down her standstill debts with France, Switzerland, and the USA after 1933, she maintained her credits from Britain at a high level. Thus while in October 1931 28 per cent of the standstill credits were British, in September 1937 the figure was 52 per cent and in February 1939 56 per cent. One explanation is that British acceptance credit was vital for the financing of German trade, but the Berlin Government also tried to encourage Germans to maintain high acceptance lines. The relatively large volume could be used to exert pressure on the City and thus on Whitehall,[90] and only in the spring of 1939 did the Bank of England feel so worried by the volume of standstill credits that it tried to reduce the lines. £34m. was still outstanding at the outbreak of war, and the debts were only fully paid off in October 1961.[91]

The problem of how to deal with Britain arose again in the summer of 1934 when at Schacht's insistence Germany defaulted on the 1924 and 1930 reparations loans too.[92] A bill was this time brought into the House of Commons in June to introduce clearing, but it was dropped once Germany agreed to continue to service the British tranche of the Dawes and Young loans (4 July). The subsequent Commons debate confirmed the German view of the kind of power structure she was dealing with in Britain: Stafford Cripps for the Labour Party angrily denounced the proposed scheme for clearing as a victory for the British *rentier*, whom he believed the Conservative Government wished to protect 'regardless of what happens

[89] Wendt, 203–7.

[90] N. Forbes, 'British Standstill Credits to Germany', paper read to Monetary History Group, 16 Mar. 1984.

[91] R. S. Sayers, *The Bank of England 1891–1944* II, Cambridge 1976, 508–11.

[92] BAK R43II/783, 7 June 1934 meeting.

to the interests of the manufacturers or producers'.[93] Whereas the City short-term loans were dealt with quickly, during 1934 and 1935 Lancashire yarn and textile manufacturers encountered great difficulty in recovering outstanding German debts and found that the British Government was not willing to help them.[94]

In the summer of 1934 Schacht was actually so confident of his influence over Norman that he did not believe that the concessions of 4 July over the reparations loans had been necessary, and was furious with Neurath for having introduced them. He explicitly stated that none of the international central bankers in Basel had expected the German concession, which had only demonstrated how National Socialist Germany could be bullied by parliaments: 'One only needs to deal firmly with Germany, then everything can be achieved. Softness and reconciliation are out of place. Germany only responds to pressure. Nothing has changed since the old régime.'[95]

After the New Plan there was some revival of Anglo-German trade, and some British exporters benefited from this: coal and herring exports did particularly well. But this expansion of trade was only possible because of the generous help of the Bank of England in financing export deals. Already in January 1934 the Bank had been prepared to assist with the costly downwards conversion of outstanding German debt. In December 1934 it began the export credit operation with a sum of £750 000.[96] In other words, in the absence of a clearing agreement, the Bank of England acted like those central banks in south-east Europe which bought German claims and thus financed expanding trade with Germany.

In the case of Switzerland, Germany carried out a very similar exercise of tapering policy according to perceptions of social structure. German diplomats concluded that real power in the Alpine state lay in the hands of bankers and hotel-owners. In consequence, Germany gave priority to keeping the bank (standstill) creditors happy. At first the long-term bond creditors were also treated relatively well. The October 1933

93 *Hansard*: 292 HC Deb. 5s, 866 25 June 1934 Debate.

94 Wendt, 235.

95 BAK R43II/783, 10 July 1934 Schacht to Hitler.

96 BAK R43II/782a, 22 Jan. 1934 Schacht to State Secretary Lammers. C. R. S. Harris, 71; Sayers, 492; Wendt, 176, 342.

German-Swiss agreement allowed for a complete transfer of the value of Swiss scrips issued under the banker protection decrees in return for Swiss acceptance of a large German export surplus. Soon it was clear that this scheme was unworkable. Other states resented the favourable treatment of the Swiss. More importantly, there was less cash available as Germany's exports fell and her imports rose with recovery. In May 1934 a new agreement gave priority in the allocation of foreign exchange to German tourists who wanted to go to the Alps, rather than German debtors who wanted to service bonds. Payments to the 60–80 000 bond-holding creditors (usually small time investors) were cut back further and further on the principle that 'Work goes before capital'. They were fobbed off with ever wilder schemes. Bonds were serviced with new bonds ('funding bonds'). In 1936 these were available for specified uses within Germany (tourism, new investment), but they could also be used, at a heavy discount, not to buy Swiss francs but to obtain hotel coupons allowing Swiss bondholders to stay in Swiss holiday hotels. The bond creditors complained again and again of their impotence *vis-à-vis* the powerful and well-organised hoteliers' lobby.

It was the Swiss bankers who worked out and implemented these plans, and defused criticism by paying off the hoteliers. They were always frightened of losing the interest on their standstill debt, and also of the confiscation of the 800–900m. s.f. Swiss deposits in Germany. The Swiss banks had reinvested a large proportion of flight capital in Germany and this now made Switzerland very vulnerable to German blackmail.[97]

Whereas the financial interests of the City and of banks were crucial in Germany's dealings with Britain and Switzerland, another strategy was required for the USA. Here too the bankers, who held almost all the short-term loans to Germany, were keen to ignore the long-term creditors, the bondholders who had moved into the risky German market often on the advice of the Wall Street houses. In the spring of 1932 a prominent New York banker privately told the German Government that 'German credit would suffer much more if

[97] See E. Kellenberger, *Theorie und Praxis des Schweizerischen Geld-, Bank- und Börsenwesens seit Ausbruch des Weltkrieges. Heft 3. Kapitalexport und Zahlungsbilanz II. Im Konjunkturzyklus der dreißiger Jahre*, Bern 1942, 220–1, 230–1.

non-payment forced a large number of American banks into liquidation than if bond-holders were paid in Marks rather than in hard currency.'[98] But after 1932 Wall Street bankers did not have the political leverage of their City of London equivalents: even Hoover had been very suspicious of the influence in politics of the Wall Street bankers. Roosevelt, whose presidency began in March 1933, was downright hostile. He thought that New York was more to blame than Germany for the catastrophe of 1931. When Schacht was invited to the USA in May in order to discuss preparations for the London World Economic Conference, he told Roosevelt that he was preparing to block the service on dollar loans. Roosevelt laughed and said, 'Serves the Wall Street bankers right.' The day after this conversation with the President, Schacht sent a telegram to Berlin ordering an immediate suspension of transfers, but had to countermand the order when Secretary of State Cordell Hull called Schacht in to tell him how 'profoundly shocked' Americans were by Schacht's dishonest and dishonourable ideas.[99]

In fact the American line continued to be nearer to Roosevelt's first impulsive reaction rather than to Hull's morning-after reflections. Roosevelt continued to think that 'the bankers have gotten themselves into this'.[1] He appointed William Dodd as Ambassador to Berlin, a man who believed that New York financiers were swindlers; and he himself said that the American bankers had 'made exorbitant profits when in 1926 they loaned large sums to German corporations and cities and succeeded in selling bonds to thousands of citizens with interest at six and seven per cent'.[2] Dodd, who hated National Socialism, nevertheless believed that the Nazi economic programme was sensible ('very similar to the Recovery programme in the United States'),[3] and that American bankers were crazy.

Germans concluded naturally that no notice needed to be

[98] IfZ ED93/19, 22 Mar. 1932 diary entry: statement of Gannon (Chase Bank).

[99] Dodd, 19. Peterson, 209. S. Schuker, 'American "Reparations" to Germany 1919–1933', in (ed.) G. D. Feldman, *Die Nachwirkungen der Inflation auf die deutsche Geschichte 1924–1933*, Munich 1985, 335–83. G. Weinberg, 'Schachts Besuch in den USA im Jahre 1933', *VfZ* 11, 1963, 166–80.

[1] Dodd, 87. [2] Ibid., 19. [3] Ibid., 26.

taken of Wall Street. There was no hope of new capital imports: it was solely this possibility that had made it so important for Germany to cultivate good relations with the United States in the 1920s. On the other hand, despite the bonds story and Nazi Germany's anti-Semitism, trade relations remained good with the USA for two or three years after 1933. It was only the increasing German control of south-east European markets and even more the active German trade policy in South America, that finally pushed the Americans away from Germany. The beginnings of the change in American attitudes occurred in late 1934. The President's Special Adviser on Foreign Trade, George Peek, devised a programme for selling more agricultural goods abroad. There was to be a bilateral exchange of US cotton and German wine and beer. Schacht encouraged the scheme since it helped to tackle the German shortage of textile fibres, and allowed Bremen import houses to form a Cotton Exchange Company. A quota of cotton would be bought at a premium of 25 per cent over the American domestic prices; but only a quarter of this sum would be paid in dollars. With the rest, American importers would be able to buy German goods at an effective discount.[4] Here was a solution of a different case to that of German dealings with the UK: in the American case financial interests were to be sacrificed while the exporter was treated sympathetically.

On the other hand, the fact that the Schacht–Peek scheme eventually collapsed indicates the limits on German policy. The State Department had always been suspicious of Roosevelt's pet projects, distrustful of the abandonment of MFN trading, and sceptical about Schacht. Hull intervened in person to destroy the Peek project, and the State Department drew up a long list of complaints about German duplicity:

> We feel that with Germany discriminating against our creditors in the matter of bond payments, against our commerce by means of quotas, and in general showing an unfriendly point of view it is not the time to give them the comfort that . . . even a small indirect credit would prove to be. However, Peek and Mooney see nothing but a

[4] H. J. Schroeder, *Deutschland und die Vereinigten Staaten 1933–1939: Wirtschaft und Politik in der Entwicklung des deutsch-amerikanischen Gegensatzes*, Wiesbaden 1970, 152–7. Dodd, 93.

good Yankee horse trade and claim that the President is enthusiastic. Mooney, I think, has been thoroughly taken in by Schacht![5]

German policy was less successful in dealing with the USA than with Britain because of a constant uncertainty about who was making American policy. If Schacht had been right in thinking that New Deal foreign policy was just made by Rooseveltians who hated Wall Street, he might have been more successful. But the assumption was a wrong one, and the Germans, who thought in very crude terms (finance versus industry; exporters versus creditors), could not really grasp this. Economic policy was also not very effective a weapon in dealing with France, although Schacht occasionally tried to emphasise his personal desire for *rapprochement* and *détente* across the Rhine. This *détente* could never be an attractive or realistic proposition because of Nazi Germany's clearly revisionist aims in the West. On the other hand, the antagonism did not really matter that much, because of the international weakness of France in the 1930s: once the reparations issue had disappeared France no longer had the capacity to obstruct any international action which did not conform to her wishes and interests.

The successes of the German version of economic appeasement did not appear to be great. Schacht himself began to appreciate that the German policy of instrumentalising economic policy in the interests of diplomacy was not working as effectively as it had in the earlier 1930s. In 1936, when the requirements of industrial rearmament and the demands of the RNS for larger fodder imports produced a new exchange crisis, Schacht joined Price Commissar Karl Goerdeler and argued the case for a liberal solution, involving devaluation and a relaxation of trade and exchange regulation. By now, however, there was a fund of Mittelstand resentment against Schacht's supposedly pro-big-business management of economic control, and there was also a substantial bureaucratic vested interest in keeping the mechanisms of export and import regulation and exchange restriction going. Schacht lost his job as Economics Minister, at the same time as Neurath, the major proponent of

[5] Quoted H. J. Schroeder, 155–6.

the now failed course of making foreign policy by means of economic policy, also went.

INNOVATION AND CONSERVATISM IN RECOVERY

Between 1934 and 1936 economic circumstances demanded a range of political choices: over farm pricing, labour demands, the size of enterprise, and the kind of competition allowed, and over trade policy and foreign debts. Making these choices involved fierce personal and ideological debates within the ranks of the Nazi leadership. Before the decisions had been taken it is possible to detect a great degree of policy continuity with Weimar, and in that early phase there was little that was specifically Nazi about the German economy. There are economic as well as political reasons for this limitation on the room for Nazi decision-making at the beginning of the Third Reich.

The economic recovery which took place between 1932 and 1934 looked like a return to many aspects of the Weimar status quo. The revival of consumer spending was particularly impressive: textile production was above the 1928 level for several months (from February to July) in the first half of 1934, before the New Plan cut short the textiles boom. Leather shoe production in 1934 was 4 per cent above the 1928 level, chocolate production 35 per cent greater, cigarettes 10 per cent, and coffee 12 per cent. Motor car production was 36 per cent over 1928 levels, and more oil and petroleum products were sold.[6] Farmers, department stores, and Mittelstand producers all benefited from the consumer boom which derived partly from the ending of the price deflation and partly too from the increases in public employment. In 1934 Hitler might still be confident that Germans were becoming more prosperous.

Recovery in producer goods industries was slower and entrepreneurs here more pessimistic for longer. Machine tool production only rose above the 1928 level in the first half of 1935. Even those branches which historians have always claimed to be at the heart of the German recovery did not look particularly buoyant. Investment in transport, which in 1927

[6] Wagemann 1935, 49, 50, 281.

had represented 16.7 per cent of total German investment fell off sharply during the depression. In 1933 it rose again to 15.5 per cent (partly in consequence of the relatively ambitious work-creation projects of these years), and in 1934 fell again to 13.7 per cent. There was still less public money invested in transport in 1936 (2144m. RM) than there had been in 1928 (2 234m. RM).[7] Employment in the construction industry only returned to the level of the summer of 1929 in 1935. Investment in construction accounted for 21.9 per cent of investment in Germany in 1927 and 20.5 per cent in 1928; in 1934 on the other hand it was only 18.1 per cent. House and apartment construction were particularly sluggish: the 1929 level for new flats was only reached in 1935. This was despite extensive government subsidies for private construction: up to 50 per cent for new construction, and up to 20 per cent for house repairs (though these figures were no higher than the level of communal subsidisation of housing in the Weimar Republic).[8] On the other hand the level of employment in civil engineering construction projects (*Tiefbau*) had already been reached by the beginning of 1934.

The really startling increases in investment in National Socialist Germany were classed as investments in public administration: in 1928 this accounted for 19.3 per cent of German investment; in 1932, 25.9 per cent, and in 1934, 35.7 per cent.[9] These figures reflected the number of jobs in state and party bureaucracy created as part of 'Hitler's social revolution'.[10] Like the recovery of the 'golden years' of Weimar stabilisation in the late 1920s, the initial Nazi recovery involved an expansion of the public sector. (Though there were important differences: the size of the civil service did not grow very fast in the late Weimar years, but its pay did; National Socialism maintained civil service salaries at the low levels of the Brüning era.)

There were other similarities between the upswing of 1932–4 and that of 1926–8: increasing consumption, the preservation of a fairly static balance in the German industrial structure,

[7] Calculated from Erbe, 25–6, 112–13. Wagemann 1935, 61.
[8] Guillebaud, 41–2.
[9] Wagemann 1935, 61.
[10] D. Schoenbaum, *Hitler's Social Revolution: Class and Status in Nazi Germany 1933–1939*, New York 1966.

and the emergence of balance of trade problems. In the 1920s the balance of trade difficulties were solved by importing foreign capital, but in the 1930s this solution was not realistic even if Hitler and his party had been less unsympathetic to international finance. Some communal politicians in 1933 were still talking about selling municipal enterprise to the Americans, but they were hardly being realistic.[11]

What was unique about the National Socialist management of the economy was not the existence of recovery but rather the nature of the political reaction when that recovery began to show the usual signs of difficulty. The year 1934 represented a testing ground for policy and for ideas about the economy in a way that 1932 or 1933 had not done. It was then, for the first time, that a German government really had a substantial freedom of manoeuvre.

The consumer boom was controlled by import restrictions, rather than by a price mechanism. Price controls led to some scarcities, but at first principally to quality deterioration. Textiles had now very high synthetic elements, were less attractive, and less in demand. Blatant consumerism, Weimar-style, stopped in 1934. Even the automobile boom suffered a slight check in 1934, as part of the mini-crisis in the consumer boom: but fast rates of growth resumed again in 1935.[12] After 1934, the economic recovery of Germany was concentrated in investment goods industries: their development has always been rightly described as vital to the Third Reich's economy.[13]

A second major difference resulted from the limitation of wage demands. Here Brüning's December 1931 Emergency Decree provided a model by cutting through the very complicated conflicts over wage contracts which had marked 1930 and 1931. Wage rates barely moved after 1932: this was largely a consequence of the destruction of the bargaining mechanism of Weimar. As recovery took place after the crisis, wages fell as a proportion of National Income (see Table XL).

In consequence, there was a real transfer to firms of resources, which were not redistributed but rather were available for

[11] BAK R43II/238, 13 June 1933 Vosberg (Vereinigte Elektrizitätswerke Westfalen) to H. Lammers (State Secretary in Reich Chancellery).

[12] Wagemann 1935, 55.

[13] For instance, Guillebaud, 239; Overy 1982, 33–5.

Table XL: Wages as a Proportion of National Income 1927–1939 (%)

1927	55.0	1934	55.5
1928	56.6	1935	54.6
1929	56.7	1936	53.5
1930	56.7	1937	52.7
1931	58.1	1938	52.4
1932	57.0	1939	51.8
1933	56.0		

Sources: Wagemann 1935, 95; Petzina 1977, 122.

internal investment. Self-financing in industry was further encouraged by the restriction of dividend payments to 6 per cent (the Anleihestockgesetz, 4 December 1934).[14] Dividend restriction weakened the stock exchange as a source of new capital. There were few new issues by firms, and by and large the capital market after 1933 was reserved for public bonds.[15] The December 1934 Law was designed explicitly to prevent a speculative boom in corporate equities following the economic recovery.

Although interest rates fell from 1931 levels, and were driven down further by the ability of the Reichsbank from October 1933 openly to engage in open market operations in securities,[16] bank loans to industry were slow to respond to recovery, and only increased after 1936.[17] 1935–6 was a turning point on the capital market: after April 1935, when a major conversion was launched, interest rates for long-term loans were cut. In 1935 bonds of credit institutions with a coupon of 6 per cent or over were more or less forcibly converted down to 4.5 per cent (bondholders could refuse to agree to the conversion, but the old unconverted bonds would not be tradeable on the bourse and could not be used as security for Reichsbank loans). The operation was a success in that the price of the converted bonds barely changed, and it became possible for industrial bor-

[14] RGBl 1934 I 1222.

[15] See table in Lurié, 88.

[16] J. Soudek, 'Funktionswandel der Offen-Markt-Politik', *Die Wirtschaftskurve* 13, 1934, 383–90.

[17] F. Reinhart, 'Stand und Entwicklung der Aktienbanken im Dritten Reich', *Bank-Archiv* 35, 1936, 149–52. Monthly statements in *Die Bank*.

rowers to stage similar conversions, and also to borrow at cheaper rates. Unlike the forcible conversion of Brüning's December 1931 Emergency Decree, the measure did not weaken investment confidence.[18] From 1935–6 larger sums became available on the loan market because of 'forced saving': quality deteriorations and price control meant that private households saved more of their income. Most of these additional savings were in fact channelled through savings banks to the state, and not taken up by private borrowers on the capital market.[19] Thus the expansion of state spending after 1935 reflected a solution to the problem of what to do in an economy where price controls instituted in the name of an anti-inflationary policy produce large savings ratios.

There were some funds that were directed by the state into industrial investments: in early 1934 state guarantees were given for the development of synthetic textiles, petroleum products, chemicals, and for native iron ore resources,[20] and state investment funds became more important as part of the operation of the Four Year Plan after 1936.[21] But most industrial finance in the Third Reich was self-finance. Given the very conservative way in which the free capital market had operated in the 1920s, this may not have put more of a brake on change than had already been applied.

It did not, however, produce a technical revolution of the kind perhaps envisaged by Hitler when he dreamt of a fully automated society. The Weimar boom had run into trouble because of wage pressure and because of the political reactions to that pressure. Nazi policy after 1934/5 ran into a different set of problems. Price control and an effective limitation of wages produced a continual worsening of qualities in consumer goods. The deterioration of textile qualities was particularly evident to the public. If, we may speculate, there had been no war, Nazi policy would have produced a society with low wages and high savings ratios manufacturing ever cheaper and shoddier goods. These features of a low-wage economy would

[18] Guillebaud 76–9.

[19] *Der deutsche Volkswirt* 10, 1935/6, Sonderbeilage 'Die Wirtschaft im neuen Deutschland, Folge 13: Unkosten und Rentabilität im deutschen Bankgewerbe' (28 Feb. 1936), 28–30, F. Reinhart, 'Die privaten Banken als Kapitalversorger der Wirtschaft'; 43–5, E. Mosler, 'Investitionen, Emissionen und Börse'.

[20] BAK R43II/238, Jan. 1934 memorandum.

[21] Petzina 1968, 96–8.

have in the end endangered Germany's position on world export markets just as surely as the combination at the end of the 1920s of a gold standard fixed exchange rate regime with wage rises had done then. In these circumstances investment would have dried up eventually in the absence of ever higher levels of state spending. As a result of decisions taken in 1933 but principally later, between 1934 and 1936, Germany had locked herself into a situation where increasing government expenditure was not only politically desirable but also economically necessary.

This analysis of the Nazi economy and of the rather limited nature of the recovery (full employment as a consequence of falling wage costs, but little restructuration) suggests, as the study of the Weimar economy has done, that there was a structural crisis in the inter-war years. In part this followed from the shock to the economy of the 1914–18 war. But the crisis also represented an inheritance from that period of rapid economic growth which between 1850 and 1914 had turned Germany from an impoverished area with a per capita income half of Britain's into one of the world's most powerful economies. In the course of this process, the state's share of national income expanded. Agriculture began to clamour for protection. Banks, which had initially been a powerful motor of growth, became more conservative in vision. The powerful industrial structures—large corporations, trusts, and cartels—which had developed were also locked into more cautious, anti-entrepreneurial courses. Labour unions grew in strength. In short, Germany was beginning to develop the institutional ossification characteristic of an old economy. In Weimar, this low growth and ossification, acted as a constraint on government action, though the pattern of government action itself was also responsible for some of the ossification.

A recent and influential attempt to provide a theoretical explanation of the development over long periods of time of special interest groups, and interventionist responses, presents this conclusion: 'The economy that has a dense network of narrow special interest organisations will be susceptible during periods of deflation or disinflation to depression or stagflation', since 'involuntary unemployment can only be explained in terms of the interests and policies that rule out mutually advantageous bargaining between those who have their own labour or other goods to sell and those who will gain from buying what is offered'.[22]

Low growth in Weimar produced increasing distributional conflicts. These destroyed first the corporate interest groups, then also Weimar democracy. At first it looked as if the Nazi state could suppress these distributional conflicts. But they re-emerged as clashes *within* the Nazi party: in 1934, 1936, and again later, in 1943/4, economic tensions led to profound political upheavals. Fundamentally, the Nazis 'solved' only one economic problem: unemployment. We should be sceptical about other Nazi claims. Controlled prices, worsening qualities, and artificial foreign exchange rates mean that published figures on the rise of national income during the 1930s are misleadingly high (this is a notorious problem in measuring output changes in any controlled economy). In fact the Third Reich was incapable of dealing with the profound structural problems posed by industrial rigidification. Only the complete destruction, in and after 1945, not of physical capital (much of which survived the war) but of the institutions and social habits that had produced the low-growth society, made it possible for more rational combinations of labour and capital to produce faster development and, with this, a way out of distributional conflict.

Under the Nazi dictatorship, a highly interventionist state faced regular strain and political turmoil as the interventionist mechanism went wrong and as the expectations built around interventionist promises were disappointed. But the tragedy of this story of interventionism was that every breakdown produced yet more interventionism. No wonder that Schacht thought the whole world was crazy.

[22] M. Olson, *The Rise and Decline of Nations: Economic Growth, Stagflation, and Social Rigidities*, New Haven 1982, 216, 229.

BIBLIOGRAPHY

I. UNPUBLISHED SOURCES

GERMAN DEMOCRATIC REPUBLIC

Zentrales Staatsarchiv, Potsdam, Abteilung Sozialismus und Historische Abteilung I (ZStA)

21.01 *Reich Finance Ministry (RFM)*
B776, B777–80, B7710.

25.01 *Reichsbank: Volkswirtschaftliche und Statistische Abteilung*
6348, 6430, 6461, 6471, 6536, 6546, 6631, 6703, 6704, 6706, 6708, 6709, 6720, 6724, 6735, 6778, 6783, 7694.

31.01 *Reich Economics Ministry (RWiM)*
15059, 15160, 15345–6, 15477, 15538–40, 15544, 15586–8, 18542–3, 18564, 18566–7.

Provisional Reich Economic Council (RWiR)
616–18.

GERMAN FEDERAL REPUBLIC

Bundesarchiv Koblenz

R2 *Reich Finance Ministry*

Reich Debt 1929–32:
2150–1, 2153, 2450, 2455, 3192–3, 3208, 3277–8, 3328, 3360, 3377–9, 3783–8, 3883–4, 4088.

Länder and Communes:
2003, 2022–3, 4067–9, 4093–9, 19980–3, 20132–51, 20195–6.

Interest Rates:
2424, 2547, 13595–6, 13640–54, 13682–4, 14519–30, 14662–8.

Reparations:
2928, 2932–4, 3066, 3539, 3540.

Budget Policy in the Third Reich:
3269–70, 3845, 3847, 3884–5, 21779, 21781, 21782, 21903–8.

R7 *Reich Economics Ministry*
3441, 4571, 4627–8, 4657–8, 4727–30.

R11 *Deutscher Industrie- und Handelstag*
1371, 1378, 1383–5.

R13I *Verein Deutscher Eisen- und Stahlindustrieller*
253, 255–6, 277, 372, 601–2, 610–13.

R26I *Commissary for Four Year Plan*
11, 36.

R28 *Reichsbank*
25–58, 133.

R43I *Reich Chancellery*
633–43, 644–9, 651, 652–61, 663, 671–3, 1206, 1457, 1549, 2045–6, 2357–60, 2362–77, 2388–90, 2392, 2436–8, 2447.

R43II *Reich Chancellery*
237–9, 244, 529–37, 540–1, 781–6, 805–7.

R45II *Deutsche Volkspartei (DVP)*
40–7, 58–9, 60, 67.

R58 *Reichssicherheitshauptamt*
447, 561, 576, 599, 604, 656, 660, 1126–8, 1569–71, 1585.

R111 *Bankers Trust Company, Berlin Branch*
20–4, 211, 214, 218–19, 230, 240–1, 244–5.

NS 6 *NSDAP Party Archive*
101, 395, 652, 703.

NS 26 *NSDAP Main Archive*
1365, 2021, 2045–6, 2050–3, 2082.

Personal Papers in Bundesarchiv
Moritz Julius Bonn, 18, 29.
Hermann Dietrich, 223–4, 318.
Eduard Dingeldey, 35, 36, 39, 42, 44, 45, 57, 62, 70, 75, 83, 90, 93.
Rudolf ten Hompel, 1, 2, 11, 18, 21–3, 29, 32.
Alfred Hugenberg, 36, 38, 86, 87, 130.
Joseph Goebbels, 64, 65, 82.
Ludwig Kastl, 4–5, 6, 7–8, 9, 10–14, 15–27, 28–9, 34, 35.
Wilhelm Lautenbach, 31.
Hans Luther, 336–59, 364, 365–70, 425, 426.
Karl Passarge, 4–6.

Herman Pünder, 88, 91–2, 93, 99, 101, 104, 107, 120, 126, 128–30, 131–4, 137–45, 149, 151, 173.
Friedrich Saemisch, 149, 151, 173.
Hjalmar Schacht, 1–7.
Paul Silverberg, 228–33, 234, 248–50, 302–4, 308–9, 334–5, 416–17, 438–44, 639–46.
Rudolf Wissell, 8.

Bundesarchiv Militärarchiv Freiburg/Breisgau (BAF)

RHS v. 897
v. 919–20.
v. 935
v. 940–3
v. 957
v. 959
v. 1004
v. 1766
Wi/IF 5.326
5.346
5.383
5.1196
5.3322
Kurt von Schleicher Papers 20–6.

Politisches Archiv des Auswärtigen Amtes, Bonn (PA/AA)

(See catalogue: George A. Kent, *A Catalogue of Files and Microfilms of the German Foreign Ministry Archives 1920–45*, 4 vols, Stanford 1962–72.)

Büro of State Secretary Schubert:
Discussions with Parker Gilbert
Dillon Read Loan
German-Russian Trade Negotiations
MinDir. Trautmann Handakten (Personal Files):
Russian Credit
Sonderreferat Wirtschaft:
Finanzwesen 1 German Finances
Finanzwesen 2 Foreign Loans
Finanzwesen 16 Foreign Currency
Finanzwesen 20 Reichsbank
Wirtschaft Reparationen:
German Loans Abroad.
Peace Treaty: Friedensvertrag Allg. 20: BIS and Reichsbank.

Länder Group II Wirtschaft: France Trade with Germany.
Länder Group IV Wirtschaft: USSR Economic Relations.

Bayerisches Staatsarchiv, Munich (BStA)

Aussenministerium (MA):
103327, 103349, 103352, 103383, 103412, 103420, 103425, 103461–70, 103734, 103857–62.
Economics Ministry (MW):
256, 262, 264–8, 270, 275, 318–19, 369, 483, 5946.
Finance Ministry (MF):
66816, 66826, 67430, 67498–556.

Prussian State Archive (Stiftung Preussischer Kulturbesitz), Berlin-Dahlem (PrSA)

State Ministry (Rep. 90):
853, 1172–3, 1346–8, 1687.
Seehandlung (Rep. 109):
1097–1100, 5526, 6016.
Finance Ministry (Rep. 151):
1689–91, 1692–5.

Berlin Stadtarchiv

Archiv des Deutschen Städtetags (DST):
B1412, B1796, B2729–31, B2746, B2784, B2796, B2846, B2879, B2910, B3238, B3465, B3748, B3778, B4157, B4159, B4472.

Institut für Zeitgeschichte, Munich (IfZ)

ED93 Papers and Diary of Hans Schäffer.
ZS/A–20 Schwerin von Krosigk Diaries 1932–3.
F40/1–2 General Ludwig Beck Papers.

Friedrich-Ebert-Stiftung, Archiv der Sozialen Demokratie, Bonn (FES)
Papers of Otto Braun, Carl Severing, Wladimir Woytinsky, and Hermann Müller.

Industrial and Bank Archives

Bayerische Vereinsbank, Munich
Akten der Bayerischen Staatsbank, Bd. 153.

Historisches Archiv der Gutehoffnungshütte AG: (HA/GHH)
4001012024/3–11, 4001012025/0–5, 400101220/0–13, 400101221/1–3, 40010124/11–14, 400101250/0–1, 400101251/0–3, 400101290, 400101293/9–14, 400101293/15–18, 400123/0–12, 400127/0–3.

Fried. Krupp GmbH, Essen (HA Krupp)
FAH IV C and IV E: FAH IV C 73, IV C 89, IV C 168, IV E 84, IV E 92, IV E 152, IV E 176–9, IV E 184–5, IV E 202–3, IV E 209.
WA: IV 1960 S2, IV 1961, IV 2887, 41/2 238–61.

Werner von Siemens Institut für die Geschichte des Hauses Siemens, Munich
4/Lf: 529, 563, 591, 599, 635, 670, 683, 685, 716, 811.
11/Lb: 97, 98, 102, 117–18, 305, 322, 344.
11/Lf: 100, 374, 430.
14/La: 773.
14/Lg: 120.
29/Ls: 774.
49/Ls: 163, 264–5.
61/Lf: 109.

Max M. Warburg Papers (Property of Herr Eric M. Warburg, Hamburg)
MS Memoirs, Correspondence; Papers of Carl Melchior.

Private papers
Dr Franz Hayler.

GREAT BRITAIN

Bank of England
OV9/60, OV34/72–82, 108, 117–21, 130–2, 146–61.

Public Records Office, Kew
Foreign Office: FO 371.
Treasury:
T160/386–7, 403, 425, 436–9, 450.

Public Records Office, Chancery Lane
Treasury Solicitor:
TS26/900, 901.

NETHERLANDS

International Institute for Social History, Amsterdam
Papers of Paul Hertz and Otto Braun.

UNITED STATES OF AMERICA

National Archives, Washington DC
Record Group 39, *Records of the Bureau of Accounts, Treasury*
County File 'Germany' 64, 67, 102–4, 106.

Record Group 59, *General Records of the Department of State*
Decimal File: 862.00.
862.51.
M679.

Federal Reserve Bank, New York

Benjamin Strong papers.
George Leslie Harrison Papers.
German Government, Credit and Finance.
Reichsbank.
Standstill.

Private Papers

George Leslie Harrison Papers, Butler Library, Columbia University, New York.
Thomas W. Lamont Papers, Baker Library, Harvard Graduate School of Business Administration, Mass.
Thomas H. McKittrick Papers, Baker Library, Harvard Graduate School of Business Administration, Mass.

II. OFFICIAL PUBLICATIONS

GERMANY

Akten zur deutschen auswärtigen Politik, 1918–1945. Aus dem Archiv des Auswärtigen Amtes. Edited by Hans Rothfels and others. Series B: 1925–1933, Göttingen 1966– (ADAP)
Akten der Reichskanzlei, Weimarer Repulik, Die Kabinette Marx I und II, 2 vols. Edited by G. Abramowski, Boppard 1973.
Akten der Reichskanzlei, Weimarer Republik, Die Kabinette Luther I und II, 2 vols. Edited by K. H. Minuth, Boppard 1977.
Akten der Reichskanzlei, Weimarer Republik, Das Kabinett Müller II, 2 vols. Edited by M. Vogt, Boppard 1970.
Akten der Reichskanzlei, Weimarer Republik, Die Kabinette Brüning I und II, 2 vols. Edited by T. Koops, Boppard 1982.
Ausschuß zur Untersuchung der Erzeugungs- und Absatzbedingungen der deutschen Volkswirtschaft (Enquête-Ausschuß).
I. *Die deutsche Schuhindustrie* (1930).
Die deutsche Eisen- und Stahlwarenindustrie (1930).
Entwicklungslinien der industriellen und gewerblichen Kartellierung (1930).
II. *Untersuchungen über Landarbeitsverhältnisse* (1929).
Untersuchung zur Lage der Landwirtschaft in den Provinzen Pommern, Niederschlesien, Oberschlesien und Grenzmark Posen-Westpreußen (1930).

III. *Die deutsche Kohlenwirtschaft* (1929).
Die deutsche chemische Industrie (1930).
Die deutsche eisenerzeugende Industrie (1930).
Die deutsche Elektrizätswirtschaft (1930).
Einzelhandel mit Bekleidung I und II (1930).
Der deutsche Wohnungsbau (1931).

IV. *Arbeitszeit, Arbeitslohn und Arbeitsleistung im Hochofenbetrieb* (1929).
Die Arbeitsleistung in der Textilindustrie in den Jahren 1913 bis 1927 (1930).
Die Arbeitsleistung in landwirtschaftlichen Betrieben und ihre Abhängigkeit von Arbeitszeit, Arbeitslohn, und anderen Faktoren (1930).
Zusammenfassender Bericht (1930).

V. *Die Reichsbank* (1929).
Der Bankkredit (1930).

Gutachten zur Arbeitslosen-Frage (Brauns-Kommission), Veröffentlichung des Reichsarbeitsblatts, Berlin 1931.

Statistisches Jahrbuch für das Deutsche Reich, Berlin, yearly.

Verhandlungen des Reichstags, Stenographische Berichte.

Wirtschaft und Statistik.

GREAT BRITAIN

Documents on British Foreign Policy, 1918–1939 (DBFP):

Series 1A (edited by W. N. Medlicott, D. A. Dakin, M. E. Lambert), 7 vols. London, 1966, 1966–75.

Series 2 (edited by E. L. Woodward and Rohan Butler, and others), 18 vols. London, 1946–80.

Command Papers:

Cmd. 3995 *Report of the Special Advisory Committee convened under the Agreement with Germany concluded at the Hague on January 20 1930*, Basle, 22 December 1931.

Cmd. 4126 *Final Act of the Lausanne Conference*, July 1932.

SWITZERLAND

Documents Diplomatiques Suisses 1848–1945, 10. 1.1.1930–31.12.1933, (DDS), Bern, 1982.

UNITED STATES OF AMERICA

Department of State: *Papers Relating to the Foreign Relations of the United States 1924–1933*, Washington DC, 1939–50 (FRUS).

OTHER

Reparation Commission: *Report of the Agent-General for Reparation Payments*, Berlin, 1925–1930.

III. NEWSPAPERS AND PERIODICALS

GERMANY

Berliner Börsenblatt
Deutsche Allgemeine Zeitung
Deutsche Bergwerkszeitung
Berliner Tageblatt
Frankfurter Zeitung
Völkischer Beobachter
Vossische Zeitung

Die Arbeit
Die Bank
Das Bank-Archiv
Der Deutsche Volkswirt
Die deutsche Volkswirtschaft
Jahrbuch für nationalsozialistische Wirtschaft
Schmollers Jahrbuch
Währung und Wirtschaft
Weltwirtschaftliches Archiv
Wirtschaftsdienst
Die Wirtschaftskurve
Wochenberichte des Instituts für Konjunkturforschung

GREAT BRITAIN

The Times
The Economist

Press Cuttings Files of the HWWA—Institut für Wirtschaftsforschung, Hamburg.

IV. SECONDARY WORKS CITED

(Titles of contemporary newspaper or periodical articles cited only once are omitted.)

Abelshauser, W. (1980) 'Staat, Infrastruktur und regionaler Wohlstandsausgleich im Preussen der Hochindustrialisierung', in (ed.) Blaich 1980, 26–34.

Aeroboe, F. (1928) *Agrarpolitik: Ein Lehrbuch*, Berlin.

Abernon, Viscount d' (1929) *An Ambassador of Peace*, London.
Abraham, D. (1981) *The Collapse of the Weimar Republic: Political Economy and Crisis*, Princeton.
Achterberg, E. (1962) *Hundert Jahre Deutsche Hypothekenbank*, n.p.
Aldcroft, D. M. (1977) *From Versailles to Wall Street*, London.
Allen, W. S. (ed.) (1976) *The Infancy of Nazism: the Memoirs of ex-Gauleiter Albert Krebs 1923–1933*, New York.
Anderson, M. (1965) 'The Myth of the Two Hundred Families', *Political Studies* 13, 163–78.
Andic, S. and Veverka, J. (1964) 'The Growth of Government Expenditure in Germany since the Unification', *Finanzarchiv* 23, 169–278.
Arndt, H. (ed.) (1960) *Die Konzentration in der Wirtschaft*, Berlin.
Aubin, H. and Zorn, W. (eds) (1976) *Handbuch der deutschen Wirtschafts- und Sozialgeschichte*, Stuttgart.
Bagehot, W. (1873) *Lombard Street: A Description of the London Money Market*, London.
Balderston, T. (1977) 'The German Business Cycle in the 1920s', *EcHR* 30, 159–61.
—— (1979) 'Cyclical Fluctuations in Germany 1924–1929', Edinburgh Ph.D.
—— (1982) 'The Origins of Economic Instability in Germany 1924–30: Market Forces versus Economic Policy', *VSWG* 69, 488–512.
—— (1983) 'The Beginning of the Depression in Germany 1927–1930: Investment and the Capital Market', *EcHR* 36, 395–415.
Balogh, T. (1932) 'Some theoretical Aspects of the Central European Credit and Transfer Crisis', *International Affairs* 11, 346–63.
—— (1938) 'The National Economy of Germany', *EcJ* 48, 461–97.
Bankenquête (1908) *Stenographische Berichte: Die Verhandlungen der Gesamtkommission zu den Punkten I bis V des Fragebogens*, Berlin.
Bariéty, J. and Bloch, C. (1968) 'Une tentative de réconciliation franco-allemande et son échec 1932–33', *Revue d'histoire moderne et contemporaine* 15, 433–65.
Barkai, A. (1977a) *Das Wirtschaftssystem des Nationalsozialismus: Der historische und ideologische Hintergrund 1933–1936*, Cologne.
—— (1977b) 'Sozialdarwinismus und Antiliberalismus in Hitlers Wirtschaftskonzept: Zu Henry A. Turner', *GG* 3, 406–17.
Baudis, D. and Nussbaum, H. (1978) *Wirtschaft und Staat in Deutschland vom Ende des 19. Jahrhunderts bis 1918/19*, Berlin.
Beitel, W. and Nötzold, J. (1979) *Deutsch-sowjetische Wirtschaftsbeziehungen in der Zeit der Weimarer Republik: Eine Bilanz im Hinblick auf gegenwärtige Probleme*, Baden-Baden.

Bennett, E. W. (1962) *Germany and the Diplomacy of the Financial Crisis 1931*, Cambridge, Mass.
—— (1979) *German Rearmament and the West 1932–33*, Princeton.
Bentin, L.-A. (1973) *Johannes Popitz und Carl Schmitt: Zur wirtschaftlichen Theorie des totalen Staates in Deutschland*, Munich.
Benz, W. and Graml, H. (1976) *Aspekte deutscher Außenpolitik im 20. Jahrhundert. Aufsätze Hans Rothfels zum Gedächtnis*, Stuttgart.
Berend, I. T. and Ranki, G. (1974) *Economic Development in East-Central Europe in the 19th and 20th Centuries*, New York.
Berghahn, V. (1971) *Der Tirpitz-Plan: Genesis und Verfall einer innenpolitischen Krisenstrategie unter Wilhelm II*, Düsseldorf.
Bergmann, C. (1930) *Deutschland und der Young-Plan*, Berlin.
Berndt, R. (1975) 'Wirtschaftliche Mitteleuropapläne des deutschen Imperialismus 1926–1931', in (ed.) Ziebura 1975, 305–34.
Bessel, R. (1978) 'Eastern Germany as a Structural Problem in the Weimar Republic', *Social History* 3, 199–218.
—— and Feuchtwanger, E. J. (1981) *Social Change and Political Development in Weimar Germany*, London.
Besson, W. (1959) *Württemberg und die deutsche Staatskrise 1928–1933: Eine Studie zur Auflösung der Weimarer Republik*, Stuttgart.
Blackbourn, D. (1980) *Class, Religion, and Local Politics in Wilhelmine Germany: the Centre Party in Württemberg before 1914*, New Haven.
Blaich, F. (1973) 'Die "Fehlrationalisierung" in der deutschen Automobilindustrie 1924 bis 1929', *Tradition* 18, 18–33.
—— (1976) 'Die "Grundsätze nationalsozialistischer Steuerpolitik" und ihre Verwirklichung im Dritten Reich', in (ed.) Henning 1976, 99–117.
—— (1977) *Die Wirtschaftskrise 1925–26 und die Reichsregierung: Von der Erwerbslosenfürsorge zur Konjunkturpolitik*, Kallmünz.
—— (1978) *Grenzlandpolitik im Westen 1926–1936: Die Westhilfe zwischen Reichspolitik und Länderinteressen*, Stuttgart.
—— (1979) *Staat und Verbände in Deutschland zwischen 1871 und 1945*, Wiesbaden.
—— (ed.) (1980) *Staatliche Umverteilungspolitik in historischer Perspektive: Beiträge zur Entwicklung des Staatsinterventionismus in Deutschland und Oesterreich*, Berlin.
Blatz, J. (1971). *Die Bankenliquidität im Run 1931. Statistische Liquiditätsanalyse der deutschen Kreditinstitutsgruppen in der Weltwirtschaftskrise 1929–1933*, Cologne.
Bloomfield, A. (1959) *Monetary Policy under the International Gold Standard 1880–1914*, New York.
Böhret, C. (1966) *Aktionen gegen die 'Kalte Sozialisierung' 1926–1930: Ein Beitrag zum Wirken ökonomischer Einflussverbände in der Weimarer Republik*, Berlin.

Boelcke, W. A. (1983) *Die deutsche Wirtschaft 1930–1945: Interna des Reichswirtschaftsministeriums*, Düsseldorf.

Bombach, G., Ramser, H.-J., Timmermann, M., and Wittmann, W. (eds) (1976) *Der Keynesianismus I: Theorie und Praxis keynesianischer Wirtschaftspolitik: Entwicklung und Stand der Diskussion*, Berlin.

—— (eds) (1976) *Der Keynesianismus II: Die beschäftigungspolitische Diskussion vor Keynes in Deutschland*, Berlin.

Bombach, G., Netzband, K.-B., Ramser, H.-J., and Timmermann, M. (eds) (1981) *Der Keynesianismus III: Die geld- und beschäftigungstheoretische Diskussion in Deutschland zur Zeit von Keynes*, Berlin.

Bonn, M. J. (1931) *The World Crisis and the Teaching of the Manchester School*, London.

Bopp, K. R. (1939) *Hjalmar Schacht, Central Banker*, Columbia.

Borchardt, K. (1976) 'Wachstum und Wechsellagen 1914–1970', in (eds) Aubin and Zorn 1976, 685–720.

—— (1979) 'Zwangslagen und Handlungsspielräume in der grossen Wirtschaftskrise der frühen dreißiger Jahre: Zur Revision des überlieferten Geschichtsbildes', *Jahrbuch der Bayerischen Akademie der Wissenschaften*, 85–132.

—— (1980) 'Zur Frage der währungspolitischen Optionen Deutschlands in der Weltwirtschaftskrise', in (eds) K. Borchardt and F. Holzheu, *Theorie und Politik der internationalen Wirtschaftsbeziehungen, Hans Möller zum 65. Geburtstag*, Stuttgart, 165–81.

—— (1982a) *Wachstum, Krisen, Handlungsspielräume der Wirtschaftspolitik: Studien zur Wirtschaftsgeschichte des 19. und 20. Jahrhunderts*, Göttingen.

—— (1982b) "Zur Aufarbeitung der Vor- und Frühgeschichte des Keynesianismus in Deutschland: Zugleich ein Beitrag zur Position von W. Lautenbach', *JNS* 197, 359–70.

—— (1983a) 'Die deutsche Katastrophe', *FAZ* 24 (29 Jan.).

—— (1983b) 'Noch einmal: Alternativen zu Brünings Wirtschaftspolitik', *HZ* 237, 67–83.

Born, K. E. (1967) *Die deutsche Bankenkrise 1931: Finanzen und Politik*, Munich.

Boyle, A. (1967) *Montagu Norman: A biography*, London.

Bracher, K. D. (1971[5]) *Die Auflösung der Weimarer Republik: Eine Studie zum Problem des Machtverfalls in der Demokratie*, Königstein/Taunus.

Brady, R. A. (1933). *The Rationalisation Movement in German Industry: A Study in the Evolution of Economic Planning*, Berkeley.

Brasch, A. v. (1935). *Das Rohstoffproblem der deutschen Woll- und Baumwollindustrie*, Berlin.

Braun, O. (1940) *Von Weimar zu Hitler*, New York.

Brauns, H. (1976) *Katholische Sozialpolitik im 20. Jahrhundert: Ausge wählte Aufsätze und Reden*, Mainz.

Brecht, A. (1967) *Mit der Kraft des Geistes: Lebenserinnerungen 1927–1967*, Stuttgart.

Bresciani-Turroni, C. (1953) *The Economics of Inflation: A Study of Currency Depreciation in Postwar Germany 1914–1923*, London.

Brinkmann, R. (1939) *Wirtschaftspolitik aus nationalsozialistischem Kraftquell: Eine Sammlung ausgewählter Vorträge, Reden und Ansprachen*, Jena.

Brüning, H. (1932) *Zwei Jahre am Steuer des Reichs: Reden aus Brünings Kanzlerzeit*, Cologne.

—— (1970) *Memoiren 1918–1934*, Stuttgart.

—— (ed. C. Nix) (1974a) *Briefe und Gespräche 1934–1945*, Stuttgart.

—— (ed. C. Nix) (1974b) *Briefe 1946–1960*, Stuttgart.

Brunner, K. (ed.) (1981) *The Great Depression Revisited*, Boston.

Bry, G. (1960) *Wages in Germany 1871–1945*, Princeton.

Buchta, B. (1959) *Die Junker und die Weimarer Republik: Charakter und Bedeutung der Osthilfe in den Jahren 1928–1933*, Berlin.

Bullock, A. (1962) *Hitler, a Study in Tyranny*, Harmondsworth.

Burk, K. (ed.) (1982) *War and the State: The Transformation of British Government 1914–1919*, London.

Büsch, O. (1960) *Geschichte der Berliner Kommunalwirtschaft in der Weimarer Epoche*, Berlin.

—— and Feldman, G. D. (eds) (1978) *Historische Prozesse der deutschen Inflation 1914 bis 1924: ein Tagungsbericht*, Berlin.

Büttner, U. (1982) *Hamburg in der Staats- und Wirtschaftskrise 1928–1931*, Hamburg.

Cairncross, A. and Eichengreen, B. (1983) *Sterling in Decline: The Devaluations of 1931, 1949, and 1967*, Oxford.

Caron, F. (trans. B. Bray), (1979) *An Economic History of Modern France*, London.

Cassel, G. (1931) *The Monetary Character of the Present Crisis* (Institute of Bankers), London.

—— (1932a[5]) *Theoretische Sozialökonomie*, Leipzig.

—— (1932b) *The Crisis of the World's Monetary System*, Oxford.

—— (1933) *Die Krise im Weltgeldsystem*, Berlin-Charlottenburg.

—— (1937) *Der Zusammenbruch der Goldwährung*, Leipzig.

Chandler, A. D. and Daems, H. (eds) (1980) *Managerial Hierarchies: Comparative Perspectives in the Rise of Modern Industrial Enterprise*, Cambridge, Mass.

Chandler, L. V. (1958) *Benjamin Strong, Central Banker*, Washington, DC.

Childers, T. (1983) *The Nazi Voter: the Social Foundations of Fascism in Germany 1919–1933*, Chapel Hill.

Clarke, S. V. O. (1967) *Central Bank Cooperation 1924–1931*, New York.

Clay, H. (1957) *Lord Norman*, London.
Cline, P. (1982) 'Winding Down the War Economy: British Plans for Peacetime Recovery 1916–1919', in (ed.) Burk 1982, 157–81.
Colm, G. and Neisser, H. (eds) (1930) *Kapitalbildung und Steuersystem: Verhandlungen und Gutachten der Konferenz in Eilsen*, Berlin.
Conze, W. (1964) 'Brünings Politik unter dem Druck der grossen Krise', *HZ* 199, 529–50.
—— (1967) 'Die politischen Entscheidungen in Deutschland 1929–1933', in (eds) Conze and Raupach 1967, 176–252.
—— and Raupach, H. (eds) (1967) *Die Staats- und Wirtschaftskrise des Deutschen Reiches 1929–33*, Stuttgart.
—— (1972) 'Brüning als Reichskanzler: Eine Zwischenbilanz', *HZ* 214, 310–34.
Costigliola, F. (1972) 'The Other Side of Isolationism: the Establishment of the first World Bank', *JAmH* 59, 602–20.
Cullity, J. P. (1967) 'The Growth of Government Employment in Germany 1882–1950', *Zeitschrift für die gesamte Staatswissenschaft* 123, 201–17.
Curtius, J. (1948) *Sechs Jahre Minister der Deutschen Republik*, Heidelberg.
Czada, P. (1969) *Die Berliner Elektroindustrie in der Weimarer Republik: Eine regionalstatistische-wirtschaftshistorische Untersuchung*, Berlin.
—— (1973) 'Ursachen und Folgen der großen Inflation', in (ed.) Winkel 1973, 9–43.
Czichon, E. (1967) *Wer verhalf Hitler zur Macht? Zum Anteil der deutschen Industrie an der Zerstörung der Weimarer Republik*, Cologne.
Dalberg, R. (1926) *Deutsche Währungs- und Kreditpolitik 1923–1926*, Berlin.
Dauphin-Meunier, A. (1936) *La Banque 1919–1935*, Paris.
Dawes, C. G. (1939) *A Journal of Reparations*, London.
Day, R. B. (1981) *The 'Crisis' and the 'Crash': Soviet Studies of the West (1917–1939)*, London.
Desai, A. V. (1968) *Real Wages in Germany 1871–1913*, Oxford.
Deutsche Bundesbank (1976) *Deutsches Geld- und Bankwesen in Zahlen 1876–1975*, Frankfurt.
—— (1976) *Währung und Wirtschaft in Deutschland 1876–1975*, Frankfurt.
Die deutsche Sozialpolitik: Eine Materialsammlung (1926), Berlin.
Deutsche Sozialpolitik: Erinnerungsschrift des Reichsarbeitsministeriums (1929), Berlin.
Deutschnationale Schriftenreihenstelle (1929) *Rüstzeug Nr. 12: Sozialpolitische Praxis der Deutschnationalen*, Berlin.
Dieckmann, H. (1960) *Johannes Popitz, Entwicklung und Wirksamkeit in der Zeit der Weimarer Republik*, Berlin.

Diehl, K. (ed.) (1932) *Wirkungen und Ursachen des hohen Zinsfußes in Deutschland*, Jena.
Dodd, W. E. Jr. and Dodd, M. (eds) (1941) *Ambassador Dodd's Diary*, London.
Döhn, L. (1970) *Politik und Interesse: Die Interessenstruktur der Deutschen Volkspartei*, Meisenheim am Glan.
Doering, D. (1969) 'Deutsche Außenwirtschaftspolitik 1933–1935: Die Gleichschaltung der Außenwirtschaft in der Frühphase des nationalsozialistischen Regimes', Berlin Ph.D.
Domarus, M. (1965) *Hitler: Reden und Proklamationen 1932–1945, kommentiert von einem deutschen Zeitgenossen*, Munich.
Eichholtz, D. (1969) *Geschichte der deutschen Kriegswirtschaft I*, Berlin.
Einzig, P. (1930) *The Bank for International Settlements*, London.
—— (1934) *Germany's Default: The Economics of Hitlerism*, London.
Ellis, H. S. (1934) *German Monetary Theory*, Cambridge, Mass.
—— (1941) *Exchange Control in Central Europe*, Cambridge, Mass.
Elster, L., Weber, A., and Wieser, F. (eds) (1923–9), 4th ed. *Handwörterbuch der Staatswissenschaften*, Jena.
Engeli, C. (1971) *Gustav Böß, Oberbürgermeister von Berlin 1921 bis 1930*, Stuttgart.
Erbe, R. (1958) *Die nationalsozialistische Wirtschaftspolitik 1933–1939 im Lichte der modernen Theorie*, Zürich.
Falkus, M. E. (1975) 'The German Business Cycle in the 1920s', *EcHR* 23, 451–65.
Farquharson, J. E. (1976) *The Plough and the Swastika: the NSDAP and Agriculture in Germany 1928–1945*, London.
Feder, E. (1971) *Heute sprach ich mit ... Tagebücher eines Berliner Publizisten 1926–1932*, Stuttgart.
Feldman, G. D. (1966) *Army, Industry, and Labour in Germany 1914–1918*, Princeton.
—— (1969) 'The Social and Economic Policies of German Big Business 1918–1929', *AmHR* 75, 47–55.
—— (1977) *Iron and Steel in the German Inflation 1916–1923*, Princeton.
—— (1978) 'Aspekte deutscher Industriepolitik am Ende der Weimarer Republik 1930–1932', in (ed.) Holl 1978, 103–25.
—— and Steinisch, I. (1978) 'Die Weimarer Republik zwischen Sozial- und Wirtschaftsstaat: Die Enstcheidung gegen den Achtstundentag', *AfS* 18, 353–439.
—— (ed.) (1982) *Die deutsche Inflation: Eine Zwischenbilanz. Beiträge zu Inflation und Wiederaufbau in Deutschland und Europa 1914–1924*, Berlin.
—— (ed.) (1985) *Die Nachwirkungen der Inflation auf die deutsche Geschichte*, Munich.
Fick, H. (1932) *Finanzwirtschaft und Konjunktur*, Jena.

Fiederlein, F. M. (1966) 'Der deutsche Osten und die Regierungen Brüning, Papen und Schleicher', Würzburg Ph.D.

Fischer, W. (1968³) *Deutsche Wirtschaftspolitik*, Opladen.

Flechtner, H. J. (1959) *Carl Duisberg: Vom Chemiker zum Wirtschaftsführer*, Düsseldorf.

Fleisig, H. (1976) War-related Debts and the Great Depression', *AmEcR* 66, 52–8.

François-Poncet, A. (1948) *Als Botschafter in Berlin 1931–1938*, Mainz.

Föhl, C. (1937) *Geldschöpfung und Wirtschaftskreislauf*, Munich, Leipzig.

Friedländer-Prechtl, R. (1926) *Chronische Arbeitskrise, ihre Ursprünge, ihre Beseitigung*, Berlin.

—— (1932) *Die Wirtschaftswende: Die Arbeitslosenkrise und deren Bekämpfung*, Leipzig.

Friedman, M. (ed.) (1956) *Studies in the Quantity Theory of Money*, Chicago.

—— and Schwartz, A. J. (1963) *Monetary History of the USA*, Princeton.

Fürstenberg, H . (1965) *Erinnerungen: Mein Weg als Bankier und Carl Fürstenberg's Altersjahre*, Wiesbaden.

Galbraith, J. K. (1976) *Money, whence it came, where it went*, Harmondsworth.

Garrett, G. (1931) *Other People's Money! The Great American Racket*, New York.

—— (1932) *A Bubble that broke the World*, Boston.

Garvy, G. (1975) 'Keynes and the economic Activists of pre-Hitler Germany', *JPolEc* 83, 391–405.

Gaulle, C. de (1944²) *Le Fil de l'épee*, Paris.

Geiger, T. (1932, 1967) *Die soziale Schichtung des deutschen Volkes: Soziographischer Versuch auf statistischer Grundlage*, Stuttgart.

Gerschenkron, G. (1970) 'Reflections on European Socialism', in (ed.) G. Grossman, *Essays in Socialism and Planning in Honor of Carl Landauer*, Englewood Cliffs, NJ, 1970, 1–17.

Gessner, D. (1976a) *Agrarverbände in der Weimarer Republik: Wirtschaftliche und soziale Voraussetzungen agrarkonservativer Politik vor 1933*, Düsseldorf.

—— (1976b) *Agrardepression, Agrarideologie und konservative Politik in der Weimarer Republik: Zur Legitimationsproblematik konservativer Politik in der Zwischenkriegszeit*, Wiesbaden.

—— (1977) *Agrardepression und Präsidialregierungen in Deutschland 1930–1933: Probleme des Agrarprotektionismus am Ende der Weimarer Republik*, Düsseldorf.

Geyer, M. (1980) *Aufrüstung oder Sicherheit: Die Reichswehr in der Krise der Machtpolitik 1924–1936*, Wiesbaden.

Glismann, H. H., Rodemer, F., and Wolter, F. (1978a) *Zur Natur der Wachstumsschwäche in der Bundesrepublik Deutschland: Eine empirische Analyse langer Zyklen wirtschaftlicher Entwicklung*, Kieler Diskussionsbeiträge 55, Kiel.

—— (1978b) *Zur empirischen Analyse langer Zyklen wirtschaftlicher Entwicklung in Deutschland: Datenbasis und Berechnungsmethoden*, Kieler Arbeitspapiere 72, Kiel.

Gordon, R. J. and Wilcox, J. A. (1981) 'Monetarist Interpretations of the Great Depression: and Evaluation and Critique', in (ed.) Brunner 1981, 49–107.

Gossweiler, K. (1971). *Großbanken, Industriemonopole und Staat. Oekonomie und Politik des staatsmonopolistischen Kapitalismus in Deutschland 1914–1932*, Berlin.

Grebing, H. (1970) *Geschichte der deutschen Arbeiterbewegung: Ein Ueberblick*, Munich.

Grebler, L. (1937) 'Work-Creation Policy in Germany 1932–35', *International Labour Review* 35, 329–51, 505–27.

Groh, D. (1973) *Negative Integration und revolutionärer Attentismus: Die deutsche Sozialdemokratie am Vorabend des Ersten Weltkrieges*, Frankfurt.

Grotkopp, W. (1954) *Die große Krise: Lehren aus der Ueberwindung der Wirtschaftskrise 1929–32*, Düsseldorf.

Grübler, M. (1982) *Die Spitzenverbände der Wirtschaft und das erste Kabinett Brüning: Vom Ende der Großen Koalition 1929/30 bis zum Vorabend der Bankenkrise 1931. Eine Quellenstudie*, Düsseldorf.

Grunberger, R. (1974) *A Social History of the Third Reich*, Harmondsworth.

Guillebaud, C. W. (1939) *The Economic Recovery of Germany*, Cambridge.

Gutachten über die gegenwärtige Lage des rheinisch-westfälischen Steinkohlenbergbaus. Dem Reichswirtschaftsminister erstattet durch Prof. Dr Schmalenbach u.a. (1928), Berlin.

Habedank, H. (1981) *Die Reichsbank in der Weimarer Republik. Zur Rolle der Zentralbank in der Politik des deutschen Imperialismus*, Berlin.

Haber, L. F. (1971) *The Chemical Industry 1900–1930: International Growth and Technical Change*, Oxford.

Hahn, L. A. (1928) *Aufgaben und Grenzen der Währungspolitik: Eine Kritik der deutschen Währungspolitik seit der Stabilisierung*, Jena.

—— (1931) *Kredit und Krise*, Tübingen.

—— (1963) *Fünfzig Jahre zwischen Inflation und Deflation*, Tübingen.

Hansen, E. W. (1978) *Reichswehr und Industrie: Rüstungswirtschaftliche Zusammenarbeit und wirtschaftliche Mobilmachungsvorarbeiten 1923–1932*, Boppard.

Hansmeyer, K.-H. (ed.) (1973) *Kommunale Finanzpolitik in der Weimarer Republik*, Stuttgart.

Hardach, G. (1970) 'Reichsbankpolitik und wirtschaftliche Entwicklung 1924–1931', *Schmollers Jahrbuch* 90, 563–92.

—— (1973) 'Währungskrise 1931: Das Ende des Goldstandards in Deutschland', in (ed.) Winkel 1973, 121–33.

—— (1974) 'Die beiden Reichsbanken: Internationales Währungssystem und nationale Währungspolitik 1924–1931', in (eds) H. Mommsen *et al.* 1974, 375–86.

—— (1976) *Weltmarktorientierung und relative Stagnation: Währungspolitik in Deutschland 1924–1931*, Berlin.

Harms, B. (1928) *Strukturwandlungen der deutschen Volkswirtschaft*, Berlin.

Harris, C. R. S. (1935) *Germany's Foreign Indebtedness*, London.

Hartwich, H.-H. (1967) *Arbeitsmarkt, Verbände und Staat 1918–1933: Die öffentliche Bindung unternehmerischer Funktionen in der Weimarer Republik*, Berlin.

Hayek, F. (1931) *Preise und Produktion, Beiträge zur Konjunkturforschung* 3, Vienna.

Heinrichsbauer, A. (1948) *Schwerindustrie und Politik*, Essen.

Helbich, W. J. (1962) *Die Reparationen in der Aera Brüning: Zur Bedeutung des Young-Plans für die deutsche Politik 1930 bis 1932*, Berlin.

Henning, F. W. (1973) 'Die Liquidität der Banken in der Weimarer Republik', in (ed.) Winkel 1973, 43–92.

—— (ed.) (1976) *Probleme der nationalsozialistischen Wirstschaftspolitik*, Berlin.

—— (ed.) (1981) *Düsseldorf und seine Wirtschaft: Zur Geschichte einer Region*, II, Düsseldorf.

Hentschel, V. (1978) *Weimars letzte Monate: Hitler und der Untergang der Republik*, Düsseldorf.

Herbst, L. (1982) *Der totale Krieg und die Ordnung der Wirtschaft: Die Kriegswirtschaft im Spannungsfeld von Politik, Ideologie und Propaganda 1939–1945*, Stuttgart.

Hermens, F. A. and Schieder, T. (eds) (1967) *Staat, Wirtschaft und Politik; Festschrift für Heinrich Brüning*, Berlin.

Herrmann, W. (1962) 'Otto Wolff', *Rheinisch-Westfälische Wirtschaftsbiographien* 8, Münster, 123–56.

Hertz, P. and Seidel, R. (1923) *Arbeitszeit, Arbeitslohn und Arbeitsleistung*, Berlin.

Hertz-Eichenrode, D. (1982) *Wirtschaftskrise und Arbeitsbeschaffung: Konjunkturpolitik 1925/6 und die Grundlagen der Krisenpolitik Brünings*, Frankfurt.

Heupel, E. (1981) *Reformismus und Krise: Zur Theorie und Praxis von SPD, ADGB und AfA-Bund in der Weltwirtschaftskrise 1929–1932/3*, Frankfurt.

Hilferding, R. (1910; repr. 1968), *Das Finanzkapital*, Frankfurt.

Hilferding, R. (1924) 'Probleme der Zeit', *Die Gesellschaft* I/1 1–17.
—— (1926) 'Politische Probleme: Zum Aufruf Wirths und zur Rede Silverbergs', *Die Gesellschaft* III/1 289–302.
Hobsbawm, E. (1959) *Primitive Rebels: Studies in Archaic Forms of Social Movement in the 19th and 20th Centuries*, Manchester.
Hoffmann, W. G. (with F. Grumbach and H. Hesse) (1965) *Das Wachstum der deutschen Wirtschaft seit der Mitte des 19. Jahrhunderts*, Berlin.
Hofmann, H. H. (1968) 'Ländliches Judentum in Franken', *Tribüne: Zeitschrift zum Verständnis des Judentums*, 2890–904.
Hofmann, W. (1966) *Städtetag und Verfassungsordnung: Position und Politik der Hauptgeschäftsführer eines kommunalen Spitzenverbandes*, Stuttgart.
—— (1974) *Zwischen Rathaus und Reichskanzlei: Die Oberbürgermeister in der Kommunal- und Staatspolitik des Deutschen Reiches von 1890 bis 1933*, Stuttgart.
Holl, K. (ed.) (1978) *Wirtschaftskrise und liberale Demokratie: Das Ende der Weimarer Republik und die gegenwärtige Situation*, Göttingen.
Holtfrerich, C.-L. (1980) *Die deutsche Inflation 1914–1923: Ursachen und Folgen in internationaler Perspektive*, Berlin.
—— (1982) 'Alternativen zu Brünings Wirtschaftspolitik in der Weltwirtschaftskrise?', *HZ* 235, 605–31.
—— (1983) 'Zu hohe Löhne in der Weimarer Republik? Bemerkungen zur Borchardt-These', *GG* 10, 122–41.
Homburg, H. (1978) 'Anfänge des Taylorsystems in Deutschland vor dem Ersten Weltkrieg: Eine Problemskizze unter besonderer Berücksichtigung der Arbeitskämpfe bei Bosch 1913', *GG* 4, 170–98.
Howson, S. (1975) *Domestic Monetary Management in Britain 1919–1928*, Cambridge.
—— and Winch, D. (1977) *The Economic Advisory Council 1930–1939*, London.
Hubatsch, W. (1978) *Entstehung und Entwicklung des Reichswirtschaftsministeriums 1880–1933: Ein Beitrag zur Verwaltungsgeschichte der Reichsministerien, Darstellung und Dokumentation*, Berlin.
Hughes, B. A. (1969) 'Owen D. Young and American Foreign Policy 1919–1929', Wisconsin Ph.D.
Hüllbüsch, U. (1967) 'Die deutschen Gewerkschaften in der Weltwirtschaftskrise', in (eds) Conze and Raupach 1967, 126–54.
Hunt, J. C. (1974) 'Peasants, Grain Tariffs, and Meat Quotas: Imperial German Protection reexamined', *CEH* 7, 311–31.
Hutchinson, T. W. (1978) *On Revolutions and Progress in Economic Knowledge*, Cambridge.
Industrie- und Handelskammer Berlin (1928) *Die Bedeutung der Rationalisierung für das deutsche Wirtschaftsleben*, Berlin.

International Military Tribunal (1949) *Trial of the Major War Criminals*, XLI, Nuremberg.

Irving, D. (1973) *The Rise and Fall of the Luftwaffe: The Life of Luftwaffe Marshal Erhard Milch*, London.

Jackson, J. (1982) 'The Politics of Depression in France 1932–1936', Cambridge Ph.D.

Jäckel, E. (trans. H. Arnold) (1974) *Hitler's Weltanschauung: A Blueprint for Power*, Middletown, Conn.

James, H. (1981) 'Rudolf Hilferding and the Application of the Political Economy of the Second International', *HJ* 24, 847–69.

—— (1984) 'The Causes of the German Banking Crisis of 1931', *EcHR* 37, 68–87.

—— (1985a) *The Reichsbank and Public Finance in Germany 1924–1933: A Study of the Politics of Economics during the Great Depression*, Frankfurt.

—— (1985b) 'Did the Reichsbank draw the right Lessons from the Great Inflation?', in (ed.) Feldman 1985, 211–30.

Jasper, G. (ed.) (1976) *Tradition und Reform in der deutschen Politik: Gedenkschrift für Waldemar Besson*, Frankfurt.

Jeanneney, J.-N. (1975) *François de Wendel en République. L'Argent et le pouvoir 1914–1940*. Thèse présentée devant l'université de Paris X, le 12 mars 1975.

—— (1981) *L'Argent caché: Milieux d'affaires et pouvoirs dans la France au XXe siècle*, Paris.

Jochmann, W. (1960) *Im Kampf um die Macht: Hitlers Rede vor dem Hamburger Nationalklub von 1919*, Frankfurt.

—— (1978) 'Brünings Deflationspolitik und der Untergang der Weimarer Republik', in (eds) Stegmann, Wendt, and Witt 1978, 97–112.

—— (ed.) (1980) *Adolf Hitlers Monologe im Führerhauptquartier 1941–1944: Die Aufzeichnungen Heinrich Heims*, Hamburg.

Jones, L. E. (1972) '"The Dying Middle": Weimar Germany and the Fragmentation of Bourgeois Politics', *CEH* 5, 23–54.

—— (1979) 'Inflation, Revaluation, and the Crisis of Middle-Class Politics: A Study in the Dissolution of the German Party System 1923–1928', *CE* 12, 146–68.

Kahn-Freund, O. (eds. R. Lewis and J. Clark) (1981) *Labour Law and Politics in the Weimar Republic*, Oxford.

Kaiser, D. E. (1980) *Economic Diplomacy and the Origins of the Second World War. Germany, Britain, France, and Eastern Europe 1930–1939*, Princeton.

Kater, M. H. (1983) *The Nazi Party: A Social Profile of Members and Leaders 1919–1945*, Oxford.

Keese, D. (1967) 'Die volkswirtschaftlichen Gesamtgrößen für das

Deutsche Reich 1925–1936', in (eds) Conze and Raupach 1967, 35–81.
Keil, W. (1919) *Flugschriften der Revolution Nr. 1: Die Rettung aus dem finanziellen Elend*, Berlin.
—— (1948) *Erlebnisse eines Sozialdemokraten*, Stuttgart.
Kershaw, I. (1983) *Popular Opinion and Political Dissent in the Third Reich: Bavaria 1933–1945*, Oxford.
Keynes, J. M. (1919) *The Economic Consequences of the Peace*, London.
—— (1923) *A Tract on Monetary Reform*, London.
—— (1929) 'The German Transfer Problem', *EcJ* 39, 1–7.
—— (1936) *The General Theory of Employment, Interest and Money*, London.
—— (1972) *Collected Writings IX: Essays in Persuasion*, London.
—— (1978) *Collected Writings XVIII, Activities 1922–1932: The End of Reparations*, London.
Kindleberger, C. P. (1973) *The World in Depression*, London.
—— (1978) *Manias, Panics, and Crashes: a History of Financial Crises*, New York.
—— and Laffargue, J.-P. (eds) (1982) *Financial Crises: Theory, History, and Policy*, Cambridge.
Klein, B. H. (1959) *Germany's Economic Preparations for War*, Cambridge, Mass.
Klein, J. J. (1956) 'German Money and Prices 1932–44', in (ed.) Friedman 1956, 121–59.
Kocka, J. (1973) *Klassengesellschaft im Krieg 1914–1918*, Göttingen.
—— (1978) 'Entrepreneurs and Managers in German Industrialisation', in (eds) Mathias and Postan 1978, 492–589.
—— (ed.) (1979) *Emil Lederer: Klassenstruktur und Probleme der Demokratie in Deutschland 1910–1940*, Göttingen.
—— (1980) 'The Rise of Modern Industrial Enterprise in Germany', in (eds) Chandler and Daems 1980, 77–116.
Köhler, Heinrich (ed. J. Becker) (1964) *Lebenserinnerungen eines Politikers und Staatsmannes 1878–1949*, Stuttgart.
Köhler, Henning (1973) 'Sozialpolitik von Brüning bis Schleicher', *VfZ* 21, 146–50.
—— (1974) 'Das Verhältnis von Reichsregierung und Grossbanken 1931', in (eds) H. Mommsen *et al.* 1974, 868–77.
Köttgen, C. (1925) *Das wirtschaftliche Amerika*, Berlin.
Kohlhaas, W. (n.d. 1964?) *Chronik der Stadt Stuttgart*, Stuttgart.
Krohn, C.-D. (1974) *Stabilisierung und ökonomische Interessen: Die Finanzpolitik des Deutschen Reiches 1923–1927*, Düsseldorf.
—— and Stegmann, D. (1977) 'Kleingewerbe und Nationalsozialismus in einer agrarisch-mittelständischen Region: Das Beispiel Lüneburg 1930–1939', *AfS* 17, 41–98.

—— (1981) *Wirtschaftstheorien als politische Interessen: Die akademische Nationalökonomie in Deutschland 1918–1933*, Frankfurt.

Kroll, G. (1958) *Von der Weltwirtschaftskrise zur Staatskonjunktur*, Berlin.

Kuczynski, J. (1960–72) *Die Lage der Arbeiter unter dem Kapitalismus*, 38 vols, Berlin.

Kuczynski, R. (1928) *Deutsche Anleihen im Ausland 1924–1927*, Berlin.

Kuczynski, T. (1972) 'Das Ende der Weltwirtschaftskrise in Deutschland 1932/33', Berlin-Karlshorst Ph.D.

Kunz, A. (1982) 'Stand versus Klasse: Beamtenschaft und Gewerkschaften im Konflikt um den Personalabbau 1923/4', *GG* 8, 55–86.

Landes, D. (1969) *The Unbound Prometheus: Technological Change and Industrial Development in Western Europe from 1750 to the Present*, Cambridge.

Lauren, F. G. (1976) *Diplomats and Bureaucrats: The first institutional responses to twentieth century diplomacy in France and Germany*, Stanford.

Lautenbach, W. (1952) *Zins, Kredit und Produktion*, Tübingen.

Leffler, M. (1972) 'The Struggle for Stability: American Policy towards France 1921–1933', Ohio State University Ph.D.

Leith-Ross, F. (1968) *Money talks: Fifty Years of International Finance*, London.

Leopold, J. A. (1977) *Alfred Hugenberg: The radical Nationalist Campaign against the Weimar Republic*, New Haven.

Leuschen-Seppel, R. (1981) *Zwischen Staatsverantwortung und Klasseninteresse: Die Wirtschafts- und Finanzpolitik der SPD zur Zeit der Weimarer Republik unter besonderer Berücksichtigung der Mittelphase 1924–1928/9*, Bonn.

Levy, H. (1935) *Industrial Germany: A Study of its Monopoly Organisations and their Control by the State*, Cambridge.

Lewis, C. (1938) *America's Stake in International Investments*, Washington, DC.

Lewis, W. A. (1949) *Economic Survey 1919–1939*, London.

Liebe, W. (1956) *Die deutschnationale Volkspartei 1918–1924*, Düsseldorf.

Liefmann, R. (trans. D. H. Macgregor) (1932) *Cartels, Concerns, and Trusts*, London.

Lindenlaub, D. (1982) 'Maschinenbauunternehmen in der Inflation 1919–1923: Unternehmenshistorische Ueberlegungen zu einigen Theorien der Inflationswirkungen und Inflationserklärung', in (ed.) Feldman 1982, 49–106.

Link, W. (1970) *Die amerikanische Stabilisierungspolitik in Deutschland 1921–1932*, Düsseldorf.

Lochner, L. P. (1955) *Die Mächtigen und der Tyrann: Die deutsche Industrie von Hitler bis Adenauer*, Darmstadt.

Long, R. C. (1928) *The Mythology of Reparations*, London.

Lüke, R. E. (1958) *Von der Stabilisierung zur Krise*, Zürich.
Lurié, S. (1947) *Private investment in a Controlled Economy: Germany 1933–1939*, New York.
Luthardt, W. (ed.) (1978) *Sozialdemokratische Arbeiterbewegung und Weimarer Republik: Materialien zur gesellschaftlichen Entwicklung 1927–1933*, 2 vols, Frankfurt.
Luther, H. (1930) *Kredit und Zins im Zeichen der Krise*, Berlin.
—— (1932) *Wirtschaftsfragen der Gegenwart*, Jena.
—— (1964) *Vor dem Abgrund 1930–1933: Reichsbankpräsident in Krisenzeiten*, Berlin.
—— (1970) *Politiker ohne Partei: Erinnerungen*, Stuttgart.
Lyttleton, A. (1973) *The Seizure of Power: Fascism in Italy 1919–1929*, London.
Macgregor, D. H. (1934) *Enterprise, Purpose, and Profit*, Oxford.
Machlup, F. (1932) 'Die Theorie der Kapitalflucht', *Weltwirtschaftliches Archiv* 36, 512–29.
Mack Smith, D. (1969^2) *Italy: a Modern History*, Ann Arbor.
Maddison, A. (1977) 'Phases of Capitalist Development', *Banca Nazionale del Lavoro Quarterly Review* 30, 103–37.
—— (1979) 'Long Run Dynamics of Productivity Growth', *Banca Nazionale del Lavoro Quarterly Review* 32, 3–43.
—— (1982) *Phases of Capitalist Development*, Oxford.
Maier, C. S. (1975) *Recasting Bourgeois Europe. Stabilisation in France, Germany, and Italy in the Decade after World War I*, Princeton.
Maizels, A. (1963) *Industrial Growth and World Trade: An empirical Study of Trends in Production, Consumption, and Trade in Manufactures from 1899–1959 with a Discussion of possible future Trends*, Cambridge.
Mantoux, E. (1946) *The Carthaginian Peace or the Economic Consequences of Mr Keynes*, London.
Marcon, H. (1974) *Arbeitsbeschaffungspolitik der Regierungen Papen und Schleicher: Grundsteinlegung für die Beschäftigungspolitik im Dritten Reich*, Frankfurt.
Marks, S. (1969) 'Reparations Reconsidered: a Reminder', *CEH* 2, 356–65.
Marquand, D. (1977) *Ramsay MacDonald*, London.
Maschke, E. (1969) *Es ensteht ein Konzern: Paul Reusch und die GHH*, Tübingen.
Mason, T. (1966) 'Der Primat der Politik: Politik und Wirtschaft im Nationalsozialismus', *Das Argument* 8, 473–94.
—— (1977) *Sozialpolitik im Dritten Reich: Arbeiterklasse und Volksgemeinschaft*, Opladen.
Mathias, P. and Postan, M. M. (eds) (1978) *Cambridge Economic History of Europe*, VII/1, Cambridge.

Matthews, R. C., Feinstein, C. H., and Odling-Smee, J. C. (1982) *British Economic Growth 1856–1973*, Oxford.

Matzerath, H. (1970) *Nationalsozialismus und kommunale Selbstverwaltung*, Stuttgart.

Maurer, I. (1973) *Reichsfinanzen und Große Koalition: Zur Geschichte des Reichskabinetts Müller 1928–1930*, Bern.

—— and Wengst, U. (eds) (1980) *Politik und Wirtschaft in der Krise 1930–1932: Quellen zur Aera Brüning*, Düsseldorf.

Menges, F. (1971) *Reichsreform und Finanzpolitik: Die Aushöhlung der Eigenstaatlichkeit Bayerns auf finanzpolitischem Wege in der Zeit der Weimarer Republik*, Berlin.

Mensch, G. (1979) *Stalemate in Technology*, Cambridge, Mass.

Meyer, R. H. (1970) *Bankers' Diplomacy: Monetary Stabilisation in the 1920s*, New York.

Minsky, H. P. (1976) *John Maynard Keynes*, New York.

—— (1982) 'The Financial-Instability Hypothesis: Capitalist Processes and the Behaviour of the Economy', in (eds) Kindleberger and Laffargue 1982, 13–39.

Mises, L. (1929) *Kritik des Interventionismus: Untersuchungen zur Wirtschaftspolitik und Wirtschaftsideologie der Gegenwart*, Jena.

—— (1931) *Die Ursachen der Wirtschaftskrise: Ein Vortrag*, Tübingen.

Mitchell, B. R. (1978) *European Historical Statistics 1780–1970*, London.

Mitchell, W. C. (1913) *Business Cycles*, Berkeley.

Möller, A. (1971) *Im Gedenken an Reichsfinanzminister Rudolf Hilferding*, Bonn.

Moeller, R. G. (1982) 'Winners and Losers in the German Inflation: Peasant Protest over the Controlled Economy', in (ed.) Feldman 1982, 263–75.

Moggridge, D. E. (1972) *British Monetary Policy 1924–1931: the Norman Conquest of $4.86*, Cambridge.

Mommsen, H. (1973) 'Die Stellung der Beamtenschaft in Reich, Ländern und Gemeinden in der Aera Brüning', *VfZ* 21, 151–65.

—— Petzina, D., and Weisbrod, B. (eds) (1974) *Industrielles System und politische Entwicklung in der Weimarer Republik*, Düsseldorf.

—— (1976) 'Staat und Bürokratie in der Aera Brüning', in (ed.) Jasper 1976, 81–137.

—— (1979) *Arbeiterfrage und nationale Frage: Ausgewählte Aufsätze*, Göttingen.

Mommsen, W. J. (ed.) (1981) *The Emergence of the Welfare State in Britain and Germany*, London.

Moreau, E. (1954) *Souvenirs d'un Gouveneur de la Banque de France: Histoire de la Stabilisation du Franc 1926–1928*, Paris.

Morgan, K. O. (1971) *Consensus and Disunity: The Lloyd George Coalition Government*, Oxford.

Morsey, R. (1975) *Zur Entstehung, Authentizität und Kritik von Brünings Memoiren 1918–1934*, Opladen.

—— (ed.) (1977) *Verwaltungsgeschichte. Aufgaben, Zielsetzungen, Beispiele, Vorträge und Diskussionsbeiträge der verwaltungsgeschichtlichen Arbeitstagung 1976 der Hochschule für Verwaltungsgeschichte Speyer*, Berlin.

Moses, J. A. (1982) *Trade Unionism in Germany from Bismarck to Hitler 1869–1933*, London.

Mühlen, N. (1938) *Der Zauberer: Leben und Anleihen des Dr Hjalmar Schacht*, Zürich.

Müller, H. (1973) *Die Zentralbank—eine Nebenregierung. Reichsbankpräsident Schacht als Politiker der Weimarer Republik*, Opladen.

Müller-Jabusch, M. (1938) *Oskar Schlitter: Zum 10. Januar 1938*, Berlin.

—— (1939) *Franz Urbig: Zum 23 Januar 1939*, Berlin.

Naphtali, F. (1928) *Konjunktur, Arbeiterklasse und sozialistische Wirtschaftspolitik*, Berlin.

—— (1930) *Wirtschaftskrise und Arbeitslosigkeit*, Berlin.

Nathan, O. (1945) *The Nazi Economic System: Germany's Mobilisation for War*, Durham, NC.

Neal, L. (1979) 'The Economics and Finance of Bilateral Clearing Agreements: Germany 1934–38', *EcHR* 32, 391–404.

Neebe, R. (1981) *Großindustrie, Staat und NSDAP 1930–1933: Paul Silverberg und der Reichsverband der Deutschen Industrie in der Krise der Weimarer Republik*, Göttingen.

—— (1983) 'Unternehmerverbände und Gewerkschaften in den Jahren der Großen Krise', *GG* 9, 302–29.

Netzband, K.-B. and Widmaier, H.-P. (1964) *Währungs- und Finanzpolitik der Aera Luther 1923–25*, Tübingen.

Neuburger, H. and Stokes, H. T. (1974) 'German Banks and German Growth: an empirical view', *JEcH* 34, 710–31.

Neumann, S. (1932, 1965) *Die Parteien der Weimarer Republik*, Stuttgart.

Neumark, F. (1932) 'Der öffentliche Haushalt, insbesondere der Reichshaushalt, unter den Einwirkungen der bestehenden Kreditschwierigkeiten', in (ed.) Diehl 1932, 573–637.

Nocken, U. (1974) 'Inter-industrial Conflicts and Alliances as exemplified by the AVI-Agreement', in (eds) H. Mommsen *et al.* 1974, 693–704.

Northrop, M. B. (1938) *Control Policies of the Reichsbank 1924–1933*, New York.

Nussbaum, M. (1978) *Wirtschaft und Staat in Deutschland während der Weimarer Republik*, Berlin.

Ohlin, B. (1929) 'The Reparation Problem: A Discussion', *EcJ* 39, 172–8.

Olson, M. (1980) *The Rise and Decline of Nations: Economic Growth, Stagflation, and Social Rigidities*, New Haven.

Osmond, J. (1982) 'Peasant farming in South and West Germany during War and Inflation 1914 to 1924: Stability and Stagnation', in (ed.) Feldman 1982, 289–307.

Otruba, G. (1976) 'Die Wirtschafts- und Gesellschaftspolitik des Nationalsozialismus im Spiegel der österreichischen Gesandtschaftsberichte 1933/34', in (ed.) Henning 1976, 43–97.

Overy, R. J. (1975) 'Cars, Roads, and Economic Recovery in Germany 1932–38', *EcHR* 28, 466–83.

—— (1979) 'The German Motorisierung and Rearmament: a Reply', *EcHR* 32, 107–13.

—— (1982) *The Nazi Economic Recovery 1932–1938*, London.

—— (1984) *Goering: The 'Iron Man'*, London.

Palyi, M. (1972) *The Twilight of Gold 1914–1936: Myths and Realities*, Chicago.

Peacock, A. J. and Wiseman, J. (1961) *The Growth of Public Expenditure in the United Kingdom*, Princeton.

Pedersen, J. and Laursen, K. (1964) *The German Inflation 1918–1923*, Amsterdam.

Pentzlin, H. (1980) *Hjalmar Schacht: Leben und Wirken einer umstrittenen Persönlichkeit*, Berlin.

Peterson, E. N. (1954) *Hjalmar Schacht, For and Against Hitler*, Boston.

Petzina, D. (1967) 'Hauptprobleme der deutschen Wirtschaftspolitik 1932/33', *VfZ* 15, 18–55.

—— (1968) *Autarkiepolitik im Dritten Reich: Der nationalsozialistische Vierjahresplan*, Stuttgart.

—— (1973) 'Elemente der Wirtschaftspolitik in der Spätphase der Weimarer Republik', *VfZ* 21, 127–33.

—— and Abelshauser, W. (1974) 'Zum Problem der relativen Stagnation der deutschen Wirtschaft in den zwanziger Jahren', in (eds) H. Mommsen *et al.* 1974, 57–76.

—— (1977) *Die deutsche Wirtschaft in der Zwischenkriegszeit*, Wiesbaden.

—— (1980) 'Staatliche Ausgaben und deren Umverteilungswirkungen. Das Beispiel der Industrie- und Agrarsubventionen in der Weimarer Republik', in (ed.) Blaich 1980, 59–105.

Phelps Brown, E. H. (1973) 'Levels and Movements of Industrial Productivity and Real Wages internationally compared', *EcJ* 83, 58–71.

Pinner, F. (1925) *Deutsche Wirtschaftsführer*, Charlottenburg.

Plum, G. (1972) *Gesellschaftsstruktur und politisches Bewußtsein in einer katholischen Region 1928–1933: Untersuchung am Beispiel des Regierungsbezirks Aachen*, Stuttgart.

Pohl, K.-H. (1979) *Weimars Wirtschaft und die Außenpolitik der Republik 1924–1926: Vom Dawes-Plan zum Internationalen Eisenpakt*, Düsseldorf.

Pohl, M. (1974) 'Die Liquiditätsbanken von 1931', *Zeitschrift für das gesamte Kreditwesen* 27, 928–32.

—— (1975) *Die Finanzierung der Russengeschäfte zwischen den beiden Weltkriegen: Die Entwicklung der 12 grossen Russlandskonsortien, Tradition*, 9. Beiheft, Frankfurt.

Popitz, J. (1930) *Der Finanzausgleich und seine Bedeutung für die Finanzlage des Reichs, der Länder und Gemeinden*, Berlin.

Preller, L. (1949) *Sozialpolitik in der Weimarer Republik*, Stuttgart.

Pridham, G. (1973) *Hitler's Rise to Power: The Nazi Movement in Bavaria 1923–1933*, New York.

Priester, H. (1931) *Das Geheimis des 13. Juli*, Berlin.

—— (1936) *Das deutsche Wirtschaftswunder*, Amsterdam.

Prion, W. (1931) *Selbstfinanzierung der Unternehmungen*, Berlin.

Protokoll über die Verhandlungen des Sozialdemokratischen Parteitages Heidelberg 1925 (1925), Berlin.

Protokoll über die Verhandlungen des Sozialdemokratischen Parteitages Kiel 1927 (1927), Kiel.

Pünder, H. (ed. T. Vogelsang) (1961) *Politik in der Reichskanzlei: Aufzeichnungen aus den Jahren 1929–1932*, Stuttgart.

Puhle, H. J. (1975) *Politische Agrarbewegungen in kapitalistischen Industriegesellschaften: Deutschland, USA und Frankreich im 20. Jahrhundert*, Göttingen.

Rathenau, W. (1925[2]) *Von kommenden Dingen*, Berlin.

Rauschning, H. (1940) *Gespräche mit Hitler*, New York.

Rebentisch, D. (1975) *Ludwig Landmann: Frankfurter Oberbürgermeister der Weimarer Republik*, Wiesbaden.

—— (1976) 'Städte und Monopol. Privatwirtschaftliches Ferngas oder kommunale Verbundswirtschaft in der Weimarer Republik', *Zeitschrift für Stadtgeschichte, Stadtsoziologie und Denkmalpflege* 3, 38–80.

—— (1977) 'Kommunalpolitik, Konjunktur und Arbeitsmarkt', in (ed.) Morsey 1977, 107–57.

Reichskreditgesellschaft, *Deutschlands wirtschaftliche Entwicklung* (half-yearly reports).

Reichsverband der Deutschen Industrie (1925) *Deutsche Wirtschafts- und Finanzpolitik*, Berlin.

—— (1929) *Aufstieg oder Niedergang?* Berlin.

—— (1930) *Beiträge zu einem Agrarprogram*, Berlin.
Remarque, E. M. (1929) *Im Westen nichts Neues*, Berlin.
Reulecke, J. (1985) 'Die Auswirkungen der Inflation auf die städtischen Finanzen', in (ed.) Feldman 1985, 97–116.
Reuter, F. (1934) *Schacht*, Leipzig.
Röpke, W. (1929) *Finanzwissenschaft*, Berlin.
—— (1931) *Der Weg des Unheils*, Berlin.
—— (1932) *Krise und Konjunktur*, Leipzig.
—— (1933) 'Trends in German Business Cycle Policy', *EcJ* 43, 427–41.
—— (ed. Eva Röpke) (1976) *Briefe 1934–1966: Der innere Kompass*, Zürich.
Rosenbaum, E. and Sherman, A. J. (1979) *M. M. Warburg & Co. 1798–1938: Merchant Bankers of Hamburg*, London.
Rosenhaft, E. (1983) *Beating the Fascists? The German Communists and Political Violence 1929–1933*, Cambridge.
Royal Institute of International Affairs (1931) *The International Gold Problem*, Collected Papers, London.
—— (1938) *Slump and Recovery 1929–1937*, London.
Rüstow, A. (1978) 'Entstehung und Ueberwindung der Wirtschaftskrise am Ende der Weimarer Republik und die gegenwärtige Rezession', in (ed.) Holl 1978, 126–51.
Saldern, A. (1966) *Herman Dietrich: Ein Staatsmann der Weimarer Republik*, Boppard.
Salin, E. (1928) *Staatliche Kreditpolitik*, Tübingen.
—— (ed.) (1929) *Das Reparationsproblem*, 2 vols, Berlin.
Sanmann, H. (1965) 'Daten und Alternativen der deutschen Wirtschafts- und Finanzpolitik in der Aera Brüning', *Hamburger Jahrbuch für Wirtschafts- und Gesellschaftspolitik* 10, 109–40.
Sauvy, A. (1967) *Histoire économique de la France entre les deux guerres*, 2 vols, Paris.
Sayers, R. S. (1976) *The Bank of England 1891–1944*, 3 vols, Cambridge.
Schacht, H. H. G. (1927) *Eigene oder geborgte Währung* (Bochum speech), Leipzig.
—— (1927) *Die Stabilisierung der Mark*, Berlin. (Trans. R. Butler, *The Stabilisation of the Mark*, London 1927.)
—— (1929) *Memorandum zum Young Plan*, Berlin.
—— (1931) *Das Ende der Reparationen*, Oldenburg. (Trans. L. Gannett, *The End of Reparations: The Economic Consequences of the World War*, London 1931.)
—— (1932) *Grundsätze deutscher Wirtschaftspolitik* (Kassel speech), Oldenburg.

—— (1934a) *Nationale Kreditwirtschaft*, Berlin.

—— (1934b) *Interest or Dividend? A Question Propounded to the World. 11 December 1933 Address delivered before the German Chamber of Commerce in Switzerland, Basle District Group*, Berlin.

—— (1935) *Deutschland und die Weltswirtschaft*, Berlin.

—— (1937) *Schacht in seinen Aeusserungen* (Volkswirtschaftliche und statistische Abteilung der Reichsbank), Berlin.

—— (1948) *Abrechnung mit Hitler*, Stuttgart.

—— (trans. P. Erskine) (1967) *The Magic of Money*, London.

Schäfer, D. (1966) *Der deutsche Industrie- und Handelstag als politisches Forum der Weimarer Republik*, Hamburg.

Schäffer, H. (1977) 'Erinnerungen Hans Schäffers an Ernst Trendelenburg', *VfZ* 25, 865–88.

Schiemann, J. (1980) *Die deutsche Währung in der Weltwirtschaftskrise: Währungspolitik und Abwertungskontroverse unter den Bedingungen der Reparationen*, Bern.

Schiller, K. (1936) *Arbeitsbeschaffung und Finanzordnung in Deutschland*, Berlin.

Schindler, R. (1978) *Die Marktpolitik des Roheisenverbandes während der Weimarer Republik*, Bielefeld.

Schmalenbach, E. (1937[6]) *Finanzierungen*, Leipzig.

Schmidt, C. T. (1934) *German Business Cycles 1924–1933*, New York.

Schmidt, E. W. (1957) *Männer der Deutschen Bank und der Disconto-Gesellschaft*, Düsseldorf.

Schmidt, G. (1981) *England in der Krise: Grundzüge und Grundlagen der britischen Appeasement-Politik*, Opladen.

Schmidt, P. (1949) *Statist auf diplomatischer Bühne 1923–45: Erlebnisse des Chefdolmetschers im Auswärtigen Amt mit den Staatsmännern Europas*, Bonn.

Schmukler, N. and Marcus, E. (eds) (1983) *Inflation through the Ages: Economic, Social, Psychological, and Historical Aspects*, New York.

Schneider, M. (1975a) *Das Arbeitsbeschaffungsprogramm des Allgemeinen Deutschen Gewerkschaftsbundes: Zur gewerkschaftlichen Politik in der Weimarer Republik*, Bonn.

—— (1975b) *Unternehmer und Demokratie: Die freien Gewerkschaften in der unternehmerischen Ideologie der Jahre 1918 bis 1933*, Bonn.

—— (1982) *Die christlichen Gewerkschaften 1894–1933*, Bonn.

Schöck, E. (1977) *Arbeitslosigkeit und Rationalisierung: Die Lage der Arbeiter und die kommunistische Gewerkschaftspolitik 1920–1928*, Frankfurt.

Schoenbaum, D. (1966) *Hitler's Social Revolution: Class and Status in Nazi Germany 1933–1939*, New York.

Schröder, E. (1964) *Otto Wiedfeldt: Eine Biographie*, Essen.

Schroeder, H. J. (1970) *Deutschland und die Vereinigten Staaten 1933–1939: Wirtschaft und Politik in der Entwicklung des deutsch-amerikanischen Gegensatzes*, Wiesbaden.

Schuker, S. A. (1976) *The End of French Predominance in Europe: The Financial Crisis of 1924 and the Adoption of the Dawes Plan*, Chapel Hill.

—— (1978) 'Finance and Foreign Policy in the Era of the German Inflation: British, French, and German Strategies for Economic Reconstruction after the First World War', in (eds) Büsch and Feldman 1978, 343–61.

—— (1985) 'American "Reparations" to Germany 1919–1933', in (ed.) Feldman 1985, 335–83.

Schulz, G. (1963) *Zwischen Demokratie und Diktatur: Verfassungspolitik in der Weimarer Republik*, Berlin.

—— (1980) 'Reparationen und Krisenprobleme nach dem Wahlsieg der NSDAP 1930: Betrachtungen zur Regierung Brüning', *VSWG* 67, 200–22.

Schulze, H. (1977) *Otto Braun, oder Preußens demokratische Mission: Eine Biographie*, Berlin.

Schumpeter, J. A. (trans. R. Opie) (1934) *The Theory of Economic Development: An Inquiry into Profits, Capital, Credit, Interest, and the Business Cycle*, Cambridge, Mass.

—— (1939) *Business Cycles*, 2 vols, London.

Schweitzer, A. (1964) *Big Business in the Third Reich*, London.

Schwerin von Krosigk, L. (1951) *Es geschah in Deutschland*, Tübingen.

—— (1974) *Staatsbankrott: Die Geschichte der Finanzpolitik des letzten Deutschen Reiches von 1920 bis 1945, geschrieben vom letzten Reichsfinanzminister*, Göttingen.

Seebold, G. H. (1981) *Ein Stahlkonzern im Dritten Reich: Der Bochumer Verein 1927–1945*, Wuppertal.

Seidenzahl, F. (1970) *Hundert Jahre Deutsche Bank*, 1970.

Sering, M. (1932) *Die deutsche Landwirtschaft unter volks- und weltwirtschaftlichen Gesichtspunkten* (Reichs- und Preußisches Ministerium für Ernährung und Landwirtschaft, Berichte über Landwirtschaft NF Sonderhefte 50), Berlin.

—— (with F. Neuhaus and F. Schlömer) (1934) *Deutsche Agrarpolitik auf geschichtlicher und landeskundlicher Grundlage*, Leipzig.

Severing, C. (1950) *Mein Lebensweg II. Im Auf und Ab der Republik*, Cologne.

Shaplen, R. (1950) *Kreuger—Genius and Swindler*, New York.

Siegrist, H. (1980) 'Deutsche Großunternehmen vom späten 19. Jahrhundert bis zur Weimarer Republik', *GG* 6, 60–102.

Siemens, G. (1961) *Der Weg der Elektrotechnik: Geschichte des Hauses Siemens II*, Munich.

Simpson, A. E. (1969) *Hjalmar Schacht in Perspective*, The Hague.
Solmssen, G. (1934) *Beiträge zu deutsche Politik und Wirtschaft 1900–1933: Gesammelte Aufsätze und Vorträge*, 2 vols, Berlin.
Solta, J. (1968) *Die Bauern der Lausitz: Eine Untersuchung des Differenzierungsprozeßes der Bauernschaft im Kapitalismus*, Bautzen.
Sombart, W. (1927) *Das Wirtschaftsleben im Zeitalter des Hochkapitalismus: Der moderne Kapitalismus III*, Munich.
—— (1929) 'Die Wandlungen des Kapitalismus', *Verhandlungen des Vereins für Socialpolitik in Zürich 1928*, Munich 1929, 23–40.
Speer, A. (1971) *Inside the Third Reich*, London.
Spenceley, G. (1979) 'R. J. Overy and the Motorisierung: A Comment', *EcHR* 32, 100–6.
Spiethoff, A. (1925) 'Krisen', in (eds) Elster, Weber, and Wieser VI 1925, 8–91.
Spindler, M. (ed.) (1974) *Handbuch der Bayerischen Geschichte IV/1*, Munich.
Spree, R. (1978) *Wachstumstrends und Konjunkturzyklen in der deutschen Wirtschaft von 1820 bis 1913*, Göttingen.
Stachura, P. D. (1983) *Gregor Strasser and the Rise of Nazism*, London.
Stegmann, D. (1973) 'Zum Verhältnis von Großindustrie und Nationalsozialismus 1930–1933', *AfS* 13, 399–482.
—— (1974) 'Die Silverberg-Kontroverse 1926: Unternehmerpolitik zwischen Reform und Restauration', in (ed.) Wehler 1974, 594–610.
—— (1978) '"Mitteleuropa" 1925–1934: Zum Problem der Kontinuität deutscher Außenhandelspolitik von Stresemann bis Hitler', in (eds) Stegmann, Wendt, and Witt 1978, 203–21.
—— Wendt, B.-J., and Witt, P.-C. (eds) (1978) *Industrielle Gesellschaft und politisches System. Beiträge zur politischen Sozialgeschichte. Festschrift für Fritz Fischer zum 70. Geburtstag*, Bonn.
Stehkämper, H. (ed.) (1970) *Konrad Adenauer, Oberbürgermeister von Köln*, Cologne.
Stollberg, G. (1981) *Die Rationalisierungsdebatte 1908–1933: Freie Gewerkschaften zwischen Mitwirkung und Gegenwehr*, Frankfurt 1981.
Stolle, U. (1980) *Arbeitspolitik im Betrieb: Frauen und Männer, Reformisten und Radikale, Fach- und Massenarbeiter bei Bayer, BASF, Bosch und in Solingen 1900–1933*, Frankfurt.
Stolper, T. (1960) *Gustav Stolper 1888–1947: Ein Leben in Brennpunkten unserer Zeit*, Tübingen.
Stoltenberg, G. (1962) *Politische Strömungen im schleswig- holsteinischen Landvolk 1918–1933: Ein Beitrag zur politischen Meinungsbildung in der Weimarer Republik*, Düsseldorf.
Stone, N. (1980) *Hitler*, London.

Strandmann, H. Pogge von (1976) 'Grossindustrie und Rapallopolitik: Deutsch-sowjetische Handelsbeziehungen in der Weimarer Republik', *HZ* 222, 265–341.

—— (1978) 'Widersprüche im Modernisierungsprozess Deutschlands: Der Kampf der verarbeitenden Industrie gegen die Schwerindustrie', in (eds.) Stegmann, Wendt, and Witt 1978, 225–40.

—— (1981) 'Industrial Primacy in German Foreign Policy? Myths and Realities in Russian-German Relations at the End of the Weimar Republic', in (eds) Bessel and Feuchtwanger 1981, 241–67.

Stresemann, G. (ed. H. Bernhard) (1932) *Vermächtnis: Der Nachlaß in drei Bänden*, Berlin.

Stucken, R. (1964^3) *Deutsche Geld- und Kreditpolitik 1914–1963*, Tübingen.

Stürmer, M. (1967) *Koalition und Opposition in der Weimarer Republik 1924–1928*, Düsseldorf.

—— (1973) 'Der unvollendete Parteienstaat: Zur Vorgeschichte des Präsidialregimes am Ende der Weimarer Republik', *VfZ* 21, 119–26.

Sundhaussen, H. (1976) 'Die Wirtschaftskrise im Donau-Balkan Raum und ihre Bedeutung für den Wandel der deutschen Außenpolitik im 20. Jahrhundert', in (eds) Benz and Graml 1976, 121–64.

Svennilson, I. (1954) *Growth and Stagnation in the European Economy*, Geneva.

Sweezy, M. Y. (1941) *The Structure of the Nazi Economy*, Cambridge, Mass.

Tammen, H. (1978) *Die IG Farbenindustrie Aktiengesellschaft 1925–1933: Ein Chemiekonzern in der Weimarer Republik*, Berlin.

Taylor, F. W. (1911a) *Shop Management*, New York.

—— (1911b) *Principles of Scientific Management*, New York.

Teichova, A. (1974) *An Economic Background to Munich: International Business and Czechoslovakia 1918–1938*, Cambridge.

Temin, P. (1971) 'The Beginning of the Depression in Germany', *EcHr* 24, 240–8.

—— (1976) *Did Monetary Forces cause the Great Depression?* New York.

Thimme, A. (1961) *Stresemann und die Deutsche Volkspartei*, Lübeck.

Thomas, G. (ed. W. Birkenfeld) (1966) *Geschichte der deutschen Wehr- und Rüstungswirtschaft 1918–1943/4*. Boppard.

Timm, H. (1952) *Die deutsche Sozialpolitik und der Bruch der Großen Koalition im März 1930*, Düsseldorf.

Tirrell, S. R. (1968) *German Agrarian Politics after Bismarck's Fall: The Formation of the Farmers' League*, New York.

Toniolo, G. (1980) *L'economia dell'Italia fascista*, Rome.

Trachtenberg, M. (1980) *Reparation in World Politics: France and European Economic Diplomacy 1918–1923*, New York.

Treue, W. (1967) 'Der deutsche Unternehmer in der Weltwirtschaftskrise 1928 bis 1933', in (eds) Conze and Raupach 1967, 82–125.

Treviranus, G. R. (1968) *Das Ende von Weimar: Heinrich Brüning und seine Zeit*, Düsseldorf.

Tschirbs, R. (1982) 'Der Ruhrbergbau zwischen Privilegierung und Statusverlust: Lohnpolitik von der Inflation bis zur Rationalsierung (1919 bis 1927)', (ed.) Feldman 1982, 308–45.

—— (1984) 'Tarifpolitik im Ruhrbergau 1918–1933', Bochum Ph.D.

Turner, H. A. (1970) 'The Ruhrlade: Secret Cabinet of Heavy Industry' *CEH* 3, 195–228.

—— (1972) *Faschismus und Kapitalismus in Deutschland: Studien zum Verhältnis zwischen Nationalsozialismus und Wirtschaft*, Göttingen.

—— (1976) 'Hitlers Einstellung zu Wirtschaft und Gesellschaft vor 1933', *GG* 2, 89–117.

—— (ed.) (1978) *Hitler aus nächster Nähe: Aufzeichnungen eines Vertrauten 1929–1932*, Frankfurt.

Turner, J. (ed.) (1984) *Businessmen and Politics*, London.

Uhlig, H. (1956) *Die Warenhäuser im Dritten Reich*, Cologne.

Ullmann, P. (1977) *Tarifverträge und Tarifpolitik in Deutschland bis 1914*, Frankfurt.

United Nations (1949) *National and International Measures for Full Employment*, New York.

Untersuchung des Bankwesens 1933 (1933–1934) *Teil I: Vorbereitendes Material*, 2 vols, Berlin 1933. *Teil II: Statistiken*, Berlin 1934.

Ursachen und Folgen (n.d.) *Vom deutschen Zusammenbruch 1918 und 1945 bis zur staatlichen Neuordnung Deutschlands in der Gegenwart: Eine Urkunden- und Dokumentensammlung zur Zeitgeschichte*, Berlin.

Varga, E. (1974) *Die Krise des Kapitalismus und ihre politischen Folgen*, Frankfurt.

Verhandlungen des VI. Allgemeinen Deutschen Bankiertages in Berlin 14–16 September 1925, Berlin 1925.

Verhandlungen des VII. Allgemeinen Deutschen Bankiertages in Köln 9–11 September 1928, Berlin 1928.

Vocke, W. (1973) *Memoiren*, Stuttgart.

Vogt, M. (1974) 'Die Stellung der Koalitionsparteien zur Finanzpolitik 1928–1930', in (eds) H. Mommsen *et al.* 1974, 439–62.

Wagemann, E. (1932a) *Geld- und Kreditreform*, Berlin.

—— (1932b) *Was ist Geld?* Oldenburg.

—— (1935) *Konjunkturstatistisches Jahrbuch 1936*, Berlin.

Wagenführ, H. (1933) 'Kartelpreise und Tariflöhne im Konjunkturverlauf', *JfN* 138, 501–17.

Wagenführ, R. (1936) *Die Bedeutung des Aussenmarktes für die deutsche Industriewirtschaft: Die Exportquote der deutschen Industrie von 1870 bis 1936*, Sonderhefte des Instituts für Konjunkturforschung 51, Berlin.
Wagner, A. (1877[2]) *Finanzwissenschaft I*, Leipzig.
Waite, R. G. L. (1952) *Vanguard of Nazism: the Free Corps Movement in Postwar Germany 1918–1923*, New York.
Wandel, E. (1971) *Die Bedeutung der Vereinigten Staaten für das deutsche Reparationsproblem 1924–1929*, Tübingen.
—— (1974) *Hans Schäffer: Steuermann in wirtschaftlichen und politischen Krisen*, Stuttgart.
Webb, S. (1982) 'Government Spending, Taxes and Reichsbank Policy in Germany 1919–1923', University of Michigan (unpublished paper).
Weber, Adolf (1921[3]) *Der Kampf zwischen Kapital und Arbeit: Gewerkschaften und Arbeitgeberverbände in Deutschland*, Tübingen.
—— (1924) *Das Gutachten der Sachverständigen und die Volkswirtschaft*, Munich.
—— (1928) *hat Schacht recht? Die Abhängigkeit der deutschen Wirtschaft vom Ausland*, Munich.
—— (1929) *Reparationen, Youngplan, Volkswirtschaft*, Berlin.
—— (1930[3]) *Ende des Kapitalismus*, Munich.
—— (1931) 'Gewerkschaften und Kartelle als Marktverbände', *JfN* 79, 704–23.
—— (1938) *Depositenbanken und Spekulationsbanken*, Munich.
Wegerhoff, S. (1982) 'Die Stillhalteabkommen 1931–33: Internationale Versuche zur Privatschuldenregelung unter den Bedingungen des Reparations- und Kriegschuldensystems', Munich Ph.D.
Wehler, H.-U. (ed.) (1974) *Sozialgeschichte heute. Festschrift für Hans Rosenberg zum 70. Geburtstag*, Göttingen.
Weidenfeld, W. (1973) 'Gustav Stresemann: Der Mythos vom engagierten Europäer', *GWU* 24, 740–50.
Weiher, S. v. and Goetzeler, H. (1981[3]) *Weg und Wirken der Siemens-Werke im Fortschritt der Elektrotechnik 1847–1980*, Munich.
Weinberg, G. (ed.) (1961) *Hitlers Zweites Buch: Ein Dokument aus dem Jahr 1928*, Stuttgart.
—— (1963) 'Schachts Besuch in den USA im Jahre 1933', *VfZ* 11, 166–80.
Weisbrod, B. (1978) *Schwerindustrie in der Weimarer Republik: Interessenpolitik zwischen Stabilisierung und Krise*, Wuppertal.
—— (1979) 'Economic Power and Political Stability Reconsidered: Heavy Industry in Weimar Germany', *Social History* 4, 241–63.
—— (1981) 'The Crisis of German Unemployment Insurance 1928/

29 and its political Repercussions', in (ed.) W. J. Mommsen 1981, 188–204.

Wendt, B.-J. (1971) *Economic Appeasement: Handel und Finanz in der britischen Deutschland-Politik 1933–1939*, Düsseldorf.

Wengst, U. (1977) 'Unternehmerverbände und Gewerkschaften in Deutschland im Jahre 1930', *VfZ* 25, 99–119.

—— (1980) 'Der Reichsverband der Deutschen Industrie in den ersten Monaten des Dritten Reiches', *VfZ* 28, 94–110.

Wenzel, G. (1929) *Deutsche Wirtschaftsführer: Lebensgänge deutscher Wirtschaftspersönlichkeiten*, Hamburg.

Werner, K. (1932) *Die deutschen Wirtschaftsgebiete in der Krise: Statistische Studie zur regional vergleichenden Konjunkturbetrachtung*, Jena.

Wilhelms, C. (1938) *Die Uebererzeugung im Ruhrkohlenbergbau 1913 bis 1932*, Jena.

Williamson, P. (1984) 'Financiers, the Gold Standard, and British Politics 1925–1931', in (ed.) Turner 1984, 106–29.

Winkel, H. (ed.) (1973) *Währungs- und Finanzpolitik der Zwischenkriegszeit*, Berlin.

Winkler, H. A (1969) 'Unternehmerverbände zwischen Ständeideologie und Nationalsozialismus', *VfZ* 17, 341–71.

—— (1972) *Mittelstand, Demokratie und Nationalsozialismus: Die politische Entwicklung von Handwerk und Kleinhandel in der Weimarer Republik*, Cologne.

Witt, P.-C. (1970) *Die Finanzpolitik des Deutschen Reiches von 1903 bis 1913: Eine Studie zur Innenpolitik des Wilhelminischen Deutschlands*, Lübeck.

—— (1974a) 'Finanzpolitik und sozialer Wandel', in (ed.) Wehler 1974, 565–74.

—— (1974b) 'Finanzpolitik und sozialer Wandel in Krieg und Inflation', in (eds) H. Mommsen *et al.* 1974, 395–426.

—— (1982) 'Finanzpolitik als Verfassungs- und Gesellschaftspolitik: Ueberlegungen zur Finanzpolitik des Deutschen Reiches in den Jahren 1930 bis 1932', *GG* 8, 386–414.

—— (1983) 'Tax Policies, Tax Assessment and Inflation: towards a Sociology of Public Finances in the German Inflation 1914–1923', in (eds) Schmukler and Marcus 1983, 450–72.

—— (1985) 'Die Auswirkungen der Inflation auf die Finanzpolitik des Deutschen Reiches 1924–1935', in (ed.) Feldman 1985, 43–94.

Wolfe, M. (1955 'The Development of Nazi Monetary Policy', *JEcH* 15, 392–402.

Wolffsohn, M. (1977) *Industrie und Handwerk im Konflikt mit staatlicher Wirtschaftspolitik? Studien zur Politik der Arbeitsbeschaffung in Deutschland 1930–1934*, Berlin.

Woytinsky, E. S. (1962) *So much alive: The Life and Work of Wladimir S. Woytinsky*, New York.

Ziebura, G. (ed.) (1971) *Grundfragen der deutschen Aussenpolitik seit 1871*, Darmstadt.

Zollitsch, W. (1982) 'Einzelgewerkschaften und Arbeitsbeschaffung: Zum Handlungsspielraum der Arbeiterbewegung in der Spätphase der Weimarer Republik', *GG* 8, 87–115.

Zumpe, L. (1980) *Wirtschaft und Staat in Deutschland 1933 bis 1945*, Berlin.

Index